Exploring

America's

Past

JOHN A. GARRATY

Gouverneur Morris Professor Emeritus of History
Columbia University

HOLT, RINEHART AND WINSTON
Harcourt Brace & Company

Austin • New York • Orlando • Atlanta • San Francisco • Boston • Dallas • Toronto • London

John A. Garraty is a distinguished historian and writer and the Gouverneur Morris Professor Emeritus of History at Columbia University. His books include the widely adopted college textbook *The American Nation.* He has held Guggenheim, Ford, and Social Science Research Council Fellowships. Professor Garraty is a former president of the Society of American Historians, editor of the forthcoming *American National Biography,* and coeditor of the *Encyclopedia of American Biography.*

Executive Editor
Sue Miller

Managing Editor
Jim Eckel

Editorial Staff

Pupil's Edition
Steven L. Hayes, *Editor*
Hadley Lewis Watson, *Associate Editor*
Margaret Thompson, *Associate Editor*
Melissa Langley, *Assistant Editor*

Multimedia
Tracy C. Wilson, *Editor*
Joni Wackwitz, *Associate Editor*
Edward D. Connolly, Jr., *Associate Editor*
Christopher J. Parker, *Associate Editor*
Robert A. Partain, *Associate Editor*
Dwonna N. Goldstone, *Assistant Editor*
Kevin N. Christensen, *Assistant Editor*
Laura H. Twohey, *Assistant Editor*

Fact Checking
Bob Fullilove, *Associate Editor*

Copy Editing
Nancy Katapodis Hicks, *Copy Editor*
Joseph S. Schofield IV, *Copy Editor*

Ancillaries
W. H. Bass III, *Editor*
Anthony Pozeck, *Associate Editor*

Editorial Permissions
Ann Farrar

Art, Design, and Photo
Diane Motz, *Art Director, Book*
Candace Moore, *Senior Designer*
Tonia Klingensmith, Lisa Walston, *Designers*
Bob Prestwood, Holly Trapp, Anne Wright, *Design Staff*
Debra Schorn, *Image Services*
Susan Michael, *Art Director, Multimedia*
Peggy Cooper, *Photo Research Manager*
Bob McClellan, Mavournea Hay, Kristin Hay, Sam Dudgeon, Victoria Smith, *Photo Team*
Cortex Communications Inc., *Photo Permissions*
Joe Melomo, *Design Manager, Media*

Production and Manufacturing
Gene Rumann, *Production Manager*
Leanna Ford, *Production Assistant*
Nancy Hargis, *Senior Production Coordinator*
Shirley Cantrell, *Production Coordinator*
Jenine Street, *Manufacturing Coordinator*
Laura Cuellar, *Manufacturing Assistant*

Electronic Publishing
Carol Martin, *EP Manager*
Kristy Sprott, *Project Manager*
Barbara Hudgens, *EP Supervisor*
JoAnn Brown, David Hernandez, Heather Jernt, Mercedes Newman, Rina May Ouellette, Michele Ruschhaupt, Charles Taliaferro, Ethan Thompson, *EP Staff*

Multimedia
Randy Merriman, *Vice President*
Kate Bennett, *Associate Director*
Debra Dorman, *Sr. Technology Projects Editor*
Lydia Doty, *Technology Projects Editor*
William L. Clark, *Associate Technology Project Editor*
Virgil McCullough, *Production Manager*
Armin Gutzmer, *Manager of Training and Technical Support*
Cathy Kuhles, *Technical Assistant*
Kathy Blanchard, *Executive Secretary*
Roslyn Degollado, *Intern*

Management of Information Systems
Ian Christopher, *Sr. System Support Specialist*

Book cover: *background scenic,* Kathleen Norris Cook; *eagle,* Art Wolfe/Tony Stone Images; *flag,* SuperStock

Printed in the United States of America

ISBN 0-03-011634-1

1 2 3 4 5 6 7 8 9   032   00 99 98 97

REVIEWERS

Sterling Stuckey
University of California, Riverside
African American

Michael M. Benedict
Ohio State University
*Civil War and Reconstruction,
American constitutional*

Beverly Jones
North Carolina Central University
Reconstruction

William Bravman
University of Maryland
Africa, social and cultural

Paul A. Gilje
University of Oklahoma
Colonial America

Herbert T. Hoover
University of South Dakota
American West, American Indian

Dorothee E. Kocks
University of Utah
American West

Robert Remini
University of Notre Dame
American studies

Marvin Lunenfeld
State University of New York
Spain

Jan E. Lewis
Rutgers University
America to 1830, family, women

Neil Foley
University of Texas at Austin
Southwestern, borderlands, Texas

Carl H. Moneyhan
University of Arkansas at Little Rock
South, Civil War and Reconstruction

Wyatt Wells
Harvard University
U.S. economic

Mary C. Brennan
Southwest Texas State University
Postwar U.S.

Raymond M. Hyser
James Madison University
Gilded Age, Progressive Era, business

Julie Greene
University of Colorado at Boulder
U.S. political and labor

Noel Pugach
University of New Mexico
U.S. diplomatic

Maureen Flanagan
Michigan State University
20th-century U.S.

Eileen Boris
Howard University
*American women, U.S. social
and cultural*

H. W. Brands
Texas A&M University
U.S. diplomatic

Marilyn Young
New York University
U.S.-East Asian relations

Nan Elizabeth Wookruff
Penn State University
20th-century U.S.

Thomas A. Schwartz
Vanderbilt University
U.S. foreign relations

David Helgren
San Jose State University

Mark C. Smith
University of Texas at Austin
American studies

Linda A. Boaen
Baird Magnet School
Fresno, California

Daniel E. Fee
South Jefferson Central
School District
Adams, New York

Marilyn Kretzer
Johnston Middle School
Houston, Texas

Jeri Goodspeed-Gross
Grass Middle School
West St. Paul, Minnesota

Tom Harris
Oak Park Middle School
Leesburg, Florida

Maureen Lewis
Yelm Middle School
Yelm, Washington

James H. Curtis
Corbett Junior High School
Schertz, Texas

Pat Tobbe
Newburg Middle School
Louisville, Kentucky

David Burns
Thomas A. Edison High School
Alexandria, Virginia

Tammy Kowalczyk
Corbett Junior High School
Schertz, Texas

Nancy Lehmann-Carssow
Lanier High School
Austin, Texas

Donny L. Branam
Dobie Middle School
Austin, Texas

Irving Kohn
Fort Myers Middle School
Fort Myers, Florida

Jacqueline Lazenby
Marysville Middle School
Marysville, Ohio

Deborah K. Lofton
Blackstock Junior High School
Oxnard, California

Roberta D. Martinez
Blackstock Junior High School
Oxnard, California

Michelle Susberry Range
Hudtloff Junior High School
Tacoma, Washington

Trisha Sims
Hyde Park Baptist High School
Austin, Texas

Kristin Truman
Hunterdon Central Regional
High School
Flemington, New Jersey

Roberto C. Vasquez
Covington Middle School
Austin, Texas

Devon I. Weyler
Lamberton Middle School
Carlisle, Pennsylvania

Lisa M. Williams
Lamberton Middle School
Carlisle, Pennsylvania

Barry Bienstock
Horace Mann School
Bronx, New York

Exploring America's Past

CONTENTS

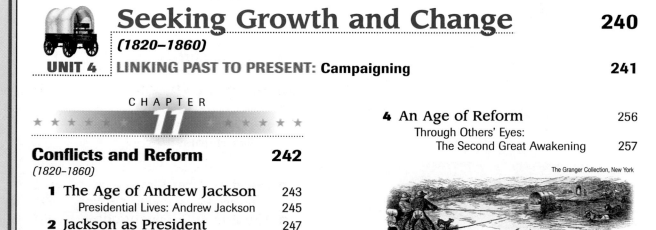

The Granger Collection, New York

Americans on the Oregon Trail

Albert Bierstadt's Emigrants Crossing the Plains

The National Cowboy Hall of Fame

Division and Reunification   286
(1848–1900)

UNIT 5   LINKING PAST TO PRESENT: Black History Month   **287**

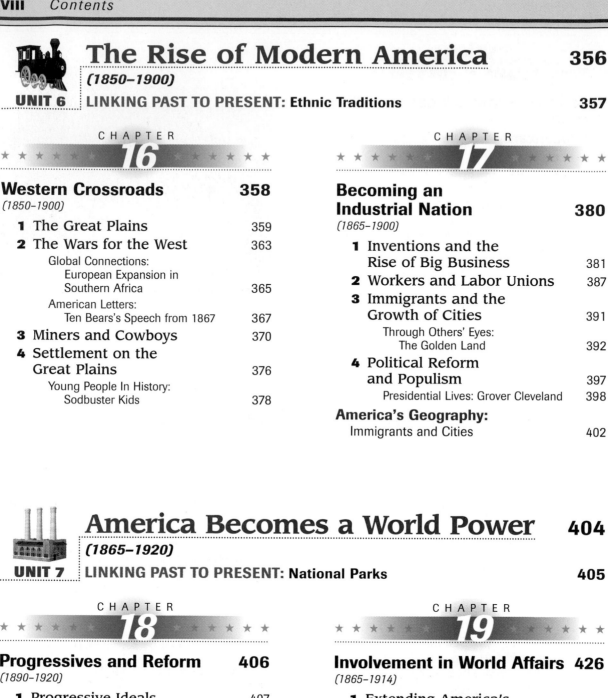

CHAPTER
20

America and the Great War   446
(1914–1920)

Spreading America's Wings

Good Times and World Crises   470
(1919–1945)

UNIT 8 ⦙ **LINKING PAST TO PRESENT: History Within a Lifetime   471**

CHAPTER
21

A Decade of Change   472
(1919–1929)

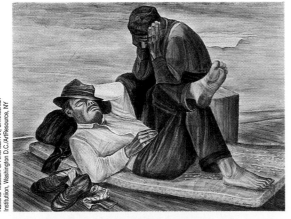

Americans in the Great Depression

CHAPTER
22

The Great Depression   496
(1929–1939)

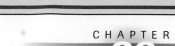

The Battle of Midway

Assuming Global Responsibilities   544
(1945–1969)

Senator Joseph McCarthy "sweeps" Communists out of the Capitol.

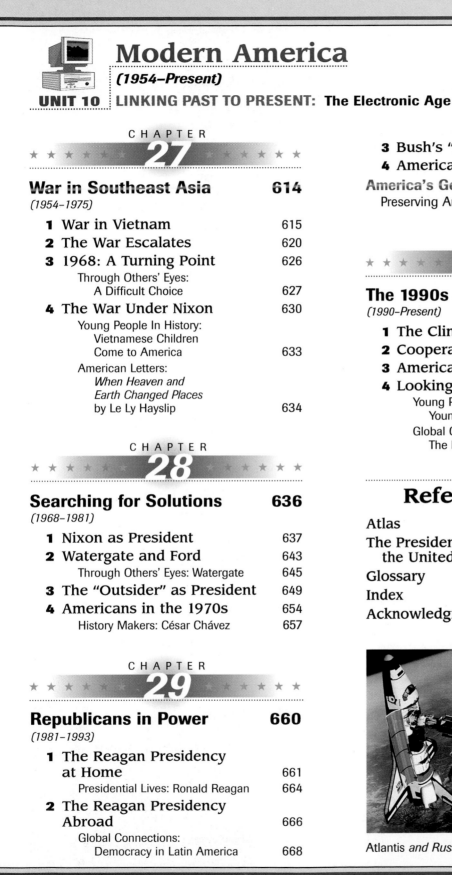

Modern America **612**
(1954–Present)

UNIT 10 LINKING PAST TO PRESENT: **The Electronic Age** **613**

Atlantis and Russian space station Mir

★ ★ ★ ★ ★ *MAPS* ★ ★ ★ ★ ★

SPANISH AMERICA, c. 1650

SPANISH MISSIONS

GEORGIA

Present-day boundaries   FLORIDA

SPANISH MISSIONS

ARIZONA   Santa Fe

NEW
MEXICO
Socorro

RIO Grande

TEXAS

Present-day boundaries

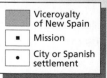

Viceroyalty
of New Spain

■ Mission

• City or Spanish
   settlement

★ ★ ★ ★ CHARTS ★ ★ ★ ★

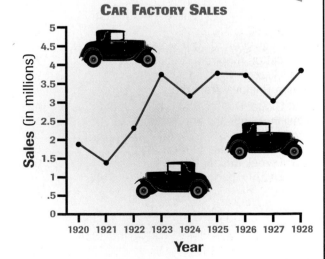

The Modern Household

CAR FACTORY SALES

Source: *Historical Statistics of the United States*

★ ★ ★ FEATURES ★ ★ ★

To the Student

Exploring America's Past is a multimedia program. Your textbook is one piece of that program. The program also includes CD-ROMs and videodiscs. As you look through your textbook, you will notice references to material on the CD-ROM. Each resource's location is indicated by a component button and a key word or phrase.

COMPONENT BUTTON ———— **Profile**

KEY PHRASE ———— • **Abraham Lincoln**

▶ Locating Items on the CD–ROM

Follow these easy steps to locate material on the *Exploring America's Past CD-ROM:*

1. Select the appropriate unit on the CD-ROM **Timescape** by clicking on the image that matches the one that appears next to the Themes in American History box at the beginning of each textbook chapter. Then click on the appropriate chapter:

 UNIT 1
Chapters 1, 2, 3, and 4

 UNIT 2
Chapters 5, 6, and 7

 UNIT 3
Chapters 8, 9, and 10

 UNIT 4
Chapters 11 and 12

 UNIT 5
Chapters 13, 14, and 15

 UNIT 6
Chapters 16 and 17

 UNIT 7
Chapters 18, 19, and 20

 UNIT 8
Chapters 21, 22, and 23

 UNIT 9
Chapters 24, 25, and 26

 UNIT 10
Chapters 27, 28, 29, and 30

2. When the **Tool Book** appears, select the component that matches the button in the chapter:

 Media Bank

 Readings

Biographies

 Glossary

Atlas

 Simulation

Interactive Map

 Gazetteer

Profiles

 Skill Builder

Time Line

3. If you have selected an Interactive Map, a Time Line, or a Simulation, you will arrive at the beginning of the activity.

4. For all other components, you will arrive at a base screen. To find a specific item, click on the word LIST to view a menu of items. When you have located the title that matches the key word or phrase in your textbook, click the item and it will appear on the screen.

▶ Searching On-Line

The **Tool Book** is a good way to access material when you know the specific database item you want. But what about when you want to find information on a general topic? There are two methods you can use to search for information on the *Exploring America's Past CD-ROM*. The first method is through a menu-driven search. The second method is through a free search. These methods can be used alone or in combination with each other.

The Menu-Driven Search. The menu-driven search enables you to access the database through six broad search categories: TIME PERIOD, REGION, THEMES, MEDIA/ COMPONENT, CHAPTER, and KEY TOPIC. Although it is possible to search the database using only one category, your search will be very general. If, for example, you select Chapter 1 from the CHAPTER category, you will get a list of every database item associated with Chapter 1. That would be a very long list!

You can narrow your search by using AND and OR to combine up to three search categories. AND and OR are known as Boolean operators. Boolean operators help you narrow or expand your search. In most cases you will want to begin your search by using AND to find specific matches. If this search is unsuccessful, you can use OR to broaden the search. You will come up with different search results depending on how you position AND and OR. Let's look at an example to see what we mean.

Suppose that you want to collect information on Abraham Lincoln's presidency. There are several ways that you can build a search. One possibility would be to use AND to combine the following search categories:

TIME PERIOD: 1850–1900
AND
REGION: United States
AND
KEY TOPIC: Presidents/Presidency

This search will find any database item that meets *all three* criteria. The diagram on the next page presents this idea graphically. The gray area represents the items that meet all three criteria—that is, any item associated with a U.S. president who served between 1850 and 1900.

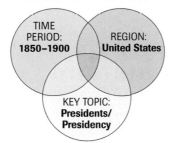

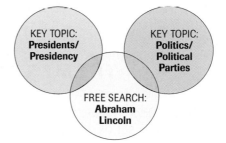

Items related to Abraham Lincoln's presidency fall in the gray area and would thus be included on the search-results list. However, the list will also include items on *any president* who served between 1850 and 1900.

Using Free Search to Narrow Your Search. If your first search attempt yields too much information that is not directly related to your search topic, you can narrow your search by changing one of the categories to FREE SEARCH. In the above example, for instance, you might replace the REGION category with FREE SEARCH: Abraham Lincoln.

> TIME PERIOD: 1850–1900
> **AND**
> KEY TOPIC: Presidents/Presidency
> **AND**
> FREE SEARCH: Abraham Lincoln

This search will locate only those items related to Abraham Lincoln's presidency.

Expanding Your Search. Since the above search includes the KEY TOPIC: Presidents/Presidency category and the AND Boolean operator, it will not call up information on Lincoln's life before he ran for president. Suppose that you decide you want more information on Abraham Lincoln's political life than just his years as president. You can broaden your search by using the OR operator:

> KEY TOPIC: Presidents/Presidency
> **OR**
> KEY TOPIC: Politics/Political Parties
> **AND**
> FREE SEARCH: Abraham Lincoln

As the diagram at the top of the next column illustrates, this search will locate any items related to Lincoln's political career.

Using all ORs will yield very different results. For example, if you replace the AND in the above search with an OR, you will locate all of the items on the database related to the presidency and individual presidents, all of the items related to politics and political parties, and all of the items related to Abraham Lincoln, regardless of time period or region of the world:

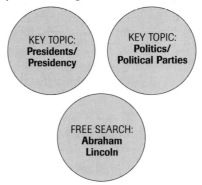

Tips for Using Free Search. How you phrase your FREE SEARCH entry will determine whether your search is broad or narrow. If you type in Presidents you will locate all of the items that are associated with any of the presidents. However, if you type in President Abraham Lincoln, you will locate only those items associated with President Lincoln.

If for some reason there are no exact matches to what you typed in, FREE SEARCH will automatically alert you to this fact and break your search down into the separate words. It will then retrieve every item associated with President, every item associated with Abraham, and every item associated with Lincoln.

One final note about FREE SEARCH—it does not care whether you use lowercase or uppercase letters. PRESIDENTS, PrEsIdEnTs, presidents, and PRESidents will all be treated the same.

Have **FUN** using the CD-ROM!

THEMES IN AMERICAN HISTORY

Exploring America's Past begins every chapter with a set of theme questions. These questions are drawn from seven broad themes central to American history: Global Relations, Constitutional Heritage, Democratic Values, Technology and Society, Geographic Diversity, Cultural Diversity, and Economic Development. These themes provide a framework for the historical events in each chapter. This framework will help you understand the connections between historical events and see how past events relate to the social, political, and economic challenges our nation faces today.

As you begin each chapter, examine the theme questions and answer them based on your own experiences or prior knowledge. As you read the chapter, explore how the theme questions relate to the chapter's history. By tracing the themes through the book, you will be able to see how each theme has developed over time.

• Global Relations

From the time thousands of years ago, when the first Asian nomads crossed a land bridge to the North American continent, America has been involved in global events. The Global Relations theme invites you to trace ways in which our nation's political, social, and economic development has affected—and been affected by—other countries and their people.

• Constitutional Heritage

No study of American history would be complete without examining the U.S. Constitution, the document that provides the legal framework for our democratic government. The Constitutional Heritage theme will help you understand the Constitution's origins and how it has evolved through constitutional amendments, Supreme Court rulings, and congressional actions. This theme also explores how individuals and different groups in the nation's history have influenced the Constitution and have been affected by it. Finally, this theme asks you to consider how the relationship between Americans and their government has changed over time.

• Democratic Values

Throughout our history, Americans have struggled to define, possess, and protect individual rights and personal freedoms, such as the freedom of speech and religion, the right to vote, and the right to privacy. The Democratic Values theme examines how changing social, economic, and political conditions have influenced the theory and practices of these rights and freedoms. This theme also explores the many conflicts that have arisen over these democratic values, and Americans' attempts to resolve these conflicts.

• Technology and Society

From the Hopi and Zuñi Indians' use of adobe bricks in building cliff villages hundreds of years ago to the computers that help you with school assignments and personal projects today, technology has influenced every aspect of our culture and society. The Technology and Society theme explores technological developments and their influence on the U.S. economy and life.

• Geographic Diversity

The Geographic Diversity theme explores ways in which the nation's vast and diverse geography has played an important role in American history. The theme examines how the development of the nation's resources has helped shape its economy, society, and politics. In addition, the Geographic Diversity theme traces how public and government attitudes about resources and the environment have changed over time.

• Cultural Diversity

Our nation's rich and unique culture comes from its many different ethnic, racial, and religious groups. The Cultural Diversity theme examines America's experiences in dealing with diverse culture groups from the time of the Spanish explorers to recent immigration from around the world.

• Economic Development

President Calvin Coolidge said in 1925 that "the business of America is business." The Economic Development theme asks you to explore the close relationship between history and economics that has shaped the United States. This theme traces the relationship between government, business, and labor in America. It examines how the growth of a strong national economy has influenced the country's domestic and foreign politics, as well as individual lives and American society in general.

GEOGRAPHY THEMES

History and geography share many common elements. History describes the events that have taken place from ancient times until the present day. Geography describes how physical environments affect human events and how people influence the environment around them. To describe a series of events without placing them in their physical settings is to tell only part of the story. Geographers have developed five themes—location, place, region, movement, and human-environment interaction—to organize information.

▶ **Location** describes a site's position. This is the spot on the earth where something is found, often expressed in terms of its position in relation to other places.

▶ **Place** refers to the physical features and human influences that define a particular site on the earth and make it different from other sites. Physical features include landscape, climate, and vegetation. Human

influences include land use, architecture, and population size.

▶ **Region** is the common cultural or physical features of an area that distinguishes it from other areas. One region may be different from another area because of physical characteristics, such as landforms or climate, or because of cultural features, such as dominant languages or religions.

▶ **Movement** describes the way people interact as they travel, communicate, and trade goods and services. Movement includes human migration as well as the exchange of goods and ideas.

▶ **Human-environment interaction** deals with the ways in which people interact with their natural environments, like clearing forests or building cities. This theme is particularly important to the study of history in that it shows how people shape and are shaped by their surroundings.

AMERICAN BEGINNINGS (BEGINNINGS–1763)

Courtesy of the Witte Museum, San Antonio, Texas

This painting shows how one artist imagined an early American Indian settlement might have looked before the Indians came into contact with Europeans.

LINKING PAST TO PRESENT
American Indian Rituals

Every year around July 4th a group of middle-school-aged girls gather in brightly colored clothing to participate in a ritual that has been practiced in their community for centuries. Although the girls live in the United States, this celebration does not focus on American independence from Great Britain. Instead, these Apache girls are celebrating their passage from childhood into adulthood. For four days, all the members of the local Apache community will sing, dance, eat, make crafts, and perform traditional rituals.

Throughout the United States many young American Indians participate in similar rituals that celebrate the passage through four stages of life—infancy, childhood, adulthood, and old age. The Apache ceremony signifies the important place that women have traditionally held in the community. Apache children trace their heritage through their mother's family line.

The process of carrying on the Apache traditions often requires memorizing hours of songs and stories. The songs sung over the four-day ceremony are never written down or recorded because they are considered to be sacred. These songs must be memorized by the performers and passed down verbally from one generation to the next.

In continuing to participate in these types of ceremonies, modern American Indians try to maintain a link to a world that was changed forever when Europeans came to the Native Americas around 1500. As you read this unit, you will learn what little we know about Native American civilizations before that time and how they were changed by contact with Europeans.

It is hard to be certain how closely modern rituals follow those of American Indians before 1500. Many of the rituals that are performed today have probably changed gradually over time. The July date of the Apache ceremony, for example, was determined by events in the late 1800s. At that time the Apaches were only allowed to gather in large groups around the time of American Independence Day. As you will learn, however, we do know that many parts of such rituals, including stories told, food prepared, crafts made, and styles of dances performed, resemble those observed by the first Europeans who encountered Native Americans some 500 years ago.

Many young American Indians, like this girl from Oklahoma, wear traditional clothing for special ceremonies.

Travelpix/FPG International

CHAPTER **1**

Worlds Meet
(Beginnings–1500)

THEMES IN AMERICAN HISTORY

Cultural Diversity:
How might cross-cultural interactions change a society?

Geographic Diversity:
How might people adapt to their physical environment?

Global Relations:
How might the growth of trade affect a society's development?

• Video Opener
• Skill Builder

*I*n his novel Alaska, *writer James A. Michener imagined what the first travelers to North America were like:*

"**On small sleds with runners of antler and bone, the travelers dragged behind them . . . bone needles, skins not yet sewn into clothing, shallow bowls carved from heavy wood or bone, long-handled cooking spoons of ivory. . . . Men and women alike knew hundreds of rules for surviving an arctic winter.**"

image above: *Early Native American pottery*

Section 1
THE FIRST AMERICANS

Multimedia Connections
Explore these related topics and materials on the CD–ROM to enrich your understanding of this section:

 Gazetteer

• Bering Strait
• Mesoamerica
• North America
• South America

 Media Bank

• Tlingit Artifact
• American Indian Music

 Profiles

• Leif Eriksson

 Atlas

• American Landscape

 Readings

• Creation Myths

Sometime around A.D. 1000, European explorer Leif Eriksson established a camp in Newfoundland. Eriksson visited many nearby areas, including a region with "wheatfields growing wild . . . also those trees which are called maple." Could this have been part of what is now the United States? We do not know. We do know, however, that the explorers met people in this land. These people were descendants of ancient travelers who arrived long before the Europeans.

As you read this section you will find out:
▶ **How the first Americans arrived, and where they came from.**
▶ **How hunter-gatherers differed from farming communities.**
▶ **What some early American societies were like.**

The Great Migration

Today Asia is separated from North America by the Bering Strait, a body of water between Alaska and Siberia more than 50 miles wide. When the first people arrived in North America from Asia, however, instead of water there was dry land. The earth was then passing through a great **Ice Age**, a period when the weather was much colder than it is now. During the Ice Age, moisture that in warmer times would have fallen as rain and drained back into the oceans fell as snow instead.

Gradually, far more snow piled up in the northern regions of the earth than could melt. Vast ice fields called **glaciers** formed. So much water was trapped in these glaciers that the water level of the oceans dropped sharply, exposing a land bridge across what is now the Bering Strait.

Eventually, animals and plants passed across the land bridge and spread throughout North America. The bones of ancient Asian elephants, called mammoths, have been found in dozens of places in the United States. Following the animals came people—the first Americans. No one knows exactly when the first Americans arrived because no historian made written records of the adventures of these pioneers. The early Americans were probably following the great herds of wild game.

Scholars disagree as to when these overland crossings began. Estimates range from 12,000 to more than 50,000 years ago. They ended about 10,000 years ago as melting glaciers signaled the end of the Ice Age. Although the Bering land bridge gradually disappeared beneath the rising ocean, some **migration**, or movement from one place to another, continued in small boats until possibly as late as 1000 B.C.

Early Societies

Once in North America, the first Americans and their descendants moved slowly to the south and east, following the game animals. They eventually settled in places as far apart as present-day New England and the southern tip of South America. Thousands of years and many generations passed before they spread over all this land.

As they advanced, the early Americans formed **societies**, each with its own distinct **culture**. Societies are groups of people that live and work together and that have common values and customs. The culture of a society consists of those common values and customs—such as language, government, and family relationships. The objects that the people create are also part of their culture.

Whenever these early Americans migrated, they

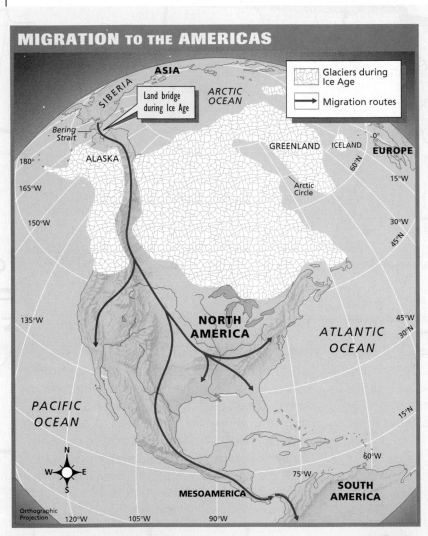

MIGRATION TO THE AMERICAS

Glaciers during Ice Age

Migration routes

Learning from Maps.
Early nomadic peoples from Asia took thousands of years to spread throughout the Americas.

• Maps

▶ **Movement.** What geographical feature enabled the nomadic peoples from Asia to travel to the Americas?

had to adapt to the different environments they encountered. Some groups made their homes in fertile valleys, others in tropical rain forests. Some settled in the mountains or in deserts. Some hunted game and gathered wild plants, roaming constantly in search of food. These **hunter-gatherers**, as they are now known, generally traveled in small groups. Their homes were usually natural shelters like caves, or tepees they carried with them as they wandered. Where climate and soil were favorable, others took up farming. Farmers soon built permanent shelters and gradually gave up their roaming ways. Farming communities were generally larger than the communities of hunter-gatherers.

Maize, or corn, was the most important food crop grown in the Americas. Groups in present-day Mexico were growing it perhaps as early as 8000 B.C. As supplies of maize increased, the farmers began to trade the surplus with other communities. Around 3500 B.C. the desert people of what is now the southwestern United States also began to grow maize. Experts believe that these early farmers learned this technique from contact with their southern neighbors.

The Maya built many detailed statues in Mesoamerica such as this one, which still stands in Honduras.

The success of agriculture in Mexico and Central America—the region often known as Mesoamerica—enabled the area to support many millions of people. As the population grew, large cities and complex societies gradually formed.

One of the most important Mesoamerican societies was that of the Maya, who thrived from about A.D. 300 to 800. The Maya developed a complex irrigation system that enabled them to produce enough food to support their large population. They also had a system of writing that used **glyphs**, or pictures. Researchers who study these glyphs have uncovered much of the history of the Maya and other early peoples.

• **Uncovering the past**

North American Societies

Scholars believe that by 1492 there were 1 to 2 million people living in what is now the United States and Canada. Today we refer to these people and their descendants as Native Americans or American Indians. They were not a single group with a common culture, however. Native Americans were organized into a wide variety of tribes, each with its own culture. Because environment had a strong effect on cultural development, tribes within a common geographic area tended to share many characteristics. For that reason, experts often group tribes by **culture area**. A culture area is a geographic region whose residents share common cultural traits.

The eastern culture areas. The Cayuga, Mohawk, Oneida, Onondaga, and Seneca

Early Native Americans used arrowheads like these to hunt big game.

• **Mammoth**

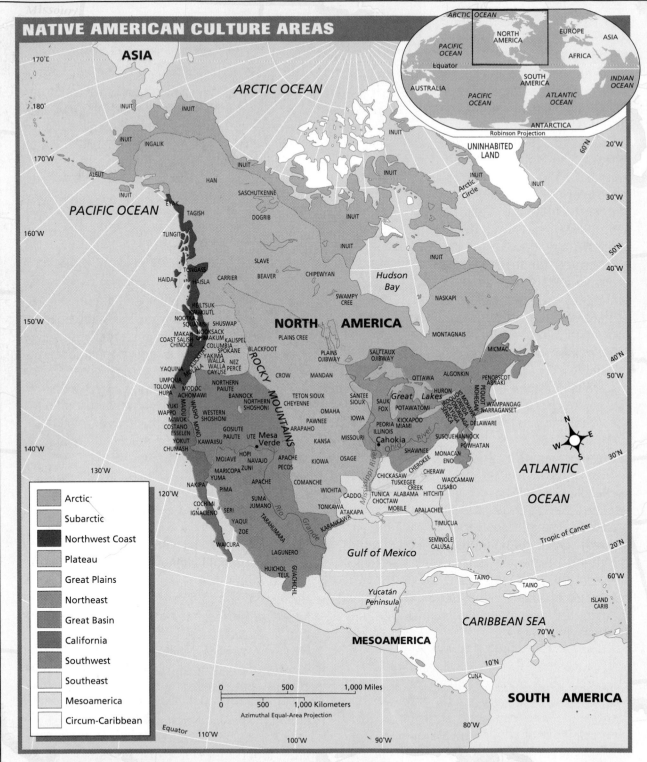

NATIVE AMERICAN CULTURE AREAS

ASIA

ARCTIC OCEAN

PACIFIC OCEAN

NORTH AMERICA

Hudson Bay

Great Lakes

ATLANTIC OCEAN

Gulf of Mexico

Yucatán Peninsula

CARIBBEAN SEA

MESOAMERICA

SOUTH AMERICA

Legend:
- Arctic
- Subarctic
- Northwest Coast
- Plateau
- Great Plains
- Northeast
- Great Basin
- California
- Southwest
- Southeast
- Mesoamerica
- Circum-Caribbean

0   500   1,000 Miles
0   500   1,000 Kilometers
Azimuthal Equal-Area Projection

Learning from Maps. Before 1500, many different Native American cultures inhabited the Americas. Many of these thriving cultures had adapted to a wide range of climatic and geographical regions.

▶ **Human-environment interaction.** How might the geography of an area influence the culture that develops there?

• Maps

tribes of the *Northeast* culture area lived in the densely wooded central region of what is now New York State. Later, they banded together as the Five Nations, or **Iroquois League**.

The Iroquois League was powerful because of its brave warriors and the alliances among its communities. As in many tribes, Iroquois men usually hunted while the women farmed. Iroquois women also played important roles in tribal decision making. For example, women were in charge of nominating members to the tribal council. They also had a voice in declaring war and making treaties.

The various peoples of the *Southeast* culture area were mostly farmers. They lived in the lower Mississippi River valley. Europeans later called these groups the "Five Civilized Tribes," which included the Cherokee, Chickasaw, Choctaw, Creek, and Seminole.

These peoples used timber from the dense forests around them to make everything from farming tools to fences to small houses. They also wove fine baskets. The Creek formed well-organized towns, with their homes arranged around a public square and a council house.

The western culture areas. In the *Southwest* culture area the Hopi and the Zuni people built with adobe—sun-baked brick plastered with mud. Their homes looked somewhat like modern apartment buildings. Some were four stories high and contained quarters for perhaps 1,000 people, along with storerooms for grain and other crops. These homes were usually built against cliffs, both to make construction easier and to help with defense against enemies. Later European explorers called these adobe homes **pueblos**, meaning "towns."

This ruin of a cliff dwelling at Mesa Verde, Colorado, is one of the most well-preserved examples of an ancient southwestern community. Over the years the cliffs helped protect the structure from harm.

● **Indian Ruins**

In the *California* culture area, groups such as the Miwok and the Hupa lived off acorns, fish, deer, and other plants and animals. This area was so fertile that it supported the densest population in what is now the United States. Most of the people lived in groups so small they are often called tribelets rather than tribes.

The Kwakiutl, Nootka, and Chinook of the *Northwest Coast* culture area lived mostly on salmon and other fish. Magnificent forests of redwood, pine, and cedar supplied lumber for their homes, canoes, and totem poles.

Farther inland, the *Plateau* culture area lay between the Cascade and Rocky Mountains. The people of this region, such as the Modoc, Nez Percé, and Cayuse, lived in small villages along the numerous, fast-flowing mountain rivers of the region. They ate mostly fish. Although their villages were independent, the people stayed in close contact with one another through river trade.

The *Great Basin* culture area was also located in mountainous country, but life was much harsher than in the Plateau area. Tribes such as the Shoshoni and the Ute wandered in small bands through dry, rugged lands. They gathered berries and nuts and hunted small animals such as rabbits and snakes. The Great Basin peoples are sometimes referred to as the "diggers" because they often had to dig for roots to survive.

The Great Plains and far north. In the 1400s most of the residents of the dry, treeless grassland known as the *Great Plains* were traveling farmers and hunters of small game. This included groups such as the Pawnee. When the soil in one spot wore out, they moved on. This changed after European explorers and settlers intro-duced horses to the Americas. Horses transformed the Great Plains tribes into hunting societies that lived off the mighty buffalo.

Far to the north lived the people of the *Arctic* and *Subarctic* culture areas. They included the Inuit, who became known to Europeans as Eskimos, an Indian word meaning "eaters of raw meat." They hunted seals, walruses, and whales. Some groups fished for salmon and hunted caribou. Because trees did not grow that far north, the Inuit often lived in igloos built of blocks of packed snow. The Inuit were probably the people Leif Eriksson and his followers met when they first arrived in North America.

• **Viking Sagas**

This finely crafted gold, silver, and bronze jewelry was worn by a person from the native land of Leif Eriksson, one of the first known Europeans to visit North America. Well known as great warriors and explorers, the Scandinavians were also skilled craftspeople.

The Granger Collection, New York

Section 1 Review

• **Glossary**

IDENTIFY and explain the significance of the following: Ice Age, glaciers, migration, societies, culture, hunter-gatherers, maize, glyphs, culture area, Iroquois League, pueblos

LOCATE and explain the importance of the following: Bering Strait, Mesoamerica

• **Gazetteer**

REVIEWING FOR DETAILS
1. How did hunter-gatherer and farming societies differ?
2. What were some of the main traits of people in each culture area?

REVIEWING FOR UNDERSTANDING
3. **Geographic Literacy** Describe how the first North Americans arrived on the continent.
4. **Writing Mastery:** *Describing* Imagine you are a member of an early American society. Write a poem describing some aspects of your daily life.
5. **Critical Thinking:** *Cause and Effect* Why did lifestyles in the Native American culture areas vary so much?

Section 2

THE LURE OF TRADE

Multimedia Connections

Explore these related topics and materials on the CD–ROM to enrich your understanding of this section:

 Atlas

- Medieval Trade Routes

 Gazetteer

- Europe
- Africa
- Asia

 Media Bank

- Medieval Church
- Medieval Life
- Marco Polo
- Western Africa
- Medieval Warfare
- Astronomy
- Astrolabe
- Manorial Life
- Diamond Sutra
- Italian Port

 Profiles

- Ibn Battuta
- Mansa Musa
- Marco Polo
- Zheng He

 Readings

- Marco Polo
- King Mbemba

n 1271 the emperor of China invited Italian merchants Niccolò and Maffeo Polo to visit his country. Niccolò's teenage son, Marco, went along. They returned home some 25 years later with amazing stories about the places they had been. As Europeans read Marco Polo's account of his travels, their interest in Asian goods grew. Many years passed, however, before Europe took a leading role in trade and exploration.

As you read this section you will find out:

▶ **Where global trade was most active before A.D. 1000.**

▶ **How religion influenced the growth of trade and cross-cultural interactions.**

▶ **How the Commercial Revolution and new technologies affected Europe.**

Europe in the Year 1000

If Leif Eriksson's crew could make their way to North America, why did no other Europeans do so for such a long time? There were several reasons for the delay.

Nations as we know them did not yet exist. True, there were kings of regions like England and France, but these rulers had relatively little power. Instead, land was divided up into sections called **manors**, which were ruled by nobles known as lords.

Each manor was a tiny world in itself. Peasants called **serfs** worked the lord's fields. Serfs labored to feed themselves and their families, but a large part of what they produced went to the lord of the manor. The manors were practically independent—the manor community produced nearly everything its members ate, wore, or used.

The residents of the manors also had to help protect the land from outside invaders. Between A.D. 600 and 1000 the manors faced constant attacks from Scandinavians and eastern European groups.

Manor life did have advantages. Everyone knew what to expect of everyone else. But it was a narrow existence in a small world. Most people lacked not only the wealth and free time to explore but also the urge to do so.

African Trading Kingdoms

While Europeans and the people of the Americas were living in relative isolation, people in Africa and Asia were exploring new lands and establishing extensive trade networks. By the 700s some Africans on the east coast were trading with Arab peoples across the Red Sea.

Other trade routes brought the desert peoples of the north into contact with the inhabitants of West Africa. Merchants from North Africa traveled south across the Sahara Desert to the kingdoms of Ghana and Mali. In these kingdoms, the merchants exchanged cloth, salt, and copper for gold and also for slaves needed to work in desert salt mines. According to one African historian, merchants from the Arabian Peninsula, attracted by gold, "came with many caravans of camels" to the trading cities.

Trade with these Arab peoples had a great influence on life in the African kingdoms, and African cultures had a strong influence on the Arabs. On the African east coast, for example, new languages developed. One of the most important was Swahili (swah-HEE-lee), a mixture of African Bantu languages and Arabic.

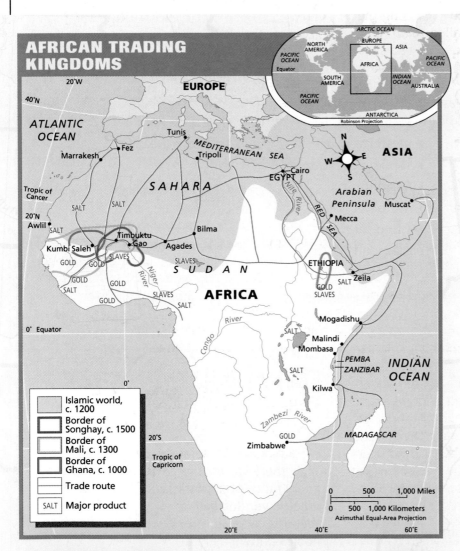

AFRICAN TRADING KINGDOMS

Legend:
- Islamic world, c. 1200
- Border of Songhay, c. 1500
- Border of Mali, c. 1300
- Border of Ghana, c. 1000
- Trade route
- SALT Major product

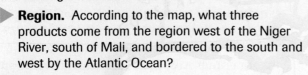

Learning from Maps.
The African trade routes allowed the exchange of goods and knowledge between cultures.

• **Maps**

▶ **Region.** According to the map, what three products come from the region west of the Niger River, south of Mali, and bordered to the south and west by the Atlantic Ocean?

The most significant cultural change resulting from these trading ties, however, was the spread of the Islamic religion.

Islam and Trade

In 610 Muhammad, a merchant who lived in the Arabian Peninsula, reported experiencing a holy vision. He founded a religion called Islam and dedicated his life to preaching the message of God, whom he called Allah. Like Judaism and Christianity, Islam emphasized the existence of only one god, honor toward parents, and kindness to others. Above all, the faith stressed devotion to Allah. Islam soon attracted many followers, who became known as **Muslims**.

After Muhammad's death, his followers organized his teachings into a holy book called the Qur'an (kuh-RAN), which Muslims carried with them as they spread the faith through trade and conquest. Muslim merchants soon controlled trade between Asia and Africa.

Sometimes the spread of the Muslim faith and culture caused problems. The powerful African empire of Ghana became divided over religion as the number of Muslim residents increased. The king, Tunka Manin, supported Ghana's traditional religion, which taught that the world was run by numerous spirits found in nature. This idea conflicted with the Muslim belief in one supreme god.

In 1076 Muslims from North Africa invaded the kingdom of Ghana and made it a Muslim nation. Internal religious conflict continued, however. As Ghana declined, it was gradually replaced by the Muslim kingdom of Mali.

The Granger Collection, New York

Trade caravans like this one moved Asian goods across the desert to Europe. Although demand for Asian goods was high, the journey to get such goods was often difficult.

• Commerce

Mali reached its peak under the leadership of Mansa Musa, a Muslim who ruled from 1307 to 1332. In 1324 Mansa Musa made a **pilgrimage**, or religious journey, to Mecca, the holy city of Islam. He also used the trip to show off Mali's great wealth and to expand its trading connections. Ibn Fadl Allah al Omari (ib-uhn FAHD AH-lah ah oo-MAHR-ee), an attendant to the Egyptian pharaoh, recalled his impression of Mansa Musa:

> **"He is the king who is the most powerful, the richest, the most fortunate, and the most feared by his enemies and the most able to do good to those around him."**

Stories of Mansa Musa's magnificent kingdom spread as far as western Europe. An atlas prepared for King Charles V of France pictured Mansa Musa, sitting on a throne holding a large gold nugget.

Cultures Cross

The growth of trade brought many different cultures into contact. In their vast travels, Muslim traders took elements of their culture to distant lands. They also brought new ideas back to their own civilization. Knowledge gained from Muslim mapmakers improved the

This early brass statue from Benin, West Africa, shows an African man blowing a horn.

• Mansa Musa   • Views of Africa

maps of the known world. The city of Timbuktu (tim-buhk-TOO) in Mali became a center of learning in the Muslim world. It contained 180 Islamic schools and three universities. The university libraries housed large collections of Greek, Roman, and Arabic manuscripts on subjects such as religion, poetry, astronomy, and medicine.

Muslims also came into contact with other Asian cultures. Ideas from China and India, for example, helped Arab mathematicians perfect their numbering system and advance the study of algebra. As in Africa, such knowledge spread across Asia largely as a result of cross-cultural trade.

Contact between China and the Arab world existed for centuries along a network of trade routes known as the **Silk Road**. However, China's rulers tried to keep foreign contacts to a minimum, so few outsiders were allowed to enter the country and few Chinese ever left. Thus, most merchants did not travel over the entire Silk Road. Instead, goods passed from one trader to another in the numerous towns that grew up along the routes.

Camel caravans carried Chinese silk, tea, spices, porcelain, and cotton linens over mountains and deserts, all the way to the Mediterranean Sea. When Europeans encountered all the products of this vast trading network, they began to expand their interest in world trade.

The Crusades

What helped thrust Europeans into further contact with the rest of the world, however, was the **Crusades**, a series of religious wars. These wars were fought for control of Palestine, an area in Southwest Asia that was sacred to Muslims, Jews, and Christians.

Since the early 600s Palestine had been ruled by Muslims. Around the year 1000, the Muslim ruler of Palestine began persecuting Christians in the region. In 1095 Pope Urban II summoned Catholics to launch a crusade (from the Latin word for "cross") to drive the Muslims out of Palestine.

Thousands of European people eagerly responded to the pope's call. They sewed crosses to their garments and marched off to Palestine. This Crusade failed, but in 1099, a second wave of Crusaders captured the city of Jerusalem. However, the Muslims did not willingly give up a region that was equally holy to their faith. On and off for the next 200 years, war raged in and around Palestine.

Gradually, the Muslims pushed the Christians back. The Muslim sultan

Through Others' Eyes
Chinese Trading Voyages

In the early 1400s the emperor of China sponsored seven large naval expeditions to expand trade and increase China's reputation in the world. These voyages spanned Southeast Asia and reached west to the Arabian Peninsula and Africa. Although the Chinese typically viewed other peoples as "barbarians," they were favorably impressed by Islamic culture. In 1432 one expedition member recorded his impressions of Mecca, one of the most important cities in the Muslim world:

> *"The people of this country are stalwart [strong] and fine-looking. . . . The customs of the people are pacific [peaceful] and admirable. There are no poverty-stricken families. They all observe the precepts [rules] of their religion, and law-breakers are few. It is in truth a most happy country."*

Although China's naval expeditions ended in 1433, they had a lasting effect on Europe. The Chinese voyages increased European explorers' desire to find a water route for trade with East Asia.

Saladin's forces recaptured the city of Jerusalem in 1187. Europeans organized several more crusades to try to regain the lost territory. Finally, Acre, the last Christian city in the region, surrendered to the Muslims in 1291.

These Crusades caused great changes in how Europeans thought and acted. The Crusaders returned from Palestine with new interests and tastes, which they communicated to friends and family. In addition, Europeans had been trading for Asian goods in the eastern Mediterranean for many years. With increasingly more contact between Europeans and Asians, the desire for Asian goods such as spices, cotton and silk cloth, and Chinese plates and vases quickly spread across Europe.

Christians and Muslims fought many bloody battles during the Crusades.

• Crusades

Europe Stirs to New Ideas

In the 1300s shortly after the end of the last Crusade, the first of many waves of a deadly disease known as the **Black Death** struck Europe. The Black Death swept across the continent, killing somewhere between 25 and 50 percent of Europe's population.

Economic recovery. By the 1400s, however, Europeans had begun to recover from this terrible disaster. Trade revived between Europe and Asia and fed a growing European economy. To pay for desired Asian products, Europeans produced more goods of their own. They manufactured more woolen cloth, trapped more fur-bearing animals, and cut more lumber. This rapid growth in the European economy produced what became known as the **Commercial Revolution**.

Other factors also contributed to the Commercial Revolution. With the great decrease in population caused by the Black Death, by the 1400s it took fewer farmers to produce enough food to meet society's needs. Since farming now required fewer workers, many people left the manors for towns. Towns grew into cities filled with **artisans**, people who crafted items by hand.

Life generally became more exciting—and also more uncertain and dangerous. Trade between East and West made merchants and bankers more important. They needed strong rulers who would build roads, protect trade routes against robbers, and keep the peace. Merchants and bankers lent money to these rulers, who used the funds to raise armies to protect their lands.

Merchants and kings helped one another. The kings became more powerful, and the merchants grew richer. As a result, the European economy expanded. At the same time, the power of the Catholic Church began to decline, but the religious ideals that inspired the Crusades were not forgotten.

Printing. Advances in printing technology during the 1450s made by Johannes Gutenberg of Germany helped to break down some barriers for people. (Printing was originally a Chinese invention.) With Gutenberg's press, a printer could make any number of copies of a book simply by setting the type once. It was no longer necessary to copy manuscripts by hand. Books became much cheaper. As a result, many more people learned to read. They improved their minds with the powerful new knowledge found in books.

The Granger Collection, New York

This engraving shows how Europeans made books after the printing press was invented. Although the printing press made the process faster, it still took many workers to make books.

• **Medieval Technology**

New technologies. Leif Eriksson and his crew had crossed the Atlantic with just a few crude instruments to guide them by the stars and sun. In cloudy weather they could only guess their location and hope for the best. By the 1400s great improvements had been made in designing and sailing ships. The compass had been invented in China and introduced to European mariners by Arab traders. Its magnetized needle always pointed north, which enabled sailors to know their direction even when the sun and stars were hidden by clouds.

Sailors were also using the **astrolabe**, an instrument that helped them figure out a ship's **latitude**—that is, its distance north or south of the equator. These instruments made navigation more accurate. Soon larger ships were being designed and built. The stage was set for Europeans to explore many other parts of the world.

Section 2 Review

• **Glossary**

IDENTIFY and explain the significance of the following: manors, serfs, Muslims, Mansa Musa, pilgrimage, Silk Road, Crusades, Black Death, Commercial Revolution, artisans, astrolabe, latitude

LOCATE and explain the importance of the following: Ghana, Mali, Timbuktu

• **Gazetteer**

REVIEWING FOR DETAILS

1. What regions were most active in world trade before A.D. 1000?
2. How did religion affect trade and cross-cultural interactions?
3. What impact did the Commercial Revolution and new technologies have on Europe?

REVIEWING FOR UNDERSTANDING

4. **Geographic Literacy** How might the location of the Arabian Peninsula have helped increase the role of Muslim merchants in world trade?
5. **Critical Thinking:** *Drawing Conclusions* Why might the existence of manors have discouraged trade among various parts of Europe?

Section 3

EUROPEANS LOOK TO THE SEA

Multimedia Connections

Explore these related topics and materials on the CD–ROM to enrich your understanding of this section:

 Gazetteer

- Portugal
- Spain
- Hispaniola

 Media Bank

- *Niña, Pinta,* and *Santa María*
- Vasco da Gama

 Readings

- Taino

 Profiles

- Bartolomeu Dias
- Kublai Khan
- Prince Henry
- Queen Isabella
- Vasco da Gama

As Europeans extended their trading ties, they began to look for other routes to East Asia. At first, they sought a water route around Africa. Some bold adventurers had different ideas, however. They talked of reaching the East by sailing west. An Italian sailor who worked for Spain actually tried to prove it could be done. The unexpected outcome to his voyage secured his place in history and changed the world forever.

As you read this section you will find out:

▶ **Why Europeans wanted to find a water route to East Asia.**

▶ **How Columbus planned to get to East Asia.**

▶ **What Columbus thought about the land and peoples he encountered.**

Getting Around Africa

Italian merchants had long held control over Europe's trade with Asia. Ships sailed from Venice, Naples, and other Italian ports carrying products such as cloth and furs to Constantinople. They brought back the silks, spices, and other Asian goods that had arrived there over the Silk Road.

By the 1300s Asian wars began to disrupt this trade by making travel extremely dangerous. The trading caravans had to crawl through bandit-filled mountain passes and trek across burning deserts where roving bands of robbers might strike at any time.

Some Europeans thought that they could avoid these dangers and not have to deal with Italian merchants if they could find an all-water route around Africa to East Asia. No one had ever sailed from Europe all the way to

East Asia. Furthermore, no European they knew of had ever seen the southwest coast of Africa.

Prince Henry of Portugal, later known as Henry the Navigator, created a research center for navigators and sailors. Geographers and mapmakers came there from many lands. Their information about tides and the position of the stars in different regions was of great value to Henry's captains.

Armed with this information and financed by Henry, brave Portuguese sailors gradually explored the African coast. In 1445 one of them, Dinís Dias, reached the great western bulge where Africa's coast turns to the east and then to the south.

By the 1470s, Portuguese ships had reached and crossed the equator. In 1488 Bartolomeu Dias managed to sail around the southern tip of the continent, only to turn back when the crew panicked, afraid to venture into the unknown seas ahead. Finally, in 1498, Vasco da Gama sailed around southern Africa and on to India.

Columbus's Voyage

Meanwhile, another explorer traveled in a different direction. His name was Cristoforo Colombo, or as we know him today, Christopher Columbus. Instead of sailing around Africa, Columbus thought he could reach Asia by sailing west. By the late 1400s few

Vasco de Gama and his crew met with the representatives of India. They arrived there after sailing around Africa.

• **Prince Henry**

educated people believed that the world was flat. They did not think that a ship sailing too far to the west would reach the edge and "fall off." They did not know, however, that there was land between Europe and East Asia.

By most navigators' estimates it was at least 10,000 miles by sea from Europe to Asia. A western voyage seemed out of the question because no ship could carry enough food and water to make such a journey across the open ocean. Columbus disagreed; he thought (incorrectly) that it was barely half that distance. He approached the rulers of several countries, hoping to find a sponsor. Finally, the Spanish monarchs, Ferdinand and Isabella, agreed to fund the voyage.

On Friday, August 3, 1492, Columbus's little fleet, the *Niña,* the *Pinta,* and the *Santa María,* set sail from Palos, Spain. After a stopover in the Canary Islands, off the coast of northwestern Africa, the ships headed into the unknown. For more than a month they sailed westward, always toward the setting sun, always alone, never another sail in sight.

As one day followed another into October, Columbus's crew began to grumble. They had not seen land for more than three weeks, and before them lay only the endless ocean. They urged Columbus to turn back. He refused.

Soon the breeze freshened and the three ships picked up speed. Then, broken branches, land birds, and other hopeful signs began to appear. Excitement mounted, in part because Ferdinand and Isabella had promised a large cash reward to the sailor who first sighted land.

Christopher Columbus in his later years.

• **Columbus**

At last, by moonlight at around 2:00 A.M. on October 12, the *Pinta*'s lookout, Rodrigo de Triana, spotted the white foam of waves breaking on a distant shore. *"Tierra! Tierra!"* he shouted. "Land! Land!"

Encounters in America

When day broke, Columbus and his companions approached the land, which was a small island in what we now call the Bahamas. He was certain that he had reached the Indies, the name the Europeans gave to the lands and islands of East Asia. Now he would earn the title promised him by Ferdinand and Isabella—Admiral of the Ocean Sea. He named the island San Salvador, or "Holy Savior," out of gratitude for reaching it safely. Columbus, however, found no spices there, no silks or rugs. Except for tiny bits that some inhabitants wore in their noses, he found none of the gold he expected.

The local inhabitants called the island Guanahaní (gwahn-uh-HAHN-ee). Because Columbus thought that he was in the Indies, he called them Indians—a label by which all Native Americans were thereafter mistakenly described. The Indians came forth bearing gifts. Columbus in turn gave them some beads, bits of cloth, and tiny brass bells. "They have so little to give," Columbus recorded, "but will give it all for whatever we give them."

By hand gestures the Indians told Columbus that many other islands lay to the west and south. He pushed on. Everywhere they went, Columbus and his men were thrilled by the strange new plants and animals they saw, including beautiful, multicolored parrots. In a letter later sent to a friend, Columbus described the terrain:

"These islands are of a beautiful appearance and . . . adorned [decorated] with a great variety of exceedingly lofty trees . . . as verdant [green] and flourishing as they exist in Spain in the month of May, some covered with flowers, others loaded with fruit."

The explorers soon reached Cuba. At every harbor, Columbus expected to find an Asian merchant fleet. Some of the local people told him that gold could be found at *Cubanacan,* by which they meant "in the middle of Cuba." Columbus thought they were saying *El Gran Can*—in Spanish, "the Great Khan"—so he sent a delegation headed by

History Makers

Isabella (1451–1504)

The Granger Collection, New York

The queen who co-sponsored Christopher Columbus's voyage was one of Spain's most important rulers. The beautiful queen with the reddish blond hair and blue-green eyes dazzled Columbus. For many years Isabella remained equally impressed by the dashing explorer. As his voyages failed to produce the wealth she hoped for, however, the queen became less supportive. No topic brought more conflict between Isabella and Columbus than did treatment of Native Americans.

Columbus believed that the best way to convert Indians to Christianity was to enslave them. Isabella disagreed. She thought that the Indians should want to become Christians, not be forced to do so. One of her last wishes before her death was that future Spanish rulers treat the Native Americans "without any injury to them or their subjects, but command that they are treated well."

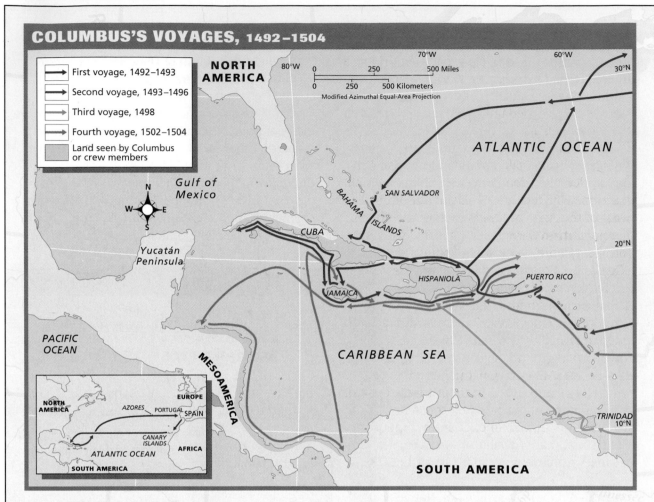

COLUMBUS'S VOYAGES, 1492–1504

First voyage, 1492–1493
Second voyage, 1493–1496
Third voyage, 1498
Fourth voyage, 1502–1504
Land seen by Columbus or crew members
NORTH AMERICA
80°W
70°W
60°W
30°N
20°N
10°N
0 250 500 Miles
0 250 500 Kilometers
Modified Azimuthal Equal-Area Projection
ATLANTIC OCEAN
Gulf of Mexico
N
S
E
W
SAN SALVADOR
BAHAMA ISLANDS
CUBA
Yucatán Peninsula
HISPANIOLA
PUERTO RICO
JAMAICA
PACIFIC OCEAN
CARIBBEAN SEA
MESOAMERICA
TRINIDAD
SOUTH AMERICA
NORTH AMERICA
EUROPE
AZORES
PORTUGAL
SPAIN
CANARY ISLANDS
AFRICA
ATLANTIC OCEAN
SOUTH AMERICA

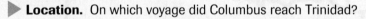

Learning from Maps. During his four voyages, Columbus became familiar with the lands in and around the Caribbean Sea.

▶ **Location.** On which voyage did Columbus reach Trinidad?

• **Maps**

interpreter Luis de Torres to pay his respects to the emperor of China, Kublai Khan! Of course, they found only tropical forests and a small village.

In December 1492 Columbus reached an island that he named Hispaniola (his-puhn-YOH-luh), the "Spanish Isle." It is the present site of Haiti and the Dominican Republic. There the inhabitants had large amounts of gold. One chief even gave Columbus a belt with a solid gold buckle.

The Spaniards could not find the source of the gold, but there was enough of it to convince them that there must be mines nearby. When the *Santa María* ran aground and had to be abandoned, Columbus left some of his crew on the island and ordered them to build a fort with the remains of the ship. He then sailed home on the *Niña*.

Reaction in Europe

When Columbus landed at Palos, Spain, on March 15, 1493, crowds lined his route. People gazed in wonder at the Indians, birds, and plants he brought to show the king and queen. When he reached Barcelona, Ferdinand and Isabella showered honors upon him. They appointed him their **viceroy**, or representative, in the Indies.

No one yet had a clear picture of where these new territories were. Columbus had claimed them for Spain, but the Portuguese, who already owned the Azore Islands, insisted that any lands found west of Africa and south of the Canary Islands belonged to them.

The two Catholic countries turned to Pope Alexander VI to decide the issue. In May 1493 the Pope divided the ocean about 400 miles west of the Azores. Lands west of the **Line of Demarcation** were to belong to Spain, those to the east to Portugal. In 1494 Spain and Portugal signed the **Treaty of Tordesillas** (tawrd-uh-SEE-uhs), which moved the line about 700 miles farther west. When Brazil, which extends well east of the Line of Demarcation, was first explored in 1500, it became Portuguese.

Columbus made three more round-trips across the Atlantic. On one he claimed the island of Trinidad off the northern coast of South America. On another trip he explored the coast of Central America from Honduras to Panama and spent several months stranded on the island of Jamaica. He obtained some

This engraving shows Native Americans meeting Columbus and his crew after the Europeans landed on Cuba.

wealth, but far less than he had hoped for. Eventually, the king took away much of his power. The explorer died, almost forgotten, in 1506. He never accepted the fact that he had not reached Asia.

Section 3 Review

• Glossary

IDENTIFY and explain the significance of the following: Henry the Navigator, Bartolomeu Dias, Vasco da Gama, Christopher Columbus, Ferdinand and Isabella, viceroy, Line of Demarcation, Treaty of Tordesillas

LOCATE and explain the significance of the following: San Salvador, Hispaniola

• Gazetteer

REVIEWING FOR DETAILS

1. Why did Europeans want to find a way to reach East Asia by sea?
2. How did Columbus plan to reach East Asia?

REVIEWING FOR UNDERSTANDING

3. **Geographic Literacy** How did Columbus's voyage change many people's ideas about the earth's geography?

• Time Line

4. **Writing Mastery:** *Expressing* Imagine that you are Christopher Columbus. Write a journal entry expressing your feelings about the land and the people you have encountered.

5. **Critical Thinking:** *Drawing Conclusions* When Columbus first returned to Europe, he was hailed as a hero, yet he died almost forgotten. Why might some people have considered his explorations a failure?

CHAPTER 2

Empires in the Americas (1500–1700)

THEMES IN AMERICAN HISTORY

Cultural Diversity:
Why might conflicts develop between different cultures?

Economic Development:
How might owning overseas colonies affect a country's economy?

Global Relations:
Why might nations compete to establish overseas colonies?

Before one Spanish expedition sailed to the Americas, a man approached its captain with a request. "[Take] my son Antonio among your troops," he pleaded, "that when he is old, he may have a tale to tell." Like young Antonio, countless other Spaniards participated in the conquest of the Americas. The tales they sent back to Spain told of a world that would be changed forever.

• **Video Opener**

• **Skill Builder**

image above: *Diego Rivera's* Colonial Domination

Section 1

SPANISH CONQUEST IN THE AMERICAS

Multimedia Connections

Explore these related topics and materials on the CD–ROM to enrich your understanding of this section:

 Media Bank

- Vasco Núñez de Balboa
- Cortés Meets Moctezuma
- Francisco Pizarro

 Gazetteer

- Spain
- Florida
- Panama
- Brazil
- Guam
- Pacific Ocean
- Mexico

 Profiles

- Hernán Cortés
- Malintzin
- Moctezuma II

 Readings

- Aztec and Inca

The Spanish artisan looked up at the dark sky and nodded. Finally, no moonlight, all the better to shape the glowing red steel as it left the fire. When done, he passed the new blade to his young assistant, who rubbed it with a fresh animal kidney to darken the metal. Later, the engraver carved a fancy pattern on the base, and the craft worker added a heavy handle. A sword was born! Using such weapons, the Spaniards conquered a land later called "America."

As you read this section you will find out:

▶ **How America got its name.**

▶ **How the explorations of Balboa and Magellan contributed to Spain's knowledge of the world.**

▶ **How Spaniards conquered the Aztec.**

A New Name for an Old Land

In the years following Columbus's voyage, other explorers ventured across the ocean and gradually came upon more lands. One of these navigators was an Italian named Amerigo Vespucci (vuh-SPOO-chee), who made at least two trips along the coast of present-day South America.

Vespucci's written description of his adventures attracted the attention of many mapmakers and geographers. He called the places he had visited a "New World, because our ancestors had no knowledge of them." In 1507 the German mapmaker who published Vespucci's account suggested that the "new land" be called America in his honor. The idea caught on, and by 1600 most Europeans referred to the new regions as America.

The Conquistadores

Soldier-explorers, or **conquistadores**, helped Spain establish and expand its empire in the Americas. They conquered and claimed vast new lands for the Spanish monarch.

The conquistadores had different reasons for undertaking this dangerous work. Simple desire for wealth encouraged many. As one conquistador announced upon his arrival in the Americas in 1504, "I came here to get gold, not to till the soil like a peasant." Once they actually found "gold and precious stones" in the new region, some conquistadores became incredibly greedy.

Many conquistadores also had religious goals. They felt a deep sense of mission, or special purpose—a belief that God had appointed them to convert Native Americans to Christianity. These conquistadores were determined to carry out this task, even if completing it meant using deadly force.

Others sought adventure. They enjoyed the challenge of exploration. When one conquistador landed in present-day Florida, he exclaimed, "Thanks be to Thee, O Lord, Who has permitted me to see something new."

Conquistadores faced almost unimaginable dangers in the Americas—Indians determined to protect their lands and cultures, tropical diseases, and exhausting marches. Many soldiers died in this "New World" far from their homes. Those who survived, however, often reaped political, financial, and emotional rewards.

Balboa's Journey

Two other explorers soon added to Amerigo Vespucci's knowledge of the Americas. The first was Vasco Núñez de Balboa (NOON-yays day bahl-BOH-uh), the governor of a Spanish settlement in what is now Panama.

In 1513 Balboa set out with about 200 Spanish soldiers and several hundred American Indians to explore the area. The party had to cross deep rivers and trudge through rain forests swarming with insects and poisonous snakes. After marching for more than three grueling weeks, they finally neared the top of some mountains. Balboa ordered the men to stop and he hiked alone to the summit. Before him, glittering in the sun as far as he could see, stretched a seemingly endless ocean.

After giving thanks to God, the expedition pushed onward until it reached the shore. Balboa waded into the sea with his sword in hand and took possession of the "new" ocean for Spain.

Balboa's discovery that another great body of water lay beyond the Americas suggested that it was in fact a very long way from Europe to Asia. To get there by sailing west, a captain would have to find a passage through the **isthmus**, or small neck of land, that connected the larger land masses. The Isthmus of Panama was relatively narrow, so it seemed likely that somewhere a water passage, or strait, led from the Atlantic to the ocean that Balboa had discovered.

Many maps used by Spanish explorers, like this one of Central America, placed the Southern Hemisphere at the top.

The Granger Collection, New York

Magellan's Voyage

In 1519 a clever Portuguese explorer named Ferdinand Magellan (muh-JEL-uhn) learned even more about the Americas when he set out to claim a group of islands in the Indies for Spain. He hoped to find a strait through the "New World" to shorten his long voyage.

Magellan was a short and powerful man. He wore a full beard and, because of an old battle wound, walked with a noticeable limp. One impressed sailor described him as "tough, tough, tough."

In September 1519 Magellan left Spain with five ships and about 240 sailors. They crossed the Atlantic Ocean to present-day Brazil, then sailed southward along the coast, searching always for a water passage to the West.

The captains of the other ships eventually became angry with Magellan, claiming that he would not discuss his plans with them. A **mutiny**, or rebellion, soon broke out. Magellan quickly crushed the revolt and put some of the leaders to death. Then he continued to sail on.

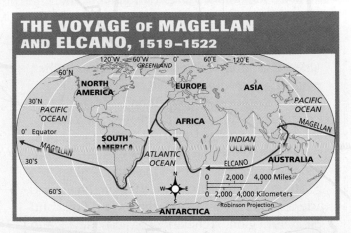

THE VOYAGE OF MAGELLAN AND ELCANO, 1519–1522

Learning from Maps.
After Ferdinand Magellan died in the Far East, Juan Sebastián de Elcano became the fleet's new leader.

● **Maps**

▶ **Movement.** How many miles did the Magellan-Elcano expedition sail on their voyage?

Ferdinand Magellan said good-bye to his wife and son—for the last time—shortly before he began his risky voyage.

Finally, the voyagers reached a break in the coast near the southern tip of South America. As the fleet entered a narrow passage between the shore and the island of *Tierra del Fuego,* or "the land of fire," fierce storms and huge waves tossed the ships around wildly. The sailors on one ship, shaken and discouraged, fled homeward.

The other ships battled strong winds and powerful currents for 38 days. At last they made it through the passage, which we now call the Strait of Magellan, into a broad and calm sea. Magellan broke down and cried with joy when he saw the smooth water. He named this ocean *el Mar Pacífico,* which means "the peaceful sea," because it seemed so calm.

Magellan then pointed his fleet northwest. For more than three long months the explorers sailed on, spotting only two islands, both uninhabited. Food supplies ran dangerously low. One sailor recorded:

" We ate biscuit . . . swarming with worms. . . . We drank yellow water that had been putrid [polluted] for many days. . . . Rats were sold

for a half ducat [gold coin] apiece, and even so, we could not always get them."

Although not very tasty, the stringy rat meat provided essential vitamins and minerals. When even this food ran out, the hungry sailors ate leather from the rigging, then sawdust. Many died, most of them from a disease called scurvy.

In early March 1521 the ships reached the island known today as Guam. After getting food and water from the inhabitants, Magellan pushed on to the present-day Philippine Islands. He became involved in a local war and died during battle. Juan Sebastián de Elcano (el-ᴋᴀʜɴ-oh) then took command.

Elcano's fleet wandered in the western Pacific for many months. Eventually, only one ship remained to sail across the Indian Ocean, around the southern tip of Africa, and home to Spain. In September 1522, almost three years after the expedition had set out, Elcano and 17 other surviving European sailors reached Spanish soil once again. They were the first to **circumnavigate**, or travel around, the entire earth. Their great sea voyage proved that sailing west from Europe to Asia was more dangerous, much farther, and more expensive than anyone had imagined.

Cortés and the Aztec

While Magellan and Elcano sailed around the world, Spain extended its presence in the "New World." By 1519 Spaniards had explored most of the islands in the Caribbean Sea and had collected much information about Indians there and in Mesoamerica.

The Aztec Empire. By the early 1500s the Aztec Empire was the most powerful Indian state in Mesoamerica. Its territory stretched from the Gulf of Mexico to the Pacific Ocean and from present-day Guatemala to the center of modern Mexico.

The Aztec had a written language and a wide knowledge of mathematics, astronomy,

Mercado/AMI/Art Resource, NY

The Aztec held many of their religious services and sacred ceremonies at stone temples. This embroidered cloth shows a soaring temple in Tenochtitlán.

• **Sports and Pastimes**

and architecture. Great stone temples dotted many of their tidy, well-run towns. Their capital city, Tenochtitlán (tay-NAWCH-tee-TLAHN), housed about 300,000 people.

The Aztec dominated other local Indians. In the Aztec religion, human sacrifices had to be offered to the gods to ensure their goodwill. For this purpose, Aztec rulers killed thousands of captives taken in wars. They also forced other Indians they had defeated to make large payments of crops or gold.

Cortés and Moctezuma.
In 1519 a conquistador named Hernán Cortés set out to explore Mesoamerica and possibly make contact with the Aztec. He sailed from present-day island of Cuba with about 600 soldiers. Shortly after Cortés landed, he met a young Aztec woman called Malintzin (mah-LINT-suhn). She became his interpreter, guide, and adviser. Malintzin told Cortés that many Indians in the area hated the Aztec and might fight against them.

With this valuable information, Cortés led his large force inland from the coast. Many Indians who resented Aztec rule joined him on the way, just as Malintzin had predicted. By the time Cortés neared Tenochtitlán, he commanded a very large army.

The Aztec emperor at that time, Moctezuma (MAWK-tay-soo-mah) II, was a delicate, well-mannered man of about 40. His people treated him with great respect. They spoke to him with eyes lowered, not daring to look at his face.

Like many Mesoamericans, Moctezuma may have believed in the prophecy of Quetzalcoatl (ket-SAHL-kwaht-uhl). This legend told of a powerful god who would someday come from the east to rule the Aztec. Moctezuma may have thought that Cortés, with his steel armor and large warhorses, was Quetzalcoatl.

In an effort to persuade Cortés to turn back from Tenochtitlán, Moctezuma sent the Spaniards a large disc of gold and some valuable jewelry. This tactic backfired. An Aztec account described the Spaniards' reaction:

"They picked up the gold and fingered it like monkeys; they seemed to be transported by joy. . . . They longed and lusted for gold. Their bodies swelled with greed . . . ; they hungered like pigs for that gold."

When Cortés and his men finally reached Tenochtitlán, Moctezuma did not openly resist

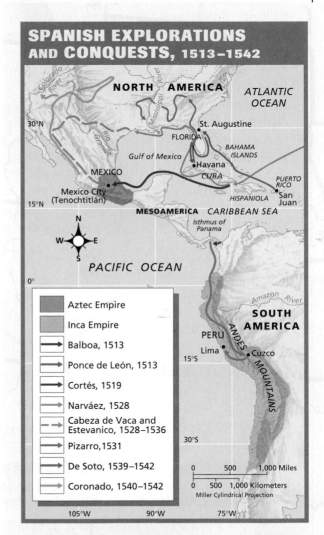

SPANISH EXPLORATIONS AND CONQUESTS, 1513–1542

| Aztec Empire |
| Inca Empire |
| Balboa, 1513 |
| Ponce de León, 1513 |
| Cortés, 1519 |
| Narváez, 1528 |
| Cabeza de Vaca and Estevanico, 1528–1536 |
| Pizarro, 1531 |
| De Soto, 1539–1542 |
| Coronado, 1540–1542 |

Learning from Maps.
Spanish explorers claimed lands from Peru in South America to the Rio Grande in North America.

• Maps

▶ **Region.** Which Spanish explorer first claimed the western coast of South America?

them. He gave them lodging in one of his palaces and provided them with delicious food. Cortés responded to this hospitality by taking Moctezuma prisoner. Although the quiet emperor remained on the throne, in reality Cortés controlled the Aztec Empire.

In 1520 the Aztec rebelled and drove the invaders out of the city. Moctezuma died during the harsh fighting. The Spaniards soon regrouped, however. Aided by their Indian allies, they recaptured Tenochtitlán roughly a year later. Cortés renamed the capital Mexico City and destroyed Aztec artifacts, houses, and temples. By 1539 Cortés controlled much of present-day Mexico. Spanish soldiers would continue to conquer more of the region in the years to come.

• **Aztec Warriors**

Aztec weapons such as this gold inlaid spear-thrower were no match against the Spanish.

Courtesy Trustees of The British Museum

One powerful but unexpected factor aided the Spaniards' conquest of the Aztec and other Mesoamerican Indians— the introduction of diseases from Europe. Indians in the Americas had no **immunity**, or resistance, to European illnesses like smallpox, measles, and typhus. Once struck and weakened, Indians found it almost impossible to defend themselves. The Spaniards took advantage of this weakness and gained huge amounts of land and gold as a result.

A new chance for conquest. Cortés's adventures caused a sensation in Spain. When conquistador Francisco Pizarro (puh-ZAHR-oh) reported the existence of another rich Indian society on the western coast of present-day South America, the Spanish king hoped for another profitable conquest. He gave Pizarro permission to explore the land, a region that Pizarro and other conquistadores had named "Peru" on an earlier visit. The rulers of this region, a people called the Inca, suffered much the same fate as the Aztec.

• **Pizarro and the Inca**

Section 1 Review

• **Glossary**

IDENTIFY and explain the significance of the following: Amerigo Vespucci, conquistadores, Vasco Nuñez de Balboa, isthmus, Ferdinand Magellan, mutiny, circumnavigate, Hernán Cortés, Malintzin, Moctezuma II, immunity

LOCATE and explain the importance of the following: Isthmus of Panama, Tenochtitlán

• **Gazetteer**

REVIEWING FOR DETAILS
1. Where did the name "America" come from?
2. How did Cortés conquer the Aztec Empire?

REVIEWING FOR UNDERSTANDING
3. **Geographic Literacy** How did the explorations of Balboa and Magellan expand Europeans' geographic knowledge?
4. **Writing Mastery:** *Describing* Imagine that you are a Spanish conquistador in Mexico during the conquest of the Aztec. Write a letter to your family describing your experiences.
5. **Critical Thinking:** *Cause and Effect* How did the Aztec treatment of their Indian subjects contribute to the fall of their empire?

Section 2

SPAIN AND NEW SPAIN

Multimedia Connections

Explore these related topics and materials on the CD–ROM to enrich your understanding of this section:

 Profiles

- Alvar Núñez Cabeza de Vaca
- Bartolomé de Las Casas
- Estevanico

 Readings

- *El Dorado*
- Fiery Sermon

 Atlas

- De Soto's Explorations
- Wealth of Spanish America

 Gazetteer

- New Spain
- Arkansas
- Texas
- Arizona

- New Mexico
- California

 Media Bank

- Spanish Medieval Music
- Treasure from the Americas
- Spanish Explorer
- Bartolomé de Las Casas

O ne observant priest noticed that Europeans were always hungry in the Americas. "In Spain . . . a man's stomach will hold out from meal to meal . . . ," he commented, "but in Mexico and other parts of America we found that two or three hours after a good meal . . . our stomachs would be ready to faint." Although he spoke of the Spaniards' hunger for food, the same could be said for the conquistadores' always unsatisfied appetite for more land and riches.

As you read this section you will find out:

▶ **How Spain governed and expanded its American empire.**

▶ **What daily life was like in New Spain.**

▶ **Why the Golden Age of Spain ended.**

Governing New Spain

The Spaniards created a system of government for their colonies to help control their vast American empire. The monarch ruled over Spain itself and the entire Spanish Empire. Royal assistants made up the **Council of the Indies**. Based in Spain, the group nominated colonial officials and drafted and administered laws relating to Spain's colonies in the Americas.

Viceroys ruled the Spanish colonies. The viceroy for New Spain—a territory that included Mexico and parts of the present-day United States—lived in Mexico City. As the monarch's personal representatives, viceroys had great power. This included the ability to issue local orders and regulations. In addition to this authority, a wide ocean separated the viceroys from Spain.

In practice they did more or less as they wanted. As one worried Spaniard wrote:

> "Our people, transported across an ocean to such strange, changing, and distant worlds . . . leave [Spain] meeker than lambs, [but] change as soon as they arrive there [America] into wild wolves, forgetting all the royal commands."

The Spanish Empire in North America

As viceroys established local governments in the Americas, conquistadores pushed further into lands that now make up part of the United States. They planted their social and cultural traditions as they went.

The Southeast. The earliest recorded Spanish landing in the present-day United States took place in the spring of 1513, when Juan Ponce de León (PAWN-say day lay-AWN) arrived to look for precious metals. He called the lush green area Florida, after *Pascua florida,* the Feast of Flowers at Easter time.

Ponce de León may have heard an Indian tale about the Fountain of Youth, a spring that supposedly prevented its bathers from growing old. Searching for this miraculous water was almost certainly not his main objective in the Americas, however. He explored the eastern shore of Florida and gradually made his way south and west around the tip of the huge peninsula. Then he returned home.

Hernando de Soto, a Spanish conquistador who had acquired a fortune while serving in Peru, led a large force through the country beyond Florida between 1539 and 1542. De Soto's expedition included a small number of women. While fighting almost constant battles with local Indians, de Soto journeyed north into present-day Georgia and the Carolinas and west through what would later become Tennessee, Alabama, Mississippi, and Arkansas.

In 1565 a Spanish conquistador named Pedro Menéndez de Avilés (may-NAYN-days day

Though the Fountain of Youth was only a myth, Juan Ponce de León's search for it had a powerful hold on artists' imaginations.

● **European Exploration**

ah-BEE-lays) founded the town of St. Augustine on the northeastern coast of Florida. St. Augustine is believed to be the oldest permanent European settlement in the present-day United States.

The Southwest. Spanish conquistadores also began to explore the area that now makes up the southwestern United States. In 1528 Pánfilo de Narváez (PAHM-fee-loh day nahr-BAH-ays) landed on the western coast of Florida with about 400 soldiers. He marched north, planning to collect gold along the way and then meet his ships at a harbor on the Gulf of Mexico. He soon ran into trouble. Illness and fierce fighting with Apalachee Indians greatly reduced his force, and when Narváez reached the coast, he could not find his fleet.

Hoping to reach distant Mexico, the Spaniards built five rickety boats, using old shirts as sails. Many died as they slowly drifted westward. A little over a month after setting out, the survivors washed ashore on or near present-day Galveston Island, Texas. Local Karankawa Indians soon attacked them.

No one knows the exact fate of the vast majority of these explorers. Only four ever returned to Spanish civilization. Among the tiny group were Álvar Núñez Cabeza de Vaca (kah-BAY-sah day BAH-kah), the treasurer of the original party, and Estevanico (e-stay-bah-NEE-koh), a North African. They spent roughly seven years traveling across southern Texas and northeastern Mexico. Acting as medicine men, they journeyed through Indian lands and reached Mexico City in 1536.

In 1540 Francisco Vásquez de Coronado led a force of Spaniards and Mexican Indians through what would become Arizona, New Mexico, Texas, Oklahoma, and Kansas. As with some other Spanish expeditions, his large group contained a number of women. Coronado hoped to find the mythical Seven Cities of Cibola, said to be full of gold, but he never succeeded.

Over time, Spanish influence spread farther into the desert regions north of Mexico. In 1598 Juan de Oñate (ohn-YAH-tay) the son of a very wealthy conquistador, journeyed there to settle in what is now New Mexico with about 400 soldiers, some accompanied by their families.

After his soldiers fought and defeated the Indians who lived in the Acoma pueblos, Oñate claimed a huge area for Spain. That same year he founded San Gabriel, which was the only Spanish settlement in the area for nearly a decade. Sometime around 1610 the Spaniards built Santa Fe, which became the area's capital. Today it is the oldest capital city in the United States.

California. As the Spanish conquered land and built settlements in the regions that now make up the southwestern United States, they also began to explore present-day California. Juan Rodríguez Cabrillo (kah-BREE-yoh) explored parts of the California coast for Spain around 1542, reaching the bays at present-day San Diego and Monterey.

Hoping to establish firm control over California, the Spaniards began to think of building colonies there. By 1602 Sebastián Vizcaíno (bees-kah-EE-noh), a wealthy Spanish merchant, had sailed up the Pacific coast as far north as Monterey Bay. He recommended that the Spaniards establish a military base there to protect their claim to the region.

History Makers

Estevanico (?–1539)

The Granger Collection, New York

Though historians know little about Estevanico's early life, most agree that he was from North Africa. He arrived in the Americas during 1528 as part of Spain's ill-fated Narváez expedition. Estevanico acted as a scout and healer on the survivors' long, difficult journey to Mexico City.

When the four weary explorers reached Spanish civilization in 1536, they reported that Indians along their route had described rich cities to the north. The viceroy begged Cabeza de Vaca and the other Spaniards to go and find them, but the men refused. Only Estevanico volunteered for the dangerous job.

Estevanico led a small expedition through Mexico and into present-day New Mexico, where Zuni Indians killed him for crossing a sacred cornmeal line. Estevanico was the first African to explore what is now the United States, and his journeys helped later explorers traveling through the Southwest.

Spanish America

As Spanish explorers spread throughout New Spain, a Hispanic American civilization slowly developed. It included some elements from the Catholic religion, Indian agriculture, and Spanish military and political organizations.

Missions. As the frontier of Spanish settlement expanded north of Mexico, Catholic priests founded church communities called **missions**. They hoped to use the missions to convert the Indians, develop distant territories, and provide a structure of Spanish government. By 1630 these priests had established some 25 missions north of the Rio Grande.

The missions were towns unto themselves, each built around a church. As time passed, large Indian villages clustered around the missions. Indians did the vast majority of the work that supported the missions. They tended large herds of cattle and grew various crops. They also wove woolen cloth and made products such as leather goods, wine, and soap.

Life for mission Indians was hard and strict. They had to give up their own religions, become Catholics, and obey the priests' orders. Those who did not willingly fit into this system often felt the lash of the whip.

Colonial life. Some Spanish soldiers eventually became civilian **colonists**, or people who leave their home countries to establish new settlements elsewhere. Using the labor of Indians and enslaved Africans, these colonists ran farms, ranches, and mines. They were joined by other Spaniards, who flooded into the Americas during the 1500s and 1600s.

• **Labor in Spanish America**

The Spanish social structure in New Spain was based largely on race. Those with Spanish blood—*peninsulares* (pay-neen-soo-LAHR-es), or Spaniards born in Spain, and *criollos* (kree-OHL-yohs), their American-born descendants—formed the upper class. *Mestizos* (me-STEE-zohs), people of mixed Spanish and Indian blood, fell beneath them. Next came Indians who had adopted Spanish ways, then mulattoes (muh-LA-tohs), or people of mixed European and

SPANISH AMERICA, c. 1650

SPANISH MISSIONS
GEORGIA
Present-day boundaries
FLORIDA

NORTH AMERICA
ROCKY MOUNTAINS
Mississippi River
APPALACHIAN MOUNTAINS
Santa Fe
Socorro
Rio Grande
Ures
FLORIDA
St. Augustine
Monterrey
Gulf of Mexico
Guadalajara
Vera Cruz CUBA   HISPANIOLA
Mexico City
—PUERTO RICO
PACIFIC OCEAN
Guatemala City
CARIBBEAN SEA
ATLANTIC OCEAN
15°N
Granada
Portobello
0   750   1,500 Miles
0   750   1,500 Kilometers
Miller Projection
Tropic of Cancer
Antioquia
Cali
Santa Fe de Bogotá
Equator 0°
Quito *Amazon River*
Piura
SOUTH AMERICA
PERU
Cajamarca
Lima
ANDES MOUNTAINS
La Paz
15°S
Arica
Salta
Tucumán
Asunción
Tropic of Capricorn 30°S
Córdoba
Mendoza
Buenos Aires
Río de la Plata
Conception
45°S
TIERRA DEL FUEGO
Cape Horn
120°W   105°W   90°W   75°W   60°W   45°W

SPANISH MISSIONS
Santa Fe
ARIZONA
NEW MEXICO
Socorro
Rio Grande
TEXAS
Present-day boundaries

Viceroyalty of New Spain
★ Capital of viceroyalty
Viceroyalty of Peru
■ Mission
• City or Spanish settlement

Learning from Maps.
By the mid-1600s the Spanish had claimed a vast area and established many cities and missions in the Americas.

• **Maps**

▶ **Location.** How far was it between the northernmost and southernmost Spanish cities?

Although isolated, church complexes like the San Jose Mission in Texas helped the Spaniards control the frontier.

• **Junípero Serra**

African ancestry. Free or enslaved black Africans were at the bottom.

On the northern frontier of New Spain, however, these divisions were somewhat less rigid. Talented and energetic people from the lower ranks of society could, with persistence and luck, sometimes achieve positions of wealth and influence.

Women occupied an important role in New Spain. They helped men settle the land and shared all the hardships of pioneering. An observer remembered one woman's difficult journey to her new home in Spanish America:

> **"She forced herself to ride in a chair atop a saddled mule, and she rode over the rough places and bad passes in these roads as easily and successfully as any of the company."**

In New Spain, married women could legally possess property and pass it to their heirs. Some women even owned and operated large ranches. In New Mexico Juana Luján (loo-HAHN) maintained an enormous spread with pastures, a garden, fields, an orchard, and livestock corrals.

Few women in New Spain ran big estates or owned large amounts of property, however. Most women worked hard inside homes owned by their fathers, husbands, or brothers. The high death rate for men in New Spain

meant that women often had to take control if one of their close male relatives died suddenly.

Many wealthy Spanish women were educated at home or in convent schools, where they learned to read and write. This privilege did not extend to all women in New Spain, however. Most Indian, African, and *mestizo* women never received any schooling. Even women from the upper classes did not have access to colleges or universities. Those who wanted to concentrate on their studies often entered convents and became nuns, such as Mexican poet Juana Inés de la Cruz.

Some Spanish children in New Spain spent their days in school. Others worked with their parents. A young boy sometimes joined his father in the fields or on errands. A young girl often helped with shopping or baking. If the family was wealthy, Indian servants or enslaved Africans did most of these jobs.

Members of a mestizo *family work together in this 1775 oil painting.*

The Granger Collection, New York

• **Women in New Spain**

The End of the Golden Age

The Golden Age of Spain began in the early 1500s and brought the country great prosperity. By the 1530s Spain ruled a greater empire than any other European nation. The Portuguese controlled the enormous region that would become Brazil, but the red and gold Spanish flag flew on staffs all over the West Indies and from present-day Argentina to New Mexico. With a huge empire, a strong army, and a thriving artistic life, the Spanish Empire seemed all-powerful.

There were some flaws with Spain's success, however. Spain's own economy, particularly its ability to produce goods, was weak and inefficient.

Denied the chance to study at a university, Juana Inés de la Cruz entered a convent in the mid-1600s and became a nun and poet.

• **Juana Inés de la Cruz**

Because of poor soil and bad farming methods, Spanish farmers did not raise enough food to support the rest of the population. Spain even had to purchase wheat from other parts of Europe.

Manufactured articles also had to be imported, because Spain had almost no industry. Instead of using gold and silver from its colonies to finance manufacturing, the Spanish government bought what it needed abroad. It paid for these imports with its treasure. In addition, all this gold and silver often caused severe **inflation**, or a sharp rise in prices.

As long as the precious metals from abroad continued to stream in, Spain could cope with its problems. When the flow slowed to a trickle in the mid-1600s, Spain's Golden Age came to an end.

Section 2 Review

• **Glossary**

IDENTIFY and explain the significance of the following: Council of the Indies, Juan Ponce de León, Hernando de Soto, Pedro Menéndez de Avilés, Álvar Núñez Cabeza de Vaca, Estevanico, Francisco Vásquez de Coronado, Juan de Oñate, Juan Rodríquez Cabrillo, Sebastián Vizcaíno, missions, colonists, Juana Inés de la Cruz, inflation

• **Gazetteer**

LOCATE and explain the importance of the following: Mexico City, Florida, St. Augustine, Santa Fe, Rio Grande

REVIEWING FOR DETAILS

1. How did Spain control its new territories and enlarge its empire in the Americas?
2. What was daily life like for the residents of New Spain?
3. Why did Spain's Golden Age come to an end?

REVIEWING FOR UNDERSTANDING

4. **Writing Mastery:** *Creating* Imagine that you are an Indian living at a Spanish mission. Create a poem or short story about your experiences there.
5. **Critical Thinking:** *Synthesizing Information* How might Spain's distance from its colonies have affected government in New Spain?

Section 3

THE STRUGGLE FOR EMPIRES

Multimedia Connections

Explore these related topics and materials on the CD–ROM to enrich your understanding of this section:

 Atlas

- Early European Settlements

 Readings

- French and Dutch in America

 Media Bank

- New Amsterdam, c. 1626
- Virginia Coastal Map

 Profiles

- Sir Walter Raleigh

 Biographies

- Queen Elizabeth

As reports of Spain's success in the Americas spread through Europe, other countries began to think of establishing their own settlements across the ocean. But what room had Spain left for other nations? One English observer surveyed the situation and wrote sadly, "[If only] they that be Englishmen/Might have been the first of all." Despite Spain's head start, many European countries soon decided to enter the race for empire.

As you read this section you will find out:

▶ **How England clashed with Spain in Europe and the Americas.**

▶ **How the English attempted to build a colony in North America.**

▶ **How the arrival of Europeans affected American Indians.**

England Enters America

When the news of Columbus's explorations reached England, Spain seemed too powerful to be challenged directly. The English concentrated on looking for a northern sea route to East Asia instead.

Early explorations in North America. In 1497 John Cabot, an Italian employed by the king of England, searched for such a passage along the coast of Newfoundland. A year later he sailed south, possibly as far as Chesapeake Bay. Cabot's voyages gave England a claim to regions in North America. The king rewarded Cabot by granting him trade privileges and a small financial reward.

English fishers also reached America about the same time, sailing in the icy waters near Newfoundland. Some may have established temporary camps ashore to salt or dry their catch. Though they did not build permanent settlements, they helped establish an English presence in North America that the country would draw on in the years to come.

Conflicts with Spain.

The English only became seriously interested in colonizing North America after Queen Elizabeth I inherited the English throne in 1558. Ruling England in a world dominated by men, the red-headed Elizabeth was a careful, clever leader. Well aware of England's limited strength compared to Spain's, she proceeded with a great deal of caution.

A talented leader and diplomat, Queen Elizabeth I spoke four languages.

England could weaken Spain without actually going to war by striking Spanish merchant ships on the high seas. In those days, a ship far from land was at the mercy of any more-powerful vessel. There was no way to call for help if suddenly attacked. A fast English ship could easily overtake a slow Spanish vessel loaded with treasure. Then Elizabeth's eager sailors could swarm aboard, kill the crew, remove the gold and silver, and sink the ship.

The Spanish considered such attackers pirates, and rightly so. Ignoring this opinion, Elizabeth encouraged English captains to roam the trade routes between Spain and its American colonies in search of easy prey. Besides weakening Spain, these attacks provided England with a great deal of gold and silver.

Francis Drake was one of the most famous of what the English affectionately called their "**sea dogs**," or sailors who preyed on Spanish ships. In 1578 Drake sailed through the Strait of Magellan on a handsome ship he later named the *Golden Hind*. In the Pacific Ocean, he captured a Spanish galleon carrying a fortune in silver. Then he went up the west coast of the Americas, possibly as far as present-day Vancouver, before crossing the Pacific and sailing home.

When Drake reached England in 1580, the *Golden Hind* was packed with Spanish treasure. Spain's forceful king, Philip II, demanded that Drake be punished. Instead, Elizabeth made him a knight.

Drake, now Sir Francis Drake, sailed again in 1585. This time he terrorized Spanish towns in the Caribbean Sea. Philip was furious! He disliked Elizabeth and he feared economic competition from the English. Philip also wanted the Protestant England to become Catholic, like Spain. So he collected what was probably the most powerful fleet the world had yet seen—some 130 ships armed with more than 3,000 cannons and carrying nearly 30,000 men. In 1588 this mighty **Spanish Armada** sailed from Spain to invade England.

As the Spanish fleet approached, Elizabeth urged her sailors to fight for the glory of England:

"I have placed my chiefest strength and safeguard in the loyal hearts and good will of my subjects. . . . By your valor [courage] in the field, we shall shortly have a famous

The Granger Collection, New York

The Vanguard, *an English warship, attacks the Spanish Armada in a surprising show of strength and strategy.*

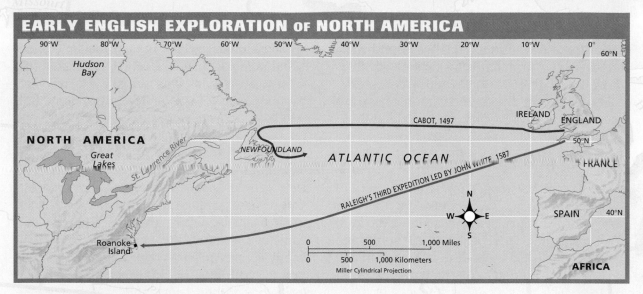

EARLY ENGLISH EXPLORATION of NORTH AMERICA

Learning from Maps. Despite threats from Spain and the failure of the Roanoke settlement, the English continued to explore North America.

▶ **Location.** What body of land did Cabot reach on his voyage to North America?

• Maps

victory over the enemies of my God, of my kingdom, and of my people."

The English ships were smaller than the Spanish vessels and easier to maneuver. They sank many of the Spanish vessels, and storms finished off still more. Only about half of the Armada struggled back to Spanish ports, and most of these ships were too damaged to be of any use. Now England was ready to carve a place for itself in the Americas.

A False Start at Roanoke Island

Even before the defeat of the great Spanish Armada, Elizabeth had begun to think of building a colony in North America. In 1578 she issued a **charter**, or document granting certain rights and powers, to an English navigator named Sir Humphrey Gilbert. This charter gave him permission to establish a settlement in the

Americas. Gilbert and a small party of colonists landed on Newfoundland in 1583, but they did not stay. Gilbert drowned on the way home when his ship went down in a storm.

In 1585 Gilbert's half-brother, Sir Walter Raleigh, sent about 100 men to the Americas. They landed on an island off of present-day North Carolina and named it Roanoke. The settlers soon built a fort, but they made no effort to plant crops. When Sir Francis Drake stopped by in 1586 after his raid on the Spanish in the Caribbean, most of the colonists went back to England with him.

The next year Raleigh sent about 118 settlers—including a number of women—to Roanoke. Most of them knew nothing of the country and had no previous experience as colonists. Just a few weeks after

The Granger Collection, New York

John White led the second Roanoke expedition. To show others what the land was like, he painted watercolors of American animals, like this land crab.

they had arrived, their leader sailed back to England for more supplies. He intended to return promptly, but the crisis caused by the attack of the Armada delayed him. When he did get back in 1591, the island was deserted. No one has ever discovered what happened to the inhabitants of Roanoke's "lost colony."

Indian-European Relations

When Columbus stepped onto San Salvador in October 1492, he gave thanks for the safe arrival of his ships. Then he claimed the land for Ferdinand and Isabella. He did so despite the obvious fact that the island already belonged to someone—the "Indians" gathered on the beach.

Later explorers—French, Dutch, Swedish, and English—dismissed the Native Americans they encountered in much the same way. What many people have called the "discovery" of a "New World" was actually the invasion and conquest of the land where Indians had lived for thousands of years.

First contact. We must use historical imagination to picture the first contacts between Europeans and American Indians. In these "new" lands, Europeans must have felt 10 feet tall. Here were discoveries to be made, fame and fortune to be won. At the beginning, many Europeans felt confident that Indians could offer little or no effective resistance. How could they resist good Christians, the Europeans asked. Of what use were spears and arrows against soldiers wearing steel and armed with guns and cannons?

It is possible that many Indians believed that the Spaniards, with their prancing war horses and shiny armor, represented the god Quetzalcoatl. The powerful European strangers might have looked down from their huge floating fortresses on the Indians' frail canoes. In contrast to the Indians' simple weapons, the foreigners had flaming, roaring "firesticks" that could strike down an animal or human across great distances.

The Columbian Exchange. In reality, of course, Europeans were not so mighty, and Indians were not so powerless. Each had things to teach and learn. The result was what historian Alfred Crosby, Jr., has called the **Columbian Exchange**. This term refers to the transfer of ideas, plants, animals, and diseases between the Americas and Europe, Africa, and Asia.

Europeans learned vital survival skills from Indians—how to live, travel, hunt, and fight in a different environment. Europeans also gained

Through Others' Eyes

The Race for Empires

Like the English, the French envied the success of the Spanish in the Americas. How, they asked, had Spaniards managed to "steal" the "New World" for themselves when the French could sail and hunt and fight better than any other people? Some French leaders feared that Spain would control the world if other European nations did not build their own colonies overseas. One French scholar of the time explained why his nation decided to enter the colonial race:

"The French above all were spurred [motivated] by a desire to do likewise in areas that had not been reached by [the Spaniards], for the French did not esteem [consider] themselves less than [the Spaniards], neither in navigation . . . nor in any other calling. The French persuaded themselves that [the Spaniards] had not discovered all, and that the world was large enough to reveal even stranger things than those already known."

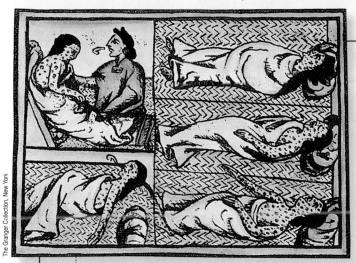

In this book illustration from the 1500s, a medicine man attempts to cure an Aztec of the smallpox he caught from the Spaniards. Diseases were the greatest threat to Indians.

battle trying to resist the European conquest of the Americas. The introduction of European diseases, however, accounted for many more Indian deaths than did Spanish military campaigns.

The germs that caused these diseases came to the Americas from Europe, where people had suffered from them for countless generations. Although many people in Europe died each year from diseases like smallpox, most Europeans had developed considerable immunity to them. The native inhabitants of the Americas lacked such immunity. One European described the result:

> "**Within a few days after our departure from every such town, the people began to die very fast . . . in some towns about 20, in some towns 40, . . . in one six score [120]. The disease also was so strange, that they neither knew what it was, nor how to cure it.**"

There are no records of early Indian populations, so it is difficult to know exactly how many Indians died from European diseases. Estimates of deaths run in the millions.

important new plants, like corn and potatoes, from Indians.

Indians also received new knowledge and material from Europeans. They acquired highly useful devices, like shovels and steel traps, from European settlers.

Disease played a tragic role in the Columbian Exchange. Many Indians died in

Section 3 Review

• Glossary

IDENTIFY and explain the significance of the following: John Cabot, Elizabeth I, Sir Francis Drake, sea dogs, Spanish Armada, Sir Walter Raleigh, charter, Columbian Exchange

LOCATE and explain the importance of the following: Newfoundland, Roanoke Island

• Gazetteer

REVIEWING FOR DETAILS

1. How did England and Spain come into conflict in the Americas and Europe, and what was the result?

2. What kind of efforts did England make to establish a permanent settlement in North America?

3. How did contact with Europeans affect American Indians?

• Time Line

REVIEWING FOR UNDERSTANDING

4. **Geographic Literacy** How did the Europeans both adapt to America's environment and change it?

5. **Critical Thinking:** *Drawing Conclusions* Why do you think the English experienced so much difficulty building a permanent colony on Roanoke Island?

The Columbian Exchange

The exchange of goods across the Atlantic Ocean that Christopher Columbus started in 1492 changed the world forever. Not since the Bering land bridge was covered by water in ancient times had there been any exchange to speak of between the Western Hemisphere (the Americas) and the Eastern Hemisphere (Europe, Asia, and Africa). Plants and animals developed that were unique to each hemisphere.

When people began to journey between the hemispheres they transported goods with them. Many plants and animals we consider "American" today were actually brought over by Europeans, Asians, and Africans. Likewise, many items we now associate with other countries actually originated in the Americas.

The state of Kentucky has long been known as the "Bluegrass State" because of the 8,000-square-mile region where the bluish-green grass grows. Kentucky Bluegrass originated as a European pasture and meadow grass. It was transplanted to North America in the 1700s.

NORTH AMERICA

SOUTH AMERICA

The Americas

Food Plants
corn, white potatoes, tomatoes, pumpkins/squash, beans (navy, lima, kidney, string), peppers (bell, chili), pineapples, peanuts, pecans, cashews, avocados, papayas, cocoa beans, vanilla beans, sweet potatoes, wild rice, cassava roots (tapioca)

Other Plants
cotton, tobacco, marigolds

Animals and Insects
turkeys, hummingbirds, rattlesnakes, gray squirrels, guinea pigs, muskrats, potato beetles

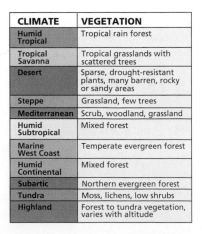

Today dogs and cats are the most common domestic pets in America. For centuries before contact with Europeans, American Indians kept dogs as companions and helpers. People in the Eastern Hemisphere raised both dogs and cats. There were no domestic cats in North America, however, until the first common "house cats" were brought over by Europeans around 1750.

CLIMATE	VEGETATION
Humid Tropical	Tropical rain forest
Tropical Savanna	Tropical grasslands with scattered trees
Desert	Sparse, drought-resistant plants, many barren, rocky or sandy areas
Steppe	Grassland, few trees
Mediterranean	Scrub, woodland, grassland
Humid Subtropical	Mixed forest
Marine West Coast	Temperate evergreen forest
Humid Continental	Mixed forest
Subartic	Northern evergreen forest
Tundra	Moss, lichens, low shrubs
Highland	Forest to tundra vegetation, varies with altitude

NUTRITIONAL VALUE OF CROPS (in millions of calories per acre)

Chief Crops of the Americas		Chief Crops of Europe, Asia and Africa	
Cassava roots (tapioca)	24.45	Rice	18.03
White potatoes	18.56	Oats	13.59
Corn	18.03	Barley	12.60
Sweet potatoes and yams	17.54	Wheat	10.37

Many American plants were more nutritious than were many of the major food crops of Europe, Asia, and Africa. **Human-Environment Interaction:** What effect might raising new crops with higher nutritional values have on the population of a region?

Source: The Columbian Exchange

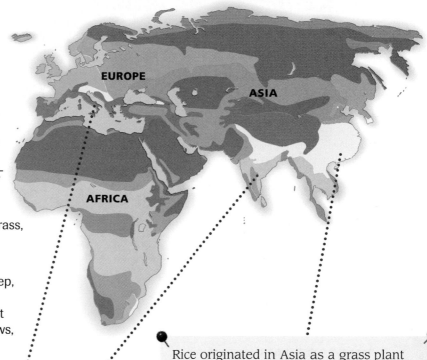

Europe, Asia, and Africa

Food Plants
wheat, oats, barley, soybeans, Asian rice, radishes, lettuce, onions, okra, chickpeas, olives, grapes, peaches, pears, oranges, lemons, coffee, watermelons, bananas, sugarcane

Other Plants
dandelions, crabgrass, couchgrass, bluegrass, roses, daisies

Animals and Insects
cows, horses, hogs, goats, sheep, chickens, rabbits, elephants, house cats, Mediterranean fruit flies, Japanese beetles, sparrows, starlings, mice, rats

Rice originated in Asia as a grass plant and became an important food source throughout the Eastern Hemisphere. Eventually, rice also became a popular food product in the Americas. **Place:** Rice grows particularly well in both East Asia and southeastern North America. Why might that be so?

Many popular Italian and Indian dishes today include tomatoes and peppers, products imported from the Americas. Although tomatoes were transplanted to Europe in the 1500s, few Europeans ate them until after 1800. People thought the colorful plants were poisonous and grew them only for decoration.

To learn more about the Columbian Exchange, go to the interactive map, "The Columbian Exchange," on the CD-ROM.

• **Columbian Exchange**

CHAPTER 3

The English Colonies
(1607–1752)

THEMES IN AMERICAN HISTORY

Global Relations:
How might events in one country affect the founding of colonies overseas?

Cultural Diversity:
Why might a country's colonies develop different cultures?

Geographic Diversity:
How might a region's geography affect the development of a colony?

 • **Video Opener**    • **Skill Builder**

he men, women, and children were sick and weary from their long voyage. Finally, in November 1620, these colonists reached America. One colonist, William Bradford, later described their landing: "They fell upon their knees and blessed the God of Heaven who had brought them over the vast and furious ocean." Bradford wondered, "What could now sustain them but the Spirit of God and His grace?"

image above: *Henry Bacon's* Landing of Pilgrims

Section 1

JAMESTOWN

Multimedia Connections

Explore these related topics and materials on the CD–ROM to enrich your understanding of this section:

 Gazetteer

- Virginia
- Jamestown
- Roanoke Island

 Simulation

- Building a Colony

 Readings

- Colonial Narrative Accounts

 Profiles

- John Rolfe
- John Smith
- Pocahontas

 Media Bank

- John Smith
- Woodlands Indian Pipe
- Population of Jamestown

Before returning to England, Captain Newport made sure that the colonists were settled into the place they had named Jamestown. Just a few days after Newport left, the colony's president, Edward Wingfield, wrote that "an Indian came to us from the great Powhatan with the word of peace." The Powhatan messenger reassured Wingfield "that he desired greatly our friendship . . . that we should sow and reap in peace." Whether the colonists and American Indians could live together peacefully remained to be seen.

As you read this section you will find out:

▶ **How Jamestown was financed.**

▶ **What hardships early settlers faced.**

▶ **What the relationship was between the colonists and the local American Indians.**

Merchant Adventurers

Despite the setback of the failed Roanoke colony, many people in England, particularly wealthy merchants, remained interested in colonization. The experiences of men like Humphrey Gilbert and Walter Raleigh had proven that founding a colony was expensive and risky. Most English merchants and manufacturers were cautious businesspeople, not daring adventurers or court favorites. Instead of outfitting expeditions as individuals, they organized what they called **joint-stock companies**. These companies were ancestors of modern-day corporations. They were owned by many stockholders who shared in the profits and losses.

In 1606 James I, who had become king after the death of Queen Elizabeth I, gave the joint-stock London Company a charter to develop a huge area of North America. The region was named Virginia in honor of Elizabeth, who, because she had never married, was known as the Virgin Queen. By 1609 the London Company's grant of land extended along the Atlantic coast from the Hudson River in present-day New York to North Carolina, and west "from Sea to Sea"—that is, all the way to the Pacific Ocean!

• **New Hopes in America**

The Settlement of Jamestown

A few days before Christmas 1606, three London Company ships set sail for Virginia. The voyage had three purposes—to prepare the way for larger groups of colonists, to search for precious metals, and to find a trade route to East Asia. The ships reached the coast of Virginia in April 1607. They sailed up a river, which the settlers named after King James. Then the 105 men who decided to stay in the new colony built a fort, which they called Jamestown.

From the start, life at Jamestown was an endless series of troubles. The settlement was easy to defend, but it was also swampy and infested with disease-bearing mosquitoes. Illness soon struck the colonists who were already weak and sick from the long ocean voyage. By the end of the summer, almost half of the settlers were dead, and many of the rest were sick with malaria. When the first supply ship arrived in December, fewer than 40 colonists were alive to greet it.

The ship brought 120 more English settlers to Jamestown, but few of the newcomers survived for very long. They were poorly prepared for the challenge of living in a wilderness, and they had few of the practical skills needed by pioneers, such as carpentry and farming. Expecting to find that wealth practically grew on trees, they did not realize that it was necessary to work hard merely to stay alive.

John Smith. Luckily, one colonist, John Smith, had the courage to take command. Smith was a short, bearded man of action. Although he was only in his mid-twenties, Smith had seen far more of the world than had the other settlers. He had fought in several wars against the Turks in

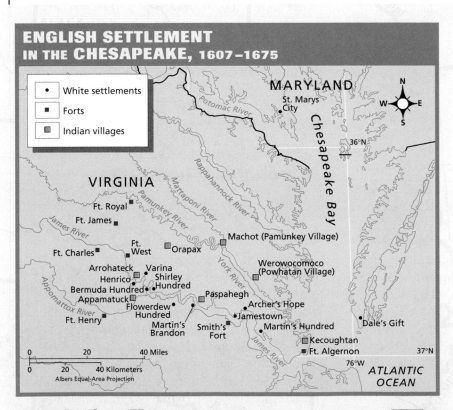

ENGLISH SETTLEMENT IN THE CHESAPEAKE, 1607–1675

- • White settlements
- ■ Forts
- ▢ Indian villages

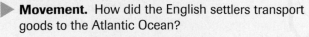

Learning from Maps. Early English settlments and forts often were located near Indian villages. This brought the cultures into close contact, and conflicts frequently erupted.

• **Maps**

▶ **Movement.** How did the English settlers transport goods to the Atlantic Ocean?

NOVA BRITANNIA.

OFFERING MOST

Excellent fruites by Planting in
VIRGINIA.

Exciting all such as be well affected
to further the same.

The London Company continually tried to rebuild Jamestown's declining population by recruiting new settlers. Posters such as this one appealed to potential colonists' hope of financial gain and sense of adventure.

eastern Europe. In one battle, he was captured and sold into slavery. However, he managed to kill his master and escape. After many other remarkable adventures, he found himself in Virginia.

Smith put all his worldly experience and resourcefulness to work in Jamestown. After becoming president of the colony's council in 1608, Smith made hard work and strict discipline the rule. He stopped the colonists from searching for gold and obtained food for them by trading with the 32 tribes of the powerful Powhatan Confederacy.

The Powhatan. The Powhatan possessed the food and knowledge of the land that the colonists lacked. The Indians showed them how to catch fish and how to grow corn. Without this help, Jamestown might not have survived.

In spite of the colonists' need for friendship with the Powhatan, relations between the two groups soon became strained. When the Powhatan no longer wanted to help Jamestown, the settlers forced their cooperation by threatening them. Smith even took food from them at gunpoint! The Powhatan responded by raiding Jamestown and killing settlers who ventured too far into the forest.

Hard Times in Jamestown

In 1609 the London Company again tried to help the struggling colony. It sent about 500 more settlers, including the first women, to Jamestown. This did not solve the colony's problems, however.

The starving time. Conditions in Jamestown continued to worsen. The winter of 1609–10 became known as the "starving time." As Smith described it, there remained only:

> **"sixtie men, women and children, most miserable and poore creatures; and those were preserved for the most part, by roots, herbes, acornes, walnuts, berries, now and then a little fish . . . yea, even the very skinnes of our horses."**

At one point, the colonists almost decided to abandon the settlement and return to England.

Things began to improve in 1611 when Thomas Dale, a military man with a reputation for sternness, arrived to run the colony. During the next five years, Jamestown was more like a military camp than a civilian community.

Around 1619, women started coming to Jamestown in greater numbers. Single women often married male settlers in mass wedding ceremonies.

The Granger Collection, New York

The colonists disliked Dale, but under his leadership they did essential work like plant corn and repair the fort. The colony survived but remained unprofitable.

New hopes. Among their other problems, the colonists struggled to produce something they could sell in Europe. They had hoped to find gold, but there was none. Instead, they found another type of "gold"—a native plant called tobacco.

American Indians had been growing and smoking tobacco for centuries. In the late 1500s Sir Walter Raleigh had made smoking fashionable in English high society. Many people, however, argued that smoking was unhealthy. King James published *Counterblaste to Tobacco,* which criticized smoking as:

> **"This filthie noveltie . . . a custome loath-some [disgusting] to the eye, hatefull to the Nose, harmefull to the braine, [and] dangerous to the Lungs."**

Thousands of English people ignored his warning, and the demand for tobacco soared.

The type of tobacco native to Virginia was too bitter for English taste. Colonist John Rolfe solved that problem in 1612 when he introduced a sweeter variety from the West Indies. The settlers now had something they could sell in England. Large farms called **plantations** gradually developed because of the great profits made by growing tobacco.

Bloodshed in Jamestown

The tobacco economy grew partly because of the relatively peaceful relations with the Powhatan. The tensions between the settlers and the Powhatan had eased in 1614, when John Rolfe married Pocahontas, a daughter of the Powhatan chief. Tobacco farming and the arrival of new settlers in Virginia, however, resulted in demands for more and more Indian land.

The strained relationship between the English and the Powhatan began to worsen, particularly after the deaths of Pocahontas and her father. Pocahontas's uncle, Opechancanough (OH-puh-chan-kuh-noh), then became the new Powhatan leader.

Historians have attempted to piece together Opechancanough's long and fascinating life. They believe that in 1561, when Opechancanough was a

History Makers
Pocahontas

Pocahontas, also known as Matoaka, was one of Jamestown's most famous figures. The daughter of a Powhatan chief, Pocahontas led a life of adventure.

In 1608 her father captured John Smith. The Powhatan were ready to kill him, but Pocahontas begged her father to spare Smith's life. Smith lived to tell the tale of his rescue by the daring 13-year-old.

Later, in 1612, English settlers took Pocahontas hostage to ensure peace with the Powhatan. In Jamestown she converted to Christianity and took the name Rebecca. She also fell in love with tobacco planter John Rolfe. Their marriage in 1614 brought a truce between the Powhatan and the colony. When the newlyweds visited England, Pocahontas was treated with the respect due a princess and was presented to the English king and queen. Tragically, Pocahontas died of smallpox in England at the age of 22.

teenager, Spanish explorer Pedro Menéndez de Avilés stopped in the Chesapeake area. Menéndez was impressed by Opechancanough and persuaded his father to let the youth sail to Spain. He promised that the boy would return with riches.

Over time, the young Indian learned Spanish, became a Catholic, and acquired the Spanish name Don Luis. After many years, he persuaded the authorities to send him back to his homeland as a missionary. He arrived with a group of priests in 1570.

Once back in the Chesapeake area, however, he gave up Christianity. After several conflicts with the priests, he killed them and then changed his name to Opechancanough.

Later, Opechancanough watched the growth of Jamestown with deep concern. By 1620 there were more than 2,000 settlers in the colony. Their increasing numbers were beginning to threaten the Powhatan's control of the region. In 1622 Opechancanough launched a sudden attack that killed almost a third of the settlers, including John Rolfe. War followed, and the English struck back with equal fierceness.

This bloodshed and other problems caused King James to cancel the London Company's charter in 1624. He put Virginia under royal control, but the fighting continued. Finally, in 1644, when Opechancanough was about 100 years old, the English captured and killed him. This ended the last Powhatan resistance.

C. Smith taketh the King of Pamaunkee prisoner 1608

Courtesy of the John Carter Brown Library at Brown University

Some historians believe this sketch—from John Smith's account of his life in Virginia—shows him threatening Opechancanough.

Section 1 Review

• **Glossary**

IDENTIFY and explain the significance of the following: joint-stock companies, James I, John Smith, John Rolfe, plantations, Pocahontas, Opechancanough

LOCATE and explain the importance of the following: Virginia, Jamestown

REVIEWING FOR DETAILS

1. How was settlement in Jamestown financed?
2. How would you describe the relationship between the Virginia colonists and American Indians?

• **Gazetteer**

REVIEWING FOR UNDERSTANDING

3. **Geographic Literacy** What hardships did early settlers in Virginia face?
4. **Writing Mastery:** *Persuading* Imagine that you are a leader of Jamestown during the "starving time." Write a speech convincing the settlers not to abandon the colony.
5. **Critical Thinking:** *Generalizations and Stereotypes* What ideas or opinions might the Virginia colonists have held about American Indians that would have led them to believe they had a right to Indian land?

Section 2

THE NEW ENGLAND COLONIES

Multimedia Connections

Explore these related topics and materials on the CD–ROM to enrich your understanding of this section:

 Gazetteer

- Boston
- Connecticut
- New Hampshire
- Plymouth

 Profiles

- William Bradford

 Readings

- Mayflower Compact

 Biographies

- Anne Bradstreet

 Atlas

- Great Migration

 Media Bank

- Anne Bradstreet
- Founding of Connecticut
- Puritan Meeting House
- Puritan Life
- Puritans in England
- Settling New England

In the 1630s merchant ships leaving for Massachusetts regularly sailed out of the ports of England. Colonists heading for New England packed the decks of ships such as the *Bevis*. In 1638 the *Bevis* sailed from Southampton. On board were Abigail and Benjamin Carpenter from the small village of Hartwell. Their four sons, all under the age of 10 years old, and Benjamin's elderly father traveled with them. Would they survive the voyage and prosper in Massachusetts?

As you read this section you will find out:

▶ **Who the Pilgrims were, and why they came to America.**

▶ **How Puritan communities were organized.**

▶ **What role religion played in New England.**

Religion and Colonization

While many people came to America for economic reasons, others had religious motives. In the early 1500s, almost a century before the first English colonists arrived in Jamestown, a religious movement called the **Reformation** had swept through Europe.

Catholics and Protestants. Before the Reformation, most western Europeans were Catholics. In 1517 Martin Luther, a German monk, published criticisms of many of the Roman Catholic Church's ideas and practices. Thousands of people supported his attempt to reform Catholicism. These protesters became known as Protestants.

Protestants founded a variety of new Christian churches. In England, King Henry VIII established the Church of England, also known

Squanto showed the Pilgrims how to fertilize their fields with fish remains to produce a larger crop yield.

The Granger Collection, New York

as the Anglican Church. The Church of England retained many Catholic ceremonies, including the mass, however.

Some English Protestants thought that the Anglican Church was still too Catholic. They wanted to "purify" it by removing all traces of Catholicism. These people became known as **Puritans**. Even more radical Protestants wanted to separate from the Church of England entirely. These **Separatists**, as they were called, eventually founded **sects**, or new religious groups.

Members of these sects, as well as Catholics, were often persecuted in England because of their beliefs. Some of them began to think of America as a place where they might practice their faith openly.

Pilgrims found Plymouth.

The **Pilgrims** were the first English Separatists to come to America seeking religious freedom. (A pilgrim is someone who has religious motives for making a journey.) They had left England for Holland in 1608 to escape persecution, but life in Holland disappointed them. After they obtained permission to settle within the London Company's grant, they returned to England. In September 1620 a party of 35 Pilgrims and 66 other colonists sailed on the *Mayflower,* bound for Virginia.

They never reached their destination. On November 9 they sighted land on Cape Cod in present-day Massachusetts. A few of the

Pilgrams had read John Smith's description of the area, which he had called New England. They decided to settle on Cape Cod because winter was approaching. They were outside the London Company's grant, so the Pilgrims drew up a document, the **Mayflower Compact**, to provide a legal basis for their colony, which they named Plymouth. As had happened in Jamestown, disease swept through the community. Within six months almost half of the colonists had died.

Fortunately, the Pilgrims had the help of two English-speaking American Indians, Samoset (SAM-uh-set), a Pemaquid Indian, and Squanto (SKWAHN-toh), a Pawtuxet Indian. They taught the Pilgrims how to plant corn, showed them where to hunt and fish, and helped them arrange a peace treaty with the powerful Wampanoag tribe. The Pilgrims worked hard,

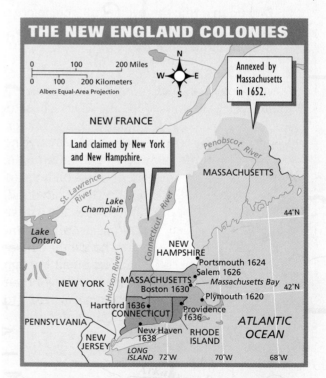

THE NEW ENGLAND COLONIES

0   100   200 Miles
0   100   200 Kilometers
Albers Equal-Area Projection

N W E S

Annexed by Massachusetts in 1652.

NEW FRANCE

Land claimed by New York and New Hampshire.

St. Lawrence River

Lake Champlain

Penobscot River

MASSACHUSETTS

44°N

Lake Ontario

NEW HAMPSHIRE

Connecticut River

Hudson River

Portsmouth 1624
Salem 1626

NEW YORK   **MASSACHUSETTS**   *Massachusetts Bay*   42°N
Boston 1630
Plymouth 1620

Hartford 1636   Providence 1636

PENNSYLVANIA   CONNECTICUT

ATLANTIC OCEAN

New Haven 1638   RHODE ISLAND

NEW JERSEY

LONG ISLAND   72°W   70°W   68°W

Learning from Maps.
Within 20 years, colonists settled throughout New England.

• Maps

▶ **Location.** What town is near the Connecticut River?

planted crops, and in the autumn gathered a good harvest. The settlers then came together to give thanks for their survival.

• Pilgrims

The Puritans

In addition to the Plymouth colony, a few English fishing settlements and trading posts had been established along the New England coast. Large-scale colonization did not begin in the region until the Puritans arrived in the 1630s, however.

Unlike the Separatist Pilgrims, the Puritans wanted only to reform the Anglican Church. But as persecution in England increased, they came to doubt that reform was possible. John Winthrop, a Puritan leader, hoped to build a model Christian community in America:

"We must consider that we shall be like a City upon a Hill; the eyes of all people are on us. . . . We shall be made a story and a byword throughout the world."

In 1629 King Charles I gave a group of Puritan merchants permission to organize a joint-stock company called the Massachusetts Bay Company. One year later, a 17-ship convoy carrying almost 1,000 Puritan men, women, and children arrived in New England. While few of these Puritans were wealthy, most had some education and had enough money to pay for their own passage and to later set themselves up in the new colony.

Anne Pollard immigrated to America when she was a child. She prospered in the Puritan colony, living to be 105 years old.

The climate in Massachusetts was very different from that in Virginia. New England winters were harsh, but the cold weather discouraged the spread of malaria and other diseases that killed so many Virginians. After a difficult first year, the Puritans prospered. Most lived longer than people in England or Virginia.

The colder climate also meant that New Englanders could not grow semitropical crops, such as tobacco. This discouraged the development of large plantations like those in Virginia. Although New England land was stony and hilly, it was very fertile. Many people who lived inland became farmers. Those in seacoast towns often became merchants, craftspeople, or fishermen.

Puritan groups that wanted to found new towns received large tracts of land from the colonial government. They centered their towns around a plot of public grazing land called a **common**. Each town usually had a school and a meetinghouse, which often served as both a church and a town hall. Each

John Winthrop, the first colonial governor of Massachusetts, founded the settlement that became Boston. His son and grandson were both colonial governors of Connecticut.

• John Winthrop

family received a small plot of land for a house. Outside the town lay fields where townspeople grew crops. The rest of the land remained town property, to be given out to new settlers as the town grew.

The Puritans founded several communities centered around their chief town, Boston. By 1640 more than 20,000 people had come to New England. They were part of a movement called the **Great Migration**. They eventually settled other colonies in Connecticut, Rhode Island, New Hampshire, and Long Island, New York.

Church and Community

Puritans believed that they had formed a **covenant**, or sacred agreement, with God to build a society based on the Bible's teachings. They worked and worshiped together, seeking to create such an ideal community. The church, family, education, and government were institutions the Puritans used to create and sustain their vision of a perfect godly society.

The church was the most important part of the Puritan community. On Sundays, everyone was expected to attend. Services, which included praying and listening to long sermons, lasted much of the day.

Unlike the early colonists in Jamestown, who were mostly single men, Puritans encouraged families to emigrate. The head of a family, usually the father, was responsible for making sure that its members lived up to Puritan ideals.

Puritans also used education as a way of maintaining social and religious unity. They wanted everyone to be able to read the Bible and understand Puritan ways. For this reason, Massachusetts required towns with at least 50 families to establish a public school.

Providing well-educated ministers for future generations was particularly important

Global Connections

The Great Migration

The Puritans who went to New England were part of a larger movement known as the Great Migration. Life in England was increasingly difficult for Puritans after 1625. King Charles I forced them out of positions in the Anglican Church and the government. In 1629 he dissolved Parliament and ruled alone for 11 years. During that time some 60,000 Puritans left England. Only about one third went to New England, however. Another 20,000 settled colonies in the Caribbean, and the rest went to other countries in Europe.

While some Puritans built colonies in America, others remained in England to challenge royal authority. When Charles summoned a new Parliament in 1640 to raise taxes, Puritan members demanded reforms. Charles resisted, and England soon plunged into civil war. Parliament's army, led by Puritan Oliver Cromwell, defeated the king in 1646. The Puritans held power in England for the next 12 years. During this time, their colonies in America continued to grow and prosper.

to Puritans. Therefore, in 1636 they founded Harvard, the first college in all the English colonies.

The Puritans discussed community issues at town meetings. This idea of political participation also extended to the colony's government. At first, all political power was in the hands of the General Court, made up of a small group of men from the colony. The General Court, however, soon gave greater privileges, including the right to vote for governor and for members of the Court, to all male church members. This gave Puritans in Massachusetts much more political influence than people had in England at the time.

• Roger
Williams

The Narragansett Indians sheltered Roger Williams after he was exiled. He bought land from them and founded Providence, Rhode Island.

The Granger Collection, New York

Conflicts in New England

Although the Puritans had left England to obtain religious freedom, they did not tolerate **dissenters**, people who disagreed with commonly held opinions. Religious dissenters were no more welcome in the Massachusetts colony than they were in England. Members of other religious sects were often expelled from the colony and sometimes were even executed.

Roger Williams. Even among themselves, Puritans had little liking for disagreement. Roger Williams, a minister, questioned many Puritan ways. He insisted that the colonists

had no right to land in Massachusetts until either they or the king purchased it from local American Indians. To the authorities, Williams's argument threatened the colony's existence.

In 1635 the Massachusetts General Court ordered Williams to leave. He went south and the next year founded Rhode Island. There he put his ideas about religious freedom and fair treatment of Indians into practice. In 1644 he received a charter for his colony.

Anne Hutchinson. Anne Hutchinson led another major dissent against Puritan beliefs. She held meetings in her home to discuss religious questions. For example, she argued that going to church and praying were less important than leading a holy life.

Hutchinson began to attract a number of followers, including important members of the colony. One supporter described her as "a woman that preaches better . . . than any . . . learned scholars." Hutchinson's teachings and popularity greatly alarmed Puritan officials. They felt even more

Anne Hutchinson was tried by the Massachusetts General Court for her religious views. The record of her trial still exists today.

• Anne
Hutchinson

threatened because a woman expressing such independent ideas challenged the authority of Puritan men. One minister called her:

> **"a dangerous instrument of the Devil, raised up by Satan amongst us. . . . The misgovernment of this woman's tongue has been a great cause of this disorder."**

In 1637 Hutchinson was expelled from Massachusetts. She and her followers then joined the Williams group in Rhode Island. Later, she and her six youngest children moved to the Dutch colony of New Netherland. In 1643 she was killed by Indians. Some Puritans believed her death was divine punishment for her sins.

Salem. One of the most extreme examples of the Puritans' attempt to maintain absolute control over their community was in the Salem witch trials of 1692. Like most people in the 1600s, Puritans believed in the existence of witchcraft. The trouble began in Salem when several girls began to act strangely. Three women were accused of bewitching the girls and were arrested. Soon, other townspeople reported that evil forces were tormenting them. Hundreds of people—mostly women—were accused of being witches. Some 30 were found guilty, and 19 were hanged before Governor William Phips stopped the trials and forbade further executions.

The Salem panic severely shook the colony. A few years later, ashamed officials issued a public apology. The Salem witch trials had highlighted some of the worst aspects of Puritan New England—suspicion, intolerance, and the community's pressure on residents to follow a strict code of behavior.

Massachusetts Historical Society

• **Salem Witch Trials**

Cotton Mather was an important minister in Boston. He wrote on religious matters, including this pamphlet, The Wonders of the Invisible World. *His writings and views on witchcraft had an impact on the Salem witch trials.*

Section 2 Review

• **Glossary**

• **Gazetteer**

IDENTIFY and explain the significance of the following: Reformation, Puritans, Separatists, sects, Pilgrims, Mayflower Compact, John Winthrop, common, Great Migration, covenant, dissenters, Roger Williams, Anne Hutchinson

LOCATE and explain the importance of the following: Massachusetts, Rhode Island, Salem

REVIEWING FOR DETAILS

1. Why did the Pilgrims come to America?
2. How did the Puritans organize their communities?
3. What role did religion play in Puritan society?

REVIEWING FOR UNDERSTANDING

4. **Geographic Literacy** Where did the Puritans spread in North America, and why did they move there?
5. **Critical Thinking:** *Cause and Effect* How can the Protestant Reformation be linked to the colonization of America? Explain your answer.

Section 3
THE SOUTHERN COLONIES

Multimedia Connections

Explore these related topics and materials on the CD–ROM to enrich your understanding of this section:

 Gazetteer

- Florida
- Maryland
- Georgia
- North Carolina
- South Carolina

 Readings

- Making the Atlantic Crossing

 Profiles

- James Oglethorpe

 Media Bank

- Colonial Savannah
- Colony of Maryland
- Life in the Carolinas
- Settling the Southern Colonies

n 1669 widows were among the few women who could claim economic independence. Unlike single and married women, widows could own property. To remarry meant that widows would risk losing their independence. Margaret Preston took steps to protect her property before she remarried. Her future husband, William Perry, signed a document guaranteeing that some of her money, a slave, her household goods, and a horse would remain hers to do with as she pleased.

As you read this section you will find out:

▶ **How the Virginia colony developed.**

▶ **What changes Bacon's Rebellion brought to Virginia.**

▶ **What new southern colonies were founded.**

Life in Virginia

Life in Virginia was very different from life in a New England community. There were few towns in Virginia because planters relied on rivers for transporting goods. Oceangoing vessels could sail up the James and other rivers, bringing European products directly to the plantations and taking away cured tobacco for sale in England. The plantations could be widely separated because the buying and selling of goods took place on each planter's dock. There were few schools because the population was so scattered. In fact, most families educated their children at home.

In general, most early Virginia settlers were more concerned with making money than in establishing families. Those interested in forming a family faced several difficulties, including the fact that there were about six times as many men as women. The high death rate also affected family life. It was common for one marriage partner to die and for the surviving partner to marry a second or even a third time.

Children frequently were raised by step-parents or, if orphaned, by strangers. Because life was short and uncertain, most parents were careful to make arrangements for their children in their wills. Colonist Susan English, who had three children, provided:

> **"whereas there wilbe charge in bringing upp the abovesaid Children both for diet Cloathing and scooling I desire . . . that whosoever bringeth upp the children unto the age of discresion [good judgment] with all things necessary and fitting shall have the male cattle for soe long tyme as the Children be with them."**

The London Company realized that families were essential if Virginia was to prosper, so it worked hard to bring over female settlers. Over time men no longer outnumbered women and a stable family life developed.

Labor Problems in Virginia

The London Company campaigned constantly to attract settlers. It gave colonists who paid their own way or that of others 50 acres of land for each "head" (person) transported. This grant was called a **headright**.

Many people who could not afford the cost of passage to America got there by becoming **indentured servants**. They signed contracts called indentures, agreeing to work for a period of time—generally four or five years—to pay for the voyage. These contracts could be bought and sold. About 75 percent of the early Virginia colonists were at one time under indenture.

Indentured servants had to work without wages for whoever owned their indentures.

Life in early Virginia involved hard work for the entire family. Women were usually responsible for child care.

The owner also received the headright for bringing the newcomer to Virginia. In other words, the person who paid the servant's passage received both land and the labor needed to farm it.

When servants completed their time of service, their employers were supposed to provide them with clothes, food, and other basic supplies. In the early years, disease killed more than two thirds of the indentured servants before their contracts expired. Despite the risks, people still came to Virginia in search of economic opportunity.

Indenture was not the only labor system in Virginia. In 1619 a Dutch ship arrived with 20 Africans on board. Historians are not sure whether these first Africans were sold as indentured servants or as slaves. As more Africans were brought to Virginia, however, many were treated as slaves. In this way, race began to be a factor in determining one's status in the colony, and the institution of slavery took root in Virginia.

Until the 1690s planters preferred indentured servants to enslaved Africans as a labor source, in part because it cost much more to buy a slave. However, planters soon found that using indentured servants had drawbacks.

Once the servants worked off their debt, many became independent planters who competed with their former employers.

The newly independent planters often found that they only had access to poor land. In addition, the increase in crop production caused the price of tobacco to fall. This left many small planters in debt and dissatisfied. They had come to America seeking a better way of life but were not getting what they expected.

Bacon's Rebellion

The discontent of small planters in Virginia erupted in 1676. They had begun to eye land that was guaranteed to the Powhatan in a 1646 treaty. Fighting soon broke out between the farmers and the Indians. Nathaniel Bacon, a newcomer to the colony, raised a large force and asked the governor of Virginia, Sir William Berkeley, to authorize him to begin a war with the Indians. Berkeley, however, wanted to keep peace with the Indians and refused Bacon's request.

Defying the governor, Bacon's force massacred peaceful Indians and attacked others at random. When Berkeley declared him a rebel, Bacon and his men turned against the government. Bacon drove the governor out of Jamestown and burned the town. In October 1676, however, Bacon became ill and died, and **Bacon's Rebellion** soon collapsed.

The Granger Collection, New York

Nathaniel Bacon (right) confronts Sir William Berkeley (left), Virginia's governor. Bacon was only 29 years old when he led the rebellion against Berkeley's government.

Although the rebellion failed to get more land for the settlers, it led to major changes in Virginia. In 1619 most male settlers had been given the right to vote for representatives to an assembly called the **House of Burgesses**. This was the first elected English governmental body in the colonies. Since 1661, however, Berkeley had refused to call an election. As a result of Bacon's Rebellion, new elections finally were held.

The rebellion also contributed to increased use of enslaved Africans by many tobacco farmers. Planters became less willing to employ indentured servants who might later become troublemakers like Bacon's rebels. Instead, planters increasingly used slaves, who could never become economic competitors. Planters also realized that the children of slaves would provide labor for the future.

Slavery was common in the Spanish and English colonies in the Caribbean. In early Virginia, some Africans were enslaved. Others, however, were indentured servants who would eventually become independent planters.

Colonial Williamsburg Foundation

Gradually, Virginia became almost entirely dependent on slave labor.

New Colonies in the South

Although it had a shaky start, Virginia was much more stable by the mid-1630s. By 1641 the colony's population had reached 7,500 and tobacco exports were topping 1 million pounds a year. Virginia's prosperity encouraged other English developers to found new colonies in the region.

Maryland. In 1632 King Charles I gave several million acres of land around Chesapeake Bay to a Catholic noble named George Calvert, Lord Baltimore. Most colonies were controlled by joint-stock companies. Lord Baltimore, however, was the **proprietor**, or single owner, of his colony.

In 1634 the first settlers arrived in the colony, which was named Maryland after Queen Mary, the wife of Charles I. After Calvert died, his son, Cecilius, Second Lord Baltimore, founded Maryland as a refuge for Catholics, but Protestants were also admitted. The Maryland **Toleration Act of 1649** guaranteed religious freedom to all Christians.

Although the death rate among the early settlers was high, life in Maryland was somewhat easier than it had been for the first colonists at Jamestown. The Maryland colony was successful because its settlers carefully planned their activities and avoided many of the mistakes that Jamestown colonists had made. Following the example of the Virginia planters, the settlers in Maryland turned to growing tobacco.

The Carolinas. In 1663 Charles II, who had become king after the death of his father, gave the land between Virginia and Spanish Florida to eight noblemen, including Sir George Carteret. The proprietors called this colony Carolina, Latin for "Charles." They hoped to attract settlers from the more established colonies. Although a number of Virginians did drift into the northern part of

the grant, settlement there was scattered. There were few roads and practically no towns, churches, or schools.

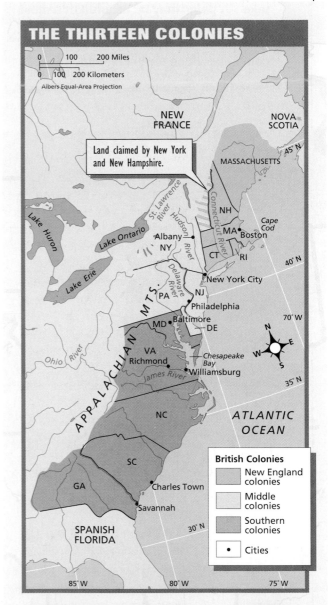

THE THIRTEEN COLONIES

Land claimed by New York and New Hampshire.

British Colonies
- New England colonies
- Middle colonies
- Southern colonies
- • Cities

Learning from Maps. English settlements filled the Atlantic coast between the borders of Spanish Florida and New France.

• Maps

▶ **Movement.** What geographical barrier stopped westward expansion in the southern colonies?

The proprietors then brought settlers from the West Indies to the southern part of their grant, promising them that:

> **"any man whatever that is but willing to take . . . pains may be assured of a most comfortable subsistence [life], and . . . raise his fortunes far beyond what he could ever hope for in England."**

Charles Town (now Charleston) was founded in 1670. It soon became a busy trading center, as well as the social and political center of the new colony.

In 1719, however, the settlers rebelled against the proprietors' government and asked the king to take control of the colony. Ten years later the area was officially separated into two royal colonies, North and South Carolina.

Georgia. The last of the southern colonies was not founded until 1733. A group of charitable Englishmen, led by James Oglethorpe, hoped Georgia would be a colony where debtors and other poor people could make a new start in life.

Few English settlers came to Georgia, however. Some prospective settlers feared the Spanish, who also claimed the region. Others resented Oglethorpe's strict rules, which included bans on liquor and slaves. In 1752 the colony's trustees turned Georgia over to the Crown.

Maryland Historical Society, Baltimore

In 1648 Margaret Brent became the first woman to demand the vote in the English colonies. A major landowner, she was active in colonial affairs and served as attorney for important colonists.

Section 3 Review

IDENTIFY and explain the significance of the following: headright, indentured servants, Bacon's Rebellion, House of Burgesses, proprietor, Cecilius Calvert, Toleration Act of 1649, James Oglethorpe

• **Glossary**

LOCATE and explain the importance of the following: Maryland, Charles Town, North Carolina, South Carolina, Georgia

REVIEWING FOR DETAILS

1. How did Bacon's Rebellion change life in Virginia?

• **Gazetteer**

2. What new southern colonies were founded, and why?

REVIEWING FOR UNDERSTANDING

3. **Geographic Literacy** How did the geography of Virginia influence the colony's development?

4. **Writing Mastery:** *Creating* Imagine that you are a proprietor of a colony. Create an advertisement to attract settlers.

5. **Critical Thinking:** *Making Comparisons* What were the major differences between the Virginia and Massachusetts colonies?

Section 4
THE MIDDLE COLONIES

Multimedia Connections

Explore these related topics and materials on the CD–ROM to enrich your understanding of this section:

 Media Bank

- Life in Colonial New York
- Settling the Middle Colonies

 Atlas

- Middle Colonies

 Profiles

- William Penn

 Gazetteer

- New York
- New Jersey
- Pennsylvania
- Delaware

Four English warships anchored in the harbor. The Dutch waited to see if the ships would fire on the town. The arrival of the English was not unexpected. Other countries had threatened New Netherland before, but up until now the Dutch had managed to drive out the Swedish and hold off the English. Governor Peter Stuyvesant (STY-vi-suhnt) was determined to unite the New Netherland colonists and fight off the enemy. Tension mounted as a crowd of colonists gathered in the harbor.

As you read this section you will find out:

▶ **How New Netherland became New York.**

▶ **Why Pennsylvania was settled.**

▶ **What colonies were created from parts of New York and Pennsylvania.**

England Seizes the Dutch Colonies

The English claimed the entire area between Newfoundland and Florida on the basis of John Cabot's 1497 voyage. They considered the Dutch in their colony of New Netherland to be intruders on English soil. The fact that Dutch merchants were buying Virginia tobacco and selling it elsewhere irritated English tobacco merchants, who felt that the tobacco trade was rightfully theirs.

In 1664 King Charles II gave his brother James, the Duke of York, a grant that included New Netherland. Then he sent four English warships to attack the colony's capital of New Amsterdam.

New Netherland was governed by Peter Stuyvesant, a colorful character with a long military career. In one battle, he had been wounded in the right leg, which had to be amputated. As a result, he walked on a decorated wooden leg.

For 17 years, Stuyvesant ruled New Netherland. Because its settlers came from many regions, numerous languages were spoken there. This diversity sometimes created cultural conflicts. New Netherland also had financial troubles. Over the years, Stuyvesant's attempts to raise taxes and to create a solidly Dutch society angered some of the colonists.

When the English warships arrived in 1664, New Amsterdam's inhabitants pushed Stuyvesant aside and surrendered the town without firing a shot. Most of the residents, including ex-governor Stuyvesant, continued to live in the colony, which was renamed New York in honor of James of York.

James then handed out generous land grants to his friends. The largest grant, which included all the land between the Hudson and Delaware Rivers, went to Sir George Carteret, who had just become one of the proprietors of Carolina, and to Lord John Berkeley. This grant became the colony of New Jersey.

To attract settlers, Carteret and Berkeley offered land on easy terms. They also promised settlers religious freedom and the right to elect a legislature. In the 1670s members of a

The Wrath of Peter Stuyvesant, painting by Asher B. Durand from The Collection of The New-York Historical Society.

Peter Stuyvesant, the governor of New Netherland, had a commanding presence. He had spent much of his life in leadership positions in military and political service.

● **Peter Stuyvesant**

religious sect known as **Quakers** purchased the western part of the colony. The proprietors sold the rest of the colony in 1684. In 1702 the two sections were combined.

Quakers Found Colonies

In 1681 Charles II awarded another large grant in America to an unlikely candidate, William Penn. Although he was wealthy and of high social status, Penn was also a Quaker.

William Penn took an active role in the founding of his colony. He visited it twice, making sure that the colony was developing as he had planned. One of his most important accomplishments was the signing of the treaty shown in this painting. Penn's treaty with these American Indians established a friendly relationship between the colonists and their Indian neighbors.

Quakers stressed religious tolerance, simplicity, and kindness toward others. They were opposed to warfare and any use of force. They also emphasized the authority of the individual in religious, social, and political matters. Because of this belief, many English people thought the Quakers were religious radicals. Therefore, Quakers were often imprisoned, tortured, or even hanged.

To protect Quakers from such persecution, Penn wanted to create a refuge for them in America. Charles II was agreeable because he owed a large sum of money to Penn's father, who had died in 1670. To cancel this debt, Charles gave Penn the region between New Jersey and Maryland, suggesting that it be called Pennsylvania in honor of Penn's father.

Penn was deeply religious. He decided to make Pennsylvania "a holy experiment" in Christian living and self-government. In his plan for the settlement of the colony, Penn declared:

"**Governments, like clocks, go from the motion men give them; and as governments are made and moved by men, so by them they are ruined. . . . Let men be good, and the government cannot be bad; if it be ill, they will cure it.**"

Like Roger Williams, Penn insisted that Indians be paid for their land and be treated fairly by the colonists. Unlike most proprietors, Penn came to America to oversee the laying-out of his colony's capital, Philadelphia, an ancient name meaning "brotherly love."

To attract settlers to his colony, Penn wrote glowing accounts of its soil and climate and circulated them throughout Europe. These, along with his promises of a voice in government and religious liberty, lured settlers from many lands. Among them were large numbers of Germans, who became known as the Pennsylvania Dutch because of the way English settlers pronounced *Deutsch*, meaning "German."

Pennsylvania prospered from the beginning. Farmers produced large crops of wheat and other foodstuffs. In 1682 Penn obtained another grant of land on Delaware Bay. When Pennsylvania expanded westward, this region received the right to have its own colonial assembly in 1704. It eventually became the colony of Delaware.

Section 4 Review

• Glossary

IDENTIFY and explain the significance of the following: Peter Stuyvesant, Quakers, William Penn

LOCATE and explain the importance of the following: New York, New Jersey, Pennsylvania, Philadelphia (See the map on page 55.)

• Gazetteer

REVIEWING FOR DETAILS
1. How and why did England take the Dutch colony of New Netherland?
2. Why was Pennsylvania founded?

REVIEWING FOR UNDERSTANDING

• Time Line

3. **Geographic Literacy** What colonies were created from New York and Pennsylvania?
4. **Writing Mastery:** *Informing* Write a paragraph telling settlers what to expect if they come to William Penn's colony.
5. **Critical Thinking:** *Making Comparisons* How was English treatment of Dutch settlers in New Netherland similar to English treatment of American Indians in the colonies? How did treatment of the two groups differ?

CHAPTER 4

Colonial Life and Government (1650–1763)

THEMES IN AMERICAN HISTORY

Constitutional Heritage:
How might one society's system of government influence another's?

Economic Development:
How might trade affect government policies and foreign relations?

Democratic Values:
How might shared experiences help create a common culture?

In 1729 writer Daniel Defoe described the great importance of international trade:

"**How miserable, how dejected [sad], do a People look, (however prosperous before,) if by any Accident of an unprosperous *War*, or an *ill manag'd Peace*, Trade receives a Blow! And how cheerfully do men Fight in a War, and Work in a Peace, if the Channels of Trade are but kept open, and a free Circulation of Business is preserved!**"

• Video Opener

• Skill Builder

image above: *A colonial family*

Section 1

THE ENGLISH COLONIAL SYSTEM

Multimedia Connections

Explore these related topics and materials on the CD–ROM to enrich your understanding of this section:

 Gazetteer

• Boston, Massachusetts

 Media Bank

• Virginia House of Burgesses
• Regional Trade
• Colonial City
• English History, 1625–1765

 Readings

• Frontier and City Life

Early one April morning in 1689, a group of angry citizens gathered in Boston. They planned to rebel against new laws that English officials had forced on them without their consent. The colonists were upset because they had come to expect a certain degree of freedom in governing their own affairs. Although colonial policies were still shaped by the needs of the Crown, in general England allowed the colonists to rule themselves.

As you read this section you will find out:

▶ **Who carried out the English Crown's policies in the colonies.**

▶ **Why the Dominion of New England failed.**

▶ **How the English government tried to control trade in the colonies.**

Governing the Colonies

Technically, the English colonies belonged to the king or queen personally, not to the government. Of course, the king or queen did not personally manage the affairs of the colonies. Colonial policy was set by the royal advisers, who made up what was called the **Privy Council**. This council, in turn, was subject to **Parliament**, the lawmaking body of England.

Each colony also had a government that carried out English policies and enforced the laws of England. Colonial governments were modeled after the English government and attended to all sorts of local matters that were of no direct concern to England. At the head of each colony was a governor who represented the king and made sure that English laws were enforced. Some governors were American-born, but most were sent over from England.

The Granger Collection, New York

Sir Richard Onslow leads a meeting of the English House of Commons in London's Westminster Hall around 1700.

Colonial governors received orders and policies from London and put them into effect. When local problems arose, however, the government had the power to handle them directly.

Governors were assisted by councils that had roughly the same powers and duties that the Privy Council had in England. In most of the colonies, members of the councils were appointed, not elected by the voters.

Elected bodies made local laws. These colonial assemblies, or legislatures, were modeled on the House of Commons, the elected branch of Parliament. On paper, they had only limited powers. The colonial governor or the government in England could cancel any law passed by a colonial assembly.

In practice, however, the assemblies had a great deal of power. Since they set taxes in the colonies, the assemblies controlled how money was raised and spent. Frequently, this power to tax and spend gave a colonial assembly control over the governor. For example, an assembly could refuse to spend money on projects that the governor wanted unless he agreed to approve laws that the assembly supported. An assembly might even attach a sentence providing money for the governor's salary to a bill he had threatened to disallow, or cancel. Then if the governor disallowed the bill, he did not get paid!

Governors, however, could call the assemblies into session and dismiss them without explanation. A governor could also order new elections for the legislators. The governor could not, however, make the legislators pass a law that a majority did not want to support.

The Dominion of New England

Most colonists liked the fact that England's empire was divided into so many separate parts. The system allowed each colony a great deal of control over its own affairs. But English leaders felt differently. They believed that combining the colonies into a few regional groups would make them easier to manage.

The most serious attempt to unify a group of colonies occurred after the death of King Charles II in 1685. Since Charles had no children who could be heirs to the throne, his brother James became king. In 1686 James created the **Dominion of New England**, which included Connecticut, Massachusetts, Rhode Island, and New Hampshire. Two years later, New York and New Jersey were added.

Sir Edmund Andros, a soldier who had formerly been colonial governor of New York, was appointed governor of the Dominion. Andros had a great deal of power. He could enact laws on his own, including tax laws. He ruled almost like a dictator, deciding by himself most questions of importance.

The colonists in the Dominion resented this loss of their independence. One angry New Englander described what life was like under Andros:

"It was now plainly affirmed [declared true], both by some in open Council, and by the same in private . . . , that the people in New England were all slaves, and the only difference between them and slaves is their not being bought and sold."

Fortunately for the citizens of the Dominion, Andros did not last very long. King James II proved to be extremely unpopular in England. He ignored laws that Parliament had passed and adopted a strongly pro-Catholic policy that alarmed many Protestants.

When James's second wife, Queen Mary of Modena, gave birth to a son who would be raised a Catholic, leaders in Parliament staged a revolt that soon became known as the **Glorious Revolution**. They invited James's Protestant daughter Mary and her Dutch husband, William of Orange, to be crowned king and queen of England.

James fled first to France and then to Ireland. Meanwhile, William and Mary crossed the English Channel from the Netherlands in November 1688 to take the throne. News of the Glorious Revolution did not reach Boston until the following April, but when word finally arrived, it encouraged the colonists to take action. Angry colonists arrested Andros and other Dominion officials. Leading citizens took over the government. The Dominion soon fell apart. English authorities gave up the idea of a united Dominion of New England.

The Navigation and Trade Acts

Although the colonists enjoyed a great deal of local self-government, the English continued to establish general policies for their American possessions. Colonies were expected to benefit the countries that owned them. One way the colonies did this was by strengthening their home country's **balance of trade**, the

• Dominion

Many colonists were pleased when William and Mary were crowned the new rulers of England. This 1689 woodcutting illustrating their coronation was re-created on song-sheets and other items celebrating the event.

The Granger Collection, New York

Goods came in and out of busy shipping ports like this one in Bristol Quay, England. The men in this picture are probably unloading sugar products.

relationship between what a nation buys from and what it sells to foreign countries (not including its own colonies). The goal was to maintain a favorable balance of trade—to **export**, or sell, more than it would **import**, or buy, from other countries.

Regulating trade. The economic program designed to achieve a favorable balance of trade was called **mercantilism**. Mercantilists hoped to maintain their country's wealth by tightly controlling trade. To make sure that the colonies produced and sold things that England needed, Parliament passed many laws regulating the buying and selling of goods. These laws were known as the **Navigation and Trade Acts**. The first act was passed in 1651, and they continued to be enacted up through the mid-1700s.

These regulations required that all goods passing between England and the colonies be transported in ships built either in the colonies or in England. The owners of the ships also had to be English or American, as did the captain and most of the crew. For example,

a Boston merchant could own a ship made in Philadelphia or London and carry goods from Virginia to New York or to any port in England or the English West Indies. The merchant, however, could not use a Dutch-made ship or hire a French captain.

European goods could be brought into the American colonies only after being taken to an English port. American colonists could import French wine, for instance, but it had to be taken to England first. Of course, once in England the wine could only be carried to the colonies in an English or colonial ship.

Colonial producers could sell certain products only within English territory. These **enumerated articles**, as they were called, were things that England needed but could not produce at home. Sugar, tobacco, furs, timber, and cotton were among the most important enumerated articles. The restrictions on these goods applied to both the colonies and to England. English sugar planters in the West Indies and tobacco planters in Virginia and Maryland could not sell their crops in France, Spain, or the Netherlands. In return, consumers in England could not buy sugar or tobacco produced in the French, Spanish, or Dutch colonies. Many colonial products, such as fish and wheat, were not enumerated because England already produced enough of them. Colonists could sell them anywhere.

Parliament also put restrictions on a few colonial handmade products that competed with similar English goods. For example, colonists could make fur hats and woolen cloth for local sale, but they were not allowed to export these products.

The English argued that these laws were fair to both the home country and the colonists. If the colonies produced raw materials that England needed, and if England manufactured items that the colonies needed, each would benefit.

Smuggling in the colonies.

This trade system worked reasonably well for many decades. The success of the trading system was partly because most colonists were farmers, and many others worked as fishers, shipbuilders, or merchants. These colonists did not produce large amounts of manufactured goods. England, on the other hand, was one of the leading producers of manufactured goods in the world.

The Navigation and Trade Acts were not enforced very strictly, however, and smuggling was common. The colonies were far from England. America had a long coastline with many out-of-the-way harbors and tiny coves where small ships could slip in under cover of night and unload illegal goods.

For many years the English government did not try very hard to prevent smuggling. England was getting all the colonial products it needed. It hardly seemed worth the cost and effort to stop shippers who tried to sneak past the English navy with tobacco bound for the West Indies, or with French wine or silk that had not been taken first to England. Thus, while on paper the English government had great power, in practice it allowed the colonies a great deal of independence.

Many colonial American women spun their own yarn from wool. Since wool was an enumerated article, colonists could not export any extra yarn or cloth they produced. They could sell such products locally, however.

Courtesy of the Free Library of Philadelphia

Section 1 Review

• Glossary

IDENTIFY and explain the significance of the following: Privy Council, Parliament, Dominion of New England, Edmund Andros, Glorious Revolution, balance of trade, export, import, mercantilism, Navigation and Trade Acts, enumerated articles

REVIEWING FOR DETAILS
1. Who was responsible for carrying out the Crown's policies in the colonies?
2. Why was the Dominion of New England unsuccessful?
3. How did the English government try to control colonial trade?

REVIEWING FOR UNDERSTANDING
4. **Writing Mastery:** *Expressing* Imagine that you are a citizen of the Dominion of New England. Write a letter to a member of Parliament expressing why you are unhappy living under the Dominion.
5. **Critical Thinking:** *Drawing Conclusions* Overall, do you think the Navigation and Trade Acts limited the colonial economy? Explain your answer.

Section 2

THE COLONIAL ECONOMY

Multimedia Connections

Explore these related topics and materials on the CD–ROM to enrich your understanding of this section:

 Media Bank

- Colonial Exports
- Colonial Tobacco
- West Indies Sugar Production

 Gazetteer

- West Africa
- British West Indies
- Great Britain

 Readings

- Slavery in the West Indies

 Profiles

- Eliza Lucas Pinckney

 Atlas

- Atlantic Slave Trade
- British West Indies

One of the first truly "self-made" Americans was the multitalented Benjamin Franklin. He started his career at age 12, working in a print shop. At 42 he was rich enough to retire from his business. In his essay "Advice to a Young Tradesman," Franklin explained how to earn a fortune in America. "The way to wealth," he wrote, ". . . is as plain as the way to market." Franklin's words were timely indeed. By the mid-1700s commerce was becoming a key to prosperity in the colonies.

As you read this section you will find out:

▶ **What the major economic products of the colonies were.**

▶ **Why trade networks developed.**

▶ **What life was like on the Middle Passage.**

The Southern Economy

The colonists needed manufactured goods such as farm tools, furniture, guns and ammunition, pots and pans, books, and glassware. They had to get most of these goods by producing crops that England or other countries could use. Crops that farmers raise in large quantities to sell are called **staple crops**.

The southern colonies had an advantage in growing staple crops because of their warm climate. Tobacco provided a staple crop for the colonists of Virginia, Maryland, and North Carolina. When American tobacco first became popular in England, its price was very high. For a time, anyone with even a small plot of land could make a good living growing tobacco. Although tobacco prices eventually fell, farmers were still able to make good profits from the crop.

In parts of South Carolina and later in Georgia, rice was the chief staple crop. Since rice needs plenty of water, it grew well in the swamps and low-lying lands along the Atlantic coast. The fields were flooded by building locks and dams to trap river water.

Slaves provided the main source of labor in the rice fields. Plantation owners tried to purchase slaves from West Africa. West African farmers were highly skilled and knowledgeable about growing rice. West Africans also seemed to have more resistance to the tropical diseases common in the rice fields.

South Carolina farmers also grew indigo, a plant that produced a blue dye used by English cloth manufacturers. Indigo was first grown in the South by Eliza Lucas (later Pinckey), whose father was a colonial official in the English West Indies. While still in her teens, Lucas ran three large plantations owned by her father.

Lucas experimented with many crops. It took her several years to perfect southern indigo. By 1746, however, she and other South Carolina planters were exporting 40,000 pounds of the crop. The following year that amount more than doubled.

The Northern Economy

The economy of the northern colonies was more diverse than that of the southern colonies. The climate from Pennsylvania to Massachusetts Bay and New Hampshire was too cold to grow most of the southern staple crops. Throughout most of the colonial period, there was no demand in Europe for wheat and other grains that grew well in the northern colonies.

One northern product that *was* highly valued in Europe was fur. Colonists hunted and trapped beavers, raccoons, foxes, and other animals for their own use, for sale locally, and for export. They sold the pelts in Europe, where they were made primarily into coats or hats. In addition, the colonists traded with the Indians for furs.

Northerners also did a great deal of fishing to earn a living, particularly in the waters off Newfoundland. Many English sailors fished that area too, so there was no market in England for fish exported from the colonies. However, dried and salted fish could be sold easily in southern Europe for good profits, and fish was not an enumerated article.

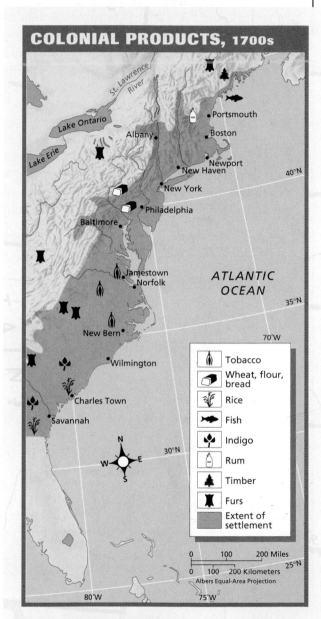

COLONIAL PRODUCTS, 1700s

Legend:
- Tobacco
- Wheat, flour, bread
- Rice
- Fish
- Indigo
- Rum
- Timber
- Furs
- Extent of settlement

0   100   200 Miles
0   100   200 Kilometers
Albers Equal-Area Projection

Learning from Maps.
The thirteen colonies provided Great Britain with a wide variety of raw materials.

• Maps

▶ **Region.** What were the southern colonies' greatest resources?

Shipbuilding and foreign commerce were also important economic activities in the northern colonies. Merchants and shipowners in Boston, New York, and Philadelphia competed vigorously with English shippers for the trade with Europe. Northern cities such as New York and Boston also became centers of the slave trade in the mainland colonies.

This northern concentration on trade developed because northern colonists generally produced much more food than they could eat. Since there was no market for American grain in England, they began to look elsewhere for buyers. The most promising market seemed to be the sugar-producing islands of the West Indies. From there a complex system of trade developed that linked many parts of Great Britain's empire. (In 1707 England and Scotland united to form the United Kingdom of Great Britain.)

Trade Networks and Slavery

The islands in the Caribbean were all small. Nearly every acre of the fertile soil in these islands was devoted to raising sugarcane. Since producing sugar required a great deal of labor, the islands were heavily populated, mostly by enslaved Africans. This large population required large amounts of food.

Most sugar planters drove their slaves mercilessly. Many slaves were literally worked to death. As a result, West Indian plantation owners also needed a constant supply of new slaves from Africa.

Colonial merchants and ship captains soon discovered that they could make good profits by shipping grain and fish to the sugar islands. Merchants also sold cattle for plowing and hauling, and lumber for building. They could invest their profits in sugar and carry it to England. Then the merchants could buy English manufactured goods for sale at home for yet another profit.

Complex trade networks soon developed, linking the northern colonies, England, the sugar islands, the southern colonies, and Africa. There were many types of trade routes. For example, American merchants frequently bought molasses in the West Indies instead of sugar. Molasses is what is left over after the sugar has been boiled out of sugarcane juice. It was considered almost a waste product in the islands and so it was very inexpensive.

The Americans took this molasses to the mainland, most often to Rhode Island and Massachusetts, where it was

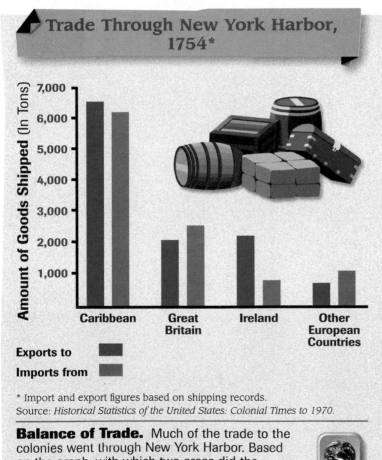

Trade Through New York Harbor, 1754*

Amount of Goods Shipped (In Tons)

7,000 / 6,000 / 5,000 / 4,000 / 3,000 / 2,000 / 1,000

Caribbean | Great Britain | Ireland | Other European Countries

Exports to
Imports from

* Import and export figures based on shipping records.
Source: *Historical Statistics of the United States: Colonial Times to 1970.*

Balance of Trade. Much of the trade to the colonies went through New York Harbor. Based on the graph, with which two areas did the colonies seem to be maintaining a favorable balance of trade in 1754?

• Graphs

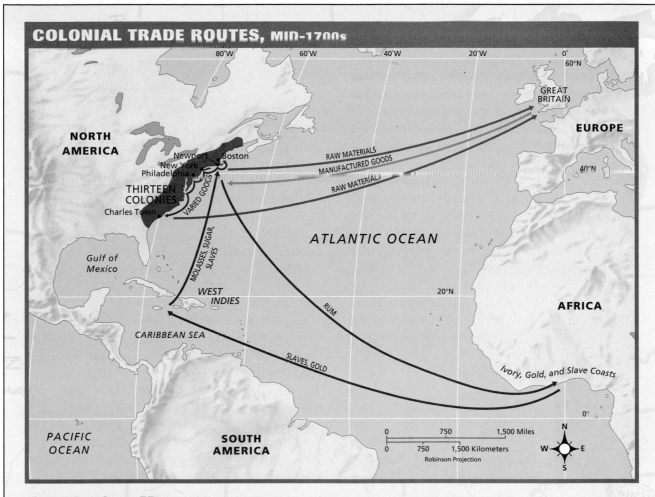

COLONIAL TRADE ROUTES, MID-1700s

NORTH AMERICA

Newport · Boston
New York
Philadelphia

THIRTEEN COLONIES

Charles Town

Gulf of Mexico

WEST INDIES

CARIBBEAN SEA

PACIFIC OCEAN

SOUTH AMERICA

ATLANTIC OCEAN

GREAT BRITAIN

EUROPE

AFRICA

Ivory, Gold, and Slave Coasts

RAW MATERIALS
MANUFACTURED GOODS
RAW MATERIALS
VARIED GOODS
MOLASSES, SUGAR, SLAVES
RUM
SLAVES, GOLD

0   750   1,500 Miles
0   750   1,500 Kilometers
Robinson Projection

Learning from Maps. The thirteen colonies exported raw materials such as timber, tobacco, and furs to Great Britain. The colonies took the molasses and sugar they imported from the West Indies and made them into rum, which the colonists then shipped to Africa.

▶ **Region.** What did Great Britain export?

• Maps

made into rum, a powerful liquor. The rum was then shipped to West Africa, where it was traded for slaves. The slaves, in turn, were taken to the West Indies.

The Middle Passage

The transporting of enslaved Africans to the Americas was called the **Middle Passage**. This trip, which normally took between six and nine weeks, was a horrifying experience for the Africans. Most captains packed as many Africans as possible below deck. Although Parliament set limits on the number of slaves

that could be carried on the ships, such regulations were rarely enforced.

On some ships there was hardly any room for the chained people to move once they were all below deck. Under such conditions, the death toll was often very high, particularly if smallpox or some other disease broke out. Olaudah Equiano (oh-LOW-duh ek-wee-AHN-oh), a slave who later bought his freedom, recalled his experience on the Middle Passage around 1755:

"The closeness of the place and the heat of the climate, added to the number in the

ship, which was so crowded that each had scarcely room to turn himself, almost suffocated us. . . . The air soon became unfit for respiration from a variety of loathsome [disgusting] smells, and brought on a sickness among the slaves, of which many died. . . . The shrieks of the women and the groans of the dying rendered [made] the whole a scene of horror."

On some ships nearly half the Africans died before reaching the colonies. Many who survived the passage never fully recovered their health. Some historians estimate that less than half of the more than 10 to 15 million people removed from Africa ever became useful workers in the Americas. The others either died during the passage or were disabled for the rest of their lives.

This cutaway of a slave ship shows how the crew planned to pack as many enslaved Africans as possible in the hold below deck. Many people died as the result of this "tight-pack" system.

• Middle Passage

Overcrowding could be bad business as well as terribly cruel and inhumane. Contagious disease on board ship could strike enslaved Africans as well as captains and crew. Despite the death rate on the Middle Passage, however, the trade networks proved very profitable for most of the merchants involved. Profits ranged anywhere from 10 to 100 percent. To those Europeans and colonists involved in the slave trade, African lives were far less important than the money the traders made.

Sailor and former slave Olaudah Equiano wrote a book about his life entitled Equiano's Travels.

• Equiano

Section 2 Review

IDENTIFY and explain the significance of the following: staple crops, Eliza Lucas, Middle Passage, Olaudah Equiano

• Glossary

REVIEWING FOR DETAILS
1. What major economic goods were produced by the southern colonies and the northern colonies?
2. Why did colonial trade networks develop?

REVIEWING FOR UNDERSTANDING
3. **Geographic Literacy** Why did the northern colonies not grow large amounts of tobacco, indigo, and rice?
4. **Writing Mastery:** *Describing* Imagine that you are an enslaved African transplanted to the colonies. Write a paragraph describing your experiences on the Middle Passage.
5. **Critical Thinking:** *Synthesizing Information* If most slaves wound up in southern colonies, how did northern cities such as New York and Boston become centers of the slave trade?

Section 3

AN AMERICAN CULTURE

Multimedia Connections

Explore these related topics and materials on the CD–ROM to enrich your understanding of this section:

 Media Bank

- Colonial Population
- Orrery
- Benjamin Franklin
- Sir Issac Newton

 Biographies

- Benjamin Banneker

 Profiles

- Jonathan Edwards

 Readings

- Religion in the Colonies
- Sermons of the Great Awakening
- Franklin's Kite Experiment

George Whitefield lifted his finger and paused. The crowd grew tense. Then a clap of thunder crashed. Whitefield fell to his knees in prayer. When the storm passed, the sun revealed a magnificent rainbow. This dramatic scene in 1740 was one of many that took place after George Whitefield arrived from Europe to spread Christianity. This religious movement, along with many new scientific ideas from Europe, challenged how colonists viewed the world around them.

As you read this section you will find out:

▶ **What impact the Great Awakening had on the colonies.**

▶ **How the Scientific Revolution shaped American thought and culture.**

▶ **How colonists gained an education with few schools available.**

The Great Awakening

The Christian religion had played an important part in the founding of several colonies and in the lives of many colonists, particularly the Quakers and the Puritans. In other areas, however, religious faith had little impact on daily life. Then in the 1730s a series of events later called the **Great Awakening** sparked new interest in Christianity.

Whitefield and Edwards. In 1739 a young minister from Great Britain named George Whitefield visited America. Over the next 30 years, Whitefield traveled to America several more times. During his visits, he preached in towns and cities large and small, from Savannah, Georgia, to York, Maine. He became one of the most popular voices of the Great Awakening.

The talented preacher George Whitefield gained followers and influenced ministers throughout the colonies.

Detail from the National Portrait Gallery, Smithsonian Institution, Washington, DC/Art Resource, NY

Whitefield was a small, fair-skinned man with deep-blue eyes. While preaching, he radiated energy and enthusiasm. He spread a message that anyone could be saved by repenting of his or her sins and trusting in Jesus Christ. He stirred intense religious emotion in his listeners everywhere. During his sermons, thousands of colonists confessed their sins and promised to try to lead better lives.

Next to Whitefield, one the best-known preachers of the Great Awakening was New England minister Jonathan Edwards. In his most famous sermon, "Sinners in the Hands of an Angry God," Edwards compared humans to the lowliest of creatures found in nature. He warned his listeners:

> **"The God that holds you over the pit of hell, much as one holds a spider or some loathsome insect over the fire, . . . is dreadfully provoked: His wrath [anger] towards you burns like fire."**

As his listeners trembled, Edwards told them the good news that God was also merciful and would still allow them into Heaven if they accepted God's forgiveness for their sins.

Effects of the Awakening. Many ministers followed in the steps of Whitefield and Edwards. As they did, waves of religious enthusiasm swept through towns from Georgia to New England.

On the frontier, where the settlers were spread thinly over wide areas, people traveled for miles to attend religious services. In Virginia and the Carolinas, and later in western Pennsylvania and New York, frontier ministers rode from place to place on horseback. They preached and held meetings wherever a group could be brought together. Methodist and Baptist preachers were particularly successful at gaining converts on the frontier.

African Americans were among the many Methodist and Baptist converts. Until the Great Awakening there had been few efforts to convert slaves to Christianity. The message of the Great Awakening offered the hope of salvation even to those who were enslaved.

The religious excitement of the Great Awakening continued until about the 1770s. The movement had important political consequences. People who came to realize that they had choices in their religious lives began to seek the same freedom in their political activities.

The Search for Knowledge

By the 1750s many colonists were also caught up by the spirit of a European movement known as the **Scientific Revolution**. This movement, which had begun in the 1500s, encouraged people to improve themselves and the world around them by careful study.

Two great scientific advances set the stage for the Scientific Revolution. One was the improvement of the telescope by the Italian scientist Galileo in 1609, which

Scala/Art Resource, NY

Galileo Galilei's telescope helped people to see the stars and encouraged other scientists to examine the mysteries of the universe.

American Letters

Benjamin Franklin's *Autobiography*

Benjamin Franklin's life story has been one of the best-selling autobiographies of all time. In the following passage, Franklin reveals how he developed a formula to help people improve themselves. The book was originally published as a series that came out in parts over several years.

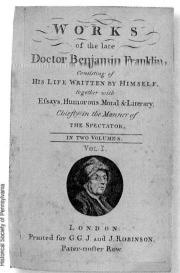

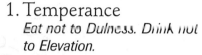

An early volume of Benjamin Franklin's best-selling Autobiography

Historical Society of Pennsylvania

It was about this time that I conceiv'd the bold and arduous [difficult] Project of arriving at moral Perfection. I wish'd to live without committing any Fault at anytime; I would conquer all that either Natural Inclination [tendency], Custom, or Company might lead me into. As I knew, or thought I knew, what was right and wrong, I did not see why I might not *always* do the one and avoid the other. But I soon found I had undertaken a Task more Difficulty than I had imagined: while my Care was employ'd in guarding against one Fault, I was often surpris'd by another. Habit took the Advantage of Inattention. Inclination was sometimes too strong for Reason. I concluded at length, . . . that the contrary Habits must be broken and good Ones acquired and established, before we can have any Dependence on a steady uniform Rectitude of [virtuous] Conduct. For this purpose I therefore contriv'd [developed] the following Method.

. . . I included after . . . Names of Virtues all that at that time occurr'd to me as necessary or desirable, and annex'd to each a short Precept [rule], which fully express'd the Extent I gave to its Meaning.

These Names of Virtues with their Precepts were:

• **Franklin**

1. Temperance
   Eat not to Dulness. Drink not to Elevation.

2. Silence
   Speak not but what may benefit others or your self. Avoiding trifling [unimportant] Conversation.

3. Order
   Let all your Things have their Places. Let each Part of your Business have its Time.

4. Resolution
   Resolve to perform what you ought. Perform without fail what you resolve.

5. Frugality
   Make no Expense but to do good to others or yourself: i.e. [that is] Waste nothing.

6. Industry
   Lose no Time. Be always employ'd in something useful. Cut off all unnecessary Actions.

7. Sincerity
   Use no hurtful Deceit. Think innocently and justly; and, if you speak, speak accordingly.

8. Justice
   Wrong none, by doing Injuries or omitting the Benefits that are your Duty.

9. Moderation
   Avoid extremes. Forbear [keep from] resenting Injuries so much as you think they deserve.

10. Cleanliness
    Tolerate no Uncleanliness in Body, Clothes or Habitation.

made it easier to study the universe. The other advance, late in the 1600s, was Sir Isaac Newton's development of theories about motion. These theories explained why the stars and planets behave as they do.

The work of Galileo, Newton, and other scientists changed the way educated people thought and the value they gave to knowledge. The orderly movements of the planets suggested that the universe was like a gigantic clock. It was complicated, but it operated according to fixed laws of nature. If laws or rules governed the universe, many people argued, surely no mystery of nature was beyond human understanding.

Self-Taught Americans

In America, it was easy to believe that thought and study would push the frontiers of knowledge forward. Explorers and scientists were finding rivers, mountains, plants, and animals that were new to them. Americans were developing new ideas and ways of doing things.

Much of this learning took place outside of organized schools. Colonial America had only a few colleges. Most Americans taught themselves or were taught at home. Benjamin Franklin, one of the greatest American thinkers of the colonial period, had only two years of formal schooling.

Early writers. Benjamin Franklin, who first gained fame as a printer and publisher, advised Americans, "Either write things worthy [of] reading, or do things worth the writing." Many Americans, such as Mary Katherine Goddard, were doing both. At various times Goddard managed newspapers in Providence, Baltimore, and Philadelphia. In 1775 she became postmaster of Baltimore, probably the first colonial woman to hold such a position.

Phillis Wheatley, a slave in Boston, began writing poetry at an early age. She was the first African American woman to have a collection of her work published. In one of her earliest poems, "To the University of Cambridge, in New England," she celebrated the value of learning:

> **"Students, to you 'tis giv'n to scan the heights**
> **Above, to traverse [cross] the etheral [heavenly] space,**
> **And mark the systems of revolving worlds."**

Young People In History

Apprentices

The Granger Collection, New York

A master potter teaches the skills of the craft to a group of apprentices.

Many children in colonial America learned trades by working with a skilled craftsperson. These trainees were called apprentices. Although most apprentices were boys, some were girls. Children usually began apprenticeships at about age 13 or 14, and their training might last as long as seven or eight years. The craftsperson, called a master, taught the apprentice the skills needed in their trade. The young pupil practiced by working alongside the master. At first, apprentices might work as assistants. As their skills grew they worked on their own under the masters' watchful eyes.

Even Benjamin Franklin started out as an apprentice—first in candlemaking and then in printing. While few apprentices enjoyed Franklin's success, apprenticeship offered a young person with no land and little education a way to earn a living in the colonies.

Detail from The Pierpont Morgan Library/Art Resource, NY

Poet Phillis Wheatley's works encouraged learning, good moral character, and religious devotion—three subjects of interest to many colonial Americans.

• **Phillis Wheatley**

Colonial scientists. Phillis Wheatley's poem reflects the Scientific Revolution's focus on education. Even many colonial scientists, however, had little or no formal education.

Benjamin Banneker, whose father was a slave and whose mother was a free African American, taught himself astronomy and surveying. Banneker also produced a widely used almanac that helped farmers plan their crops. Later in his career, Banneker helped lay out the boundaries of the District of Columbia.

Another surveyor and astronomer of the period was David Rittenhouse, a clockmaker from Pennsylvania. During the course of his work, he improved the making of clocks, telescopes, and other instruments. He also built a mechanical model that closely copied the movements of the sun and planets.

John Bartram traveled far and wide collecting unusual plants for his garden outside Philadelphia. He sent carefully packed samples of his discoveries to the leading European naturalists and they sent him their own unusual finds. Distinguished visitors from Europe often came to see Bartram's collection, as did many well-known Americans like Benjamin Franklin. Such sharing of information was another way colonists spread their knowledge throughout the colonies.

The Granger Collection, New York

The Franklin stove was one of many new inventions for use in American colonial homes. Ben Franklin himself sketched this design of the stove.

Section 3 Review

• **Glossary**

IDENTIFY and explain the significance of the following: Great Awakening, George Whitefield, Jonathan Edwards, Scientific Revolution, Benjamin Franklin, Mary Katherine Goddard, Phillis Wheatley, Benjamin Banneker

REVIEWING FOR DETAILS
1. How did the Great Awakening affect the colonies?
2. What effects did the Scientific Revolution have on American thought and culture?
3. With few schools in America, how did colonists gain an education?

REVIEWING FOR UNDERSTANDING
4. **Writing Mastery:** *Creating* Imagine that you are an early American writer. Write a poem or short story that expresses the importance of learning in the American colonies.
5. **Critical Thinking:** *Synthesizing Information* How might shared experiences such as the Great Awakening and the Scientific Revolution have contributed to the creation of a common American culture?

Section 4

EXPANDING WESTWARD

Multimedia Connections

Explore these related topics and materials on the CD–ROM to enrich your understanding of this section:

 Gazetteer

- Ohio River valley
- Great Lakes
- Pittsburgh
- Quebec

 Atlas

- King Philip's War
- North America in 1754
- French and Indian War

 Readings

- Seven Years' War

 Media Bank

- Yankee Doodle Dandy
- Battle of Quebec

 Profiles

- Metacom

On July 7, 1742, the Iroquois leader Canassateego headed a delegation of Indians meeting with Pennsylvania officials who wanted to expand British settlement into the Ohio River valley. The British knew that French leaders had similar desires. Fearing that the French were gaining the loyalty of American Indians in the valley, the Pennsylvanians tried with little success to secure the delegates' trust. Tensions over this region would eventually end in war.

As you read this section you will find out:

▶ **How trade influenced relations among American Indian groups.**

▶ **What events led to the French and Indian War.**

▶ **How the French and Indian War affected Great Britain's empire.**

Conflict Over Land and Trade

As the British colonists expanded westward, they met resistance from both American Indians and French colonists. Of course, conflict with Indians was not new. In Puritan New England, the Wampanoag led by Metacom, whom the Puritans called King Philip, attempted in 1675 to halt settlement after several of their warriors were killed by settlers. In a series of deadly raids, they destroyed some 12 villages. The colonists struck back with equal force. In August 1676 Metacom was killed, and the war was soon over.

The colonists' final victory in what the British later called King Philip's War was aided by the Mohawk, who were members of the Iroquois League. In the mid-1600s the Iroquois, who at that time were allies of the Dutch in New Netherland, had gained control

Through Others' Eyes
Colonial Traders

By the mid-1700s many tribes in the Ohio River valley were suffering the ill effects of contact with some French and British traders. For this reason, many opposed white settlement in the area for fear it would destroy their culture. Particularly damaging had been the introduction of alcohol. In 1753 Oneida chief Scarouady pled with his British allies to prevent dishonest traders from ruining the tribes:

> *"The rum ruins us. We beg you would prevent its coming in such quantities by regulating the traders. When these whisky traders come they bring thirty or forty caggs [kegs] and put them down before us and make us drunk, and get all the skins that should go to pay the debts we have contracted for goods bought of the fair traders, and by this means we not only ruin ourselves but them [the traders] too. These wicked whisky sellers, when they have once got the Indians in liquor, make them sell their very clothes from their backs. In short, if this practice be continued we must inevitably [certainly] be ruined."*

Trouble in Ohio Country

In 1718 Alexander Spotswood, then lieutenant governor of Virginia, had warned British authorities, "The French have built so many forts that the British settlements almost seem surrounded." He advised the British to protect their claims by encouraging settlement along the Great Lakes. Likewise, by 1750 French Canadians were complaining about British activities on Lake Ontario:

> **"It is there that the English hand out rum to the Indians, even though the King of France has forbidden this trade. It is there that the English try to win over all the Indian nations. . . . As long as the English occupy Fort Oswego, we must distrust even those Indians who are most loyal to the French."**

Although the Great Lakes area continued to be a source of conflict between the two sides, it was only after each tried to establish military posts deep in the Ohio River valley that a final, decisive war broke out.

Conflict over forts. In 1752 the French governor of Canada, the Marquis Duquesne de Menneville, ordered the construction of a new chain of forts running from Lake Erie south to the Ohio River, in what is now western Pennsylvania. The French actions alarmed many people in the British colonies, including

of the trade in beaver pelts in the northeast. In 1649 the Iroquois had defeated the Huron, who were allies of the French.

For decades thereafter the Iroquois prospered through a mixture of war, diplomacy, and trade policy. They acted as middlemen in the profitable fur trade, gathering pelts from other tribes and selling them to the English. However, they also cooperated with the French when Iroquois leaders felt it was in their best interest to do so.

Native Americans from many tribes traded valuable beaver pelts with Europeans. Sometimes this trade led to wars between tribes.

The Granger Collection, New York

Lieutenant Governor Robert Dinwiddie of Virginia.

When Dinwiddie learned what the French were doing, he sent a planter and land surveyor named George Washington to warn them that they were trespassing on Virginia property. In November 1753 Washington set out with a party of six to find the French commander. After weeks of tramping through icy forests, Washington encountered the French and delivered Dinwiddie's message. Duquesne rejected it with disgust.

Fort Duquesne. In early 1754 Dinwiddie sent another group of Virginians to build a British fort where the Monongahela and Allegheny Rivers join to form the Ohio River. Dinwiddie then appointed Washington as lieutenant colonel of the Virginia **militia**, a group of citizens organized for military service. He ordered Washington to lead a force to protect the incomplete post against French attack.

Before Washington could reach the site, the French drove off the construction party. Then they completed the post themselves, naming it Fort Duquesne. Washington marched toward Fort Duquesne. Along the way he won a brief battle with a small French party. The main French force then advanced against Washington. He set up a defensive post, Fort Necessity, but the French easily surrounded it. After an all-day battle Washington had to surrender. The French commander then allowed Washington and his men to go free. They returned to Virginia, leaving the disputed territory in French hands.

• **Years of War**

The French and Indian War

After Washington's retreat the war began in earnest. In all of North America there were no more than 70,000 French settlers. The population of the British colonies was about 1.5 million. This gave the British a definite advantage. For about two years, however, the French won most of the battles. Many of the Indians sided with them, because, unlike the British, the French usually did not try to force the Indians to give up their lands or their ways of life.

The British were not easily discouraged, however. The tide began to turn after a brilliant British politician, William Pitt, took over management of the war effort. British troops finally captured Fort Duquesne in 1758. They changed its name to Fort Pitt, which is why the modern city on the site is named Pittsburgh.

Gradually, other key French posts were taken. The most decisive battle occurred at the French city of Quebec in 1759. The battle took place outside of the city on a field called the Plains of Abraham. Both the British commander, General James Wolfe, and the

NORTH AMERICA IN 1763

British
French
Spanish
Russian
Unclaimed

ARCTIC OCEAN

UNCLAIMED

Hudson Bay

NEWFOUNDLAND

140° W

PACIFIC OCEAN

Disputed

CANADA

Great Lakes

FRENCH

40° N

LOUISIANA

Mississippi River

Ohio River

THIRTEEN COLONIES

60° W

ATLANTIC OCEAN

FLORIDA

NEW SPAIN

Gulf of Mexico

WEST INDIES

20° N

CARIBBEAN SEA

Rio Grande

N W E S

0   500   1,000 Miles
0   500 1,000 Kilometers
Azimuthal Equal-Area Projection

120° W   100° W   80° W

60° N   40° W

40° N

Learning from Maps.
Wars in Europe soon spilled over into North America and radically changed the colonial borders.

• **Maps**

▶ **Place.** What country had the smallest land claims in 1763?

British general Edward Braddock was killed trying unsuccessfully to recapture Fort Duquesne in 1755.

• **Fort Duquesne**

War. Spain entered the conflict on the side of France in 1762, only to see its colonies in Cuba and the Philippine Islands overwhelmed by the British.

The British were victorious almost everywhere. When the war ended in 1763, the British were able to redraw the map of the world. France had to surrender Canada and most of its claims in the Mississippi and Ohio River valleys. Spain turned over Florida and the Gulf Coast as far as the Mississippi River to the British. The British colonists were delighted. The French threat to the Ohio River valley had been removed. Spain had been pushed back from the southern frontier.

All was not yet settled, however. Although some of the colonies had contributed men and money to the conflict, British soldiers and sailors had done most of the fighting. The Royal Treasury paid most of the bills. In the long run, these and other factors would cause growing conflict between the British government and its colonists. Yet in 1763 most colonists felt loyal to the king and grateful to Great Britain.

French commander, General Louis Joseph de Montcalm, were killed in the fight, which ended with the surrender of the city to the British.

By this time, the conflict had spread throughout the world, including Europe, where it became known as the Seven Years'

Section 4 Review

• **Glossary**

IDENTIFY and explain the significance of the following: Metacom, Marquis Duquesne de Menneville, George Washington, militia

LOCATE and explain the importance of the following: Ohio River valley, Great Lakes

• **Gazetteer**

REVIEWING FOR DETAILS

1. How did trade increase conflict among American Indian groups?
2. What triggered the French and Indian War? How did the war affect control of North America?

REVIEWING FOR UNDERSTANDING

• **Time Line**

3. **Geographic Literacy** Why might the Ohio River valley have become an area of conflict between the French and the British?
4. **Writing Mastery:** *Persuading* Imagine that you are an American Indian from the Ohio River valley. Write a speech persuading your tribe to side with either the French or the British.
5. **Critical Thinking:** *Recognizing Point of View* Most descriptions of the early Iroquois come from the French and their Indian allies, who described the Iroquois as brutal warriors. Why might such sources be biased?

unit 2

THE NEW AMERICAN NATION (1755–1801)

Betsy Ross and her assistants make the first American flag in 1776. The "Stars and Stripes" was officially adopted as the flag of the United States in 1777.

LINKING *P*AST TO PRESENT
American Principles

"I pledge allegiance to the flag of the United States of America." Millions of American middle-school students recite these words every day before classes begin. Many started out memorizing these words as soon as they were old enough to go to school, at which point the students often did not quite understand what the words meant. "With liberty and jelly for all," recited one elementary student at the end of the Pledge.

The Pledge of Allegiance originated in 1892, when Francis Bellamy wrote it to celebrate the 400th anniversary of Columbus's voyage. Almost immediately, students began to recite the Pledge in schools. Before long, all students were required to say the Pledge, but controversy soon followed.

In the 1930s members of certain religious groups said that reciting the Pledge went against their sacred beliefs. In 1943 the U.S. Supreme Court ruled that forcing people to recite the Pledge against their religious beliefs was contrary to the principles upon which this nation was founded. Although some political leaders today still support the idea of requiring students to say the Pledge, it remains a voluntary action.

The issues the Pledge has raised and the process by which these issues have been debated would never have been imaginable to people 300 years ago. As you read this unit, you will learn how a group of people living in North America under European rule joined together to create a system of government unlike anything the world had

These teenagers are observing artwork in the rotunda of the U.S. Capitol Building in Washington, D.C.

Paul S. Conklin

witnessed before. They founded a nation based on two things—individual freedom of expression and government by the people.

In most societies before 1776, if a ruler ordered the people to recite a pledge they had little choice but to obey or be severely punished. There was no system by which they could challenge the word of the ruler. As you will learn, however, in the eastern part of North America those principles of government began to change with a rebellion that started in the late 1700s.

CHAPTER **5**

The Granger Collection, New York

Americans Seek Independence (1755–1783)

THEMES IN AMERICAN HISTORY

Economic Development:
How might economic conditions contribute to political revolution?

Democratic Values:
Why might colonists break away from their home country?

Global Relations:
Why might nations support a revolution in another country's colonies?

The spring of 1775 did not dawn hopeful for James Thacher, a young doctor who lived near Boston. British soldiers had "actually commenced [started] hostilities against our people," he confided to his journal. He went on to describe the call that echoed through colonial towns: "To Arms! To Arms!" The American Revolution had begun.

• Video Opener

• Skill Builder

image above: Washington Crossing the Delaware

Section 1

RESISTING BRITISH RULE

Multimedia Connections

Explore these related topics and materials on the CD–ROM to enrich your understanding of this section:

 Media Bank

- Samuel Adams
- Keeping the People Informed

 Atlas

- Pontiac's Rebellion

 Profiles

- Pontiac
- Samuel Adams

 Gazetteer

- Great Britain
- Appalachian Mountains
- New York
- Massachusetts

"We will not submit to any tax!" rebel leader Samuel Adams shouted. "We are free, and we want no King!" Shortly after his radical speech, British warships sailed into Boston's harbor. The vessels carried troops, sent to put down a revolt in Massachusetts. This alarmed Boston's citizens, most of whom supported the king. Their loyalty would be tested as Britain tried to force the colonists into line.

As you read this section you will find out:

▶ **How the end of the French and Indian War affected Native Americans and colonists.**

▶ **How Britain attempted to raise money in America.**

▶ **How the colonists resisted British attempts to control them.**

Conflict Across the Appalachians

The end of the French and Indian War changed the lives of American Indians living west of the Appalachian Mountains. After his country's victory, the British commander in the colonies raised the price of goods traded to Indians. He also refused to give presents or feasts in exchange for trade and the use of Indian land, standard practices with the French. These policies angered the Seneca, Ottawa, Miami, and other Indians of the Ohio River valley. The tribes also had to deal with white settlers, who began pouring into the area after the French defeat in North America.

In 1763 Pontiac, an Ottawa chief, organized Indians to protect their land. They began a war to drive the settlers back across the Appalachians. The Indian force fought for about two years, destroying most of the British forts along the frontier. After their siege of Fort Detroit failed, however, the Indians soon halted their attacks. **Pontiac's Rebellion** came to an end.

Realizing that it would be difficult to protect settlers, the British government issued the **Proclamation of 1763**, which closed the area west of the Appalachian Mountains to newcomers. This initially benefited Indians, but it frustrated colonists who believed that the frontier was their only opportunity to own land. Many simply ignored the new policy and continued to move into the region.

Pontiac urged Indians from different tribes in the Ohio River valley to work together against the British. The rebellion slowed British settlement in the area.

Paying for Defense

The British soon found themselves in financial trouble. Great Britain had borrowed huge sums to pay for the French and Indian War and had stationed more than 10,000 soldiers in the colonies to enforce the Proclamation of 1763. To ease the burden, British officials wanted the colonists to start paying for their own protection and government.

New taxes. In April 1764 Parliament passed what became known in America as the Sugar Act. This law set **duties**, or import taxes, on foreign sugar, textiles, and other goods entering the colonies. Britain also

cracked down on smuggling to make sure that everyone paid the duties.

In March 1765 Parliament approved the **Stamp Act**. The law enabled the British to collect money by selling stamps, which had to be purchased and attached to all printed matter in the colonies. This even applied to common items like land deeds, marriage licenses, and newspapers.

Angry protests. The colonies erupted in opposition when colonists learned the terms of the Stamp Act. They were outraged about being taxed without having representatives in Parliament and began to take up the cry, "No taxation without representation."

In October 1765, representatives from nine colonies attended the Stamp Act Congress in New York City. This organization issued a statement that colonists could be taxed only by those legislatures in which they had direct representation. Many colonists also refused to import some British goods.

Opponents of the Stamp Act began to join groups called Sons of Liberty and Daughters of Liberty. Like many other colonists, members of these organizations believed in action rather than talk. Protests over the Stamp Act led to riots in several colonies.

The repeal of the Stamp Act. The colonists' refusal to import certain goods was

The Stamp Act was Britain's first direct tax on its American colonies. Enraged by the law, many colonists burned the stamps in public to show their displeasure.

Many colonists celebrated the "death" of the hated Stamp Act, whose "funeral" is shown in this cartoon. Members of Parliament grieve while carrying a small coffin.

so effective that British merchants urged Parliament to back down. In March 1766 Parliament decided to **repeal**, or officially withdraw, the hated Stamp Act. Parliament did not want this to seem like a surrender, so it passed the Declaratory Act. This law stated that the colonies remained under Parliament's control. Many colonists ignored the new act's message, however. They did not accept the principle that Parliament was supreme.

American Resistance Grows

After repealing the Stamp Act, Britain needed a new supply of money. Thus, Charles Townshend, the country's finance minister, attempted to tax the colonies yet again.

The Townshend Acts. In 1767 Parliament passed the **Townshend Acts**, which placed duties on some items colonists imported from Great Britain—glass, lead, paper, paint, and tea. Customs officials used **writs of assistance**, or special search warrants, to help them collect the taxes and stop smuggling. These writs of assistance allowed agents to search any ship, warehouse, or home without reason.

Many colonists saw Parliament's move as another violation of their rights. They decided to **boycott**, or refuse to buy, British goods. Colonial merchants stopped importing British products. Colonial women began spinning and weaving cloth in their homes rather than purchasing British cloth. The Sons of Liberty also staged more protests.

In New York further conflict arose when townspeople refused to obey the Quartering Act, which required colonists to quarter, or house and supply, British soldiers. In response, Britain suspended the New York assembly.

The largest protest came from Boston, where the Massachusetts legislature called on the colonies to resist the Townshend Acts. Britain dismissed the Massachusetts assembly and moved a large number of soldiers, called "Redcoats" because of their bright red uniforms, into Boston.

The Boston Massacre. The soldiers' presence soon led to trouble. On March 5, 1770, a large crowd began yelling insults at a squad of Redcoats guarding the customhouse. People hurled snowballs, some packed around stones. The British soldiers panicked and fired

Trouble often broke out when British soldiers gathered in colonial towns to enforce Parliament's laws.

● **Poor Old England**

into the mob. Three colonists were killed, and two others died later. An African American sailor named Crispus Attucks was among the dead. Boston's radicals, led by Samuel Adams, called this incident the **Boston Massacre**. Shortly afterward, the British commander and eight soldiers were arrested and charged with murder. Despite angry calls for revenge, the soldiers received a fair trial. Boston lawyer John Adams, Samuel Adams's cousin and himself a critic of British policy, defended the

● **Crispus Attucks**

Many colonists blamed the British for the terrible violence in Boston. In this painting of the Boston Massacre by Paul Revere, British troops fire on the colonists.

soldiers. Most were found to have acted in self-defense.

Trouble Over Tea

In March 1770 Parliament repealed all the Townshend duties except the tax on tea. This helped restore calm in the colonies. The new British prime minister, Lord North, also promised not to raise any more money by taxing the colonists.

Many colonial radicals like Samuel Adams remained active, however. Adams and his supporters believed that:

> **"among the natural rights of the colonists are these: first, a right to life; second, to liberty; third, to property; together with the right to support and to defend them in the best manner they can."**

Adams thought Britain's actions threatened the colonists' rights. He and other colonists formed **Committees of Correspondence** to share information about resistance to the British. Similar groups sprang up in other colonies. Without intending to, these committees gradually became a kind of informal central government for the colonies.

The tea business. After a few years of peace, new problems erupted in the colonies. The British East India Company, an important business, was in financial trouble. It had a huge amount of unsold tea in its warehouses. In May 1773 Parliament passed a **Tea Act**

allowing the firm to sell its product directly to the American colonies. Using its own agents, the company bypassed American tea sellers and saved the money that merchant "middlemen" normally took.

Americans greatly resented the Tea Act. Local tea merchants lost business. Other colonists thought the law set a terrible example—that Parliament had the power to give a British business control of an industry and disrupt trade in America. Despite its popularity, colonists began to boycott tea.

When ships carrying the British East India Company's tea arrived in America, public protest soared to new heights. In Charleston, South Carolina, a crowd persuaded the firm's tea agents to resign. The tea went into storage, but it could not be sold without an agent. In New York and Philadelphia the captains of the tea ships did not even try to unload their cargo. Rather than risk trouble, they sailed back to England.

Samuel Adams worried that the British East India Company's cheap tea would be a temptation to colonists. To destroy the tea he helped organize the Boston Tea Party.

The Boston Tea Party. Massachusetts governor Thomas Hutchinson was determined that Boston would accept tea from the British East India Company. When three tea ships arrived in November, he insisted that their captains prepare to unload the cargo soon for public sale.

While the vessels lay at anchor in Boston Harbor, Samuel Adams and other activists stirred up the public at mass meetings. Angry crowds gathered in the streets, and the tension grew for more than two weeks. Finally, on the night of December 16, 1773, townspeople disguised as Mohawk Indians boarded the ships. Bostonian George Hewes described the daring event that became known as the **Boston Tea Party**:

"**In about three hours . . . we had thus broken and thrown overboard every tea chest to be found in the ship, while those in the other ships were disposing of the tea in the same way.**"

The protesters continued their work until they had destroyed huge amounts of the British East India Company's tea.

The Intolerable Acts

Britain's reaction to the Boston Tea Party was swift and severe. Parliament passed four new laws to reclaim its control and punish Massachusetts. Many colonists called these the **Intolerable Acts**.

Under the first law, no ship could enter or leave Boston Harbor until the townspeople had paid for the tea they had ruined. The second act canceled Massachusetts's charter.

Now town meetings could be held only with the governor's permission. The third law moved trials involving Massachusetts officials charged with criminal activity to Britain. Lastly, a new Quartering Act required residents of Boston to shelter British soldiers in their homes. To enforce all of these laws, General Thomas Gage, commander of the British troops in North America, soon replaced Thomas Hutchinson as the governor of Massachusetts.

Even though the British government's response was aimed primarily at Massachusetts, it outraged people from all the colonies. Increasingly, British actions seemed to threaten the colonists' liberty. In June 1774 the Massachusetts Committee of Correspondence sent out a call for a meeting of colonial leaders.

Many colonists saw King George III as an uncaring leader who was out of touch with colonial problems.

The Granger Collection, New York

● **King George III**

Three months later, delegates from all the colonies except Georgia met in Philadelphia for the **First Continental Congress**. The Congress expressed its loyalty to Britain but demanded the repeal of all British taxation laws. The group banned all trade with Britain until Parliment met its demands.

The delegates set up a Continental Association to enforce this ban. They also advised the colonists to begin forming militias and agreed to meet again the following May if their demands had not been met. Their meeting concluded with this warning: "We have for the present only resolved to pursue . . . peaceable measures." In Britain, King George III, who had lost all patience with the colonists, summed up the crisis. "The Colonies," he wrote, "must either submit or triumph."

Section 1 Review

● **Glossary**

IDENTIFY and explain the significance of the following: Pontiac's Rebellion, Proclamation of 1763, duties, Stamp Act, repeal, Townshend Acts, writs of assistance, boycott, Samuel Adams, Boston Massacre, Committees of Correspondence, Tea Act, Boston Tea Party, Intolerable Acts, First Continental Congress

REVIEWING FOR DETAILS

1. What conflicts arose between American Indians and colonists after the end of the French and Indian War, and what was the outcome?
2. How did Britain try to use its colonies to make money?
3. How did the colonists respond to British attempts at control?

REVIEWING FOR UNDERSTANDING

4. **Writing Mastery:** *Informing* Imagine that you live in Boston. Write a letter to a friend agreeing or disagreeing with colonists' actions at the Boston Tea Party.
5. **Critical Thinking:** *Recognizing Point of View* Why do you think the British believed they were justified in their new colonial policies?

Section 2

LIBERTY OR DEATH

Multimedia Connections

Explore these related topics and materials on the CD–ROM to enrich your understanding of this section:

 Media Bank

- "The Pennsylvania Song"
- Two Continental Congresses
- Revolutionary War Soldiers

 Readings

- Revolutionary War Armies

 Profiles

- Patrick Henry
- Peter Salem

 Gazetteer

- Lexington
- Concord
- Boston

The Redcoats had driven the rebels from Breed's Hill! Bostonians loyal to the British cheered when they heard the news. Their celebration ended, however, when the British soldiers straggled back to town. That evening the wounded filled the streets, and the consequences of war became clear to everyone. As Henry Hulton explained, "The lamentations [grief-filled cries] of the women and children over their husbands and fathers, pierced one to the soul."

As you read this section you will find out:

▶ **Why the battles at Lexington and Concord were significant.**

▶ **What role the Second Continental Congress played.**

▶ **How geography influenced the colonists' military strategy in Boston.**

Lexington and Concord

Conflict over the Intolerable Acts turned Massachusetts into an armed camp. General Gage and his troops occupied Boston. Citizens in the surrounding towns and villages responded by forming militia companies. Parliament soon declared Massachusetts to be in a state of rebellion. The British government sent 6,000 more soldiers to join Gage and ordered him to arrest the rebel leaders.

The "shot heard round the world." On the night of April 18, 1775, Gage sent 700 troops to destroy a militia's supply of weapons in Concord, a town west of Boston. He wanted his soldiers to stop in nearby Lexington and capture rebels Samuel Adams and John Hancock on the way. The colonists learned of these plans. Paul Revere and

Paul Revere was a silversmith and artist who became active in the independence movement. He became famous after his "midnight ride" to warn colonists of a British attack.

The Granger Collection, New York

William Dawes rode through the night, calling out, "The British are coming!" to warn the nearby towns.

The first British soldiers reached Lexington at dawn. Waiting for them were about 70 **Minutemen**—members of rebel militias who were ready for action on a minute's notice. British major John Pitcairn rode forward and ordered them to move off, sneering "Disperse [leave] . . . rebels! You dogs, run!" Suddenly, someone—no one knows who—fired "the shot heard round the world." More shots followed, and when the smoke cleared, eight Minutemen lay dead. Ten other rebel colonists and one British soldier were also wounded.

The British retreat. The British marched on to Concord. After more fighting they destroyed whatever supplies the colonists had not carried off or hidden. Then the British turned back toward Boston. Outside Concord, Minutemen from nearby towns rapidly gathered. All along the road to Boston the angry colonists hid behind trees and in hollows, showering the British with bullets when they passed. Thousands of local citizens picked up their muskets and followed the sound of gunfire to join in the fight. One British soldier described the terrifying journey:

"**All the hills on each side of us were covered with rebels . . . so that they kept the road always lined and a very hot fire on us without intermission. We . . . returned their fire as hot as we received it; but when we arrived within a mile of Lexington our ammunition began to fail, and the light companies were so fatigued . . . they were scarce able to act.**"

By the time they reached Boston, the British had more than 270 **casualties**—people killed, wounded, or missing. The colonists lost less than 100 of some 3,800 militiamen. The battles at Lexington and Concord marked the beginning of the American Revolution.

The Second Continental Congress

Less than a month after the bitter clashes at Lexington and Concord, delegates to the

Trying to frighten and confuse the Minutemen waiting on the Lexington town green, the British troops screamed loudly as they went into battle.

The Granger Collection, New York

Second Continental Congress met in Philadelphia. Massachusetts radicals Samuel Adams, John Adams, and John Hancock joined the assembly, as did Benjamin Franklin of Pennsylvania. Virginia sent its fiery speaker Patrick Henry, who had recently urged the colonists to take up arms against the British in a dramatic speech:

> "Gentlemen may cry peace, peace—but there is no peace. The war is actually begun! . . . Is life so dear, or peace so sweet, as to be purchased at the price of chains and slavery? Forbid it, Almighty God! I know not what course others may take; but as for me, give me liberty, or give me death!"

Henry favored immediate independence from Great Britain, but not all the delegates took such an extreme position. Given the number of conflicting opinions, the Congress decided not to break away from Britain. The delegates did issue a "Declaration of the Causes and Necessity of Taking Up Arms" and also created an official military force, the **Continental Army**. The Congress appointed Virginia delegate George Washington to command the army.

Washington accepted this new assignment eagerly and set out at once for Massachusetts. Before he reached the colony, however, word came that an important battle had just occurred.

The Battle of Bunker Hill

On June 16, 1775, the colonial militia moved in on Bunker Hill and Breed's Hill, which overlooked Boston from the north. The colonists spent the night digging an earthen fort to protect their position on Breed's Hill. The British discovered their presence the next morning. General William Howe, who had replaced Gage, quickly sent British troops to drive the rebels from the hill.

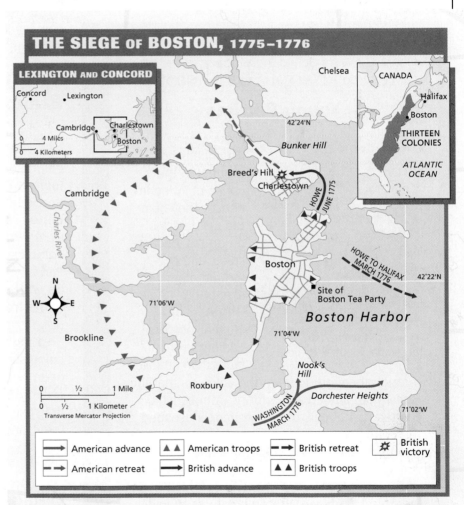

THE SIEGE OF BOSTON, 1775–1776

LEXINGTON AND CONCORD

Concord • Lexington

Cambridge • Charlestown
Boston

0   4 Miles
0   4 Kilometers

Chelsea

CANADA
Halifax
Boston

THIRTEEN COLONIES

ATLANTIC OCEAN

42°24'N

Bunker Hill

Breed's Hill
Charlestown

HOWE JUNE 1775

Cambridge

Charles River

Boston

HOWE TO HALIFAX MARCH 1776

42°22'N

Site of Boston Tea Party

Boston Harbor

71°06'W

71°04'W

N W E S

Brookline

Nook's Hill

Roxbury

Dorchester Heights

WASHINGTON MARCH 1776

71°02'W

0   ½   1 Mile
0   ½   1 Kilometer
Transverse Mercator Projection

| → | American advance | ▲▲ | American troops | ⇢ | British retreat | ☼ | British victory |
| ⇠ | American retreat | → | British advance | ▲▲ | British troops | | |

Learning from Maps.

After the British drove the American forces from Breed's Hill, the Americans took up positions around Boston. When Washington's troops occupied Dorchester Heights in March 1776, the British decided to retreat by sea.

• Maps

▶ **Location.** What does Dorchester Heights overlook?

The colonists on Breed's Hill were tired and hungry after their night's work. They expected fresh militia to come and reinforce them, but none arrived. Now these civilian soldiers faced professional British troops.

Across the bay, hundreds of Bostonians watched from their windows and rooftops as the battle began. The British, loaded down with heavy packs, advanced up the hill in three broad lines. To save ammunition, an American commander ordered his men: "Don't one of you fire until you see the whites of their eyes." When the Americans finally did shoot, their musket balls tore through the enemy. The British fell back, leaving the field littered with dead and dying men.

Twice more the British charged with fixed bayonets. Inside the fort the Americans ran low on ammunition. They loaded their guns with nails and pieces of glass and fired off one last round of shots. Then the British came over the wall, forcing the Americans to retreat. The British victory at what became known as the **Battle of Bunker Hill** was a very costly one. More than 1,000 British soldiers and some 400 American militiamen were killed or wounded.

The Olive Branch Petition

Despite the bloodshed at Lexington, Concord, and Bunker Hill, many colonists still hoped for peace. In July 1775, after much debate, the Second Continental Congress sent the **Olive Branch Petition** to King George III. It asked him to protect the colonies against further actions by Parliament until a compromise could be worked out. The document got its name from the olive branch, a traditional symbol of peace.

King George was furious with the colonists and declared them to be in open rebellion. To isolate America, he ordered a **blockade**, or naval measure that used ships to cut off a country's trade and supplies. Now it was up to Washington and his army to fight the British.

Washington's First Victory

After Washington arrived in Boston with his army, he pinned down the British troops. He decided not to attack the city until he had better artillery.

Young People In History
Young Patriots

A young drummer boy accompanies older Patriots.

Many young Americans contributed to the cause of independence. They beat the call to arms on drums, became spies, and performed other acts of bravery.

In April 1777, 16-year-old Sybil Ludington rode more than 30 miles through the night to warn the colonists that the British had landed at Danbury, Connecticut. Alerted by her call, the townspeople escaped the enemy advance.

As a teenager, James Forten signed on an American ship and carried gunpowder to the deck during battle. When the British captured his vessel, he faced a terrible danger. Would they enslave him because he was African American? The captain's son, however, liked Forten and asked for his release. Forten chose to be imprisoned with his fellow Americans, saying, "I'm a prisoner for my country, and I'll never be a traitor to her."

In May 1775 Ethan Allen and the "Green Mountain Boys," a militia from present day Vermont, had captured Fort Ticonderoga in northern New York. This gave the rebels a valuable supply of cannons—if they could move them to Boston. Colonel Henry Knox, a young artillery officer, hoped to do so. He and his men dragged about 50 cannons nearly 300 miles, using sleds and oxen. They reached Washington's camp with the heavy equipment in January 1776.

Overjoyed, Washington had the cannons hauled up Dorchester Heights, overlooking Boston from the south. From this position the colonists could bombard the British in the city below. General Howe realized that his troops were in a dangerous position. On March 17, 1776, the entire British army sailed off to Britain's naval base in Nova Scotia. More than 1,000 colonists went with the British army. They preferred exile to rebellion against king and country. Some also feared for their lives if they remained. For the time being, Washington had driven British troops from the American colonies.

As British troops struggled up Breed's Hill in the humid June heat, Bostonians streamed to the city's rooftops to watch the important battle unfold.

● **Home Front**

Section 2 Review

● **Glossary**

● **Gazetteer**

IDENTIFY and explain the significance of the following: Minutemen, casualties, Second Continental Congress, Patrick Henry, Continental Army, William Howe, Battle of Bunker Hill, Olive Branch Petition, blockade

LOCATE and explain the importance of the following: Lexington, Concord, Bunker Hill, Breed's Hill

REVIEWING FOR DETAILS

1. What was significant about the fighting at Lexington and Concord?
2. What actions did the Second Continental Congress take?

REVIEWING FOR UNDERSTANDING

3. **Geographic Literacy** How did Boston's geography influence the colonists' military strategy against the British?
4. **Writing Mastery:** *Persuading* Imagine that you are part of the militia that fought in Lexington. Draw up a flyer persuading other colonists to take up arms against the British.
5. **Critical Thinking:** *Drawing Conclusions* If you had been a delegate to the Second Continental Congress, would you have favored immediate independence or a more cautious approach? Explain your answer.

Section 3

DECLARING INDEPENDENCE

Multimedia Connections

Explore these related topics and materials on the CD–ROM to enrich your understanding of this section:

 Media Bank

- Harassing Loyalists
- Loyalist Recruiting Poster

 Readings

- *Common Sense*

 Profiles

- Thomas Paine

 Gazetteer

- Virginia
- South Carolina
- Connecticut

Caesar Rodney rode hard through the night to reach Philadelphia. His word would decide Delaware's position in the congressional vote on independence. He had to make it in time! Rodney soon got the chance to give his "voice in the matter of Independence." Like so many others, he voted to break away from Britain. The Americans had made their fateful choice.

As you read this section you will find out:

▶ **What effect Thomas Paine's *Common Sense* had on colonists.**

▶ **What the main parts of the Declaration of Independence are.**

▶ **How the Declaration of Independence has affected the United States and other countries.**

The Impact of *Common Sense*

By early 1776 the call for independence was gaining ground. A few colonists still believed that King George III was under the influence of bad advisers. More people in the colonies, however, thought George was cruel and unfair.

Thomas Paine, an Englishman who had recently come to America, helped convince the colonists that the king was wrong. In January 1776 he published a pamphlet called *Common Sense*. In it, Paine attacked not only the king but also the whole idea of monarchy. Americans had a natural right to rule themselves, Paine insisted:

"**A government of our own is our natural right; and when a man seriously reflects on the precariousness [uncertainty] of human** affails, he will become convinced that it is infinitely wiser and safer to form a consti tution of our own in a cool, deliberate manner, while we have it in our power, than to trust such an interesting event to time and chance."

Common Sense was an immediate best-seller throughout the colonies. As a colonist from South Carolina explained, "It made independents of the majority of the country."

Congress Burns Its Bridges

By June 1776 nearly all the members of the Second Continental Congress were ready to act. On June 7 Richard Henry Lee of Virginia introduced a resolution for independence. Before passing it, the Congress appointed a committee to prepare a statement that explained the need for independence. The committee members were Benjamin Franklin, John Adams, Roger Sherman of Connecticut, Robert Livingston of New York, and Thomas Jefferson of Virginia. Jefferson was the main author of this statement, the **Declaration of Independence**.

On July 2 the delegates approved Lee's resolution. Two days later, on July 4, many of them signed the Declaration of Independence. They were burning their bridges behind them. "I am well aware of the toil and blood and treasure that it will cost us," Adams wrote to his wife Abigail, "to maintain this declaration and support and defend these states."

In the colonies, reaction to the Declaration was mixed. People who supported the British, called **Loyalists** or Tories, strongly opposed the Declaration. They regarded the **Patriots**, people who favored independence, as rebels. To the Patriots, however, a Tory was "a creature whose head is in England, [and] whose body is in America."

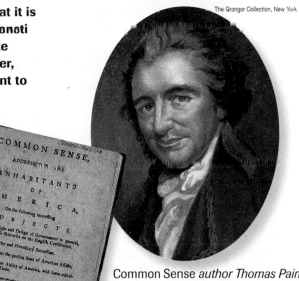

The Granger Collection, New York

Historical Society of Pennsylvania

Common Sense author Thomas Paine lived in poverty in England before meeting Benjamin Franklin, who convinced him to try life in America.

In British eyes, the Declaration's signers were traitors. If the "Americans" lost the war, these rebel leaders could expect the treatment commonly given traitors—death.

The Declaration of Independence

The Declaration of Independence is one of the best-known and most influential political documents ever written. It consists of two parts. The first restates the ideas of English philosopher John Locke. He believed human beings formed governments to protect their natural rights. If a government failed to do its job, or fulfill its "contract," the people could abolish it and create a new one—by force if necessary. The second part of the Declaration leveled several charges against George to prove that he had broken this "contract" with the colonists.

The Declaration includes the famous words, "all men are created equal." Over the years, people have debated what Jefferson meant by this phrase. Jefferson's noble principle did not apply to everyone in the 1700s. Despite their many contributions to the Revolution, women lacked full legal equality. So did African Americans, free and enslaved. Many African Americans had joined the fight for American independence before the delegates even signed the Declaration. Caesar Ferrett, Samuel Craft, and Prince Estabrook, for example, were among the militiamen at Lexington. Nevertheless, Jefferson's equality did not apply to African Americans, thousands of whom were held in slavery. New Englander Samuel Hopkins noted:

> **"Our struggle for liberty . . . while the poor Negroes look on and hear . . . that slavery is more to be dreaded than death, and [that] we are resolved to live free or die, . . . leads them to attend to their own wretched situation more than otherwise they could."**

Despite these contradictions between its intent and practice, the Declaration's case for equality deeply influenced political thinking. Later American reformers used Jefferson's words in their arguments to abolish slavery and to increase rights for women and African Americans. The Declaration also inspired people in many other countries as they struggled for freedom.

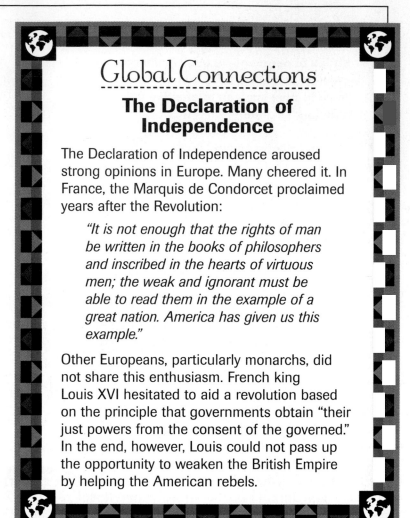

Global Connections

The Declaration of Independence

The Declaration of Independence aroused strong opinions in Europe. Many cheered it. In France, the Marquis de Condorcet proclaimed years after the Revolution:

> *"It is not enough that the rights of man be written in the books of philosophers and inscribed in the hearts of virtuous men; the weak and ignorant must be able to read them in the example of a great nation. America has given us this example."*

Other Europeans, particularly monarchs, did not share this enthusiasm. French king Louis XVI hesitated to aid a revolution based on the principle that governments obtain "their just powers from the consent of the governed." In the end, however, Louis could not pass up the opportunity to weaken the British Empire by helping the American rebels.

Section 3 Review

• Glossary

IDENTIFY and explain the significance of the following: Thomas Paine, Thomas Jefferson, Declaration of Independence, Loyalists, Patriots, John Locke

REVIEWING FOR DETAILS

1. How did the colonists react to Thomas Paine's *Common Sense*?
2. What are the two main sections of the Declaration of Independence?
3. How has the Declaration of Independence affected political thinking in the United States and other countries?

REVIEWING FOR UNDERSTANDING

4. **Writing Mastery:** *Persuading* Imagine that you are a political writer. Produce a short pamphlet persuading colonists to revolt against the British or to remain loyal.
5. **Critical Thinking:** *Determining the Strength of an Argument* How strong an argument did Jefferson present to justify a revolution against British rule in the colonies? Explain your answer.

DECLARATION OF INDEPENDENCE

IN CONGRESS, JULY 4, 1776
THE UNANIMOUS DECLARATION OF THE
THIRTEEN UNITED STATES OF AMERICA,

When in the Course of human events, it becomes necessary for one people to dissolve the political bands which have connected them with another, and to assume among the Powers of the earth, the separate and equal station to which the Laws of Nature and of Nature's God entitle them, a decent respect to the opinions of mankind requires that they should declare the causes which impel them to the separation.

Thomas Jefferson wrote the first draft of the Declaration of Independence in a little more than two weeks.

In the first paragraph, the signers state that it is important to justify why the colonists must break their political ties with Britain.

impel: force

endowed: provided

We hold these truths to be self-evident, that all men are created equal, that they are endowed by their Creator with certain unalienable Rights, that among these are Life, Liberty and the pursuit of Happiness. That to secure these rights, Governments are instituted among Men, deriving their just powers from the consent of the governed, That whenever any Form of Government becomes destructive of these ends, it is the Right of the People to alter or to abolish it, and to institute new Government, laying its foundation on such principles and organizing its powers in such form, as to them shall seem most likely to effect their Safety and Happiness. Prudence, indeed, will dictate that Governments long established should not be changed for light and transient causes; and accordingly all experience hath shown, that mankind are more disposed to suffer, while evils are sufferable, than to right themselves by abolishing the forms to which they are accustomed. But when a long train of abuses and usurpations, pursuing invariably the same Object evinces a design to reduce them under absolute Despotism, it is their right, it is their duty, to throw off such Government, and to provide new Guards for their future security.—Such has been the patient sufferance of these Colonies; and such is now the necessity which constrains them to alter their former Systems of Government. The history of the present King of Great Britain is a history of repeated injuries and usurpations, all having in direct object the establishment of an absolute Tyranny over these States. To prove this, let Facts be submitted to a candid world.

usurpations: wrongful seizures of power

despotism: unlimited power

tyranny: oppressive power used by a government or ruler

candid: fair

Here the Declaration lists the charges that the colonists had against King George III. How does the language in the list appeal to people's emotions?

He has refused his Assent to Laws, the most wholesome and necessary for the public good.

He has forbidden his Governors to pass Laws of immediate and pressing importance, unless suspended in their operation till his Assent should be obtained; and when so suspended, he has utterly neglected to attend to them.

He has refused to pass other Laws for the accommodation of large districts of people, unless those people would relinquish the right of Representation in the Legislature, a right inestimable to them and formidable to tyrants only.

relinquish: release, give up
inestimable: priceless
formidable: causing dread

Why do you think the king had his legislatures in the colonies meet in places that were hard to reach?

He has called together legislative bodies at places unusual, uncomfortable, and distant from the depository of their Public Records, for the sole purpose of fatiguing them into compliance with his measures.

He has dissolved Representative Houses repeatedly, for opposing with manly firmness his invasions on the rights of the people.

He has refused for a long time, after such dissolutions, to cause others to be elected; whereby the Legislative Powers, incapable of Annihilation, have returned to the People at large for their exercise; the State remaining in the mean time exposed to all the dangers of invasion from without, and convulsions within.

annihilation: destruction

convulsions: violent disturbances

naturalization of foreigners: the process by which foreign-born persons become citizens

He has endeavored to prevent the population of these States; for that purpose obstructing the Laws of Naturalization of Foreigners; refusing to pass others to encourage their migration hither, and raising the conditions of new Appropriations of Lands.

appropriations of land: setting aside land for settlement

He has obstructed the Administration of Justice, by refusing his Assent to Laws for establishing Judiciary Powers.

tenure: term

He has made Judges dependent on his Will alone, for the tenure of their offices, and the amount and payment of their salaries.

He has erected a multitude of New Offices, and sent hither swarms of Officers to harass our People, and eat out their substance.

He has kept among us, in times of peace, Standing Armies without the Consent of our legislature.

He has affected to render the Military independent of and superior to the Civil Power.

He has combined with others to subject us to a jurisdiction foreign to our constitution, and unacknowledged by our laws; giving his Assent to their acts of pretended legislation:

For quartering large bodies of armed troops among us:

For protecting them, by a mock Trial, from Punishment for any Murders which they should commit on the Inhabitants of these States:

For cutting off our Trade with all parts of the world:

For imposing taxes on us without our Consent:

For depriving us in many cases, of the benefits of Trial by Jury:

For transporting us beyond Seas to be tried for pretended offences:

For abolishing the free System of English Laws in a neighboring Province, establishing therein an Arbitrary government, and enlarging its Boundaries so as to render it at once an example and fit instrument for introducing the same absolute rule into these Colonies:

For taking away our Charters, abolishing our most valuable Laws, and altering fundamentally the Forms of our Governments:

For suspending our own Legislature, and declaring themselves invested with Power to legislate for us in all cases whatsoever.

He has abdicated Government here, by declaring us out of his Protection and waging War against us.

He has plundered our seas, ravaged our Coasts, burnt our towns, and destroyed the lives of our people.

He is at this time transporting large armies of foreign mercenaries to complete the works of death, desolation and tyranny, already begun with circumstances of Cruelty & perfidy scarcely paralleled in the most barbarous ages, and totally unworthy the Head of a civilized nation.

He has constrained our fellow Citizens taken Captive on the high Seas to bear Arms against their Country, to become the executioners of their friends and Brethren, or to fall themselves by their Hands.

He has excited domestic insurrections amongst us, and has endeavored to bring on the inhabitants of our frontiers, the merciless Indian Savages, whose known rule of warfare, is an undistinguished destruction of all ages, sexes and conditions.

In every stage of these Oppressions We have Petitioned for Redress in the most humble terms: Our repeated Petitions have been answered only by repeated injury. A Prince, whose character is thus marked by every act which may define a Tyrant, is unfit to be the ruler of a free People.

Nor have We been wanting in attention to our British brethren. We have warned them from time to time of attempts by their legislature to extend an unwarrantable jurisdiction over us. We have reminded them of the circumstances of our emigration and settlement here. We have appealed to their native justice and magnanimity, and we have conjured them by the ties of our common kindred to disavow these

---

a multitude of: many

What wrongful acts does the Declaration state have been committed by the king and the British Parliament?

quartering: lodging, housing

The "neighboring Province" that is referred to here is Quebec.

arbitrary: not based on law

render: make

abdicated: given up

foreign mercenaries: soldiers hired to fight for a country not their own

perfidy: violation of trust

insurrections: rebellions

Notice that the Declaration has 18 paragraphs beginning with "He has" or "He is." What is the effect of this repetition?

petitioned for redress: asked formally for a correction of wrongs

unwarrantable jurisdiction: unjustified authority

magnanimity: generous spirit

conjured: urgently called upon

consanguinity: common ancestry
acquiesce: consent to

rectitude: rightness

In this paragraph, the signers state their actual declaration of independence. What rights would the new United States of America now have as an independent nation?

Congress adopted the final draft of the Declaration of Independence on July 4, 1776. A formal copy, written on parchment paper, was signed on August 2, 1776.

About two months before his participation on the committee to prepare the Declaration, John Adams received a letter from his wife, Abigail Adams. The last sentence said, "If particular care and attention is not paid to the ladies, we are determined to foment [start] a rebellion and will not hold ourselves bound by any laws in which we have no voice, or representation." Did the writers of the Declaration listen to her advice?

usurpations, which, would inevitably interrupt our connections and correspondence. They too have been deaf to the voice of justice and of consanguinity. We must, therefore, acquiesce in the necessity, which denounces our Separation, and hold them, as we hold the rest of mankind, Enemies in War, in Peace Friends.

We, therefore, the Representatives of the united States of America, in General Congress, Assembled, appealing to the Supreme Judge of the world for the rectitude of our intentions, do, in the Name, and by Authority of the good People of these Colonies, solemnly publish and declare, That these United Colonies are, and of Right ought to be Free and Independent States; that they are Absolved from all Allegiance to the British Crown, and that all political connection between them and the State of Great Britain, is and ought to be totally dissolved; and that as Free and Independent States, they have full Power to levy War, conclude Peace, contract Alliances, establish Commerce, and to do all other Acts and Things which Independent States may of right do. And for the support of this Declaration, with a firm reliance on the Protection of Divine Providence, we mutually pledge to each other our Lives, our Fortunes and our sacred Honor.

John Hancock
Button Gwinnett
Lyman Hall
George Walton
William Hooper
Joseph Hewes
John Penn
Edward Rutledge
Thomas Heyward, Jr.
Thomas Lynch, Jr.
Arthur Middleton
Samuel Chase
William Paca
Thomas Stone
Charles Carroll of Carrollton
George Wythe
Richard Henry Lee
Thomas Jefferson
Benjamin Harrison
Thomas Nelson, Jr.
Francis Lightfoot Lee
Carter Braxton
Robert Morris
Benjamin Rush
Benjamin Franklin
John Morton
George Clymer
James Smith

George Taylor
James Wilson
George Ross
Caesar Rodney
George Read
Thomas McKean
William Floyd
Philip Livingston
Francis Lewis
Lewis Morris
Richard Stockton
John Witherspoon
Francis Hopkinson
John Hart
Abraham Clark
Josiah Bartlett
William Whipple
Matthew Thornton
Samuel Adams
John Adams
Robert Treat Paine
Elbridge Gerry
Stephen Hopkins
William Ellery
Roger Sherman
Samuel Huntington
William Williams
Oliver Wolcott

Section 4

INDEPENDENCE IS WON

Multimedia Connections

Explore these related topics and materials on the CD–ROM to enrich your understanding of this section:

 Biographies

- John Paul Jones

 Media Bank

- Mercy Otis Warren
- John Paul Jones
- Joseph Brant
- Baron Fredrick von Steuben

- Battle of Trenton
- Francis Marion

 Gazetteer

- Saratoga
- Yorktown

 Atlas

- Victories of John Paul Jones

 Readings

- Indians and the War
- Occupied New York

 Profiles

- Benedict Arnold
- Bernardo de Gálvez
- Deborah Sampson
- Mercy Otis Warren
- Nathan Hale

t was September 1776. Lord Richard Howe, a British naval officer, waited for his guests. He had invited the Patriots to informal peace talks. The Americans sent Benjamin Franklin, John Adams, and Edward Rutledge to meet with him. As they talked, relations became strained. "Is there no way of turning back this step of independence?" Howe asked. The Americans said that things had gone too far. Disappointed, Howe thanked them for coming. The war would continue.

As you read this section you will find out:

▶ **How Washington's army fared in the middle colonies.**

▶ **Why the Battle of Saratoga was the turning point in the Revolution.**

▶ **How the British were defeated in the South.**

Americans at War

The Patriots had declared their independence, and now they would have to fight for it. This task went to George Washington's Continental Army. Washington soon turned his inexperienced troops into orderly units. At first, there were 28 regiments, each with eight companies of about 90 men. Washington removed officers who could not maintain discipline and appointed new ones. He made the soldiers construct barracks and taught them to march in step. Washington's endless list of tasks and stern approach made him unpopular with many troops. Some Europeans, including Count Casimir Pulaski and Thaddeus Kosciusko of Poland, and Baron Friedrich von Steuben of Prussia, helped train the army.

More than 5,000 African Americans served in the Continental Army. Jehu Grant, the escaped slave of a Loyalist, described why he enlisted:

> **"When I saw . . . the people all engaged for the support of freedom, I could not but . . . be pleased with such [a] thing. . . . These considerations induced me to enlist into the American army, where I served faithful about ten months."**

Women also contributed to the Continental Army's success. In addition to those who ran farms and businesses, many women acted as nurses, did laundry, and cooked for the soldiers. Some even fought in the ranks. Among them were Mary Ludwig Hays and Deborah Sampson. Hays carried water to the troops, earning her the nickname Molly Pitcher. When her husband fell in battle, she took his place loading cannons. Sampson disguised herself as a man in order to enlist with Washington's troops and became the most famous woman to fight in the Continental Army.

Mary Ludwig Hays showed great courage when she loaded cannons and carried water during battle.

• **Deborah Sampson**

• **Molly Pitcher**

America's Darkest Hour

After they retreated from Boston, the British decided to capture New York. If successful, this would crush the Revolution by splitting the colonies in two.

A loss at New York. In late June 1776, General Howe sailed just south of New York City with about 10,000 troops. Two months later the British attacked Long Island, where Washington had moved much of his army. Howe outmaneuvered the Patriots and struck from two directions. Washington barely managed to withdraw his battered troops across the East River to safety on Manhattan Island. Howe then drove the Americans to the north end of Manhattan and took control of New York City. Large numbers of Loyalists welcomed the British with open arms. After further fighting, Washington retreated across the Hudson River into New Jersey. Many of his soldiers had been captured, and others had deserted. Just weeks after the Patriots had declared their independence, their cause seemed doomed!

Victories at Trenton and Princeton. During this dark hour, Washington devised a daring plan. Howe had settled down for the winter in New York City, but he left about 1,400 soldiers in Trenton, New Jersey. These **mercenaries**, or hired fighters, were called Hessians because some of their leaders came from the German state of Hesse-Cassel.

On Christmas night, in the middle of a snowstorm, Washington led his troops across the ice-choked Delaware River, nine miles north of Trenton. At dawn the American soldiers overwhelmed the astonished Hessians and took more than 900 prisoners. The surprise was so complete that only about 30 Hessians and few, if any, Patriots died in the brief **Battle of Trenton**.

American Letters

The Crisis

Thomas Paine

In late 1776 the American cause seemed almost hopeless. Washington's appeals for more troops and supplies went unheard. Thomas Paine, author of Common Sense, *traveled with the army on its long retreat. In December he wrote a new pamphlet,* The Crisis, *to rouse Americans to the cause of freedom.*

These are the times that try men's souls. The summer soldier and the sunshine patriot will, in this crisis, shrink from the service of his country; but he that stands it now deserves the love and thanks of man and woman. Tyranny, like hell, is not easily conquered; yet we have this consolation [comfort] with us— that the harder the conflict, the more glorious the triumph. What we obtain too cheap, we esteem [honor] too lightly: It is dearness only that gives everything its value. Heaven knows how to put a proper price upon its goods; and it would be strange indeed if so celestial [heavenly] an article as freedom should not be highly rated. Britain, with an army to enforce her tyranny, has declared that she has a right not only to tax but "to bind us in all cases whatsoever," and if being bound in that manner is not slavery, then there is not such a thing as slavery upon earth. . . .

. . . I turn . . . to those who have nobly stood and are yet determined to stand the matter out. I call not upon a few, but upon all; not in this state or that state, but on every state. Up and help us. . . . Throw not the burden of the day upon Providence, but "show your faith by your works," that God may bless you. It matters not where you live, or what rank of life you hold, the evil or the blessing will reach you all. . . . The heart that feels not now is dead; the blood of his children will curse his cowardice who shrinks back at a time when a little might have saved the whole. . . . But he

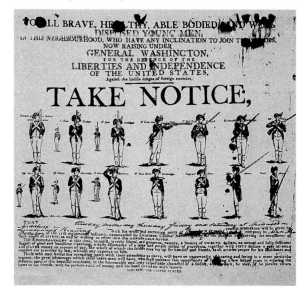

Recruitment poster for the Continental Army, led by General Washington

whose heart is firm, and whose conscience approves his conduct, will pursue his principles unto death. . . .

There are cases which cannot be overdone by language, and this is one. There are persons, too, who see not the full extent of the evil which threatens them; they solace [assure] themselves with hopes that the enemy, if he succeed, will be merciful. It is the madness of folly to expect mercy from those who have refused to do justice. . . .

. . . By perseverance [determination] and fortitude [endurance] we have the prospect of a glorious issue [result]; by cowardice and submission, the sad choice of a variety of evils—a ravaged country—a depopulated city— habitations [homes] without safety and slavery without hope. . . . Look on this picture and weep over it! And if there yet remains one thoughtless wretch who believes it not, let him suffer it unlamented [without grief].

Washington quickly struck again, this time at nearby Princeton, where he drove two British regiments from the town. Then he made camp for the winter at Morristown, New Jersey, about 30 miles west of New York. Washington's victories at Trenton and Princeton did wonders to raise American spirits during this difficult time.

A New British Strategy

The war began again in the spring of 1777. The British developed a complicated strategy for the upcoming battles. A British army under the command of General John "Gentleman Johnny" Burgoyne would march south from Canada into New York. At the same time, Howe would march north from New York City to meet Burgoyne. The British hoped this would threaten New England and draw Washington's Continental Army northward, where large numbers of Redcoat forces could defeat the Patriots.

Howe never fully understood his role in the plan, however, and did not carry it out. He decided to attack Philadelphia, home of the rebel Congress, instead. Howe moved his troops by sea to Delaware Bay and soon landed in Pennsylvania. Washington hurried south as soon as he learned of Howe's location.

When the two armies clashed just southwest of Philadelphia at Brandywine Creek, the Americans lost very badly. Howe then marched into Philadelphia. The American cause of independence once again seemed to be in danger of defeat.

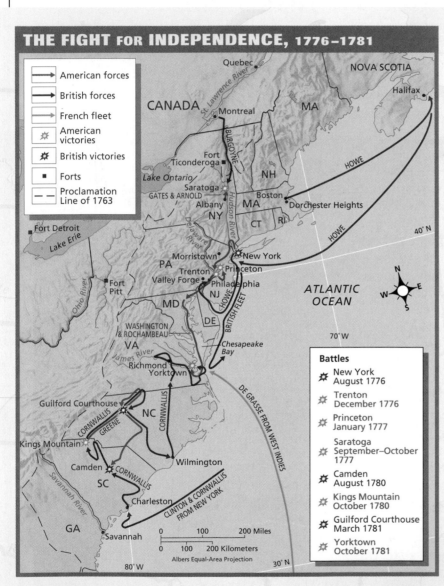

THE FIGHT FOR INDEPENDENCE, 1776–1781

Legend:
- American forces
- British forces
- French fleet
- ☆ American victories
- ✦ British victories
- ■ Forts
- Proclamation Line of 1763

Battles
- ✦ New York August 1776
- ☆ Trenton December 1776
- ☆ Princeton January 1777
- ☆ Saratoga September–October 1777
- ✦ Camden August 1780
- ☆ Kings Mountain October 1780
- ☆ Guilford Courthouse March 1781
- ☆ Yorktown October 1781

0   100   200 Miles
0   100   200 Kilometers
Albers Equal-Area Projection

Learning from Maps.
The Revolutionary War was fought across the vast area of the thirteen colonies. British troops could be transported on ships of the British fleet, while the American army had to move on foot.

• **Maps**

▶ **Region.** Where did most of the later battles of the war take place?

• **Battle of Saratoga**

Dressed in a fancy uniform, General John "Gentleman Johnny" Burgoyne surrenders to the Patriots. American and British officers later marked the event with a formal dinner.

Turning Point at Saratoga

Meanwhile, General Burgoyne, unaware that Howe would not be meeting him, marched southward from Canada with more than 7,200 troops. Burgoyne's army recaptured Fort Ticonderoga on July 5. Then their advance slowed to a crawl. The retreating Patriots burned bridges and chopped down huge trees to block the paths through the heavily forested region. With each passing day, more and more American militias gathered near Saratoga, New York, under the command of American general Horatio Gates.

On September 19 and October 7, 1777, Gates delivered crushing blows to Burgoyne's force. Baroness von Riedesel, whose husband commanded the German troops with the British, described the defeated army's retreat:

> **"Fires had been kindled in every direction, and many tents left standing to make the enemy believe that the camp was still there. We traveled continually the whole night. Little Frederica [von Riedesel's daughter] was afraid and would often begin to cry. I was therefore obliged to hold a pocket handkerchief over her mouth, lest our whereabouts should be discovered."**

With supplies running low and no help in sight, Burgoyne surrendered his force on October 17. The **Battle of Saratoga** proved to be the turning point in the war.

New Hopes and Hard Times

The Battle of Saratoga again raised the hopes of many Americans. It also brought aid from abroad. Without this assistance, the United States might never have been born.

Aid from abroad. When news of Saratoga reached Paris in early 1778, France officially recognized the government of the United States of America. France also signed a treaty of alliance and declared war on Great Britain.

The French were eager to weaken Britain, their longtime enemy. They had been helping the rebels with loans and supplies from the start of the war, and many French officers had already come to America to fight. After the Battle of Saratoga the French army and navy joined in the American Revolution directly, greatly strengthening the forces against the British.

Spain also declared war on Great Britain. Bernardo de Gálvez, the governor of Spanish Louisiana and Florida, sent weapons, supplies, and money. Later he captured the British fort at Pensacola, Florida.

The winter at Valley Forge.   Before much aid reached the colonies, Washington's army had to get through the winter of 1777–78 at Valley Forge, near Philadelphia. Supplies of food and clothing were scarce. One Patriot described the difficult, painful experience:

> **"Thousands were without blankets, and were obliged to warm themselves over fires all night. . . . It was not uncommon to track the march of the men over ice and frozen ground by the blood from their naked feet."**

In spite of such hardships, the tattered army made it through the winter.

Supplies ran so low at Valley Forge that many soldiers did not have enough clothing to leave their tents. Roughly 25 percent of the troops died during the cold winter.

● **Valley Forge Diary**

The March Toward Victory

After Saratoga, the British concentrated their efforts in the South. The Americans had control of New England and by 1779 they had won major victories in the West. The British thought they would have a better chance in the South, which reportedly contained many Loyalist militia units. Using their great navy, the British captured the ports of Savannah, Georgia, in 1778 and Charleston, South Carolina, in 1780. General Lord Charles Cornwallis had the responsibility of conquering the rest of the southern colonies. In August 1780 he defeated an American army at Camden, South Carolina.

Cornwallis soon faced trouble, however. Roving bands of Patriot **guerrillas**, or fighters who use hit-and-run tactics, began picking away at the British forces. These bands were led by Francis Marion and Thomas Sumter. Marion was called the "Swamp Fox" because he and his soldiers usually disappeared into the nearest swamp when the British attacked.

In March 1781 Cornwallis defeated an American force at Guilford Courthouse in North Carolina. It was a costly victory. Cornwallis lost about one third of his soldiers in the battle and became short of supplies. He quickly retreated to the coast, where the British navy could support him.

● **Heroes and Traitors**

Victory at Yorktown

By May 1781 Cornwallis had marched north into Virginia. He established his army at Yorktown, choosing a peninsula with harbor access at the mouth of the York River. A Patriot force under French general Lafayette took up positions outside Yorktown.

Washington, and Comte de Rochambeau (raw-shahm-boh) a French general, gave up a plan to attack New York City and marched south to Yorktown. Their combined forces arrived in September 1781. Over 16,000 French and American troops on the peninsula stood ready to prevent the more than 7,000 British soldiers from escaping over land. Off the coast, French warships blocked any help or escape by sea.

On October 9 Washington's artillery began to batter the British position in the **Battle of Yorktown**. Cornwallis sent off a last, desperate message to his commander. "If you cannot relieve me very soon, you must be prepared to hear the worst."

No assistance came. On October 19 Cornwallis surrendered. His troops marched out of Yorktown, while the band played "The World Turned Upside Down."

The fighting was over. The British still controlled New York City, Charleston, Savannah, and some frontier posts, but they no longer had the will to continue the war. In Great Britain, public opposition to the war had grown. In March 1782 Parliament voted, in effect, to give up "farther prosecution of offensive war on the continent of North America." About two weeks later Lord North resigned as prime minister. Although they still had to sign a peace treaty with the British, the Americans had won their independence.

General Charles Cornwallis surrenders at the Battle of Yorktown. The Americans had defeated the British!

Section 4 Review

IDENTIFY and explain the significance of the following: mercenaries, Battle of Trenton, John Burgoyne, Horatio Gates, Battle of Saratoga, Charles Cornwallis, guerrillas, Francis Marion, Battle of Yorktown

• **Glossary**

REVIEWING FOR DETAILS

1. What successes and failures did Washington's army have in New York, New Jersey, and Pennsylvania?

2. In what way can the Battle of Saratoga be considered the turning point in the American Revolution?

• **Time Line**

REVIEWING FOR UNDERSTANDING

3. **Geographic Literacy** Why was Washington able to defeat the British at Yorktown?

4. **Writing Mastery:** *Creating* Imagine that you are a soldier in Washington's army. Write a journal entry, song lyric, or poem about your experiences at New York, Trenton, or Valley Forge.

5. **Critical Thinking:** *Drawing Conclusions* Do you think the Patriots could have won the Revolution without help from foreign nations? Give facts to support your opinion.

Loyalists in America

A variety of people in the colonies supported the British during the Revolutionary War. It is difficult, however, to estimate exactly how many American colonists remained loyal to Britain. Some Patriots considered any person who did not actively support their cause to be a Loyalist. As a result, many people who tried to stay neutral during the war, including religious groups like the Quakers, were considered Loyalists.

Other Loyalist activity was very direct. Loyalist newspapers were published throughout the colonies. Loyalist military units, called Provincial Corps, were organized in several areas. New York was the leading colony for Loyalist activity, with five Loyalist newspapers and 18 Provincial Corps.

Many Loyalists fled the colonies during the war. After the British surrendered, thousands more Loyalists emigrated to escape persecution by Patriots. The majority went to Canada, while others went to Great Britain and the Caribbean Islands.

Sites of Loyalist Activity, 1775–1783

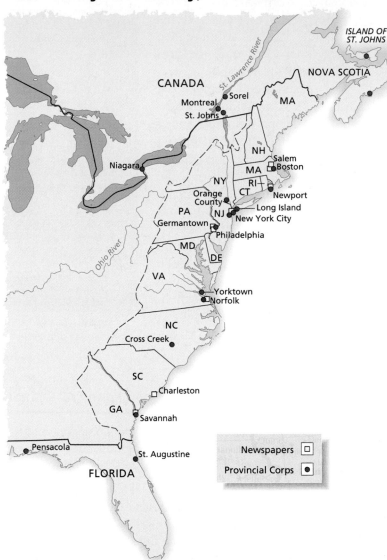

Some cities with many Loyalists had both newspapers and Provincial Corps. **Place:** Which colonial cities housed both Loyalist newspapers and Provincial Corps? What was the primary Loyalist activity in cities outside of the thirteen colonies?

Loyalist Resettlement, 1770–1780s

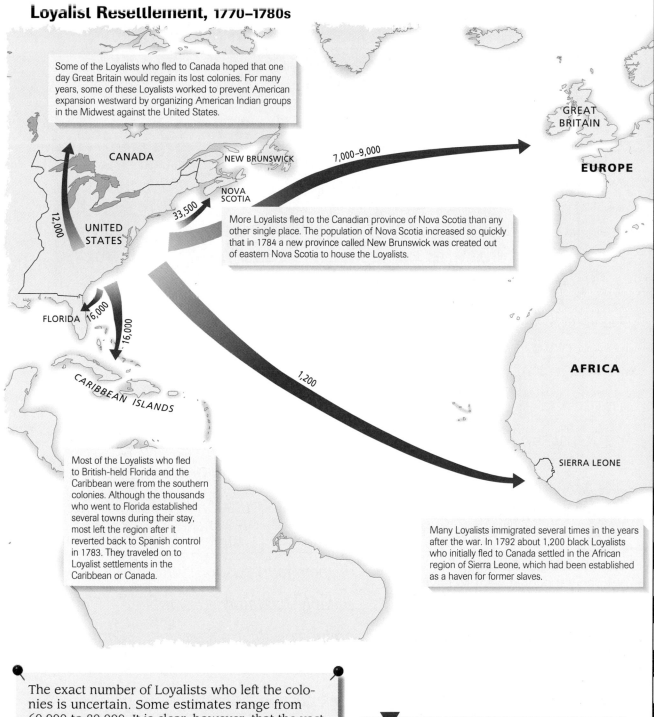

Some of the Loyalists who fled to Canada hoped that one day Great Britain would regain its lost colonies. For many years, some of these Loyalists worked to prevent American expansion westward by organizing American Indian groups in the Midwest against the United States.

CANADA

NEW BRUNSWICK

NOVA SCOTIA

GREAT BRITAIN

EUROPE

7,000–9,000

12,000

33,500

UNITED STATES

More Loyalists fled to the Canadian province of Nova Scotia than any other single place. The population of Nova Scotia increased so quickly that in 1784 a new province called New Brunswick was created out of eastern Nova Scotia to house the Loyalists.

FLORIDA 16,000

16,000

CARIBBEAN ISLANDS

1,200

AFRICA

SIERRA LEONE

Most of the Loyalists who fled to British-held Florida and the Caribbean were from the southern colonies. Although the thousands who went to Florida established several towns during their stay, most left the region after it reverted back to Spanish control in 1783. They traveled on to Loyalist settlements in the Caribbean or Canada.

Many Loyalists immigrated several times in the years after the war. In 1792 about 1,200 black Loyalists who initially fled to Canada settled in the African region of Sierra Leone, which had been established as a haven for former slaves.

The exact number of Loyalists who left the colonies is uncertain. Some estimates range from 60,000 to 80,000. It is clear, however, that the vast majority stayed in North America. **Movement:** Why might more Loyalists have gone to Canada or the Caribbean Islands rather than to Great Britain?

To learn more about the Loyalists in America, go to the interactive map, "The Loyalists," on the CD-ROM.

• Loyalists

CHAPTER 6

Nebraska State Historical Society

Forming a New Nation (1776–1789)

THEMES IN AMERICAN HISTORY

Constitutional Heritage:
Why might people want to have a basic set of written laws with which to govern their country?

Democratic Values:
Why might people choose a democratic form of government?

Economic Development:
How might economic issues influence people's political beliefs?

 • Video Opener

 • Skill Builder

ℬenjamin Franklin acknowledged that the U. S. Constitution had flaws. "When you assemble . . . men to have the advantage of their joint wisdom," he wrote, "you inevitably [certainly] assemble . . . all their prejudices, their passions. . . . Can a perfect production be expected?" Whatever its imperfections, Franklin concluded, the document gave the young nation a government it badly needed.

image above: Drafting the Constitution

Section 1

MOVING TOWARD SELF-GOVERNMENT

Multimedia Connections

Explore these related topics and materials on the CD–ROM to enrich your understanding of this section:

 Readings

- Iroquois Great Law of Peace
- What Is an American?

 Media Bank

- Ohio River Flatboat

 Profiles

- Benjamin Franklin

 Glossary

- English Bill of Rights
- Magna Carta
- town meetings

 Gazetteer

- Great Britain
- Virginia
- Maryland
- Appalachian Mountains

Many Americans realized that victory in the American Revolution would allow them to create an entirely new form of government. Patriot John Adams called this chance "a phenomenon [remarkable event] in the political world." He observed, "We must realize the theories of the wisest writers, and invite the people to erect the whole building with their own hands." The American experiment in the tricky art of self-government had begun.

As you read this section you will find out:

▶ **What traditions and ideas influenced government in America.**

▶ **What elements many of the first state constitutions had in common.**

▶ **Why state leaders created a national government but limited its power.**

Thinking About Government

Even before the Revolution ended, Americans began to develop an independent system of government, one shaped by many political and intellectual traditions. Some of these traditions were based in English experience. In 1215 English nobles had forced King John to sign Magna Carta, a document that limited the power of the monarch. It declared that the monarch could not collect taxes without the consent of an advisory body. Magna Carta thus provided the basis for establishing parliamentary democracy in Great Britain. Another model for American government was the English Bill of Rights of 1689, which declared that the monarch could not make or suspend any law, create any tax, or maintain an army in peacetime without the consent of Parliament.

Voting rights varied greatly from state to state. While most state constitutions did not extend the vote to women, for example, New Jersey gave women the vote between 1790 and 1807.

The Granger Collection, New York

Other ideas came from European philosophy. The **Enlightenment**, a movement during the 1700s that grew out of the Scientific Revolution, influenced many American leaders. Philosophers of the Enlightenment used reason to investigate and to try to improve government and society. For example, in his book *The Social Contract,* philosopher Jean-Jacque Rousseau (roo-soh) studied many different forms of government and concluded that the best was one in which everyone was equal.

American leaders also drew on colonial traditions, such as New England town meetings. In these gatherings, ordinary citizens participated in community government by voicing their opinions on important issues.

State Governments and Constitutions

During the Revolution, Patriots wanted to make the colonies into independent states. In order to remove British political controls, leaders in each colony either revised their old royal charter or wrote a new state **constitution**—a set of laws that defines the basic structure and powers of a government.

Under the new constitutions, powerful state legislatures replaced the colonial assemblies. Because the colonists feared government abuses, however, most constitutions put some controls on the legislature. Many established short terms of office, in part so that

voters could quickly get rid of unpopular representatives. One North Carolina man expressed many colonists' fears of a powerful central government:

> "The more experience I acquire, the stronger is my conviction [belief] that *unlimited power can not be safely trusted* to any man or set of men on earth. . . . Power of all kinds has an irresistible propensity [tendency] to increase a desire for itself."

The new constitutions assigned little power to the state executive. In addition, most state constitutions limited the power of judges by placing them under the control of the legislature.

Many of the state constitutions contained a bill of rights. These guaranteed that the state governments would not violate the rights and freedoms of their citizens.

The constitutions reflected Americans' desire for a **republican** form of government, or one in which the people hold the power and give elected representatives the authority to make and carry out laws. The constitutions greatly expanded **suffrage**, or voting rights, for white men. Suffrage varied from state to state, even for white men. In Pennsylvania, for example, all free men who paid taxes could vote. But in South Carolina, men had to own a certain amount of property to vote.

Most of the states did not extend suffrage to African Americans, American Indians, and women. During the next few decades, however, supporters of the antislavery movement convinced most northern states to ban slavery in their territory and to give voting rights to free African American men.

The Articles of Confederation

Setting up the state governments proved easier than forming a central structure. This was an old problem. In 1754 Benjamin Franklin had drafted the **Albany Plan of Union**, a proposal for permanently uniting the colonies. He believed that common interests made it worthwhile for the colonies to have some sort of common government. At the time, his plan attracted little support.

During the 1760s and 1770s, however, citizens responded to the need for group action with the Stamp Act Congress and the boycott of British goods. When the Revolution finally came, Franklin made the case for unity. "We must all hang together," he said, "or assuredly we shall all hang separately."

The Second Continental Congress eventually agreed with Franklin. It became, in effect, America's first government. It operated a postal service, planned finances, and even printed paper money. The Congress also appointed American **diplomats**, or officials who conducted government relations with foreign countries.

By November 1777 Congress had also written a constitution called the **Articles of Confederation**. This document was America's first national constitution. The Articles stressed the independence of the separate states. It established the United States of America as only "a firm league of friendship"—a loose alliance of states.

The Articles of Confederation created a single national governing body called the **Confederation Congress** and generally gave it the powers that had been granted to the Second Continental Congress. Each of the 13 states had one vote in Congress and was

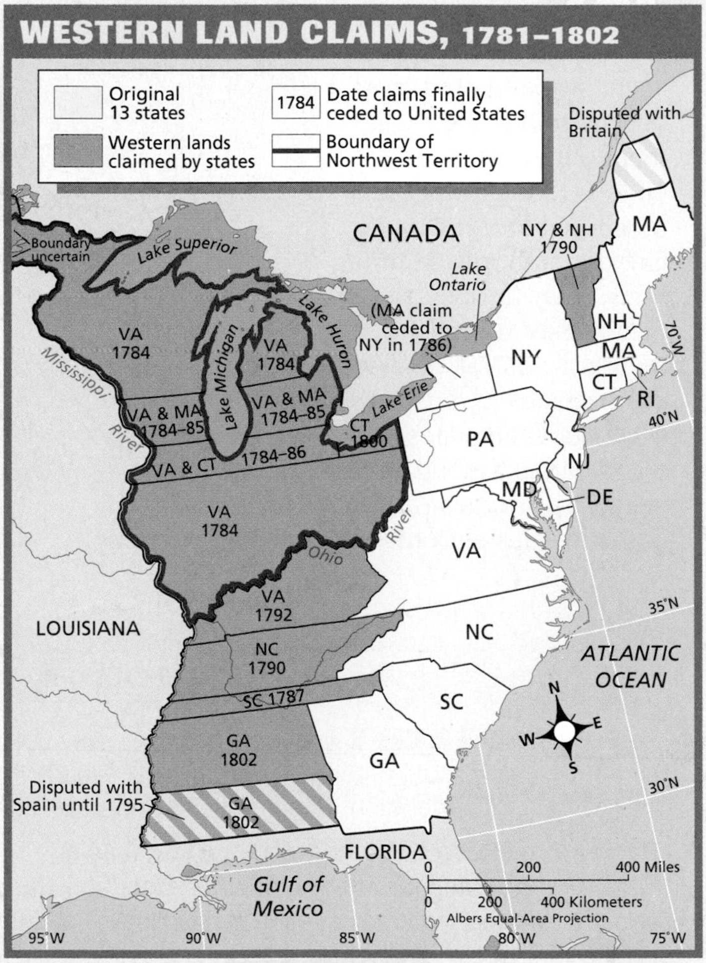
WESTERN LAND CLAIMS, 1781–1802
Original 13 states
Western lands claimed by states
1784 Date claims finally ceded to United States
Boundary of Northwest Territory
Disputed with Britain
CANADA
MA
NY & NH 1790
Boundary uncertain
Lake Superior
Lake Ontario
(MA claim ceded to NY in 1786)
Lake Huron
Lake Michigan
VA 1784
VA 1784
NH
NY
MA
CT
RI
Mississippi River
VA & MA 1784–85
VA & MA 1784–85
Lake Erie
CT 1800
PA
VA & CT 1784–86
NJ
MD
DE
VA 1784
Ohio River
VA
VA 1792
LOUISIANA
NC
NC 1790
ATLANTIC OCEAN
SC 1787
SC
GA 1802
GA
Disputed with Spain until 1795
GA 1802
FLORIDA
Gulf of Mexico
0 200 400 Miles
0 200 400 Kilometers
Albers Equal-Area Projection
95°W
90°W
85°W
80°W
75°W
70°W
40°N
35°N
30°N
N
S
E
W

Learning from Maps. Many of the original 13 states had western land claims, some of which were larger than the states themselves. Most of these claims were eventually ceded to the United States.

▶ **Location.** What state claimed the greatest amount of western land?

• **Maps**

supposed to contribute money for national defense and other expenses.

The Articles had serious weaknesses, however. Congress could not take action on certain important matters, such as declaring war or making treaties, without approval by nine states. The Articles also did not specify how Congress was to exercise or enforce many of the powers it did have. For example, Congress could decide how much money it needed and how much each state should pay, but it could not make them pay.

The states reserved other powers as well, like the authority to print their own money. They could also establish their own policies for **interstate commerce**, or business and trade between states.

Rivalries among several states held up **ratification**, or formal approval, of the Articles of Confederation. After deciding that the document could not go into effect until all the states had accepted it, Congress distributed copies in late 1777. Maryland and other states without large western land holdings would not ratify it until all state claims to lands beyond the Appalachian Mountains were turned over to the new United States. Virginia and a few other states with huge land claims refused to do so, unwilling to lose money from western land sales. Eventually, only two states—Maryland and Virginia—continued to fight over this issue. In January 1781 Virginia finally agreed to give up some of its claims in a bid for national unity. Maryland then ratified the Articles soon after.

The Granger Collection, New York

Benjamin Franklin, a scientist and political leader, conducted electrical experiments with lightning.

Section 1 Review

• **Glossary**

IDENTIFY and explain the significance of the following: Enlightenment, constitution, republican, suffrage, Albany Plan of Union, diplomats, Articles of Confederation, Confederation Congress, interstate commerce, ratification

REVIEWING FOR DETAILS

1. What did many of the first state constitutions have in common?
2. Why did state leaders establish a national government but limit its power?

REVIEWING FOR UNDERSTANDING

3. **Geographic Literacy** Why might different amounts of western land ownership lead to conflict between states?

4. **Writing Mastery:** *Informing* Imagine that you are a historian. Write a paragraph explaining how Magna Carta, the English Bill of Rights of 1689, the Enlightenment, and New England town meetings influenced American government.

5. **Critical Thinking:** *Synthesizing Information* How did the state constitutions and the Articles of Confederation display Americans' fear of powerful government?

Section 2

EXPERIMENTS IN SELF-GOVERNMENT

Multimedia Connections

Explore these related topics and materials on the CD–ROM to enrich your understanding of this section:

 Media Bank

- Shays at the Court
- Defeat of Shays's Rebellion
- Town of Cincinnati in 1800
- Classroom Equipment

 Simulation

- The Democracy Project

 Gazetteer

- Ohio
- Indiana
- Illinois
- Michigan
- Wisconsin
- Massachusetts

 Profiles

- Daniel Shays

 Readings

- Schooling in Early America

John Adams expressed his concerns about the new experiment in self-government. "Our Country . . . is not yet out of Danger," he wrote. ". . . The Prospect before Us is joyful, but there are Intricacies [difficulties] in it, which will perplex [puzzle] the wisest Heads and wound the most honest hearts." Though excited by the chance to build a new government and society, Americans faced the future with more than a little fear.

As you read this section you will find out:

▶ **How the United States developed the territory beyond the Appalachian Mountains.**

▶ **What economic problems the new nation faced.**

▶ **Why Massachusetts farmers revolted against their state government.**

The Confederation Congress Succeeds

Despite its initial failure to secure ratification, the Confederation Congress had some successes. For example, it appointed diplomats to work out a complicated treaty with Great Britain and developed western lands.

The Treaty of Paris of 1783. One of Congress's most important achievements was the **Treaty of Paris of 1783**. Negotiated by an American delegation in France, it officially ended the Revolutionary War and signaled Britain's recognition of U.S. independence. It also enlarged American territory.

The Treaty of Paris required the British to remove their armed forces from the new country. In return, the United States agreed to restore the rights of American Loyalists.

Congress also promised to ask the states to return seized Loyalist property, although few states actually did. Finally, the United States promised to let British subjects try to recover prewar debts owed them by Americans.

Once the treaty established the borders of the United States, Congress turned to organizing the Trans-Appalachian West, or the land between the Appalachian Mountains and the Mississippi River. To do this, Congress passed laws called land ordinances.

The Land Ordinance of 1785.
Congress established a plan for the orderly sale of the country's western territory with the **Land Ordinance of 1785**. The law called for the land to be surveyed and divided into townships six miles on a side. Each township was split into sections of 640 acres. These pieces could then be sold. The law also required that one particular section per township be reserved to support a public school.

The Northwest Ordinance.
The Land Ordinance of 1787, better known as the **Northwest Ordinance**, was a plan to create a government for the region north of the Ohio River and west of Pennsylvania. This area became known as the Northwest Territory.

The law provided that the land be divided into smaller territories. After 5,000 free men of voting age had settled in a territory, they could then elect a legislature and send a nonvoting delegate to Congress. The Northwest Ordinance outlined the next step:

> **"Whenever any of the said States shall have sixty thousand free inhabitants therein, such State shall be admitted . . . into the Congress of the United States, on an equal footing with the original States in all respects whatever."**

In addition, the law required new states to establish a republican form of government. It provided that "there shall be neither slavery nor involuntary servitude in the [Northwest Territory] otherwise than in the

NORTH AMERICA IN 1783

- Hudson Bay
- ATLANTIC OCEAN
- NEWFOUNDLAND
- Disputed
- CANADA
- Disputed
- Mississippi River
- Ohio River
- Trans-Appalachian West
- APPALACHIAN MTS.
- UNITED STATES
- LOUISIANA
- Rio Grande
- Disputed
- FLORIDA
- NEW MEXICO
- Gulf of Mexico
- WEST INDIES
- PACIFIC OCEAN
- NEW SPAIN
- CARIBBEAN SEA
- 140°W
- 40°N
- 20°N
- 120°W
- 100°W
- 80°W
- 60°W
- 40°W
- 60°N

	United States
	French
	Spanish
	British
	Russian
	Unclaimed

0   500   1,000 Miles
0   500   1,000 Kilometers
Azimuthal Equal-Area Projection

Learning from Maps.
The Treaty of Paris granted the United States territory that included the original 13 states and lands west of the Appalachian Mountains.

• Maps

▶ **Place.** What was the western boundary of the United States in 1783?

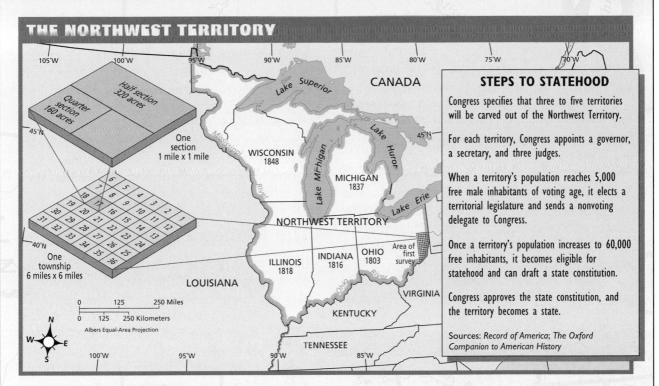

THE NORTHWEST TERRITORY

STEPS TO STATEHOOD

Congress specifies that three to five territories will be carved out of the Northwest Territory.

For each territory, Congress appoints a governor, a secretary, and three judges.

When a territory's population reaches 5,000 free male inhabitants of voting age, it elects a territorial legislature and sends a nonvoting delegate to Congress.

Once a territory's population increases to 60,000 free inhabitants, it becomes eligible for statehood and can draft a state constitution.

Congress approves the state constitution, and the territory becomes a state.

Sources: *Record of America; The Oxford Companion to American History*

Learning from Maps. The Northwest Territory was divided into townships of six square miles. Each township was subdivided into 36 sections of 640 acres.

▶ **Place.** What river is the southern boundary of the Northwest Territory?

● **Maps**

punishment of crimes." This represented a great triumph for Americans who opposed slavery. However, it also showed the need to compromise with those who favored the institution because the ordinance allowed the return of slaves who had escaped into the Northwest Territory.

Under the Northwest Ordinance, the states of Ohio, Indiana, Illinois, Michigan, and Wisconsin eventually were formed. As the nation expanded westward, it used the same basic method to admit new states.

Trade Problems

Peace quickly brought out the weaknesses of a national government that was only a "league of friendship" among the states. Instead of helping each other, as friends would, the states competed fiercely.

Interstate commerce. Under the Articles of Confederation, Congress had no power to regulate trade between states. Each state set its own interstate commerce policies, which sometimes clashed with those of its neighbors. By the mid-1780s there were 13 different sets of trade regulations in the United States!

Like many other American businesspeople, a group of concerned Philadelphia merchants argued that Congress should be given the power to oversee interstate commerce. They insisted that national considerations must be placed ahead of state interests in order to avoid quarrels:

"If Congress should think fit to act upon it, . . . a regard to *national interest* [well-being] may get the better of that jealous spirit which on other occasions has hitherto [until now] defeated the wisest

plan for redeeming our *national credit & character.*"

To give Congress authority over interstate commerce, all the states would have to approve **amendments**, or official changes, to the Articles. Political leaders could not reach unanimous agreement, however, and the trade problem continued.

International trade. The Articles also denied Congress the power to collect **tariffs**, or taxes on imported goods. This affected international trade and hurt many American businesses.

During the war, British manufacturers did not sell their products in America. Colonial businesses therefore had started supplying goods. With peace restored, the British began to offer their manufactured items in the United States at low prices in order to win back customers. Americans might have controlled this trend by taxing British imports. Again, Congress lacked the power to do so. The states could not stop the practice, either. If one state taxed the goods, British merchants could simply ship their products to a state that had no tariff laws.

The Money Problem

Under the Articles, states were supposed to cover the expenses of the national government. This system never worked well, however. Most states tended to pay only for things that benefited them directly. For example, North Carolina and Georgia, both open to attacks by American Indian or Spanish forces, agreed to contribute money for defense along the frontier. South Carolina, however, was geographically protected from these dangers by North Carolina and Georgia and thus refused to pay.

Since Congress could not force the states to contribute money, it soon had serious financial problems. Desperate to pay its bills, Congress printed more and more paper money. Under the Articles, state governments could issue paper currency too, and all did so. Because there was so much money in circulation, it fell in value. Fearing that merchants and bankers would refuse to accept the new money, people lost confidence in it. When the central or state governments printed large amounts of paper money, steep inflation resulted.

Not all Americans disliked this inflation, however. It helped **debtors**, or people who owe money, pay off their accounts. For example, a farmer who borrowed $10 when wheat sold for 25 cents a bushel had to sell

Global Connections

American Trade with China

The end of the American Revolution brought peace—and conflict—to American merchants. Resentful at the war's outcome and determined to prevent the new nation from succeeding, Great Britain closed markets formerly open to American businesses. Britain also restricted trade between the United States and the British West Indies, a large market for American goods of all sorts.

American merchants soon found a new trading partner—China. Before the Revolution, Great Britain had refused to allow American ships to sail to China. Independence removed that obstacle, of course, and American merchants quickly took advantage of their new opportunity. The *Empress of China* left the Atlantic coast in 1784 carrying ginseng, a root popular in China. After sailing for several months, it reached the trading city of Canton, becoming one of the first American ships ever to enter Chinese waters. This voyage launched a profitable trading relationship between the United States and China.

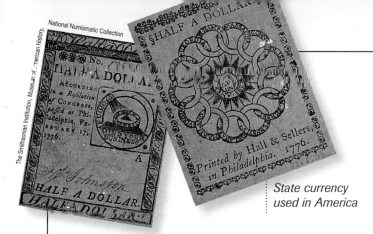

State currency used in America

40 bushels to pay the $10 back. If inflation drove the price of wheat up to 50 cents a bushel, the farmer had to sell only 20 bushels to pay the debt. This meant that **creditors**, or people to whom money is owed, would be repaid with currency that had only half the purchasing power of that which they had lent.

Shays's Rebellion

Events in Massachusetts soon gave many Americans more cause to worry. Unlike other state governments, the Massachusetts legislature would not print enough paper money to meet popular demands. In addition, state leaders raised taxes, a move that particularly hurt small property owners. Poor farmers who could not pay these taxes had their farms seized by the government. Anger grew, and farmers began to demonstrate peacefully against what they called the "gross [terrible] mismanagement of our rulers."

Daniel Shays eventually emerged as a leader of the protests. He was a former Patriot who had fought at Ticonderoga, Bunker Hill, and Saratoga. In September 1786 Shays gathered a group of protesters in Springfield, Massachusetts. They forced the state supreme court to shut down, hoping to postpone or end legal judgments against poor farmers. Then in January 1787 Shays and his followers attacked the Springfield **arsenal**, or arms storage center, to get weapons. The governor sent more than 4,000 militia to guard the building and defeated the rebel force. Shays lost later battles as well and fled to Vermont. By late February the uprising had collapsed.

Although **Shays's Rebellion** failed in the short run, it led to improvements for many Massachusetts farmers. Soon after the disturbance, the state legislature enacted some of the rebels' demands.

Section 2 Review

IDENTIFY and explain the significance of the following: Treaty of Paris of 1783, Land Ordinance of 1785, Northwest Ordinance, amendments, tariffs, debtors, creditors, arsenal, Shays's Rebellion

• **Glossary**

LOCATE and explain the importance of the following: Trans-Appalachian West, Northwest Territory

REVIEWING FOR DETAILS

• **Gazetteer**

1. How did Congress develop the region beyond the Appalachian Mountains?
2. What economic problems did the United States encounter after the Revolution?

REVIEWING FOR UNDERSTANDING

3. **Geographic Literacy** How might the acquisition of the Northwest Territory have benefited the United States?

4. **Writing Mastery:** *Persuading* Imagine that you are a poor Massachusetts farmer. Write a short letter to convince your neighbors to join in Shays's Rebellion.

5. **Critical Thinking:** *Cause and Effect* How did weaknesses in the Articles of Confederation cause economic and political problems?

Section 3

"WE THE PEOPLE"

Multimedia Connections

Explore these related topics and materials on the CD-ROM to enrich your understanding of this section:

 Profiles

- James Madison
- George Washington
- William Paterson
- Edmund Randolph

 Media Bank

- Federal System
- Requirements for Federal Office
- Dolley Madison
- Abigail Adams
- James Madison
- Edits to the Constitution
- Remember the Ladies

 Biographies

- Abigail Adams
- Benjamin Banneker

 Glossary

- Electoral College

B efore long, many American leaders concluded that their first experiment in self-government was not working well. In 1787 they met in Philadelphia to try to find some solutions. Philadelphia was a crowded, hot, smelly city. The humidity was almost unbearable, and biting flies swarmed everywhere. Some delegates had occasional outbursts of temper, but by the end of the steamy summer, they had created a very important document—the U.S. Constitution.

As you read this section you will find out:

▶ **Why political leaders decided to hold the Constitutional Convention.**

▶ **How the delegates settled major disagreements.**

▶ **How the delegates viewed the role of each branch of government.**

A Meeting in Philadelphia

Along with widespread economic problems, Shays's Rebellion forced some Americans to consider the future of the Confederation Congress and republican government itself. They referred to life under the Articles of Confederation as a "parade of horribles" and asked some difficult questions. Did allowing the people to rule mean that they would resort to violence whenever their government did something they disliked? Would debtors try to get out of paying their debts whenever they gained control of the legislature?

These concerns led some political leaders and businesspeople to consider **reforms**, or improvements, to the Articles. After a series of meetings, they called for a gathering of representatives from all the states to discuss the national government.

Congress reluctantly approved this proposal, and every state but Rhode Island agreed to send delegates to the meeting. Like many other leaders, George Washington

• **Road to Philadelphia**

was pleased with this development. In a letter to a friend, he wrote of his hope that the delegates would closely examine the Articles:

> **"My wish is that the Convention . . . probe the defects [faults] of the Constitution [the Articles] to the bottom, and provide radical [extreme] cures, whether they are agreed to or not. A conduct like this will stamp wisdom and dignity on the proceedings."**

On May 25, 1787, the delegates gathered for the first session of what became known as the **Constitutional Convention**. They met at the Pennsylvania State House in a simply furnished room described as "neat but not elegant."

The delegates elected Washington as the presiding officer of the gathering. They also decided to keep the proceedings secret until they had completed their work. This encouraged people to speak frankly about difficult issues. Despite the secrecy, Virginia delegate James Madison decided to keep careful notes. A leading Patriot, he had helped write Virginia's constitution and knew the impor-

tance of precise record-keeping. Madison's notes give us a thorough account of the speeches and events at the convention.

Representation: Conflict and Compromise

Just four days after the start of the convention, Virginia delegate Edmund Randolph presented a set of resolutions that would create a new system of government instead of merely revising the Articles of Confederation. Drafted in part by Madison, this **Virginia Plan** proposed that the "league of friendship" among the states become a truly national government.

The Virginia Plan provided for a central government with three separate branches. There was to be an executive and a **bicameral**, or two-house, legislature. The plan also mentioned a system of national courts.

The Virginia Plan suggested that state population determine representation in both houses of the legislature. Members of the legislature would then choose the executive. Not surprisingly, delegates from states with large populations favored the Virginia Plan because it gave them a great deal of influence. The plan, however, made those from states with small populations very uneasy. They feared that the heavily populated states would take control of the new government.

In mid-June, William Paterson offered the **New Jersey Plan**, a set of resolutions written by delegates from states with small populations. This plan proposed to continue the one-state, one-vote system used under the Articles. After just a few days of debate, however, the delegates rejected the New

George Washington oversees the Constitutional Convention.

• **Signing of the Constitution**

Jersey Plan and decided to continue their discussions using the Virginia Plan as the model for the new government.

This defeat of the New Jersey Plan did not mean that all was well. The delegates from the smaller states dug in their heels on the question of representation by population. The fight dragged on for weeks and threatened to break up the convention. The delegates finally accepted what is often called the **Great Compromise**. It established that population would determine representation in the national legislature's lower house, while each state would have an equal vote in the legislature's upper house.

The Question of Slavery

Even after approving the Great Compromise, the delegates continued to clash over whether or not slaves should be counted in a state's population. Many northern delegates felt that allowing southerners to include slaves gave the slave states an unfair political advantage and encouraged slavery. Southern delegates insisted that slaves be counted in a state's population. They hoped this would give the South more votes in the legislature.

After a heated debate, the delegates agreed to the **Three-Fifths Compromise**. It established a system of counting "the whole Number of free Persons" and three fifths of "all other Persons," meaning slaves, for the purposes of representation. In another compromise related to slavery, the delegates permitted the importation of slaves until 1808. The delegates also wrote a clause that required states to return any "Person held to Service or Labor" who managed to escape into their territory.

It is clear today that when the delegates spoke of "We the People," they were not referring to slaves. Nowhere did the U.S. Constitution contain the words *slave* or *slavery*.

Some of the participants at the convention probably felt uneasy about allowing slavery to exist in a nation that proclaimed "all men are created equal." Others, however, believed that African Americans were inferior. Along with the delegates, nearly all white people at the time shared this **prejudice**, or unreasonable opinion unsupported by facts. Many delegates also thought that individual states should decide the issue of slavery. Of course, some delegates—northern and southern—were themselves slaveholders. Whatever their personal feelings about slavery, they voted to protect their own economic and political interests.

History Makers

Roger Sherman (1721–1793)

Few delegates at the Constitutional Convention could match the public service of Connecticut's

The Granger Collection, New York

Roger Sherman. As a member of the Second Continental Congress, Sherman had helped draft both the Declaration of Independence and the Articles of Confederation. Sherman regarded the convention as fundamentally important to the nation's future.

His commitment to continuing the fragile convention led Sherman to help write and to introduce in early June 1787 what became known as the Great Compromise. He did not offer much explanation of the plan, however, and at first it received little attention. After weeks of standstill, however, the delegates looked at the proposal again. They adopted the Great Compromise in mid-July and went on to complete the U.S. Constitution.

This antislavery painting shows "Liberty" extending knowledge to freed slaves.

In the end, many delegates believed that they had to accept the existence of slavery if they wanted to form a truly united nation. The delegates feared that if they threatened slavery or its supporters, some of the southern states would not join the Union.

The delegates' actions at Philadelphia led some free African Americans to step up their work against slavery and the slave trade. They argued that all African Americans should be free. A few years after the convention, black scientist Benjamin Banneker expressed regret that the nation's leaders showed so little concern for African Americans:

"If your love for . . . those inestimable [very great] laws . . . was founded on sincerity, you could not but be solicitous [concerned], that every individual, of whatever rank or distinction, might with you equally enjoy the blessings thereof."

Forming a Government

The delegates eventually wrote a constitution that described the powers and shape of the new government. It would consist of three main parts: a **legislative branch** to write the laws; an **executive branch** to carry out the laws; and a **judicial branch** to interpret the laws. The Constitution also outlined various processes and procedures, such as making treaties and electing government officials.

The legislature. The delegates at the convention intended to make the national legislature the most powerful part of the new government. They were determined to prevent it from being controlled by a monarch or prime minister.

The delegates assumed that the lower house, or the **House of Representatives**, would act on behalf of the people. They intended that the upper house, or the **Senate**, would give the executive advice and consent on appointments and foreign treaties.

The presidency. One of the most important results of the convention was the creation of a powerful executive branch. When the delegates thought about the new office, they were torn in different directions. Some did not even want an executive official. Others wanted a national leader, but not one who was too powerful. Nor did they want a figurehead, someone who appeared to rule but had no real

In the early 1790s, Benjamin Banneker published a popular almanac and also wrote a well-known letter defending the intellectual capabilities of African Americans.

power. The delegates finally decided on a strong executive—a president who would act as the head of state.

Everyone expected that the first president would be George Washington. This was one reason why the delegates gave the presidency so much power. They admired and trusted him so much that they made the office worthy of his talents. Washington could not be president forever, of course. To create a way of

The Articles of Confederation and the Constitution

ARTICLES	CONSTITUTION
Executive Branch	
• No executive to administer and enforce legislation; Congress had sole authority to govern	• President administers and enforces federal laws
• Executive committee to oversee government when Congress out of session	
Legislative Branch	
• A unicameral (one-house) legislature	• A bicameral (two-house) legislature
• Each state had one vote, regardless of population	• Each state has equal representation in the Senate; each state represented according to population in the House of Representatives
• Nine votes (of the original 13) to enact legislation	• Simple majority to enact legislation
Judicial Branch	
• No national court system	• National court system, headed by Supreme Court
• Congress to establish temporary courts to hear cases of piracy	• Courts to hear cases involving national laws, treaties, the Constitution, cases between states, between citizens of different states, or between a state and citizens of another state
Other Matters	
• Admission to the Confederation by 9 votes (of 13)	• Congress to admit new states; all must have a republican form of government
• Amendment of Articles by unanimous vote	• Amendment of the Constitution by two-thirds vote of both houses of Congress or by national convention and ratified by three fourths of the states
• The states retained independence	• The states accept the Constitution as the supreme law of the land

A Better Foundation. The Constitution fixed some of the weak points of the Articles of Confederation. How did the documents differ in terms of the executive branch? How might the Constitution's provisions regarding the executive branch have remedied some of the weaknesses of the Articles?

choosing his successor, the delegates worked out a complicated system called the Electoral College. (See the Constitution Handbook on page 141.)

The judiciary. The Constitution established a system of national courts that would be separate from those of the individual states. The document specifically mentioned only a "supreme" court, but it also allowed for the creation of lower courts. The delegates left it up to Congress to determine the number of judges on the Supreme Court and the actual structure of the lower courts.

"The Supreme Law of the Land"

A brief article in the Constitution established the document as "the supreme Law of the Land." It replaced the Articles' "league of friendship" with a national government.

The Constitution divided power between state and national governments in a system known as **federalism**. For example, the delegates gave the national government the authority to collect tariffs and other taxes on goods, regulate interstate and international trade, coin money, and maintain an army and a navy. The delegates allowed states to keep many of their powers. The states still had the right to tax their citizens, control public education, punish criminals, and make all sorts of local regulations.

The U.S. Constitution fixed many problems of the Articles. The Constitution's Preamble neatly summarized the intent of these changes. The "People" were creating "a more perfect Union." It would "promote the general Welfare" by supplying the national unity lacking under the Articles.

The noble bald eagle became a symbol for the United States.

Section 3 Review

• Glossary

IDENTIFY and explain the significance of the following: reforms, Constitutional Convention, James Madison, Virginia Plan, bicameral, New Jersey Plan, Great Compromise, Three-Fifths Compromise, prejudice, legislative branch, executive branch, judicial branch, House of Representatives, Senate, federalism

REVIEWING FOR DETAILS
1. What factors encouraged political leaders to hold the Constitutional Convention?
2. How did the delegates decide major disputes?
3. What were to be the roles of each branch of government?

REVIEWING FOR UNDERSTANDING
4. **Writing Mastery:** *Expressing* Write a paragraph expressing your opinion about the way the delegates dealt with slavery at the Constitutional Convention.
5. **Critical Thinking:** *Drawing Conclusions* Why did the delegates create a system of government based on federalism?

Section 4

THE "MORE PERFECT UNION"

Multimedia Connections

Explore these related topics and materials on the CD–ROM to enrich your understanding of this section:

 Gazetteer

• New York City

 Biographies

• Alexander Hamilton

 Profiles

• John Hancock
• Paul Revere

 Atlas

• Federalists and Antifederalists

 Media Bank

• *Federalist Papers*
• Samuel Adams

As states ratified the new Constitution, many Americans rejoiced at what they hoped would finally be a successful attempt at self-government. Celebrations often began with large, noisy parades. Some cities lit towering bonfires. Philadelphia threw a huge party for its citizens. An observer reported that 17,000 people gathered "to celebrate . . . the constitution of the United States, and that they separated at an early hour, without intoxication, or a single quarrel."

As you read this section you will find out:

▶ **Why Federalists supported the Constitution.**

▶ **Why Antifederalists opposed the Constitution.**

▶ **How the first presidential election took place.**

Federalists and Antifederalists

In September 1787 the delegates completed the Constitution and sent copies to each state. The document would become law when 9 of the 13 states had ratified it.

In the months following the Constitutional Convention, popular interest in the document was high. People everywhere read and discussed the proposal. They elected representatives to state ratifying conventions, where the final decision to approve or disapprove the Constitution would be made.

Different opinions. Since the Constitution involved so many important changes, it did not have everyone's approval. Supporters of the new Constitution called themselves **Federalists**. Many were wealthy lawyers, merchants, and planters. Those who opposed the new Constitution became known as **Antifederalists**. They tended to come from rural areas and were generally less wealthy than Federalists.

The Federalists argued that the Constitution would strike a good balance between national unity and state independence. They believed that a strong central government would help prevent disturbances like Shays's Rebellion. Federalists also thought that the Constitution represented a new age of democracy. For example, one New Jersey farmer declared:

> "**What a glorious spectacle would the adoption of this constitution exhibit!** . . . **We should probably have the honor of teaching mankind** . . . THAT **MAN** HIMSELF IS ACTUALLY CAPABLE OF GOVERNING HIMSELF.**"**

The Antifederalists disapproved of the Constitution because they felt the powerful new central government might destroy the states' independence. They also feared the power of the wealthy over poorer citizens. As one Massachusetts Antifederalist described the situation, if the Federalists win, "they will swallow up all us little folks." The Constitution, another excited Antifederalist wrote, was "a beast, dreadful and terrible," which "devours, breaks into pieces, and stamps [the states] with his feet."

A bill of rights. Like the Articles of Confederation, the Constitution did not contain a bill of rights to guarantee certain freedoms. Foremost among these rights were freedom of speech, freedom of the press, and freedom of religion. Under the Articles, the central government had been weak. In addition, many of the state constitutions contained bills of rights. A national bill of rights had not seemed important, but now some people feared for their freedoms.

Ratifying the Constitution

As political leaders considered the new Constitution, no one knew what to expect. In some states the Federalists had a clear majority, but in others the Antifederalists ruled public opinion.

An easy start. Delaware was the first state to ratify the Constitution. In December 1787 Delaware delegates voted unanimously to approve the document. By early January 1788 Pennsylvania, New Jersey, Georgia, and Connecticut also had ratified the Constitution by large margins.

Ratification by just nine states would be enough to adopt the Constitution. But how effective could the government be if populous states like Massachusetts, New York, and Virginia refused to join the United States?

The Pennsylvania Packet, *and* Daily Advertiser.

[Price Four-Pence.] WEDNESDAY, SEPTEMBER 19, 1787. [No. 2690.]

WE, the People of the United States, in order to form a more perfect Union, establish Justice, insure domestic Tranquility, provide for the common Defence, promote the General Welfare, and secure the Blessings of Liberty to Ourselves and our Posterity, do ordain and establish this Constitution for the United States of America.

ARTICLE I.

Sect. 1. ALL legislative powers herein granted shall be vested in a Congress of the United States, which shall consist of a Senate and House of Representatives.

Sect. 2. The House of Representatives shall be composed of members chosen every second year by the people of the several states, and the electors in each state shall have the qualifications requisite for electors of the most numerous branch of the state legislature.

No person shall be a representative who shall not have attained to the age of twenty-five years, and been seven years a citizen of the United States, and who shall not, when elected, be an inhabitant of that state in which he shall be chosen.

Representatives and direct taxes shall be apportioned among the several states which may be included within this Union, according to their respective numbers, which shall be determined by add-

This Pennsylvania newspaper was one of many that reprinted the full text of the Constitution for its readers. The preamble to the Constitution is shown here.

Citizens of New York City celebrate the state's ratification of the U.S. Constitution on July 26, 1788.

Difficult battles. The Massachusetts convention met in January 1788 and debated the Constitution for nearly a month. At first, the Antifederalists seemed to have a majority. Samuel Adams and John Hancock were delegates. Because they were famous supporters of states' rights, many people thought they were Antifederalists.

The Federalists, however, proved to be clever politicians. They eventually convinced Hancock to support the Constitution. He even made an important suggestion that helped persuade delegates in Massachusetts and other states to ratify it. If there were objections to the Constitution, he proposed, delegates should accept it and later submit amendments to improve the document.

In Boston Paul Revere organized a mass meeting to urge ratification. This show of support in Samuel Adams's home district helped sway him to approve the Constitution in spite of his doubts. After some additional negotiation between Hancock and Adams, the Massachusetts convention voted 187 to 168 to ratify. By late June, Maryland, South Carolina, and New Hampshire had also voted to accept the document. At last the Constitution had been ratified! Shortly thereafter, by a close margin, Virginia became the tenth state to join the Union. By the beginning of July only New York, North Carolina, and Rhode Island had yet to approve the document.

New York was most important. Because of the state's location, the nation would be split into two parts if New York did not ratify the Constitution and enter the Union. However, the Antifederalists outnumbered the Federalists at the New York ratifying convention by more than two to one! Defeat for the ratification of the Constitution seemed certain.

A number of factors helped the New York Federalists improve their chances of success. A series of newspaper essays, now known as the *Federalist Papers,* explained and defended the Constitution. They were written by Alexander Hamilton and John Jay, both New York Federalists, and James Madison of Virginia.

• *Federalists Papers*

New York's central location also placed the Antifederalists there in a difficult position. They realized that New York needed the United States as much as the United States needed New York. Moreover, popular opinion in New York City favored the Constitution. Local leaders threatened to break away from the state and join the Union on their own if the New York delegates rejected the Constitution. In late July 1788 enough Antifederalists supported the Constitution to ratify it, 30 to 27.

Orphaned as a teenager, Alexander Hamilton worked as a store clerk in the West Indies. Friends and relatives, impressed by his intelligence, decided to send him to school in America.

The Granger Collection, New York

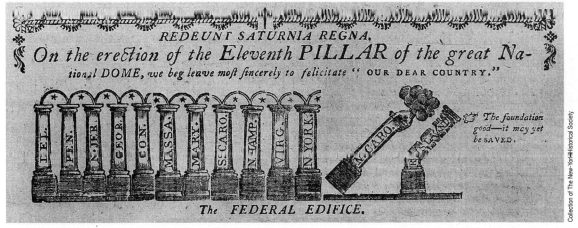

REDEUNT SATURNIA REGNA.
On the erection of the Eleventh PILLAR of the great National DOME, we beg leave most sincerely to felicitate "OUR DEAR COUNTRY."

The foundation good—it may yet be SAVED.

The FEDERAL EDIFICE.

Collection of The New-York Historical Society

This cartoon celebrates ratification while also criticizing North Carolina's and Rhode Island's refusal to ratify the Constitution.

The United States of America

Now the new system of federal government would have its chance. Although North Carolina did not ratify the Constitution until November 1789, and Rhode Island held out until May 1790, by that time the new government had been firmly established.

The states began to select their representatives and senators in the fall of 1788. By January 1789 almost all of the state legislatures had chosen their presidential electors. On April 6 the new Congress gathered for the formal counting of the electoral votes in New York City, the temporary national capital. No one was surprised that George Washington was the unanimous choice of the electors. John Adams became vice president.

In late April, Washington stood on the balcony of Federal Hall, at the corner of Broad and Wall Streets, and took the oath of office as president. When he finished, the city rang with the sound of church bells, and the evening sky blazed with the largest display of fireworks the nation had ever seen. The 13 states had at last become one country! What would Americans make of their new Union?

Section 4 Review

• Glossary

IDENTIFY and explain the significance of the following: Federalists, Antifederalists, John Hancock, Alexander Hamilton, John Jay, John Adams

REVIEWING FOR DETAILS

1. Why did Federalists favor the Constitution?
2. Why did Antifederalists dislike the Constitution?
3. When was the new government launched? Who served as the first president?

• Time Line

REVIEWING FOR UNDERSTANDING

4. **Geographic Literacy** Why was ratification of the Constitution by New York so important?
5. **Critical Thinking:** *Making Comparisons* How was the fight for ratification in Massachusetts similar to that in New York?

CONSTITUTION HANDBOOK

The delegates who assembled in the spring of 1787 to revise the Articles of Confederation included many of the most capable leaders in the country. Convinced that the Confederation was not strong enough to bring order and prosperity to the new nation, the delegates abandoned all thought of revising the Articles. Instead, they proceeded to draw up a completely new Constitution. Patrick Henry called this action "a revolution as radical as that which separated us from Great Britain." Out of their long political experience, their keen intelligence, and their great learning, these framers of the Constitution created a blueprint for a truly united nation—the new United States of America.

An observer once referred to the U.S. Constitution as "the most wonderful work ever struck off at a given time by the brain and purpose of man." Revised, modified, and amended, the Constitution has served the American people for more than 200 years. It has become a model for representative government throughout the world. The Constitution has successfully survived the years for two reasons. First, it lays down rules of procedure and guarantees of rights and liberties that must be observed, even in times of crisis. Second, it is a "living" document, capable of being revised to meet changing times and circumstances.

"To Form a More Perfect Union"

The framers of the Constitution wanted to establish a strong central government, one that could unite the country and help it meet the challenges of the future. At the same time, however, they feared a government that was too strong. The memories of the troubled years before the American Revolution were still fresh. The framers knew that uncontrolled power in the hands of individuals, groups, or branches of government could lead to tyranny.

The framers' response was to devise a system of government in which power is divided between the states and the federal government and then further divided within each government. In *The Federalist* Number 51, James Madison described the advantages of such a system:

> *"In the compound republic of America, the power surrendered by the people is first divided between two distinct governments, and then the portion allotted [given] to each subdivided among distinct and separate departments. Hence a double security arises to the rights of the people. The different governments will control each other, at the same time that each will be controlled by itself."*

The seven Articles that make up the first part of the Constitution provide the blueprint for this system. The framers divided the government into three branches—the legislative branch (Congress), the executive branch (the president and vice president), and the judicial branch (the federal courts)—each with specific powers. As a further safeguard, the framers wrote a system of checks and balances into the Constitution. Articles I, II, and III outline the checks and balances and the powers of each branch of government.

Article IV outlines the relations between the states and between the states and the federal government. Among the issues addressed are each state's recognition of other states' public records and citizens' rights, the admission of new states, and the rights and responsibilities of the federal government in relation to the states.

Article V specifies the process by which the Constitution can be amended. The framers purposely made the process slow and difficult. They feared that if the amendment process was too easy, the Constitution—the fundamental law of the land—would soon carry no more weight than the most minor law passed by Congress.

Article VI includes one condition that addressed the immediate concerns of the framers and two conditions that have lasting significance. The short-term condition promises that the United States under the Constitution will honor all public debts entered into under the Articles of Confederation. The two long-term conditions declare the Constitution is the "supreme Law of the Land" and prohibit religion being used as a qualification for holding public office.

Article VII is the framers' attempt to ensure ratification of the Constitution. Under the Articles of Confederation, amendments had to be approved by all 13 original states. Realizing that it would be difficult to get the approval of all the states, the framers specified that the Constitution would go into effect after ratification by only nine states.

Protecting Individual Liberty

The framers' opposition to a strong central government was in part a concern over states' rights. It was also rooted in the desire to protect individual liberties. American colonists had always insisted on the protection of their civil liberties—their rights as individuals.

The Articles of the Constitution contain many important guarantees of civil liberties. On a broad level, the separation of powers and the system of checks and balances help safeguard citizens against the abuse of government power. The Articles also contain conditions that speak directly to an individual's right to due process of law. For example, Section 9 of Article I prohibits both *ex post facto* laws and bills of attainder.

An *ex post facto* law is a law passed "after the deed." Such a law sets a penalty for an act that was not illegal when it was committed. A bill of attainder is a law that punishes a person by fine, imprisonment, or seizure of property without a court trial. If Congress had the power to adopt bills of attainder, lawmakers could punish any American at will, and that person could do nothing to appeal the sentence. Instead, the Constitution provides that only the courts can impose punishment for unlawful acts, and then only by following the due process of law.

Section 9 of Article I also protects a citizen's right to the writ of *habeas corpus.* The writ of *habeas corpus* is a legal document that forces a jailer to release a person from prison unless the person has been formally charged with, or convicted of, a crime. The Constitution states that "the Privilege of the Writ of Habeas Corpus shall not be suspended, unless when in Cases of Rebellion or Invasion the public Safety may require it."

The Constitution also gives special protection to people accused of treason. The framers of the Constitution knew that the charge of treason was a common device used by rulers to get rid of people they did not like. Rulers could bring the charge of treason against people who merely criticized the government. To prevent such use of this charge, Section 3 of Article III carefully defines treason and the circumstances under which a person may be charged with it:

> *"Treason against the United States, shall consist only in levying War against them, or in adhering to their Enemies, giving them Aid and Comfort. No Person shall be convicted of Treason unless on the Testimony of two Witnesses to the same overt [obvious] Act, or on Confession in open Court."*

The Article also protects the relatives of a person accused of treason. Only the convicted person can be punished. No penalty can be imposed on the person's family.

The Bill of Rights

Despite the safeguards written into the Articles of the Constitution, some states initially refused to ratify the document because it did not offer greater protection to the rights of individuals. These states finally agreed to ratification after they had been promised that a bill of rights would be added to the Constitution by amendment.

In 1789 the first Congress of the United States wrote the ideals of the Declaration of Independence into the Bill of Rights, the first 10 amendments to the Constitution. Among other things, the Bill of Rights protects persons against any action by the federal government that may deprive them "of life, liberty, or property, without due process of law."

Among the guarantees of liberty in the Bill of Rights, several are particularly important. The First Amendment guarantees freedom of religion, speech, the press, and assembly, and the right to petition. The Fourth Amendment forbids "unreasonable searches and seizures" of any person's home. The Fifth, Sixth, and Eighth Amendments protect individuals from random arrest and punishment by the federal government. The Bill of Rights was ratified by the states in 1791. It has remained one of the best-known features of the Constitution.

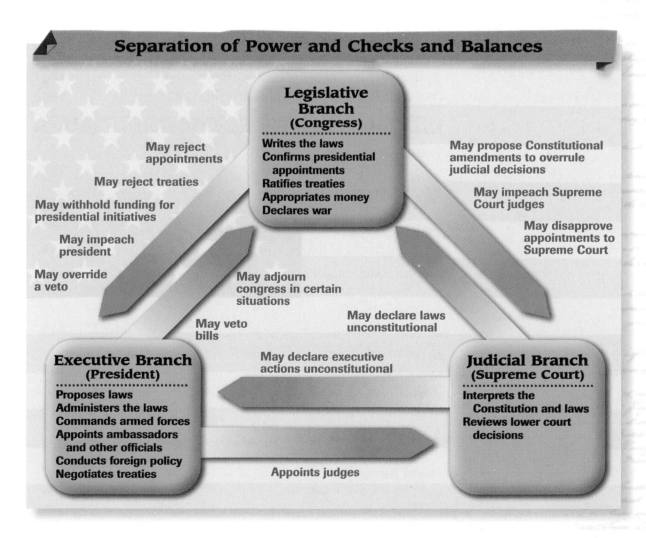

Separation of Power and Checks and Balances

Legislative Branch (Congress)
- Writes the laws
- Confirms presidential appointments
- Ratifies treaties
- Appropriates money
- Declares war

May reject appointments

May reject treaties

May withhold funding for presidential initiatives

May impeach president

May override a veto

May propose Constitutional amendments to overrule judicial decisions

May impeach Supreme Court judges

May disapprove appointments to Supreme Court

May adjourn congress in certain situations

May veto bills

May declare laws unconstitutional

May declare executive actions unconstitutional

Executive Branch (President)
- Proposes laws
- Administers the laws
- Commands armed forces
- Appoints ambassadors and other officials
- Conducts foreign policy
- Negotiates treaties

Judicial Branch (Supreme Court)
- Interprets the Constitution and laws
- Reviews lower court decisions

Appoints judges

CONTENTS

OF THE CONSTITUTION

PREAMBLE

WE THE PEOPLE OF THE UNITED STATES, IN ORDER TO FORM A MORE PERFECT UNION, ESTABLISH JUSTICE, INSURE DOMESTIC TRANQUILITY, PROVIDE FOR THE COMMON DEFENCE, PROMOTE THE GENERAL WELFARE, AND SECURE THE BLESSINGS OF LIBERTY TO OURSELVES AND OUR POSTERITY, DO ORDAIN AND ESTABLISH THIS CONSTITUTION FOR THE UNITED STATES OF AMERICA. "

*Parts of the Constitution that have been ruled through are no longer in force or no longer apply because of later amendments.

Preamble
The short and dignified Preamble explains the goals of the new government under the Constitution.

ARTICLE I

Section 1. All legislative Powers herein granted shall be vested in a Congress of the United States, which shall consist of a Senate and House of Representatives.

Section 2. The House of Representatives shall be composed of Members chosen every second Year by the People of the several States, and the Electors in each State shall have the Qualifications requisite for Electors of the most numerous Branch of the State Legislature.

No Person shall be a Representative who shall not have attained to the Age of twenty five Years, and been seven Years a Citizen of the United States, and who shall not, when elected, be an Inhabitant of that State in which he shall be chosen.

Representatives and direct Taxes shall be apportioned among the several States which may be included within this Union, according to their respective Numbers, which shall be determined by adding to the whole Number of free Persons, including those bound to Service for a Term of Years, and excluding Indians not taxed, three fifths of all other Persons. The actual Enumeration shall be made within three Years after the first Meeting of the Congress of the United States, and within every subsequent Term of ten Years, in such Manner as they shall by Law direct. The Number of Representatives shall not exceed one for every thirty Thousand, but each State shall have at Least one Representative; and until such enumeration shall be made, the State of New Hampshire shall be entitled to chuse three; Massachusetts eight; Rhode Island and Providence Plantations one; Connecticut five; New York six; New Jersey four; Pennsylvania eight; Delaware one; Maryland six; Virginia ten; North Carolina five; South Carolina five; and Georgia three.

When vacancies happen in the Representation from any State, the Executive Authority thereof shall issue Writs of Election to fill such Vacancies.

The House of Representatives shall chuse their Speaker and other Officers; and shall have the sole Power of Impeachment.

Section 3. The Senate of the United States shall be composed of two Senators from each State, chosen by the Legislature thereof, for six Years; and each Senator shall have one Vote.

Immediately after they shall be assembled in Consequence of the first Election, they shall be divided as equally as may be into three Classes. The Seats of the Senators of the first Class shall be vacated at the Expiration of the second Year, of the second Class at the Expiration of the fourth Year, and of the third Class at the Expiration of the sixth Year, so that one third may be chosen every second Year; and if Vacancies happen by Resignation, or otherwise, during the Recess of the Legislature of any State, the Executive thereof may make

Legislative Branch
Article I explains how the legislative branch, called Congress, is organized. The chief purpose of the legislative branch is to make the laws. Congress is made up of the Senate and the House of Representatives. The decision to have two bodies of government solved a difficult problem during the Constitutional Convention. The large states wanted the membership of Congress to be based entirely on population. The small states wanted every state to have an equal vote. The solution to the problem of how the states were to be represented in Congress became known as the Great Compromise.

The number of members each state has in the House is based on the population of the individual state. Each state has at least one representative. In 1929 Congress fixed the size of the House at 435 members. Today, if each member of the House were to represent only 30,000 Americans, the House would have more than 8,600 members.

Every state has two senators. Senators serve a six-year term. Every two years, one third of the senators reach the end of their terms. In any election, at least two thirds of the senators stay in office. This system ensures that there are experienced senators in office at all times.

The only duty that the Constitution assigns to the vice president is to preside over meetings of the Senate. Modern presidents have given their vice presidents more responsibilities.

The House charges a government official of wrongdoing, and the Senate acts as a court to decide if the official is guilty.

Congress decided that elections will be held on the Tuesday following the first Monday in November of even-numbered years. The Twentieth Amendment states that Congress shall meet in regular session on January 3 of each year. The president may call a special session of Congress whenever it is necessary.

Congress makes most of its own rules of conduct. The Senate and the House each have a code of ethics that members must follow. It is the task of each house of Congress to discipline its own members. Each house keeps a journal, and a daily, unofficial publication called the *Congressional Record* details what happens in congressional sessions. The general public can learn how their representatives voted on bills by reading the *Congressional Record*.

The framers of the Constitution wanted to protect members of Congress from being arrested on

~~temporary Appointments until the next Meeting of the Legislature, which shall then fill such Vacancies.~~

No Person shall be a Senator who shall not have attained to the Age of thirty Years, and been nine Years a Citizen of the United States, and who shall not, when elected, be an Inhabitant of that State for which he shall be chosen.

The Vice President of the United States shall be President of the Senate, but shall have no Vote, unless they be equally divided.

The Senate shall chuse their other Officers, and also a President pro tempore, in the Absence of the Vice President, or when he shall exercise the Office of President of the United States.

The Senate shall have the sole Power to try all Impeachments. When sitting for that Purpose, they shall be on Oath or Affirmation. When the President of the United States is tried, the Chief Justice shall preside: And no Person shall be convicted without the Concurrence of two thirds of the Members present.

Judgment in Cases of Impeachment shall not extend further than to removal from Office, and disqualification to hold and enjoy any Office of honor, Trust or Profit under the United States: but the Party convicted shall nevertheless be liable and subject to Indictment, Trial, Judgment and Punishment, according to Law.

Section 4. The Times, Places and Manner of holding Elections for Senators and Representatives, shall be prescribed in each State by the Legislature thereof; but the Congress may at any time by Law make or alter such Regulations, except as to the Places of chusing Senators.

~~The Congress shall assemble at least once in every Year, and such Meeting shall be on the first Monday in December, unless they shall by Law appoint a different Day.~~

Section 5. Each House shall be the Judge of the Elections, Returns and Qualifications of its own Members, and a Majority of each shall constitute a Quorum to do Business; but a smaller Number may adjourn from day to day, and may be authorized to compel the Attendance of absent Members, in such Manner, and under such Penalties as each House may provide.

Each House may determine the Rules of its Proceedings, punish its Members for disorderly Behaviour, and, with the Concurrence of two thirds, expel a Member.

Each House shall keep a Journal of its Proceedings, and from time to time publish the same, excepting such Parts as may in their Judgment require Secrecy; and the Yeas and Nays of the Members of either House on any question shall, at the Desire of one fifth of those Present, be entered on the Journal.

Neither House, during the Session of Congress, shall, without the Consent of the other, adjourn for more than three days, nor to any other Place than that in which the two Houses shall be sitting.

Section 6. The Senators and Representatives shall receive a Compensation for their Services, to be ascertained by Law, and paid out of the Treasury of the United States. They shall in all Cases, except Treason, Felony and Breach of the Peace, be privileged from Arrest during their Attendance at the Session of their respective Houses, and in going to and returning from the same; and for any Speech or Debate in either House, they shall not be questioned in any other Place.

No Senator or Representative shall, during the Time for which he was elected, be appointed to any civil Office under the Authority of the United States, which shall have been created, or the Emoluments whereof shall have been encreased during such time; and no Person holding any Office under the United States, shall be a Member of either House during his Continuance in Office.

Section 7. All Bills for raising Revenue shall originate in the House of Representatives; but the Senate may propose or concur with Amendments as on other Bills.

Every Bill which shall have passed the House of Representatives and the Senate, shall, before it become a Law, be presented to the President of the United States; If he approve he shall sign it, but if not he shall return it, with his Objections to that House in which it shall have originated, who shall enter the Objections at large on their Journal, and proceed to reconsider it. If after such Reconsideration two thirds of that House shall agree to pass the Bill, it shall be sent, together with the Objections, to the other House, by which it shall likewise be reconsidered, and if approved by two thirds of that House, it shall become a Law. But in all such Cases the Votes of both Houses shall be determined by yeas and Nays, and the Names of the Persons voting for and against the Bill shall be entered on the Journal of each House respectively. If any Bill shall not be returned by the President within ten Days (Sundays excepted) after it shall have been presented to him, the Same shall be a Law, in like Manner as if he had signed it, unless the Congress by their Adjournment prevent its Return, in which Case it shall not be a Law.

Every Order, Resolution, or Vote to which the Concurrence of the Senate and House of Representatives may be necessary (except on a question of Adjournment) shall be presented to the President of the United States; and before the Same shall take Effect, shall be approved by him, or being disapproved by him, shall be repassed by two thirds of the Senate and House of Representatives, according to the Rules and Limitations prescribed in the Case of a Bill.

Section 8. The Congress shall have Power To lay and collect Taxes, Duties, Imposts and Excises, to pay the Debts and provide for the common Defence and general Welfare of the United States; but all Duties, Imposts and Excises shall be uniform throughout the United States;

To borrow Money on the credit of the United States;

To regulate Commerce with foreign Nations, and among the several States, and with the Indian Tribes;

To establish an uniform Rule of Naturalization, and uniform Laws on the subject of Bankruptcies throughout the United States;

To coin Money, regulate the Value thereof, and of foreign Coin, and fix the Standard of Weights and Measures;

To provide for the Punishment of counterfeiting the Securities and current Coin of the United States;

To establish Post Offices and post Roads;

false charges by political enemies who did not want them to attend important meetings. The framers also wanted to protect members of Congress from being taken to court for something they said in a speech or in a debate.

The power of taxing is the responsibility of the House of Representatives. The framers felt that because members of the House are elected every two years, representatives would listen to the public and seek its approval before passing taxes.

The veto power of the president and the ability of Congress to override a presidential veto are two of the important checks and balances in the Constitution.

The framers of the Constitution wanted a national government that was strong enough to be effective. This section lists the powers given to Congress. The last sentence in Section 8 (see page 140) contains the famous "elastic clause"—so called because it has been stretched (like elastic) to fit many different circumstances. The clause was first disputed when Alexander Hamilton proposed a national bank. Thomas Jefferson said that because the Constitution did not give Congress the power to establish a bank, it could not do so. Hamilton argued that the bank was "necessary and proper" in order to carry out other powers of Congress, such as borrowing money and regulating currency. This argument was tested in the courts in 1819 in the case of *McCulloch* v. *Maryland*, when Chief Justice Marshall ruled in favor of the federal government. Powers given to the government by the "elastic clause" are called implied powers.

To promote the Progress of Science and useful Arts, by securing for limited Times to Authors and Inventors the exclusive Right to their respective Writings and Discoveries;

To constitute Tribunals inferior to the supreme Court;

To define and punish Piracies and Felonies committed on the high Seas, and Offences against the Law of Nations;

To declare War, grant Letters of Marque and Reprisal, and make Rules concerning Captures on Land and Water;

To raise and support Armies, but no Appropriation of Money to that Use shall be for a longer Term than two Years;

To provide and maintain a Navy;

To make Rules for the Government and Regulation of the land and naval Forces;

To provide for calling forth the Militia to execute the Laws of the Union, suppress Insurrections and repel Invasions;

To provide for organizing, arming, and disciplining, the Militia, and for governing such Part of them as may be employed in the Service of the United States, reserving to the States respectively, the Appointment of the Officers, and the Authority of training the Militia according to the discipline prescribed by Congress;

To exercise exclusive Legislation in all Cases whatsoever, over such District (not exceeding ten Miles square) as may, by Cession of particular States, and the Acceptance of Congress, become the Seat of the Government of the United States, and to exercise like Authority over all Places purchased by the Consent of the Legislature of the State in which the Same shall be, for the Erection of Forts, Magazines, Arsenals, dock-Yards, and other needful Buildings; —And

To make all Laws which shall be necessary and proper for carrying into Execution the foregoing Powers, and all other Powers vested by this Constitution in the Government of the United States, or in any Department or Officer thereof.

Although Congress has implied powers, there are also limits to its powers. Section 9 lists powers that are denied to the federal government. Several of the clauses protect the people of the United States from unjust treatment. For example, Section 9 guarantees the writ of *habeas corpus* and prohibits bills of attainder and *ex post facto* laws (see page 132).

Section 9. ~~The Migration or Importation of such Persons as any of the States now existing shall think proper to admit, shall not be prohibited by the Congress prior to the Year one thousand eight hundred and eight, but a Tax or duty may be imposed on such Importation, not exceeding ten dollars for each Person.~~

The Privilege of the Writ of Habeas Corpus shall not be suspended, unless when in Cases of Rebellion or Invasion the public Safety may require it.

No Bill of Attainder or ex post facto Law shall be passed.

No Capitation, or other direct, Tax shall be laid, unless in Proportion to the Census or Enumeration herein before directed to be taken.

No Tax or Duty shall be laid on Articles exported from any State.

No Preference shall be given by any Regulation of Commerce or Revenue to the Ports of one State over those of another: nor shall Vessels bound to, or from, one State, be obliged to enter, clear, or pay Duties in another.

No Money shall be drawn from the Treasury, but in Consequence of Appropriations made by Law; and a regular Statement and Account of the Receipts and Expenditures of all public Money shall be published from time to time.

No Title of Nobility shall be granted by the United States: And no Person holding any Office of Profit or Trust under them, shall, without the Consent of the Congress, accept of any present, Emolument, Office, or Title, of any kind whatever, from any King, Prince, or foreign State.

Section 10. No State shall enter into any Treaty, Alliance, or Confederation; grant Letters of Marque and Reprisal; coin Money; emit Bills of Credit; make any Thing but gold and silver Coin a Tender in Payment of Debts; pass any Bill of Attainder, ex post facto Law, or law impairing the Obligation of Contracts, or grant any Title of Nobility.

No State shall, without the Consent of the Congress, lay any Imposts or Duties on Imports or Exports, except what may be absolutely necessary for executing its inspection Laws: and the net Produce of all Duties and Imposts, laid by any State on Imports or Exports, shall be for the Use of the Treasury of the United States; and all such Laws shall be subject to the Revision and Controul of the Congress.

No State shall, without the Consent of Congress, lay any Duty of Tonnage, keep Troops, or Ships of War in time of Peace, enter into any Agreement or Compact with another State, or with a foreign Power, or engage in War, unless actually invaded, or in such imminent Danger as will not admit of delay.

Section 10 lists the powers that are denied to the states. In our system of federalism, the state and federal governments have separate powers, share some powers, and are each denied other powers. The states may not exercise any of the powers that belong to Congress.

ARTICLE II

Section 1. The executive Power shall be vested in a President of the United States of America. He shall hold his Office during the Term of four Years, and, together with the Vice President, chosen for the same Term, be elected, as follows.

Each State shall appoint, in such Manner as the Legislature thereof may direct, a Number of Electors, equal to the whole Number of Senators and Representatives to which the State may be entitled in the Congress: but no Senator or Representative, or Person holding an Office of Trust or Profit under the United States, shall be appointed an Elector.

The Electors shall meet in their respective States, and vote by Ballot for two Persons, of whom one at least shall not be an Inhabitant of the same State with themselves. And they shall make a List of all the Persons voted for, and of the Number of Votes for each; which List they shall sign and certify, and transmit sealed to the Seat of the Government of the United States, directed to the President of the Senate. The President of the Senate shall, in the Presence of the Senate and House of Representatives, open all the Certificates, and the Votes

Executive Branch
The president is the chief of the executive branch. It is the job of the president to enforce the laws. The framers wanted the president's and vice president's term of office and manner of selection to be different from those of members of Congress. They decided on four-year terms, but they had a difficult time agreeing on how to select the president and vice president. The framers finally set up an electoral system, which varies greatly from our electoral process today. The Twelfth Amendment changed the process by requiring that separate ballots be cast for president and vice president. The rise of political parties has since changed the process even more.

~~shall then be counted. The Person having the greatest Number of Votes shall be the President, if such Number be a Majority of the whole Number of Electors appointed; and if there be more than one who have such Majority, and have an equal Number of Votes, then the House of Representatives shall immediately chuse by Ballot one of them for President; and if no Person have a Majority, then from the five highest on the List the said House shall in like Manner chuse the President. But in chusing the President, the Votes shall be taken by States, the Representation from each State having one Vote; A quorum for this Purpose shall consist of a Member or Members from two thirds of the States, and a Majority of all the States shall be necessary to a Choice. In every Case, after the Choice of the President, the Person having the greatest Number of Votes of the Electors shall be the Vice President. But if there should remain two or more who have equal Votes, the Senate shall chuse from them by Ballot the Vice President~~.

In 1845 Congress set the Tuesday following the first Monday in November of every fourth year as the general election date for selecting presidential electors.

The youngest elected president was John F. Kennedy; he was 43 years old when he was inaugurated. (Theodore Roosevelt was 42 when he assumed office after the assassination of McKinley.) The oldest elected president was Ronald Reagan; he was 69 years old when he was inaugurated.

The Congress may determine the Time of chusing the Electors, and the Day on which they shall give their Votes; which Day shall be the same throughout the United States.

No Person except a natural born Citizen, ~~or a Citizen of the United States, at the time of the Adoption of this Constitution~~, shall be eligible to the Office of President; neither shall any Person be eligible to that Office who shall not have attained to the Age of thirty five Years, and been fourteen Years a Resident within the United States.

In Case of the Removal of the President from Office, or of his Death, Resignation, or Inability to discharge the Powers and Duties of the said Office, the Same shall devolve on the Vice President, and the Congress may by Law provide for the Case of Removal, Death, Resignation or Inability, both of the President and Vice President, declaring what Officer shall then act as President, and such Officer shall act accordingly, until the Disability be removed, or a President shall be elected.

Emolument means "salary, or payment." In 1969 Congress set the president's salary at $200,000 per year. The president also receives an expense account of $50,000 per year. The president must pay taxes on both.

The oath of office is administered to the president by the chief justice of the U.S. Supreme Court. Washington added "So help me, God." All succeeding presidents have followed this practice.

The framers wanted to make sure that an elected representative of the people controlled the nation's military. Today, the president is in charge of the army, navy, air force, marines, and coast guard. Only Congress, however, can decide if the United States will declare war. This section also contains the basis for the formation of the president's cabinet. Every president, starting with George Washington, has appointed a cabinet.

The President shall, at stated Times, receive for his Services, a Compensation, which shall neither be increased nor diminished during the period for which he shall have been elected, and he shall not receive within that Period any other Emolument from the United States, or any of them.

Before he enter on the Execution of his Office, he shall take the following Oath or Affirmation:—"I do solemnly swear (or affirm) that I will faithfully execute the Office of President of the United States, and will to the best of my Ability, preserve, protect and defend the Constitution of the United States."

Section 2. The President shall be Commander in Chief of the Army and Navy of the United States, and of the Militia of the several States, when called into the actual Service of the United States; he may require the Opinion, in writing, of the principal Officer in each of the executive Departments, upon any Subject relating to the Duties of their respective Offices, and he shall have Power to grant Reprieves and Pardons for Offenses against the United States, except in Cases of Impeachment.

He shall have Power, by and with the Advice and Consent of the Senate, to make Treaties, provided two thirds of the Senators present concur; and he shall nominate, and by and with the Advice and

Consent of the Senate, shall appoint Ambassadors, other public Ministers and Consuls, Judges of the supreme Court, and all other Officers of the United States, whose Appointments are not herein otherwise provided for, and which shall be established by Law: but the Congress may by Law vest the Appointment of such inferior Officers, as they think proper, in the President alone, in the Courts of Law, or in the Heads of Departments.

The President shall have Power to fill up all Vacancies that may happen during the Recess of the Senate, by granting Commissions which shall expire at the End of their next Session.

Most of the president's appointments to office must be approved by the Senate.

Section 3. He shall from time to time give to the Congress Information of the State of the Union, and recommend to their Consideration such Measures as he shall judge necessary and expedient; he may, on extraordinary Occasions, convene both Houses, or either of them, and in Case of Disagreement between them, with Respect to the Time of Adjournment, he may adjourn them to such Time as he shall think proper; he shall receive Ambassadors and other public Ministers; he shall take Care that the Laws be faithfully executed, and shall Commission all the Officers of the United States.

Every year the president presents to Congress a State of the Union message. In this message, the president explains the legislative plans for the coming year. This clause states that one of the president's duties is to enforce the laws.

Section 4. The President, Vice President and all civil Officers of the United States, shall be removed from Office on Impeachment for, and Conviction of, Treason, Bribery, or other high Crimes and Misdemeanors.

ARTICLE III

Section 1. The judicial Power of the United States, shall be vested in one supreme Court, and in such inferior Courts as the Congress may from time to time ordain and establish. The Judges, both of the supreme and inferior Courts, shall hold their Offices during good Behaviour, and shall, at stated Times, receive for their Services, a Compensation, which shall not be diminished during their Continuance in Office.

<u>Judicial Branch</u>
The Articles of Confederation did not set up a federal court system. One of the first things that the framers of the Constitution agreed upon was to set up a national judiciary. With all the laws that Congress would be enacting, there would be a great need for a branch of government to interpret the laws. In the Judiciary Act of 1789, Congress provided for the establishment of lower courts, such as district courts, circuit courts of appeals, and various other federal courts. The judicial system provides a check on the legislative branch; it can declare a law unconstitutional.

Section 2. The judicial Power shall extend to all Cases, in Law and Equity, arising under this Constitution, the Laws of the United States, and Treaties made, or which shall be made, under their Authority;—to all Cases affecting Ambassadors, other public Ministers and Consuls;—to all Cases of admiralty and maritime Jurisdiction;—to Controversies to which the United States shall be a Party;—to Controversies between two or more States;— ~~between a State and Citizens of another State~~;—between Citizens of different States;—between Citizens of the same State claiming Lands under Grants of different States, ~~and between a State, or the Citizens thereof, and foreign States, Citizens or Subjects~~.

In all Cases affecting Ambassadors, other public Ministers and Consuls, and those in which a State shall be Party, the supreme Court shall have original Jurisdiction. In all the other Cases before mentioned, the supreme Court shall have appellate Jurisdiction, both as to Law and fact, with such Exceptions, and under such Regulations as the Congress shall make.

The Trial of all Crimes, except in Cases of Impeachment, shall be by Jury; and such Trial shall be held in the State where the said Crimes shall have been committed; but when not committed within any State, the Trial shall be at such Place or Places as the Congress may by Law have directed.

Congress has the power to decide the punishment for treason, but it can punish only the guilty person. "Corruption of Blood" means punishing the family of a person who has committed treason. It is expressly forbidden by the Constitution.

Section 3. Treason against the United States, shall consist only in levying War against them, or in adhering to their Enemies, giving them Aid and Comfort. No Person shall be convicted of Treason unless on the Testimony of two Witnesses to the same overt Act, or on Confession in open Court.

The Congress shall have Power to declare the Punishment of Treason, but no Attainder of Treason shall work Corruption of Blood, or Forfeiture except during the Life of the Person attainted.

ARTICLE IV

The States
States must honor the laws, records, and court decisions of other states. A person cannot escape a legal obligation by moving from one state to another.

Section 1. Full Faith and Credit shall be given in each State to the public Acts, Records, and judicial Proceedings of every other State. And the Congress may by general Laws prescribe the Manner in which such Acts, Records and Proceedings shall be proved, and the Effect thereof.

Section 2. The Citizens of each State shall be entitled to all Privileges and Immunities of Citizens in the several States.

A Person charged in any State with Treason, Felony, or other Crime, who shall flee from Justice, and be found in another State, shall on Demand of the executive Authority of the State from which he fled, be delivered up, to be removed to the State having Jurisdiction of the Crime.

~~No Person held to Service of Labour in one State, under the Laws thereof, escaping into another, shall, in Consequence of any Law or Regulation therein, be discharged from such Service or Labour, but shall be delivered up on Claim of the Party to whom such Service or Labour may be due~~.

Section 3 permits Congress to admit new states to the Union. When a group of people living in an area that is not part of an existing state wishes to form a new state, it asks Congress for

Section 3. New States may be admitted by the Congress into this Union; but no new State shall be formed or erected within the Jurisdiction of any other State; nor any State be formed by the Junction of two or more States, or Parts of States, without the Consent of the Legislatures of the States concerned as well as of the Congress.

The Congress shall have Power to dispose of and make all needful Rules and Regulations respecting the Territory or other Property belonging to the United States; and nothing in this Constitution shall be so construed as to Prejudice any Claims of the United States, or of any particular State.

Section 4. The United States shall guarantee to every State in this Union a Republican Form of Government, and shall protect each of them against Invasion; and on Application of the Legislature, or of the Executive (when the Legislature cannot be convened) against domestic Violence.

ARTICLE V

The Congress, whenever two thirds of both Houses shall deem it necessary, shall propose Amendments to this Constitution, or, on the Application of the Legislatures of two thirds of the several States, shall call a Convention for proposing Amendments, which, in either Case, shall be valid to all Intents and Purposes, as Part of this Constitution, when ratified by the Legislatures of three fourths of the several States, or by Conventions in three fourths thereof, as the one or the other Mode of Ratification may be proposed by the Congress; Provided that no Amendment which may be made prior to the Year One thousand eight hundred and eight shall in any Manner affect the first and fourth Clauses in the Ninth Section of the first Article; and that no State, without its Consent, shall be deprived of its equal Suffrage in the Senate.

ARTICLE VI

All Debts contracted and Engagements entered into, before the Adoption of this Constitution, shall be as valid against the United States under this Constitution, as under the Confederation.

This Constitution, and the Laws of the United States which shall be made in Pursuance thereof; and all Treaties made, or which shall be made, under the Authority of the United States, shall be the supreme Law of the Land; and the Judges in every State shall be bound thereby, any Thing in the Constitution or Laws of any State to the Contrary notwithstanding.

then write a state constitution and offer it to Congress for approval. The state constitution must set up a representative form of government and must not in any way contradict the federal Constitution. If a majority of Congress approves of the state constitution, the state is admitted as a member of the United States of America.

The Amendment Process
America's founders may not have realized just how enduring the Constitution would be, but they did set up a system for changing or adding to the Constitution. They did not want to make it easy to change the Constitution. There are two different ways in which changes can be proposed to the states and two different ways in which states can approve the changes and make them part of the Constitution.

National Supremacy
One of the biggest problems facing the delegates to the Constitutional Convention was the question of what would happen if a state law and a federal law conflicted. Which law would be followed? Who would decide? The second clause of Article VI answers those questions. When a federal law and a state law disagree, the federal law overrides

the state law. The Constitution is the "supreme Law of the Land." This clause is often called the "supremacy clause."

The Senators and Representatives before mentioned, and the Members of the several State Legislatures, and all executive and judicial Officers, both of the United States and of the several States, shall be bound by Oath or Affirmation, to support this Constitution; but no religious Test shall ever be required as a Qualification to any Office or public Trust under the United States.

ARTICLE VII

Ratification
The Articles of Confederation called for all 13 states to approve any revision to the Articles. The Constitution required that 9 out of the 13 states would be needed to ratify the Constitution. The first state to ratify was Delaware, on December 7, 1787. Almost two and a half years later, on May 29, 1790, Rhode Island became the last state to ratify the Constitution.

The Ratification of the Conventions of nine States, shall be sufficient for the Establishment of this Constitution between the States so ratifying the Same.

Done in Convention by the Unanimous Consent of the States present the Seventeenth Day of September in the Year of our Lord one thousand seven hundred and Eighty seven and of the Independence of the United States of America the Twelfth. In witness whereof We have hereunto subscribed our Names,

George Washington—
President and deputy from Virginia

NEW HAMPSHIRE
John Langdon
Nicholas Gilman

DELAWARE
George Read
Gunning Bedford, Jr.
John Dickinson
Richard Bassett
Jacob Broom

MASSACHUSETTS
Nathaniel Gorham
Rufus King

MARYLAND
James McHenry
Daniel of St. Thomas
*   Jenifer*
Daniel Carroll

CONNECTICUT
William Samuel
*   Johnson*
Roger Sherman

NEW YORK
Alexander Hamilton

VIRGINIA
John Blair
James Madison, Jr.

NEW JERSEY
William Livingston
David Brearley
William Paterson
Jonathan Dayton

NORTH CAROLINA
William Blount
Richard Dobbs
*   Spaight*
Hugh Williamson

PENNSYLVANIA
Benjamin Franklin
Thomas Mifflin
Robert Morris
George Clymer
Thomas FitzSimons

Jared Ingersoll
James Wilson
Gouverneur Morris

SOUTH CAROLINA
John Rutledge
Charles Cotesworth
*   Pinckney*
Charles Pinckney
Pierce Butler

GEORGIA
William Few
Abraham Baldwin

Attest:
William Jackson,
*   Secretary*

The delegates signed the Constitution in the Independence Hall Assembly Room. The room has been preserved so it looks much like it would have in 1787.

THE AMENDMENTS

Articles in addition to, and Amendment of the Constitution of the United States of America, proposed by Congress, and ratified by the Legislatures of the several States, pursuant to the fifth Article of the original Constitution.

[The First through Tenth Amendments, now known as the Bill of Rights, were proposed to the states for ratification on September 25, 1789, and declared in force on December 15, 1791.]

First Amendment

Congress shall make no law respecting an establishment of religion, or prohibiting the free exercise thereof; or abridging the freedom of speech, or of the press; or the right of the people peaceably to assemble, and to petition the Government for a redress of grievances.

Bill of Rights
One of the conditions set by several states for ratifying the Constitution was the inclusion of a Bill of Rights. Many people feared that a stronger central government might take away basic rights of the people that had been guaranteed in state constitutions. If the three words that begin the preamble—"We the people"—were truly meant, then the rights of the people needed to be protected.

The First Amendment protects—among other freedoms—freedom of speech—and forbids Congress to make any "law respecting an establishment of religion" or restraining the freedom to practice religion as one chooses.

Second Amendment

A well regulated Militia, being necessary to the security of a free State, the right of the people to keep and bear Arms, shall not be infringed.

Third Amendment

No Soldier shall, in time of peace, be quartered in any house, without the consent of the Owner, nor in time of war, but in a manner to be prescribed by law.

Fourth Amendment

A police officer or sheriff may only enter a person's home with a search warrant, which allows the law official to look for evidence that could convict someone of committing a crime.

The right of the people to be secure in their persons, houses, papers, and effects, against unreasonable searches and seizures, shall not be violated, and no Warrants shall issue, but upon probable cause, supported by Oath or affirmation, and particularly describing the place to be searched, and the persons or things to be seized.

Fifth Amendment

The Fifth, Sixth, and Seventh Amendments describe the procedures that courts must follow when trying people accused of crimes. The Fifth Amendment guarantees that no one can be put on trial for a serious crime unless a grand jury agrees that the evidence justifies doing so. It also says that a person cannot be tried twice for the same crime.

No person shall be held to answer for a capital, or otherwise infamous crime, unless on a presentment or indictment of a Grand Jury, except in cases arising in the land or naval forces, or in the Militia, when in actual service in time of War or public danger; nor shall any person be subject for the same offence to be twice put in jeopardy of life or limb; nor shall be compelled in any criminal case to be a witness against himself, nor be deprived of life, liberty, or property, without due process of law; nor shall private property be taken for public use, without just compensation.

Sixth Amendment

The Sixth Amendment makes several guarantees, including a prompt trial and a trial by a jury chosen from the state and district in which the crime was committed. The Sixth Amendment also states that an accused person must be told why he or she is being tried and promises that an accused person has the right to be defended by a lawyer.

In all criminal prosecutions, the accused shall enjoy the right to a speedy and public trial, by an impartial jury of the State and district wherein the crime shall have been committed, which district shall have been previously ascertained by law, and to be informed of the nature and cause of the accusation; to be confronted with the witnesses against him; to have compulsory process for obtaining witnesses in his favor, and to have the Assistance of Counsel for his defence.

Seventh Amendment

The Seventh Amendment guarantees a trial by jury in cases that involve more than $20, but in modern times, usually much more money is at stake before a case is heard in federal court.

In Suits at common law, where the value in controversy shall exceed twenty dollars, the right of trial by jury shall be preserved, and no fact tried by a jury, shall be otherwise re-examined in any Court of the United States, than according to the rules of the common law.

Eighth Amendment

Excessive bail shall not be required, nor excessive fines imposed, nor cruel and unusual punishments inflicted.

Ninth Amendment

The enumeration in the Constitution, of certain rights, shall not be construed to deny or disparage others retained by the people.

The Ninth and Tenth Amendments were added because not every right of the people or of the states could be listed in the Constitution.

Tenth Amendment

The powers not delegated to the United States by the Constitution, nor prohibited by it to the States, are reserved to the States respectively, or to the people.

Eleventh Amendment

[Proposed March 5, 1794; declared ratified January 8, 1798]
The Judicial power of the United States shall not be construed to extend to any suit in law or equity, commenced or prosecuted against one of the United States by Citizens of another State, or by Citizens or Subjects of any Foreign State.

Twelfth Amendment

[Proposed December 9, 1803; declared ratified September 25, 1804]
The Electors shall meet in their respective states, and vote by ballot for President and Vice-President, one of whom, at least, shall not be an inhabitant of the same state with themselves; they shall name in their ballots the person voted for as President, and in distinct ballots the person voted for as Vice-President, and they shall make distinct lists of all persons voted for as President, and of all persons voted for as Vice-President, and of the number of votes for each, which lists they shall sign and certify, and transmit sealed to the seat of the government of the United States, directed to the President of the Senate;—The President of the Senate shall, in the presence of the Senate and House of Representatives, open all the certificates and the votes shall then be counted;—The person having the greatest number of votes for President, shall be the President, if such number be a majority of the whole number of Electors appointed; and if no person have such majority, then from the persons having the highest numbers not exceeding three on the list of those voted for as President, the House of Representatives shall choose immediately, by ballot, the President. But in choosing the President, the votes shall be taken by states, the representation from each state having one vote; a quorum for this purpose shall consist of a member or members from two-thirds of the states, and a majority of all the states shall be necessary to a choice. And if the House of Representatives shall not choose a President whenever the right of choice shall devolve upon them, before the fourth day of March next following, then the Vice-President shall act as President, as in the case of the death or other constitutional disability of the President. —The person having the greatest number of votes as Vice-President, shall be the Vice-President, if such number be a majority of the whole number of Electors appointed, and if no person have a majority, then from the two highest numbers on the list, the Senate shall Choose the Vice-President; a quorum for the purpose shall consist of two-thirds of the whole number

The Twelfth Amendment changed the election procedure for president and vice president. This amendment became necessary because of the growth of political parties. Before this amendment, electors voted without distinguishing between president and vice president. Whoever received the most votes became president, and whoever received the next highest number of votes became vice president. A confusing election in 1800, which resulted in Thomas Jefferson's becoming president, caused this amendment to be proposed.

of Senators, and a majority of the whole number shall be necessary to a choice. But no person constitutionally ineligible to the office of President shall be eligible to that of Vice-President of the United States.

Thirteenth Amendment
[Proposed January 31, 1865; declared ratified December 18, 1865]

Although some slaves had been freed during the Civil War, slavery was not abolished until the Thirteenth Amendment took effect.

Section 1. Neither slavery nor involuntary servitude, except as a punishment for crime whereof the party shall have been duly convicted, shall exist within the United States, or any place subject to their jurisdiction.

Section 2. Congress shall have power to enforce this article by appropriate legislation.

Fourteenth Amendment
[Proposed June 16, 1866; declared ratified July 28, 1868]

In 1833 the Supreme Court ruled that the Bill of Rights limited the federal government but not the state governments. This ruling was interpreted to mean that states were able to keep African Americans from becoming state citizens: if African Americans were not citizens, they were not protected by the Bill of Rights. The Fourteenth Amendment defines citizenship and prevents states from interfering in the rights of citizens of the United States.

Section 1. All persons born or naturalized in the United States, and subject to the jurisdiction thereof, are citizens of the United States and of the State wherein they reside. No State shall make or enforce any law which shall abridge the privileges or immunities of citizens of the United States; nor shall any State deprive any person of life, liberty, or property, without due process of law; nor deny to any person within its jurisdiction the equal protection of the laws.

Section 2. Representatives shall be apportioned among the several States according to their respective numbers, counting the whole number of persons in each State, ~~excluding Indians not taxed~~. But when the right to vote at any election for the choice of electors for President and Vice President of the United States, Representatives in Congress, the Executive and Judicial officers of a State, or the members of the Legislature thereof, is denied to any of the ~~male~~ inhabitants of such State, ~~being twenty-one years of age~~, and citizens of the United States, or in any way abridged, except for participation in rebellion, or other crime, the basis of representation therein shall be reduced in the proportion which the number of such ~~male~~ citizens shall bear to the whole number of ~~male~~ citizens ~~twenty-one years of age~~ in such State.

Section 3. No person shall be a Senator or Representative in Congress, or elector of President and Vice President, or hold any office, civil or military, under the United States, or under any State, who, having previously taken an oath, as a member of Congress, or as an officer of the United States, or as a member of any State legislature, or as an executive or judicial officer of any State, to support the Constitution of the United States, shall have engaged in insurrection or rebellion against the same, or given aid or comfort to the enemies thereof. But Congress may by a vote of two-thirds of each House, remove such disability.

Section 4. The validity of the public debt of the United States, authorized by law, including debts incurred for payment of pensions and bounties for services in suppressing insurrection or rebellion, shall not be questioned. But neither the United States nor any State shall assume or pay any debt or obligation incurred in aid of insurrection or rebellion against the United States, ~~or any claim for the loss of emancipation of any slave~~; but all such debts, obligations and claims shall be held illegal and void.

Section 5. The Congress shall have power to enforce, by appropriate legislation, the provisions of this article.

Fifteenth Amendment

[Proposed February 27, 1869; declared ratified March 30, 1870]

Section 1. The right of citizens of the United States to vote shall not be denied or abridged by the United States or by any State on account of race, color, or previous condition of servitude.

Section 2. The Congress shall have power to enforce this article by appropriate legislation.

The Fifteenth Amendment extended the right to vote to African American men.

Sixteenth Amendment

[Proposed July 12, 1909; declared ratified February 25, 1913]
The Congress shall have power to lay and collect taxes on incomes, from whatever source derived, without apportionment among the several States, and without regard to any census or enumeration.

Seventeenth Amendment

[Proposed May 13, 1912; declared ratified May 31, 1913]
The Senate of the United States shall be composed of two Senators from each State, elected by the people thereof, for six years; and each Senator shall have one vote. The electors in each State shall have the qualifications requisite for electors of the most numerous branch of the State legislatures.

When vacancies happen in the representation of any State in the Senate, the executive authority of such State shall issue writs of election to fill such vacancies: *Provided,* That the legislature of any State may empower the executive thereof to make temporary appointments until the people fill the vacancies by election as the legislature may direct.

~~This amendment shall not be so construed as to affect the election or term of any Senator chosen before it becomes valid as part of the Constitution.~~

The Seventeenth Amendment required that senators be elected directly by the people instead of by the state legislature.

Eighteenth Amendment

[Proposed December 18, 1917; declared ratified January 29, 1919; repealed by the Twenty-first Amendment December 5, 1933]

~~**Section 1.** After one year from the ratification of this article the manufacture, sale, or transportation of intoxicating liquors within, the importation thereof into, or the exportation thereof from the United States and all territory subject to the jurisdiction thereof for beverage purposes is hereby prohibited.~~

Although many people felt that prohibition was good for the health and welfare of the American people, the amendment was repealed 14 years later.

Section 2. The Congress and the several States shall have concurrent power to enforce this article by appropriate legislation.

Section 3. This article shall be inoperative unless it shall have been ratified as an amendment to the Constitution by the legislatures of the several States, as provided in the Constitution, within seven years from the date of the submission hereof to the States by the Congress.

Nineteenth Amendment

[Proposed June 4, 1919; declared ratified August 26, 1920]

The right of citizens of the United States to vote shall not be denied or abridged by the United States or by any State on account of sex.

Congress shall have power to enforce this article by appropriate legislation.

Twentieth Amendment

[Proposed March 2, 1932; declared ratified February 6, 1933]

Section 1. The terms of the President and Vice-President shall end at noon on the 20th day of January, and the terms of Senators and Representatives at noon on the 3d day of January, of the years in which such terms would have ended if this article had not been ratified; and the terms of their successors shall then begin.

Section 2. The Congress shall assemble at least once in every year, and such meeting shall begin at noon on the 3d day of January, unless they shall by law appoint a different day.

Section 3. If, at the time fixed for the beginning of the term of the President, the President elect shall have died, the Vice-President elect shall become President. If a President shall not have been chosen before the time fixed for the beginning of his term, or if the President elect shall have failed to qualify, then the Vice-President elect shall act as President until a President shall have qualified; and the Congress may by law provide for the case wherein neither a President elect nor a Vice-President elect shall have qualified, declaring who shall then act as President, or the manner in which one who is to act shall be selected, and such person shall act accordingly until a President or Vice-President shall have qualified.

Section 4. The Congress may by law provide for the case of the death of any of the persons from whom the House of Representatives may choose a President whenever the right of choice shall have devolved upon them, and for the case of the death of any of the persons from whom the Senate may choose a Vice-President whenever the right of choice shall have devolved upon them.

Section 5. Sections 1 and 2 shall take effect on the 15th day of October following the ratification of this article.

Section 6. This article shall be inoperative unless it shall have been ratified as an amendment to the Constitution by the legislatures of three-fourths of the several States within seven years from the date of its submission.

Abigail Adams was disappointed that the Declaration of Independence and the Constitution did not specifically include women. It took almost 150 years and much campaigning by suffrage groups for women to finally achieve voting privileges.

In the original Constitution, a newly elected president and Congress did not take office until March 4, which was four months after the November election. The officials who were leaving office were called "lame ducks" because they had little influence during those four months. The Twentieth Amendment changed the date that the new president and Congress take office. Members of Congress now take office on January 3, and the president takes office on January 20.

Twenty-first Amendment

[Proposed February 20, 1933, declared ratified December 5, 1933]

Section 1. The eighteenth article of amendment to the Constitution of the United States is hereby repealed.

Section 2. The transportation or importation into any State, Territory, or possession of the United States for delivery or use therein of intoxicating liquors, in violation of the laws thereof, is hereby prohibited.

~~**Section 3.** This article shall be inoperative unless it shall have been ratified as an amendment to the Constitution by conventions in the several States, as provided in the Constitution, within seven years from the date of the submission hereof to the States by the Congress.~~

The Twenty-first Amendment is the only amendment that has been ratified by state conventions rather than by state legislatures.

Twenty-second Amendment

[Proposed March 21, 1947; declared ratified February 26, 1951]

Section 1. No person shall be elected to the office of the President more than twice, and no person who has held the office of President, or acted as President, for more than two years of a term to which some other person was elected President shall be elected to the office of the President more than once. ~~But this Article shall not apply to any person holding the office of President when this Article was proposed by the Congress, and shall not prevent any person who may be holding the office of President, or acting as President, during the term within which this Article becomes operative from holding the office of President or acting as President during the remainder of such term.~~

~~**Section 2.** This article shall be inoperative unless it shall have been ratified as an amendment to the Constitution by the legislatures of three-fourths of the several States within seven years from the date of its submission to the States by the Congress.~~

From the time of President Washington's administration, it was a custom for presidents to serve no more than two terms of office. Franklin D. Roosevelt, however, was elected to four terms. The Twenty-second Amendment made into law the old custom of a two-term limit for each president, if re-elected.

Twenty-third Amendment

[Proposed June 16, 1960; declared ratified March 29, 1961]

Section 1. The District constituting the seat of Government of the United States shall appoint in such manner as the Congress may direct:

A number of electors of President and Vice-President equal to the whole number of Senators and Representatives in Congress to which the District would be entitled if it were a State, but in no event more than the least populous state; they shall be in addition to those appointed by the States, but they shall be considered, for the purposes of the election of President and Vice-President, to be electors appointed by a State; and they shall meet in the District and perform such duties as provided by the twelfth article of amendment.

Section 2. The Congress shall have power to enforce this article by appropriate legislation.

Until the Twenty-third Amendment, the people of Washington, D.C., could not vote in presidential elections.

Twenty-fourth Amendment

[Proposed August 27, 1962; declared ratified January 23, 1964]

Section 1. The right of citizens of the United States to vote in any primary or other election for President or Vice-President, for electors for President or Vice-President, or for Senator or Representative in Congress, shall not be denied or abridged by the United States or any State by reason of failure to pay any poll tax or other tax.

Section 2. The Congress shall have power to enforce this article by appropriate legislation.

Twenty-fifth Amendment

[Proposed July 6, 1965; declared ratified February 10, 1967]

The illness of President Eisenhower in the 1950s and the assassination of President Kennedy in 1963 were the events behind the Twenty-fifth Amendment. The Constitution did not provide a clear-cut method for a vice president to take over for a disabled president or upon the death of a president. This amendment provides for filling the office of the vice president if a vacancy occurs, and it provides a way for the vice president to take over if the president is unable to perform the duties of that office.

Section 1. In case of the removal of the President from office or of his death or resignation, the Vice-President shall become President.

Section 2. Whenever there is a vacancy in the office of the Vice-President, the President shall nominate a Vice-President who shall take office upon confirmation by a majority vote of both Houses of Congress.

Section 3. Whenever the President transmits to the President pro tempore of the Senate and the Speaker of the House of Representatives his written declaration that he is unable to discharge the powers and duties of his office, and until he transmits to them a written declaration to the contrary, such powers and duties shall be discharged by the Vice-President as Acting President.

Section 4. Whenever the Vice-President and a majority of either the principal officers of the executive departments or of such other body as Congress may by law provide, transmit to the President pro tempore of the Senate and the Speaker of the House of Representatives their written declaration that the President is unable to discharge the powers and duties of his office, the Vice-President shall immediately assume the powers and duties of the office as Acting President.

Thereafter, when the President transmits to the President pro tempore of the Senate and the Speaker of the House of Representatives his written declaration that no inability exists, he shall resume the powers and duties of his office unless the Vice-President and a majority of either the principal officers of the executive department or of such other body as Congress may by law provide, transmit within four days to the President pro tempore of the Senate and the Speaker of the House of Representatives their written declaration that the President is unable to discharge the powers and duties of his office. Thereupon Congress shall decide the issue, assembling within forty-eight hours for that purpose if not in session. If the Congress, within twenty-one days after receipt of the latter written declaration, or, if Congress is not in session, within twenty-one days after Congress is required to assemble, determines by two-thirds vote of both Houses that the President is unable to discharge the powers and duties of his office, the Vice-President shall continue to discharge the same as Acting President; otherwise, the President shall resume the powers and duties of his office.

Twenty-sixth Amendment

[Proposed March 10, 1971; declared ratified July 5, 1971]

Section 1. The right of citizens of the United States, who are eighteen years of age or older, to vote shall not be denied or abridged by the United States or by any State on account of age.

Section 2. The Congress shall have power to enforce this article by appropriate legislation.

Twenty-seventh Amendment

[Proposed September 25, 1789; declared ratified May 7, 1992]
No law, varying the compensation for the services of the Senators and Representatives, shall take effect, until an election of Representatives shall have intervened.

The Voting Act of 1970 tried to set the voting age at 18. But the Supreme Court ruled that the act set the voting age for national elections only, not state or local elections. This ruling would make necessary several different ballots at elections. The Twenty-sixth Amendment gave 18-year-old citizens the right to vote in all elections.

Federalism

Powers Delegated to the National Government	Powers Shared by National and State Governments	Powers Reserved for the States
Declare war	Maintain law and order	Establish and maintain schools
Maintain armed forces	Levy taxes	Establish local governments
Regulate interstate and foreign trade	Borrow money	Conduct corporate laws
Admit new states	Charter banks	Regulate business within the state
Establish post offices	Establish courts	Make marriage laws
Set standard weights and measures	Provide for public welfare	Provide for public safety
Coin money		Assume other powers not delegated to the national government or prohibited to the states
Establish foreign policy		
Make all laws necessary and proper for carrying out delegated powers		

Sharing Power. Under the system of federalism, the national and state governments share political power. "Delegated powers" are given to the national government. "Reserved powers" are given to the states. Why might it be beneficial to have the national government establish post offices? Why might it be beneficial to have the state governments establish and maintain schools?

CHAPTER 7

From the Collections of Henry Ford Museum & Greenfield Village

Launching the United States (1789–1801)

THEMES IN AMERICAN HISTORY

Constitutional Heritage:
Why might people disagree over the interpretation of the Constitution?

Global Relations:
How might conflict between two countries affect a third country?

Economic Development:
Why might one country loan money to other countries?

 • Video Opener

 • Skill Builder

*F*rench immigrant Michel Guillaume Jean de Crèvecoeur expressed his views on his new home and its citizens:

"**Americans are the western pilgrims who are carrying along with them that great mass of arts, sciences, vigor, and industry which began long since in the east; they will finish the great circle. The Americans . . . are incorporated into one of the finest systems of population which has ever appeared.**"

image above: *Passing the cup of freedom*

Section 1

FIRST STEPS

Multimedia Connections

Explore these related topics and materials on the CD–ROM to enrich your understanding of this section:

 Atlas

• U.S. Regions, 1790

 Profiles

• George Washington

 Biographies

• Alexander Hamilton

 Readings

• African Americans in the 1700s
• Children in the New Republic

 Media Bank

• Amending the U.S. Constitution
• Bill of Rights Stamp
• Alexander Hamilton

P resident George Washington would have preferred to serve without pay, as he had during the Revolutionary War. Congress, however, voted him an annual salary of $25,000 and rented him a three-story mansion in New York City, the new national capital. Martha Custis Washington described the house as "handsomely furnished, all new." The Washingtons lived in grand style, serving the best food at official dinners and driving around town in a horse-drawn carriage.

As you read this section you will find out:

▶ **How the president and Congress launched the new government.**

▶ **How Alexander Hamilton planned to strengthen the nation's finances.**

▶ **Why Hamilton and Jefferson clashed over the need for a national bank.**

The New Nation

New York City was still a small town of about 30,000 people in 1789. Like other towns in the United States, New York City was alive with excitement as the new government took office. People wondered what the future would bring. Americans had their constitution, but what would they do with democracy?

This new government seems simple when compared to the enormous federal government of today. It was not so simple, however, to design and staff it in 1789.

Establishing precedents. Washington had few **precedents**, or earlier examples, to follow. He knew that as the first president, every time he made a decision he was establishing a precedent for future presidents. This was a big responsibility.

Many people lined the streets of Trenton, New Jersey, to watch George Washington on his way to New York City to be inaugurated as the first president of the United States.

The Constitution had given the office of president a great deal of power. A strong and determined leader, Washington wanted to use this power to the fullest to ensure liberty and order in the new nation. Yet he also wanted to calm citizens who were worried about the possible misuse of presidential power. For that reason, Washington was particularly careful not to overstep his authority. He sincerely believed in the separation of powers. It was the job of Congress to make the laws. His job as the chief executive was to execute, or carry out, those laws.

The cabinet. Washington's first task was to appoint officials to run the government departments. He also had to decide what jobs needed to be done and how the work should be organized and supervised. This task required cooperation with Congress, which had to pass laws to create government positions and to provide money to pay salaries. It was also up to the Senate to approve Washington's appointments.

In 1789 Congress created three main executive departments: a Treasury Department, a State Department, and a War Department. Each department was headed by a secretary appointed by the president. Washington soon began to meet with the department secretaries for advice. This small group of department heads became the first **cabinet**.

Today the State Department is in charge of government relations with foreign countries. In 1789, however, it also had to manage all domestic affairs except those handled by the War and Treasury Departments. Yet Thomas Jefferson, the first secretary of state, had a staff of only five clerks! The War Department, headed by General Henry Knox, maintained a small army and navy. In peacetime just a few people were needed to carry out military functions. Only the Treasury Department, run by Alexander Hamilton, had a fairly large staff. It collected taxes and tariffs. Under Hamilton's direction, the department made a farsighted economic plan for the United States.

President Washington and his cabinet (left to right) Henry Knox, Alexander Hamilton, Thomas Jefferson, and Edmund Randolph

Washington also made several other important executive appointments. Attorney General Edmund Randolph served as the president's legal adviser, and Postmaster General Samuel Osgood ran the Post Office.

Jefferson and Hamilton

At cabinet meetings, Jefferson was very independent minded and often disagreed with Hamilton. Hamilton was a bundle of energy with wide-ranging interests. He was eager to increase his influence. Knox tended to agree with Hamilton's suggestions. Gradually, Hamilton became Washington's most important adviser.

Hamilton's ideas about government and human nature were controversial and remain so today. He had a low opinion of the average person's honesty and judgment. He believed that most people were selfish and easily misled by sly, power-hungry leaders.

Hamilton favored the rich but did not trust them much more than what he called "the mass of the people." If the rich had power, they would control the rest of society, Hamilton believed. If the poor had power, they would use it to seize the property of the rich. A good government, he thought, was one that balanced rival interests between rich and poor. This attitude was not unusual. However, Hamilton went beyond most political thinkers of his day. He thought that the selfish desires of the rich could be used to strengthen the government and the whole nation.

Although Jefferson found much to admire in Hamilton, he strongly criticized Hamilton's political beliefs:

"Hamilton was, indeed, a singular [unique] character. Of acute [sharp] understanding, disinterested, honest, and honorable in all private transactions, amiable [friendly]

in society, and duly [properly] valuing virtue in private life, yet so bewitched [fascinated] and perverted [misguided] by the British example as to be under thorough conviction [belief] that corruption [dishonesty] was essential to the government of a nation."

Presidential Lives

George Washington

George Washington was considered by many to be very dignified. After one visit with the president, Abigail Adams wrote,

"I found myself much more deeply impressed [by the Washingtons] than I ever did before their Majesties of Britain."

To many people, Washington seemed too formal to be a real person. He was more like a statue on a pedestal than a human being. This was because he was so aware of his responsibilities that he could hardly ever relax. Americans considered him the greatest hero of the Revolution. He felt that he had to live up to this high image.

Such expectations made Washington's life difficult. After his inauguration he wrote a friend, "I greatly fear that my countrymen will expect too much from me." He often complained about the burdens of his office. He looked forward to the day when he could retire to Virginia. Washington never neglected his duties, however. He was probably the best first president the nation could have had.

First Lady Martha Washington entertained many important political leaders at the presidential mansion in New York City.

● **Martha Washington**

Jefferson believed that Hamilton wished to undo the gains of the Revolution and go back to a less democratic form of government. He even thought that Hamilton wanted to make the United States into a monarchy, perhaps with George Washington as king.

Jefferson wanted to keep the government as small as possible. In his opinion, the best way to keep government small was to keep society simple. He believed that the United States was a free country because it was a nation of farmers. The population was spread out and people managed their own affairs. Countries with crowded seaports and industrial towns needed more government controls to preserve order. "When we get piled upon one another in large cities," Jefferson said, "we shall become corrupt."

Hamilton, on the other hand, disagreed with this idea. He wanted the nation to have a mixed economy, and he did everything in his power to encourage business growth.

Financing the New Nation

One of the main reasons government leaders had decided to strengthen the national government by crafting the Constitution had been the poor financial condition of the United States. During and after the Revolution, the government had accumulated a **national debt**. The amount of the debt the country owed was estimated at $77 million. This national debt included loans from foreign countries and treasury certificates. These certificates, often called **bonds**, represented money that the government borrowed from private citizens. Bond holders could cash in the bonds at a later date to earn a profit. The debt also included payments promised to soldiers and money owed to merchants and manufacturers. Many other countries hesitated to make any new loans to the United States because they were not sure if the American experiment in government would succeed.

New taxes. Using its new power to tax, Congress placed tariffs of about 5 percent on many foreign goods entering the country. This law was quite similar to the measures Parliament had employed in the 1760s to raise money in America. Those laws had been a major cause of the Revolution. Americans paid these new taxes, although somewhat reluctantly, because these taxes were passed by their representatives, not an outside power.

These taxes were used to meet the day-to-day expenses of the government. They did not raise enough money to pay off all the national debt, however.

Hamilton's plan.   It was the responsibility of Secretary of the Treasury Hamilton to find a way to pay off the national debt. He proposed gradually raising enough money through **excise taxes**—taxes on goods produced and consumed inside the country.

Hamilton also had the task of restoring the credit of the government. Investors were afraid the government would not be able to pay off its debts. Some investors even doubted that the U.S. experiment in democracy would succeed. They considered the United States a poor credit risk and were unwilling to lend it money. As a result, government bonds had fallen far below face value. Many people sold their bonds at a loss—sometimes selling a $1,000 bond for as little as $150—to investors who were willing to take a risk. Such buyers, called **speculators**, were gambling that someday the government would be able to pay off its bonds at full value. If this happened, they would make huge profits.

Hamilton proposed doing just that. A speculator who had bought a $1,000 bond for $500 would receive the full $1,000. Hamilton believed that paying off the nation's debts at face value would restore the nation's credit. He also reasoned that his plan would encourage investment in the United States and thus boost the economy.

Some Americans believed this policy was unfair to former soldiers and other Patriots who had sold their bonds cheaply. Hamilton pointed out, however, that the speculators had paid what the bonds were worth at the time they bought them. They had taken the risks and were entitled to the profits. After some hesitation, Congress approved Hamilton's proposal and passed it into law.

Hamilton also wanted the United States to take over $21.5 million of the $25 million in debts owed by individual states. Jefferson and most southern congressmen opposed this idea. The largest state debts were owed by New England states. Most southern states had already managed to pay off their debts and did not want the federal government to take on the debts of those states that had not yet paid.

Jefferson and other southerners went along with Hamilton's plan only after he agreed to use his influence to get Congress to locate the permanent national capital in the South. Maryland and Virginia donated land for the new capital. Despite this compromise, the controversy over the debt revealed a growing split between Hamilton, a New Yorker, and Jefferson, a Virginian.

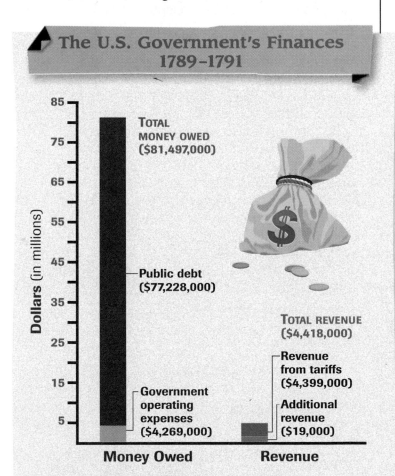

The U.S. Government's Finances 1789–1791

TOTAL MONEY OWED ($81,497,000)

Public debt ($77,228,000)

Government operating expenses ($4,269,000)

TOTAL REVENUE ($4,418,000)

Revenue from tariffs ($4,399,000)

Additional revenue ($19,000)

Money Owed

Revenue

Dollars (in millions)

Source: *Historical Statistics of the United States.*

Government Finances.   One of the most pressing problems of Washington's administration was the federal government's finances. How much more money did the government owe than it took in between 1789 and 1791?

The Bank of the United States. Jefferson also objected to Hamilton's proposal to create the **Bank of the United States**, a national bank with branches in major American cities. In 1790 there were very few banks of any kind in the country. Hamilton argued that the government could deposit money received from taxes into the bank. The bank would print paper money, called **bank notes**, to represent the money it had on deposit. It could also make loans to merchants and manufacturers, which might expand trade. Hamilton believed that this bank would benefit the entire nation.

In 1791 Congress passed a bank bill, but Washington did not sign it immediately. He could find nothing in the Constitution authorizing Congress to create a bank. So he asked his advisers if they thought the bill was constitutional. Hamilton said the bill was constitutional. He believed that Congress could establish a bank as long as the Constitution did not clearly oppose it. This interpretation of the Constitution is known today as **loose construction**. Jefferson, on the other hand, insisted that Congress could not form the bank, because the Constitution did not specifically say that Congress had the power to do so. This interpretation is known today as

The First Bank of the United States was built in Philadelphia. Alexander Hamilton fought a long battle to have this bank established.

strict construction. Washington decided to support Hamilton and sign the bank bill.

• Construction

Hamilton was a financial genius. Under his guidance, the national debt was financed and the credit of the United States was soon as good as that of any nation in the world. Many people found the national bank to be a valuable institution. Hamilton was second only to Washington in establishing the shape and power of the new federal government.

Section 1 Review

• Glossary

IDENTIFY and explain the significance of the following: precedents, cabinet, national debt, bonds, excise taxes, speculators, Bank of the United States, bank notes, loose construction, strict construction

REVIEWING FOR DETAILS
1. What actions did the president and Congress take to launch the new government?
2. What was Hamilton's plan to handle the national debt and strengthen the nation's finances?
3. Why did Hamilton favor a national bank and Jefferson oppose it?

REVIEWING FOR UNDERSTANDING
4. **Writing Mastery:** *Expressing* Imagine that you are a newspaper editor. Tell your readers whether or not Hamilton's plan to repay the bonds at their full value is fair.
5. **Critical Thinking:** *Making Comparisons* Why do you think Jefferson and Hamilton had different views about society and government?

BILL OF RIGHTS

FIRST AMENDMENT   Guarantees freedom of speech, religion, and the press and the right to assemble peacefully and to petition the government.

SECOND AMENDMENT   Acknowledges the necessity of state militias and the right of people to keep and bear arms.

THIRD AMENDMENT   Forbids troops being quartered in a person's home without consent as stated by law.

FOURTH AMENDMENT   Forbids search and seizures without a warrant, which may be issued only with probable cause.

FIFTH AMENDMENT   Ensures that a person must be indicted by a grand jury before being tried for a serious criminal offense; prohibits persons from being tried twice for the same crime; protects people from being forced to testify against themselves; and guarantees that no person be denied life, liberty, or property without due process of law.

SIXTH AMENDMENT   Guarantees the right to a speedy trial with an impartial jury in all criminal cases, the right to know all charges, the right to obtain and question all witnesses, and the right to legal counsel.

SEVENTH AMENDMENT   Guarantees a trial in most civil cases.

EIGHTH AMENDMENT   Prohibits excessive bail or fines and forbids cruel and unusual punishment.

NINTH AMENDMENT   Protects individual rights not stated in the Constitution.

TENTH AMENDMENT   Reserves for the states and the people the powers not specifically delegated to the government or prohibited by the Constitution.

Section 2

A TIME OF TROUBLES

Multimedia Connections

Explore these related topics and materials on the CD–ROM to enrich your understanding of this section:

 Gazetteer

- Haiti

 Atlas

- Ohio Valley, 1750–1811

 Media Bank

- Northwest Indian Life
- Battle of Fallen Timbers

 Readings

- Indian Confederacy

 Profiles

- Toussaint L'Ouverture
- Edmond Genet
- Thomas Pinckney
- Anthony Wayne

n the summer of 1794, David Bradford and his neighbors gathered to debate a new tax on whiskey. To these farmers in western Pennsylvania, the new tax seemed as unjust as British taxes before the Revolution. In the spirit of 1776, local farmers vowed resistance. Like the Patriots of that earlier time, the farmers threatened tax collectors and formed militias. Britain's King George III had used troops against the rebel Patriots. Many wondered if President Washington would treat these Pennsylvania farmers any differently.

As you read this section you will find out:

▶ **How the French Revolution affected American politics.**

▶ **Why western farmers rebelled.**

▶ **What parting advice President Washington gave to the nation.**

Trouble Abroad

Events on the other side of the Atlantic Ocean intensified the political conflicts that developed over Hamilton's economic policies. The American Revolution had been popular in France, in part because it weakened France's chief rival, Great Britain. It also seemed a great step forward for the republican ideals that many French people supported.

The French Revolution. The American Revolution, along with Enlightenment ideas of personal liberty, helped inspire the **French Revolution**, which began in 1789. The French Revolution, in turn, was greeted with enormous enthusiasm in America.

This enthusiasm slackened, however, after Revolutionary extremists, or radicals, gained control of France. The extremists began to

Global Connections

The American Revolution

Inspired in part by the ideas and success of the American Revolution, the French demanded more rights from their government. When their demands were not met, the angry citizens revolted. On July 14, 1789, Parisians stormed the Bastille—a hated prison-fortress. This marked the beginning of the French Revolution. The monarchy was toppled and replaced by a republican government.

In 1791 the freed slave François-Dominique Toussaint L'Ouverture (TOO-san loo-vuhr-TOOHR) led slaves and free people of African-European ancestry to rise up against France on the Caribbean colony they named Haiti. Other revolutions were also brewing in Latin America. In Mexico in 1810 a creole priest named Miguel Hidalgo y Costilla led a rebellion against the Spanish government. Simon Bolívar and José de San Martín led uprisings against the Spanish Crown in South America between 1809 and 1824. Out of their efforts came independence for the countries of Venezuela, Ecuador, Colombia, Argentina, Chile, and Peru.

help had made it possible for America to win its independence. In fact, the 1778 treaty of alliance with France was still in effect. The United States seemed duty-bound to side with France. Other Americans, including Alexander Hamilton, considered the leaders of the French Revolution too radical and favored the British.

American neutrality. Washington took a more balanced view. He issued the **Neutrality Proclamation**, warning Americans not to favor either side. The United States would try to be "friendly and impartial [fair]" to both. He did not believe the United States would benefit from war with either France or Great Britain.

Maintaining neutrality proved difficult. The French government ignored Washington's proclamation and sent over a special diplomatic representative, Edmond Genet (zhuh-ne). He arrived in America in April 1793. Genet quickly persuaded a number of Americans who owned merchant ships to become **privateers**—armed private ships authorized to attack enemy shipping—and to attack British ships on the high seas. Genet even tried to organize private American

make harsh changes to the society. They executed thousands of men and women, including King Louis XVI and Queen Marie Antoinette. As one French noble described:

> "Troops of women and men armed with pikes [long spears] and muskets were everywhere hunting the men of the [king's] Bodyguard. . . . The barbarous horde [crowd] manifested [showed] a savage pleasure, some of them . . . dancing round the bodies."

Then in 1793 war broke out between France and Great Britain. Many Americans, including Thomas Jefferson, were sympathetic to France. French

This anti-French cartoon shows President Washington in his federal chariot heading off an invasion of French Revolutionary leaders.

Detail from the original, courtesy of The Historic New Orleans Collection

Spain's refusal to allow Americans to load and unload cargo at the important seaport of New Orleans greatly affected the trade of western farmers.

• **Spanish Land Claims**

armies to attack British Canada and Spanish Florida and Louisiana, because France was at war with Spain as well as Great Britain. Washington finally demanded that the French government recall Genet.

Washington's troubles were not over. The navies of both France and Great Britain began to seize American merchant ships on the Atlantic. Both countries ignored U.S. claims of neutrality. In a single year, several hundred American vessels loaded with valuable goods were captured. As time passed this disruption caused serious financial problems for many Americans involved in trade overseas.

New Treaties

In 1794 Washington sent John Jay to Britain to try to work out a solution to all the conflicts that had developed between the two nations. Jay had done well negotiating the Treaty of Paris that ended the American Revolution.

Jay's Treaty. Jay got the British to agree to withdraw their troops from forts on the western frontier of the United States. Britain also promised to improve trade relations and to pay damages to the shipowners whose vessels had been seized. In turn, the United States agreed to pay debts owed to British merchants prior to the Revolution.

These terms, however, failed to meet the expectations of many Americans. The British ignored the American view of the rights of neutral nations during wartime and continued seizing American merchant ships. In addition, the British would not agree to pay for slaves they had taken during the Revolutionary War.

Many Americans disliked **Jay's Treaty**. Mobs of angry citizens gathered to protest its ratification. Nevertheless, Washington decided to accept the treaty. He realized that the United States had made some gains in the treaty and that time was on the nation's side. With each year the United States became richer and stronger. A war with Great Britain, or any other European nation, would cost much and could gain little. After a long debate, the Senate accepted these arguments and voted to ratify the treaty.

Pinckney's Treaty. The United States obtained an additional and very unexpected benefit from Jay's Treaty. It improved relations with Spain. Before the war, relations between the two

People opposed to Jay's Treaty express their feelings by burning an image of John Jay.

• **John Jay**

countries had not been good. The Spanish government had refused to recognize the boundary between Florida and the United States. Spain also controlled the west bank and mouth of the Mississippi River, including the city of New Orleans.

The Spanish refused to allow Americans to load and unload cargo freely at New Orleans. This was an economic burden on western farmers who needed to transfer their farm products from river craft to oceangoing ships. The farmers wanted Spanish authorities to grant them the **right of deposit**—the right to transfer their goods without paying a duty.

When Spanish authorities read Jay's Treaty, they suspected that the published version was incomplete because many treaties of the time had secret clauses. Perhaps there was a clause calling for a British-American alliance. Spain decided to try to improve relations with the United States.

In 1795 Spain signed a treaty accepting the American version of the Florida boundary line. The treaty also recognized Americans' right to navigate freely on the Mississippi River and granted them the right of deposit at New Orleans. This agreement became known as **Pinckney's Treaty** because it was negotiated for the United States by Thomas Pinckney.

The Treaty of Greenville. On the western frontier, American settlers were pushing past the Appalachian Mountains. The Indian tribes of the region north of the Ohio River resisted the invasion of American settlers who moved into the area after 1783. The tribes joined together in a confederacy and pledged not to sell any territory to the settlers. By the late 1780s, however, 10,000 settlers were pouring into the Ohio Valley each year. They disregarded the fact that the land had always been owned by Indians. These settlers demanded that the U.S. government protect them.

The leader of the Indian confederacy was Michikinikwa (mi-chee-ken-EEK-wah), or Little Turtle, chief of the Miami. He successfully defeated the troops Washington sent to the region in 1790 and 1791. In August of 1794 the

Chief Little Turtle tried to negotiate a settlement with General Anthony Wayne in 1794 before bloody fighting resumed between the Indians and American troops.

• Little Turtle

confederacy, now led by the Shawnee chief Blue Jacket, was defeated in the **Battle of Fallen Timbers**. After the battle, American commander "Mad Anthony" Wayne ordered his troops to set the Indians' cornfields and homes on fire. The Indians lost everything. In 1795 more than 90 leading chiefs were forced to sign the **Treaty of Greenville**, turning over the entire southern half of present-day Ohio to the American settlers.

The Whiskey Rebellion

Washington faced a much different problem when western farmers protested an excise tax Congress had placed on whiskey that was distilled, or manufactured, in the United States. The tax was one of the measures designed by Hamilton to raise money to pay off the nation's debts. It triggered what is known as the **Whiskey Rebellion**.

The tax angered frontier farmers who usually distilled a large part of their surplus rye and other grain into whiskey. The farmers did this because whiskey was cheaper to ship to market than bulky farm products.

Farmers in western Pennsylvania rioted in 1794 to protest the whiskey tax. They bullied tax collectors, tried to prevent courts from meeting, and marched on Pittsburgh.

Washington promptly called 12,900 militia troops to duty. He put Virginia governor Henry Lee in charge of the military, with Alexander Hamilton as the civilian leader. When the soldiers finally reached the troubled area, however, not a single "rebel" could be found. No one dared to stand up before this huge force, which was larger than any American army had been during the Revolutionary War! The "rebellion" had ended, or perhaps it would be more accurate to say that it had disappeared.

Some historians believe that Washington overreacted to the Whiskey Rebellion. Perhaps he did. Still, there was a difference between his swift and painless enforcement of the law and the bloodshed of Daniel Shays's rebellion only eight years earlier. This time there was a strong central government backed by the new Constitution.

Washington's Farewell Address

By 1796 Washington could justly feel that he had set the United States well on its way as an independent nation. Jay's and Pinckney's Treaties had improved American relations with Great Britain and Spain. The new nation was growing. Kentucky had enough people to become a state by 1792. Tennessee entered the Union in 1796, and Ohio would soon follow.

Besides his sense of having completed his main tasks, Washington was tired after serving two terms as president. Political bickering was beginning to affect his reputation as a national hero. Although he surely could have been elected to a third term had he wished to be, Washington decided to retire.

His Farewell Address of September 1796 was drafted with the help of Hamilton and James Madison. It contained his parting advice to the American people. That advice can be boiled down to three ideas—unity at home, good national credit, and neutrality abroad. To prevent political disunity, Washington warned:

"**In contemplating [thinking about] the causes which may disturb our Union, it occurs as matter of serious concern that any ground should have been furnished for characterizing [political] parties by geographical discriminations [divisions]: Northern and Southern; Atlantic and Western; whence [from where] designing [scheming] men may endeavor [try] to**

During the Whiskey Rebellion some Pennsylvania farmers tarred and feathered tax inspectors to show their dissatisfaction with the new tax laws.

excite a belief that there is a real difference of local interests and views."

Washington advised the government to use the nation's credit "as sparingly [little] as possible . . . by shunning [avoiding] occasions of expense." He urged Americans not to pass on to future generations "the burden which we ourselves ought to bear."

As for neutrality, Washington advised, "Observe good faith and justice toward all nations. Cultivate peace and harmony with all." Washington supported fair dealings with all foreign countries rather than a permanent policy of alliances or isolation.

As the first president, Washington made decisions that shaped the highest office in the land. He set up a cabinet of advisers. He restored the credit of the United States and avoided foreign wars. When he left office, he recommended neutrality and national unity. Would those who came after him be able to follow this advice?

This oil painting from 1810 illustrates the association many Americans made between George Washington and the ideals of liberty.

Section 2 Review

• Glossary

IDENTIFY and explain the significance of the following: French Revolution, Neutrality Proclamation, Edmond Genet, privateers, Jay's Treaty, right of deposit, Pinckney's Treaty, Battle of Fallen Timbers, Treaty of Greenville, Whiskey Rebellion

REVIEWING FOR DETAILS
1. Why did Americans disagree over the nation's policy toward France?
2. What advice did Washington give to the nation as he left office?

REVIEWING FOR UNDERSTANDING
3. **Geographic Literacy** Why might western Pennsylvania farmers have opposed the whiskey tax more strongly than similar farmers in a less mountainous area?
4. **Writing Mastery:** *Expressing* Write a short speech supporting or criticizing Edmond Genet's actions.
5. **Critical Thinking:** *Synthesizing Information* How might the fact that Great Britain was a more powerful nation than Spain have affected Jay's and Pinckney's Treaties?

Section 3

JOHN ADAMS'S PRESIDENCY

Multimedia Connections

Explore these related topics and materials on the CD–ROM to enrich your understanding of this section:

 Readings

- What Is an American?
- Election of 1796
- John Adams

 Media Bank

- Settlers Moving West
- Clothing Styles, 1776–1812
- Farm Life
- Abigail Adams

 Profiles

- John Adams

C harles Pinckney (Thomas's brother), John Marshall, and Elbridge Gerry listened to the French secret agents' list of demands. The three Americans had been sent to France to iron out the two nations' differences. But instead of negotiating, the French agents demanded a bribe! The Americans were furious. This was not how things were done in America. Finally, one of the Americans burst out angrily, "No, no! Not a sixpence!"

As you read this section you will find out:

▶ **How the rise of political parties affected government.**

▶ **What problems the nation had overseas during John Adams's presidency.**

▶ **How Americans' rights and freedoms were threatened at home.**

The Election of 1796

The election of a president to succeed Washington was the first in which **political parties** played a role. Political parties are groups of people who organize to help elect government officials and to try to influence government policies.

The first political parties developed around Alexander Hamilton and Thomas Jefferson. Members of Congress who favored Hamilton's financial policies took the name of the **Federalist Party**. The Federalists began to vote as a group on most issues.

Those who opposed Hamilton and his ideas began to call themselves the **Democratic-Republican Party**, or Republicans for short. (This party has no historical connection to the Republican Party of today.) Jefferson was one of their best-known leaders.

By 1796 Hamilton was probably the most powerful figure in the Federalist Party. Because he had been born in the West Indies, however, he could not, under the Constitution, run for president. Therefore, the Federalists settled on Vice President John Adams as their candidate for president. Jefferson was the Republican favorite.

For vice president, the Federalist leaders decided to run Thomas Pinckney of South Carolina, who had negotiated the treaty with Spain. The Republican candidate for vice president was Senator Aaron Burr of New York.

The campaign to succeed Washington was a bitter one. A typical campaign advertisement for Jefferson ran:

"*Who shall be President of the United States?. . . THOMAS JEFFERSON is a firm REPUBLICAN,—JOHN ADAMS is an avowed [openly declared] MONARCHIST. . . . Will you, by your votes, contribute to [help] make the avowed friend of monarchy, President? . . . Adams is a fond admirer of* the British Constitution, and says it is the first wonder of the world. *Jefferson likes* better our Federal Constitution, and thinks the British full of deformity, corruption, and wickedness."

Hamilton also disliked Adams. This was partly because as vice president, Adams had opposed some of Hamilton's ideas. However, Hamilton dared not openly oppose his party's presidential candidate. Instead, he worked out a clever but shady scheme. He persuaded a few Federalist electors in South Carolina not to vote for Adams. Then, if Pinckney got even one more electoral vote than Adams, he would be president and Adams vice president!

Unfortunately for Hamilton, news of his plan leaked out. A large number of Federalist electors who were friendly to Adams reacted by not voting for Pinckney. When the electoral votes were counted, Adams had 71 and Pinckney only 59. Jefferson, who had the united support of the Republican electors, received 68 votes. So Jefferson, not Pinckney, became the new vice president!

The 1796 election revealed that the Constitution's method for electing a president did not work well in a system that had political parties. It put two rivals, Adams and Jefferson,

Some Americans feared that the Federalist-Republican rivalry threatened to tear down the very foundations that the new country was built upon.

Although John Adams won the presidency in 1796, he had to deal with the Republicans, not only in Congress but also in his own administration. His vice president, Thomas Jefferson, was from the opposing party.

Agents in France.

Washington had tried without success to reach an agreement with France, but Adams decided to try again. In October 1797, three U.S. diplomats arrived in France to meet with the French foreign minister, Charles-Maurice de Talleyrand.

Instead of meeting with Talleyrand, the Americans met and exchanged letters with three of his secret agents. These agents said that Talleyrand would not discuss the issues until he received a large bribe. In addition, he expected the United States to make a large loan to France and to apologize for harsh remarks about France that Adams had made in a speech to Congress.

Adams was very upset by the diplomats' report, which substituted the letters X, Y, and Z for the names of the agents. Adams shared the report with the members of Congress, who became angry and made it public.

News of the **XYZ affair** created a public outcry. "Millions for defense, but not one cent for tribute [forced payment]" became a Federalist slogan. Popular feeling against France grew bitter. For the next two years the United States and France waged an undeclared naval war in the Atlantic.

Congress began making preparations for war. It created a Department of the Navy and set aside money for new warships. It also

in the uncomfortable position of serving together as president and vice president.

The XYZ Affair

From the beginning of his presidency, John Adams had to deal with the same international problems that had troubled George Washington. France was still at war with Great Britain. French leaders were angry at the United States for agreeing to Jay's Treaty. French warships and privateers were stopping American merchant ships on the high seas and seizing their cargoes.

This cartoon of American diplomats refusing a bribe from the "monster" France expressed the general outrage over the XYZ affair.

The United States dismantled most of its military forces after the Revolution. International events, however, proved the need for continuous military forces. As tensions increased between the United States and France, President Adams moved to increase the strength of American naval forces. This etching from 1800 shows workers building the warship Philadelphia.

The Granger Collection, New York

increased the size of the army. Washington came out of retirement to command this force, with Hamilton second in command. Suddenly, Adams, who had been elected president by a close vote, became a national hero.

War or peace. Adams wanted to be re-elected president in 1800. He knew that his strong stand on the XYZ affair had made him very popular. Americans saw him as the defender of the nation's honor. If he could win the dispute with France, he would almost certainly be re-elected. Adams was not willing to rush into a war with France, however. When he learned that Talleyrand was eager to repair the damage caused by the XYZ affair, Adams decided to negotiate.

Late in 1799 he sent three new diplomats to Paris. After months of discussion they signed a treaty known as the Convention of 1800. Adams had stopped the threat of a full-fledged war with France. He had also seriously divided his political party, however, because many Federalists wanted the conflict to continue so that Adams would gain more public support and be re-elected.

The Alien and Sedition Acts

Taking advantage of the war scare and the public anger over the XYZ affair, in the summer of 1798 the Federalists pushed several laws through Congress. These laws are known as the **Alien and Sedition Acts**. They were aimed at foreigners in the United States and at Republicans who were supposedly trying to weaken the government.

One of these laws increased the length of time foreigners had to live in the United States before they could become citizens. Others gave the president the power to jail or to **deport**—order out of the country—foreigners he considered "dangerous to the peace and safety of the United States."

Just as severe was the Sedition Act. This law made it a crime for anyone to "write, print, utter, or publish" statements discrediting the government, members of Congress, or the president. The Sedition Act was an attempt to frighten the Republicans into silence. In practice, it was used to protect Adams but allowed the press to attack Jefferson freely.

This engraved cartoon from 1798 illustrates the level of hostile debate the Sedition Act caused in Congress. Representative Roger Griswold (right) is shown attacking Matthew Lyon, who was one of many Republicans prosecuted under the new law.

The Granger Collection, New York

Such an attack on freedom of speech and the press was a threat to everything the American Revolution had sought to protect. In 1798 the American experiment in republican government was little more than 20 years old. Was it about to come to an end?

Attacks on the Alien and Sedition Acts

Vice President Jefferson reacted swiftly against the Alien and Sedition Acts, which he believed were unconstitutional. He wrote several statements called resolutions that explained his reasoning. The Kentucky legislature, where the Republicans had a majority, voted to approve the first resolution in November 1798. The Virginia legislature passed a similar resolution written by James Madison.

The **Virginia and Kentucky Resolutions** argued that the federal government had overstepped its power. When Congress went beyond its legal powers, what could be done?

Jefferson had a simple answer. The Constitution, he wrote, was a contract made by the separate states that gave certain powers to the federal government. If Congress passed a law the Constitution did not give it the power to pass, any state could declare the law unconstitutional.

If put into practice, this idea could have put an end to the United States as one nation. If any state could refuse to obey a law of Congress, the national government might soon collapse. Fortunately, the other states, which were mostly controlled by Federalists, did not respond favorably to Jefferson's resolutions. Federalists believed that no state should have the power to decide whether a law was unconstitutional.

Congress eventually repealed the Alien and Sedition Acts. The Virginia and Kentucky resolutions are important, however, because they put forth an argument for **states' rights**— the belief that the states, not the federal government, hold ultimate political power.

The Election of 1800

Republicans used the Alien and Sedition Acts to attack Adams and the Federalists during the hotly contested presidential election of 1800. The Republican Party once again nominated Jefferson for president and Aaron Burr for vice president. The Federalists ran Adams and Charles Pinckney.

In the campaign the Republicans were united, the Federalists badly divided. Hamilton disliked Adams so much that he published the pamphlet "The Public Conduct and Character of John Adams," in which he described Adams as jealous, conceited, and ill-tempered. According to Hamilton, Adams was totally unfit to be president. Adams returned Hamilton's dislike in full.

Hamilton, of course, had no intention of helping Adams get re-elected. Once again he tried to manage the Federalist electors so that the Federalist candidate for vice president got more votes than Adams. Again this trick failed. Adams received 65 electoral votes, Pinckney only 64. However, Jefferson beat them both with 73 votes.

Although victorious, the Republicans faced a problem. Because they were well organized, all their electors had voted for Burr as well as Jefferson. He, too, had 73 electoral votes. The electors had intended that Burr be vice president. A tie meant that the House of Representatives would have to choose between them. For an entire week the House could not come to a decision. Finally, a few representa-

The Granger Collection, New York

This campaign banner was used by Jefferson supporters in the election of 1800. It read, "Thomas Jefferson—President of the U.S.A." and "John Adams—no more."

tives changed their votes, giving Jefferson the presidency. Burr became vice president.

To avoid future ties for president and vice president, the Twelfth Amendment was added to the Constitution. Thereafter, the electors voted separately for president and vice president. Despite the problems that plagued the election of 1800, the young nation was able for the first time to transfer power peacefully between different parties.

Section 3 Review

IDENTIFY and explain the significance of the following: political parties, Federalist Party, Democratic-Republican Party, XYZ affair, Alien and Sedition Acts, deport, Virginia and Kentucky Resolutions, states' rights

• Glossary

REVIEWING FOR DETAILS

1. What effect did the rise of political parties have on government?

2. What foreign problems did the United States face during John Adams's presidency?

• Time Line

3. How did the Federalists try to control criticism of their policies?

REVIEWING FOR UNDERSTANDING

4. **Writing Mastery:** *Expressing* Imagine that you are the campaign manager for one of the political parties. Write a short paragraph either attacking or defending Adams's presidency.

5. **Critical Thinking:** *Cause and Effect* What problems might have arisen from choosing a president and vice president from different parties?

unit 3

BUILDING A STRONG NATION (1790–1860)

This image shows a busy urban marketplace in the 1800s. Such marketplaces developed along with the rise of cities after the Revolutionary War.

LINKING *P*AST TO PRESENT
Young Consumers

"And now a word from our sponsor. . . ."

The commercial shows middle-school-aged students using some product that the sponsoring company would like viewers to buy. Such advertisements can be found every day on television and in print advertisements. They are increasingly common today as Americans between the ages of 6 and 14 together have billions of dollars in spending money.

Many students earn spending money by doing chores at home. As a result, more and more teenagers have become consumers, or buyers of products, in recent years. Many teenagers read consumer magazines like *Zillions,* which offers comparisons of products and tips on money management for its readers.

Young consumers spend their money on a wide variety of products. Some even invest for future earnings. Some do both,

like the young consumers who recently purchased "collector's editions" of a popular comic book. Many bought one copy to read and a second one to preserve so that it would increase in value over time.

The students who earn money and buy products are all participating in a type of economy that came to dominate American society in the early 1800s. As you read this unit, you will learn that until that time, the economy was largely driven by the ownership of land, not the earning of wages and the buying of manufactured products.

Most Americans who lived around 1800 made or traded everything they needed. They spent most of their time working on their own land and in their homes. As you will learn, however, changes began to take place in the northern American economy that eventually made wage earning and consumer purchasing the norm.

This girl is helping her mother buy food at an outdoor market.

CHAPTER **8**

The Granger Collection, New York

Expansion and War
(1801–1830)

THEMES IN AMERICAN HISTORY

Cultural Diversity:
How might cultural differences lead to unrest within a country?

Global Relations:
Why might governments find it difficult to maintain control of overseas territories?

Economic Development:
How might economic issues affect U.S. relations with other nations?

• Video Opener

• Skill Builder

In less than 25 years, the young American government had gained a huge amount of land. Louisiana, once a French property, was now part of the United States, as was Florida, a former Spanish settlement. Even decades later, travelers marveled at the diversity of America. "There are many soils and many climates included within the . . . United States," one British woman remarked, ". . . many countries."

image above: *New Orleans around 1800*

Section 1

JEFFERSON AS PRESIDENT

Multimedia Connections

Explore these related topics and materials on the CD–ROM to enrich your understanding of this section:

 Biographies

- Sacagawea

 Profiles

- Thomas Jefferson
- Zebulon Pike

 Media Bank

- Clark's Buffalo-Skin Shirt
- Slave Revolt in Saint Domingue
- Lewis & Clark Meeting Indians
- Drawings from Clark's Journal
- Bird from Clark's Journal

- President Thomas Jefferson
- Burr-Hamilton Duel
- Chief Justice John Marshall

 Readings

- Jefferson's Inaugural Address

T he Shoshoni Indian girls bent over the berries that grew on the banks of the Missouri River. Suddenly a war party of Hidatsa Indians swept down. They captured the girls, keeping some and selling others. Sacagawea (sak-uh-juh-WEE-uh) was among those sold by the Hidatsa. Drawing on her skills as an interpreter, Sacagawea later became "the outstanding Indian woman in the West," guiding an important American expedition through dangerous territory.

As you read this section you will find out:

▶ **Why President Jefferson clashed with the Supreme Court.**

▶ **Why the Louisiana Purchase was important to the United States.**

▶ **What the Lewis and Clark expedition achieved.**

The Republicans in Charge

Thomas Jefferson viewed his election as a kind of second American Revolution. In his opinion, it had halted the Federalists' attempt to make the United States a monarchy. In his inaugural address, Jefferson emphasized unity by pointing out how important majority rule was in a democracy like the United States. He reminded victorious Republicans, however, that minority groups had rights too, and that "to violate [them] would be oppression." Political differences, he said, could be smoothed over by discussion and compromise, "Let us, then, fellow-citizens, unite with one heart and one mind. . . . We are all Republicans, we are all Federalists."

In practice, Jefferson made few drastic changes in the direction of the national government. Some Federalist laws, such as the

Alien and Sedition Acts and the Whiskey Tax, were either repealed or allowed to expire. President Jefferson came to recognize that some Federalist laws provided many benefits for the nation. Jefferson continued Alexander Hamilton's policy of paying off the national debt to ensure good credit. He also made no effort to do away with the Bank of the United States, which had proven to be a useful financial institution.

Presidential Lives

Thomas Jefferson

When Thomas Jefferson became president, he was nearly 58 years old. He was a tall, lanky man. His red hair was streaked with gray.

The Granger Collection, New York

Although he had been born a Virginia aristocrat, Jefferson looked more like a country squire than the leader of a nation. He had always been painfully shy, which sometimes caused him to appear reserved. However, when Jefferson discussed such topics as science, mathematics, architecture, music, and art, his eyes lit up and he talked with great ease.

Jefferson had little taste for fancy ceremony. He once greeted the French representative to the United States wearing a dressing gown and slippers! At that time, important government officials usually dressed in powdered wigs, satin coats covered with medals, and silver-buckled shoes. Jefferson saw ordinary citizens and foreign diplomats each in their turn. He told them all, "Nobody shall be above you, nor you above anybody."

Jefferson and the Courts

One problem Jefferson encountered in his first term involved the courts. He was annoyed that so many judges were Federalists. Since the judges had been appointed before Jefferson took office, there was little he could do about the situation.

Supreme Court Chief Justice John Marshall, whom Jefferson particularly disliked, had been appointed by President John Adams after he had been defeated in the election of 1800 but before Jefferson had taken office. At the same time, Adams had appointed many other judges and court officials who were unfriendly to the Republicans. Some of these officials were called the "midnight judges" because Adams had signed the papers appointing them during the final hours of his presidency.

In the confusion of Adams's last hours, however, some of these papers had not been distributed, and Jefferson refused to let them be released to the appointees. William Marbury, whom Adams had appointed as a justice of the peace, asked the Supreme Court to order Jefferson's secretary of state, James Madison, to issue his appointment papers.

The case of **Marbury v. Madison** in 1803 provided a great test for the Court. The chief justice ruled that he could not force the president to give the appointment to Marbury. Marshall explained that the part of the Judiciary Act of 1799 that allowed the Supreme Court to give such an order was **unconstitutional**, or in violation of the Constitution.

• Marshall Court

Marshall established for the Court the power of **judicial review**—the right to declare an act of Congress unconstitutional. This meant that the Supreme Court had the final say in interpreting the Constitution.

The Louisiana Territory

Jefferson's most important accomplishment as president was to roughly double the size of the United States. This became possible when the United States purchased Louisiana, a huge area between the Mississippi River and the Rocky Mountains.

Napoleon and Louisiana. In 1800 Spain secretly agreed to give New Orleans and the rest of Louisiana back to France. French leader Napoleon Bonaparte had a plan to make Louisiana the center of a great new empire in the Western Hemisphere.

Americans became greatly alarmed at the prospect of France controlling the mouth of the Mississippi. If France cut off Americans' right of deposit in New Orleans, American trade would suffer tremendously. To solve the problem, Jefferson instructed Robert R. Livingston, the U.S. minister in Paris, to persuade France to cede New Orleans to the United States. Jefferson also sent his trusted adviser James Monroe to assist Livingston.

In order to build a naval base to protect his new empire, Napoleon needed to take control of Haiti, a nation on the Caribbean island of Hispaniola. Up until 1791 Haiti had been a French colony called Saint Domingue. Then former slave Toussaint L'Ouverture (TOO-san loo-vuhr-TOOHR) led a successful revolt against France. Although an attack in 1801 led to L'Ouverture's capture, the French forces were wiped out by Haitian rebels and disease. Napoleon soon gave up his dream of a Western empire.

● **Revolution**

The Louisiana Purchase. Jefferson had instructed Livingston and Monroe to offer France $10 million for New Orleans and West Florida. In April 1803, however, Napoleon offered to sell not only New

Among his many talents, President Thomas Jefferson was a fine architect. He designed his magnificent home, called Monticello, in Charlottesville, Virginia.

● **Thomas Jefferson**

Orleans but all of Louisiana to the United States! The astonished American diplomats quickly seized the opportunity, offering $15 million for the entire territory, a price of roughly four cents per acre. Although Jefferson was not sure if the Constitution allowed him to make the purchase, he decided to go ahead with the deal, which became known as the **Louisiana Purchase**.

Life in Louisiana. Most of the residents of this vast territory were American Indians, including the Osage, Kansa, Shoshoni, Cheyenne, and many other

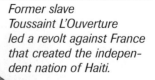
Former slave Toussaint L'Ouverture led a revolt against France that created the independent nation of Haiti.

● **Toussaint L'Ouverture**

The Granger Collection, New York

tribes. The region's residents of European descent tended to live in small settlements. One of the oldest of these settlements was Arkansas Post in what is now southeastern Arkansas. In 1800 this hunting and trading post had about 400 inhabitants of various backgrounds.

Many Louisianans also lived in larger settlements like New Orleans. By 1803 this city was home to about 4,000 Europeans and some 4,000 Africans, about 1,300 of whom were free. The city had lighted streets, two banks, a horse-powered sawmill, a French-language newspaper, and several churches and stores. The heavy merchant traffic that passed through New Orleans made this city important to the commercial needs of the United States.

The Lewis and Clark Expedition

Even before Spain officially returned Louisiana to France, President Jefferson had asked Congress for money to explore it. After Congress supplied him with $2,500, he appointed his private secretary, a former soldier named Meriwether Lewis, to head an expedition. Lewis persuaded another soldier, his friend William Clark, to join him

• Exploring

as co-leader of the expedition. Jefferson gave the explorers detailed instructions. They were to make maps of the country, to keep careful records of climate and soil conditions, to look for valuable minerals, and to collect plant and

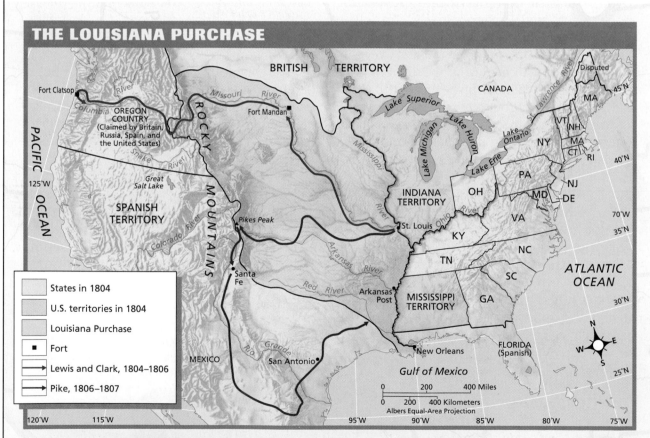

THE LOUISIANA PURCHASE

Learning from Maps. The Louisiana Purchase almost doubled the size of the United States. President Jefferson sent Lewis and Clark to explore this new territory.

▶ **Movement.** What rivers did Lewis and Clark follow from St. Louis on their way to the Pacific Ocean?

• Maps

animal samples. He also instructed them to gather information about the Indians.

Lewis and Clark prepared for more than a year. They gathered the necessary equipment, such as guns, warm clothing, gifts for the Indians, and medicines. They also chose the 45 members of what they called their Corps of Discovery. One member was a half-French, half-Indian interpreter who was skilled in Indian sign language.

Finally, in the spring of 1804 the **Lewis and Clark expedition** set out from St. Louis, near the junction of the Mississippi and Missouri Rivers. During their nearly two and a half years of travel they acquired an enormous amount of information. American Indians, particularly Sacagawea, greatly helped the explorers on their journey. Sacagawea served as an interpreter and helped the expedition survive in the harsh environment.

The Lewis and Clark expedition gave the United States a firmer claim to the Oregon Country, a region also claimed by Britain, Russia, and Spain that lay in the northwest. The success of Lewis and Clark also encouraged other explorations. In 1806 Zebulon Pike explored the southern part of the Louisiana

The Granger Collection, New York

Shoshoni interpreter Sacagawea played a crucial role in Lewis and Clark's expedition through the Louisiana Territory.

• **Meriwether Lewis** • **Lewis's Journal**

Purchase. His party traveled up the Arkansas River, and in November Pike sighted the mountain in present-day Colorado that was later named Pikes Peak.

Section 1 Review

IDENTIFY and explain the significance of the following: John Marshall, *Marbury* v. *Madison*, unconstitutional, judicial review, Toussaint L'Ouverture, Louisiana Purchase, Lewis and Clark expedition, Zebulon Pike

• **Glossary**

LOCATE and explain the importance of the following: Arkansas Post, St. Louis, Pikes Peak

REVIEWING FOR DETAILS

1. Why did Thomas Jefferson clash with the Supreme Court?

2. What did the Lewis and Clark expedition accomplish?

• **Gazetteer**

REVIEWING FOR UNDERSTANDING

3. **Geographic Literacy** Why was the Louisiana Purchase significant?

4. **Writing Mastery:** *Describing* Imagine that you are a member of the Lewis and Clark expedition. Write several journal entries describing your travels.

5. **Critical Thinking:** *Drawing Conclusions* What do you think were the long-term consequences of the *Marbury* v. *Madison* case?

Section 2

THE THREAT OF WAR

Multimedia Connections

Explore these related topics and materials on the CD–ROM to enrich your understanding of this section:

 Gazetteer

- New Orleans
- Canada
- Northwest Territory

 Atlas

- Barbary Coast

 Profiles

- Tecumseh

 Readings

- Barbary Wars

 Media Bank

- U.S. Imports and Exports
- New Orleans Street Scene
- Map of New Orleans, c. 1800
- Red Eagle Surrenders

Betsy Beauchamp wrote a letter to President Thomas Jefferson. "I am under the obligation," she began, "to inform you that I am in a distressed situation." She explained that her beloved brother Isack Moore, a sailor on an American merchant ship, had been forced into the service of the British! Her attempts to free him had cost her much time and money, but still her brother remained a captive. She begged Jefferson to do something to help.

As you read this section you will find out:

▶ **How Great Britain and France interfered with American rights.**

▶ **What policies Jefferson adopted to defend America's neutrality.**

▶ **Why people on the frontier pushed hardest for war with Great Britain.**

New Challenges to Neutral Rights

Just a few weeks after selling Louisiana, France was again at war with Great Britain. As in the past, the United States avoided taking sides. Both countries, however, challenged America's neutrality.

The nation's prosperity depended to a large extent on foreign trade. Americans still needed foreign manufactured goods, and farmers sold a great deal of their produce abroad. Because this trade was valuable to both sides, French and British warships and privateers set out to capture American merchant ships bound for each other's ports.

These attacks on American shipping were not only costly but also a blow to American pride. Many American merchants continued to trade in Europe despite the dangers. Even more alarming to most Americans than the loss of ships and cargoes was the loss of American sailors.

As the war in Europe continued, Great Britain stepped up its longtime practice of **impressment**—forcing sailors suspected of being British subjects to serve in the Royal Navy. Conditions in the British navy were terrible. Sailors had to live in extremely cramped quarters and obey strict rules of conduct. As a result, the desertion rate was very high. British warships often stopped American merchant ships on the high seas to search for deserters.

• **Trouble**

American relations with Great Britain became even more strained in June 1807. The British frigate *Leopard* stopped the *Chesapeake,* an American naval ship. The British claimed that four men aboard were British deserters. When the American commander refused to allow the British to search his ship, the *Leopard* opened fire. The *Chesapeake* surrendered, and the British snatched the four sailors off the ship. Only one turned out to be a British deserter. The incident encouraged many Americans to call for war.

among sailors and among workers who had been making goods that were usually exported. The busy American shipbuilding industry nearly came to a halt.

New Englanders particularly resented the Embargo Act. One man who signed himself "A lover of his Country" wrote to Jefferson on July 4, 1808:

> **"Mr. President if you know what is good for your future welfar[e] you will take off the embargo that is now such a check upon American commerce. . . . Your friend as long as you act with propriety [properness] toward your country but when you depart from that I am your enehmy [enemy]."**

Because many Americans considered the embargo unwise and unfair, they did not hesitate to break the law. Trade by sea between one American port and another was allowed. Therefore, many captains claimed that they were making such a voyage but went to Europe or the West Indies instead.

Despite these violations and the smuggling of American goods into Canada, the Embargo Act seriously hurt the American economy. The value of goods imported into the United States

The Embargo Act

Instead of going to war, Jefferson tried to put economic pressure on both Great Britain and France. In December 1807 he persuaded Congress to pass the **Embargo Act**. An **embargo** is a government order prohibiting trade—in this case, all exports from the United States. Jefferson hoped that by depriving Britain and France of goods they needed, the embargo would make them stop violating America's neutral rights. He also reasoned that if American ships did not carry goods on the high seas, no American sailor could be forced into a foreign navy.

This was, of course, an extreme measure to avoid war. Stopping foreign trade caused massive unemployment

The Granger Collection, New York

The British impressment of American sailors aboard the Chesapeake *increased support for a war against Great Britain.*

in 1808 was less than half what it was in 1807. Exports dropped from $108 million in 1807 to $22 million in 1808.

Drifting Toward War

Early in 1809, after James Madison had been elected president, Congress responded to the protests over loss of trade. Congress replaced Jefferson's earlier Embargo Act with the **Non-Intercourse Act**. This law restored trade with all foreign countries *except* France and Great Britain and ports under their control. It also gave the president the power to open trade with either France or Great Britain if such trade "shall cease to violate the neutral commerce of the United States."

The Non-Intercourse Act was just as hard to enforce as the Embargo Act. A ship's captain could, for example, set out officially for the Netherlands and when he reached the English Channel change course for Great Britain or France. Finally, in 1810 Congress removed all restrictions on trade with Great Britain and France. However, Congress provided that if either nation stopped attacking American merchant ships, the president could cut off trade with the other nation.

Kentucky senator Henry Clay was one of the most outspoken War Hawks in Congress.

This action was an attempt to get each side to be the first to respect American neutral rights. The British, however, ignored the new American policy and continued to impress American sailors. The policies of Jefferson and Madison had failed. More and more Americans began calling for war with Great Britain.

The War Hawks

Most of the people who favored war were southerners and westerners. Their leaders belonged to a new breed of young Republicans in Congress known as **War Hawks**. Two of the most famous were John C. Calhoun of South Carolina and Henry Clay of Kentucky. In a speech to the Senate in February 1810, Clay made his views clear. "I prefer the troubled ocean of war," he said, "to the calm, decaying pool of dishonorable peace."

Although many War Hawks were angered by the impressment of American sailors, they were more concerned with expanding the boundaries of the United States. Some hoped to take Florida from Spain, now Great Britain's ally in the long war against Napoleon. Others hoped to gobble up British-owned Canada. The War Hawks

The Plumb-pudding in danger, —or State Epicures taking un Petit Souper. "the great Globe itself, and all which it inherit," is too small to satisfy such insatiable appetites.

During the early 1800s many countries such as the United States were caught in the middle as the British and the French "carved up the world" between them.

also blamed the Spanish and British for help-ing Indians resist the advance of American settlers.

The situation was particularly tense in the Northwest Territory. The huge area that American Indians turned over to land-hungry settlers in the Treaty of Greenville of 1795 was not enough to satisfy the settlers for long. One of the settlers' leaders was General William Henry Harrison, governor of the Indiana Territory. Harrison considered Indians to be "wretched savages" who were blocking the forward march of what he called "civilization." He used trickery, bribery, and military force to push Indians off their land.

In 1809 Harrison reached a treaty agreement with the chiefs of a few Indian tribes in the territory. The tribes gave up 3 million acres in return for about $10,000—less than half a cent an acre. The U.S. government was selling similar land for at least $2 an acre.

Tecumseh and the Prophet

Even before Harrison made this deal, a brilliant leader had been rising among the Indians of the Ohio Valley. He was Tecumseh (tuh-KUHM-suh) of the Shawnee nation. Tecumseh was furious when he heard how the Native Americans had been cheated. He believed that God, "the Great Spirit," had created the land for Indians to *use* but not to *own*. At a meeting with Harrison, Tecumseh argued that Indians had no right to sell the land. "Sell a *country!*"

he cried. "Why not sell the air, the clouds and the Great God!"

Tecumseh offered Indian support in any war against the British if the United States would give up its claims to the lands purchased by the 1809 treaty. Harrison told Tecumseh frankly that the president would never agree to this.

Despite this rejection, however, Tecumseh continued his efforts to unite all the Indian nations east of the Mississippi to resist white expansion. He was a marvelous speaker and worked tirelessly for his cause. Even Harrison admitted that Tecumseh was "one of those . . . geniuses which spring up occasionally to produce revolutions."

Tecumseh traveled up and down the frontier of the United States talking to the Sauk, the Fox, and the Potawatomi in the north as well as the Creek, the Choctaw, and the Cherokee in the south. Everywhere he spoke for unity among Native Americans:

"**White people . . . have driven us from the great salt water, forced us over the mountains, and would shortly push us into the lakes. But we are determined to go no farther. The only way to stop this evil is for all red men to unite.**"

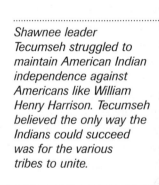

Shawnee leader Tecumseh struggled to maintain American Indian independence against Americans like William Henry Harrison. Tecumseh believed the only way the Indians could succeed was for the various tribes to unite.

The brutal Battle of Tippecanoe severely weakened American Indian control over land in the Midwest. Among white settlers, however, it made a hero of General William Henry Harrison.

Tecumseh was aided in his crusade by his brother Tenskwatawa (ten-SKWAHT-uh-wah), known as the Prophet. The Prophet attracted many Indians to the confederacy, but he was an ineffective leader. General Harrison marched with about 1,000 troops toward Tenskwatawa's village of Prophetstown in the fall of 1811. Tecumseh, who was away at the time, had cautioned Tenskwatawa to avoid a fight until the confederacy was ready. But the Prophet attacked anyway.

The **Battle of Tippecanoe** took place in present-day Indiana, near where Tippecanoe Creek joins the Wabash River. The battle was fierce and extremely bloody, but Harrison defeated the Indians. The returning Tecumseh was stricken with grief and anger. He knew that the defeat had destroyed his confederacy.

Section 2 Review

• Glossary

IDENTIFY and explain the significance of the following: impressment, Embargo Act, embargo, Non-Intercourse Act, War Hawks, William Henry Harrison, Tecumseh, Battle of Tippecanoe

REVIEWING FOR DETAILS

1. How did Great Britain and France threaten American neutrality?
2. How did Jefferson and Madison try to defend America's neutrality?
3. Why was the push to declare war on Great Britain strongest on the frontier?

REVIEWING FOR UNDERSTANDING

4. **Geographic Literacy** How was the American Indian view of land different from that of the white settlers? What conflicts arose from this difference?
5. **Critical Thinking:** *Generalizations and Stereotypes* What stereotype of Indians did William Henry Harrison hold? How might this view have influenced the way he treated them?

Section 3

THE WAR OF 1812

Multimedia Connections

Explore these related topics and materials on the CD–ROM to enrich your understanding of this section:

 Gazetteer

- Fort Detroit
- Lake Erie
- Potomac River

 Media Bank

- Time Line: War of 1812
- Battles of the War of 1812
- Naval Warfare, War of 1812
- Bombardment of Fort McHenry

 Profiles

- Oliver Hazard Perry

Maryland lawyer and poet Francis Scott Key had been on board the British warship for days. Now he watched as British vessels gleefully bombed Baltimore's Fort McHenry. Would the fort or the American flag that flew overhead survive the attack? Dawn revealed the stars and stripes, tattered but proud! A few days later Key recalled the battle in a poem. It began with, "Oh, say, can you see, by the dawn's early light. . . . " His stirring words eventually became the national anthem.

As you read this section you will find out:

▶ **How the early battles progressed.**

▶ **How British attacks in America affected the course of the war.**

▶ **Why the Battle of New Orleans was significant.**

Early Battles

In June 1812 Congress finally declared war on Great Britain. The first American victories in the War of 1812 occurred at sea. Great Britain was still fighting France, so the Royal Navy could not spare its entire fleet to fight the Americans. Its Atlantic fleet was still much larger than the American navy.

Early in the war, however, the tiny American navy won some important victories against the British. For example, in August 1812, the frigate *Constitution* defeated the British frigate *Guerrière* in a battle off the Maine coast. Then it defeated the British frigate *Java* in another famous battle.

After these early losses, British captains avoided single-ship battles with American frigates. Instead, the British established a naval blockade just as it had during the Revolution.

The Fight for Canada

At the start of the war, Canada seemed an easy target to some Americans. The population of Canada was small, compared to that of the United States. Yet when an American force commanded by General William Hull crossed into Canada from Fort Detroit in July 1812, Indians led by Tecumseh attacked the soldiers. Hull then withdrew to Fort Detroit, pursued by a small Canadian force under General Isaac Brock. Hull soon surrendered. By the end of 1812, the British controlled Lake Erie and most of present-day Indiana and Illinois.

In light of these setbacks, President Madison put General Harrison in command of the army on the northwest frontier. Before a new American invasion of Canada could be launched, however, a British naval squadron had to be cleared from Lake Erie.

The U.S. troops who accomplished this task were under the command of Oliver Hazard Perry. At least 10 percent of these sailors were African American. In September 1813, in the **Battle of Lake Erie**, Perry's force defeated the British forces. "We have met the enemy, and they are ours," Perry informed Harrison.

Now Harrison was able to recapture Fort Detroit and advance into Canada. At the Thames River in southern Canada he defeated the British and their Indian allies on October 5, 1813.

The **Battle of the Thames** allowed the United States to win back the Great Lakes region. Perhaps more significantly, however, the battle resulted in the death of Tecumseh. Without this great leader, the Indian confederacy collapsed.

Southern Battles

In March, 1814, Creek Indian forces that had been aiding the British were defeated by the Tennessee militia. American general

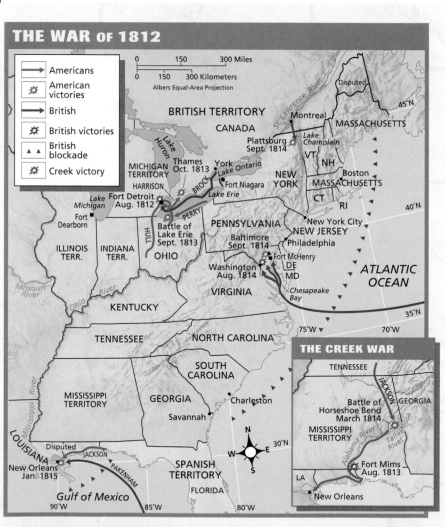

• Maps

Learning from Maps.
The War of 1812 lasted nearly three years. Battles took place all over the United States.

▶ **Place.** Which forts were located on the Great Lakes? What battles were fought on the Great Lakes?

Andrew Jackson led a force of 2,000 troops in a series of armed conflicts that ended with the **Battle of Horseshoe Bend**. After this defeat, in which about 750 Creek people were killed, the tribe was forced to give up 20 million acres of land that they controlled.

The defeats suffered by the British were humiliating. The greatest blow to British pride was when U.S. forces burned York, the capital of British Canada. Afterward, the British set out to inflict the same on the U.S. capital and to draw U.S. forces away from Canada. In August 1814 a force of some 4,000 British troops came ashore southeast of Washington. The troops marched into Washington and set fire to all the public buildings, including the Capitol and the White House.

President James Madison was out with the forces trying to halt the British advance. He escaped by fleeing up the Potomac River. First Lady Dolley Madison, protected by a slave, got away from the White House minutes before the British entered. She wrote to her sister as she was leaving:

> **"We have had a battle . . . and here I am still, within sound of the cannon! Mr. Madison comes not. May God protect us! A wagon has been procured [found], and I have had it filled with . . . the most valuable portable articles. . . . I insist on**

The Granger Collection, New York

This engraving shows the burning of Washington after the British marched through the city.

• Early View

> **waiting until the large picture of General Washington is secured, and it requires to be unscrewed from the wall."**

The British had no intention of stopping in Washington. On September 13, British warships opened fire on Fort McHenry, which guarded the entrance to Baltimore Harbor. After a whole day and night of firing on the fort with no success, the British fleet withdrew. Baltimore was safe.

The Battle of New Orleans

After being stopped at Baltimore, the British unleashed a greater attack aimed at New Orleans. In late 1814 a force of 7,500 British troops landed on the Louisiana coast and marched through the swampy country without being discovered.

On December 23, 1814, about 2,000 British troops were only seven miles from New Orleans when a muddied messenger burst in to warn General Andrew Jackson, who was in

First Lady Dolley Madison helped save many articles from the White House before it was burned by the British.

• Dolley Madison

charge of defending the city. Although somewhat surprised, Jackson declared, "Gentlemen, the British are below. We must fight them tonight!" He ordered every available unit forward—a total of about 2,400 men. They included Jackson's regular troops, along with hastily organized militia units. Among the militia were several hundred free African Americans, a band of Choctaw Indians, and a group of pirates.

Jackson's troops attacked the British at about 8:00 P.M. After two hours of fighting, he decided to fall back before the British could receive reinforcements. His men built an earthen defensive wall behind a canal only five miles from New Orleans.

When the British commander, General Edward Pakenham, finally attacked on January 8, 1815, his men were mowed down by a hail of iron and lead. Over 2,000 British soldiers were killed or wounded. When the smoke cleared, even the toughest veterans were stunned by the sight of the battlefield. "The field was entirely covered with . . . bodies," one Kentucky soldier reported. Only 71

The Granger Collection, New York

The Battle of New Orleans was the greatest victory for the United States in the War of 1812, even though the war was officially over by the time the battle took place.

Americans were killed or wounded, however, in this **Battle of New Orleans**.

The loss of life at New Orleans was particularly tragic because the war was officially over before the battle was even fought! This important news had not even reached the United States, however, because communications were slow. Nevertheless, Jackson and his men had won the greatest land victory of the war, and it made the general a popular hero.

Section 3 Review

• **Glossary**

IDENTIFY and explain the significance of the following: Battle of Lake Erie, Battle of the Thames, Battle of Horseshoe Bend, Dolley Madison, Andrew Jackson, Battle of New Orleans

LOCATE and explain the importance of the following: Fort Detroit, Lake Erie, Fort McHenry

• **Gazetteer**

REVIEWING FOR DETAILS
1. What was the outcome of early battles at sea?
2. How did British strategy affect the course of the war?

REVIEWING FOR UNDERSTANDING
3. **Geographic Literacy** British forces invaded the United States in three places. How might geography have made this strategy difficult to carry out?
4. **Writing Mastery:** *Describing* Imagine that you are a newspaper reporter after the Battle of New Orleans. Write an article describing the battle's significance.
5. **Critical Thinking:** *Making Comparisons* How was the War of 1812 similar to the American Revolution? How were the two conflicts different?

Section 4
PEACE AND NEW BOUNDARIES

Multimedia Connections

Explore these related topics and materials on the CD–ROM to enrich your understanding of this section:

 Media Bank

- *The County Fair*
- Map of New Orleans, 1815
- American Patriotism

 Gazetteer

- Belgium

 Atlas

- Territorial Expansion, 1820

 Readings

- Adams-Onís Treaty
- Monroe Doctrine
- Washington Irving

James Gallatin felt a little shy. Imagine him, just a teenager, at a Christmas dinner to celebrate the treaty that would end the War of 1812! He quickly reminded himself that he was there to assist his father, Albert Gallatin, one of the American diplomats who had negotiated the deal with British officials. After the elaborate meal, which featured roast beef, he described the event in his diary. "It was a scene to be remembered," he wrote. "God grant that there may be always peace between the two nations."

As you read this section you will find out:

▶ **What effects the War of 1812 had on the United States.**

▶ **How the United States annexed Florida.**

▶ **Why the Monroe Doctrine was significant.**

Negotiating Peace

In August 1814, British and American diplomats met at Ghent in Belgium to negotiate an end to the war. The discussions dragged on for months. Finally, everyone realized that the reasons for fighting had disappeared. With Napoleon temporarily defeated, the British no longer needed to stop American ships from carrying goods to Europe or to impress American sailors into the Royal Navy. On Christmas Eve 1814, the delegates signed the **Treaty of Ghent**. Though neither side could claim victory, peace was restored. The treaty did not even mention the issues of neutral rights and impressment. Indeed, it had few concrete terms, but it was generally popular among Americans.

News of the treaty came shortly after the Hartford Convention, a meeting of New

This image of the signing of the Treaty of Ghent on Christmas Eve 1814 was painted by Amedee Forestier 100 years after the signing. The treaty set the terms for the end of the War of 1812.

National Museum of American Art, Washington, DC/Art Resource, NY

England Federalists called in December 1814 to protest the war. With peace restored, the goals of the convention were pointless. The Federalists appeared out of date and almost unpatriotic, and their power gradually declined. In the 1816 presidential election, the Federalist candidate, Rufus King, got only 34 votes in the Electoral College to James Monroe's 183 votes.

The War of 1812 not only helped bury the Federalists, it also convinced the nations of Europe that the United States was here to stay. The British in particular began to treat America with greater respect. After the war, conflicts between the two nations were solved by diplomats.

In 1815 Great Britain and the United States signed an agreement ending certain restrictions on America's trade with the British Empire. In 1817 the two nations signed the **Rush-Bagot Agreement**, which provided that neither country would maintain a fleet of warships on the Great Lakes. The **Convention of 1818** set the boundary between the Louisiana Purchase and British Canada at 49° north latitude from northern Minnesota to the Rocky Mountains. The agreement also called for joint control of the disputed area of Oregon Country.

The Annexation of Florida

The Florida question, however, was not as easy to settle. Southerners had hoped that the War of 1812 would pry Florida from Spanish control. By the end of the war, the United States had staked a claim to an area called West Florida, though Spain disputed the claim.

Settlers who lived along the southern frontier of the United States complained of raids by Seminole Indians from Spanish Florida. The settlers also complained that many of their slaves were escaping to Spanish territory.

Late in 1817, President James Monroe sent General Jackson to defeat the Seminole. Ignoring the boundary line, Jackson pursued them into Florida at the head of an army of 2,000 U.S. troops. When the Seminole fell back, avoiding a battle, a furious Jackson seized two British traders and put them on trial for encouraging the Seminole raids. The two men were found guilty and executed. Jackson then captured two Spanish forts, including Pensacola, the capital of West Florida.

Luis de Onís, the Spanish minister to the United States, bitterly protested Jackson's behavior. Most Americans, however, supported Jackson's actions. President Monroe did not want to go against popular sentiment.

Therefore, Secretary of State John Quincy Adams told Onís that Jackson had only acted to protect the security of the United States. Adams also suggested that if Spain could not control what went on in its colony of Florida, it should turn the colony over to the United States.

In the **Adams-Onís Treaty**, signed in February 1819, Spain gave up claims to West Florida and agreed to **cede**, or surrender, the rest of Florida to the United States. Spain also abandoned its claims to the Oregon Country. In return, the United States agreed to pay the $5 million in claims for damages that Americans had against the Spanish government in Florida. In addition, the United States agreed to a boundary between the Louisiana Purchase and Spanish Mexico, giving up any claims to the land that would later become Texas.

The Adams-Onís Treaty was a great triumph for the United States. Adams later said that the day he and Onís signed the treaty was "the most important day of my life." In little more than 40 years the young nation had grown from a string of settlements along the Atlantic coast to a huge country nearly an entire continent wide. Adams believed "the whole continent appears to be destined . . . to be peopled by one nation."

Revolution in Latin America

The Adams-Onís Treaty was just one sign that the great Spanish Empire in the Americas was falling apart. Revolutionary leaders like Simón Bolívar in Venezuela, José de San Martín in what became Argentina, Bernardo O'Higgins in Chile, and Miguel Hidalgo y Costilla in Mexico inspired the people to throw off their colonial masters. By 1822 most of Spain's colonies in the Americas had declared their independence.

These revolutions delighted many people in the United States. The new nations seemed to be copying the example of their North American neighbor. Once free from Spain's control, these new nations would be open to ships and goods from the United States.

Great Britain also profited from Spain's declining influence by greatly increasing its trade with the new republics. British leaders soon found themselves in a difficult position,

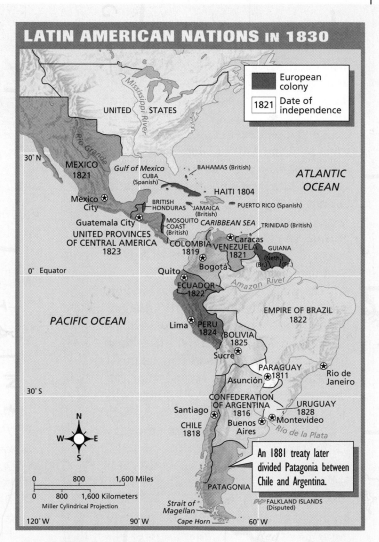

LATIN AMERICAN NATIONS IN 1830

An 1881 treaty later divided Patagonia between Chile and Argentina.

Learning from Maps.
Many countries in Latin America became independent in the early 1800s.

▶ **Place.** Which nations became independent from 1820 to 1825?

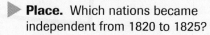

Many Latin American leaders like Simón Bolívar of Venezuela helped their countries break free from Spanish rule.

● **Simón Bolívar**

"**that the American continents, by the free and independent condition which they have assumed and maintain, are henceforth not to be considered as subjects for future colonization by any European powers.**"

Monroe went on to say that the United States would "consider any attempt" by the European powers to create new colonies in the Americas "as dangerous to our peace and safety." In return, America would not become involved in European affairs.

European leaders were both amused and annoyed by Monroe's declaration. They knew that British seapower was really what would

however. They worried about the possibility that other European monarchs might help the king of Spain regain control of his colonies.

In 1823 British foreign minister George Canning proposed that the United States and Great Britain issue a joint declaration. This statement would declare that the two countries would not try to annex any of Spain's former or current colonies and would warn other nations not to try to restore Spanish control in Latin America.

Canning's statement, however, was not one the United States wished to make. The island of Cuba was still a Spanish colony. Someday, the United States might be interested in taking it over. Canning's plan would rule out this possibility. The United States was also reluctant to do anything to help the British increase trade with the new Latin American republics.

The Monroe Doctrine

John Quincy Adams advised President Monroe to issue a statement of his own that dealt with entirely American interests. On December 2, 1823, in a speech to Congress, the president announced what came to be known as the **Monroe Doctrine**. Its main point declared:

Through Others' Eyes
The Test of Time

The Monroe Doctrine continued to influence U.S.–Latin American relations into the 1900s. While some U.S. presidents ignored the policy, others used it as an excuse to interfere in Central and South America. Although Europeans and some Latin Americans protested against U.S. involvement, other people from Latin America believed the Monroe Doctrine was important to their countries' protection. For example, in 1916, Simón Planas Suárez, a Venezuelan diplomat, expressed his support for the Monroe Doctrine:

"If all our republics were great Powers, strong and wealthy, the Monroe Doctrine would . . . probably be unnecessary. . . . But unfortunately such is not the case. . . . Consequently, the shield which has protected the Latin-American people against possible conquests of their territory by European nations has been the Monroe Doctrine, which . . . faithfully represents the sentiment of all America without distinction of race or latitude."

keep the European monarchies out of the Americas. The new Latin American nations generally approved of Monroe's ideas and hoped he was sincere. However, some Latin Americans wondered if the United States could really help them in times of crisis.

At the time, the Monroe Doctrine merely announced that America was taking its place on the world diplomatic stage. Later, when the United States became powerful enough to back its words with actions, it was clear that President Monroe had issued a kind of second Declaration of Independence. This one said to the nations of Europe: "Hands off the Western Hemisphere." The Monroe Doctrine became one of the most important statements of U.S. foreign policy ever issued.

The Era of Good Feelings

The Monroe Doctrine was one sign of **nationalism**, or national pride, that swept the United States after the War of 1812. Albert Gallatin, America's minister to France, described this mood:

> **"The war had renewed & reinstated the National feelings & character, which the Revolution had given. . . . The people . . . are more American: they feel & act more as a Nation."**

President Monroe seemed to symbolize the emergence of this national spirit. He had been elected in 1816 without major opposition in part because the Federalists were so unpopular after the War of 1812. When Monroe ran for re-election four years later, no one ran against him. The Federalist Party soon collapsed.

In 1817 President Monroe made a good-will tour of New England, which had been a Federalist strong point. Yet everywhere he went, enthusiastic crowds greeted the president warmly. As one Boston newspaper wrote, an "Era of Good Feelings" had begun.

National Portrait Gallery, Smithsonian Institution, Washington, DC/Art Resource, NY

President Monroe

• **James Monroe**

Section 4 Review

• **Glossary**

• **Time Line**

IDENTIFY and explain the significance of the following: Treaty of Ghent, James Monroe, Rush-Bagot Agreement, Convention of 1818, Adams-Onís Treaty, cede, Monroe Doctrine, nationalism

REVIEWING FOR DETAILS

1. What were the results of the War of 1812?
2. What was the significance of the Monroe Doctrine?

REVIEWING FOR UNDERSTANDING

3. **Geographic Literacy** How did the location of Florida contribute to its annexation by the United States?

4. **Writing Mastery:** *Expressing* Write a letter to a friend expressing the feelings that swept the nation in the years following the War of 1812.

5. **Critical Thinking:** *Drawing Conclusion* What factors might have led President Monroe to decide to issue the Monroe Doctrine?

CHAPTER 9

THE FIRST LOCOMOTIVE IN AMERICA

The North and Manufacturing (1790–1860)

THEMES IN AMERICAN HISTORY

Technology and Society:
How might new technology affect the growth of industry?

Economic Development:
What impact might the growth of industry have on a country's economy?

Global Relations:
How might immigration affect the development of a society?

• Video Opener

• Skill Builder

𝒫oet Thomas Man described the early effects of factories in the United States:

"**For Liberty our fathers fought,**
 Which with their blood, they dearly
  bought.
 The factory system sets at naught.
 A slave at morn, a slave at eve,
 It doth my innermost feelings grieve;
 The blood runs chilly from my heart,
 To see fair Liberty depart."

image above: *American steam locomotive, 1829*

Section 1

FROM FARMS TO FACTORIES

Multimedia Connections

Explore these related topics and materials on the CD–ROM to enrich your understanding of this section:

 Media Bank

- Inventions, 1760–1850
- Making Straw Hats
- Cooper's Shop

 Gazetteer

- Rhode Island

 Biographies

- Samuel Slater

 Readings

- *American Notes*

 Profiles

- Eli Whitney

In 1801 a young inventor named Eli Whitney took 10 guns to Washington. Before an amazed group of officials, Whitney took the guns apart. He mixed the parts so that it was not possible to know which trigger went with which barrel, and so on. Then, choosing pieces at random, he reassembled the parts into 10 new guns. This demonstration began a new era of industrial expansion that dramatically changed the American way of life.

As you read this section you will find out:

▶ **How and where the Industrial Revolution began.**

▶ **Why most American factories were located in the Northeast.**

▶ **How mass production changed industry.**

The Turn Toward Manufacturing

Since the first English settlements were established in the 1600s, land had been the chief source of wealth in America. This was still the case in the early 1800s. Most people wanted to own land, even if only a small plot. Owning land was a sign of freedom, independence, and stability in society. It seemed as if Americans' preference for farm life might prohibit interest in expanding industry.

Support for manufacturing. The American Revolution had brought the nation political independence. Economic independence was more complicated, however. As soon as the Revolution ended, the British began selling cloth, chinaware, and every sort of manufactured product at bargain prices to win back

American customers. American consumers eagerly purchased these goods, and American producers lost business.

A small but very determined group of Americans saw the advantages of developing manufacturing. Alexander Hamilton was an important spokesperson for this group. Hamilton and others favored a mixed economy, one in which manufacturing existed side by side with agriculture. Some people argued that manufacturing would make America independent of European suppliers.

Because the United States was mainly an agricultural nation, Americans continued to depend on foreign-made goods for many years. However, the conflicts with Britain that led to the War of 1812 made overseas trade almost impossible. As foreign products became less available, quick profits could be made by anyone who could manufacture goods that previously had been imported.

Many Americans came to believe that manufacturing should be an important part of the economy. They realized that if Americans could produce more manu-

Americans imported many items from overseas, such as this British-made water pitcher, which celebrates the first U.S. census in 1790.

factured goods, they would be less dependent on foreign sources. Even Thomas Jefferson, who had opposed government assistance to industry, wrote in 1816:

> **"To be independent for the comforts of life we must fabricate [make] them ourselves. We must now place the manufacturer by the side of the agriculturist. . . . Shall we make our own comforts or go without them at the will of a foreign nation? . . . Experience has taught me that manufactures are now as necessary to our independence as to our comfort."**

The Industrial Revolution. Great Britain had been able to dominate the world market for many years because British manufacturers had largely shifted their work from hand tools to power-driven machinery. Historians have labeled this shift the **Industrial Revolution**, a period of great industrial expansion.

The process began in Great Britain in the 1700s. The first steps toward industrialization came in the **textiles**, or cloth, industry. Before industrialization, most families made much of their own clothing. Almost every home had a spinning wheel for making thread, and some also had a loom for weaving cloth. It took much longer to spin thread, however, than it took to weave the thread into cloth. This meant that one weaver used all the thread that several spinners could produce.

Sometime around 1764 James Hargreaves, a British weaver, built a hand-operated mechanical spinning wheel called the spinning jenny. Some people say the machine was named after Hargreaves's wife. Others say the name came from "gin," a short form of the word *engine*. Spinning jennies were relatively small, inexpensive, and easy to build. Before long, many textile manufacturers had adopted Hargreaves's useful invention.

The spinning jenny increased output, but it did not greatly reduce the price of cotton cloth. Because cotton fibers were not very strong, cotton could not be used very easily to make long threads for weaving cloth. By 1769 a former barber named Richard Arkwright solved this problem. He invented a spinning machine, called a water frame, that produced much stronger cotton thread. With the widespread use of the water frame, the price of textiles fell dramatically.

Arkwright's spinning machine was much too large to fit into people's homes, however. He set up his machines in mills along streams, where water could be used to power the new

James Hargreaves's spinning jenny greatly improved cloth production. This woman is working with an advanced version of Hargreaves's jenny.

equipment. Instead of taking the work to the people in their homes, Arkwright brought people to the work in the mills. In this way, Arkwright and others like him created Britain's first factories.

The Factory Comes to America

Arkwright's spinning machines proved so successful that British cloth was soon being exported to every part of the world. The British government had no intention of losing the competitive advantage that resulted from its new industrial methods. The British would not allow the export of textile-making machinery, and workers who were familiar with the machines could not leave the country.

Despite government opposition, a number of skilled workers did manage to make their way to America. One of the most important was Samuel Slater, who at one time had worked for Arkwright. When Slater decided to come to America, he memorized the designs for the new cotton-spinning machinery.

Slater arrived in New York in 1789. He soon met Moses Brown, whose family had been engaged in commerce and small-scale manufacturing in Providence, Rhode Island,

for generations. Slater formed a partnership with Brown and another investor, William Almy, who was Brown's son-in-law. Slater agreed to produce cotton-spinning machines in Pawtucket, Rhode Island. By 1793 the task was complete.

Slater's machines spun cotton thread that was better than homespun cotton. Soon, Slater was operating his own factories as well as designing them for other people.

Slater's factories made nothing but thread. Brown and Almy sold some of this thread at their store in Providence. The rest of the thread was supplied to workers, who wove it into cloth on looms in their homes. The weavers returned the cloth to Brown and Almy, who paid them a set price per yard for the cloth they wove. Brown and Almy then sold the cloth in their store. This system of take-home work remained an important part of production long after factories became widespread. In addition to cloth, many products such as hats and shoes were produced in a similar manner.

Encouraged by Slater's success with these textile producers, other Americans began to build factories. Much of this early industry developed in the northeastern United States. The location of the new factories and the towns

Samuel Slater's factory in Pawtucket, Rhode Island, relied on nearby waterfalls for power. Most early factories were built in similar locations to take advantage of waterpower.

that grew up around them was influenced by the region's geography.

Since the machinery in the factories was driven by waterpower, the factories were built beside swiftly moving streams and rivers, where waterwheels turned the machinery. Particularly ideal were sites in the Northeast where rivers drop from the Appalachian foothills to the Atlantic Coastal Plain in small waterfalls. Owners built factories all along the northeastern seaboard to take advantage of this power source.

Mass Production

America contained vast reserves of many natural resources that were useful to the manufacturing process. Forests provided lumber for buildings and machines, and iron could be used to make tools and nails. Although the natural resources existed in good supply, changes had to take place before manufacturers could produce large numbers of identical goods in great quantities, a process known as **mass production**.

Industrial **technology**—the use of tools to produce goods or to do work—used in the late 1700s seems quite inefficient by modern standards. Most items were made by skilled artisans, thus each item was slightly different from the other. If part of an item broke, it took a long time to fix because an artisan would have to craft a new part from scratch. In some cases the entire item would have to be rebuilt.

Using this system of production, most manufacturing was very slow. For example, it took the new government arsenal at Springfield, Massachusetts, two years to turn out only 245 muskets. When war threatened between the United States and France in the 1790s, Congress purchased 7,000 muskets from foreign sources. At this point, several inventors, the most famous of whom was Eli Whitney, stepped in to try to improve the nation's industrial technology.

Whitney believed that he could manufacture muskets by using **interchangeable parts** This meant that all the parts for a certain model of the gun would be exactly the same and could be used with the pieces of any other gun of the same model. Thus, when a part on a gun broke, that part could be fixed more quickly than before. Whitney explained the key to his strategy:

"**One of my primary objects is to form the tools so the tools themselves shall fashion the work and give to every part its just proportion—which when once accomplished, will give expedition [speed], uniformity [sameness], and exactness to the whole.**"

In 1798 Whitney signed a government contract and received an advance payment of $5,000 to get his business started. It took him over two years to build the equipment that would enable him to turn out identical parts. Within a few months of starting production, his shop near New Haven, Connecticut, had produced 500 muskets.

Whitney's and others' demonstrations of the importance of interchangeable parts revolutionized manufacturing in America. Soon, machine parts could be replaced with relative ease, making industrial production more efficient and economical.

Before the invention of interchangeable parts, most mechanical items had to be forged by hand by artisans like these. It took them a long time to craft new items from scratch when one broke. The process saved time and labor.

Section 1 Review

• Glossary

IDENTIFY and explain the significance of the following: Industrial Revolution, textiles, Samuel Slater, mass production, technology, Eli Whitney, interchangeable parts

REVIEWING FOR DETAILS

1. How and where did the Industrial Revolution begin?
2. How did mass production change the way goods were made?

REVIEWING FOR UNDERSTANDING

3. **Geographic Literacy** Why did most early American factories develop in the Northeast?
4. **Writing Mastery:** *Classifying* Write a paragraph explaining the advantages and disadvantages of having workers produce goods in factories rather than in their homes.
5. **Critical Thinking:** *Making Comparisons* How do mass-produced items differ from products crafted by artisans? What might have been some advantages and disadvantages of the two types of production?

Section 2

LIFE IN THE FACTORIES

Multimedia Connections

Explore these related topics and materials on the CD–ROM to enrich your understanding of this section:

 Profiles

- Sarah Bagley
- Francis Cabot Lowell

 Media Bank

- Cyrus H. McCormick
- Chuck Factory
- Mill Workers

 Readings

- Rules for Boardinghouses

 Simulation

- Choosing a Factory Site

n the 1830s Sarah Monroe helped launch one of the first organizations for female workers. Monroe explained, "If it is unfashionable for the men to bear oppression in silence, why should it not also become unfashionable with the women?" As factories increased production, many workers grew unhappy with labor conditions. Some organized to protest wage cuts or increased working hours. Although few of these early efforts were very successful, they provided workers with a way to voice their concerns about the new industrial era.

As you read this section you will find out:

▶ **Who worked in factories.**

▶ **What working and living conditions were like for mill workers.**

▶ **Why workers organized unions.**

Recruiting a Labor Force

The northeastern section of the United States—the New England states, plus New York, New Jersey, and Pennsylvania—soon became the nation's major manufacturing area. In large cities like New York and Boston, one could find a variety of industries. In smaller factory towns, the economy often centered around one industry. For example, Lynn, Massachusetts, was a center for the shoe industry, while Danbury, Connecticut, focused on hat manufacturing.

In the 1790s the first American factories were just being built. The question of who would work in these factories soon arose. In Great Britain most early factory jobs were filled by tenant farmers who had been thrown out of work when owners fenced the land in order to raise sheep. This process has come to be known as the **enclosure movement**. In America, however, most farmers still owned their own land. Most artisans, such as carpenters and shoemakers, owned their own workshops. Few Americans worked for wages, and still fewer were willing to work in factories.

The early textile manufacturers solved this problem in two ways. One was by employing children. Samuel Slater's first spinning machines were operated by seven boys and two girls ranging in age from 7 to 12. Slater employed these children because their small hands could operate the machinery easily. He paid them between 25 and 55 cents a week, much less than adults in Rhode Island, who usually earned over $3 a week.

Child labor seemed perfectly reasonable to most people. Farm children had always worked, and poor families were delighted to have any money their children could earn. Factories sometimes employed entire families.

The Lowell Girls

Another method of attracting factory workers was developed by Francis Lowell, a Boston merchant. In 1810 Lowell went to Britain, where he spent the next two years visiting spinning and weaving mills. He was deeply impressed by their efficiency. Like Slater, he carefully memorized the layout of the mills, hoping to be able to reproduce them in New England.

By the time Lowell returned to the United States, the War of 1812 had broken out. British goods were no longer available. Lowell organized a group of investors called the Boston Associates and hired a young engineer named Paul Moody to help him build power looms copied from designs he had seen in Britain.

The Associates built a factory at Waltham, Massachusetts, where they could use the waterpower of the Charles River. The looms were finished in 1814, and production started the following year. This factory spun cotton into thread and also wove it into cloth with machines.

Lowell was determined not to employ poor families. Instead, he hired young unmarried women from nearby farms. Many of these young women planned to work for wages for only a short time to earn extra money for their families before they got married.

Young People In History
Factory Workers

"Families wanted—Ten or Twelve good respectable families consisting of four or five children each, from nine to sixteen years of age, are wanted to work in a cotton mill." This was the text of an 1828 advertisement in Rhode Island. Such ads were quite common in the early 1800s. During that time, many children worked in factories to help their families make ends meet.

Some early textile mills preferred to hire children to work in the same mills as their parents. That way the parents could oversee their children's work. Some reformers, however, worried that mill life was unhealthy for children, as it kept them out of school and exposed them to dangerous working conditions. Children were often mistreated by factory supervisors. Others lost limbs and some were even killed in industrial accidents. Still, child labor continued in many factories until the 1900s.

The Granger Collection, New York

Young workers head to the factory.

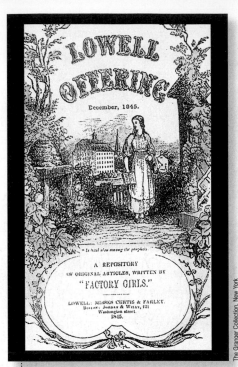

Many women wrote articles for the Lowell Offering, *a magazine produced by female factory workers.*

At first, life in the factory community seemed both profitable and interesting to many **Lowell girls**, as the female workers were called. They lived in company dormitories, where their activities were closely supervised. Lucy Larcom began working at Lowell when she was about 11 years old. "I liked it better than going to school," she recalled years later. Larcom added:

• **Home to Factory**

"**I regard it as one of the privileges of my youth that I was permitted to grow up among those active, interesting girls. . . . They were earnest and capable, ready to undertake anything that was worth doing. . . . They gave me a larger, firmer ideal of womanhood.**"

The success of Lowell's business system encouraged other manufacturers to construct similar mills. Conditions varied from mill to mill. As time passed, however, living and working conditions in many mill towns became harsh as owners tried to increase profits by demanding more work from employees. Some workers became unhappy with their situation. In 1845 a Lowell girl, now known only as Julianna, expressed what many factory workers were feeling:

"**Crowded into a small room, which contains three bed and six females, . . . what chance is there for *studying?* and much less so for thinking and reflecting? . . . Incarcerated [Held captive] within the walls of a factory . . . drilled there from five [A.M.] until seven o'clock [P.M.], year after year . . . what *will* be the natural, rational result? What but ignorance, misery, and *premature decay* of both *body* and *intellect?***"

Efforts to Help Workers

Sarah Bagley, another Lowell girl, became so unhappy with the system that in 1844 she founded the Lowell Female Labor Reform Association to campaign for laws improving working conditions in factories. Bagley organized branches of the Association in other New England factory towns. She also published articles attacking the "cotton lords" who controlled the textile mills.

A group called the Lowell Female Labor Reform Association was one of many new **labor unions**, or organizations workers form to improve their conditions. Although there had been some labor

Young women like these often learned how to make thread at home before going off to work in textile mills.

• **Working Conditions**

The Granger Collection, New York

organizations since the colonial period, few had been very successful. In the 1830s and 1840s, however, many skilled workers joined unions. They protested long hours and low wages or wage reductions.

Sometimes workers would stage a **strike**— a refusal to work until their demands for improved conditions were met. Few early strikes were successful, however. The courts and other authorities tended to view unions as illegal attempts to "control" wages. They usually sided with the employers.

The harsh conditions and long hours of factory work caused a number of reformers to try to improve the lives of these workers. Seth Luther, a carpenter and textile worker, was one of the most outspoken critics of the factory system. In particular, he criticized the employment of children in factories. Instead of working, he argued, every child should receive a good education at public expense. Luther also called for shorter work hours and better working conditions for all laborers.

Many less-radical reformers supported the movement to reduce the workday from the usual dawn-to-darkness routine to 10 hours. Employers, however, had much more influence with legislators, and the 10-hour movement made slow progress. In 1840, however, the federal government did set a 10-hour limit on the workday of its employees.

Many people in Lynn, Massachusetts, showed up to express their support for a strike by shoe-factory workers. The strike parade included some 800 female workers, some 4,000 male workers and firefighters, a military unit, and a band.

The Granger Collection, New York

Section 2 Review

• **Glossary**

IDENTIFY and explain the significance of the following: enclosure movement, Francis Lowell, Lowell girls, Sarah Bagley, labor unions, strike, Seth Luther

REVIEWING FOR DETAILS
1. What groups of people worked in early factories?
2. What were working and living conditions like at the mills?
3. Why did some workers organize unions?

REVIEWING FOR UNDERSTANDING
4. **Writing Mastery:** *Creating* Write a poem or short story expressing how some Lowell girls might have felt about their lives.
5. **Critical Thinking:** *Recognizing Point of View* What might have been some of the factors affecting Seth Luther's view of the factory system?

Section 3

LIFE IN THE CITIES

Multimedia Connections

Explore these related topics and materials on the CD–ROM to enrich your understanding of this section:

 Gazetteer

- Germany
- Ireland

 Media Bank

- Immigrant Music
- Occupations, Boston, 1850
- Cartoon of Immigrant Woman
- Immigrant Culture

 Atlas

- Boston, 1850

Shortly after moving to America, Englishwoman Alice Barlow wrote to her family overseas to describe her new home. "Tell my old friends," she declared, ". . . if they were here, they would know nothing of poverty." The new home she described was overflowing with opportunity. Barlow's husband had already found a job in a textile factory. The nation's cities attracted thousands of people like the Barlows who were seeking prosperity and a better life.

As you read this section you will find out:

▶ **Why Irish and German immigration increased.**

▶ **What problems emerged as urban population grew.**

▶ **How the rise of a middle class affected women.**

Immigration from Europe

Sometimes when early factory workers organized strikes, they were replaced by **immigrants**—foreign-born people who had recently moved to the United States. The number of immigrants, particularly Europeans, coming to America was increasing yearly.

Between 1790 and 1820, only about 234,000 immigrants had entered the United States. During the next 30 years almost 2.5 million people crossed the Atlantic bound for America. Nearly all of these immigrants came to the United States because they were poor and hoped to earn a better living.

The majority came from Ireland, Germany, and Great Britain. In the 1840s disease destroyed most of the potato crop in Ireland. Facing starvation, thousands of Irish people came to the United States. Many Germans moved to escape political turmoil caused by a failed revolution in 1848. Others came to gain religious freedom or better jobs.

Most immigrants settled among people of similar national, religious, and ethnic backgrounds. While about half the German immigrants were Protestant, about one third were Catholic and one fifth were Jewish. Most Irish immigrants were Catholic. They established many new Catholic churches in the nation's large cities. By the mid-1800s Catholicism was one of the largest religious denominations in the United States.

Some Americans opposed unlimited immigration because they believed that too many newcomers would destroy American institutions. They were called **nativists** because they wanted to keep the country for "native Americans." They conveniently forgot, however, that the only real native Americans were American Indians. Fear of competition for jobs fueled the anger of many nativists, such as Boston resident Jesse Chickering, who complained in 1850:

> **"The increased competition for employment has diminished the facility [ease] of obtaining it. . . . In many employments the foreigners, at first compelled [forced] by necessity to labor for small wages, have at length almost excluded the natives."**

Most nativists were members of various Protestant churches. They were particularly hostile to the Irish Catholics, who were arriving in large numbers. Most of the Irish immigrants were poor, unskilled, and willing to work for less money than most native-born workers.

In 1834 a nativist mob burned a Catholic convent near Boston. Similar violent incidents occurred in other parts of the country. In 1849 some nativists went so far as to form a new, anti-immigrant political party, later known as

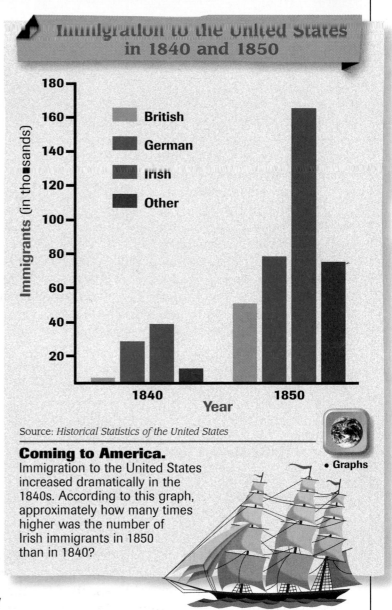

Immigration to the United States in 1840 and 1850

Immigrants (in thousands)

Source: *Historical Statistics of the United States*

• Graphs

Coming to America. Immigration to the United States increased dramatically in the 1840s. According to this graph, approximately how many times higher was the number of Irish immigrants in 1850 than in 1840?

the American Party. Members of the secretive organization were often called **Know-Nothings** because when asked about the organization, they replied, "I know nothing about it."

City Life in America

While many immigrants who came to America between 1820 and 1850 became farmers, a significant number settled in the cities of the Northeast. They were not the only people coming to the cities, however.

By the mid-1800s, many cities were becoming very crowded. This painting shows downtown New York City around the 1850s. At that time, New York was already becoming a bustling city.

Urban growth. When they grew up, many children of American farmers moved to towns and cities. The expanding industrial economy offered them many new job opportunities in all areas of trade and commerce.

Free African Americans also came to the northern cities in large numbers. However, many white factory employers refused to hire black workers for well-paying, skilled jobs. Most unions excluded black workers entirely. Thus, many urban African Americans worked in service industries instead of factories. In New York, Philadelphia, and Boston, many African American men found jobs as house servants, waiters, barbers, coachmen, shoe shiners, and porters. African American women often worked as laundresses, dressmakers, seamstresses, and cooks.

• **African Americans in the North**

With all these new arrivals, the number of people living in towns and cities rose from about 5 percent of the U.S. population in 1790 to about 18 percent in 1850. In 1790 there were only 24 urban centers in the United States with a population of 2,500 or more. By 1850 there were about 235.

Urban problems. American cities underwent many growing pains during this period. As cities grew, slums developed because the cities could not absorb people as fast as the newcomers arrived. Large apartment buildings were broken up into many small units. People even lived in attics and cellars.

In these buildings several families often lived crowded together in single dwellings. Rents were usually low, but because there were so many apartments in each building, the owners could make very large profits. Little, if any, of the profits went to keeping the buildings in repair. They were often unsanitary and unsafe.

Since few city streets were paved, there was always mud in rainy weather. This gave rise to an often-told joke about the poor condition of city streets: A passing citizen offers

Global Connections

German Immigrants

The immigrants we refer to as "Germans" were not all from a single country known as Germany. In the mid-1800s Germany as we know it was not yet a unified nation like France or Great Britain. Instead, it was a group of independent countries in which the citizens spoke a common German language.

When French emperor Napoleon tried to conquer Europe in the early 1800s, many people in the German-speaking countries realized how vulnerable they were on their own. One group in particular, known as Liberals, wanted to create a unified government under a constitutional system.

In 1848 Liberals launched a revolution for constitutional reform. Anti-Liberals not only defeated the revolutionaries but also began a campaign to silence Liberal supporters. To escape harsh new restrictions, thousands of "Germans" fled their homelands for the United States.

help to a man who has sunk up to his neck in a huge mud puddle. "No need to worry," replies the man. "I have a horse under me."

Polluted water and the lack of sanitation often led to epidemics of contagious diseases. One of the most dreaded diseases was cholera, which attacks the intestinal system. During cholera epidemics, poor people living in dirty, crowded apartments died by the thousands. Some people, therefore, thought the disease was a punishment for poverty.

Most American cities did not have police or fire departments. Even the largest cities had no more than a few police officers, who usually did not have uniforms to identify them. Volunteer fire companies put out fires. Cash prizes were sometimes awarded to the companies that responded most quickly to alarms, causing much competition between these associations. When fires broke out, fire companies sometimes fought each other rather than the blaze.

Urban attractions. Despite its problems, many people found the hustle and bustle of city life exciting. The cities were the cultural centers of American life. More theaters and concert halls were built. Book and magazine publishing prospered. Cafes, taverns, and libraries attracted artists, writers, and crowds of ordinary people searching for excitement, adventure, and jobs.

The Middle Class

The beginnings of industrialization had both positive and negative effects on families living in cities. As the American economy moved steadily from an agricultural base to manufacturing, family life changed. The industrial changes in the Northeast brought dramatic improvements in the average family's standard of living. By 1840 the industrial surge had increased personal income in the region about 35 percent above the national average. As a result of this change, a new social class developed between the rich and the poor—the **middle class**.

Middle-class families were usually headed by a father who owned a small business or worked in a management or other professional job created by the new economy. Middle-class wives usually did not work

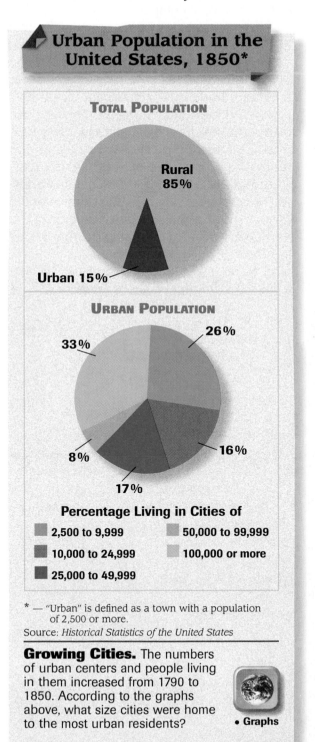

Urban Population in the United States, 1850*

TOTAL POPULATION

Rural 85%

Urban 15%

URBAN POPULATION

26%

33%

16%

8%

17%

Percentage Living in Cities of

2,500 to 9,999

10,000 to 24,999

25,000 to 49,999

50,000 to 99,999

100,000 or more

* — "Urban" is defined as a town with a population of 2,500 or more.

Source: *Historical Statistics of the United States*

Growing Cities. The numbers of urban centers and people living in them increased from 1790 to 1850. According to the graphs above, what size cities were home to the most urban residents?

• Graphs

outside of the home. A middle-class woman's lifestyle was normally determined by her husband's wealth and by the type of job he held.

• Household Chores

The wives of wealthy city husbands had a great deal of leisure time compared to farm women or working-class women. This was because they could employ servants and buy items they needed.

The fact that many middle-class women had more time on their hands increased their interest in education. Several all-female academies were founded to educate women. One of the best was Catharine Beecher's school in Hartford, Connecticut.

Beecher wrote and lectured extensively on women's education. She also founded the American Women's Educational Association and other teacher-education institutions. Beecher's goal was to establish teacher-training schools run by master teachers. As she explained in 1835 in *An Essay on the Education of Female Teachers*:

> **"When these teachers shall have succeeded in training classes of teachers on the best system their united wisdom can devise, there will be instructors prepared for other seminaries [schools] . . . ; and thus a regular and systematic course of education can be disseminated [spread] through the nation."**

Beecher and other supporters of female education believed that the future of the nation lay in the hands of its women.

A middle-class family relaxes at home around 1840. Many prosperous and educated families would entertain themselves in the evenings by having one member of the family read to everyone else.

Section 3 Review

• Glossary

IDENTIFY and explain the significance of the following: immigrants, nativists, Know-Nothings, middle class, Catharine Beecher

REVIEWING FOR DETAILS

1. Why did many Irish and German immigrants come to America?
2. How did the rise of a middle class affect women's lives?

REVIEWING FOR UNDERSTANDING

3. **Geographic Literacy** What were some of the problems that emerged as urban areas grew?
4. **Writing Mastery:** *Describing* Imagine that you are an immigrant living in an American city. Write a letter to a family member overseas describing your new community.
5. **Critical Thinking:** *Generalizations and Stereotypes* "Look at the hordes of . . . Irish thieves and vagabonds roaming about our streets," exclaimed a nativist in the 1840s. How does this statement reflect a use of stereotypes?

Section 4

TRANSPORTATION AND GROWTH

Multimedia Connections

Explore these related topics and materials on the CD–ROM to enrich your understanding of this section:

 Gazetteer

- Lake Erie

 Profiles

- Daniel Boone
- Robert Fulton

 Atlas

- National Road

 Media Bank

- St. Louis Waterfront
- First Locomotive
- Transportation Methods
- Tom Thumb and Horse Car

Writer Mark Twain described one of the many inventions that radically altered American life in the 1800s: "She is long and sharp and trim and pretty. She has two fancy-topped chimneys . . . and a fanciful pilothouse. . . . The furnace doors are open and the fires glaring bravely." The mysterious creature was a steamboat. Such improvements in transportation encouraged the growth of business and brought the nation's people closer together.

As you read this section you will find out:

▶ **How the government tried to improve overland transportation.**

▶ **What effect canals and steamboats had on water travel.**

▶ **What advantages railroads offered over other forms of travel.**

New Roads and Turnpikes

As cities expanded, they became so large that it was no longer easy to walk from one end to the other. By the 1830s New York City had dozens of carriages, each drawn by two or four horses with seating for 12 passengers. In the winter some drivers replaced their wheels with runners, turning the carriages into sleighs. Carriages could soon be found in most cities, and service between many cities was also available.

In the countryside, nearly all roads were unpaved. They turned into seas of mud after every heavy rain and were bumpy and rough in dry weather. Most long roads were built by private companies. The builders collected tolls, or fees, from people who used them. The tollgate was usually a pike, or pole, blocking the road. When the traveler paid the toll, the

The National Road made travel overland much easier, as these travelers experienced in the 1850s. As a result, thousands more people moved west of the Appalachian Mountains.

pike was raised or turned aside to let the traveler pass. These toll roads were thus called **turnpikes**.

Overland travel was both expensive and slow. In the early 1800s it cost more to haul a ton of goods several miles overland than to bring the same ton all the way across the Atlantic Ocean! This was one reason why rebellious Pennsylvania farmers in the 1790s turned their surplus corn into whiskey.

To improve overland transportation, the federal government began construction of the **National Road** in 1811 at Cumberland, Maryland. The route crossed over the mountains in southwestern Pennsylvania and ended at the site of present-day Wheeling, West Virginia. Gradually, it was extended west to Vandalia, Illinois.

The road was a remarkable engineering achievement. It had a foundation of solid stone and a top of gravel, and it carried countless numbers of wagons and carts. The road was constructed so well that some of its bridges are still in use today.

This engraving shows a section of the Erie Canal at Lockport, New York, in 1838.

Canals

The easiest means of moving goods and people was by water. The problem was that few American rivers and lakes were connected. Fortunately, many could be joined by digging **canals**, or artificial waterways.

Goods were carried along canals on barges. These barges were towed by horses or mules, which walked alongside the canal. It was much easier for animals to pull heavy loads on canal barges than it was to pull them over dry land. Thus, canal transportation was much cheaper than transportation by road.

Canals were expensive to build, however, and could not be constructed without great financial support. In 1817 New York governor DeWitt Clinton, who had been a member of the state canal commission, persuaded the state legislature to build a canal running from the Hudson River across the state all the way to Lake Erie. As Clinton explained it, the canal:

"will create the greatest inland trade ever witnessed. The most fertile and extensive regions of America will avail [make use] themselves of its facilities for a market. All their surplus . . . will concentrate in the city of New York."

The route of the **Erie Canal** would pass through the Mohawk Valley, a gap in the Appalachian Mountains where the land was fairly level. This meant that the water would not have to be raised and lowered very much by canal locks.

In 1817 work on "Clinton's Big Ditch" began. Much of the digging was done by Irish immigrants. The first section was opened in 1819. In 1825 the Erie Canal was completed. The canal was an engineering wonder: some 363 miles long, 40 feet wide, and 4 feet deep. It cost the state $7 million, an enormous amount of money at the time.

However, as Clinton had predicted, the canal attracted so much traffic that the tolls collected soon paid its cost. The cost of shipping goods fell from $100 a ton before the canal was built to $5 a ton afterward. The canal became the busiest route for goods and people moving west.

When people in other states saw how profitable the Erie Canal was, they hurried to build canals of their own. By 1840 more than 3,300 miles of canals had been built throughout the country, farther than the distance across the continent.

The canals united the different sections of the country and stimulated their economies. Farm crops could now be shipped cheaply to distant markets. Products manufactured in the East no longer had to be lugged over the Appalachian Mountains by wagon.

Steamboats

Although much more economical, travel by canal was slow—mules pulling a barge could only cover about one mile an hour. What water transportation needed was a new

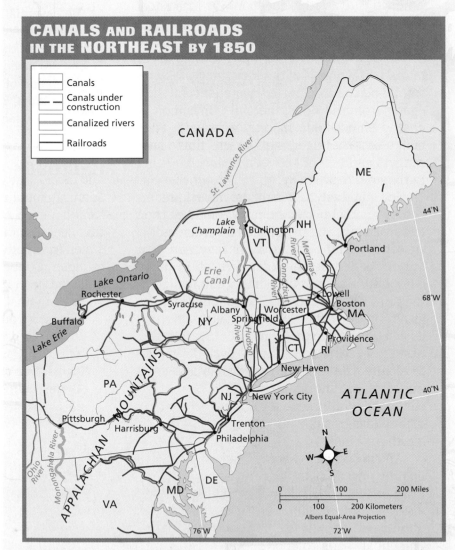

CANALS AND RAILROADS IN THE NORTHEAST BY 1850

Canals
Canals under construction
Canalized rivers
Railroads

Learning from Maps.

By 1850 much of the Northeast was connected by railroads and canals. People and goods could move more easily.

▶ **Place.** Which port cities were connected to inland sites by canals?

• Maps

source of power. British technology supplied the answer. In the 1760s a Scottish man named James Watt invented a practical steam engine. Watt's invention, which used the energy of burning wood and coal, was used to run machines in factories. Steam power meant that factories no longer had to be located near dams or swiftly moving rivers.

If steam could drive machines, could it also be used to move boats? One of the first Americans to ask this question was John Fitch, a silversmith and clockmaker. In 1787 Fitch launched a steamboat propelled by 12 paddles on the Delaware River. Among the many spectators who witnessed the launching of Fitch's smoke-belching monster were several delegates from the Constitutional Convention in nearby Philadelphia. Shortly afterward, Fitch built a second, larger boat, which carried passengers and freight between Philadelphia and Burlington, New Jersey.

For another 20 years, however, steamboats were neither efficient nor reliable. Then Robert Fulton, an artist turned inventor, built a steamboat on the East River in New York City. Fulton called it the *Clermont*, but those who had watched it being built called it "Fulton's Folly," believing it would never work. In August 1807 the *Clermont* made its first voyage, up the Hudson River from New York City to Albany. The 130-mile trip took 32 hours, compared to a time of four days by sailing ship.

An associate of Fulton's, Nicholas Roosevelt, built the *New Orleans* in Pittsburgh in 1811. This boat soon made the 1,950-mile trip from Pittsburgh to New Orleans in just 14 days. Previously the journey had taken four to six weeks. An even more dramatic breakthrough occurred in 1815 when the steamboat *Enterprise* sailed up the Mississippi River from New Orleans to Pittsburgh against the current. Before that time, a trip upstream from New Orleans to Pittsburgh took more than four months. Soon, dozens of steamboats were churning up and down the western rivers of the United States.

By the 1830s steamboats had become an important part of the transportation system. One European traveler noted:

> "The essential point is . . . that they should be numerous; . . . well commanded or not, it matters little, if they move at a rapid rate, and are navigated at little expense. The circulation of steamboats is as necessary to the West, as that of the blood is to the human system."

Railroads

Soon after the canals and steamboats, there came an even more significant transportation advance—the railroad. One of the first steam-driven locomotives, the Tom Thumb, was built by Peter Cooper for the Baltimore & Ohio Railroad in 1830. Cooper raced the Tom Thumb against a horse-drawn coach. The locomotive swept ahead right from the start. It broke down before the finish line, however, and the horse won the race.

Despite this unimpressive beginning, trains had many advantages over canals and steamboats. They could go practically anywhere that tracks could be put down. They were much faster,

Many steamboats like these traveled the Mississippi River in the mid-1800s. Steam travel also decreased the amount of time it took to travel across the oceans.

The painting shows the potential advantages that railroads promised over other forms of land travel in the early 1800s. A train passes by quickly and easily in contrast to the farmer, who is strug gling to get his wagon and team across a muddy road.

and they could haul greater loads. Perhaps most importantly, trains could operate all year round in the northern states, where many canals and rivers were frozen solid in the winter months.

In the beginning many Americans considered trains dangerous. The sparks from the engines sometimes set fields on fire and frightened farm animals. Many early engines often jumped the tracks. The long-term advantages of railroads, however, could not be resisted. During the 1840s about 9,000 miles of track were built, mostly in the Northeast.

Railroads gave the economy a great boost. Besides reducing travel time and cost, they allowed many other businesses to expand. The demand for iron for engines and rails greatly increased the mining and smelting of iron. Remote areas boomed once the railroads reached them. Farmers increased output as railroads allowed them to quickly ship their goods to distant markets.

The railroads expanded the transportation growth that began with turnpikes. This **Transportation Revolution** made it easier for people in one region to meet and to do business with people in other regions. The Transportation Revolution began a process of linking the nation closer together that continues to the present.

Section 4 Review

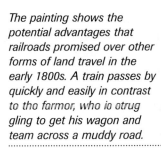

IDENTIFY and explain the significance of the following: turnpikes, National Road, canals, DeWitt Clinton, Erie Canal, Robert Fulton, Transportation Revolution

• Glossary

REVIEWING FOR DETAILS

1. What did the U.S. government do to improve overland transportation?
2. How did canals and steamboats affect transportation?
3. In what ways were railroads an improvement over other forms of transportation?

• Time Line

REVIEWING FOR UNDERSTANDING

4. **Geographic Literacy** How did geography interfere with travel by land and water? How were these obstacles overcome using technology?

5. **Critical Thinking:** *Synthesizing Information* How did the Transportation Revolution help unite the nation?

CHAPTER 10

The Granger Collection, New York

The South and King Cotton (1790–1860)

THEMES IN AMERICAN HISTORY

Cultural Diversity:
How might different people's common experiences contribute to forming a common culture?

Economic Development:
How might geography affect a regional economy?

Technology and Society:
Why might people be interested in making technological advances?

- Video Opener

- Skill Builder

African American abolitionist Henry Highland Garnet looked at the sea of faces before him. "Slavery!" he hissed. "How much misery is comprehended [included] in that single word." Garnet continued, "Awake, awake; millions of voices are calling you! Your dead fathers speak to you from their graves." He ended his speech with a singular call: "Resistance! Resistance! RESISTANCE!"

image above: *Romantic view of a plantation*

Section 1
COTTON IN THE SOUTH

Multimedia Connections

Explore these related topics and materials on the CD–ROM to enrich your understanding of this section:

 Atlas

• Agriculture and Slavery

 Readings

• Cotton Kingdom

 Profiles

• Eli Whitney
• John C. Calhoun

 Media Bank

• Pre-Civil War South

In the early 1800s cotton controlled the fortunes of most white southerners. One traveler noticed this when he stopped at a quiet Georgia inn and the manager immediately asked him about the price of cotton. "She said . . . there was an academy to which her daughter went when cotton was thirty cents per pound," he remembered. "But . . . as cotton had fallen to fifteen cents she could not afford to buy an instrument, and supposed her daughter must forget her music."

As you read this section you will find out:

▶ **What difficulties southern farmers faced in growing cotton.**

▶ **Why southern farmers moved westward.**

▶ **Why the demand for slaves rose after the invention of the cotton gin.**

The Birth of the Cotton Kingdom

In the years immediately following the American Revolution, some people thought that the falling price of tobacco signaled the end of plantation agriculture—and slavery. They believed both institutions would gradually die out in the new nation.

A troublesome crop. When there arose a new demand for cotton, however, many Americans became convinced that slavery had a future in the United States. Cotton could be grown profitably with slave labor. The efficient new spinning machines common in British factories by the 1790s had lowered the cost of cotton goods. As the price of these products went down, people could buy more of them. This increased the demand for cotton.

At first, few southern farmers could meet this demand. Not all varieties of cotton could be grown easily in the United States. Green-seed cotton, however, was hardy enough to grow almost anywhere in the South. The fibers of this plant were short and tightly woven around its seeds in pods called "bolls." It took a long time for even a skilled person to pick the seeds from a single pound of this cotton. People wished someone would invent a machine for removing the pesky seeds.

Eli Whitney and the cotton gin. In 1792, some nine years before he demonstrated his guns with interchangeable parts, Eli Whitney decided to take a job as a tutor on a Georgia plantation. There he talked with a number of farmers. They mentioned their interest in growing cotton and showed him how hard it was to remove the seeds from the bolls.

Curious, Whitney studied the cotton plant carefully. After only a short period of thinking and experimenting in the spring of 1793, he had designed and built a **cotton gin**, a machine that separated the seeds from the fibers. The machine consisted of a wooden box with a handle. When stuffed with cotton, the gin used stiff brushes and rollers fitted with wire teeth to pull the fibers through narrow slits and free them from the seeds. One person turning the handle could remove the seeds from 50 pounds of cotton in less than a day! In addition, the cotton gin was inexpensive and easy to copy. Most farmers could build their own or buy one. Whitney's gin quickly made it profitable to grow cotton in the South.

Eli Whitney's cotton gin changed the shape and direction of the American South.

This engraving shows how workers ran cotton through a gin to separate fibers from seeds.

The Cotton Boom

All over the South, farmers began to plant cotton, hoping to make money from the growing demands for the crop. In 1793 farmers grew about 10,000 bales, or large bundles. In 1801 production reached 100,000 bales, and by 1835 it had passed the 1 million mark.

A crop for the North. The availability of southern cotton soon contributed to the rapid growth of the northern textile industry. People everywhere benefited from cheap cotton clothing, which was cool in the summer and much easier to keep clean than woolen garments. Other businesses related to textiles, such as shipping, also boomed because of the ready supply of cheap southern cotton.

Cotton expands westward. As cotton farming became more profitable, people pushed westward in search of more fertile land. They flocked into Alabama, Mississippi, Tennessee, Arkansas, Louisiana, and Texas. In these areas, farmers also raised large quantities of corn, wheat, cattle, and other food products, but cotton was their key to prosperity. Before long, there was a recognizable **cotton belt**, a huge agricultural region largely devoted to the production of cotton, across the southern United States.

Although not all farmers prospered, a great many who moved westward to grow cotton became very wealthy. It was much less expensive to use slaves to work the cotton fields than to hire workers. According to one observer, these cotton farmers made "oceans of money." Cotton farmer E. N. Davis evaluated his chances of success and determined that the odds were good:

"I shall make a crop with the hands and finish the work the ensuing [following] fall and winter. My hands are doing a good business, averaging me some 200 Acres of Land per day. If . . . [the cotton] comes on the Market soon it will be a small fortune."

The whole region prospered. Southern exports of cotton to the Northeast, Great Britain, and other markets paid for badly needed manufactured goods.

Slavery expands westward. As the cotton belt expanded, the demand for slaves grew. The great cotton boom increased farmers' desire for workers who would plant, weed, and harvest the crop and then gin and bale the fluffy white fibers.

Under the terms of the compromise delegates had reached at the Constitutional Convention, Congress banned the importing of slaves in 1808. Although some illegal importation of slaves continued, the market for American-born slaves increased dramatically. This increased the price of slaves, and many slaveholders in the Upper South started to sell slaves to eager pioneers in the Lower South.

● Southern Defense

Whenever they conducted business off the plantation, many slaves had to wear tags such as these indicating their occupation.

Section 1 Review

● Glossary

IDENTIFY and explain the significance of the following: Eli Whitney, cotton gin, cotton belt

REVIEWING FOR DETAILS
1. Why was growing and selling cotton difficult for southern farmers?
2. Why did the demand for slaves rise after Whitney invented the cotton gin?

REVIEWING FOR UNDERSTANDING
3. **Geographic Literacy** Why did white southern farmers move westward in the early 1800s?
4. **Writing Mastery:** *Describing* Imagine that you are an Alabama cotton farmer. Write a letter to a relative in Massachusetts and describe how the cotton gin has changed things on your farm.
5. **Critical Thinking:** *Cause and Effect* How did the development of efficient spinning machines in Great Britain affect agriculture in the American South?

Section 2
THE WORLD COTTON BUILT

Multimedia Connections

Explore these related topics and materials on the CD–ROM to enrich your understanding of this section:

 Gazetteer

- Richmond
- Lexington
- New Orleans

 Interactive Map

- The Cotton Plantation

 Profiles

- Mary Boykin Chesnut

 Media Bank

- Southern Population, 1850
- Slaveholding Families, 1850
- Small Southern Farm

In 1860 Alabama resident Daniel R. Hundley wrote one of the first studies of the southern population. He divided southerners into groups such as "The Southern Gentlemen," "The Middle Class," "Cotton Snobs," "The Southern Yankee," "The Southern Yeoman," "Poor White Trash," and "The Negro Slaves." While Hundley's study was largely shaped by his own biased views as a wealthy landowner, his book reflected the diversity of people that could be found in southern society.

As you read this section you will find out:

▶ **What social groups existed within the white southern population.**

▶ **What kind of industries there were in the South.**

▶ **What life was like for free African Americans in the South.**

The Planters

Unlike popular images often portrayed in movies and books, most white people in the South did not live on large, beautiful plantations or hold slaves. In fact, most white southerners had no slaves at all.

A small group of slaveholders dominated southern society, however. These were the **planters**, people who owned plantations and who held more than 20 slaves. In 1850 there were about 46,000 planters in a southern population of almost 9 million. Planters were often quite rich since they usually owned a large amount of fertile land on which enslaved African Americans worked. Thus, slaves played an essential role in creating planters' large fortunes.

Planters' lives varied greatly. While most had between 20 and 50 slaves, a few held as

This engraving shows the "big house" and slave quarters on a Mississippi sugar plantation.

many as 3,000. Planters typically lived in simple two-story houses with columned front porches, but a few had mansions with fancy trim.

Katherine Lumpkin left a description of her grandfather's 1,000-acre estate in Georgia, which included a workforce of about 50 slaves. Lumpkin called the plantation "a community and business rolled into one." In addition to the "big house," or main residence, there were:

> **"slave quarters, stables, and springhouse [storage place], and the work radiating out into the fields from this hub of activity."**

Separate buildings held the carpentry shop and the smokehouse. Lumpkin's was not even a particularly large plantation!

The White Majority

Most other white southerners lived and worked in rural areas. They made up the groups below the planters on the South's social ladder.

Small farmers. Small farmers were the largest group in white southern society. Because plantations took the best soil, small farmers often had to make do with land in hilly regions or other less favorable locations.

Like the planters, small farmers' wealth and social status varied. The majority, however, had no slaves. Those who did rarely held more than one or two, or perhaps a slave family with a couple of children. This was largely because slaves were very costly. In 1850 a slave could cost $1,000. These small farmers often labored alongside their slaves in the fields.

Young People In History
Plantation Children

During the early years of childhood, white and slave children often played together. There were glaring differences between the lives of the children from the start, however. The slaveholder's children wore fancy clothing. Wealthy planters imported expensive clothes for their children from fashionable stores in Europe. Slave children made do with whatever the master gave them, often plain dresses for boys and girls alike.

These children, who lived on a wealthy southern plantation in the 1800s, were provided with the fanciest of toys.

Slavery eventually disrupted the lives of both white and slave children, causing a painful break between former playmates. Sometimes it became obvious when a black teenager had to call a slaveholder's new baby "Young Massa" or "Young Missus." Other times it became obvious when a white child left for school and a slave child went to work in the nursery or fields.

The work for small farmers and slaves was extremely difficult. Farmers and slaves spent all day in the hot sun, doing the backbreaking work of plowing, planting, and harvesting crops. In addition to cotton, most small farmers in the South raised corn or other grain, vegetables, and barnyard animals. They depended on most of these for food and sold whatever was left over. The women in the family spun cotton into thread, wove the thread on a simple loom, then turned the homespun cloth into shirts, dresses, and other garments.

Most small farmers hoped to one day be as wealthy as the planters. Many who had no slaves were enthusiastic supporters of slavery, hoping to someday have enough money to obtain slaves of their own.

Other rural whites. This was not true, however, in remote mountain valleys and in other isolated areas, where the poorest whites resented both slaves and slaveholders. Planters and small farmers commonly looked down on these poor whites. Very poor white people made up a large part of southern society. They often lived on some of the least productive soil. They survived by fishing, hunting, and tending small garden patches. One traveler described them as "poverty-stricken vagabonds [tramps] . . . without . . . reliable means of livelihood [income] . . . [and] having almost no property but their own bodies."

Manufacturing and the Urban South

Although the South devoted most of its resources to agriculture, there was some manufacturing in the region. Textiles, tobacco products, and iron played important roles in economic growth, particularly in the cities of the Upper South. Other businesses, such as sugar refineries, ropemaking companies, and cotton presses, dotted the region as well.

Many of the textile mills in the South were located on the streams and rivers of the eastern

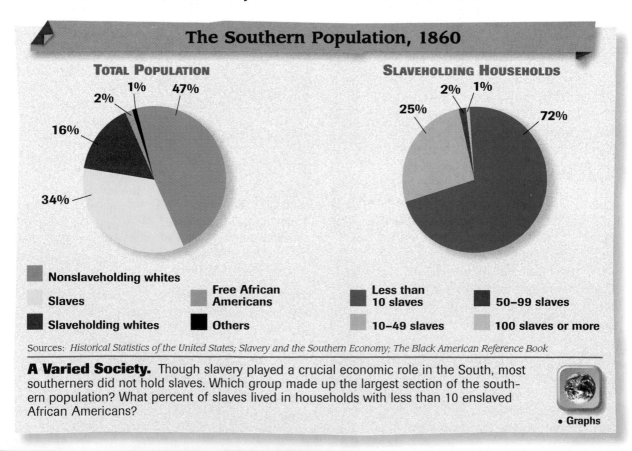

The Southern Population, 1860

TOTAL POPULATION

1% — 47%
2%
16%
34%

- Nonslaveholding whites
- Slaves
- Slaveholding whites
- Free African Americans
- Others

SLAVEHOLDING HOUSEHOLDS

2% 1%
25%
72%

- Less than 10 slaves
- 10–49 slaves
- 50–99 slaves
- 100 slaves or more

Sources: *Historical Statistics of the United States; Slavery and the Southern Economy; The Black American Reference Book*

A Varied Society. Though slavery played a crucial economic role in the South, most southerners did not hold slaves. Which group made up the largest section of the southern population? What percent of slaves lived in households with less than 10 enslaved African Americans?

• Graphs

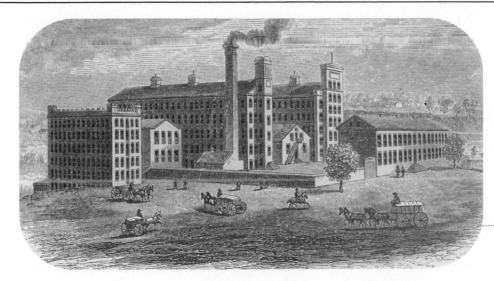

Manufacturing businesses like this textile mill in Columbus, Georgia, were rare in the South before 1860, even though the southern states produced most of the cotton used in textile mills.

slopes of the Appalachian Mountains. One of the best known and most efficient was William Gregg's cotton mill in South Carolina. It employed about 300 workers by 1850, many of them women or teenagers.

Tobacco companies were clustered in the Upper South. In the 1850s Richmond, Virginia, had about 50 companies manufacturing tobacco products. Many of the tobacco workers were slaves, either purchased by the companies or hired from individual slaveholders. Kentucky had ropemaking plants in Louisville and Lexington. Cotton presses, which compressed the fluffy crop into 500-pound bales, also existed in many southern cities. The New Orleans Levee Steam Cotton Press, which employed more than 100 slaves in 1850, was one of the largest.

Iron manufacturing was also an important industry in the South. The **Tredegar Iron Works** of Richmond was the largest iron company in the region. It made steam engines and other iron products. The Tredegar Iron Works sometimes competed successfully with northern iron mills. Like other southern firms, it used slave labor.

Many southerners dreamed of great industrial growth in their region. "With slave labor that . . . is absolutely reliable," reported a New Orleans newspaper, "manufactured fabrics can be produced so as to compete successfully with the world."

Southern cities and manufacturing grew at a slow pace, however. In 1860 the total amount of manufactured goods in all the southern states put together was less than that of Massachusetts alone! The northern states had over 10 times more people working in manufacturing.

A number of factors explained the growing economic difference between the North and South. Southerners tended to invest their wealth in land and slaves rather than in factories. In addition, the South's dependence on slave labor discouraged European immigrants from settling there. This deprived the region of many consumers and skilled workers.

Free African Americans

Not all African Americans in the South were slaves. By 1860 the region contained about 260,000 free African Americans. Some had taken on extra work while they were slaves and had saved enough money to purchase their freedom. Some had been freed voluntarily by slaveholders. Others were the children of free African Americans and had never been slaves.

Southern whites felt that the institution of slavery was threatened by the mere existence of a free black population, since it served as a constant reminder to slaves that freedom was possible. In a petition to have all free African

Americans banished from South Carolina, a group of whites wrote:

> **"[Slaves] continually have before their eyes, persons of the same color, many of whom they have known . . . freed from the control of masters, working where they please, going whither they please, and expending their money how they please."**

White southerners created legal restrictions that made life very difficult for free African Americans. They generally could not vote, carry guns, travel without a pass, speak at public meetings, or learn to write. Free African Americans also faced the possibility of being kidnapped and sold into slavery. "Though we are not slaves," one African American newspaper explained, "we are not free."

Despite such restrictions, a small number of black southerners managed to buy land and become

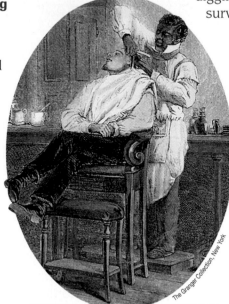

This free African American man ran his own barbershop in Richmond, Virginia. Some free African Americans who remained in the South ran similar businesses.

farmers. Some free African Americans held slaves, and a few even owned plantations.

Other free African Americans mastered skilled trades, such as printing, barbering, bricklaying, and carpentry. A few owned businesses and became wealthy. Many, however, had to accept low-paying, unskilled jobs like ditch digging and street sweeping just to survive.

Many free African Americans in the South formed strong communities, and a number of them made important contributions to American life. For example, Norbert Rillieux, who lived in New Orleans, invented a device to extract syrup from sugar and helped make syrup widely available and more affordable.

Although there were some exceptions, the lives of many free African Americans in the South were not much better than those of slaves. Most white southerners thought of them as merely slaves who had no masters.

Section 2 Review

• Glossary

IDENTIFY and explain the significance of the following: planters, William Gregg, Tredegar Iron Works, Norbert Rillieux

REVIEWING FOR DETAILS

1. What different social groups existed within the white southern population?
2. What kind of manufacturing industries existed in the South?
3. How would you describe the lives of free African Americans in the South?

REVIEWING FOR UNDERSTANDING

4. **Writing Mastery:** *Creating* Imagine that you are a reporter for a British newspaper traveling through the South. Write an article describing the region and southern society.
5. **Critical Thinking:** *Drawing Conclusions* Why might the South's dependence on slave labor have discouraged European immigrants from settling there?

Section 3

THE SLAVE SYSTEM

Multimedia Connections

Explore these related topics and materials on the CD–ROM to enrich your understanding of this section:

 Media Bank

- African American Spiritual
- Sales Bill
- Sojourner Truth

 Readings

- Spirituals
- Nat Turner's Rebellion
- Amistad Mutiny
- Cultural Borrowings
- Narrative of Sojourner Truth

 Profiles

- Nat Turner
- Sojourner Truth

In the tense days after a failed Virginia slave revolt, one African American gave a simple reason for his participation—freedom. "I have nothing more to offer than what General Washington would have had to offer, had he been taken by British officers," the man explained. "I have ventured my life . . . to obtain the liberty of my countrymen, and am a willing sacrifice to their cause." What he called a "mockery of a trial" quickly ended, and officials executed more than 30 fighters for their freedom.

As you read this section you will find out:
▶ **How slaveholders controlled slaves.**
▶ **How slaves' culture helped them survive slavery.**
▶ **How enslaved African Americans resisted slavery.**

Treatment of Slaves

By 1850 more than 3 million slaves lived in the South. Many worked in factories or city homes or on small farms, but more than half labored on plantations.

Slave control. Slaveholders' treatment of slaves differed considerably. Some masters tried to treat slaves well while others treated slaves horribly.

Almost all slaveholders used physical punishment to control and discipline slaves. When asked about her previous master, one former slave answered, "Beat women! Why sure he . . . beat women. Beat women jes lak men." Even slave children sometimes felt the lash. Hannah Davidson refused to discuss how her former master treated her. "The things that my sister May and I suffered were so terrible," she said. "It is better not to have such things in our memory."

Slave codes. White southerners also wrote laws called **slave codes** to control slaves. The slave codes outlawed a wide variety of activities: slaves could not testify against whites in court, travel without authorization, hit a white person, carry firearms, and so on. The codes varied from state to state and were not consistently enforced, but their existence helped ensure slaves' obedience.

Under the slave codes, most states made it illegal to teach slaves to read and write. Sometimes, sympathetic whites or other African Americans disobeyed this restriction and educated a few slaves. Even so, by 1860 only about 5 percent of slaves had learned to read.

The slave codes did not recognize marriages between slaves. Some slaveholders, however, allowed slaves to maintain family ties. Of course, slaveholders had the legal right to break up slave families.

Slaves who were separated from their families never stopped hoping to locate and rejoin them. Many ran away in an effort to reach loved ones. Reward notices in southern

Slave families were often separated by sale. This extended family from South Carolina represents several generations of enslaved people.

newspapers, such as this one from South Carolina, described these attempts:

> "**RUN** away . . . **HAGAR,** and her daughter called **MARY.** . . . I was since informed that the above negroes crossed the Ashley River a few days ago, and suppose they are gone to Mr. William Stoutenburg's plantation, as her relations belong to him."

Slave auctions. Perhaps no aspect of slavery brought out its inhumanity more than slave auctions. Slaves waited as buyers looked them over, poking and prodding them as they might a horse or cow. Far worse, buyers were deciding the slaves' fate and often that of the slaves' families. One former slave left this description of an auction in New Orleans:

> "[Randall] . . . was made to jump, and run across the floor, and perform many other feats, exhibiting his activity and condition. All the time . . . [his mother] Eliza was crying aloud, and wringing her hands. She besought [pleaded with] the man not to buy him, unless he also bought herself and [her daughter]. . . . The man answered that he could not afford it."

Many companies like this one in Alexandria, Virginia, earned money by selling American-born slaves after the Atlantic slave trade was banned.

Living Conditions of Slaves

The experiences of slaves living on plantations varied a great deal. Some slaves did chores inside the master's house while others worked in the fields. Slaves also worked as carpenters, blacksmiths, seamstresses, and at other skilled trades.

Plantation slaves generally lived in cabins located in a group near the "big house" of the master. These cabins were small—often two rooms and a narrow hallway for a family—and barely furnished. Many did not have beds. Most had dirt floors and fireplaces for cooking and heat. One former slave described the cabins as "but log huts—the tops partly open."

Slaves' food consisted mainly of corn meal and salt pork or bacon. This did not make for a balanced or tasty diet. Many slaveholders allowed slaves to have small vegetable gardens. Slaves also added to their bland food by fishing and by trapping small forest animals, such as rabbits and raccoons.

Slave auctions like this one were usually humiliating experiences for the people who were being sold. Buyers often treated the slaves more like livestock than people.

Slaves wore simple clothing—cotton and woolen shirts and pants or dresses, work shoes, and a hat or kerchief for protection against rain and summer heat. Such clothing rarely lasted long or protected slaves against cold weather.

The Culture of Slavery

Despite their condition, enslaved African Americans managed to develop a distinct slave culture. African American historian Thomas R. Frazier has declared that "it was in this search for freedom and self-expression that the slaves made their most important contributions to our heritage."

Religion. Although slaveholders often required their slaves to attend white churches, many slaves secretly formed their own churches. Since many of the slave codes outlawed meetings among slaves, religious services frequently occurred "way out in the woods or the bushes somewhere so that the white folks couldn't hear."

Slaves often combined Christian beliefs and traditional African practices to create a unique religion. Slave Christianity often

Slave communities created their own culture, which included music and dances that often blended African and European traditions. This tradition still influences African American music today.

stressed that slaves would find freedom in the afterlife. Many enslaved Africans believed that one day they would be led to a "promised land" that was free of slavery. This gave slaves some comfort in daily life and also reinforced the injustice of slavery to them.

An important part of religious practices among slaves were the deeply moving songs known as **spirituals**. These songs were sung in worship services, at work, and at social gatherings. The spirituals, which also blended Christian and African traditions, provided emotional comfort in the slaves' difficult lives.

Folktales. Slaves also developed other ways of expressing their dignity and humanity. Their **folktales**, or oral stories, reflect this. Some of the stories were moral fables that helped educate and set a standard of behavior for slaves to follow.

Other tales featured an animal trickster, or sneaky character, such as the famous Brer Rabbit. In these stories, the animal represented either a particular slave or a personality type who usually got the better of a more powerful but dim-witted opponent. Slaves often used this sort of folktale to triumph symbolically over a master or over slavery itself.

Rebellion and Resistance

Slave culture provided strength, hope, and a way to resist slavery. Many slaves also engaged in many other forms of resistance, however. Some protested individually, while others joined together in open rebellion.

Slave resistance. Many slaves opposed slavery with individual acts of courage that protested the system and lessened its effects on their lives. This resistance took many forms. Slaves might set fire to barns, disrupting the plantation. They might step on plants while plowing, slowing their own work and cutting into the master's profit. They might slip away at night to visit friends on nearby plantations. Some sought freedom in the North by running away.

Slaves sometimes pretended that they were sick or injured. This was a particularly successful form of resistance, since slaveholders realized that forcing "sick" slaves to work might cause permanent injury and lessen their value.

Slave revolts. A small number of slaves actually rebelled against the slave system. Very few of these revolts succeeded because of the restrictions of the slave codes. Slaveholders feared slave uprisings so much that they usually reacted to them with terrible brutality. When captured, rebellious slaves were nearly always tortured or killed.

One rebel leader was Denmark Vesey of Charleston, South Carolina. Vesey had purchased his freedom after winning some money in a lottery. After his escape, he preached against slavery.

By 1821 Vesey had developed a plot to gather thousands of slaves, steal guns, and kill

American Letters

Incidents in the Life of a Slave Girl

Harriet Jacobs

Harriet Jacobs was born into slavery in North Carolina in 1813. In 1842 she escaped to the North. She published her narrative account of slavery, Incidents in the Life of a Slave Girl, *in 1861. In this selection from her book, Jacobs relates how the slaveholders tried to use religion to control slaves. She was about 18 years old and still enslaved at the time of the events she describes.*

After the alarm caused by Nat Turner's insurrection [rebellion] had subsided [died down], the slaveholders came to the conclusion that it would be well to give the slaves enough of religious instruction to keep them from murdering their masters. The Episcopal clergyman offered to hold a separate service on Sundays for their benefit. . . .

When the Rev. Mr. Pike came, there were some twenty persons present. . . . Pious [Holy] Mr. Pike brushed up his hair till it stood upright, and, in deep, solemn tones, began: "Hearken, ye servants! Give strict heed unto my words. You are rebellious sinners. . . . Instead of serving your masters faithfully, which is pleasing in the sight of your heavenly Master, you are idle, and shirk [avoid] your work. God sees you. . . . Although your masters may not find you out, God sees you; and he will punish you. You must forsake your sinful ways, and be faithful servants. . . . If you disobey your earthly master, you offend your heavenly Master. . . ."

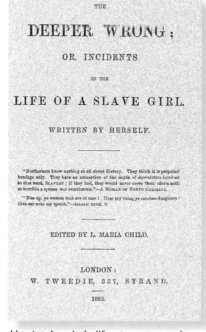

THE

DEEPER WRONG;

OR, INCIDENTS

IN THE

LIFE OF A SLAVE GIRL.

WRITTEN BY HERSELF.

"Northerners know nothing at all about Slavery. They think it is perpetual bondage only. They have no conception of the depth of *degradation* involved in that word, SLAVERY; if they had, they would never cease their efforts until so horrible a system was overthrown."—A WOMAN OF NORTH CAROLINA.

"Rise up, ye women that are at ease! Hear my voice, ye careless daughters! Give ear unto my speech."—ISAIAH xxxii, 9.

EDITED BY L. MARIA CHILD.

LONDON:

W. TWEEDIE, 337, STRAND.

1862.

Harriet Jacobs's life story was published with the help of a northern abolitionist. This edition is from 1862.

We went home, highly amused at brother Pike's gospel teaching. . . . I went the next Sabbath evening, and heard pretty much a repetition of the last discourse [discussion]. . . . I went home with the feeling that I had heard the Reverend Mr. Pike for the last time. . . .

I well remember one occasion when I attended a Methodist class meeting. I . . . happened to sit next a poor, bereaved [grieving] mother. . . . The class leader was the town constable—a man who bought and sold slaves. . . . This white-faced, black-hearted brother came near us, and said to the stricken woman, "Sister, can't you tell us how the Lord deals with your soul? Do you love him as you did formerly?"

She rose to her feet, and said, in piteous tones, "My Lord and Master, help me! My load is more than I can bear. . . . They've got all my children. Last week they took the last one. God only knows where they've sold her. . . . Pray for her brothers and sisters! I've got nothing to live for now. God make my time short!"

She sat down, quivering in every limb. I saw that constable class leader become crimson in the face with suppressed [held in] laughter, while he held up his handkerchief, that those who were weeping for the poor woman's calamity [tragedy] might not see his merriment. . . .

No wonder the slaves sing—

"Ole Satan's church is here below;
Up to God's free church I hope to go."

The Granger Collection, New York

Nat Turner and his followers plotted a massive rebellion against the slave system. Although the revolt failed to end slavery, it did strike fear in the southern white community.

became a slave minister, preaching after long days in the field. Turner hated slavery and believed that God had chosen him to seek freedom.

In 1831 Turner and his followers killed about 60 whites before being captured. This episode became known as **Nat Turner's Rebellion**. Some slaveholders responded to the revolt by carrying out their own reign of violence and terror. In the process they killed at least 120 innocent African Americans in the area.

Turner's revolt had widespread results. It fanned fear and rage throughout the white population of the South. White officials increased restrictions on slaves, making it more difficult for slaves to meet in groups outside the presence of whites. The Virginia legislature passed laws that almost completely eliminated slave preachers, slave schools, and slave religious meetings. Nat Turner's Rebellion was a lasting indication of how much slaves despised their condition and how badly they wanted to be free.

most of the white population of Charleston. At the last minute, one of Vesey's followers betrayed the plan. Officials later hanged Vesey and 35 other participants.

A Virginia slave named Nat Turner organized what proved to be the bloodiest slave uprising in America. As a young boy, Turner had taught himself to read. He eventually

Section 3 Review

• Glossary

IDENTIFY and explain the significance of the following: slave codes, spirituals, folktales, Denmark Vesey, Nat Turner's Rebellion

REVIEWING FOR DETAILS
1. What methods did slaveholders use to control slaves?
2. How did enslaved African Americans resist slaveholders?

REVIEWING FOR UNDERSTANDING
3. **Geographic Literacy** How did geographic conditions in the South make it difficult for slaves to escape?
4. **Writing Mastery:** *Creating* Write a folktale, like those told by African Americans in the 1800s, that reflects important elements of slave culture.
5. **Critical Thinking:** *Synthesizing Information* How did the slave codes make it difficult for people like Denmark Vesey and Nat Turner to mount successful revolts against slavery?

Section 4

THE CRUSADE AGAINST SLAVERY

Multimedia Connections

Explore these related topics and materials on the CD-ROM to enrich your understanding of this section:

 Biographies

- William Lloyd Garrison

 Profiles

- Angelina and Sarah Grimké
- Charles Remond
- Harriet Tubman
- Robert Purvis
- Theodore Weld

 Media Bank

- William Lloyd Garrison

Maria Stewart stepped up to the stage. Everyone in the Boston auditorium knew it was a very special day. To hear this inspiring African American abolitionist, the first native-born woman in America to deliver a political lecture—how wonderful! The crowd hushed as she spoke. "All the nations of the earth are crying out for liberty and equality," Stewart explained. "Away, away with tyranny [unjust rule] and oppression [burden]."

As you read this section you will find out:

▶ **Why some African Americans supported the colonization movement.**

▶ **How the American Anti-Slavery Society opposed slavery.**

▶ **Why some northern whites opposed the abolition movement.**

Ideas About Abolition

Even before the American Revolution, small groups of Americans began to call for **abolition**, or an end to slavery. The Quakers, for example, criticized slaveholders for supporting what they believed to be an un-Christian practice. Free African Americans in the North also formed antislavery societies and published newspapers.

The colonization movement. In the early 1800s some people explored the idea of colonizing, or settling, African Americans outside the United States. Most white sponsors of colonization had a low opinion of African Americans. This group wanted to send black people "back" to Africa, even though by this time most black Americans had been born in America.

A small group of African Americans and whites saw colonization as a way for black people to escape prejudice and abuse. Paul Cuffe, a wealthy northern African American, was one of the first to support colonization. In 1815 he transported 38 free black volunteers to West Africa at his own expense. However, Cuffe died before he could send another group.

In 1817 a number of white citizens founded the **American Colonization Society**. They bought land in what became the nation of Liberia and helped free African Americans settle there. In the late 1820s the society also began to purchase slaves, free them, and send them to Africa. By 1830 the organization had persuaded about 1,400 African Americans to make the move to Africa. Most African Americans did not want to live there, however. They viewed America, not Africa, as their home. Their opposition to colonization helped cause the movement to lose strength in the 1830s and 1840s.

Different motives, different goals. Even as support for colonization faded, more people began to consider the situation of African Americans in the United States. Gradually, more people became abolitionists.

Abolitionists opposed slavery for a variety of reasons. Some abolitionists put forth religious arguments, stressing that God saw all human beings as equals. Other abolitionists believed in the ideal of freedom. They quoted the Declaration of Independence to show that slavery violated American principles.

Abolitionists also had different goals. Some wanted African Americans to have the same rights that white people had. Others thought black people should have fewer liberties than white people.

Radical Voices Demand Action

Two radical abolitionists helped to bring attention to the growing movement against slavery. David Walker was a free African American from North Carolina. Over time he educated himself and made his way to Boston, where he operated a used-clothing store.

In 1829 Walker wrote *Appeal to the Colored Citizens of the World,* an influential pamphlet. It urged African Americans—free and slave—to protest for freedom. "Will you wait," he warned America, "until we shall . . . obtain our liberty by the crushing arm of power?" Walker secretly distributed copies of his pamphlet by sewing them into the clothes of sailors heading to the South.

William Lloyd Garrison, a white Massachusetts publisher, soon added his voice to Walker's in the call for freedom. Garrison wanted immediate abolition and criticized not only slaveholders but all Americans who allowed slavery to exist.

In 1831 Garrison began publishing an abolitionist newspaper, *The Liberator.* Supported at first mostly by African American subscribers, *The Liberator* eventually entered the homes of more and more white people, encouraging support for abolition.

Though Garrison used only nonviolent tactics, his radical position alarmed even some more conservative abolitionists. He cried "No Union with Slaveholders," urging northern

Our Country is the World, our Countrymen are all Mankind.

William Lloyd Garrison's The Liberator *became one of the most widely read abolitionist newspapers in the North.*

• Abolitionists

Former slave Harriet Tubman (far left) risked her life to help many others escape from slavery, including the people pictured here with her.

• **Underground Railroad**

states to break away from the nation. He publicly set fire to a copy of the Constitution, claiming that it was "an agreement with Hell."

group supported abolition and racial equality. The group also called for using nonviolent methods to achieve these goals. The society soon spread throughout the North and the Midwest by creating smaller regional organizations and hiring inspiring speakers.

The Underground Railroad

Like Walker and Garrison, many abolitionists sprang into action for the cause. In the 1830s a small group of abolitionists formed the **Underground Railroad**, an informal network that helped between roughly 50,000 and 75,000 slaves escape to freedom. It used more than 3,000 "conductors," or guides, to help lead slaves along different paths to liberty in Canada or in the North. They stopped at "stations"— barns, stables, and safe houses—to hide escaping slaves.

One of the most famous conductors was Harriet Tubman, who escaped slavery after suffering years of abuse as a field hand. She became a specialist in the dangerous task of helping slaves escape into the northern states. Tubman made at least 19 trips into the South and helped free more than 300 slaves.

The American Anti-Slavery Society

In 1833 Garrison and other abolitionists founded an organization called the **American Anti-Slavery Society**. The

Through Others' Eyes
The Abolition Movement

After 1833, when Great Britain ended slavery in its empire, many British abolitionists turned their attention elsewhere. Some offered advice to their American friends who were working hard to end slavery. In 1839 British historian Esther Copley reported on efforts to aid American abolition:

"We should employ every means in our power to promote the utter annihilation [destruction] of slavery. . . . Such appears to be the duty of Britain towards other nations, especially America, to whom she is most closely allied. . . . Several deputations [groups] have already been sent from Great Britain to America, to promote the great object, particularly by lecturing in the principal cities and towns of the free States, upon . . . the duty, necessity, and advantage of immediate emancipation. . . . It is a matter of heartfelt delight and congratulation, that the good cause seems to be rapidly spreading in America."

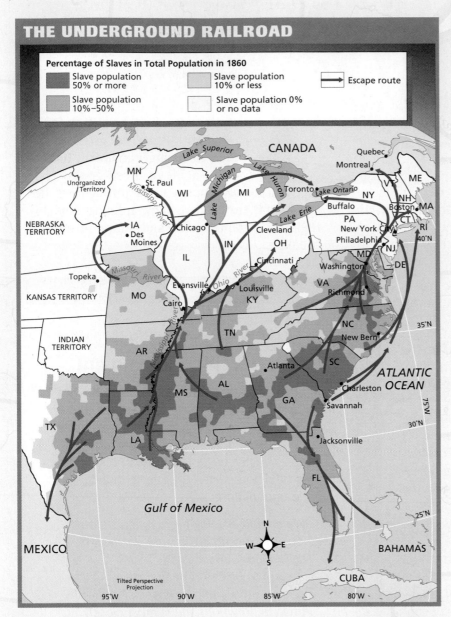

THE UNDERGROUND RAILROAD

Percentage of Slaves in Total Population in 1860

- Slave population 50% or more
- Slave population 10%–50%
- Slave population 10% or less
- Slave population 0% or no data
- → Escape route

Learning from Maps.

Conductors on the Underground Railroad helped between 50,000 and 75,000 slaves find freedom.

▶ **Movement.** How did a slave's location help determine his or her route to escape on the Underground Railroad?

• Maps

Society. They demonstrated that even some southerners hated slavery. Angelina Grimké expressed her commitment to abolition:

> **"If persecution is the means which God has ordained [ordered] for the accomplishment of this great end, [freedom]; then . . . LET IT COME; for it is my deep, solemn, deliberate conviction [belief], that this is a cause worth dying for."**

In 1836 Angelina Grimké wrote an "Appeal to the Christian Women of the South," urging southern women to "overthrow this horrible system of oppression and cruelty."

Frederick Douglass. The abolitionist movement soon added another powerful fighter to its ranks. Frederick Douglass had been a slave in Maryland for many years. In 1838 he escaped and eventually settled in Massachusetts.

One day in 1841, Douglass attended a meeting of the Anti-Slavery Society. Without preparation, he delivered a powerful speech. The members of the society were so impressed that they urged him to work full-time for abolition.

Douglass gradually began to engage in political activity. He and Martin Delany also

The Grimké sisters. The sisters Sarah and Angelina Grimké, two white abolitionists from South Carolina, traveled through New England for the American Anti-Slavery

Former slave Frederick Douglass became a powerful voice in the fight against slavery.

• Narrative

published an abolitionist paper, the *North Star.* In one article he wrote:

> **"The white man's happiness cannot be purchased by the black man's misery. . . . All distinctions founded on complexion [skin color] ought to be . . . abolished, and every right, privilege, and immunity, now enjoyed by the white man, ought to be as freely granted to the man of color."**

Different strategies. As the abolition movement gained strength, two different groups emerged. Garrison and many of his followers favored immediate **emancipation**, or freedom, for slaves. Other abolitionists supported gradual emancipation.

Opposition to Abolition

Most white southerners hated the abolition movement. Many white northerners did as well. Several factors motivated their opposition to abolition. Many white workers feared job competition from freed slaves. Some northern manufacturers thought abolition would destroy the southern economy and eventually hurt their businesses. In addition, many northerners shared a deep prejudice against all African Americans.

Like southerners, some northerners disliked the abolition movement so much that they resorted to harassment and violence. Opponents often tried to break up abolition meetings by shouting or throwing rocks. Sometimes they hurt or even killed individual abolitionists. Several times when Elijah Lovejoy published abolitionist articles in his Illinois newspaper, opponents broke into his shop and destroyed his press. When Lovejoy tried to install another press in November 1837, an angry group murdered him. Some abolitionists became discouraged by this opposition. However, they were slowly convincing the people of the North that slavery was an evil institution.

Section 4 Review

• Glossary

IDENTIFY and explain the significance of the following: abolition, Paul Cuffe, American Colonization Society, David Walker, William Lloyd Garrison, Underground Railroad, Harriet Tubman, American Anti-Slavery Society, Sarah and Angelina Grimké, Frederick Douglass, emancipation

• Time Line

REVIEWING FOR DETAILS
1. Why did some African Americans support the movement for colonization?
2. What were some of the methods the American Anti-Slavery Society used to fight slavery?
3. Why did some northern whites oppose the abolition movement?

REVIEWING FOR UNDERSTANDING
4. **Writing Mastery:** *Persuading* Create a poster for the American Anti-Slavery Society persuading people to support the abolition movement.
5. **Critical Thinking:** *Recognizing Point of View* How did some white northerners' support of the colonization movement reveal their racial prejudice?

The Cotton Kingdom

Throughout the 1800s the South continued to grow the staple crops it had relied on in the 1700s, such as tobacco, rice, and sugarcane, but those crops were quickly overshadowed in importance by cotton. The fluffy white bolls dominated the economy of the region like no other crop. The wealth of the South rose and fell according to the cotton market. It became so important to the southern economy that many people referred to it as "King Cotton."

The rise of the textile industry in the Northeast and in Europe created a huge demand for cotton. By 1860 cotton accounted for about half of the value of all major exports for the United States. This made cotton, and the South, vital to the overall economy of the nation. As tensions increased between the North and the South over slavery, some southerners thought that the importance of cotton would prevent the federal government from interfering with the slave system.

The Cotton Kingdom

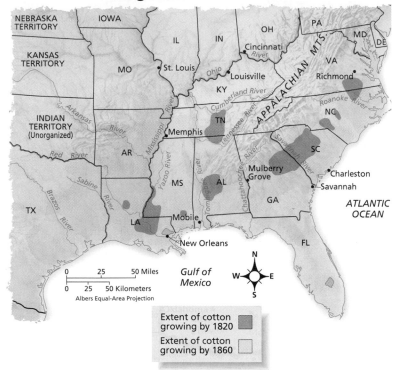

Extent of cotton growing by 1820

Extent of cotton growing by 1860

The Cotton Kingdom gradually expanded westward throughout the 1800s. **Region:** What two states began to grow cotton after 1820? What three states accounted for about 60 percent of all cotton production?

Share of Total Cotton Production by State in 1850

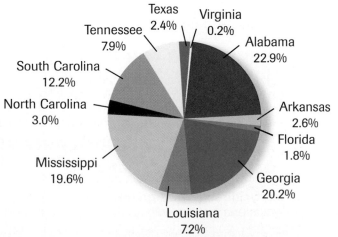

Texas 2.4%
Virginia 0.2%
Tennessee 7.9%
Alabama 22.9%
South Carolina 12.2%
Arkansas 2.6%
North Carolina 3.0%
Florida 1.8%
Mississippi 19.6%
Georgia 20.2%
Louisiana 7.2%

Source: Historical Statistics of the South, 1790–1970

Cotton Production and U.S. Exports, 1790–1850

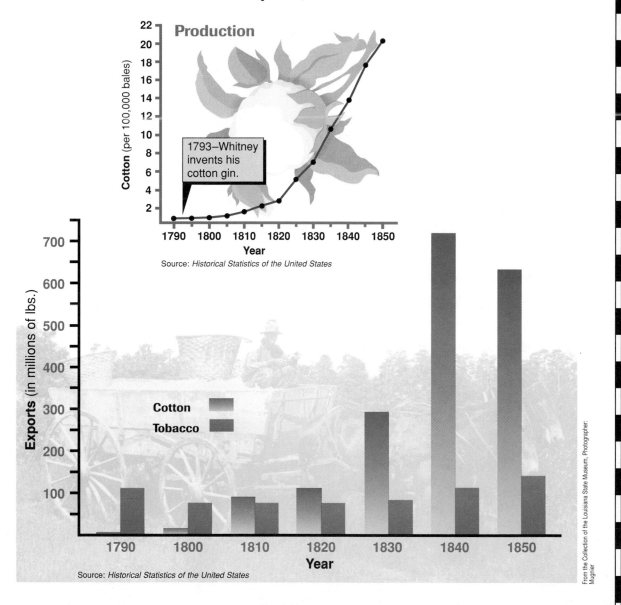

Production

Cotton (per 100,000 bales)

1793—Whitney invents his cotton gin.

Year

Source: *Historical Statistics of the United States*

Exports (in millions of lbs.)

Cotton
Tobacco

Year

Source: *Historical Statistics of the United States*

Tobacco was the country's leading export crop in 1790. Within 15 years, cotton had exceeded it. While tobacco production rose very slowly throughout the early 1800s, cotton boomed. The vast majority of this cotton was exported to Europe. **Linking Geography and History:** About how many times more cotton than tobacco was exported in 1840?

To learn more *about the Cotton Kingdom, go to the interactive map, "The Cotton Plantation," on the CD-ROM.*

• **The Cotton Plantation**

u n i t **4**

$\mathcal{S}$EEKING GROWTH AND CHANGE (1820–1860)

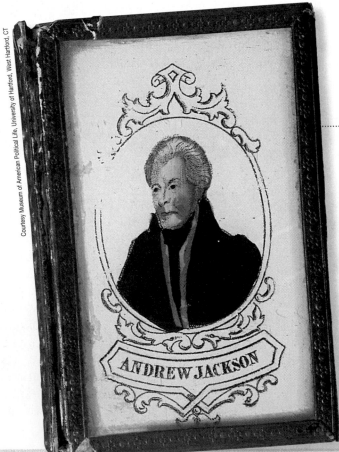

Courtesy Museum of American Political Life, University of Hartford, West Hartford, CT

Campaign items like this image of Andrew Jackson and this frog statue engraved with "Croak for the Jackson Wagon," marked a change in the way people ran for public office.

LINKING PAST TO PRESENT
Campaigning

VOTE MISSY FOR STUDENT COUNCIL PRESIDENT! This was one of the signs supporting a candidate running for office at Mena Middle School. She and her opponents all made signs, flyers, and buttons to encourage other students to vote for them. They even gathered at an assembly to give campaign speeches to the student body.

Students all across the country participate in similar campaigns every year. Their methods of carrying out campaigns reflect many of the methods that politicians use when they try to win public office. Posters, flyers, buttons, and public speeches are standard in almost all elections as each candidate tries to convince voters that he or she is the best candidate for the position. Bill Clinton and Bob Dole used these tactics to woo the voters in the 1996 presidential campaign.

American elections were not always carried out in such a manner, however. During the country's first 30 years, most candidates for public office did very little campaigning. What little they did was aimed mostly at leaders of their own political parties. As you read this unit, you will learn that things began to change in the 1820s, a period that set the standard for the way in which political campaigns would be carried out in the future.

Instead of focusing their attention only on party leaders, candidates began to appeal directly to voters. They flooded the countryside with campaign "giveaways"

Even though they may be too young to vote, these teenagers are getting involved in politics by campaigning for a candidate in a state election.

such as buttons, metal tokens, bandannas, cups, and plates. Local campaign committees encouraged voters to get involved in elections by holding high-spirited parades, barbecues, and rallies. These public parties were intended both to make politics "fun" for voters and to get them excited about a particular candidate.

Probably the most significant change brought about in the 1820s was the increasing involvement of ordinary people in politics. As you read this unit, note that even many people who could not vote became active in campaigns and sought other ways of affecting national politics. You will learn that the era of the 1820s ushered in a period of expanding democratic ideals and political participation that are still at work in America today.

CHAPTER **11**

The Granger Collection, New York

Conflicts and Reform
(1820–1860)

THEMES IN AMERICAN HISTORY

Constitutional Heritage:
How might the federal and state governments come into conflict?

Geographic Diversity:
Why might people from different regions of the country work together for political change?

Democratic Values:
How does American society reflect a belief in individual rights?

*W*riter Ralph Waldo Emerson captured the hopeful spirit of America during the presidency of Andrew Jackson:

"It is easy to see that a greater self-reliance must work a revolution in all the offices and relations of men; in their religion; in their education; in their pursuits; their modes [ways] of living; their association; in their property; in their . . . views."

 • Video Opener    • Skill Builder

image above: *Andrew Jackson on the road to his inauguration*

Section 1

THE AGE OF ANDREW JACKSON

Multimedia Connections

Explore these related topics and materials on the CD–ROM to enrich your understanding of this section:

 Gazetteer

- Maine
- Missouri

 Atlas

- Male Suffrage

 Profiles

- Andrew Jackson
- Henry Clay

 Readings

- Jefferson on Missouri

After his inaugural address, Andrew Jackson held a reception at the White House. The mansion was soon full of people. Some knocked over furniture and tracked mud over the carpets, while others consumed huge amounts of food and drink. One woman reported that "the *majesty of the people* had disappeared, and . . . [had been replaced by] a mob . . . scrambling, fighting, romping." The new president escaped out a side door and slept in a nearby hotel.

As you read this section you will find out:

▶ **Why the Missouri Compromise was important.**

▶ **How national politics changed in the 1820s.**

▶ **How Jacksonian Democracy affected government.**

The Missouri Compromise

During President Monroe's first term, the nation grew rapidly. Settlers swarmed west, and new states joined the Union. This expansion, however, raised the issue of whether slavery should be allowed in the new lands. The issue came to a crisis in 1819, when Missouri applied for admission as a **slave state**, or a state where slavery was permitted. At the time there were 11 free states and 11 slave states in the Union. Missouri would upset this balance.

Government leaders, led by Speaker of the House Henry Clay, created the **Missouri Compromise** in 1820. This agreement admitted Missouri as a slave state and Maine as a free state. The compromise outlawed slavery in the rest of the Louisiana Purchase north of 36°30′ north latitude.

THE MISSOURI COMPROMISE

Free state	Slave state
Free territory	Slave territory

MAINE

MISSOURI

Missouri Compromise Line
36° 30' N

Learning from Maps.
Under the Missouri Compromise, Maine entered the Union as a free state and Missouri as a slave state.

• Maps

▶ **Region.** After the Missouri Compromise, how many slave territories were there? How many free territories?

The Second President Adams

After the Missouri Compromise, sectional differences played an increasingly important role in national politics. No candidate had opposed President Monroe for re-election in 1820. In the following years, however, the North, South, and West each produced important leaders. When Monroe did not seek a third term, they competed for the presidency.

The election of 1824. One candidate was Secretary of State John Quincy Adams, the son of former president John Adams. The Adams name combined with his long career of public service gave John Quincy advantages, but he had few supporters outside the northeastern states. The favorite in the South was William H. Crawford of Georgia, Monroe's secretary of the treasury. The two other candi-

dates were westerners, Andrew Jackson of Tennessee and Henry Clay of Kentucky.

As a hero of the War of 1812, Jackson was a nationally popular figure. In the heated campaign of 1824, Jackson won the largest share of the popular vote. No candidate received a majority of the electoral votes, however. Therefore, according to the Constitution, the House of Representatives decided the election. Clay strongly opposed Jackson, whom he considered unqualified to become president. Clay encouraged his supporters to back Adams, who then received the votes of a majority of the states and became president. After the election, Adams appointed Clay secretary of state. Jackson and his supporters accused Adams and Clay of making a "corrupt bargain." This turn of events made an angry Jackson very eager for the next election.

Adams's presidency. President Adams was extremely hardworking. He rose every morning at 5:00. Even in the dead of winter, Adams threw open his window and took a sponge bath with ice-cold water to prepare for his day's work. He took office, he said, with:

> "**intentions upright and pure, a heart devoted to the welfare of our country, and the unceasing application of all the faculties allotted [assigned] to me to her service.**"

Adams favored a government that put national interests before sectional concerns. He would not use the

Around 1840 John Quincy Adams posed for this daguerreotype, an early form of photography.

• **John Quincy Adams**

political tactics necessary to get his programs adopted. For example, he refused to replace government officials who resisted his policies with people who supported them. As a result, his administration faced many problems.

The Election of 1828

By 1828 Adams was discouraged and depressed, but he was determined to seek re-election. This time he faced only one opponent—Andrew Jackson.

The campaign of 1828 was bitterly fought and mean-spirited. The race was, however, typical of politics at the time. Jackson's supporters split from the Democratic-Republican Party and began calling themselves Democrats. This was the formal beginning of the modern **Democratic Party**.

The Democrats said little about the political issues of the day. Instead, when they discovered that Adams had bought an ivory chess set and a billiard table for the White House, they charged him with wasting public money on gambling devices. The president's supporters replied with their own accusations. They said that Jackson was a gambler and a murderer. They also told shady stories about his wife, Rachel, and his mother. Neither these accusations nor the political issues probably had much effect on the election. Jackson won mainly because he was so popular.

Jacksonian Democracy

Jackson's victory marked a turning point in American history. He was the first westerner to occupy the White House, and his election signaled the growing importance of the West in the expanding nation.

The election also demonstrated a new democratic spirit in America that many historians have given the label **Jacksonian Democracy**. When he was running for president, Jackson presented himself as being in tune with the common person. Jackson and his supporters claimed that any ordinary person who was intelligent enough

Presidential Lives

Andrew Jackson

President Jackson was a pale, thin man who had a reputation for being very tough. His nickname was "Old Hickory," after a type of tree that produces extremely hard wood.

During the American Revolution, young Andrew had refused to polish a British officer's boots. The angry officer slashed the boy with a sword. Jackson bore the scar the rest of his life.

Later, when he was a general, Jackson showed little mercy for British or American Indian enemies. He was also tough on his personal and political opponents. His reputation as a fighter was widely known. While fighting one duel, he was shot in the chest. The bullet remained lodged there for the rest of his life.

Tough "Old Hickory" had a soft spot when it came to his wife, Rachel, however. When Rachel died just weeks before his inauguration, Jackson felt her loss deeply. He blamed her death on the vicious attacks made on her character during the 1828 campaign. "Those vile wretches," said a grief-stricken Jackson of his wife's critics. "May God Almighty forgive her murderers. . . . I never can."

The Granger Collection, New York

could be an effective leader. Good leaders did not have to come from the upper classes of society. Jackson summed it up this way:

"**The duties of all public officers are . . . so plain and simple that men of intelligence may readily qualify themselves for their**

The Granger Collection, New York

Many Americans viewed Andrew Jackson as a man of the people. While he was president, residents of upstate New York sent him a 1,400-pound wheel of cheese. The White House invited hundreds of people to consume this gift at an informal party.

performance. . . . In a country where offices are created solely for the benefit of the people, no one man has any more intrinsic [basic] right to official station [position] than another."

This faith in ordinary people had already led to important reforms. Most state governments had done away with property qualifications for voting and holding office. Presidential electors were increasingly chosen directly by the voters instead of by state legislatures.

Party leaders soon began to hold national meetings. Delegates from all over the nation attended these meetings, called **nominating conventions**, to choose their party's presidential and vice presidential candidates.

After the elections, winners generally appointed their supporters to government jobs. During Jackson's time this practice became known as the **spoils system**, from the phrase "to the victor belong the spoils." While Jackson did not make any more such appointments than most earlier presidents had, the Jacksonians added the idea of **rotation in office**. After a certain time some jobholders were replaced to give the party in power more political control.

Section 1 Review

• **Glossary**

IDENTIFY and explain the significance of the following: slave state, Henry Clay, Missouri Compromise, John Quincy Adams, Democratic Party, Jacksonian Democracy, nominating conventions, spoils system, rotation in office

REVIEWING FOR DETAILS
1. How did the presidential elections of the 1820s differ from those of earlier years?
2. What effect did Jacksonian Democracy have on government?

REVIEWING FOR UNDERSTANDING
3. **Geographic Literacy** How did the Missouri Compromise temporarily settle regional differences?
4. **Writing Mastery:** *Persuading* Imagine that you are a political leader in the 1820s. Write a short speech persuading members of your party to support a greater role for Americans in their government.
5. **Critical Thinking:** *Drawing Conclusions* What are the disadvantages of political candidates using negative personal attacks in their campaigns?

Section 2
JACKSON AS PRESIDENT

Multimedia Connections
Explore these related topics and materials on the CD–ROM to enrich your understanding of this section:

 Media Bank

- Panic of 1837
- Martin Van Buren
- National Debt

 Glossary

- balanced budget
- deficit spending
- nullification crisis

 Profiles

- Martin Van Buren
- John C. Calhoun

Davy Crockett, a frontier hero, had opposed the presidency of fellow Tennessean Andrew Jackson. He also disliked Jackson's chosen successor, Martin Van Buren. Before the 1836 presidential campaign, Crockett wrote: "I think *all* will agree, that Martin Van Buren is not the man he is cracked up to be." Some people, Crockett added, had even "used the popularity of General Jackson to abuse the country with Martin Van Buren." Crockett's words were an attempt to sway the voters.

As you read this section you will find out:
▶ **Why the North and the South disagreed about tariffs.**
▶ **What the nullification crisis was.**
▶ **How Jackson destroyed the Bank of the United States.**

The Tariff Issue

President Jackson's national popularity was not a strong enough unifying force to end sectional disagreements. The argument over tariffs was particularly troublesome. Many people in the Northeast favored **protective tariffs**, high duties on imported goods that competed with American products.

Much of the enthusiasm for protective tariffs was connected to a plan developed by Henry Clay called the **American System**. While some northerners wanted protective tariffs, many westerners wanted the government to help pay for internal improvements, such as the roads and canals needed to get western goods to market. Clay hoped that these two regions could vote as one on issues—western members of Congress would vote for high tariffs in exchange for northern

By 1821 Henry Clay, then in his mid-forties, was an able politician. His support of the Missouri Compromise had gained him the nickname "Great Pacificator" [peacemaker]. Over the next 30 years, he continued to work toward compromise.

votes for internal improvements. Clay explained that America had a:

> **"great diversity of interests: agricultural, planting, farming, commercial, navigating, fishing, manufacturing. . . . The good of each part and of the whole should be carefully consulted. This is the only mode by which we can preserve, in full vigor, the harmony of the whole Union."**

Southern states, however, which had few industries to protect, opposed protective tariffs. These tariffs would raise the price of many manufactured goods southerners had to buy from other countries.

The Nullification Crisis

Further complicating the tariff argument was the belief of some Americans that protective tariffs were unconstitutional. They argued that the Constitution gave Congress the power to tax imports to raise money but not to make foreign goods less competitive in price. Vice President John C. Calhoun of South Carolina insisted that if a state considered a law of Congress unconstitutional, the state could nullify, or refuse to accept, the law and prevent it from being enforced in that particular state.

Many Americans thought **nullification** threatened the Union. In 1830 Senator Daniel Webster of Massachusetts voiced this concern in a speech to the Senate. He closed with these rousing words: "Liberty *and* Union, now and forever, one and inseparable!"

Calhoun had expected that Congress would lower the high tariff of 1828, which many southerners called the **Tariff of Abominations** because they found it hateful. The northern manufacturers' influence in Congress was growing, however, and a new tariff passed in 1832 lowered duties only slightly.

Many southerners were extremely angry over this new tariff, and South Carolina decided to nullify it. Calhoun resigned as vice president and was elected senator from South Carolina. Jackson believed the nation would fall apart if states could reject federal laws. He threatened to march into South Carolina with U.S. troops and hang the nullifiers.

Few Americans were ready to break up the Union over tariffs, so Congress passed a new tariff that lowered duties gradually. South Carolina then repealed the Ordinance of Nullification. With this compromise, the nullification crisis passed, but the fundamental question—whether a state had the right to reject a federal law it believed to be unconstitutional—remained unanswered.

This political cartoon shows the Ordinance of Nullification blowing a hole through the wall built by the protective tariffs.

Jackson and the Bank

One reason Jackson acted so confidently in the nullification crisis was that he had just been overwhelmingly re-elected president in 1832. His popularity had risen in part because of his fight against the establishment of the Second Bank of the United States.

The charter for the First Bank of the United States had expired in 1811. In 1816 Congress had chartered a Second Bank of the United States to operate for a period of 20 years. Many Americans, including Jackson, opposed this Bank. Jackson believed that it had too much power over the nation's economy, and he favored limits on the Bank's operations.

The Bank's supporters in Congress knew that Jackson hoped to destroy it. Therefore, before the presidential election of 1832, they introduced a bill extending the Bank's existence. They hoped Jackson would sign it, or suffer the consequences of a veto in the election. Jackson vetoed the bill, explaining that the Bank had allowed a few wealthy investors to make profits from "the earnings of the American people." Most Americans were impressed by Jackson's attack on wealth. In the 1832 election Jackson defeated Henry Clay, 219 electoral votes to 49.

Jackson then began to withdraw the government's money on deposit in the Bank of the United States. He ordered that the federal government's income from taxes and land sales be deposited in various state banks.

Jackson's opponents charged that the government was showing favoritism in this matter. They called banks that received these deposits "pet banks." Many of these banks began to lend money recklessly. More bank notes were put into circulation. This, combined with other factors, caused enormous inflation. In 1837 this inflationary boom ended in a sudden collapse of prices and business activity, called the **Panic of 1837**. When people refused to accept the bank notes as payment, many banks failed. In addition, many companies throughout the country went out of business. The economies of the West and the South suffered greatly.

Some Americans opposed Jackson's policies. One person criticized Jackson's political leadership by showing "King Andrew the First" holding the presidential veto and standing on a shredded copy of the U.S. Constitution.

President Martin Van Buren

In 1836, with Jackson's strong support, the Democratic Party had nominated Martin Van Buren for president. Van Buren had been secretary of state during Jackson's first term and vice president during his second. This small, red-haired man was such a clever politician that he was frequently called "the Little Magician" or "the Red Fox." Even though three candidates ran against him, Van Buren won with little difficulty.

Van Buren's opponents in 1836 were members of a newly formed political organization known as the **Whig Party**, founded by Henry Clay in 1834. The new party did not present a serious challenge to the more established Democrats in the election of 1836, but they would play an important role in future elections.

Van Buren's presidency was hurt by the economic **depression**—a sharp drop in business activity accompanied by high unemployment— that followed the Panic of 1837. When Van Buren sought re-election in 1840, the Whigs had a sound strategy. They united behind General William Henry Harrison, who was famous for having defeated the great Indian leader Tecumseh at the Battle of Tippecanoe.

During the 1840 campaign the Whigs sang the praises of "Old Tippecanoe." They described Harrison as a simple man who lived in a log cabin and always offered a warm welcome to strangers. In contrast, the Whigs insisted that Van Buren dined off gold plates and wasted the people's money on expensive French wines. When Van Buren tried to discuss such issues as the tariff and banking policy, they shouted, "Van, Van, is a used-up man."

Voter turnout for the election of 1836 had reached close to 1.5 million. In 1840 the number of voters soared to around 2.4 million. Harrison won by an enormous margin—234 electoral votes to 60. The appeal to the common person that the Jacksonians had set in motion in 1828 had proved unbeatable.

This image captures the main elements of William Henry Harrison's campaign. To the left, Harrison and his dog give a warm welcome to the one-legged veteran. This represents Harrison's fame as a soldier and host, while atop the roof, the American flag emphasizes his patriotism.

• **William Harrison**

The Granger Collection, New York

Section **2** Review

• **Glossary**

IDENTIFY and explain the significance of the following: protective tariffs, American System, John C. Calhoun, nullification, Daniel Webster, Tariff of Abominations, Panic of 1837, Martin Van Buren, Whig Party, depression

REVIEWING FOR DETAILS

1. Why did the North and the South have different views about protective tariffs?
2. How did the nullification crisis develop, and how was it settled?
3. How did President Jackson deal with the Bank of the United States?

REVIEWING FOR UNDERSTANDING

4. **Geographic Literacy**   Why did Henry Clay's American System focus on a compromise between the West and the North rather than the West and the South?

5. **Critical Thinking:** *Making Comparisons*   What were the similarities and differences between the presidential elections of 1828 and 1840?

Section 3

INDIAN REMOVAL

Multimedia Connections

Explore these related topics and materials on the CD–ROM to enrich your understanding of this section:

 Profiles

- John Ross
- Sequoyah

 Gazetteer

- Indian Territory

 Media Bank

- Cherokee Trail of Tears

 Readings

- Trail of Tears
- Two Views of Indian Removal

Black Hawk and other Sauk returned to their Illinois home, east of the Mississippi River, for the spring planting. The time for the planting came and went, however, while they negotiated and battled with the U.S. Army. Exhausted and starving, Black Hawk and his followers decided to retreat west, back across the river. Troops came upon them and opened fire on the men, women, and children who tried desperately to swim to the safety of the far shore. They would never again return to Illinois.

As you read this section you will find out:

▶ **Why settlers wanted to remove American Indians.**

▶ **Where the government moved Indians.**

▶ **How American Indians resisted removal.**

Jackson's Indian Policy

One of the major issues during Jackson's presidency was the removal of eastern Indians to territory west of the Mississippi River. As the nation expanded, settlers slowly pushed American Indians farther and farther west.

Americans who lived far from the frontier knew very little about Indians other than what they read in novels such as James Fenimore Cooper's "Leatherstocking Tales." Settlers who wanted Indian land had no interest in learning about American Indians or their rights. They often ignored the fact that Indians' right to their land was guaranteed by treaties.

Ever since President Jefferson's time, U.S. presidents had considered relocating eastern Indians onto western territory acquired in the Louisiana Purchase. Under President Monroe, a policy of removal had been adopted to solve "the Indian Problem," and Jackson had been a supporter of Indian removal since the War of 1812. Jackson felt that Indian nations were a threat to the stability of the United States because they were not under the federal government's authority.

Jackson hoped to convince Indians to move by offering to pay eastern tribes for their lands, to transport them west at government expense, and to settle them on the frontier. The place chosen to become **Indian Territory** was in present-day Oklahoma.

Not everyone favored Indian removal. For example, some religious groups strongly objected to uprooting people from their homes. Senator Theodore Frelinghuysen of New Jersey was also a critic of the seizure of Indian lands. "We have crowded the tribes upon a few miserable acres," he said, ". . . and still, like the horse-leech, our insatiated cupidity [unsatisfied greed] cries, give! give! give!" Despite such protests, in 1830 Congress passed the **Indian Removal Act**, providing money to carry out Jackson's policy.

Indian Removal Begins

The federal government first approached the Choctaw, who lived primarily in central Mississippi. In September 1830, government agents organized a conference at Dancing Rabbit Creek. Over 5,000 Choctaw attended. The agents distributed gifts, including cash bribes. They promised to provide the Choctaw with land in the West, free transportation, expense money for a year while they were settling in their new home, and annual grants to support the tribal government.

Any Choctaw who wished to remain in Mississippi would be given a plot of land. Agents warned, however, that failure to move could mean destruction of their society. The federal government would offer the Choctaw no protection against the state of Mississippi.

The Choctaw accepted removal in the **Treaty of Dancing Rabbit Creek** and then ceded their homeland—10.5 million acres—to the United States. "Friends, my attachment to my native land is strong—that cord is now broken," one Choctaw chief said. "We must go forth as wanderers in a strange land!"

Jackson was eager to have the removal carried out quickly. The move was badly managed, however. The first Choctaw group set out during the winter of 1831–32. That winter turned out to be bitterly cold, even in Mississippi and Arkansas. Many Choctaw died of exposure and starvation.

For later Choctaw parties, the journey was somewhat better. A Choctaw named Tushpa recalled his last days spent on the eastern side of the Mississippi River.

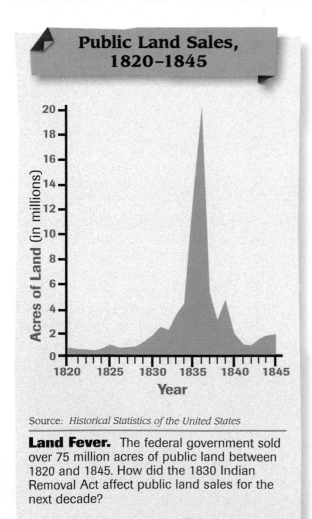

Public Land Sales, 1820–1845

Acres of Land (in millions)

Source: *Historical Statistics of the United States*

Land Fever. The federal government sold over 75 million acres of public land between 1820 and 1845. How did the 1830 Indian Removal Act affect public land sales for the next decade?

"The party put up some shelter and arranged temporary camps and prepared to stay on the banks of the river until they might

During his life Sequoyah excelled as a scholar, silver-smith, painter, and warrior. He is most noted, however, for developing the Cherokee alphabet and teaching thousands of Cherokee to read and write.

The Granger Collection, New York

cross it. On the second night of their stay a runner had announced that a fire had destroyed their former homes and everything that had been left in them, so that the last hope of remaining in this homeland was rudely snatched away. . . ."

In all, about 15,000 Choctaw settled in Indian Territory.

Resistance to Removal

The removal policy was applied to most Indians east of the Mississippi, including northern tribes. In 1832 a band of Sauk who earlier had moved to Iowa returned to Illinois under Chief Black Hawk. Army and state militia units were immediately dispatched to drive them back. The resulting Black Hawk War was short but very bloody. Black Hawk was soon captured, and his defeated followers were returned back across the Mississippi to Iowa.

More resistance to removal came from the southeastern

United States, where some 120,000 American Indians still lived. Resistance was greatest among the Cherokee and the Seminole.

Cherokee resistance. For centuries, the Cherokee had been farmers. They lived in houses grouped in small settlements or towns and worked fields owned by the entire community. Families were assigned specific plots to cultivate.

The Cherokee had adopted many elements of white culture. They had a written alphabet, a newspaper, and a constitution modeled on the U.S. Constitution. Like many white southerners, some Cherokee owned plantations and held slaves.

The Cherokee also maintained their own tribal government. Under a series of treaties with the United States, they were essentially a separate nation within the state of Georgia. It was not long, however, before Georgia authorities informed the Cherokee that they must either give up their government and submit to Georgia law or leave the state. If they refused they would be driven out by force.

Jackson believed the Cherokee should agree to move west because they were unwilling to give up their government. After all, he explained, every year thousands of Americans left family and friends "to seek new homes in distant regions." Jackson's comparison overlooked the fact that most of the settlers *wanted*

Woolaroc Museum, Bartlesville, Oklahoma

Jackson's Indian removal policy meant the dislocation of thousands of American Indians. Forced out of their homes and carrying what possessions they could, American Indians endured terrible conditions on the journey to Indian Territory.

to move west, and the Cherokee did not. Jackson also ignored the fact that the Indians' right to their lands was guaranteed by treaty.

The Cherokee took their battle to the courts. In the 1832 case of **Worcester v. Georgia**, the U.S. Supreme Court ruled in their favor. The Court declared that Georgia law did not extend to the Cherokee Nation. The Cherokee had won their case within the U.S. legal system!

President Jackson, however, did not accept the Supreme Court's ruling. He permitted Georgia, in effect, to nullify the Court's decree and use force against the Cherokee.

The Trail of Tears. In 1835, in the **Treaty of New Echota**, a small group of Cherokee leaders finally agreed to be resettled. This small group clearly did not represent a majority of the Cherokee people, but the U.S. Senate ratified the treaty by a single vote in May 1836. Chief John Ross presented the Cherokee's protest to Congress:

> **"Little did they anticipate that when taught to think and feel as the American citizen, and to have with him a common interest, they were to be despoiled by their guardian, to become strangers and wanderers in the land of their fathers."**

Two years later the Cherokee were driven from their homes by militia and were locked up in stockades. They were then marched 800 miles west through Tennessee and Arkansas to Indian Territory. Along the way, sick and tired people were left in the freezing cold to care for themselves with little or no food. Many did not survive the trip. Of the estimated 17,000 Cherokee who started the journey, about 4,000 died before they reached their destination. The Cherokee called this forced march the **Trail of Tears**.

Seminole resistance. Some Seminole Indians in Florida had also signed treaties agreeing to move west. When the majority of the Seminole refused to leave, however, the government sent in troops. The Seminole, led by Osceola, were experts at striking swiftly and then

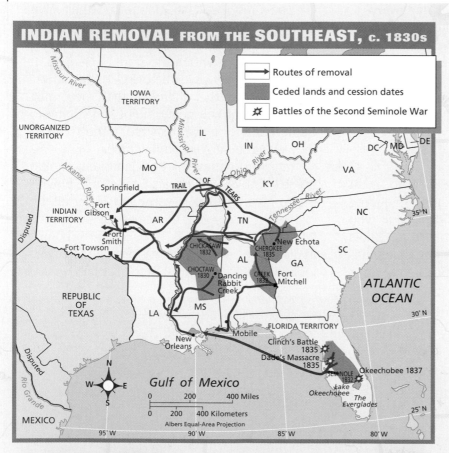

INDIAN REMOVAL FROM THE SOUTHEAST, c. 1830s

Routes of removal
Ceded lands and cession dates
Battles of the Second Seminole War

Learning from Maps.
American Indians crossed hundreds of miles and passed through several states on their forced relocation west under the Indian Removal Act.

• Maps

▶ **Location.** What states bordered Indian Territory?

melting away into swamps and thickets. For seven years they fought on, retreating deeper into the Everglades but never surrendering, despite their decreasing numbers.

By the time the second of two Seminole wars had come to an end in 1842, fewer than 3,000 Seminole had been sent to Indian Territory. Their resistance finally wore down the federal government, which had lost 1,500 regular army soldiers and $20 million trying to remove the Seminole.

The Seminole, however, were not a typical example of Indian Removal. In just over a decade, the government had resettled about 45,000 southern Indians. Removed tribes suffered heavy loss of lives, and few Indians remained north of Florida. For the time being, the survivors were free to go their own way.

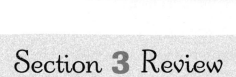

• **Osceola**

Under Osceola's leadership, the Seminole resisted removal. They continued to fight even after Osceola was captured at a peace conference. He died in an army prison in South Carolina in 1838.

The Granger Collection, New York

Section 3 Review

• **Glossary**

IDENTIFY and explain the significance of the following: Indian Territory, Indian Removal Act, Treaty of Dancing Rabbit Creek, *Worcester* v. *Georgia,* Treaty of New Echota, Trail of Tears, Osceola

REVIEWING FOR DETAILS

1. Why did white settlers support Indian removal?
2. How did Indians resist removal from their lands?

REVIEWING FOR UNDERSTANDING

• **Gazetteer**

3. **Geographic Literacy**   Where did the government relocate American Indians, and what hardships did Indians face getting there?

4. **Writing Mastery:** *Creating*   Write a short story, poem, or song that expresses how a Cherokee might have felt on the Trail of Tears.

5. **Critical Thinking:** *Generalizations and Stereotypes*   How did the attitudes of many whites toward American Indians affect the government's Indian policy?

Section 4

AN AGE OF REFORM

Multimedia Connections

Explore these related topics and materials on the CD–ROM to enrich your understanding of this section:

 Media Bank

- Shakers
- Ralph Waldo Emerson
- Hudson River School
- Seneca Falls Declaration
- Helping the Children
- Educating the Blind
- Social Reform
- Reform and Society

 Readings

- American Romantic Poets
- Reform and the Ideal World
- Women Seek Rights

 Profiles

- Emily Dickinson
- Mary Lyon
- Emma Willard

 Atlas

- Utopian Communities

 Biographies

- Ralph Waldo Emerson

 Simulation

- Reform: Making a Difference

R everend Thomas Low Nichols had been to several revivals. The crowded camps always seemed to bubble with excitement. After waking up to prayers, the camp would gather for a hearty breakfast, then more people would arrive and the camp meeting would begin. People became hysterical with joy, rolling on the ground or shouting prayers. A number of them were converted. Most would attempt to maintain the momentum and bring their spirit of reform back to their communities.

As you read this section you will find out:

▶ **What ministers preached in the Second Great Awakening.**

▶ **How Americans tried to reform society.**

▶ **Why women wanted more rights.**

The Second Great Awakening

In the 1790s a **Second Great Awakening** began in various parts of the nation. One of the most influential preachers of the Second Great Awakening was Charles Grandison Finney. He believed that **revivals**, or spirited religious meetings, were essential to spreading the word of God. Finney gave hundreds of sermons in the 1820s and 1830s. In his sermons he described a democratic heaven that seemed rather like the United States of America. "God always allows His children as much liberty as they are prepared to enjoy," Finney explained.

The revival movement swept through upstate New York, Kentucky, and Ohio with great force. People flocked to religious camp meetings, which often lasted for days.

Revival camps were full of emotion and energy as ministers preached to eager crowds.

● **Southern Camp Meetings**

Converts joined several Protestant groups, most notably Presbyterian, Baptist, and Methodist. Church attendance increased throughout the country.

The Second Great Awakening also advanced the cause of moral and social reform, which was a vital function of churches all over America. For example, many ministers outside the South became involved in the abolition movement.

Reforming Society

The hopeful spirit of the Second Great Awakening affected other movements around the country. Some New Englanders, for example, were attracted to **transcendentalism**, a philosophy that stressed an individual's ability to transcend, or rise above, material concerns, such as money or possessions. New England writers Ralph Waldo Emerson, Henry David Thoreau, and Margaret Fuller, and educator Bronson Alcott were important transcendental leaders. Americans also formed **utopian communities**, places where they tried to live out their vision of a perfect society.

● **American Romantics**

Most Americans were unwilling to live in isolated utopian communities and abandon many of the patterns of everyday life. They were, however, sincerely interested in improving society. Some devoted their energies to helping poor and disadvantaged people.

Through Others' Eyes

The Second Great Awakening

During the Second Great Awakening a young French visitor, Alexis de Tocqueville, toured the United States. He recorded his impressions of the country's religion in his book *Democracy in America*:

"It must never be forgotten that religion gave birth to Anglo-American society. In the United States, religion is therefore mingled with all the habits of the nation and all the feelings of patriotism, whence it derives a peculiar force. . . . Religious institutions have remained wholly distinct from political institutions, so that former laws have been easily changed whilst former belief has remained unshaken. Christianity has therefore retained a strong hold on the public mind in America. . . . Christian sects [groups] are infinitely diversified [spread out] and perpetually [continuously] modified; but Christianity itself is an established and irresistible fact."

Dorothea Dix dedicated her life to social reform.

● **Dorothea Dix**

Aiding the disadvantaged. Dorothea Dix, a Massachusetts schoolteacher and reformer, revolutionized the treatment of people who were mentally ill. One day in 1841 Dix taught a Sunday school class in a jail in Cambridge, Massachusetts. She discovered to her horror that mentally ill people were being kept there and treated like criminals. Dix spent months visiting prisons and then reported her findings to the Massachusetts legislature:

"I come to present the strong claims of suffering humanity . . . the miserable, the desolate [deserted], the outcast . . . to call your attention to the *present* state of insane persons confined . . . in *cages, closets, cellars, stalls, pens! Chained, naked, beaten with rods*, and *lashed into obedience*."

Thereafter, Dix worked hard to improve the care of prisoners and those who suffered from mental illness. She visited prisons all over the country and wrote reports describing conditions within them. Dix insisted that mental illness should not be treated as criminal behavior. Through her efforts, many states investigated the treatment of mentally ill persons and established facilities for their care.

Saving children. As cities grew larger, an increasing number of children and teenagers began to get into trouble with the law. Many orphans, runaways, and children who had been abandoned by their parents wandered homeless in the cities, sometimes begging and stealing to survive. When found, these children were often put into the local poorhouse along with adult debtors, drunkards, and tramps. Some people thought that a different approach should be taken with these children.

Reformers founded houses of refuge in New York, Boston, and Philadelphia. Life in these institutions was hard; discipline was strict. The children rose at dawn, and after passing inspection to make sure they were neat and clean, they had an hour or so of lessons. After breakfast, the rest of the day, except for the noon break, was spent working in shops. The boys made such things as cane chair seats, nails, and candles. The girls spent their time sewing. Evening classes went on until bedtime. Reformers hoped to change the behavior of delinquent children. They also wanted to make sure that the homeless ones were protected and taught a trade.

Attacking "Demon Rum." Still other reformers tried to get citizens to give up what they considered bad habits, such as drinking alcohol and gambling. **Temperance**, the effort to limit drinking, soon became a campaign to eliminate the consumption of alcohol. Other reformers supported the **prohibition**, or outlawing, of

The Granger Collection, New York

Reformers hoped that family life would be improved if adults signed the temperance pledge.

Students like these often found themselves taking exams under difficult conditions. One-room schoolhouses could be overcrowded and physically uncomfortable. Having students of a wide range of ages made it hard at times for teacher and student alike. Nonetheless, Americans took pride in their free public education and in the high literacy rate they achieved as a nation.

the manufacture and sale of alcoholic beverages. Many members of the American Temperance Society, which was founded in 1826, traveled around the country lecturing and distributing pamphlets promoting temperance. The campaign reached a high point in 1851 when the state of Maine outlawed the manufacture and sale of alcoholic beverages.

Educational Reforms

The fight for public education made a great deal of progress in the mid-1800s during the Age of Reform. Educational reformers argued that democracy could not prosper unless all citizens could read and write. Schools would train students to be patriotic, hardworking, and law-abiding citizens. Many Americans also supported public education because they hoped it would enable their children to succeed in the world.

Before 1839 there were no established qualifications for teachers. One man being interviewed for a job as a teacher in a mining town was asked only, "Do you retain a clear recollection of the twenty-six letters of the alphabet?" Apparently that was all the town expected him to know to "educate" the local children!

By modern standards even the best schools of the 1830s and 1840s were very uncomfortable. One-room "little red schoolhouses" were the rule. Students sat on narrow, backless benches. Sixty or more children of all ages were sometimes crowded into one classroom, and a single teacher had to deal with first graders and teenagers at the same time.

The effort to improve public education was particularly strong in Massachusetts. The Puritans had established public elementary schools in all but the smallest colonial towns, and the state built on this foundation. Thanks to Horace Mann, the first secretary of education for Massachusetts, by 1848 there were 50 well-equipped and comfortable public schools throughout the state.

The growth of public education had many far-reaching effects. By the 1860s villages, towns, and cities in other states had established free elementary schools, and most white adults in the United States could read and write. Education had become a public responsibility.

In the early 1800s, however, women had little hope of receiving much education beyond reading and writing. Free African Americans had even fewer opportunities. Many people believed that African Americans were intellectually inferior and that women could not stand the strain of studying such difficult subjects as chemistry and mathematics.

In 1833 Oberlin College in Ohio became the first college to admit women and African Americans. Four years later, Mary Lyon founded the first women's college, Mount Holyoke in Massachusetts. In 1847 the poet Emily Dickinson, then a teenager, described Mount Holyoke's high standards:

> "**Miss Lyon is raising her standard of scholarship a good deal, on account of the number of applicants this year and on account of that she makes the examinations more severe than usual. You cannot imagine how trying they are, because if we cannot go through them all in a specified time, we are sent home.**"

The Women's Rights Movement

Since the late 1700s many women had grown increasingly dissatisfied with the limitations society placed on their activities. During the 1830s and 1840s, increasing prosperity offered middle- and upper-class women more time to pursue activities outside the home. Many of

The Granger Collection, New York

Horace Mann spent his life calling for education reform—both in public schools and in teaching practices.

• **Horace Mann**

them became involved in reform movements and began to call for more rights for women.

Women and abolition. Many women became reformers and were particularly interested in the abolition movement. Women such as former slave Sojourner Truth were able to move audiences with their powerful speeches opposing slavery. When women became abolitionists, their activism often raised an awareness of their own limited rights. Female abolitionists frequently found themselves forced into secondary roles. For example, many women who tried to speak in public against slavery were prevented from doing so by male abolitionists.

Both Sarah and Angelina Grimké experienced so much resistance when they made speeches attacking slavery that they became activists for women's rights as well. Angelina Grimké wrote that "the investigation of the rights of the slave has led me to a better understanding of my own [rights]."

One argument abolitionists used against slavery was the statement in the Declaration of Independence that "all men are created equal." Supporters of women's rights argued that if slaves were entitled to equality, surely women were too. Women were still treated as second-class citizens, however. They did not have such civil rights as voting or sitting on juries. Most married women had little or no control over their own property.

The Seneca Falls Convention. Another abolitionist, Elizabeth Cady Stanton, became a women's rights leader after she was not allowed to participate in an antislavery conference in 1840. Eight years later, Stanton and Lucretia Mott organized the first American women's rights convention at Seneca Falls, New York.

In their Declaration of Sentiments at the **Seneca Falls Convention**, the delegates echoed the Declaration of Independence. Just as it had listed complaints of the colonists, the Declaration of Sentiments contained a list of women's grievances. "The history of mankind," the declaration said, "is a history of repeated injuries . . . on the part of man toward woman." These included denials of the right to vote, the right to equal educational opportunity, and the right of married women to own property. The Declaration of Sentiments also demanded that women receive "all the rights and privileges which belong to them as citizens of the United States."

In the 1850s several national women's rights conventions took place. Women were fighting for change. Susan B. Anthony organized campaigns on behalf of equal pay for female teachers and for equal property rights for women. Addressing a women's rights convention in 1855,

Lucy Stone described the inspiration for her hard work.

"In education, in marriage, in religion, in everything, disappointment is the lot of woman. It shall be the business of my life to deepen this disappointment in every woman's heart until she bows down to it no longer."

Some states began to grant women more legal rights. In 1860 New York gave women the right to sue in court and to control their earnings and property. The women's rights campaigners had achieved some of their goals, but women were unable to gain the right to vote.

Elizabeth Cady Stanton (left) and Susan B. Anthony (right) were tireless in their pursuit of women's rights.

● **Women in Jacksonian American**

Section 4 Review

● **Glossary**

IDENTIFY and explain the significance of the following: Second Great Awakening, Charles Grandison Finney, revivals, transcendentalism, utopian communities, Dorothea Dix, temperance, prohibition, Horace Mann, Mary Lyon, Elizabeth Cady Stanton, Lucretia Mott, Seneca Falls Convention, Susan B. Anthony

● **Time Line**

REVIEWING FOR DETAILS
1. What ideas did preachers express during the Second Great Awakening?
2. How did Americans try to reform society?
3. Why did women campaign for more rights?

REVIEWING FOR UNDERSTANDING
4. **Writing Mastery:** *Expressing* Write a short essay expressing the benefits of a public education system.
5. **Critical Thinking:** *Drawing Conclusions* How might working for movements such as abolition or educational reform have encouraged women to demand greater rights for themselves?

CHAPTER **12**

Americans Expand West (1820–1860)

THEMES IN AMERICAN HISTORY

Geographic Diversity:
How might natural resources stimulate the development of a region?

Cultural Diversity:
How might a people's culture reflect the particular region in which they live?

Global Relations:
In what ways might national expansion affect foreign relations?

● **Video Opener**

● **Skill Builder**

*I*n the United States, thousands of men and women of all ages took editor Horace Greeley's advice to "fly, scatter through the country, go to the Great West." The American West was not an empty land waiting to be settled, however. American Indians had lived there for centuries, and Mexicans had migrated north to the Southwest and California.

image above: *Thomas Moran's* Grand Canyon of the Yellowstone

Section 1

AMERICANS IN TEXAS

Multimedia Connections

Explore these related topics and materials on the CD–ROM to enrich your understanding of this section:

 Atlas

- Settlements in Texas, 1850

 Biographies

- Antonio López de Santa Anna

 Media Bank

- Sam Houston, Texas Hero
- Lorenzo de Zavala
- Comanche on Horseback
- Mexican Fandango
- Life in Northern Mexico
- Austin, Republic of Texas
- Texas, 1822–1845

 Profiles

- Stephen F. Austin
- Sam Houston

 Readings

- Comanche Kidnapping
- Texas

F ather Miguel Hidalgo y Costilla reached for the church bells and pulled the rope. Would history remember the bells that rang for independence on September 16, 1810? For it was on this day in the small village of Dolores, Mexico, that Hidalgo summoned Mexicans to throw off Spanish rule, embrace racial equality, and redistribute the land. Thousands of Mexicans answered this *Grito de Dolores* (Cry of Dolores), which signaled the beginning of Mexico's revolt against Spain.

As you read this section you will find out:

▶ **How Mexico treated settlers from the United States.**

▶ **Why Texans wanted independence from Mexico.**

▶ **How Texas won its independence.**

Mexican Texas

Mexico finally won its independence from Spain in 1821. The new country's territory included present-day Mexico and what today are the states of Texas, New Mexico, Arizona, California, Nevada, Utah, and portions of Colorado, Wyoming, Oklahoma, and Kansas.

The struggle for independence had taken its toll on Texas, which was inhabited mainly by Indians and **Tejanos** (tay-HAH-nohs), Texans of Mexican descent. Settlements in east Texas had been destroyed, and the region had lost almost two thirds of its Tejano population. Only about 3,000 Tejanos remained. They lived mainly on sprawling cattle ranches or in old mission towns like San Antonio.

The Mexican government hoped to rebuild Texas's population and settlements by attracting colonists from Europe and the United

States. The newcomers would become loyal citizens and would also help Mexico's economy, which was burdened by a heavy war debt and the loss of Spanish investment.

● **New Spain and Mexico**

Texas Opens to Americans

Before the Mexican Revolution, a few U.S. citizens had begun to trickle into Texas. Among them was Moses Austin of Missouri, who expected to acquire a fortune by establishing a colony of 300 American families in Texas.

Spain had given Austin a land grant, but he died of pneumonia before he could organize a group. On his deathbed, Austin asked his son Stephen to carry out his dream of establishing a colony in Texas.

In 1821 Stephen F. Austin and a group of 300 families, later known as the "Old Three Hundred," arrived in Texas. Before they could establish their settlement, Austin had to renew his father's land grant with the new Mexican government.

Austin therefore became an ***empresario***— someone who made a business of bringing in settlers. Each *empresario* received thousands of acres of land for bringing families into Texas. Each family also received a grant of land. American settlers began to pour into Texas to take advantage of this offer. Most new colonists were southerners interested in growing cotton. They often brought slaves to work their land.

Austin became a citizen of Mexico, as required by the government, and was the political leader of the American settlement in Texas. He was unsuccessful, however, in persuading other American settlers to be loyal to Mexico. Furthermore, few bothered to learn Spanish or to adapt to Mexican culture. By 1830 some 20,000 Americans had settled in Texas, outnumbering Tejanos by about five to one. Most of these colonists were beginning to feel that Texas should be *their* country, rather than part of Mexico. Others felt that their ties were to the United States.

THE TEXAS WAR FOR INDEPENDENCE, 1835–1836

Claimed by United States, Texas, and Mexico

INDIAN TERRITORY

ARKANSAS (1836)

Red River

UNITED STATES

DISPUTED TERRITORY

Sabine River

REPUBLIC OF TEXAS (1836)

LA

Colorado River

Pecos River

Brazos River

The Alamo February–March 1836

HOUSTON

San Antonio

AUSTIN'S COLONY

San Jacinto April 1836

SANTA ANNA

Goliad March 1836

28°N

Nueces River

URREA

Gulf of Mexico

→ Texan army

✦ Texan victory

→ Mexican army

✦ Mexican victory

Rio Grande

MEXICO

N W E S

26°N

0   150   300 Miles
0   150   300 Kilometers
Albers Equal-Area Projection

96°W   94°W

Learning from Maps.

The Texans won their independence from Mexico, but the Republic's border remained in dispute. Mexico considered the Nueces River to be Texas's southern boundary.

● **Maps**

▶ **Location.** How far did the Texans claim that their southern border extended?

Stephen F. Austin obtained a large land grant to establish a colony in Texas. He became a Mexican citizen, but his loyalty to Mexico was soon tested.

These developments troubled the Mexican government. One official, General Manuel Mier y Terán, warned:

> **"The department of Texas is contiguous to [borders] the most avid [greedy] nation in the world. The North Americans have conquered whatever territory adjoins them. They incite [encourage] uprising in the territory in question."**

Concerned about the situation in Texas, Mexico decided to reverse its policy and prohibited further immigration from the United States. This restriction, along with a ban on importing slaves, angered most American colonists and even many Tejanos.

Texas Gains Independence

These Texans disliked the national government in Mexico City. Most believed in the Mexican constitution of 1824, which gave the Mexican states a great deal of local control. After a new, strongly centralized Mexican government took control in the early 1830s, Mexican officials began to take away the powers guaranteed to states in the constitution. This angered the residents of Texas, who did not want people in a faraway capital to run their lives. They wanted more local power over such issues as the right to hold slaves.

Government leaders in Mexico City resented the Texans' attitude. When Austin went to Mexico City to explain the Texans' position, he was thrown in jail and held for a year without trial.

The fight for the Alamo. Finally, in 1835, Texans revolted. The Mexican government quickly reacted. President Antonio López de Santa Anna marched northward at the head of an army of 6,000 troops to put down the rebellion. In February 1836 he captured San Antonio. However, 187 rebels and about 30 townspeople retreated into the **Alamo**, an old Spanish mission that had been converted to a fort. They refused to surrender despite the overwhelming odds. In a letter addressed "To the People of Texas & all Americans in the world," rebel leader William Travis vowed "Victory or Death!"

> **"I shall never surrender or retreat. . . . I call on you in the name of Liberty, of patriotism & everything dear to the American character, to come to our aid. . . . If this call is neglected, I am determined to sustain myself as long as possible & die like a soldier who never forgets what is due to his own honor & that of his country."**

The defenders of the Alamo fought off attacks by the Mexican army for nearly two weeks, but eventually Santa Anna's troops successfully stormed the walls. Suzanna Dickenson (above) was one of the few survivors of the Battle of the Alamo.

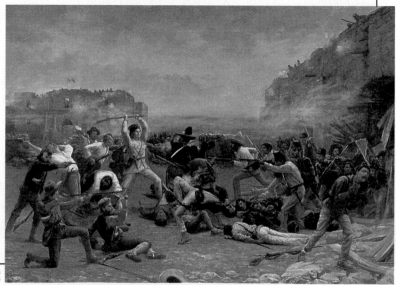

Fall of the Alamo by Robert Jenkins Onderdonk, Courtesy of Friends of the Governor's Mansion, Austin, Texas

After nearly two weeks of repeated attacks, Santa Anna's army finally overran the Alamo. Every one of its defenders died—only the lives of civilians were spared. The victory cost Santa Anna some 1,500 casualties.

Among the Alamo's dead were Davy Crockett, a colorful frontier character who had represented Tennessee in Congress, and James Bowie, for whom the Bowie knife is named. The battle set Francisco Esparza, who attacked the Alamo, against his brother, Gregorio, who died defending it. Other Tejano families were similarly divided in the conflict.

After the Alamo, another Mexican army captured the town of Goliad. However, the fighting spirit of the rebels was unbroken, particularly after they learned that Santa Anna had ordered the execution of 371 Texans captured at Goliad.

Victory at San Jacinto. On March 2, 1836, the Texans had declared independence. They set up a temporary government for their **Republic of Texas** and appointed Sam Houston commander of its army. For a time Houston retreated east-ward. Then, on April 21, 1836, he turned and attacked Santa Anna's pursuing army.

Houston had only about 800 soldiers, Santa Anna about 1,400. "Forward!" Houston shouted. The Texans rushed into the Mexican camp, the battle cry "Remember the Alamo! Remember Goliad!" on their lips. Under the Texans' fierce attack, the Mexicans fell back in disorder and were soon defeated.

Houston's victory was total. "The fierce vengeance of the Texans could not be resisted," he later explained. In less than 20 minutes more than 600 Mexicans were killed. This short **Battle of San Jacinto** had determined who would win the war. After the battle, Santa Anna was captured. Houston set Santa Anna free in exchange for his promise to grant Texas its independence. When the war ended, the Texans set up a permanent government, electing Houston, a former governor of Tennessee, president and Lorenzo de Zavala, who had served in the Mexican congress, vice president.

The Granger Collection, New York

President Antonio López de Santa Anna led the troops that came to put down the rebellion in Texas.

Section 2
THE FAR WEST

Multimedia Connections

Explore these related topics and materials on the CD–ROM to enrich your understanding of this section:

 Gazetteer

- Oregon Country

 Atlas

- Oregon Country

 Media Bank

- Oregon Settlers
- Trailblazer

 Profiles

- Marcus Whitman
- George Caleb Bingham
- George Catlin

 Interactive Map

- Mission to Metropolis

 Readings

- Two Years Before the Mast
- Settling the Northwest

Many pioneer women were eager to head west. The wagons had to be hitched and the supplies loaded, then the wagon train could get rolling and the adventure would begin. On the trail, some lost their eagerness. Lodisa Frizzel wrote:

> **"That this journey is . . . perilous [dangerous], the deaths of many will testify . . . and often as I passed the freshly made graves, I have glanced at the side boards of the wagon, not knowing how soon it might serve as the coffin for some one of us."**

As you read this section you will find out:
▶ **Why Americans went west.**
▶ **What life on the trail was like.**
▶ **How manifest destiny affected American migration.**

The Fur Trade

While some Americans were heading south to Texas, others were going west. Most of the westward-bound pioneers were involved in the fur trade. The American Fur Company, begun by John Jacob Astor, a German immigrant, controlled most of the western fur trade by the 1820s. Other fur traders built a thriving trade based in St. Louis.

Companies hired rugged **mountain men** to roam the Rocky Mountains and trap beaver and other animals. The life of a mountain man was full of hardships, and only a few got rich. The harsh climate and rugged terrain made the job risky. Trapper James Clyman reported:

> **"I think few men had stronger ideas of their bravery and disregard of fear than I had but . . . to be shot at from behind a**

This 1841 drawing shows trappers and American Indians meeting outside Fort Walla Walla in Oregon Territory. They are probably trading furs for manufactured goods from the East.

picketed Indian village was more than I had contracted for and somewhat cooled my courage."

Trapping was solitary work in remote areas far from white settlements. During the fall and spring, mountain men set and checked their traps. In July or August, they met at a **rendezvous**, a yearly gathering where they sold their furs, exchanged stories, and had a rollicking good time. In the winter, mountain men often lived with friendly American Indians who showed them how to survive and trap in the wilderness.

Beaver pelts, which were extremely popular in Europe, brought the best prices for the fur trappers. After the beaver had been trapped out of one area, the mountain men moved on. Eventually, there was no new trapping land to move on to because the beaver population was nearly extinct from over trapping. Beaver also became less fashionable in Europe. By around the 1840s, the fur trade had collapsed. But the mountain men's role in the West was not over. As one St. Louis newspaper pointed out, some trapping expeditions had clearly demonstrated "that overland expeditions in large bodies [groups] may be made to that remote region [the Far West]."

Trappers had followed Indian trails or cut new ones through the mountains. These paths were later used by westward-bound settlers who hired mountain men to guide them through the wilderness.

Settling Oregon

West of the Rocky Mountains lay Oregon Country, with its magnificent forests, fertile valleys, and rivers full of fish. Oregon, as it was commonly called in the early 1800s, stretched northward from California to the present southern boundary of Alaska. Spain, Russia, Great Britain, and the United States all claimed the region until Spain gave up its claim in 1819, and Russia withdrew in 1825. By this time the United States and Britain had agreed to joint occupation of the region.

Oregon fever.   The first U.S. settlers to move to Oregon were a few missionaries who arrived in the Willamette Valley in the 1830s. Among the first to make the six-month journey was Jason Lee, a Methodist minister sent to preach to American

• **Narcissa Whitman**

Narcissa Prentiss Whitman was one of the first white settlers in Oregon. She, along with her husband, was massacred by Cayuse Indians.

Indians. Two years later Marcus and Narcissa Whitman and another missionary couple arrived in Oregon.

These missionaries had little success in converting local Indians to Christianity. They were successful, however, in attracting more easterners, particularly farmers, to the area. By 1840 some 120 farms could be found in the Willamette Valley.

From such small beginnings came a mass movement westward. All over the eastern states, people caught what they called "Oregon fever." They gathered in groups in western Missouri to make the 2,000-mile trip over the **Oregon Trail**.

This trail followed the Platte River to Fort Laramie, a fur-trading post in present-day Wyoming, and then crossed the Rockies by way of South Pass before descending to Oregon along the Snake and Columbia Rivers.

Marcus Whitman, who had returned east on church business, led one of the first big groups of pioneers. Nearly 1,000 people set out in the spring of 1843. They rode in 120 canvas-covered wagons pulled by oxen and were accompanied by several thousand farm animals and a small army of pet dogs.

This large group was essentially a community on wheels. Because the journey was full of dangers and hardship, the caravan was ruled like an army. It had an elected council to settle disputes. A guide chose the route and decided where and when to stop for food and

Hudson River school painter Albert Bierstadt captured the West's landscape in such paintings *as this* Emigrants Crossing the Plains.

rest. A bugler summoned everyone to rise at dawn and begin the long day's journey. Each night the pioneers arranged the wagons in a great circle—in part out of fear of an attack from the American Indians whose lands the settlers crossed.

The group traveled 10 to 15 miles on an average day. Getting the entire company across a river could take as long as five days, for there were no ferries or bridges along the way. Nevertheless, progress was steady. In late November, 1843, the caravan reached the Willamette Valley safely.

Life on the trail. Over the next few years, many more settlers made the trip west. So

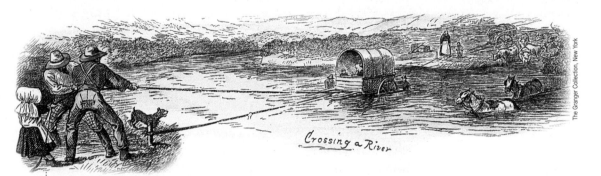

Pioneers on the Oregon Trail faced many hardships. Crossing a river was dangerous and time-consuming.

Young People In History

On the Trail

About 40,000 children—one out of every five pioneers—made the trek across the country to the Far West. These pioneer children showed great courage and responsibility. Teenagers shared chores with adults. They herded livestock, collected fuel and food, and stood guard at night. Those who lost parents often had to care for younger family members. The journey was not all hard work, however. For many children it was also a great adventure. They met Indians, made new friends, and traveled through dramatic countryside. One young pioneer even kept an antelope, Jennie, as a pet. Many who finally reached the Far West shared the same emotions that Elizabeth Keegan expressed:

Children rode on ponies and in wagons on the trek west.

> *"the feeling of those who have come that wearisome journey, the joy they feel at once more beholding and mingling with their fellow creatures."*

wagon wheel or other gear could cause serious problems for travelers. Groups heading west also had to pay careful attention to the weather. Heavy rains or snow could leave pioneers stranded for months at a time. In 1846, for example, heavy snows stranded a group of pioneers known as the Donner party in the Sierra Nevada Mountains. Members of the group were able to survive only by resorting to cannibalism.

Making the trip west required back-breaking labor. Men, women, and children all shared in the work. The men drove the wagons, herded the cattle, and scouted for Indians. Women did the cooking and washing, hauled water, and usually helped load and unload the wagons. Martha Ann Morrison, a girl of 13, remembered:

> **"The women helped pitch the tents, helped unload, and helped yoking up the cattle. . . . Many times the men were off [away from camp]. One time my father was away hunting cattle driven off by the Indians, and that left Mother and the children to attend to everything."**

In addition to the physical hardships, many pioneers also suffered emotionally from leaving friends and family behind. Elizabeth Goltra sadly noted, "I am leaving my home, my early friends and associates never to see them again." Despite these challenges, thousands of pioneers made the trip west. The ruts worn by their wagon wheels can still be seen today.

California

Not everyone on the trail was going to Oregon. Others were making their way to the Mexican province of California. From the late 1700s, American ships had sailed around South America to the California coast. Americans

long as they stayed healthy, most pioneers saw the trip as a great adventure. The trek was long, tiring, and hazardous, however. Along the way many died—most from disease, a few from Indian attacks. Settlers feared American Indians, even though they traded with them for food and information. In reality, however, few Indians attacked wagon trains.

Pioneers heading west faced many other dangers. Without the proper tools, a broken traded with the **Californios**—settlers from Mexico and their descendants—exchanging American manufactured goods for cattle hides and furs.

Few Americans intended to settle in California. Most came only to trade. One of the first such traders was John A. Sutter. Sutter had immigrated to America from Switzerland in 1834 and eventually made his way to Oregon. He then sailed to the Hawaiian Islands. From there he sailed to Alaska and finally to San Francisco.

In 1839 Sutter persuaded the Mexican governor of California to grant him a large tract of land at the junction of the American and Sacramento Rivers. He gradually built a home and a fort, which came to be called **Sutter's Fort**. The entire place was surrounded by a thick wall 18 feet high topped with cannons for protection against Indian attacks.

Sutter, like most of the Americans in California, was a merchant. His fort had an excellent location on the **California Trail**, which branched off south from the Oregon Trail. The fort attracted weary pioneers the way a magnet attracts iron.

After Mexico became independent, some Americans also traded overland following a 780-mile-long route called the **Santa Fe Trail**. This trail ran from Missouri to Santa Fe, in present-day New Mexico. A 19-year-old newlywed, Susan Shelby Magoffin, described the hardships of the trail that she and her husband, a trader, encountered:

> **"Now, about dark, we came into the mosquito regions. . . . Millions upon millions were swarming around me, and their knocking against the carriage *reminded me of a hard rain*. It was equal to any of the plagues of Egypt. I lay almost in a perfect stupor [daze], the heat and stings made me perfectly sick."**

Manifest Destiny

For 200 years moving west had seemed like climbing up a steep hill—slow and difficult work. The pioneers of the 1840s, like the mountain men who had traveled before them, had to cross rugged and dangerous country. Vast prairies, high mountains, and barren deserts lay in their path. Neither the Great Plains nor the Rocky Mountains could stop the determined pioneers, however. One enthusiastic speaker referred to the towering Rockies as "mere molehills."

Americans rushed westward eagerly, excited by the possibility that the entire continent could be theirs! One newspaper editor, John L. O'Sullivan, used the phrase **manifest destiny** to describe this nationwide feeling.

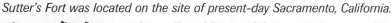

Sutter's Fort was located on the site of present-day Sacramento, California.

The Granger Collection, New York

Detail from National Museum of American Art, Washington, DC/Art Resource, NY

Emanuel Gottlieb Leutze's Westward the Course of Empire Takes its Way *shows Americans' feeling of manifest destiny in the mid-1800s. The scout points the way west for the eager settlers.*

Manifest destiny was the popular belief that the United States was destined to expand across the North American continent to the Pacific Ocean, and possibly even beyond. O'Sullivan explained that the nation was:

> **"to overspread and to possess the whole of the continent which Providence [fate] has given us for the development of the great experiment of liberty and . . . self-government."**

Many Americans agreed with O'Sullivan. Like the U.S. settlers in Texas, the Oregon and California pioneers mostly ignored the fact that they were going to areas not then part of the United States. Those who believed in manifest destiny also gave little thought to the fact that the West was not empty land but was a region alive with cultures that had existed for centuries. On the Oregon Trail people sang:

> **"The hip-hurrah for the prairie life!**
> **Hip-hurrah for the mountain strife!**
> **And if rifles must crack, if swords**
> ** we must draw,**
> **Our country forever, hurrah, hurrah!"**

Section 2 Review

IDENTIFY and explain the significance of the following: John Jacob Astor, mountain men, rendezvous, Marcus and Narcissa Whitman, Oregon Trail, Californios, Sutter's Fort, California Trail, Santa Fe Trail, manifest destiny

• **Glossary**

REVIEWING FOR DETAILS

1. Why did many Americans head west?
2. How did the idea of manifest destiny affect American migration westward?

REVIEWING FOR UNDERSTANDING

• **Gazetteer**

3. **Geographic Literacy** How would you describe life on the trail west?
4. **Writing Mastery:** *Creating* Imagine that you are a former mountain man. Create an advertisement to drum up business for your new job as a trail guide.
5. **Critical Thinking:** *Synthesizing Information* What supplies do you think someone heading west might need? Why would they need these items?

Section 3
WAR WITH MEXICO

Multimedia Connections

Explore these related topics and materials on the CD–ROM to enrich your understanding of this section:

 Profiles

- John Tyler
- Zachary Taylor
- Winfield Scott
- John Frémont

 Media Bank

- Texas Admitted to the Union
- Bear Flag Revolt
- Music of the Southwest
- Zachary Taylor and Officers

 Readings

- Course of Empire
- Opposition to the Mexican War

n the sleepy town of Sonoma, California, rebellion stirred. A pounding at the door awoke the household. The servant who went to investigate the racket found 30 armed men at the door. They demanded to see Commandante Vallejo, the local top-ranking Mexican official. Doña Francisca Vallejo turned to her husband and begged him to escape, but he refused. They arrested him and put him in jail. Vallejo suffered greatly while in custody: "I left Sacramento half dead, and arrived here [Sonoma] almost without life."

As you read this section you will find out:

▶ **What events led to war with Mexico.**

▶ **What course the fighting took during the war.**

▶ **What consequences the war had.**

Expanding the Nation's Boundaries

In the 1840s westward expansion was both a unifying and a dividing force. Many Americans believed in expanding the nation's boundaries, but each section of the country wanted a different region. Southerners had little interest in Oregon. They wanted Texas, and some even hoped to **annex**, or take control of, Cuba and parts of Central America to expand slave territory even farther. Many northerners were strongly opposed to adding Texas to the Union because that would mean opening more territory to slavery.

This was the situation when James K. Polk was elected president in late 1844. Polk, a Democrat, had promised to bring Texas and Oregon under U.S. control. In December 1845 Texas became a state. Once he took office,

Polk began diplomatic negotiations with the British about Oregon. Polk's Democratic supporters made it clear that if Great Britain did not agree to a satisfactory settlement, they were ready to take the territory by force.

In 1846, after considerable discussion, the negotiators reached a compromise. Oregon was divided by extending the existing boundary along the 49th parallel between the United States and Canada to the West Coast.

Polk also hoped to obtain New Mexico and California. However, he could not claim, as he did with Texas and Oregon, that the lands were already peopled by U.S. citizens. By 1846 there were still very few Americans living in New Mexico or California. Polk would have to find a different way to bring those territories under the control of the United States.

The Mexican War

Although Mexico had not been able to prevent Texas from gaining independence, it had never accepted the Texans' claim to land all the way to the Rio Grande, the "Great River." Mexican officials insisted that Texas extended only to the Nueces, a river farther north and east.

After Texas became part of the United States, Polk sent troops under the command of General Zachary Taylor south of the Nueces River. Then he sent a diplomat named John Slidell to Mexico City to discuss the border dispute. Polk had instructed Slidell to offer Mexico $25 million for both New Mexico and California, as well as for recognition of the United States's border claims to the Rio Grande. Mexican leaders became angry and refused to discuss the boundary issue or even acknowledge that Texas was now part of the United States.

Polk announces war. In January of 1846 President Polk ordered General Taylor to advance to the Rio Grande. Shortly after Taylor did so, a Mexican force attacked one of his

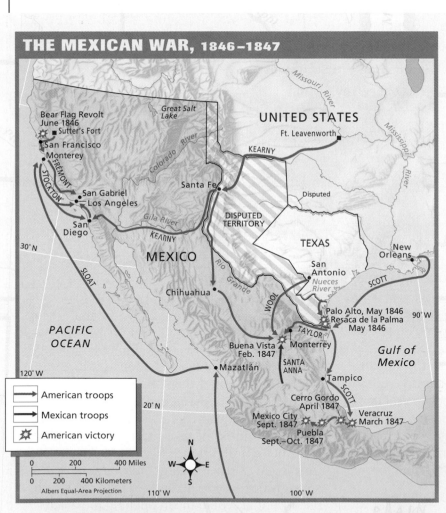

THE MEXICAN WAR, 1846–1847

American troops
Mexican troops
American victory

0   200   400 Miles
0   200   400 Kilometers
Albers Equal-Area Projection

Learning from Maps.
The U.S. troops concentrated on taking the California coast and the major cites on the way to Mexico City.

▶ **Location.** Looking at the map, in which cities south of the Rio Grande were battles fought?

• **Maps**

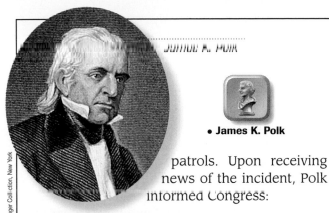

James K. Polk

● **James K. Polk**

patrols. Upon receiving news of the incident, Polk informed Congress:

> **"After reiterated [repeated] menaces [threats], Mexico has passed the boundary of the United States, has invaded our territory and shed American blood upon the American soil. . . . War exists."**

Meanwhile, on May 8 and 9, 1846, in the battles at Palo Alto and Resaca de la Palma, Taylor's troops had driven the Mexican army across the Rio Grande. Later, in the summer, General Stephen Kearny captured Santa Fe, winning control of New Mexico. Kearny's force pushed on to southern California, where it combined with a force under Robert Stockton. This force then captured San Diego, San Gabriel, and Los Angeles.

In northern California, explorer John C. Frémont and his party had joined residents of the area around Sutter's Fort to defeat the local Mexican forces. Then they designed a flag—a grizzly bear over a plain background—and declared the Republic of California. This incident became known as the **Bear Flag Revolt**.

The capture of Mexico City. In February 1847 General Taylor won a major victory over the Mexican forces at Buena Vista. After the battle, much of Mexican territory north of Mexico City was controlled by American troops. These vic-

tories contributed to General Taylor's reputation as a hero, but they created a political problem for Polk.

Taylor was a plain, unassuming soldier; his troops affectionately called him "Old Rough and Ready." Polk was afraid that Taylor might run for president on the Whig Party ticket in 1848. Polk did not plan to seek a second term, but as a loyal Democrat, he did not want Taylor to gain too much political advantage from any battlefield successes.

The president therefore put General Winfield Scott in command of the final campaign of the war to capture Mexico City. Scott lacked Taylor's easy-going style. Behind his back Scott's troops called him "Old Fuss and Feathers." Even though Scott was also a Whig, Polk thought he was less of a threat to the Democratic Party than Taylor.

Scott was an excellent general. In March 1847 he ordered 10,000 troops ashore near Veracruz on Mexico's east coast. They captured the city and then marched inland, following the same route that Hernán Cortés had taken in the 1500s. Scott's troops won an important battle at Cerro Gordo and captured the town of Puebla. By September they were at the outskirts of Mexico City.

The battle for Mexico City was brutal. The U.S. soldiers were vastly outnumbered. The Mexicans suffered much higher losses during the battle, however, and Scott's troops were victorious. The Mexicans soon asked for peace.

When General Scott captured Veracruz, he took control of one of Mexico's most important port cities.

National Portrait Gallery, Smithsonian Institution, Washington, DC/Art Resource, NY

The transcendentalist Henry David Thoreau was a critic of the Mexican War. He was imprisoned after he refused to pay his taxes in protest of U.S. actions.

The Treaty of Guadalupe Hidalgo

President Polk had assigned Nicholas P. Trist, a State Department official, to negotiate a peace treaty once Mexico had been defeated. He authorized Trist to offer to buy California and the rest of the Southwest from Mexico. Trist proved to be an excellent negotiator. The negotiations took a great deal of time, however, and Polk became impatient. Officials close to Polk advised him to demand even more territory. In his haste, Polk sent Trist a message ordering him to break off the peace negotiations with Mexico.

Trist ignored the order. He persuaded the Mexicans to cede California, Nevada, and Utah as well as parts of Arizona, New Mexico, Colorado, and Wyoming for a little more than $15 million. This huge U.S. gain of territory became known as the **Mexican Cession**. Trist completed the negotiations with the Mexican government and sent the resulting **Treaty of Guadalupe Hidalgo** back to Polk in the United States. Furious, Polk had Trist fired from his State Department job and refused to pay him for the time he had spent in Mexico.

Nevertheless, Polk had to accept the treaty. The terms, after all, were better than he had hoped for, and the war had become extremely unpopular in some parts of the country. Many people felt that a minor boundary dispute was no reason for seizing so much Mexican territory. Adding more territory where slavery might be established was another concern in the North. Polk therefore swallowed his anger and submitted the treaty to the Senate, which ratified it after heated debate.

Just a few years later, in 1853, the United States completed its territorial expansion in the Southwest when American diplomat James Gadsden negotiated the **Gadsden Purchase** with Mexico. For $10 million, the purchase added a strip of Mexican land to southern New Mexico and Arizona.

A Blending of Cultures

After the Mexican War, more and more Americans moved into the Southwest and the West. They brought their own language, laws, and ways of behaving. The cultural differences between the Americans and the Mexican Americans already in the region created problems, however.

Before the war, about 75,000 Mexicans and more than 250,000 American Indians lived in the Southwest and California. Under the Treaty of Guadalupe Hidalgo, these Mexicans received all the rights of American citizens. However, many Mexican Americans

American Indians and the Spanish worked and lived in missions like San Diego de Alcala.

The Granger Collection, New York

American Letters

The Squatter and the Don
María Amparo Ruiz de Burton

In 1880 María Amparo Ruiz de Burton began writing the novel The Squatter and the Don. *Born in 1832 to a prominent Californio family, she was well positioned to write about the Californios and their struggle to protect their land against American squatters. In the novel Doña Josefa asks, "Is it possible that there is no law to protect us; . . . is there no hope?" Her husband's response highlights the plight of the Californios.*

María Amparo Ruiz de Burton published her novel under the name "C. Loyal," meaning Ciudadano Leal, or Loyal Citizen. This name had been a way of signing official correspondence in Mexico.

Courtesy The Bancroft Library

"I remember," calmly said Don Mariano, "that when I first read the text of the treaty of Guadalupe Hidalgo, I felt a bitter resentment against my people; against Mexico, the mother country, who abandoned us—her children—with so slight a provision of obligatory stipulations [necessary requirements] for protection. But afterwards, upon mature reflection, I saw that Mexico did as much as could have been reasonably expected at the time. In the very preamble of the treaty the spirit of peace and friendship, which animated both nations, was carefully made manifest [clear]. That spirit was to be the *foundation* of the relations between the conqueror and conquered. How could Mexico have foreseen then that when scarcely half a dozen years should have elapsed the trusted conquerors would, '*In Congress Assembled*,' pass laws which were to be retroactive upon [taking away privileges already granted to] the defenseless, helpless, conquered people, in order to despoil [ruin] them? The treaty said that our rights would be the same as those enjoyed by all other American citizens. But, you see, Congress takes very good care not to enact retroactive laws for Americans; laws to take away from American citizens the property which they hold now, already, with a recognized legal title. No, indeed. But they do so quickly enough with

us—with us, the Spano-Americans, who were to enjoy equal rights, mind you, according to the treaty of peace. This is what seems to me a breach [breaking] of faith, which Mexico could neither presuppose [expect] nor prevent." . . .

[Don Mariano:] "We have had no one to speak for us. By the treaty of Guadalupe Hidalgo the American nation pledged its honor to respect our land titles just the same as Mexico would have done. Unfortunately, however, the discovery of gold brought to California the riff-raff of the world, and with it a horde [group] of land-sharks, all possessing the privilege of voting, and most of them coveting [wanting] our lands, for which they very quickly began to clamor [shout]. There was, and still is, plenty of good government land, which any one can take. But no. The forbidden fruit is the sweetest. They do not want government land. They want the land of the Spanish people, because we 'have too much,' they say. So, to win their votes, the votes of the squatters, our representatives in Congress helped to pass laws declaring all lands in California open."

lost their property when newcomers successfully challenged and took away land titles that had been granted by Spanish or Mexican authorities years before. Costly court battles forced other Mexican Americans to sell their land. Ranchers protested to Congress:

"Some, who at one time had been the richest landholders, today find themselves without a foot of ground, living as objects of charity."

Poor Mexican Americans suffered the most. Many were forced to take low-paying jobs on ranches and in mines.

Despite the hostility, however, the different groups borrowed many ideas from one another. Newcomers learned from Mexicans how to mine the ore-rich hills of the Southwest. They also learned that *churros,* the tough Mexican sheep, were better adapted to the dry lands of the Southwest than eastern breeds. Sheep raising had already changed the lives of some Indian tribes. Sheep ranching had become the center of the Navajo economy. Navajo women, who were expert weavers, made beautiful woolen blankets and traded these blankets for horses and other necessary items. Many American newcomers began to raise sheep as well.

In turn, many newcomers brought eastern tools, seeds, and livestock, as well as the latest inventions and business techniques. A new culture was formed in the Southwest that still exists today. It can be found in the local music and art, in laws and architecture, and in the clothes people wear. It is a way of life with roots in three rich cultures—Indian, Mexican, and Anglo American.

Navajo women were skilled weavers. They traded their products with both the Spanish and the Americans.

Section 3 Review

• **Glossary**

IDENTIFY and explain the significance of the following: annex, James K. Polk, Zachary Taylor, Bear Flag Revolt, Winfield Scott, Nicholas P. Trist, Mexican Cession, Treaty of Guadalupe Hidalgo, Gadsden Purchase

• **Gazetteer**

LOCATE and explain the importance of the following: Rio Grande, Santa Fe, Buena Vista, Veracruz, Mexico City

REVIEWING FOR DETAILS
1. Why did war break out between the United States and Mexico?
2. How did the United States defeat Mexico?
3. What were the consequences of the war for Mexico and the United States?

REVIEWING FOR UNDERSTANDING
4. **Geographic Literacy** What geographic conditions might have made combat and the movement of troops difficult during the Mexican War?
5. **Critical Thinking:** *Determining the Strength of an Argument* Some Americans argued that it was the nation's manifest destiny to spread into Mexico's territory. Do you think that this reasoning justified war with Mexico? Explain your answer.

Section 4
THE GOLDEN WEST

Multimedia Connections

Explore these related topics and materials on the CD–ROM to enrich your understanding of this section:

 Atlas

- Mormons, 1830–1851

 Readings

- Westward Ho!

 Media Bank

- Clipper Ship
- Indian Wars, 1840–1860

 Profiles

- Joseph Smith
- Brigham Young

I n 1848 James Marshall brought John Sutter news of a discovery that, Marshall said, "would put both of us in possession of unheard-of wealth—millions and millions of dollars." But how long could they keep Marshall's discovery a secret? They rushed to the new mill on the American River, only to find people already highly excited. Then an Indian worker picked up a shiny object and cried *"Oro! Oro!"*—gold, gold! The secret was out, and California would never be the same.

As you read this section you will find out:

▶ **Who the Mormons were, and what they achieved in the West.**

▶ **What life was like in the mining camps.**

▶ **What impact the California Gold Rush had on the region.**

The Mormons of Utah

One of the most remarkable westward migrations was undertaken by the **Mormons**. Mormons belong to the Church of Jesus Christ of Latter-Day Saints, which was founded in 1830 by Joseph Smith, a New York farmer. Smith attracted several hundred followers, saying he had discovered and translated religious revelations contained on buried golden tablets. From these, he created the Book of Mormon, the basis for the Mormon Church. The Mormons prospered, but their religious practices set them apart from their neighbors. For example, some Mormon men practiced polygamy, which permitted a spouse to have more than one mate at the same time.

Eventually, the Mormons moved to a town they called Nauvoo, in Illinois. Some people in Nauvoo found Smith too strong-willed. He

The Mormons great trek west succeeded in large part because of the organization and leadership of Brigham Young.

organized a Mormon militia and destroyed his critics' printing press. By 1844 opposition to the Mormons in Illinois led to Smith's arrest. Shortly thereafter, a mob attacked the jail and shot Smith.

Mormons head west. After Smith's murder, the Mormons decided to look for a place on the frontier far removed from other people. Brigham Young became their new leader. Young was an excellent organizer. He divided about 12,000 Mormons into small groups and began leading them west in 1846, along what became known as the **Mormon Trail**. The party proceeded slowly, stopping to build camps and to plant crops so that those who followed would have shelter and food.

In July 1847 Young and his followers reached a dry, sun-baked valley near Great Salt Lake in present-day Utah. Young decided, "If nobody on earth wants such a place, then that is the place for my people." There they built Salt Lake City as their permanent home. The Mormon settlement succeeded, largely because of its unity and Young's leadership. As head of both the church and the government, he had almost total control over the Mormon community.

African Americans joined the forty-niners' rush west. They sifted dirt and panned for gold in streams, hoping to strike it rich.

Regulating water rights. The Mormons prospered in this dry country in part because of their intelligent, cooperative use of water. Unlike the East, where water was plentiful, water was scarce in the West. For the Mormon settlers to survive in Utah they had to dam streams and flood land. In addition, they constructed canals and irrigation ditches.

The Mormons believed that the community good outweighed the good of individuals. A limited resource such as water was divided among all the people. Later, other westerners followed the Mormons' example of shared water use, and this principle has become the basis for present-day water law in all western states.

The Gold Rush

By 1848, crossing the continent was a fairly common experience. The trip was still long, tiring, and often dangerous, but the routes were well marked. There were also forts and settlements along the way where travelers could rest.

In the late 1840s California attracted many easterners. Some of them settled around Sutter's Fort on the American River. To supply lumber for new settlers, Sutter decided to build a sawmill about 35 miles up the river.

James W. Marshall was in charge of building the new mill. While inspecting the mill, Marshall noticed bits of shiny yellow metal shimmering in the water. He collected some of the metal and had it tested. It was pure gold.

This discovery took place in January 1848. Soon, other people began to **prospect**, or search for, gold. When they found gold, the miners told friends. By May of that year the town of San Francisco was buzzing with the news.

"Gold! Gold! *Gold* from the American River!" Then in December 1848 President Polk announced that the gold in California was "more extensive and valuable" than had been thought. This news triggered the **California Gold Rush** of 1849. In that year at least 80,000 people, called **forty-niners**, flocked to California.

The forty-niners. Most of the forty-niners followed the overland trails across the Rocky Mountains. Others sailed from the East to Panama, crossed the isthmus on foot, and then sailed north to San Francisco.

Still others took the all-water route around South America. Sometimes it took six months to make the long ocean voyage. But for those who could afford it, sleek, three-masted clipper ships made the trip in much less time. In 1851 the clipper *Flying Cloud* sailed from Boston to San Francisco in 89 days—a record time.

Gold fever. In 1849 about $10 million worth of gold was mined in California. By 1852 some 100,000 prospectors were mining there, and they found about $80 million worth of gold. Some miners became extremely wealthy. Two African American miners hit a deposit so rich that the site was named Negro Hill in honor of their find. In four months these two men found gold worth $80,000.

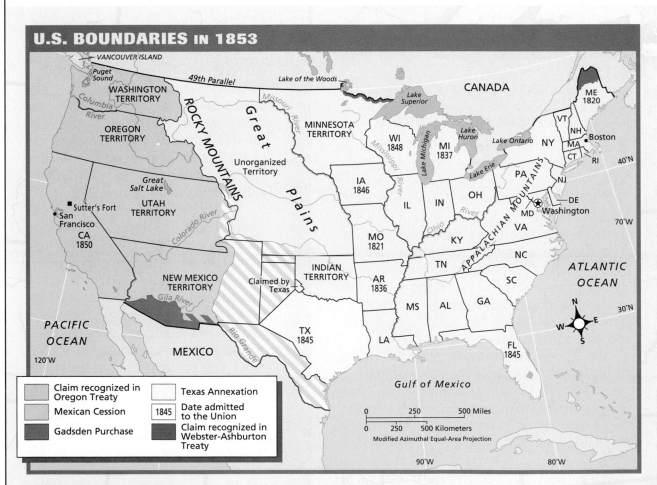

U.S. BOUNDARIES IN 1853

Legend: Claim recognized in Oregon Treaty; Mexican Cession; Gadsden Purchase; Texas Annexation; 1845 Date admitted to the Union; Claim recognized in Webster-Ashburton Treaty

Learning from Maps. By 1853 the current boundaries of the continental United States were established.

▶ **Place.** What states were admitted to the Union in 1845?

• **Maps**

Most miners, however, made little or nothing. Still, they were willing to risk all for a chance at making a fortune. When word of a new strike reached town, people rushed to the gold fields to start prospecting. Forty-niner Alonzo Delano wrote:

> **"In May, 1850, a report reached the settlements that a wonderful lake had been discovered, . . . the shores of which abounded with gold, and to such an extent that it lay like pebbles on the beach. An extraordinary ferment [activity] among the people ensued [began], and a grand rush was made from the towns. . . . Stores were left to take care of themselves, business of all kinds was dropped, mules were suddenly bought up at exorbitant [very high] prices, and crowds started off to search for the golden lake."**

Whenever miners found traces of gold, they staked a claim by driving wooden stakes in the ground to mark the spot. Soon, dozens of other prospectors would flock to the surrounding area to stake out their claims, and disputes about boundaries often broke out.

Life in Mining Camps

Villages called mining camps sprang up wherever gold was found. These camps were given colorful names, such as Whiskey Bar, Hangtown, Poker Flat, and Skunk Gulch. Life in these camps was uncomfortable, expensive, and sometimes dangerous.

A person could be flat broke one day and worth thousands of dollars the next. Such an up-and-down life, combined with the hardships the miners faced, encouraged a live-for-the-day attitude. Many miners were heavy drinkers and reckless gamblers. Fighting in the mining camps with fists, knives, and guns was common.

Mining camps attracted all sorts of thieves and tricksters, as well as clever saloon-keepers and business dealers. Merchants sold the miners everything from pickaxes and tents to fancy clothes and fine horses at sky-high prices. These townspeople made far more money than most miners.

Despite the problems of camp life, most prospectors and storekeepers were eager to build schools and churches and live peacefully. The difficulty was that most of the camps sprang up and died too quickly to establish orderly governments. When the gold ran out, prospectors abandoned camps and rushed off to strikes in other regions. The old camps became ghost towns, inhabited only by stray cats, hermits, or vagabonds.

Global Connections
Chinese Immigration

In the densely populated Guangdong province of southeastern China, the mid-1800s was a time of economic hardship. The expenses of war weakened the Chinese government and resulted in high taxes. Thousands of farmers lost their land when they could not pay these taxes. Landless farmers rarely found employment—hunger and poverty became their way of life. Even more Chinese joined the ranks of the poor when floods devastated the land and crops. In Guangdong this had a disastrous consequence—famine.

Just when conditions seemed at their worst, word spread throughout the province that "gold hills" had been found in California. Soon, young Chinese men were crossing the Pacific, hoping to find gold and return with their riches to China. It seemed as though *gam saan haak* "travelers to the golden mountain" always came back rich. In reality, of the thousands of Chinese who came to California, few found gold and many could never afford to return to their homes in China.

Building the Golden West

The California Gold Rush greatly increased both western development and the economic growth of much of the country. For Indians in California, however, it was a disaster. The movement of white settlers into the gold region crowded many American Indian tribes off their lands. In California, Indians who had not been forced to labor on the great ranches were almost wiped out by the invading settlers and miners.

People from the United States, Mexico, South America, Europe, and as far away as China and Australia flocked to California. Not all newcomers were welcome, however:

> **"The Yankee regarded every man but [an Anglo] American as an interloper [intruder], who had no right to come to California and pick up the gold of 'free and enlightened citizens.'"**

Many Mexicans and Californios were treated badly. They often had their lands seized, suffered violent attacks, and were viewed as second-class citizens. Chinese miners and free African Americans also faced discrimination. A heavy foreign miners tax was placed on Chinese prospectors, and they were not allowed to become naturalized citizens because they were not white.

Despite these obstacles and the hard mining life, the gold fields lured a huge number of people who shared the dream of "striking it rich." In a way, gold made California a land of great cultural diversity.

During the California Gold Rush, people came from as far away as China to make their fortune.

Section 4 Review

• Glossary

• Gazetteer

• Time Line

IDENTIFY and explain the significance of the following: Mormons, Joseph Smith, Brigham Young, Mormon Trail, prospect, California Gold Rush, forty-niners

REVIEWING FOR DETAILS
1. What was life like in the mining camps?
2. How did the California Gold Rush affect the region?

REVIEWING FOR UNDERSTANDING
3. **Geographic Literacy** Who were the Mormons, and what were their accomplishments in the West?
4. **Writing Mastery:** *Creating* Imagine that you are a prospector. Write a journal entry about your experiences in working your mining claim.
5. **Critical Thinking:** *Making Comparisons* What were the differences between the Mormons and the forty-niners? Describe how those differences affected their settlement patterns.

The Journey West

Although travelers to the West arrived by sailing around South America or crossing the Isthmus of Panama, the more popular routes were overland. Good trails were important in the migration westward. Travelers needed dependable sources of water, game to hunt for food, and enough grass to sustain their livestock. Some trails spread over a wide area, only narrowing to a single path at river crossings and mountain passes. Many trails had been traveled by Indians on foot and horseback long before the first wagons rumbled over the trails.

Some travelers used the southern trails originally made by the Spanish to connect missions and forts in the 1700s. By 1870 almost 400,000 people had traveled the northern routes of the Oregon, California, and Mormon Trails. These trails were longer than some of the southern trails, but were somewhat easier to cross. By the 1880s most of the overland routes had been replaced by railroads.

Major Water Routes from the East Coast to California in 1849

Both of the major water routes to the gold fields of California from the East Coast were long. Although those who went across the Isthmus of Panama had a much shorter trip, they had to travel overland about 50 miles to catch a ship that would take them the rest of the way to San Francisco. Sometimes travelers had to wait in Panama a long time until a ship arrived. Instead of waiting, some impatient travelers journeyed the rest of the way overland through Central America and Mexico. **Movement:** If you were living in New York and wanted to travel to San Francisco by boat, about how long would your trip be if you took the route around South America?

Although the main route from Fort Hall to Sutter's Fort is generally identified as the California Trail, the route actually branched off into several trails that travelers could take. The terrain and lack of a good water supply made travel along the California Trail more difficult than along the Oregon Trail. Some travelers found the route so difficult that they preferred to travel all the way to Oregon, then go south along the West Coast to get to California.

Major Overland Routes to the West in 1860

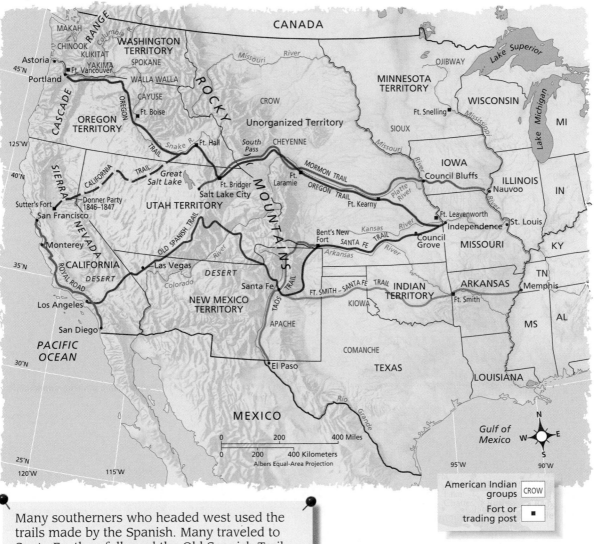

Many southerners who headed west used the trails made by the Spanish. Many traveled to Santa Fe, then followed the Old Spanish Trail, one of the first major trails established in North America. The 1,200-mile Old Spanish Trail went through some of the driest and most difficult terrain of the Southwest. **Movement:** If you were living in St. Louis, Missouri, in 1860 and wanted to travel to Monterey, California, which route would you take to get there? Why?

To learn more about the journey west, go to the interactive map, "Mission to Metropolis," on the CD-ROM.

• **Mission to Metropolis**

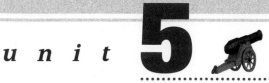

unit **5**

DIVISION AND REUNIFICATION (1848–1900)

THE FIFTEENTH AMENDMENT.
CELEBRATED MAY 19TH 1870.

This artwork celebrates the passage of the Fifteenth Amendment to the Constitution giving former slaves the right to vote. It shows some major events in African American history during the Civil War and Reconstruction Eras.

LINKING PAST TO PRESENT
Black History Month

Every February, high school students from Prince George's County, Maryland, participate in the Black Pursuits Quiz Competition. One of the sponsors of the event describes it as "an activity that pits teams . . . in an all-day academic match to determine who knows the most about black . . . history and culture." Since its creation in the 1980s, both the popularity of the contest and students' knowledge of African American history have increased.

Students all across the country focus on the achievements of African Americans during February, which is typically recognized as Black History Month. Some of the activities in which students participate include reading about African American leaders; experiencing aspects of African culture such as songs, dances, and crafts; and viewing films and museum displays on African American history.

Although many students from coast to coast observe Black History Month, the celebration is particularly significant in states like Maryland, which supported slavery in the 1800s. As you read this unit, you will learn what role the southern states played in the increasing conflict over the enslavement of African Americans.

For most people in the 1800s the study of history was the study of those who held power, meaning the study of wealthy white men. Although black labor played a central role in the development of the southern economy and culture, few people would have considered African American contributions to society worthy of study. As long as most African Americans remained property, their heritage as a people was not widely recognized.

As you will learn, this situation slowly began to change in the mid-1800s, as more and more people in power began to oppose the enslavement of African Americans. Although the battle over this issue would tear the country apart, in the end it created a society free of slavery—one that would eventually begin to recognize the important contributions of its many African American citizens.

These teenagers are learning about black history as part of their family's celebration of Kwanza, an African American holiday in December.

CHAPTER **13**

Breaking Apart
(1848–1861)

THEMES IN AMERICAN HISTORY

Constitutional Heritage:
How might differing interpretations of the Constitution cause problems?

Democratic Values:
How might individuals use the political system to express opinions?

Geographic Diversity:
Why might slavery have caused controversy when new territory was added to the United States?

A foreign observer of the growing sectional conflict in the United States asked an American what separated northerners and southerners. "The first is slavery; the second the climate. . . . Every ten years the South loses some proportion of its representation," the man observed. "Power is quickly shifting from these old centers." Would these things break up the United States? Americans would soon find out.

• Video Opener

• Skill Builder

image above: *Slave quarters in the South*

Section 1

AN UNEASY PEACE

Multimedia Connections

Explore these related topics and materials on the CD–ROM to enrich your understanding of this section:

 Biographies

- Frederick Douglass

 Profiles

- Millard Fillmore
- Harriet Beecher Stowe
- Henry Clay
- Daniel Webster
- John C. Calhoun
- James K. Polk

 Readings

- Flight to Canada

The slave catcher marched fugitive Anthony Burns into the Boston courthouse. Angry abolitionists quickly planned to rescue him. One morning several thousand people gathered around the courthouse. The abolitionists rammed the door with a huge log and fired shots. The judge was not swayed, however, and decided to return Burns to slavery. Bostonians watched as Burns marched, chained, to a waiting ship. "The funeral of liberty!" one protest sign read.

As you read this section you will find out:

▶ **Why the Mexican Cession aroused controversy between North and South.**

▶ **How the Compromise of 1850 attempted to satisfy all Americans.**

▶ **Why the Fugitive Slave Act caused controversy in the North.**

Slavery in the Mexican Cession

Victory in the Mexican War had added a huge tract of land to the United States. It also revived a national controversy over slavery in western territories, however.

The Missouri Compromise of 1820 had admitted Missouri as a slave state and Maine as a free state. It also divided the rest of the Louisiana Purchase into free and slave territory. The compromise permitted slavery in the land south of Missouri's southern border, which was marked by an imaginary line at latitude 36° 30'. It prohibited slavery in the land north of this line, with Missouri as the sole exception.

After the Treaty of Guadalupe Hidalgo, which ended the war between the United States and Mexico, some people favored extending the Missouri Compromise line all the way to the Pacific Ocean. This would split the Mexican Cession in two, allowing slavery only in areas south of the line.

Other Americans felt that none of this new territory should be open to slavery. Even before the war with Mexico had ended, Representative David Wilmot of Pennsylvania introduced the **Wilmot Proviso**. It declared that "neither slavery nor involuntary servitude shall ever exist in" any territory taken from the Republic of Mexico. Although the House of Representatives passed the measure, southerners defeated it in the Senate. Many northerners, however, hoped the terms of the Wilmot Proviso would eventually be adopted and settle the debate over slavery in the Mexican Cession.

Still other Americans proposed to end the controversy by applying a principle known as **popular sovereignty**. This process would let voters in a new territory make their own decision about slavery. They would elect proslavery or antislavery representatives, who would then decide the issue. If popular sovereignty were approved, however, it would end the Missouri Compromise.

The Election of 1848

The debate over slavery in the Mexican Cession played an important part in the heated presidential election of 1848. Since President James K. Polk did not seek a second term, the Democrats nominated Lewis Cass, a senator from Michigan. Cass was a supporter of popular sovereignty.

Many northern Democrats were unhappy about the nomination of Cass. They considered popular sovereignty a victory for supporters of slavery because it might allow slaveholders to bring slaves into new territories. Along with some antislavery Whigs, these Democrats founded a new political organization called the **Free-Soil Party**. They picked former president Martin Van Buren as their candidate. Their platform called for "free soil, free speech, free labor, and free men."

The Whig Party nominated war hero Zachary Taylor for president. Taylor refused to express an opinion on slavery, fearing that it would only divide his supporters. During the campaign, the Whigs stressed Taylor's victories in the Mexican War, his courage, and his personal honesty. This approach and the avoidance of the slavery issue worked well, and Taylor won the election.

The Compromise of 1850

The presidential election did not bring the country any closer to solving the controversy over slavery in the Mexican Cession. Developments in California finally forced Congress to resolve this difficult issue.

In 1848 Martin Van Buren and his running mate, Charles Francis Adams, ran on the first presidential ticket to represent the Free-Soil Party.

The Granger Collection, New York

Senator Henry Clay of Kentucky gives a speech convincing Congress to support his compromise plan for balancing the interests of slave and free states.

California demands an answer. The gold rush that began in 1849 greatly increased California's population. It was clear that the region would enter the Union directly as a state rather than through the usual process of territorial development. The question was whether California would be a free state or a slave state.

Most Californians did not want slavery. Few of the Spanish and Mexican families there had ever been slaveholders, and most of the American settlers came from free states. If California became a free state, however, it would upset the balance of free and slave states in the Union.

As political leaders struggled with these issues, other difficult problems complicated their debate. Many northerners had long disapproved of the existence of slavery and the slave trade in the nation's capital. Southerners had complained that the U.S. law requiring the return of fugitive slaves was too weak. Antislavery sentiment in the North made it difficult for southerners to reclaim slaves who had escaped there.

Henry Clay's solution. All the important members of Congress took part in the slavery debate. Kentucky senator Henry Clay offered a series of proposals to settle the situation. Congress should admit California as a free state, Clay urged. To further please northerners, he suggested that the slave trade should be prohibited in the District of Columbia. To satisfy southerners, Clay proposed a harsh fugitive slave bill. He also argued that the rest of the Mexican Cession should be organized into territories where popular sovereignty would decide the slavery issue.

A heated debate. Senator John C. Calhoun of South Carolina bitterly attacked Clay's compromise. His once-powerful voice broken by illness, Calhoun sat grim and silent as another senator read his speech. "How can the Union be preserved?" he asked. Since slaves were a form of property, Calhoun argued, slaveholding citizens had the right to take their "property" into all the territories of the United States. Calhoun threatened that unless Congress allowed slaveholders to bring slaves into the territories, the southern states would leave the Union.

New York senator William Seward also attacked the compromise. He spoke against making any concessions to the slave interests. Clay's compromise, he said, was "radically wrong and essentially vicious."

Daniel Webster of Massachusetts, however, delivered a powerful speech in support of Clay's compromise proposals. He warned Americans to settle their differences:

> **"I wish to speak today, not as a Massachusetts man, nor as a Northern man, but as an American. . . . Is the great Constitution under which we live . . . to be thawed and melted away . . . ? No, sir! No, sir! . . . I see it as plainly as I see the sun in heaven—I see that disruption must produce . . . a war."**

Compromise at last. The debate dragged on for weeks. In the middle of it, both Senator Calhoun and President Taylor died. Vice President Millard Fillmore, who favored Clay's compromise, succeeded Taylor. Clay's proposals finally came to a vote. All passed and together became known as the **Compromise of 1850**. California entered the Union as a free state. The rest of the Mexican Cession was formed into two territories, Utah and New Mexico, where settlers would determine slavery's status through popular sovereignty. The slave trade, but not slavery itself, was prohibited in the District of Columbia, and a stronger fugitive slave law was enacted.

Few Americans approved of all these laws. The Compromise of 1850, however, appeared to put an end to the conflict between the free and slave states. As Illinois senator Stephen A. Douglas put it, a "final settlement" had been reached—or so it seemed to many Americans in 1850.

Slave Catching

The **Fugitive Slave Act** of 1850 quickly proved that the controversy was far from over. The law was enforced even in areas where it was very unpopular. Anyone caught hiding runaway slaves faced six months in jail and a $1,000 fine per slave. All citizens were required to help capture runaway slaves when ordered to do so by a law official. Since many southern slave owners offered rewards for the return of runaway slaves, slave catchers had a good reason to snatch up as many runaways as possible. The law provided that persons accused of being escaped slaves could not testify in their own defense.

During the next few years, law officials seized some 200 African Americans, most of whom were sent into slavery. This was only a small percentage of the number who had escaped, but these cases had a powerful impact on the black community. Runaways

A MAN KIDNAPPED!

A PUBLIC MEETING AT

FANEUIL HALL!

WILL BE HELD

THIS FRIDAY EVEN'G,

May 26th, at 7 o'clock,

To secure justice for A MAN CLAIMED AS A SLAVE by a

VIRGINIA KIDNAPPER!

And NOW IMPRISONED IN BOSTON COURT HOUSE, in defiance of the Laws of Massachusetts. Shall he be plunged into the Hell of Virginia Slavery by a Massachusetts Judge of Probate?

BOSTON, May 26th, 1854.

The Granger Collection, New York

Outraged northerners considered the practices of slave catchers to be kidnapping.

Opponents of the Fugitive Slave Act of 1850 feared that it would leave all African Americans at the mercy of dishonest slave catchers.

and even African American northerners who had never been slaves felt threatened, and many left the United States for Canada.

The incidents also influenced northern whites, many of whom were prejudiced against people of African descent, free or slave. Yet in spite of these prejudices, some also sympathized with runaways who had risked their lives to win freedom. An additional concern was that free African Americans in the North would be falsely sent into slavery under the new law.

Both white and black northerners were outraged when they witnessed accused fugitive slaves being dragged off without a chance to defend themselves in court. Even white northerners who remained unmoved by stories of cruelty to slaves usually objected to the law's requirement that they help officials catch escaped slaves.

Abolitionists led the attack on the law. Frederick Douglass, an escaped slave himself, urged resistance. "The only way to make the fugitive slave law dead letter," he wrote, "is to make a half a dozen or more dead kidnappers." In Boston an angry group so threatened one slave catcher that he fled the city in fear for his life. In Pennsylvania a mob actually killed a slave catcher.

Few captured runaways gained their freedom through public protest or force. In most cases they went before a judge as the law provided. Some won freedom, but most were carried off into slavery without the public taking much notice. Nevertheless, more and more northerners were becoming troubled about the existence of slavery.

A Novel About Slavery

Northerners' discomfort with the slavery issue grew after the 1852 publication of **Uncle Tom's Cabin**, a powerful novel about slavery. The author, Harriet Beecher Stowe, was born in Connecticut but spent many years in Ohio. There she met fugitive slaves and learned about the cruel and unjust nature of slavery. While visiting a Kentucky plantation, Stowe gathered material to write her graphic account of the slave system. *Uncle Tom's Cabin* tells the story of a slave named Tom, who is sold to the cruel master of a Louisiana cotton plantation. This man has Tom beaten, and the long-suffering slave dies from his injuries. "Oh, my country!" Stowe wrote of Tom's death, "these things are done under the shadow of thy laws!"

Harriet Beecher Stowe created much controversy with her book, Uncle Tom's Cabin.

The Granger Collection, New York

Many southerners were deeply offended by *Uncle Tom's Cabin*. One minister called Stowe's novel "a filthy, lying book." The novel, however, shocked many northerners, and it became an immediate popular success. The novel was made into a play and presented in packed theaters all over the free states and territories.

Although it is not known exactly how many of the millions of people who read the book or saw the play became abolitionists as a result, *Uncle Tom's Cabin* had an unquestionable effect on northern attitudes toward slavery. One reader described the impact of the book in an anonymous letter to the author:

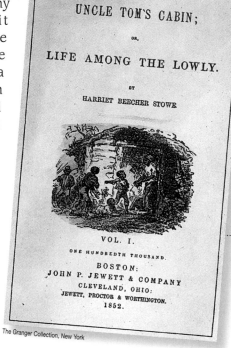

The Granger Collection, New York

"I sat up last night long after one o'clock, reading and finishing 'Uncle Tom's Cabin.' I *could not* leave it any more than I could have left a dying child; nor could I restrain an almost hysterical sobbing. . . . This storm of feeling has been raging, burning like a very fire in my bones, all the livelong night, and all through my duties this morning it haunts me,—I *cannot* do away with it."

This edition of Uncle Tom's Cabin *was the 100,000th copy of Stowe's popular novel about slavery. Within a short time there were few people unfamiliar with her story.*

Section 1 Review

• **Glossary**

IDENTIFY and explain the significance of the following: Wilmot Proviso, popular sovereignty, Free-Soil Party, Henry Clay, John C. Calhoun, Compromise of 1850, Fugitive Slave Act, *Uncle Tom's Cabin*, Harriet Beecher Stowe

REVIEWING FOR DETAILS
1. Why did the Mexican Cession cause controversy between northerners and southerners?
2. How did the Compromise of 1850 attempt to solve the problem of slavery in the Missouri Compromise?
3. Why did many northerners object to the Fugitive Slave Act?

REVIEWING FOR UNDERSTANDING
4. **Writing Mastery:** *Creating* Imagine that you are a northerner in the 1850s. Create a short poem, speech, letter, or editorial expressing your reaction to the sensation created by *Uncle Tom's Cabin*.
5. **Critical Thinking:** *Recognizing Point of View* Taking the point of view of a southerner, list from best to worst the three solutions offered to settle the issue of slavery in the Mexican Cession. Then list them as a northerner. Explain why the two lists might differ.

Section 2

THE STRUGGLE FOR KANSAS

Multimedia Connections

Explore these related topics and materials on the CD–ROM to enrich your understanding of this section:

 Gazetteer

- Nebraska
- Kansas

 Atlas

- Bleeding Kansas

 Readings

- Southerners Eye Latin America
- Violence in Congress

 Profiles

- Franklin Pierce

 Media Bank

- Slavery Compromises, 1820–1854
- John Brown

South Carolina representative Preston Brooks approached Massachusetts senator Charles Sumner. Brooks was furious about Sumner's attack on the Kansas-Nebraska Act and his personal comments about one of Brooks's relatives. The South Carolina man raised his cane and beat Sumner until the wood splintered. Sumner's blood splattered on the floor. The greatest political issue of the day—the question of expanding slavery into new territory—had erupted in violence in the U.S. Senate.

As you read this section you will find out:

▶ **What plan Stephen Douglas had for the new western territories.**

▶ **Why northerners protested Douglas's plan.**

▶ **Why trouble arose in Kansas.**

The Kansas-Nebraska Act

The controversy over slavery in the territories soon erupted again. After California entered the Union, a number of plans for building a railroad to the West Coast sprang up. Northerners generally favored a route from Chicago, while southerners wanted the railroad to run from New Orleans.

No railroad could be built through a region that did not have a territorial government, however. Hoping to secure a northern route for his Illinois voters, Senator Stephen A. Douglas introduced a bill in 1853 to create a territorial government for the region west of Missouri and Iowa.

Douglas's bill ran into trouble, however. Southerners in Congress did not want to create a northern territory. They argued that the railroad could take a southern route and cross

SOUTHERN CHIVALRY— ARGUMENT VERSUS CLUB'S.

This violent attack on Massachusetts senator Charles Sumner by South Carolina representative Preston Brooks demonstrated how hostile the congressional debate over slavery had become. Sumner never completely recovered from his injuries.

New Mexico Territory, which already existed because of the Compromise of 1850. They also feared that the proposed territory, which was north of the Missouri Compromise line, might eventually become a free state. Southerners refused to vote for Douglas's bill.

Douglas was a clever politician, however. When he realized that southern representatives disliked his bill, he came up with a new plan—allowing the settlers themselves to decide the question of slavery in the new territory. This plan was simply the principle of popular sovereignty that had already been applied in New Mexico and Utah Territories. As a further compromise, Douglas also proposed that the area be split into two territories—Kansas, west of the slave state of Missouri, and Nebraska, west of the free state of Iowa.

Douglas knew that many northerners would dislike this Kansas-Nebraska bill because Kansas might be settled by slave owners. He thought, however, that northerners would merely grumble. Douglas himself believed that the area's climate, which was unsuitable for the most profitable plantation crops, made it unlikely that slavery would be established there.

On January 4, 1854, Douglas introduced his revised bill in the Senate. Antislavery

northerners were outraged, and they responded to the proposed law with roars of protest. The bill, in effect, repealed the ban on slavery imposed by the Missouri Compromise. Some antislavery members of Congress called the Kansas-Nebraska bill "an atrocious plot" to make the area "a dreary region . . . inhabited by masters and slaves."

For months Congress debated the bill. Finally, with the votes of southerners who approved of the popular sovereignty provision, the **Kansas-Nebraska Act** passed both houses. President Franklin Pierce, who had won the office in the 1852 election, promptly signed the bill.

Conflicts in Kansas

The northerners who had opposed the Kansas-Nebraska bill grew more angry after it became law. They soon became determined to prevent slavery from spreading from Missouri into Kansas. New York senator Seward said:

"Gentlemen of the Slave States, . . . We will engage in competition for the virgin soil of Kansas, and God give the victory to the side which is . . . right."

Eli Thayer, a Massachusetts abolitionist, organized the Massachusetts Emigrant Aid Company to help pay the moving expenses of antislavery families willing to settle in Kansas.

Encouraged by people like Thayer or prompted by their own beliefs, hundreds of free-soilers rushed to Kansas. They hoped to use popular sovereignty to ban slavery in the territory. Pro-slavery citizens in Missouri also hurried to Kansas.

When the first territorial governor took a census of Kansas late in 1854, he found fewer than 3,000 voters in the territory. After officials held an election for a territorial legislature in March 1855 however, they counted more than 6,300 ballots! Missourians had crossed into Kansas to vote. Their ballots were illegal, of course, since they were not residents of the territory. Still, their votes were counted. As a result, a large majority of the delegates elected

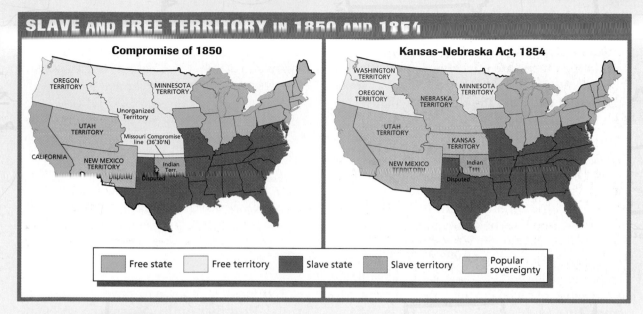

SLAVE AND FREE TERRITORY IN 1850 AND 1854

Compromise of 1850

OREGON TERRITORY

MINNESOTA TERRITORY

Unorganized Territory

UTAH TERRITORY

Missouri Compromise line (36°30'N)

CALIFORNIA

NEW MEXICO TERRITORY

Indian Terr.

Disputed

Disputed

Kansas-Nebraska Act, 1854

WASHINGTON TERRITORY

OREGON TERRITORY

NEBRASKA TERRITORY

MINNESOTA TERRITORY

UTAH TERRITORY

KANSAS TERRITORY

NEW MEXICO TERRITORY

Indian Terr.

Disputed

| | Free state | | Free territory | | Slave state | | Slave territory | | Popular sovereignty |

Learning from Maps. The Kansas-Nebraska Act led many northerners to believe that southerners wanted to expand slavery throughout the United States.

▶ **Place.** How did the Kansas-Nebraska Act extend slavery?

• **Maps**

---

to the territorial legislature were supporters of slavery.

The new legislature moved quickly to pass laws authorizing slavery in Kansas. One law even provided the death penalty for anyone giving help to runaway slaves. Free-soil Kansans were furious. They argued that the new legislature had no right to rule them, and promptly set up their own government.

With two governments claiming to rule the same territory, it is not surprising that fighting soon broke out. Both sides took up arms. Some abolitionists in the East began shipping guns to the antislavery forces so they could

Reverend Henry Ward Beecher was one of the most outspoken abolitionists of his era.

defend themselves. One such abolitionist was the Reverend Henry Ward Beecher, a brother of Harriet Beecher Stowe. He was so successful in convincing people to send guns to Kansas that people began to call the weapons "Beecher's Bibles."

In November 1855 a pro-slavery man killed a free-soil settler in an argument. The dead man's friends then set fire to the killer's cabin.

John Brown and "Bleeding Kansas"

As other such incidents occurred, the situation in Kansas grew more explosive. In the spring of 1856, antislavery settlers organized their own government and militia in Lawrence, Kansas. On May 21 a pro-slavery sheriff and a large group of armed Missourians marched into Lawrence and attacked the town. An eyewitness described the scene:

"The newspaper offices were the first objects of attack. . . . The presses were

broken down to pieces and the type carried away in the river. The papers and books were treated the same way. . . . From the printing offices the attackers went to the hotel. By evening, all that remained . . . was a part of one wall. The rest was a shapeless heap of ruins."

This engraving shows the attack on Lawrence, Kansas, by supporters of slavery. The attack shocked people throughout the country.

One person was killed in the attack. A man named John Brown soon set out to avenge the attack on Lawrence. During his 56 years Brown had tried many businesses but failed time after time. His behavior had often been on the fringes of the law, if not outside it. Yet he sincerely opposed slavery—calling it "the sum of all villainies"—and felt a deep devotion to the cause of racial equality. He had come to Kansas in October 1855 to support the antislavery movement there.

A few days after Brown learned of the attack on Lawrence, he led a party of seven men—four of whom were his sons—to a proslavery settlement near Pottawatomie Creek. In the dead of night Brown and his followers entered the cabins of unsuspecting families and murdered five people simply because they supported slavery.

This incident, known to slavery supporters as the **Pottawatomie Massacre**, brought Kansas to the verge of civil war. Free-soilers and pro-slavery men squared off to fight. Politicians and the press played up the unrest in Kansas. Soon, horror-stricken citizens were reading exaggerated newspaper reports of the situation in "Bleeding Kansas." They grew more worried about the future of the country as they read about Americans fighting each other on the Plains.

Section 2 Review

IDENTIFY and explain the significance of the following: Stephen A. Douglas, Kansas-Nebraska Act, Franklin Pierce, Henry Ward Beecher, John Brown, Pottawatomie Massacre

• **Glossary**

LOCATE and explain the importance of the following: Kansas, Lawrence, Pottawatomie Creek

REVIEWING FOR DETAILS

1. What was Stephen Douglas's controversial plan for the new territories west of Missouri and Iowa?

• **Gazetteer**

2. Why did antislavery northerners protest Douglas's plan for the new territories?

3. Why did people refer to the territory as "Bleeding Kansas"?

REVIEWING FOR UNDERSTANDING

4. **Geographic Literacy** Why did both antislavery and pro-slavery forces try to advance their respective positions in Kansas rather than Nebraska?

5. **Critical Thinking:** *Drawing Conclusions* How did the conflict in Kansas represent the issues that were dividing the entire nation?

Section 3

THE ROAD TO DISUNION

Multimedia Connections

Explore these related topics and materials on the CD–ROM to enrich your understanding of this section:

 Profiles

- Abraham Lincoln
- Stephen Douglas
- James Buchanan
- Dred Scott

 Media Bank

- Congressman Lincoln
- Poster for John C. Fremont
- Attack on Abolitionist Press

 Readings

- *Civil Disobedience*

The Michigan sun filtered through a large grove of oak trees as many of the state's leading citizens gathered "to consider . . . the measures which duty demands." So many people came to the meeting that officials moved it from a large hall to the circle of trees outdoors. Speakers criticized the Kansas-Nebraska Act and labeled slavery a great evil. A new political organization—the Republican Party—took shape.

As you read this section you will find out:

▶ **How the Kansas-Nebraska Act changed American politics.**

▶ **How the *Dred Scott* decision affected African Americans and the issue of slavery.**

▶ **How Lincoln and Douglas differed over slavery in new territories.**

Political Changes

The controversy over slavery in the territories produced major shifts in the nation's political parties. The Democratic Party, under the leadership of Stephen Douglas, had supported the Kansas-Nebraska Act. Antislavery Democrats opposed the act, and when it passed, the party lost thousands of supporters throughout the northern states.

The Whig Party, however, shattered completely. Pro-slavery southern members supported the act. Antislavery northern members opposed it. Some Whigs abandoned the party altogether and switched to the new, anti-immigrant American Party, whose members were called the Know-Nothings. The Know-Nothings supported the Kansas-Nebraska Act and won some local elections in the 1850s. The party never had much support, however.

The Granger Collection, New York

The Republican Party grew very large in a short amount of time. This engraving shows the crowds that gathered at the party's national convention in 1860. The party's main goal was to keep slavery out of the territories.

Many northern Whigs and northern Democrats joined a new organization called the **Republican Party**. It sprang up in the North after passage of the Kansas-Nebraska Act. For Republicans, the most important issue was keeping slavery out of the western territories. Dislike of slavery was not the only reason the party took this stand. In fact, some Republicans shared the racial prejudices of many other white Americans. They feared that small farmers in the territories could not compete if southerners brought their slaves there.

The election of 1856 proved just how unsettled the political situation was. All three parties offered candidates. Democrat James Buchanan won the election, but the Republican Party made a strong showing.

• **Election of 1856**

The *Dred Scott* Case

Two days after Buchanan took office, a Supreme Court decision produced yet another crisis. Americans had been anxiously awaiting the Court's ruling in an important case involv-ing a slave named Dred Scott. Very little is known about Scott's early life. He was born in Virginia and must have been a very deter-mined person, because he carried on a long struggle for his freedom.

For many years Scott was the slave of John Emerson, an army doctor. Although Emerson lived for a time in Missouri, during the course of his career, he took Scott to live in Illinois, a free state, and Wisconsin Territory, a free region. Emerson eventually sent Scott back to Missouri.

In 1846 Scott sued for his freedom in a Missouri court. He argued that since slavery was illegal in Illinois and the Wisconsin Territory, he had become free when Dr. Emerson took him to those places. Scott claimed that he could not be re-enslaved just because he had been returned to Missouri. Therefore, he believed that he was legally still free. The case eventually came to the Supreme Court for final settlement. On March 6, 1857, the Court announced the ***Dred Scott* decision**. Seven of the nine justices ruled against Scott.

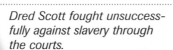

Dred Scott fought unsuccessfully against slavery through the courts.

The Chief Justice of the Supreme Court, Roger B. Taney (TAW-nee), explained the majority position. "The Negro race," he said, "were not regarded . . . as citizens" by the Constitution of the United States. Since Scott was not a citizen, he had no right to bring a suit in a federal court. Taney's statement alone was enough to keep Scott a slave. Taney, however, did not leave it at that.

Living in Illinois, he argued, had not made Scott free. Nor did his stay in Wisconsin Territory, because the Missouri Compromise, which had banned slavery in that territory, had been unconstitutional!

Taney reasoned that slaves were not persons, but property. The Fifth Amendment to the U.S. Constitution states that no person "shall . . . be deprived of life, liberty, or property, without due process of law"—that is, action by a court. Therefore, a law that prevented slaveholders from taking slaves into a territory violated the slaveholders' Fifth Amendment rights.

Slaveholders cheered the Court's decision in the *Dred Scott* case. "What are you going to do about it?" they asked northerners. Northerners responded to the *Dred Scott* decision with a storm of criticism. Abolitionists and other opponents of slavery argued that the Court was using part of the Bill of Rights to keep people in chains! Black abolitionist Robert Purvis spoke for many when he said:

> **"This atrocious [horrible] decision furnishes final confirmation of the already well-known fact that, under the Constitution and government of the United States, the colored people are nothing and can be nothing but an alien, disfranchised [powerless], and degraded class."**

Even worse to many northerners was the Court's ruling that the Missouri Compromise was unconstitutional. That law had been canceled, of course, by passage of the Kansas-Nebraska Act. The Court's action, however, implied that Congress did not have the power to stop the advance of slavery into the West. Republicans particularly objected to this part of the decision. It made their main goal—to keep slavery out of the territories—illegal.

The Lincoln-Douglas Debates

The national controversy over the *Dred Scott* decision played an important role in an 1858 Senate race in Illinois. The Republican Party nominated Abraham Lincoln to oppose

The Supreme Court decision in the Dred Scott *case shocked many northerners opposed to slavery. They felt it allowed slavery to expand throughout the United States.*

Senator Douglas. Lincoln was a prosperous lawyer who had once served a term in Congress. He had always been a loyal member of the Whig Party and seemed a rather ordinary local politician.

Lincoln takes a stand. Lincoln's status changed when the Kansas-Nebraska Act revived the question of slavery in the territories. "If slavery is not wrong," Lincoln later said, "then nothing is wrong." Still, he was not an abolitionist. Slavery was like a cancer, he said, but cutting it out might cause the patient—the United States—to "bleed to death." He was, however, firmly opposed to the extension of slavery. By 1856 Lincoln had joined the new Republican Party.

Lincoln was an excellent speaker with a remarkable gift for words. His strong position and good judgment called him to the attention of Republican leaders. Although Lincoln hated slavery, he did not hate slaveholders, and he did not blame them for the existence of the institution. He even admitted that he did not know how to do away with slavery in states where it already existed. These views appealed to moderates in the North.

A challenge. Lincoln's fine mind and clever tongue were important because Douglas was a brilliant speaker and an expert on the issues of the day. Lincoln knew it would be difficult—but not impossible—to remove Douglas from his long-held Senate seat. To boost his prospects, Lincoln challenged Douglas to debate him in different sections of Illinois. Douglas agreed. Their seven encounters around the state eventually became known as the **Lincoln-Douglas debates**.

These meetings attracted large crowds, for each was a great local occasion. Families piled into wagons and rumbled for miles over dusty roads to hear the two men speak. Because of the issues involved, newspapers all over the country reported on the debates in detail.

Douglas's side. Douglas tried to persuade the voters that Lincoln and the Republicans were dangerous radicals. He accused them of being abolitionists and of favoring equality for African Americans. Lincoln "thinks that the Negro is his brother," Douglas sneered.

As for the western territories, Douglas defended popular sover-

History Makers

Stephen A. Douglas
(1813–1861)

Stephen Douglas was full of energy and determination. He usually got what he wanted. Before the Illinois legislature elected him to the Senate, Douglas made a fortune in business and served as a state legislator, a judge, and a U.S. representative. Since he was quite short with a wide chest and booming voice, observers called him the "Little Giant." Douglas attributed his political success to his extraordinary closeness with voters.

"I live with my constituents [voters]," he once boasted. "Drink with them, lodge with them, pray with them."

Douglas had a deep commitment to national unity. When it appeared that slave states might leave the Union as a result of the election of 1860, he went on a tour to beg southerners to reconsider. His noble effort failed. Douglas died of typhoid fever soon after.

National Portrait Gallery, Smithsonian Institution, Washington, DC/Art Resource, NY

Throughout Illinois, Abraham Lincoln and Stephen Douglas debated the issue of slavery.

Lincoln's reply. Hoping to appeal to Illinois voters, Lincoln responded by distancing himself from then-radical racial beliefs: "I have no purpose to introduce political and social equality between the white and the black races." But, he added, all people had the "natural rights" described in the Declaration of Independence: the right to life, liberty, and the pursuit of happiness. Unlike Douglas, who appealed to the racism of his audience, Lincoln urged white Americans to show sympathy for African Americans and respect for their human rights.

Lincoln also stood firm on the issue of slavery's expansion. Republicans viewed "the institution of slavery as a wrong," he told audiences. "One of the methods of treating it as a wrong is to *make provision* [be sure] *that it shall grow no larger.*"

The Freeport Doctrine

During a debate at Freeport, Illinois, Lincoln attempted to use the issue of slavery in the territories against Douglas. He reminded the senator that the *Dred Scott* decision had determined that slavery could go into any territory. Since this was the case, Lincoln asked, then how could the people of a territory possibly

eignty. He also believed that climate and soil conditions would not support slavery in the western territories. Allowing slaveholders to settle in Kansas, he told the crowds, did not mean they would necessarily do so.

The situation of runaway slaves was one of the issues that fueled debates throughout the 1850s. This image shows runaway slaves from Maryland.

The Granger Collection, New York

keep slavery out of their region even through popular sovereignty?

Douglas's answer became known as the **Freeport Doctrine**. He replied:

National Portrait Gallery, Smithsonian Institution, Washington, DC/Art Resource, NY

"It matters not what way the Supreme Court may . . . decide [about slavery]; the people have the lawful means to introduce it or exclude it as they please. . . . If the people are opposed to slavery, they will elect representatives to that body [the local legislature] who will by unfriendly legislation effectually [effectively] prevent the introduction of it into

This doll was used by supporters of Stephen A. Douglas during one of his campaigns.

their midst. If, on the contrary, they are for it, their legislation will favor its extension."

Douglas meant that since territorial legislatures had the power to write local laws, they could either support slavery or make it impossible for the institution to exist.

This argument helped Douglas in Illinois, where many voters wanted to believe that popular sovereignty could work in the territories despite the *Dred Scott* decision. Douglas's speeches hurt him in the South, however, where slaveholders felt betrayed by the Freeport Doctrine. Thus, Douglas's strategy reduced his chances of achieving his greatest goal—the presidency.

On election day the Democrats carried the Illinois legislature by a small majority. Douglas was therefore re-elected to the Senate. But Lincoln probably benefited from the debates more than Douglas did. His effective speeches attracted much national attention. "It [the campaign] gave me a hearing," he said of the political race. "I believe I have made some marks."

Section 3 Review

• Glossary

IDENTIFY and explain the significance of the following: Republican Party, Dred Scott, *Dred Scott* decision, Abraham Lincoln, Lincoln-Douglas debates, Freeport Doctrine

REVIEWING FOR DETAILS

1. What impact did the Kansas-Nebraska Act have on political parties?
2. How did the *Dred Scott* decision affect African Americans and the issue of slavery in general?
3. How did Lincoln and Douglas differ in their views on the expansion of slavery into western territories?

REVIEWING FOR UNDERSTANDING

4. **Writing Mastery:** *Creating* Imagine that you are working for either the Lincoln or Douglas campaign in Illinois. Create a campaign poster expressing your candidate's ideas on slavery.
5. **Critical Thinking:** *Cause and Effect* Why had many pro-slavery southerners supported Douglas, and why did they stop supporting him after he stated his Freeport Doctrine?

Section 4
THE SECESSION CRISIS

Multimedia Connections

Explore these related topics and materials on the CD–ROM to enrich your understanding of this section:

 Gazetteer

- South Carolina

 Media Bank

- Harpers Ferry
- Secession
- Last Moments of John Brown
- Candidate Lincoln

 Readings

- South Carolina's Declaration

Two men pushed through the snowdrifts outside the mansion. They spoke in low tones of a bold, dangerous scheme— John Brown's plan to attack an arsenal in the South and to free slaves. "We cannot give him up to die alone," one man pleaded. "I will raise so many hundred dollars for him; . . . ask [your friends] to do as much." The other man finally agreed. They and their associates became the "Secret Six," a tiny group that funded Brown's raid.

As you read this section you will find out:

▶ **How Americans reacted to John Brown's raid.**

▶ **How Abraham Lincoln became president.**

▶ **Why many southerners wanted to leave the United States.**

John Brown's Raid

In October 1859 John Brown again appeared on the national scene. Outraged by the continuing existence of slavery, he decided to organize a band of armed followers and break into an arsenal in Virginia. With the captured weapons, he planned to free nearby slaves and seize land in the mountains. Apparently Brown expected slaves from all over the region to join him. With their help he would organize uprisings and launch raids to rescue more slaves.

Brown soon persuaded six important Massachusetts abolitionists to give him enough money to organize and supply his group, which included about 20 white and African Americans followers. Brown and his force targeted the federal arsenal in the town of Harpers Ferry, Virginia.

A midnight attack. On the evening of October 16, 1859, Brown and his men splashed across a stream near the arsenal. In what became known as **John Brown's raid**, they overpowered a guard and occupied both the arsenal and a government rifle factory. Brown then sent some of his followers off to capture several local slaveholders as hostages. When workers arrived at the arsenal in the morning, Brown also took some of them prisoner. Then he waited for the slaves in the area to rise up and join his rebellion.

Not one slave did so, but the local authorities reacted promptly. In a matter of hours they pinned down Brown's force in the arsenal. A detachment of U.S. Marines under the command of Colonel Robert E. Lee arrived from Washington. Brown refused to surrender. On October 18 Lee ordered his forces to attack.

Ten of Brown's men died in the attack, but Brown was taken alive. Officials charged him with conspiracy, treason, and murder. After a fair but swift trial, Brown was convicted and sentenced to be hanged.

Brown's raid might have been dismissed as the work of a lunatic had he acted like a disturbed person after his capture. But he did not do so. Instead, Brown behaved with remarkable dignity and self-discipline. When he was condemned to death, Brown said that he had acted in the name of God:

"I believe that to have interfered as I have done . . . in behalf of His despised poor, was not wrong, but right. Now, if it is deemed necessary that I should forfeit my life for the furtherance of the ends of justice . . . let it be done! . . . I feel no consciousness of guilt."

A short time later Brown was hanged.

The debate over John Brown. Although most moderate northerners condemned Brown, he was a hero to the opponents of slavery. "Our heart may grow more hopeful for humanity when it sees [his] sublime [great] sacrifice," a young African American woman wrote to Brown's wife. Many abolitionists considered Brown a noble freedom-fighter. They conveniently forgot about the bloody murders Brown had committed in Kansas.

Brown's attack terrified and enraged people throughout the South. "Our peace has been disturbed; our citizens have been imprisoned . . . ; their property has been seized by force of arms," the Virginia governor protested in a message to the state legislature. When some northerners practically made Brown a saint, southerners became even more concerned. They began to fear that northerners intended

Through Others' Eyes

John Brown's Raid

Most African Canadians responded to John Brown's attack on Harpers Ferry with enthusiasm and praise. They regarded his effort as an admirable move for freedom. Harvey C. Jackson posted the following notice just five days after Brown was executed:

"You are all aware of the excitement recently created at Harper's Ferry . . . by Captain John Brown and a few others. . . . You are also aware that their attempt was a failure. . . . But that bold attempt to liberate the slaves will be attended with the most important results. It has already enlightened public opinion more than all the anti-slavery speeches made for the last ten years. . . . Some persons may brand Brown's effort as 'rash, futile [useless], and wild,' but they must acknowledge that it will be productive of much good. . . . Brown and his confederates are martyrs to the cause of Liberty."

Believing he was called to carry out violence for the cause of abolition, John Brown made a lasting impression on the country. This mural of him was painted on the Kansas statehouse.

to destroy slavery, not merely limit its expansion. Once again, northerners and southerners looked at each other with suspicion, fear, and even hatred.

The Election of 1860

As the 1860 presidential election drew near, the Democrats became even more sharply divided over slavery. Their first nominating convention broke up after the delegates could not agree on a candidate. They gathered again a few months later, but once more they failed to agree. After the convention nominated Stephen Douglas, southern Democrats broke away. They nominated President Buchanan's vice president, John C. Breckinridge of Kentucky.

In the meantime, the Republican convention took place. To broaden the party's appeal, leaders drafted a program of economic reforms to go along with their position that slavery be kept out of the territories. New York senator Seward was the leading presidential candidate. Many, however, thought Seward was too antislavery for most northern voters. After much political "horse trading," or intense back-and-forth bargaining, the Republican delegates nominated Abraham Lincoln.

Fearing that the South might leave the Union if a Republican won the election, some southerners formed yet another political organization. They called it the **Constitutional Union Party**. Its platform was simple—"the Union as it is and the Constitution as it is." Though many members of this party supported slavery, they did not want the country to break apart over the issue.

The Constitutional Unionists nominated John Bell from Tennessee, who had served in both houses of Congress. Although he held slaves, Bell had opposed the Kansas-Nebraska Act, which made him attractive to many moderates.

The November election showed just how fragmented the nation had become. With four candidates running, no one could hope to get a majority of the popular vote. The electoral vote was a different matter. Lincoln and Douglas fought it out in the heavily populated free states. Lincoln won in most of these states, taking 180 electoral votes to Douglas's mere 12.

In the less populated slave states Breckinridge and Bell divided the vote. Breckinridge took all the states of the Lower South and some of those in the Upper South, winning 72 electoral votes. Bell carried the states of Tennessee, Kentucky, and Virginia, which netted him 39 electoral votes.

These results gave Lincoln a solid majority, 180 of the 303 electoral votes. Although he received much less than half the popular vote, he had won the presidency.

THE ELECTION OF 1860

	Electoral Vote	Popular Vote	% of Pop. Vote
Lincoln	180	1,865,593	39.8
Douglas	12	1,382,713	29.5
Breckinridge	72	848,356	18.1
Bell	39	592,906	12.6

*New Jersey cast four electoral votes for Lincoln and three for Douglas.
Source: *Historical Statistics of the United States*

Electoral Winner by State
- Lincoln (Republican)
- Douglas (Northern Democratic)
- Breckinridge (Southern Democratic)
- Bell (Constitutional Union)
- 4 Electoral votes

Learning from Maps.
Lincoln's victory in the election of 1860 increased pre-existing regional tensions and soon led to secession.

• Maps

▶ **Place.** How did the election results reflect regional interests?

The Lower South Secedes

Lincoln's victory alarmed many southerners. He had not carried a *single* slave state. Southerners recognized that Lincoln had been legally elected, but they questioned the fairness of a political system that allowed him to govern people who had not chosen him. A New Orleans newspaper editorial expressed the typical viewpoint:

"The history of the . . . Republican party of the North is a history of repeated injuries and usurpations [things taken without right], all having in direct object the establishment of absolute tyranny over the slaveholding States. . . . [The North has] capped the mighty pyramid of unfraternal [unfriendly] enormities by electing Abraham Lincoln . . . on a platform and by a system which indicates nothing but the subjugation [enslavement] of the South and the complete ruin of her . . . institutions. The South has compromised until she can compromise no farther."

For several years southerners had talked of possibly withdrawing from the United States if an antislavery Republican was ever elected president. Now southern radicals prepared to act on that threat. Within days of Lincoln's election, the legislature of South Carolina summoned a special convention to consider the question of **secession**, the act of formally withdrawing as part of the nation. Before the end of the year the delegates voted to withdraw their state from the United States of America.

Two views of secession. Though some southerners did not want to leave the Union, others used the idea of states' sovereignty to justify secession. They pointed out that the original 13 states had existed separately before they had joined together to form the United States. Representatives from the states had drafted and then approved the U.S. Constitution, southerners noted. Surely, they reasoned, each state then had the right to cancel its allegiance if its citizens so desired.

Many northerners saw secession as a challenge to the basic principles of the Constitution. The Constitution bound all the states together by mutual consent, they argued. The states had agreed to recognize the Constitution as the supreme law of the land. They had also accepted federalism—the sharing of power by the national and state governments—and the responsibility of the national government to oversee certain government functions. After years of accepting the system the slave states now proposed to cast the Constitution aside in favor of states' rights. This angered northerners.

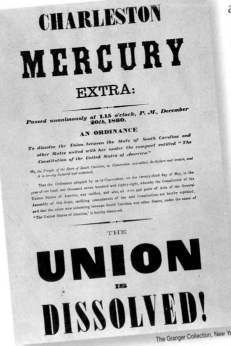

The Granger Collection, New York

Protecting the South. Southerners' belief in states' sovereignty formed their constitutional basis for secession. This does not, however, account for why so many people in the South were willing to leave the Union. Their loyalty to the region and to the slave system explain their desire for separation. The prolonged controversy over slavery had weakened southerners' loyalty to the nation as a whole.

Even though Lincoln and other moderates had no intention of trying to get rid of slavery where it already existed, southerners could not accept the idea that slavery itself was "wrong." When Lincoln's point of view triumphed and he became president of the United States, many southerners no longer wished to be part of the nation.

....

A South Carolina newspaper published this broadside on December 20, 1860, to announce that the state had seceded.

Section 4 Review

• Glossary

• Time Line

IDENTIFY and explain the significance of the following: John Brown's raid, Constitutional Union Party, secession

REVIEWING FOR DETAILS
1. How did Abraham Lincoln win the presidency?
2. Why did so many southerners want to secede?

REVIEWING FOR UNDERSTANDING
3. **Geographic Literacy** How did the election of 1860 show that the nation was divided?
4. **Writing Mastery:** *Describing* Write a short newspaper article describing reactions to John Brown's raid.
5. **Critical Thinking:** *Determining the Strength of an Argument* How did both northerners and southerners defend their positions on secession? Which position seems stronger to you?

AMERICA'S GEOGRAPHY

Balancing Political Power

Maintaining a balance of political power between the slave and free states had been a major concern in the United States since the Constitutional Convention. The balance of power in Congress was of particular concern. The free states had always had a greater representation in the House of Representatives because of their larger populations. Representation in the Senate, however, was kept in balance by ensuring that as each new free state came into the union, so did a slave state. This balance of slave and free states was upset in the 1850s when three new free states joined the Union without any new slave states being added. When Abraham Lincoln was elected president in 1860, many southerners believed that they had lost their voice in the federal government.

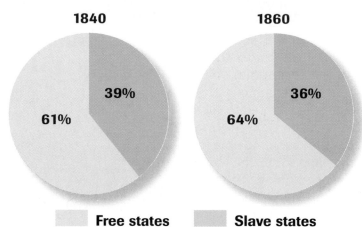

Distribution of Population Counted for Representation

1840

39%

61%

1860

36%

64%

Free states   Slave states

The delegates to the Constitutional Convention had agreed that only three fifths of the slave population would count in determining how many representatives each state would be allowed in the House. At that time, the well-populated free states enjoyed a small numerical advantage over the slave states. In the 1800s the population grew at a faster rate in the free states than in the slave states. This meant that the number of representatives for the free states increased more quickly than the number of representatives for the slave states. As a result, it became more difficult for the slave states to win decisions in the House. **Linking Geography and History:** How many seats did the free states gain in the House of Representatives between 1840 and 1860?

Representatives in the House

	Slave States	Free States
1840	88	135
1860	85	155

Admission of New States

Free States ▶   Illinois • 1818

1820   1830

Slave States ▶   Missouri • 1821

Stephen Douglas had good reason to believe that slavery was unlikely to become popular in the territories. Although the territories were the cause for much of the debate over the expansion of slavery in the 1850s, there were few slaves in the region. From the political standpoint of the South, however, the issue of whether slavery would be allowed in the territories was extremely important.

The United States in 1860

Free states
Slave states
Territories

The makeup of the Senate ensured equality among the states by allowing each state two senators. The system did not ensure equality between regions, however. Initially, the greatest concern was over equality between large and small states, but soon the struggle between slave and free states took center stage. **Linking Geography and History:** What would the total number of senators have been for the free states in 1860? For the slave states?

To learn more about balancing political power, go to the interactive map, "Balancing Political Power," on the CD-ROM.

• **Balancing Political Power**

Michigan • 1837   Iowa • 1846   Wisconsin • 1848   California • 1850   Minnesota • 1858   Oregon • 1859

1840   **1850**   **1860**

Arkansas • 1836   Florida • 1845   Texas • 1845

CHAPTER **14**

The Connecticut Historical Society, Hartford, Connecticut

The Civil War
(1861–1865)

THEMES IN AMERICAN HISTORY

Geographic Diversity:
How might geography affect the outcome of a war?

Economic Development:
How might a nation's economy affect its ability to wage war?

Constitutional Heritage:
How might a period of rebellion affect a people's civil rights?

While many Americans feared the coming of the Civil War, others were thrilled. Abolitionist Frederick Douglass saw it as a chance to end slavery, "the monster evil of the nineteenth century." "Friends of freedom," he cried, "now is your time." To many southerners the war offered a different freedom—independence from the United States! Americans on both sides soon learned the high cost of these goals.

• **Video Opener**

• **Skill Builder**

image above: *Antisecession cartoon, 1861*

Section 1

THE WAR BEGINS

Multimedia Connections

Explore these related topics and materials on the CD–ROM to enrich your understanding of this section:

 Media Bank

- Union Soldiers' Occupations
- Road to the Civil War
- Civil War Recruitment Poster
- Union and Confederate Soldiers

- Elizabeth Blackwell
- Civil War Nurses
- Susie King Taylor
- Nurse Tending a Soldier

 Readings

- Raising the Regiments

 Profiles

- Elizabeth Blackwell
- Dorothea Dix
- Abraham Lincoln
- Susie King Taylor

O n December 20, 1860, the people of Charleston, South Carolina, went wild with excitement. Their state had seceded from the Union! People poured out into the streets to spread the word. The celebrations lasted through the day and into the night. Back in Washington, President James Buchanan was at a reception. Suddenly, a South Carolina congressman rushed in with the fateful news from Charleston. The shaken president quickly left the gathering when he heard the account of South Carolina's secession.

As you read this section you will find out:
▶ **How the Confederacy was formed.**
▶ **What incident sparked the Civil War.**
▶ **What the strengths and weaknesses of each side were when the war began.**

The Confederate States of America

By February 1, 1861, Mississippi, Louisiana, Alabama, Georgia, Florida, and Texas had joined South Carolina in seceding from the Union. On February 4, delegates from the seceding states met in Montgomery, Alabama, to create their own central government, called the **Confederate States of America**—or the Confederacy for short. It took the delegates just four days to draft a constitution. This was possible because the document was based on the U.S. Constitution.

After writing their constitution, the delegates chose Jefferson Davis of Mississippi as president of the Confederacy and Alexander Stephens of Georgia as vice president. In an election later that year, southern voters confirmed their delegates' choice.

The Granger Collection, New York

Jefferson Davis had served in both the U.S. military and government.

● **Jefferson Davis**

Davis was a tall, slender man with high cheekbones, fair hair, and blue gray eyes. He was 52 years old when he became president of the Confederacy. Like Abraham Lincoln, he was born in Kentucky, the child of a pioneer family. He graduated from the United States Military Academy in 1828, but he resigned his commission in 1835 and became a cotton planter in Mississippi.

In 1845 Davis was elected to the House of Representatives. When the Mexican War broke out, however, he gave up his seat to serve as a colonel in the army. Although wounded in the Battle of Buena Vista, Davis recovered fully. In 1847 he was appointed to the U.S. Senate. When Franklin Pierce became president in 1853, he named Davis secretary of war.

Davis was an extremely hard worker, but he did not get along well with people, and he often quarreled with government officials. These traits would later create problems in the Confederate government.

Lincoln Becomes President

In early 1861, however, Davis's strengths seemed much more obvious than his weaknesses. Indeed, when Abraham Lincoln was inaugurated as president of the United States on March 4, 1861, many people thought him a far less inspiring leader than the president of the new Confederacy.

Lincoln had chosen a cabinet that included his four main Republican rivals for the presidency. His attempt to unite his party was understandable at a time of national crisis, but many people wondered whether this backwoods lawyer could control such a powerful group. Lincoln appointed one of the best-known Republicans in the United States, William H. Seward, as secretary of state. Seward did not think Lincoln was capable of

Presidential Lives
Abraham Lincoln

Shortly after the Civil War began, Abraham Lincoln faced a devastating crisis at home—the death of his beloved young son, William. Sadly, Lincoln and his wife had experienced a similar loss before. In February 1850 their three-year-old son, Edward, had died of tuberculosis. The Lincolns barely survived this tragedy, but they soon had another child.

William, their newborn son, was a smart and handsome boy. Many observers thought he was Lincoln's favorite child, though the president showed no outward preference. In January 1862 William fell sick with "bilious fever." This harsh illness might have been caused by polluted water in the White House. He died a few weeks later, plunging both the Lincolns into a deep depression. "My boy is gone—he is actually gone!" Lincoln cried upon learning the terrible news. "We loved him so," the president later reflected.

The Civil War left little time for grief, however. Lincoln struggled to lead the Union even as he mourned his son.

The Granger Collection, New York

being president. Seward was ready, he told his wife, "to save freedom and my country" by making the major decisions necessary to run the country himself.

Lincoln, however, did not intend to be dominated by Seward or anyone else. In his inaugural address, his words to the divided nation made his position clear:

> **"I have no purpose, directly or indirectly, to interfere with the institution of slavery in the states where it exists. I believe I have no lawful right to do so, and I have no inclination [intention] to do so. . . .**
>
> **We are not enemies but friends. We must not be enemies. Though passion may have strained, it must not break our bonds of affection."**

In hopes that the southern states might be persuaded to change their minds, Lincoln assured the South that he would not rush troops into the region to prevent secession. Many northerners believed that the secession crisis could be solved by yet another compromise. Nevertheless, Lincoln warned that secession was illegal. "No state, upon its own mere motion," he said, "can lawfully get out of the Union."

The immediate problem facing Lincoln was the situation at Fort Sumter. The fort was located on an island in South Carolina's Charleston Harbor. The commander of Union forces in Charleston, Major Robert Anderson, had kept control of the fort when South Carolina seceded. Anderson and his men could not hold out forever without fresh supplies, however. After considering the fort's position, Lincoln decided to send food—but no reinforcements or ammunition—to the fort. He then informed the governor of South Carolina of his intentions.

After months of standoff, the Confederates decided to capture the fort before supplies could arrive. On April 12, they began to bombard Fort Sumter. By the next day, they had nearly destroyed the fort. When the Union's ammunition was almost exhausted, Major Anderson and his weary troops surrendered. The Civil War had begun.

Preparing for War

After the attack on Fort Sumter, Lincoln called for 75,000 volunteer soldiers. The Confederate Congress quickly responded with a call for 100,000 men. News that Lincoln intended to use force against the Confederacy convinced Virginia, North Carolina, Tennessee, and Arkansas to secede and to join the other Confederate states.

Choosing sides. To strengthen support for secession in Virginia, the Confederacy shifted its capital from Montgomery, Alabama, to Richmond, Virginia. The people of western Virginia, however, held few slaves and preferred to remain in the Union. Several western counties seceded from Virginia. In 1863 they were admitted to the Union as the state of West Virginia.

Four additional slave states—Delaware, Maryland, Kentucky, and Missouri—remained in the Union. Both sides wanted the loyalty of these strategic states. Kentucky and Missouri were important for control of the Ohio and Mississippi Rivers. If Maryland seceded, the

More than 3,000 shells poured down onto Fort Sumter during the 34-hour bombardment. Miraculously, no one on either side was killed or seriously wounded in the battle.

Confederacy would surround Washington! Delaware, which had few slaves, showed the strongest support for the Union. Many people in the other three states, however, openly supported the South. Soldiers from these **border states** fought on both sides.

At times, the war set brother against brother, husband against wife, and father against son. Four of Henry Clay's grandsons fought for the South and three others fought for the North. First Lady Mary Todd Lincoln, a native of Kentucky, had four brothers in the Confederate army.

The volunteers. In both the North and the South, the recruiting of troops was left to the states. In most places, recruits came forward enthusiastically. Even a few women enlisted in the army, disguised as men. The majority of recruits, however, were men hoping for an exciting adventure that would take them far from the farm or the factory. Most southerners fought to defend what they saw as their rights, while many northerners signed up to preserve the Union. In Boston, Mary Ashton Livermore reported:

> **"Hastily formed companies marched to camps of rendezvous, the sunlight flashing from gun-barrel and bayonet. . . . Merchants and clerks rushed out from stores, bareheaded, saluting them as they passed. . . . I had never seen anything like this before."**

Soldiers were not the only type of volunteers needed by the North and South. Some civilians served as spies. One important spy for the Union was Mary Elizabeth Bowser, a slave who worked in the home of Confederate president Jefferson Davis.

Many other men and women volunteered to care for the armies' sick and wounded. Before the war, most Americans considered nursing a male profession. During the war, however, thousands of women served this role. Catholic nuns turned their convents into hospitals and treated soldiers on both sides. The well-known reformer Dorothea Dix volunteered her services and was appointed superintendent of nurses for the Union armies. To train nurses and to improve the overall state of medical conditions, Dr. Elizabeth Blackwell helped found what became the U.S. Sanitary Commission.

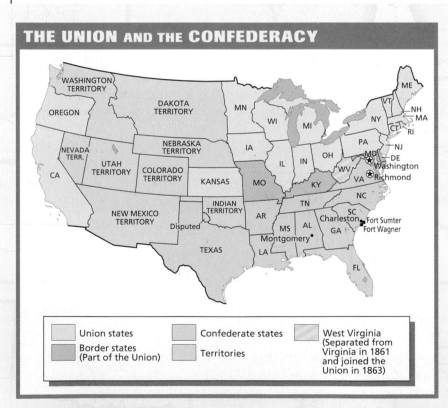

THE UNION AND THE CONFEDERACY

- Union states
- Border states (Part of the Union)
- Confederate states
- Territories
- West Virginia (Separated from Virginia in 1861 and joined the Union in 1863)

Learning from Maps.
Washington was surrounded by slave states.

▶ **Region.** What states made up the Confederacy? What states made up the Union?

• Maps

North Versus South

In numbers, the Confederacy was no match for the Union. The North had about 22 million people, the South about 9 million. About 3.5 million of the southerners were slaves. Because southerners were unwilling to arm slaves, the Confederate army could only draw from around 1 million men.

In 1860 about 85 percent of the nation's factories were in the northern states. New York, Pennsylvania, and Massachusetts each had more factories than the entire South. There were only two small gun factories in the South, and no southern factory was capable of handling the need for uniforms and shoes.

In addition, the North had more than twice as many miles of railroad tracks as the South and almost twice the number of horses, donkeys, and mules. Thus, the Union could easily move its troops and supplies. The United States already had an army and navy, as well as established ways of raising money. The Confederacy had to create these institutions from scratch.

The Confederacy, however, had important strategic advantages over the Union. The South's military tradition provided it with brilliant generals. In addition, the South did not

Women on both sides made valuable contributions to the war effort. They labored on farms, in government, and in factories. Making cartridges in arsenals was dangerous work.

• **Rating the North and South**

have to *defeat* the North. Instead, it just had to defend itself until the people in the North grew tired of fighting. Southern armies also had the advantage of usually fighting on familiar land and among friendly civilians. These factors added to their determination to fight and helped make up for the shortage of troops and supplies.

Section 1 Review

• **Glossary**

IDENTIFY and explain the significance of the following: Confederate States of America, Jefferson Davis, Abraham Lincoln, border states, Elizabeth Blackwell

REVIEWING FOR DETAILS
1. What steps did southerners take to form a new nation?
2. How did the Civil War begin?

REVIEWING FOR UNDERSTANDING
3. **Geographic Literacy** Why would the support of Maryland, Delaware, Kentucky, and Missouri have been important to each side in the Civil War?
4. **Writing Mastery:** *Expressing* Take the role of a general for the North or South and, in a short essay, explain why you think your side had the most advantages at the beginning of the Civil War.
5. **Critical Thinking:** *Drawing Conclusions* Why do you think people chose to side with the North or the South? Explain your answer.

Section 2

THE WAR: EAST AND WEST

Multimedia Connections

Explore these related topics and materials on the CD–ROM to enrich your understanding of this section:

 Atlas

- War in New Mexico
- Theaters of War, 1861–1865
- War in Missouri and Arkansas
- Southern Railroads, 1862–1865

 Media Bank

- Civil War Music 1
- Civil War Battles
- Second Battle of Bull Run
- Mary Boykin Chesnut
- Family Store
- Johnny Shiloh
- Wounded Union Soldiers
- Stonewall Jackson

 Profiles

- Mary Boykin Chesnut
- George McClellan

 Biographies

- Stonewall Jackson

It takes time to raise and train an army, but people in the North were impatient for action. "On to Richmond" was the popular cry in Washington. In July 1861, long before the Union troops were ready, General Irvin McDowell ordered them into Virginia. Laughing and joking along the way, the soldiers were joined by carriages filled with politicians, newspaper reporters, and curious onlookers. Some carried picnic lunches, anticipating an afternoon of entertainment.

As you read this section you will find out:

▶ **What the Union's war goals were in the East, and why it did not achieve them.**

▶ **How the Union pursued its war goals in the West.**

▶ **Why the Mississippi River and the city of Vicksburg were important.**

The First Battle of Bull Run

On July 21, 1861, some 35,000 poorly trained Union troops met the Confederate army of about 22,000 soldiers along a small stream called Bull Run at Manassas railroad junction in northern Virginia. The Confederates, who were not much better prepared, held the high ground above the stream. The Union general, Irvin McDowell, circled west, guessing that the Confederate line was weakest there. When he attacked, the Confederates fell back.

The Union soldiers broke the Confederate line, but Confederate troops under General Thomas J. Jackson stopped the Union advance cold. At the peak of the **First Battle of Bull Run**, a southern officer cried, "There is Jackson standing like a stone wall! Rally behind the Virginians!"—winning for Jackson the nickname "Stonewall."

When the southerners counterattacked, the Union army panicked. Hundreds of Union soldiers dropped their weapons and fled north toward Washington. The Confederates might have captured the Union capital if they had not been so disorganized. As southern General Joseph E. Johnston commented, "Our army was more disorganized by victory than that of the United States by defeat."

Following the battle, a government clerk named Clara Barton saw that many of the wounded went untreated because the army lacked medical services. Thereafter, she provided first aid and distributed supplies to Union soldiers. The soldiers labeled her "Angel of the Battlefield" because she even gave aid in the midst of battle. After the war, Barton eventually organized the American Red Cross.

After Bull Run, Americans on both sides realized that winning the war might be difficult. Southerner Mary Chesnut worried that the victory would mislead "us into a fool's paradise of conceit at our superior valor [courage]." She had cause for concern. In the North, Lincoln's secretary wrote, "The preparations for the war will be continued with increased vigor by the Government." Indeed, Congress authorized Lincoln to raise a force of 1 million soldiers to serve for three years.

The War in the East

Lincoln replaced McDowell with George B. McClellan. General McClellan then prepared to attack Richmond, located only about 100 miles south of Washington. Union leaders believed that by capturing the Confederate capital, the war would come to a quick end.

McClellan was a skilled organizer and was popular with ordinary soldiers, but he had serious weaknesses as a leader. He was vain and had too high an opinion of his own abilities. McClellan also often overestimated the strength of his enemies. Despite his dashing appearance and bold talk, he never seemed ready to march against the enemy.

After the disastrous loss at the First Battle of Bull Run, McClellan's cautious approach seemed the right policy. The Union army had to be trained and disciplined before it was ready to fight again. Yet even when this task had been accomplished, McClellan still delayed. Finally, in March 1862 he was ready to advance.

McClellan on the move. McClellan's plan for capturing Richmond was complicated but sensible. He moved his army by boat down the Potomac River and through Chesapeake Bay to the Virginia coast southeast of Richmond. He planned to take the Confederates by surprise by attacking where their defenses seemed weakest. Instead of striking swiftly as his plan called

Clara Barton

● **Clara Barton**

The Confederate soldiers broke through Union lines at Bull Run. As they charged, they let loose a terrifying scream. This later became known as the "rebel yell." The sound struck terror in the hearts of many Union soldiers.

The Granger Collection, New York

for, however, McClellan hesitated. He had more than 100,000 men—a force that was much larger than the Confederates'—yet he pleaded for more troops. Impatient for action, President Lincoln wrote an urgent letter to McClellan on April 9, 1862:

"**[Your] hesitation to move upon an intrenched [entrenched] enemy is but the story of Manassas [Bull Run] repeated. . . . I have never written you, or spoken to you, in greater kindness of feeling than now. . . . *But you must act.*"

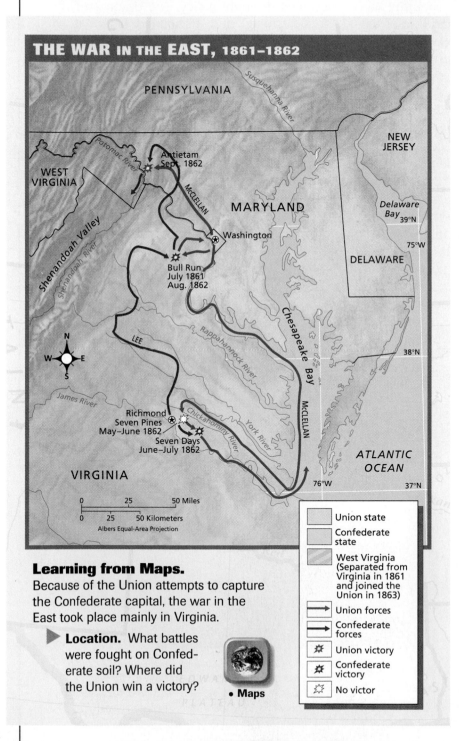

THE WAR IN THE EAST, 1861–1862

Union state

Confederate state

West Virginia (Separated from Virginia in 1861 and joined the Union in 1863)

Union forces

Confederate forces

Union victory

Confederate victory

No victor

Learning from Maps.
Because of the Union attempts to capture the Confederate capital, the war in the East took place mainly in Virginia.

▶ **Location.** What battles were fought on Confederate soil? Where did the Union win a victory?

● **Maps**

In early May, McClellan finally began a slow-moving advance. On May 31, while the Union army was crossing the Chickahominy River, Confederate general Joseph E. Johnston launched a fierce attack. Despite heavy loss of life in this **Battle of Seven Pines**, neither side gained an advantage.

Johnston was wounded in this battle and had to give up his command. Robert E. Lee, the officer who had led the 1859 capture of John Brown at Harpers Ferry, became the new commander of the southern armies.

Lee takes command. Lee, who had served brilliantly during the Mexican War, had been Lincoln's first choice to lead the Union army. He had declined. Although he opposed secession, Lee decided that his first loyalty was to his home state of Virginia.

Lee was a great addition to the Confederate army. With McClellan threatening Richmond, Lee daringly sent Stonewall Jackson's troops in northern Virginia up to threaten the defenses of Washington. Lincoln became alarmed at the southern army's presence so near the capital. He canceled the

Robert E. Lee was beloved in the South and respected in the North. His horse, Traveler, was nearly as celebrated. After the war, visitors kept hairs from his tail as souvenirs.

• **Robert E. Lee**

reinforcements requested by McClellan and ordered them to protect Washington instead. This was what Lee had wanted.

In June 1862 Lee launched an all-out attack on McClellan's forces. After a series of clashes, the Union army fell back. Lee had won the **Seven Days Battles**. More than 16,000 Union soldiers were killed or wounded, and the South lost nearly 20,000 men.

The Second Battle of Bull Run.

A discouraged Lincoln ordered General McClellan to withdraw and to combine his troops with a new army that had been formed south of Washington under the command of General John Pope.

As McClellan pulled back, Lee moved northward. He wanted to destroy this new army before McClellan's could join it. In a daring maneuver, Lee sent Stonewall Jackson's troops to hit Pope's army from the rear. Jackson marched swiftly and then struck hard, destroying Pope's supplies and supply lines. In desperation, on August 29, Pope attacked the Confederates.

This **Second Battle of Bull Run** was fought on almost the same ground as the first. Again, the Confederates drove the Union troops back toward Washington. Dismayed by Pope's failure, Lincoln gave McClellan command of Pope's army.

The War in the West

At the same time the war was raging in the East, Union forces were on the move in the West. After the First Battle of Bull Run, the Union focused on its chief objective in the West—to control the Mississippi River. This would take away the South's most important trade route to the sea and would make movement of troops and supplies within the South difficult. The South would be cut in two.

Grant on the move. The struggle for the river was long and bitter. Out of this struggle came the Union's greatest general, Ulysses S. Grant. Although Grant had been just an average student at West Point, he served well in the Mexican War. After the war, however, he found his army posting in the West lonely and boring, and he began to drink heavily.

In 1854 Grant left the army. He tried a number of different careers but succeeded in none. When the Civil War began, he quit his job in a leather shop and joined an Illinois regiment. Because of Grant's performance, he was quickly promoted to the rank of brigadier general.

Grant was a shy, small man who constantly chewed cigars

General Ulysses S. Grant

• **Ulysses S. Grant**

and rarely stood up straight. His uniforms were rumpled and ill fitting. Grant did not look like a general, yet he was brave and determined, and he turned out to be an excellent military strategist.

Grant decided that the best way to get control of the Mississippi River, which the Confederates had heavily fortified, was to attack the more vulnerable but strategically important Tennessee River. In February 1862 he organized a successful land-and-river attack on Fort Henry, a Confederate outpost on the Tennessee. Union gunboats pounded the fort into surrender before moving on to attack Fort Donelson, on the Cumberland River. When the fort's commander asked Grant the terms for surrender, Grant replied, "No terms except an unconditional and immediate surrender can be accepted." This won him the nickname "Unconditional Surrender" Grant.

The Battle of Shiloh.

Grant next marched his men farther south along the Tennessee River. He intended to capture a Confederate railroad center at Corinth, Mississippi. However, on April 6, 1862, about 20 miles north of Corinth, the Confederates surprised Grant's army at Shiloh Church in southern Tennessee. During the first day of this **Battle of Shiloh**, the Confederates drove Grant's army back.

Fortunately for Grant, 25,000 fresh Union troops arrived during the night. The next day, the Union army forced the Confederates back, but Shiloh was an extremely costly victory. In just two days, the Union suffered some 13,000 casualties. Confederate casualties were some 11,000.

The huge losses suffered by both sides had a sobering effect on the troops, their generals, and the public. After the battle one soldier reflected, "I saw more of human agony and woe than I trust I will ever again be called on to witness."

The Capture of Vicksburg

While Grant was fighting to gain control of the Tennessee River, a Union fleet commanded by Captain David Farragut captured New Orleans and Baton Rouge, Louisiana. By autumn, only a 200-mile-long stretch of the Mississippi River between Vicksburg, Mississippi, and Port Hudson,

THE WAR IN THE WEST, 1862–1863

Union state

Union occupied 1863

Confederate state

Union forces

Union victory

Confederate forces

Confederate victory

UNION STRATEGY
Control of the Mississippi would split the Confederacy and enable northern forces to reach the Deep South.

IL
IN
Louisville
KY
MO
Paducah
Ft. Donelson Feb. 1862
Cumberland River
Ft. Henry Feb. 1862
Nashville
Murfreesboro Dec. 1862–Jan. 1863
Shiloh April 1862
TN
Chattanooga Nov. 1863
Memphis
GRANT
Corinth
JOHNSTON
Tennessee River
Chickamauga Sept. 1863
Arkansas River
AR
Birmingham
Atlanta
AL
GA
MS
Vicksburg May–July 1863
Jackson
GRANT
LA
Tombigbee River
Mississippi River
TX
Sabine River
Port Hudson May–July 1863
Baton Rouge
Mobile
FL
New Orleans April 1862
30°N
FARRAGUT
Gulf of Mexico

N W E S

0   75   150 Miles
0   75   150 Kilometers
Azimuthal Equal-Area Projection

90°W   85°W

After the Union victories at Murfreesboro and Chattanooga, the Union's western armies were in position to divide the Upper and Lower South.

Learning from Maps.
The war in the West was fought largely in Mississippi and Tennessee.

▶ **Region.** What physical feature made this area strategically important?

• Maps

• War in
Indian
Territory

Confederate guns in Vicksburg, high over the Mississippi River, shell Union gunboats on the river below.

he pinned down Pemberton's troops inside Vicksburg and waited for them to surrender—a military strategy known as a **siege**. The siege of Vicksburg began in mid-May. Grant's army shelled the city almost continuously. As the Confederates ran short of food, a resident wrote in her diary:

"**We are utterly cut off from the world, surrounded by a circle of fire. . . . The fiery shower of shells goes on day and night. . . . People do nothing but eat what they can get, sleep when they can, and dodge the shells.**"

On July 4, 1863, Pemberton surrendered to Grant. Shortly afterward, Port Hudson, the last remaining southern position on the Mississippi River, also surrendered.

Even after the fall of Vicksburg and Port Hudson, the Confederates continued to control much of Louisiana, Arkansas, and Texas. However, these states were cut off from the rest of the Confederacy!

Louisiana, was still in Confederate hands. Grant then decided to attack Vicksburg, a city high on the cliffs overlooking the river. A small Confederate force, commanded by General John C. Pemberton, defended the city.

Grant first approached Vicksburg from the north in November 1862, but he soon discovered that the marshy land around the city made an infantry attack impossible. Instead,

Section 2 Review

• Glossary

• Gazetteer

IDENTIFY and explain the significance of the following: First Battle of Bull Run, Stonewall Jackson, George B. McClellan, Battle of Seven Pines, Robert E. Lee, Seven Days Battles, Second Battle of Bull Run, Ulysses S. Grant, Battle of Shiloh, siege

LOCATE and explain the importance of the following: Richmond, Potomac River, Vicksburg, Port Hudson

REVIEWING FOR DETAILS

1. What did the Union hope to accomplish in the war in the East, and why was it unable to achieve these goals?

2. How did Union forces go about winning the war in the West?

REVIEWING FOR UNDERSTANDING

3. **Geographic Literacy** Why were the Mississippi River and the city of Vicksburg important in the West?

4. **Writing Mastery:** *Describing* Imagine that you are a newspaper reporter at one of the major battles of the Civil War, such as Second Bull Run or Shiloh. Write a short article describing what you have seen.

5. **Critical Thinking:** *Making Comparisons* Compare the attempts of Generals McDowell and McClellan to capture the Confederate capital. What difficulties did each commander face?

Section 3
THE PEOPLE'S WAR

Multimedia Connections

Explore these related topics and materials on the CD–ROM to enrich your understanding of this section:

 Atlas

- Emancipation, 1863

 Profiles

- Charlotte Forten
- Robert Smalls

 Readings

- Emancipation Proclamation
- Emancipation Reactions

 Simulation

- Global Politics & the Civil War

 Media Bank

- Celebrating Emancipation
- Southern Plantation
- Northern Machine Shop

As the Civil War dragged on, most Americans—men and women, soldiers and civilians—began to feel its terrible effects. "God grant these things may soon end and peace be restored. Of this war I am heartily sick and tired," complained a Pennsylvania soldier. Confederate Mary Chesnut voiced the feelings of many civilians on both sides: "Is anything worth it? This fearful sacrifice—this awful penalty we pay for war?"

As you read this section you will find out:

▶ **How the Emancipation Proclamation changed the war.**

▶ **Why some northerners opposed the war.**

▶ **How the war affected the economy of the South.**

Antietam

General Lee believed that the South had to do more than simply defend Richmond. To end the war, it had to deliver such a stinging defeat that northerners would grow tired of the costly conflict and would lose the will to fight. So Lee decided to march north, around the defenses of Washington. On September 4, 1862, he crossed the Potomac River and entered Maryland.

Union general McClellan was unsure of Lee's exact position. Then on September 13, one of McClellan's soldiers found a copy of Lee's battle plans wrapped around some cigars in an abandoned Confederate camp. With this information, McClellan was able to track down Lee's army. The armies met in battle on September 17 at Antietam Creek, near Sharpsburg, Maryland. Lee had about

Confederate soldiers lie dead beside the ruins of a cannon following the Battle of Antietam. The high casualties at Antietam made it the bloodiest single day of the entire war.

40,000 soldiers, McClellan nearly twice that number.

The **Battle of Antietam** began at dawn. When it ended at twilight, the Confederates had lost nearly 14,000 men, the Union forces more than 12,000. Then the next night, the Confederates retreated across the Potomac River. The North could finally claim a victory in the East.

Emancipation

Even before Antietam, the high cost of lives and money had started to change northerners' view of the war. Many began to believe that the war had to do more than preserve the Union—it also had to put an end to slavery. Otherwise, a northern victory would be in vain because future conflict would be inevitable. Lincoln also believed that slavery should not continue, but he was aware of the obstacles to ending slavery. He knew that many white northerners remained prejudiced against African Americans, whether enslaved or free. He also realized that a president did not have the constitutional authority to simply end slavery.

Lincoln was a clever politician. To emancipate, or free, the Confederates' slaves, he issued a military order declaring an end to slavery in the Confederacy in order to weaken the rebels' ability to fight the war. Lincoln felt he could do this under his constitutional powers as commander-in-chief of the armed forces.

Lincoln waited to issue the **Emancipation Proclamation** until after the Union victory at Antietam. He then announced that after January 1, 1863:

"**all persons held as slaves within any state or designated part of a state, the people whereof shall then be in rebellion against the United States, shall be then, thenceforward, and forever free.**"

Of course, the Emancipation Proclamation did little to free slaves until the Union defeated

Global Connections

The Civil War

Neither Great Britain nor France entered the Civil War, but both nations leaned toward supporting the South. French ruler Napolcon III saw the war as a chance to obtain an empire in Mexico. While the North and South were fighting, French troops were overthrowing Mexico's government. Lincoln protested France's actions, but Davis did not.

Some British believed that an independent South would be a better market for industrial products. By mid-1862, Confederate victories in Virginia had increased Britain's confidence in the South. British leaders began to discuss pressuring Lincoln to end the war.

Lincoln's Emancipation Proclamation, however, ended whatever real hopes the South had for outside intervention. Slavery was illegal in Britain and France, and the British abolitionist movement was strong. Both countries might have supported southerners in a war strictly for independence. Neither nation, however, would side with a government fighting to defend its right to enslave people.

the Confederacy. Nonetheless, it was an important step. "The dawn of freedom which it heralds [declares] may not break upon us at once; but it will surely come," rejoiced abolitionist Charlotte Forten.

African Americans and the War

President Lincoln also ordered that freed slaves be encouraged to enlist in the army. Enlisting former slaves, he told General Grant, "works doubly, weakening the enemy and strengthening us."

From the beginning of the war, free African Americans and **contrabands**—escaped slaves who crossed Union lines—had tried to join the Union army. It was not until July 1862, however, that Congress authorized African Americans to join the armed forces. Furthermore, it was only after Lincoln issued the Emancipation Proclamation that African Americans officially were encouraged to enlist in fighting units. Frederick Douglass described the motivation of many of the tens of thousands of African American volunteers:

"Once let the black man get upon his person the brass letters, U.S.; let him get an eagle on his button, and a musket on his shoulder and bullets in his pocket, and there is no power on earth which can deny that he has earned the right to citizenship."

African American troops first saw major action in Port Hudson, Louisiana, in early July 1863. Later that same month, the **54th Massachusetts Infantry** won an honored place in U.S. military history during the battle for Fort Wagner, in South Carolina's Charleston Harbor. After days of trying to take the fort, the Union commander ordered a desperate frontal attack. Knowing the risks, the 54th led the charge under a storm of Confederate cannon fire. The soldiers reached the top of the fort's walls before being turned

Under steady cannon fire, the 54th Massachusetts Infantry bravely led the charge to take Fort Wagner. Over half the regiment was wounded or killed during the charge.

● African American Soldiers

back in fierce fighting. As leader of the charge, the 54th had the highest casualty rate of the battle. The regiment lost nearly half its men.

In all, some 180,000 black soldiers fought for the Union. By the end of the war there were 166 all-black regiments, and one Union soldier in eight was an African American. For much of the war, black soldiers were paid less than white soldiers, even though they performed with equal bravery. Twenty-one African Americans won the Congressional Medal of Honor and more than 30,000 gave their lives for the cause of freedom.

Liberty with her Union shield defends herself against the Copperheads, represented as snakes in this 1863 political cartoon.

Northern Opposition to the War

Not everyone in the North, however, welcomed the Emancipation Proclamation. Some northerners were unwilling to support a war to free slaves or to prevent the southern states from seceding.

The Copperheads. Northern Democrats who opposed the war were known as **Copperheads**. Many Copperheads were sympathetic to the South. Radical Copperheads organized secret societies, through which they persuaded Union soldiers to desert and helped Confederate prisoners to escape.

To stop the activities of the Copperheads and other critics of the war, Lincoln at times suspended *habeas corpus*, a constitutional protection that prevents authorities from unlawfully jailing people. Lincoln hoped to quiet criticism of the Union war effort by imprisoning protesters. During the war, the government jailed some 13,000 Americans without formal charges.

The draft. A few months after the Emancipation Proclamation went into effect, Congress established a **draft**, a system requiring men to serve in the military. Like the Confederate draft law passed in 1861, this measure allowed draftees to hire substitutes. Draftees could even avoid military service by paying the government $300. Poor men could not possibly raise $300, which was as much as some laborers earned in a year.

Draft riots soon broke out throughout the North. The worst occurred in New York City, where rioters ran wild for four days in July 1863. They burned buildings, looted shops, and attacked local African Americans. African Americans were the target of the rioters because many blamed the draft on the Emancipation Proclamation and resented having to risk their lives to free slaves. Union troops were rushed from the battlefront to New York, but more than 100 people were killed before order was restored.

Southern Shortages

While the North was facing opposition to the war, the South was struggling with economic problems. Paying for the war was among its most difficult tasks. Because the South could not raise enough funds by borrowing or taxing, it simply printed money—more than $1.5 billion. This resulted in tremendous inflation. Salt rose from $2 a bag before the war to $60 in some places by the fall of 1862. Near the end of the war, 50 Confederate paper dollars were worth less than one gold dollar.

In addition, the South's tradition of growing cotton instead of food crops resulted in food shortages in some areas. Clothing was also scarce in the South. Confederate soldiers wore ragged uniforms and sometimes marched without shoes.

Manufactured products were also scarce in the South. The region was mostly agricultural and was largely cut off from trade with Europe. Early in the war, Lincoln had established a naval blockade of southern ports. About 6,000 ships had entered and left southern ports in 1860. By the next year, however, only 800 ships managed to slip past the blockade. Each year fewer and fewer slipped through. The capture of New Orleans also cut off the whole interior of the South from international trade.

The South's shortages encouraged some ship captains to try to break through the ever-tightening northern blockade. The blockade runners' ships were small and fast. The British

Confederate blockade runners tried to slip past Union ships. As the blockade tightened, fewer Confederate ships were successful in their attempts.

island of Bermuda, in the western Atlantic Ocean, was among their favorite destinations. There they exchanged cotton or other farm products for guns, medicines, blankets, and coffee, as well as for silks and other luxuries.

The volume of these imports was too small to have much effect on the South's needs, however. In addition, the blockade runners carried whatever goods they thought would sell for the best price. Because most blockade runners were private citizens, the Confederate government could not force them to import the war supplies that southern armies so badly needed.

• **Wartime Economy**

Section 3 Review

• **Glossary**

IDENTIFY and explain the significance of the following: Battle of Antietam, Emancipation Proclamation, contrabands, 54th Massachusetts Infantry, Copperheads, *habeas corpus,* draft

REVIEWING FOR DETAILS
1. What changes did the Emancipation Proclamation bring in the war?
2. Why did some northerners object to the war?
3. How did the war affect the South's economy?

REVIEWING FOR UNDERSTANDING
4. **Writing Mastery:** *Expressing* Imagine that you are a member of the 54th Massachusetts Infantry. Write a letter back home telling why you feel it is important to fight for the Union.
5. **Critical Thinking:** *Determining the Strength of an Argument* President Lincoln believed that the need to win the war and save the Union permitted him to suspend the rights of some Americans. Do you think this was a convincing argument? Explain your answer.

Section 4

VICTORY AT LAST

Multimedia Connections

Explore these related topics and materials on the CD–ROM to enrich your understanding of this section:

 Profiles

- George Meade
- Jeb Stuart

 Readings

- Gettysburg Address

 Media Bank

- Fredericksburg
- Chancellorsville
- Wilderness
- Spotsylvania Court House
- Cold Harbor
- Sherman's Army in Atlanta

- Ruins of Atlanta
- Jeb Stuart
- Draft of Gettysburg Address

G **Glossary**

- Andersonville Prison

Confederate general James B. Longstreet studied the Union troops on the hills outside of Gettysburg. Convinced that the enemy's position was too strong, he urged Robert E. Lee not to force a fight in this place. But Lee had confidence in his soldiers. "The enemy is there," he said, "and I am going to attack him there." Longstreet remained worried, however. He sensed that Lee would not win the victory he needed outside this small Pennsylvania town.

As you read this section you will find out:

▶ **Why the Battle of Gettysburg was significant.**

▶ **What General Grant's strategy was to win the war.**

▶ **How General Sherman's march affected the South.**

The Battle of Gettysburg

By the spring of 1863 the war had raged for two long years, and the North seemed no closer to restoring the nation than when Fort Sumter fell. Reports from the front did little to raise northern spirits. On Virginia battlefields like Fredericksburg and Chancellorsville, the Confederates continued to beat back the Union armies. As the casualties continued to mount, Lincoln searched for a general who could defeat Lee and put an end to the terrible war.

● Southern Victories

Lee on the move. Lee invaded the North for a second time in June 1863. He still hoped to gain a decisive victory on northern soil and make the Union give up the struggle. As gray-clad Confederates marched through Maryland

and into Pennsylvania, Union troops raced cross-country to intercept them. General George G. Meade was in command, the fifth officer to head the Union forces in less than a year.

On July 1, some of Meade's cavalry made contact with Confederate infantry outside of Gettysburg, Pennsylvania. The southerners had come to the town looking for some much-needed shoes. Both sides quickly concentrated their armies at Gettysburg.

Meade positioned his troops south of town on Cemetery Ridge. Lee's forces occupied Seminary Ridge, almost a mile away. For the next two days, the Confederates tried to capture Cemetery Ridge. As the sun set on July 2, Union troops had turned back fierce attacks on the northern and the southern ends of their position.

Pickett's Charge. On the afternoon of July 3, Confederate artillery shelled Cemetery Ridge. Around 3:00 P.M. General George E. Pickett led a charge at the center of the Union line. Howling the eerie "rebel yell," some 15,000 southern soldiers started at a trot across about a mile of open ground into heavy Union gunfire.

For a brief moment, a handful of southerners reached the Union trenches, but the Union forces rallied and drove back **Pickett's Charge**. In 30 bloody minutes, almost half the Confederate attackers had been killed or

On average, Civil War soldiers spent about 50 days in camp for every day they spent in battle. Like many men on both sides, this soldier from the 31st Pennsylvania Infantry is joined in camp by his wife and children.

● **Soldiers of the Civil War**

wounded. Pickett described his "overwhelming heartbreak" in a letter to his wife:

"**Well, it is over now. The battle is lost, and many of us are prisoners, many are dead, many wounded, bleeding and dying. Your soldier lives and mourns. If it were not for you, my darling, he would rather . . . be back there with his dead, to sleep for all time in an unknown grave.**"

The **Battle of Gettysburg** was indeed over. The Confederates lost more than 20,000 men,

Union forces (left) defend themselves against the Confederates (right) during Pickett's Charge.

● **Battle of Gettysburg**

the Union forces some 23,000. On July 4, 1863, the very day that Vicksburg surrendered in the West, Lee began his retreat from Gettysburg. Had General Meade pursued, he might have destroyed Lee's army and ended the war. Instead, Meade delayed, and the war dragged on.

Grant Versus Lee

In March 1864 Lincoln called Grant to Washington and named him commanding general of all Union armies. Grant decided to try to end the war by mounting two great offensives. He would lead an advance toward Richmond, seeking a showdown battle with Lee's army in northern Virginia.

Another Union army commanded by General William Tecumseh Sherman would march from Chattanooga, Tennessee, into Georgia to capture the important railroad center of Atlanta. Then the two armies would march toward each other, crushing any Confederate resistance that remained.

Grant's march into Virginia met fierce resistance. In May 1864 Grant and Lee clashed in a series of bloody battles. Lee's soldiers fought hard to keep the Union forces from advancing. Grant's army, however, pressed on toward Richmond.

As Union and Confederate forces hammered away at each other, the death count rose. In seven weeks of fighting, Grant had lost

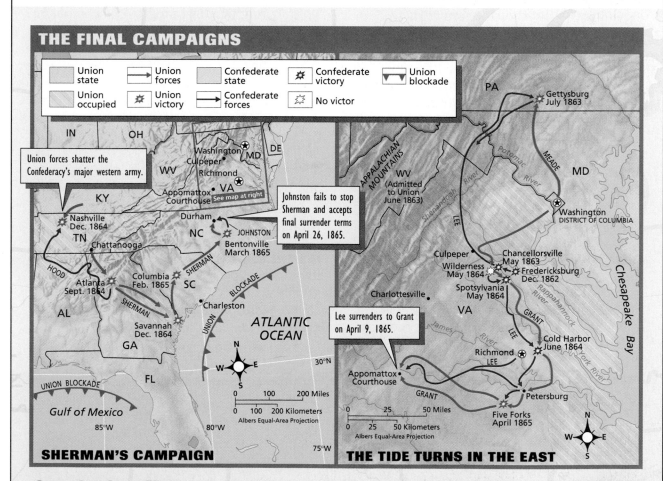

THE FINAL CAMPAIGNS

| Union state | Union forces | Confederate state | Confederate victory | Union blockade |
| Union occupied | Union victory | Confederate forces | No victor | |

SHERMAN'S CAMPAIGN

THE TIDE TURNS IN THE EAST

Learning from Maps. After Gettysburg, Lee retreated south and concentrated on stopping Grant's advance toward Richmond.

▶ **Place.** What states did Sherman's army march through after the capture of Atlanta?

• **Maps**

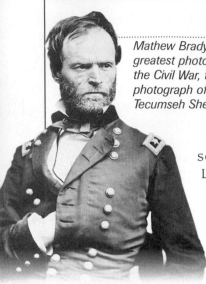

Mathew Brady, perhaps the greatest photographer of the Civil War, took this photograph of William Tecumseh Sherman.

● **William T. Sherman**

some 65,000 men to Lee's 35,000. Despite the high cost in lives, Grant was wearing down Lee's tired army. The Confederates were running short of men and equipment. Lee could no longer replace all his casualties.

In contrast, Grant was supported by a steady stream of recruits. In addition, Uion factories were turning out almost unlimited amounts of supplies. The larger population and greater resources of the North were finally tipping the scales toward the Union.

In June 1864 Grant crossed the James River and approached the town of Petersburg, an important railroad junction a few miles south of Richmond. If Grant captured Petersburg, most supplies to Richmond and to Lee's army would be cut off.

Lee's weary veterans managed to stop the Union army outside Petersburg, but Grant placed the town under siege. Trenches stretched for miles as both sides dug in. Snipers and artillery attacks took Union and Confederate lives almost daily. For nearly 10

desperate months, the Confederate defenses held firm.

Sherman's March to the Sea

While Grant was stalled outside Petersburg, Sherman advanced toward Atlanta with a force of more than 100,000 troops. Like the Shawnee chief for whom he was named, William Tecumseh Sherman was a tough and relentless soldier. John B. Hood, the Confederate general resisting him, had only 60,000 men. Hood twice attacked Sherman's advancing troops. Both attacks failed, and on September 2, the Union army marched triumphantly into Atlanta.

News of Sherman's victory reached the North during the 1864 presidential campaign. Lincoln had been renominated by Republicans and prowar Democrats on a "National Union" ticket. The vice presidential candidate was Andrew Johnson, a Tennessee Democrat who had remained loyal to the Union. The Democratic Party's presidential candidate was General McClellan. With the war dragging on, Lincoln feared he would lose the election. Sherman's success helped Lincoln, however, and he was re-elected in a landslide victory— 212 electoral votes to 21.

After the election, on November 15, Sherman's army began marching eastward from Atlanta toward Savannah, Georgia, on the Atlantic coast. As he left Atlanta, Sherman set fire to the city. He was waging what is called **total war**—a strategy to break an enemy's will to fight by destroying the

The fires ordered first by Confederate general Hood and then by Union general Sherman destroyed much of Atlanta.

● **Burning of Atlanta**

American Letters

Hospital Sketches

Louisa May Alcott

Louisa May Alcott is best known for her famous novel Little Women, *published in 1868. However, it was another novel,* Hospital Sketches, *published in 1863, that first brought her to the attention of the American public. During the Civil War Alcott worked as a volunteer nurse in a military hospital near Washington. There she helped care for the casualties that poured in from the battlefields of Virginia.* Hospital Sketches *is a fictional version of her experiences. Her descriptions were a sharp contrast to the idealistic views many Americans held about the war in its early years.*

Louisa May Alcott helped support her father and family with her writing.

• **Civil War Nurses**

"They've come! they've come! hurry up, ladies—you're wanted."

"Who have come? the rebels?"

This sudden summons in the gray dawn was somewhat startling to a three days' nurse like myself, and, as the thundering knock came at our door, I sprang up in my bed. . . .

"Bless you, no child; it's the wounded from Fredericksburg; forty ambulances are at the door, and we shall have our hands full in fifteen minutes."

. . . I had rather longed for the wounded to arrive . . . ; but when I peeped into the dusky street lined with what I at first had innocently called market carts, now unloading their sad freight at our door, . . . I indulged in a most unpatriotic wish that I was safe at home again, with a quiet day before me. . . .

. . . There they were! "our brave boys," as the papers justly call them, for cowards could hardly have been so riddled with [full of] shot and shell, so torn and shattered. . . . In they came, some on stretchers, some in men's arms, some feebly staggering along propped on rude crutches, and one lay stark and still with covered face, as a comrade gave his name to be recorded before they carried him away to the dead house. All was hurry and confusion; the hall was full of these wrecks of humanity, for the most exhausted could not reach a bed till duly ticketed and registered; the walls were lined with rows of such as could sit, the floor covered with the more disabled. . . .

. . . The house had been a hotel before hospitals were needed, and many of the doors still bore their old names; some not so inappropriate as might be imagined, for my ward was in truth a *ball-room,* if gun-shot wounds could christen it. . . . Round the great stove was gathered the dreariest group I ever saw—ragged, gaunt [very thin] and pale, mud to the knees, with bloody bandages untouched since put on days before; many bundled up in blankets, coats being lost or useless; and all wearing that disheartened [discouraged] look which proclaimed [showed] defeat. . . . I pitied them so much, I dared not speak to them, though, remembering all they had been through since the rout [defeat] at Fredericksburg, I yearned to serve the dreariest of them all.

resources of the opposing civilian population and its army. When this harsh policy was questioned, Sherman simply said, "War is cruelty."

As Sherman's army marched through Georgia, it left behind a path of destruction 60 miles wide. His troops destroyed or consumed everything in their path that could aid the southern war effort.

The Union soldiers slaughtered chickens and cattle for food. They burned barns and houses. When the troops crossed a railroad line, they tore up the tracks, burned the ties, and twisted the rails so that they were useless.

On December 21 the Union army entered Savannah, Georgia. Then Sherman marched north, destroying large sections of South Carolina and North Carolina with the same cold-blooded efficiency.

Surrender at Appomattox

On March 4, 1865, Lincoln began his second term as president. The war still raged, but it now seemed clear that the long and tragic conflict was drawing to a close. In his second inaugural address, Lincoln outlined the policy he intended to follow toward the South:

"With malice [hatred] toward none, with charity for all, with firmness in the right as God gives us to see the right, let us strive on to finish the work we are in, to bind up the nation's wounds, to care for him who shall have borne the battle and for his widow and his orphan—to do all which may achieve and cherish a just and lasting peace among ourselves and with all nations."

In early April 1865, Grant finally overran the Confederate defenses at Petersburg. Lee had to abandon both Petersburg and Richmond and retreat westward. His last hope was to escape into North Carolina and to join with the Confederate army that Sherman was driving before him. When Grant's pursuing troops sealed off his escape route, Lee made the painful decision to surrender.

Lee and Grant met at the home of Wilmer McLean in the Virginia town of Appomattox Courthouse on Sunday, April 9. It was a moving scene. Lee was dignified in defeat, Grant gracious in victory. "I met you once before, General Lee, while we were serving in Mexico," Grant said after they had shaken hands. "I think I should have recognized you anywhere."

The two generals talked briefly about that old war when they had been comrades. Then Grant sat down at a little table and wrote out the terms of surrender. Considering the loss of life on both sides—more than 350,000 Union soldiers and more than 250,000 Confederates—and the completeness of the Union

Over 40,000 Union soldiers filled the cramped and unsanitary quarters of Andersonville prison camp in Georgia. The poor living conditions resulted in the deaths of over 10,000 of its prisoners.

● **Casualties of War**

Lee and Grant signed the surrender papers at Appomattox. Grant then provided food rations to the starving Confederate troops and ordered his army not to celebrate, saying, "the rebels are our countrymen again."

• Civil War Music 2

victory, the terms were generous. The Confederates were merely to surrender their weapons and flags and depart in peace.

When General Lee hinted that his men needed to keep their horses for the spring planting, Grant said that every man who claimed to own a horse or mule could take the animal home with him. Both men signed the surrender papers. Then Grant introduced Lee to his staff. As he shook hands with Colonel Ely Parker, a Seneca Indian, Lee observed, "I am glad to see one real American here." Colonel Parker replied, "We are all Americans." Union bugler Seth M. Flint described what happened after the meeting concluded:

"**Out came General Lee, his soldierly figure erect, even in defeat. We stiffened and gave him a salute, and the man in gray courteously [politely] returned it. . . .**

After the departure of General Lee, we quickly learned the happy news of the surrender and it spread like wildfire through the army. That night was one of the happiest I have ever known.

When I sounded taps, the sweetest of all bugle calls, the notes had scarcely died away when from the distance—it must have come from General Lee's headquarters— came, silvery clear, the same call. The boys on the other side welcomed peace."

Section 4 Review

• Glossary

IDENTIFY and explain the significance of the following: George G. Meade, Pickett's Charge, Battle of Gettysburg, William Tecumseh Sherman, total war

LOCATE and explain the importance of the following: Petersburg, Atlanta, Savannah, Appomattox Courthouse

REVIEWING FOR DETAILS

1. How did the Battle of Gettysburg affect the war?
2. How did General Grant plan to win the war?

• Gazetteer

REVIEWING FOR UNDERSTANDING

3. **Geographic Literacy** How did Sherman's total war policy affect the South?
4. **Writing Mastery:** *Persuading* Imagine that you are a Confederate soldier or civilian. Write a letter to General Lee to persuade him either to surrender or to continue fighting.

• Time Line

5. **Critical Thinking:** *Drawing Conclusions* What did Lee hope to gain by invading the North?

CHAPTER 15

Reuniting the Nation

(1865–1900)

THEMES IN AMERICAN HISTORY

Constitutional Heritage:
How might amending the U.S. Constitution protect people's rights?

Democratic Values:
Why might some groups want to keep others from voting?

Economic Development:
How might people try to reshape their economy after a defeat in war?

African American poet Frances Watkins Harper described life for former slaves in the South after the Civil War:

"Well, the Northern folks kept sending
The Yankee teachers down;
And they stood right up and helped us,
Though Rebs did sneer and frown. . . .
Then I got a little cabin,
A place to call my own—
And I felt as independent
As the queen upon her throne."

• Video Opener

• Skill Builder

image above: *Former slaves during Reconstruction*

Section 1

RECONSTRUCTING THE SOUTH

Multimedia Connections

Explore these related topics and materials on the CD–ROM to enrich your understanding of this section:

 Profiles

- Thaddeus Stevens
- Ulysses S. Grant
- Andrew Johnson

 Readings

- Oh Captain! My Captain!
- Andrew Johnson's Impeachment

 Media Bank

- Lincoln's Assassination
- Reconstruction Amendments

On the evening of April 14, 1865, less than a week after the South's surrender, Abraham and Mary Todd Lincoln were attending a play at Ford's Theater in Washington. Suddenly, a shot rang out. John Wilkes Booth, an actor sympathetic to the South, had slipped into the president's box and fired a bullet into Lincoln's head. The president died the next day. Northerners were shocked and grief-stricken. For southerners, Lincoln's death heightened uncertainty about the future.

As you read this section you will find out:

▶ **What the main goal of President Johnson's Reconstruction plan was.**

▶ **What the Radical Republicans wanted from Reconstruction.**

▶ **Why Congress impeached President Johnson.**

President Andrew Johnson

President Lincoln's death left a terrible void. For months he had been involved in planning for **Reconstruction**, the rebuilding of the South's government and society after the end of the Civil War. Much now depended on Vice President Andrew Johnson, who became president after Lincoln's assassination.

Before the Civil War, Johnson had served in both houses of Congress and as governor of Tennessee. Although he was a Democrat, the Republicans had picked him to run for vice president in 1864 because he was one of the few pro-Union politicians who came from a Confederate state.

Most Republican politicians expected Johnson to make a fine president. Some disagreed, however, over how he should treat the defeated South. Many moderate Republicans

Apprenticed to a tailor as a young boy, President Andrew Johnson never had any formal education. Through hard work and the help of his wife, Eliza, he succeeded in politics, winning his first local office at the age of 19.

believed that Lincoln's idea of "malice [hatred] toward none" was the best policy. They hoped, as Lincoln had once said, "to bind up the nation's wounds" quickly.

Johnson pleased the moderate Republicans and Democrats by issuing **amnesty**, or forgiveness, to southerners who would take an oath of loyalty to the United States. The states of the former Confederacy would then eventually be allowed to hold elections and send representatives and senators to the U.S. Congress. Under Johnson's plan, southern states could still deny African Americans the right to vote.

Radical Republicans were concerned that the president's plan put too much power in the hands of former slaveholders. They were determined to protect the rights of the newly freed slaves. Radical Republicans wanted Johnson to punish the planters severely.

Congressman Thaddeus Stevens of Pennsylvania was one of the Radical leaders. He demanded that the United States seize the property of the large former slaveholders and divide it among the former slaves. There would be plenty of "rebel land," he said, to give a 40-acre farm to every adult male former slave in the South.

The Black Codes

Radicals like Stevens were deeply concerned about the way former slaves, or freedpeople, were being treated in the South. By April 1866 all the southern state governments established under President Johnson's amnesty plan had ratified the new **Thirteenth Amendment** to the Constitution, which officially abolished slavery. However, powerful white planters still formed the majority of leaders in the South and easily controlled the new governments. These "white" governments did not allow freedpeople to vote. Southern state legislatures swiftly passed regulations called **Black Codes**. These codes were designed to keep freedpeople in a slavelike condition.

The Black Codes often barred African Americans from any kind of work except farming and household service. Some states forced African Americans to sign labor contracts with landowners at the beginning of each year. If they left their jobs, they received no pay for what they had done. If they did not sign, they were charged with being vagrants. When convicted, the "sentence" often included having

Under the Black Codes, this African American man was arrested for vagrancy simply because he did not have a job. To pay his fine he was "sold" as a servant to the highest bidder.

The Granger Collection, New York

the freed person work for a landowner for a full year without pay.

The Black Codes alarmed many northerners, and the results of southern elections alarmed them even further. Southern voters chose for office many of the people who had led them during the Civil War. Several former Confederate generals were elected to Congress. In 1866 the Georgia legislature sent Alexander H. Stephens, former vice president of the Confederacy, to represent the state in the U.S. Senate, even though Stephens had only recently been paroled from prison.

Most of the newly elected representatives were members of the Democratic Party. Both houses of Congress voted not to allow them to take their seats. Even moderate Republicans were furious. Johnson's plan for bringing southern states back into the Union was rejected.

Johnson and the Republicans

The Radical Republicans in Congress then began to reconstruct the South according to their own ideas. Shortly before the end of the war, Congress had created the **Freedmen's Bureau**, an agency run by the army. Its main assignment was to care for freedpeople and **refugees**, people who had fled their homes to avoid danger. Early in 1866 Congress passed a bill increasing the ability of the Bureau to protect freedpeople. President Johnson vetoed this bill, hoping to control Congress.

In April both houses of Congress passed the **Civil Rights Act of 1866**. The bill forbade southern states from passing laws such as the Black Codes restricting freedpeople's rights. Johnson vetoed the bill, but Congress

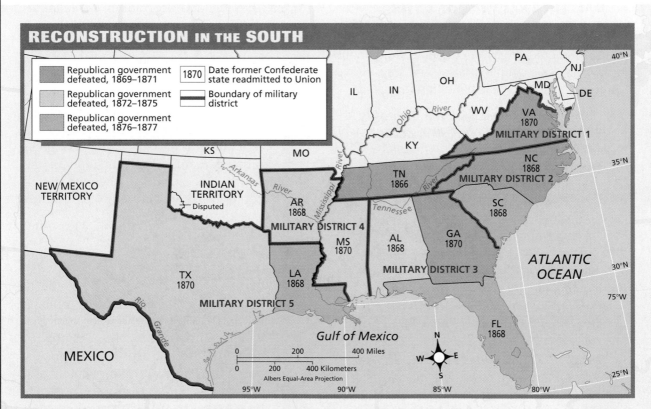

Learning from Maps. As northern support for Reconstruction declined, southern states began to vote out their Republican governments.

▶ **Place.** In military district 3, which state defeated its Republican government at the earliest date? Which state defeated its Republican government at the latest date?

● **Maps**

obtained the two-thirds majority necessary to override the veto.

Congress next passed the **Fourteenth Amendment** to the Constitution. In many ways this measure was even more important than the Thirteenth Amendment. "All persons born or naturalized [admitted as citizens] in the United States," the amendment read, ". . . are citizens of the United States and of the State wherein they reside." This gave citizenship to all African Americans in the United States. Then the amendment struck down the Black Codes by declaring:

> **"No State shall make or enforce any law which shall abridge [reduce] the privileges or immunities [freedoms] of citizens of the United States; nor shall any State deprive any person of life, liberty, or property, without due process of law; nor deny to any person . . . the equal protection of the laws."**

Most white southerners strongly objected to the Fourteenth Amendment. The southern states refused to ratify it. Without their votes, it was impossible to get the required approval of three fourths of the states. When it became clear that the southern states would not ratify the Fourteenth Amendment, Congress passed a series of **Reconstruction Acts** to pressure them. These stern measures strengthened military control of the South. They divided the former Confederacy into five military districts and stationed troops in each district.

To end army rule, each state would have to draw up a new constitution that guaranteed African Americans the right to vote. Each southern state would also have to ratify the Fourteenth Amendment. In other words, Congress ordered a military occupation of the South. Lincoln's hope that the nation could quickly bind up its wounds would not be fulfilled.

President Johnson on Trial

Republicans blamed President Johnson for much of the stubborn resistance of white southerners to the Republican plan for Reconstruction. Johnson opposed the Fourteenth Amendment and vetoed every one of the Reconstruction Acts.

Most Republicans finally became convinced that Reconstruction would never be successful unless Johnson was no longer president. In February 1868,

Through Others' Eyes

A British View of the Impeachment Crisis

Foreign journalists paid close attention to the impeachment crisis. The editors of the London *Examiner,* for example, praised the way Americans settled political differences:

"We, for our parts, think the men of 1789 were wiser Constitution builders than the Republican leaders of 1868. . . . But we have never yet heard of the Constitution of a country worth studying that has not been subjected from time to time to temporary and even perilous derangement [dangerous madness]. It may go wrong, but it will come right again. . . . Injustice for the moment may be done to Mr. Johnson by the uncontrollable violence of a party vote. But it is something after all to reflect that our descendants, when they go politically mad, do not take to political murder, as our fathers used to do. The official life of President Johnson may possibly be shortened by a few months, but even his enemies do not dream of imbruing [soaking] their hands in his blood, in this frenzy of political rage."

angry congressional leaders decided to try to remove him from office. They began the official process of **impeachment**—bringing formal charges of wrongdoing against a public official. In all, they brought 11 charges against the president. He was spared in his Senate trial because the senators fell one vote short of conviction on the strongest charges. The threat, however, was enough to end Johnson's resistance to the Radicals.

The presidential election of 1868 led to a dramatic change in the political situation. The federal troops stationed in the South prevented whites from interfering with the voting process. Naturally, African Americans overwhelmingly cast their ballots for the Republican candidate, Ulysses S. Grant. Grant won an easy victory in the electoral college—214 votes to 80 for the Democratic candidate, Horatio Seymour.

At last, in the spring of 1868, African Americans were allowed to participate in southern governments. These governments ratified the Fourteenth Amendment. The final state to complete the process was Georgia, in July 1870—more than five years after the end of the Civil War.

Early in 1869 the overwhelmingly Republican Congress drafted still another constitutional amendment that guaranteed that "the right of citizens of the United States to vote shall not be denied . . . on account of race, color, or previous condition of servitude." Within about a year this **Fifteenth Amendment** was ratified by the states. While the Fifteenth Amendment was a great victory for the rights of African American men, many women were deeply disappointed that the amendment did not extend the vote to them.

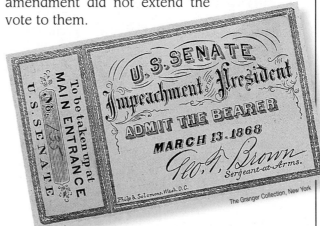

This ticket allowed public admission to the gallery box in the U.S. Senate to observe President Johnson's impeachment trial.

Section 1 Review

• **Glossary**

IDENTIFY and explain the significance of the following: Reconstruction, Andrew Johnson, amnesty, Radical Republicans, Thirteenth Amendment, Black Codes, Freedmen's Bureau, refugees, Civil Rights Act of 1866, Fourteenth Amendment, Reconstruction Acts, impeachment, Fifteenth Amendment

REVIEWING FOR DETAILS

1. What was President Johnson's main goal for Reconstruction?
2. What did the Radical Republicans hope to gain from Reconstruction?
3. Why did some members of Congress want to impeach President Johnson?

REVIEWING FOR UNDERSTANDING

4. **Writing Mastery:** *Describing* Write a brief paragraph describing the differences between Johnson's approach to Reconstruction and the Radical Republicans' approach.

5. **Critical Thinking:** *Determining the Strength of an Argument* Some Radical Republicans argued that Reconstruction could not be successful with Johnson in office. Was this argument valid? Explain your answer.

Section 2

FREEDOM AFTER SLAVERY

Multimedia Connections

Explore these related topics and materials on the CD–ROM to enrich your understanding of this section:

 Atlas

- African American Colleges

 Media Bank

- The First Vote
- African American Home Scene
- Freedmen's Bureau Office
- Fisk Jubilee Singers
- Fisk Jubilee Singers slide show

 Profiles

- Blanche K. Bruce
- Hiram Revels

Like the American Revolution, the Civil War marked a great turning point in American history. From it a dramatically different society arose. The war had destroyed the South's economy and the lifestyle of many white southerners. The social and economic positions of the former slaves also had changed. African Americans were eager to explore the boundaries of their new freedom.

As you read this section you will find out:

▶ **What changes freedpeople experienced during Reconstruction.**

▶ **Who served in Reconstruction governments.**

▶ **Why the sharecropping system was developed and what effects it had.**

The Privileges of Freedom

The Thirteenth, Fourteenth, and Fifteenth Amendments brought former slaves freedom first of all to decide what to do with their own time. It meant freedom to move about. In many cases, families that had been separated under slavery were reunited. For example, in Alabama, Nelson and Phoebe Humphrey and their five children were reunited after living on two separate plantations. The Humphreys, who had been field hands, each started their own businesses after emancipation. Phoebe Humphrey took in laundry while Nelson Humphrey did odd jobs.

Most other former slaves continued to work the land, but now their work was for their own gain, not someone else's. Older people labored less and rested more. Mothers devoted more time to their children and homes, less to planting, hoeing, and harvesting. Caroline Jones, a former house slave, reported shortly after the war that her occupation was now "caring for her family."

Another privilege of freedom was that former slaves could seek education. Very few could read and write because it had been against the law in most southern states to teach slaves to read. The Freedmen's Bureau set up schools in the South as soon as the war ended. In Charleston, South Carolina, for example, schools were established as soon as the Union army captured the city.

African American students of all ages responded eagerly to opportunities for schooling. All over the South, elderly freedpeople could be seen learning their ABCs alongside their grandchildren. Charlotte Forten, a northern African American woman who taught freed slaves in South Carolina, wrote:

"Many of the grown people are desirous of learning to read. It is wonderful how a people who have been so long crushed to the earth . . . can have so great a desire for knowledge."

By 1870 there were more than 150,000 students in Freedmen's Bureau schools. In addition to these schools, several new colleges were established for African American students. Included among these were Howard University, Fisk University, and Hampton Institute.

Freedpeople also founded new churches that attracted large congregations. Many white religious groups from the North contributed time, money, and teachers to help educate former slaves. Northern African American congregations also recruited large numbers of teachers and sent clergy to help establish new schools and churches for former slaves. Methodist, Presbyterian, and Baptist churches expanded rapidly in the South. By 1870 one of the most influential new groups, the Colored Methodist Episcopal Church, had grown large enough to appoint its first bishops, W. H. Miles and R. H. Vanderhorst. Many leaders of the black churches also played influential roles in politics.

Reconstruction Governments

The occupation of the South by the U.S. Army helped African Americans vote and hold office in all the states of the former Confederacy. Nothing made most white southerners more

Many former slaves studied at this Freedmen's Bureau school in Charleston, South Carolina.

● **Reconstruction Programs**

The Granger Collection, New York

The first African American members of Congress: (left to right) Hiram Revels, Benjamin Turner, Robert DeLarge, Josiah Wells, Jefferson Long, Joseph Rainey, and Robert Elliott.

bitter and resentful than to be "ruled" by the very people they had dominated for so long.

African American politicians.

"Rule" is not, however, the proper word to describe the role of African Americans in southern politics during Reconstruction. Between 1869 and 1901, only 22 African Americans ever served in Congress. African Americans did hold many local offices, but the only state legislature to have a black majority between 1868 and 1877 was South Carolina's.

Like their white counterparts, black politicians in the South varied widely in ability and devotion to their duties. During the 1870s white southerners who objected to African Americans holding office called attention to any cases of corruption or mistakes that came to light involving black politicians.

In reality, many African American legislators were men of great character and ability. The Reverend Henry M. Turner, who had been a Union army chaplain during the war, was elected to the Georgia legislature and later served as a postmaster. Another minister, Hiram Revels, who was born free in

North Carolina and moved north, helped recruit several black regiments during the Civil War. In 1866 he settled in Natchez, Mississippi, and became active in politics. He served briefly in the U.S. Senate, filling the unexpired term of Confederate president Jefferson Davis for the state of Mississippi. Later, Revels became president of Alcorn College.

Carpetbaggers and scalawags.

Most of the officeholders in the "Black Republican" governments, as their opponents called them, were white. Those who came from the northern states were called **carpetbaggers** because travelers of the period often carried their belongings in soft-sided bags made of carpeting. Many southerners believed that these "invaders" had come south not to put down roots but only to get rich.

Southern white Republicans were referred to scornfully by their Democratic neighbors as **scalawags**—good-for-nothing rascals. In reality, however, many of the "scalawags" were conservative, high-minded community leaders. The Confederate governor of Georgia, Joseph E. Brown, became a Republican and served as chief justice of the Georgia Supreme Court during Reconstruction.

"Carpetbaggers" and "scalawags" came from all walks of life. Some genuinely wanted

In this cartoon by James Wales, the defeated South is shown carrying the heavy burden placed on it by evil "carpetbaggers" and federal troops during the Reconstruction Era.

to improve schools for former slaves and to help them achieve political influence. Others were employees of the federal government stationed in the South. Still others hoped to obtain state political offices by attracting black votes. Most "carpetbaggers" mainly wanted to improve themselves economically. Only after establishing themselves in their new homes did some of them become involved in local politics.

The southern state governments accomplished a great deal during the Reconstruction Era. They raised taxes in order to improve public education, which had been badly neglected before 1860. They also spent large sums on roads, bridges, railroads, and public buildings damaged during the war, and they expanded public support for social services. The biggest challenge for southerners, however, was constructing a new economy that was not based on slave labor.

Sharecropping

Most black southerners had been farmworkers before emancipation. Nearly all former slaves continued to work on the land after they became free. Efforts by Radical Republicans like Thaddeus Stevens to carve up the large plantations and give each black family "forty acres and a mule" never attracted much support among northern whites, however.

According to a law passed in 1862, each former slave could get a free 160-acre farm in the West. Only a handful managed to do so, however, because the price of land was just a small part of the cost of starting a farm. Most freed families lacked the tools, seed money, and the transportation to the frontier. Therefore, most of the former slaves continued to farm land owned by whites. At first they worked for wages, but most landowners were short of

History Makers
Blanche K. Bruce
(1841–1898)

One of the most famous African American politicians of the Reconstruction era was Mississippi senator Blanche K. Bruce, who was born a slave in Virginia. Unlike most slaves, he re-

ceived a good education. During the Civil War Bruce ran away to Kansas, where he opened a school for African Americans. After the war he attended Oberlin College, then moved to Mississippi, where he became a wealthy planter.

Bruce was highly respected in the Republican Party. He held many elected and appointed positions in addition to serving in the Senate from 1875 to 1881. He worked tirelessly on issues such as economic and political reform and civil rights. In one of his most famous speeches, Bruce expressed his hopes that freedpeople would eventually be able to succeed despite racism. "I have confidence," he declared, ". . . in the endurance, capacity, and destiny of my people."

cash, and freedpeople wanted to be more independent of plantation control.

A new system called **sharecropping** was soon created. Sharecropping means sharing the crop. The landowners provided the farmers with houses, tools, seeds, and other supplies. The sharecroppers provided the skill and labor needed to grow the crops. When the harvest was gathered, it was supposed to be shared, usually half to two thirds for the landowner, the rest for the sharecropper.

This system freed black workers from the close daily supervision they had endured under slavery. Each family generally had its own cabin and tilled its own plot of land as a separate unit. At first, the system allowed freedpeople the opportunity to choose what crop to grow, rather than being forced to grow cotton or tobacco. For these reasons, many families became sharecroppers instead of working the land for wages. Sharecroppers could at least hope that by working hard and saving they might someday have enough money to buy a farm of their own someday. Then they would be truly free.

In practice, it was very difficult for sharecroppers to buy their own farms. Sharecroppers ran up bills at the general store during the growing season. When the crop was sold in the autumn, they planned to use the money to pay off this debt. If they experienced bad weather or sold their crops for less than expected, they could not pay their bills. In addition, local storekeepers often cheated sharecroppers. Frequently, the merchant added items the farmers had never purchased to the bill. Some landowners also cheated the sharecroppers when the harvest was divided. At the end of the season, many sharecroppers often found themselves much deeper in debt than they had been before the crop was planted in the spring!

Most sharecroppers who objected to the system were threatened with the loss of credit in the future, or with violence. Even when they dealt with honest landowners and merchants, it was hard to make a decent living as a sharecropper. Prices were high in the stores because the storekeepers also had to borrow to get the goods they sold. The South's economic problems and racial prejudice kept most African American sharecroppers from acquiring land of their own.

In sharecropping families, everyone had to help out with the work in the fields. These children are helping their family to pick cotton around 1870.

The Granger Collection, New York

Section 2 Review

• Glossary

IDENTIFY and explain the significance of the following: Henry M. Turner, Hiram Revels, carpetbaggers, scalawags, sharecropping

REVIEWING FOR DETAILS
1. What were some of the privileges freedpeople enjoyed during Reconstruction?
2. Who governed the states of the former Confederacy during Reconstruction?
3. Why was the sharecropping system developed? What were some of the results of this system?

REVIEWING FOR UNDERSTANDING
4. **Writing Mastery:** *Expressing* Write a poem, song, or short story expressing how you think freedpeople might have felt about life under Reconstruction.
5. **Critical Thinking:** *Making Comparisons* How would you compare life for southern African Americans before and after emancipation?

Section 3

THE END OF RECONSTRUCTION

Multimedia Connections

Explore these related topics and materials on the CD–ROM to enrich your understanding of this section:

 Media Bank

• "Exodus" Movement
• Slave Narrative

 Profiles

• Rutherford B. Hayes
• John Harlan

 Readings

• *Plessy* v. *Ferguson*

 Glossary

• southern Democrat

The grandson of former slave Charlotte Fowler cried: "Oh, grandma, they have killed my poor grandpappy!" Moments earlier Fowler's unarmed husband, Wallace, had been shot by white men in hoods. Wallace Fowler, a 70-year-old former slave, had been an open supporter of the Radical Republicans. This loyalty cost him his life. Fowler's death was just one example of how some southern whites resisted the changes brought by Reconstruction.

As you read this section you will find out:

▶ **How some southern whites resisted Reconstruction.**

▶ **Why the election of 1876 led to the end of Reconstruction.**

▶ **How the case of *Plessy* v. *Ferguson* affected society.**

Resistance to Reconstruction

The great majority of white southerners strongly resisted the changes forced upon them during Reconstruction. They did so in many ways, sometimes openly, sometimes secretly in the dead of night. In 1866 some white southerners began to form secret organizations that used violence to hold back African Americans.

The most notorious of these organizations was the **Ku Klux Klan**. Klan members were determined to intimidate white Republican leaders and to keep African Americans from voting. They tried to frighten potential voters by galloping through the night dressed in white robes, hoods, and masks, claiming to be the ghosts of Confederate soldiers. They burned black churches and schools, and

In this 1874 cartoon, artist Thomas Nast portrays the harassment African Americans faced after emancipation as worse even than life had been under slavery.

threatened terrible tortures against African Americans who dared to exercise their right to vote.

When these scare tactics did not work, the Klan often resorted to physical violence. Many hundreds of southern African Americans were assaulted. Statistics on the Reconstruction Era reveal that in one North Carolina judicial district there were 12 murders, 14 cases of arson, and more than 700 beatings. During this same period more than 150 African Americans were murdered in Jackson County, Florida.

The federal government sent troops to stop the worst Klan violence. By the early 1870s, the power of the Klan had been broken. Gradually, however, more and more white southerners joined in efforts to keep African Americans from voting. Groups in Mississippi, South Carolina, and Louisiana even formed private military companies and marched around in broad daylight. They beat African Americans whom they believed to be "uppity" or rebellious. When some victims resisted, bloody battles broke out.

The Granger Collection, New York

This Alabama member of the Ku Klux Klan poses in his robe for a formal portrait in 1868. Klan hoods hid the wearers' identities.

In 1876 Senator Blanche K. Bruce of Mississippi denounced such violence against African Americans:

> **"It is an attack by an aggressive, intelligent, white political organization upon inoffensive, law-abiding fellow-citizens; a violent method for political supremacy, that seeks . . . the destruction of the rights of the party assailed [attacked]."**

The Election of 1876

For the most part, Senator Bruce's protests went unheeded. By 1876 many white northerners had begun to lose interest in trying to control southern affairs. As long as the white southerners did not actually try to re-enslave African Americans, northerners were prepared to put Klan activities in the South out of their minds. They grew more concerned about other issues such as the condition of the national economy.

Gradually, the number of troops stationed in the southern states was reduced. Without military protection, many African Americans were afraid to vote or exercise their other rights. In state after state during the 1870s, all-white conservative parties took control of the government away from the Republicans. These political organizations resisted the changes Republicans had proposed for the South. Many of their leaders were former Confederate officials who took advantage of the Amnesty Act of 1872, which ended the Fourteenth Amendment ban on former Confederate leaders holding office.

The Republican Party was further weakened by President Grant's failure to live up to the people's expectations. Grant proved to be as poor a chief executive as Andrew Johnson, but in a different way. His administration was marked by serious scandals and corruption. Although he was easily re-elected in 1872, by 1876 the Republicans remained in control of just three southern states—Louisiana, Florida, and South Carolina.

In the heated presidential election of 1876 Democratic governor Samuel J. Tilden of New York faced Republican governor Rutherford B. Hayes of Ohio. Tilden narrowly won the popular vote. He also led in electoral college votes, but 20 of these—the electoral votes of South Carolina, Louisiana, Florida, and one single vote in Oregon—were in dispute. If all 20 votes went to Hayes, he would then have an electoral majority. Charges of election tampering flew wildly as both Tilden and Hayes claimed victory in these disputed states.

After weeks of debate, Congress appointed a special

The election of 1876 between Hayes and Tilden threatened another civil war as Tilden supporters were ready to use violence to make sure that he became president.

electoral commission made up of eight Republicans and seven Democrats to study the matter. The commission, voting along party lines, gave all the disputed votes to Hayes. Thus, Hayes won with 185 electoral votes to Tilden's 184. The Democrats felt cheated. Many remained ready to fight to make Tilden president.

• **Contested Election**

In this crisis, leaders of the two political parties worked out what is known as the **Compromise of 1877**. If the Democrats would agree to accept the electoral commission's decision, Hayes would remove all the remaining federal troops stationed in the South.

In exchange, the Democrats promised to guarantee African Americans their rights and not to prevent them from voting. After all these details had been settled, the Democrats agreed to go along with the electoral commission's decision, and Hayes was inaugurated.

Second-Class Citizens

After the Compromise of 1877, white northerners turned their backs on black southerners. At the same time, white leaders in the southern states broke their promise to treat African Americans fairly. Step-by-step, they deprived black southerners of the right to vote

Faced with increasing persecution and more limited opportunities after the Compromise of 1877, some rural African Americans, like the group pictured here, moved to southern cities hoping to find a better life.

and reduced them to second-class citizens. White southern leaders started by requiring voters to pay **poll taxes**, or taxes on individuals, which were often collected at the time of an election. In other places they required voters to pass **literacy tests**, which limited voting to those who could read well. Although these laws should have disqualified many white voters, they were directed primarily against African Americans.

One way this was done was by using so-called **grandfather clauses** as part of voting requirements. These clauses stated that literacy tests and poll taxes did not apply to persons who had been able to vote before 1867, or to their descendants. Almost all white male southerners fell into this category, but no black southerners did. Once black southerners ceased to have an influence on elections, officials paid little attention to their other rights and desires.

Along with political discrimination, the legal **segregation**, or forced separation, of the races became widespread. Starting in 1881 with Tennessee, southern states began to pass what became known as **Jim Crow laws**, which enforced segregation.

When African Americans were segregated at public places like theaters, some went to court to seek their constitutional rights. In one case, W. H. R. Agee protested against being denied a hotel room in Jefferson City, Missouri. In another case, Sallie Robinson sued because she and her nephew were forced to ride in a second-class car while traveling on a southern railroad, even though they had first-class tickets.

These and other suits, known as the *Civil Rights Cases*, were decided by the Supreme Court in 1883. The majority of the justices ruled that a previous civil rights act, which had been passed in 1875, was unconstitutional and furthermore that the Fourteenth Amendment protected against actions by state governments, not by private persons. It was therefore legal for private businesses to practice racial segregation.

In 1896 the Supreme Court heard the case of **Plessy v. Ferguson**. Homer A. Plessy, an African American from Louisiana, was arrested for taking a seat in a railroad car reserved by Louisiana law for whites. His attorneys argued that the law under which he was arrested was unconstitutional. The Court ruled against Plessy on the grounds that the railroad provided separate but equally good cars for black passengers.

Justice John Marshall Harlan objected to this separate-but-equal idea. Harlan's family had held slaves. The experiences of

Reconstruction, however, had changed his views of racial issues. In his dissent Harlan wrote.

> "[I]n the eye of the law, there is in this country no superior, dominant, ruling class of citizens. There is no caste [social class] here. Our Constitution is color-blind and neither knows nor tolerates classes among citizens. In respect of civil rights, all citizens are equal before the law."

In 1896 Harlan's was a minority opinion not only on the Court but also among white citizens in all parts of the country. Efforts to prevent segregation practically ended. African American travelers could not stay at hotels used by white guests. Theater owners herded black audiences into separate sections, usually high in the balcony. Black streetcar riders had to sit or stand in the rear sections. They could not enter "white" parks or swim at "white" public beaches. Even cemeteries were segregated. Although segregation was enforced most strongly in the South, it was also found in some northern cities.

The schools, parks, and other facilities open to black people were almost never as good as those for white people. For example, in 1876 some southern states were spending the same amount on the education of every child, black or white. By the late 1890s, however, most southern schools were required to be segregated, and most southern states were spending several times more on each white child than on each black child. The "equal" part of the separate-but-equal ruling was ignored practically everywhere.

The Granger Collection, New York

In this drawing an African American man is asked to leave the "white" section of a segregated railroad car.

Section 3 Review

• Glossary

IDENTIFY and explain the significance of the following: Ku Klux Klan, Blanche K. Bruce, Compromise of 1877, poll taxes, literacy tests, grandfather clauses, segregation, Jim Crow laws, *Plessy* v. *Ferguson*, John Marshall Harlan

REVIEWING FOR DETAILS

1. How did some southern whites resist Reconstruction policies?
2. How did the election of 1876 put an end to Reconstruction?
3. What was the impact of *Plessy* v. *Ferguson*?

REVIEWING FOR UNDERSTANDING

4. **Writing Mastery:** *Persuading* Imagine that you are a southern African American in the late 1800s. Write a letter to your state legislator persuading him to vote against a Jim Crow law.
5. **Critical Thinking:** *Cause and Effect* How did the changing attitude of many northerners affect people in the South?

Section 4
THE NEW SOUTH

Multimedia Connections

Explore these related topics and materials on the CD–ROM to enrich your understanding of this section:

 Profiles

- Booker T. Washington

 Biographies

- Ida B. Wells-Barnett

 Media Bank

- New South Rises from Ashes
- Commerce in the South
- Illiteracy in the South
- Wade Hampton
- Crop Lien System

 Readings

- A Sharecropper's Story
- Atlanta Compromise

With the following words in 1886 Atlanta journalist Henry Grady expressed what many hoped would be a better future for the troubled South after Reconstruction:

> "**The new South presents a perfect democracy . . . a hundred farms for every plantation, fifty homes for every palace—and a diversified [varied] industry that meets the complex need of this complex age.**"

As you read this section you will find out:

▶ **How the crop-lien system affected the southern economy.**

▶ **How the Redeemers tried to improve the southern economy.**

▶ **What Booker T. Washington advised African Americans to do to succeed.**

The Crop-Lien System

By the late 1800s the sharecropping system dominated southern society. Although the system started among former slaves, soon roughly half of all southern sharecroppers were white. In general, there was little difference in the standard of living among black and white sharecroppers. Before the war there had been few landless whites in the South. Economic hard times after the war, however, caused many small landowners to lose their holdings. Many turned to sharecropping. Few would ever own land again.

The shortage of money in the South made nearly everyone—landowners, sharecroppers, merchants, and manufacturers—dependent on bankers and other people with funds to invest. In order to ensure that farmers' loans were repaid after the crops had been harvested, these investors demanded that the landowners put up the future crop as security for the loan. This gave investors a claim, called a **crop lien**, against the harvest before the crop was even planted. If the borrower was unable to pay when the loan came due, the lender could take possession of the crop.

On the surface, the crop-lien system seemed fair enough. However, it had an unfortunate side effect. The lenders insisted that the borrowers grow one of the South's major cash crops, particularly cotton. There was a world market for these crops, and they could be converted into cash anywhere, anytime. If the price was low, the crops could often be stored until market conditions improved.

Both the landowners and the share-croppers would have been better off if they could have grown vegetables and fruits as well as cash crops. This concentration on just one crop rapidly exhausted the fertility of the soil. In addition, if farmers had an unusually large harvest, the price of the cash crops fell steeply because supply was greater than demand.

Everyone was caught up in the system. The bankers put pressure on the landowners and storekeepers, who in turn forced the sharecroppers to plant what the bankers wanted. Some might argue that the bankers were greedy and shortsighted, but from the bankers' point of view it would have been extremely risky to lend a farmer money to grow tomatoes, for example. Such crops had to be sold locally when they were ripe or they would rot and become worthless within a few days.

The Redeemers

Because of conditions under the crop-lien and sharecropping systems, southern agriculture remained depressed for years. Although the region was gener-ally tied to farming, a few business leaders called for the creation of a "New South" based on industry.

As a result of the Compromise of 1877, by the late 1870s political power was as much in the hands of southern whites as it had been before the Civil War. The new white leaders in most states called themselves **Redeemers**.

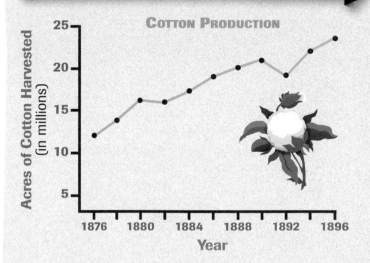

Cotton Production and Cotton Prices, 1876–1896

COTTON PRODUCTION

Acres of Cotton Harvested (in millions) vs. *Year*

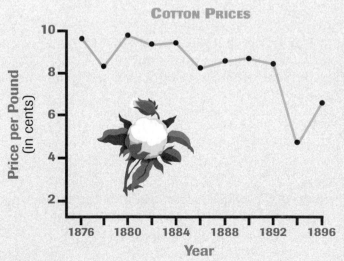

COTTON PRICES

Price per Pound (in cents) vs. *Year*

Source: *Historical Statistics of the United States*

A Cash Crop. As the sharecropping system expanded, more southern land was used to grow cotton. What general trend do you notice between the expansion of cotton production and the price of cotton from 1876 to 1896?

Redeemers hoped that the expansion of industries like this southern ironworks would improve the overall economy of the South. Agriculture would continue to dominate the southern economy, however.

They claimed that they were redeeming, or taking back, powers and duties their class had exercised before Reconstruction.

The Redeemers were forward-looking when it came to economic questions. They hoped to increase industrial production and improve the South's railroad network.

There was a great deal of talk about "out-Yankeeing" the Yankees. The South had large supplies of both cotton and poor people. Why not combine them in order to manufacture cotton goods? Between 1880 and 1900 the number of textile mill workers in the South jumped from 17,000 to 88,000. The output of these mills, most of which were in the Southeast, increased even more rapidly. The South's tobacco production also expanded rapidly because of the invention of machines that produced cigarettes in huge numbers.

Many black southerners did not benefit from the "New South." Most mill jobs were closed to African Americans. Some policies of the Redeemers led to more racial discrimination. For example, the Redeemers also made steep cuts in state taxes. Then, to

balance state budgets, they reduced spending on social services and education, particularly for African Americans.

The Atlanta Compromise

Faced with these handicaps, many black southerners took the advice of Booker T. Washington. Washington founded Tuskegee Institute, an African American trade school in Alabama. Washington was born a slave. Through dedication and study he obtained an education while also working to pay for his schooling. During Reconstruction Washington had seen firsthand what happened to most African Americans who openly fought against racial prejudice.

These experiences convinced him that African Americans could hope for fair treatment only if they made themselves essential to the South as a reliable, trained, and capable

Noted African American scientist George Washington Carver observes his chemistry students at Tuskegee Institute. Founded in 1881, the school blossomed under Booker T. Washington's leadership as he gained funding and attracted teachers like Carver.

workforce. Until they elevated themselves to this level, Washington believed that African Americans should not struggle for equal rights, particularly equal political rights. Washington became highly skilled at obtaining the financial support of wealthy whites who agreed with his philosophy. As a result of Washington's efforts, and because of its high-quality graduates, Tuskegee Institute prospered.

Washington was already well known when, in an 1895 speech at Atlanta, Georgia, he proposed what became known as the **Atlanta Compromise**. In it he argued that African Americans should accept the American system and try to get ahead within it. Thus, African American students should learn skilled trades so that they could earn more money and improve their lives. Washington believed that there was nothing shameful about working with one's hands, as he explained:

"In the great leap from slavery to freedom . . . we shall prosper in proportion as we learn to dignify and glorify common labor. . . . The opportunity to earn a dollar in a factory just now is worth infinitely more than the opportunity to spend a dollar in an opera-house."

Washington asked whites only to be fair. Help African Americans, he argued, by making sure that what was separate was really equal. Some black leaders, such as journalist Ida B. Wells-Barnett, criticized Washington. She argued that African Americans should do all they could to oppose segregation, which was never truly equal. They should insist on receiving all their rights as citizens. Most white southern leaders, however, were delighted with the Atlanta Compromise, in part because it discouraged African Americans from challenging the system.

Ida B. Wells-Barnett was born into slavery in 1862. Educated in a Freedmen's Bureau school, she first became a teacher. She went into journalism after losing her teaching job for protesting discrimination. She spent the rest of her career fighting racism.

Section 4 Review

• **Glossary**

• **Time Line**

IDENTIFY and explain the significance of the following: crop lien, Redeemers, Booker T. Washington, Atlanta Compromise, Ida B. Wells-Barnett

REVIEWING FOR DETAILS

1. How did the crop-lien system affect the economic situation in the South?
2. What did the Redeemers try to do to improve the southern economy?

REVIEWING FOR UNDERSTANDING

3. **Geographic Literacy** How did the crop-lien system affect southern land?
4. **Writing Mastery:** *Describing* Imagine that you are in the audience during Booker T. Washington's Atlanta speech. Write a letter to a friend describing Washington's advice to African Americans.
5. **Critical Thinking:** *Fact and Opinion* Booker T. Washington argued that whites would support separate but equal segregation. Why might some black leaders have questioned his opinion?

u n i t **6**

THE RISE OF MODERN AMERICA (1850–1900)

The Granger Collection, New York

This painted photograph shows an immigrant family making garments around 1900. The United States experienced one of its largest periods of immigration around this time.

LINKING PAST TO PRESENT
Ethnic Traditions

It is Christmas time in Texas, and Phyllis Salazar is gathering with her family to make tamales. Making tamales is an annual tradition that is practiced in many Mexican American families. When Phyllis was young, her mother taught her the tradition. At that time the family boiled a hog's head to get the pork needed to make the tamales. This did not appeal to young Phyllis, who now uses pork roast and chicken to fill the tasty tamales she makes.

The process for making the tamales usually takes an entire day. Sometimes cooks experiment by filling the tamales with sweet-flavored raisins or nuts and seeds. "If a new filling tastes good," says Salazar, "we use it again next year."

On New Year's Eve, some Mexican American families celebrate by making *buñuelos*, pastry items that are sometimes called "Mexican doughnuts." They are often eaten with Mexican hot chocolate, a rich, frothy drink. In recent years more and more Americans not of Mexican descent have come to enjoy such foods as well.

Food represents just one of the many items from different cultures that enrich American life. The popularity of restaurants that specialize in Chinese, Italian, Greek, and other ethnic foods illustrates how diverse American tastes have become. Mexican food in particular has become one of the most popular types of ethnic foods consumed in the United States.

As you read this unit, you will learn that many ethnic groups whose cultures influence American life today did not come to the United States in large numbers until the late 1800s. You will also learn about how Americans spread into the Southwest and were influenced by its Spanish and Mexican heritage of the region.

This Mexican American family gathers to make tamales for a Christmas celebration.

CHAPTER **16**

The Granger Collection, New York

Western Crossroads
(1850–1900)

THEMES IN AMERICAN HISTORY

Cultural Diversity:
Why might conflict arise between new settlers and people already living in an area?

Technology and Society:
How might technological advances affect new areas of settlement?

Economic Development:
What conflicts might arise between individuals and big business?

*W*hen forty-niner Jasper Hixson crossed the Great Plains, he noted that "in the best map we can get hold of, this is called the Great American Desert." Unlike many people in the United States, he saw the land's potential and predicted:

"The land is too fertile and possesses too many inducements [attractions] for settlement to remain in possession of the Indians forever."

• **Video Opener**

• **Skill Builder**

image above: *Plains Indians' tepees*

Section 1

THE GREAT PLAINS

Multimedia Connections

Explore these related topics and materials on the CD-ROM to enrich your understanding of this section:

 Glossary

- cultural assimilation
- nomad
- Sun Dance

 Gazetteer

- Great Plains
- Oregon Country

 Atlas

- Great Plains

 Media Bank

- Bison Population
- Great Plains Landscape

The men returned from the successful summer buffalo hunt, pleased that there would be food for the fall and winter. The night would be a time of feasting and celebration. A lot of hard work still lay ahead for the women, however. A mature buffalo could weigh up to 2,000 pounds, and every part of the buffalo would be used. The women had to cut off the meat, stretch it, and dry it. The fat would be boiled and saved for soup. The hide had to be scraped and dehaired before it could be tanned.

As you read this section you will find out:

▶ **How Plains Indians were organized.**

▶ **How the horse introduced by Europeans changed Plains Indian life.**

▶ **In what ways the Plains Indians were dependent on the buffalo.**

The "Great American Desert"

Today the region known as the Great Plains extends from western Texas north to the Dakotas and then on into Canada. In the 1800s, endless acres of grassland rolled westward across the Plains, gradually rising until they reached the Rocky Mountains.

The various American Indian groups that lived in this region became known as **Plains Indians**. The Blackfoot Indians, who lived in the northern Plains, described the land as being full of animal and plant life. In the Blackfoot creation story, the "Old Man" made the land and then:

"covered the plains with grass for the animals to feed on. He marked off a piece of ground, and in it he made to grow all kinds

For years, Plains Indians saw only a few explorers and fur traders cross their land. Then wagon trains filled with pioneers heading for Oregon and California began to roll across the Plains.

of roots and berries—camas [bulbs], wild carrots, wild turnips, sweet-root, bitter-root, sarvis berries, bull berries, cherries, plums, and rosebuds. He put trees in the ground. He put all kinds of animals on the ground. . . . [He] took the antelope down on the prairie, and turned it loose; and it ran away fast and gracefully."

Some early explorers had called the Plains region the "Great American Desert." Most people who had never visited the Plains thought that the region was home only for the coyote, the donkey-eared jackrabbit, the prairie dog, the antelope, and the great, shaggy buffalo. The buffalo in particular seemed the masters of the Great Plains. About 12 million buffalo were grazing there at the end of the Civil War. Despite all the active life there some reports—based on the Plains' limited rainfall and mostly treeless landscape—described the region as "a country destined to remain forever an uninhabited waste."

The Plains Indians

The Plains, of course, were not uninhabited. Nearly 30 Plains Indian tribes lived there. The Apache lived in present-day western Texas, Arizona, and northern Mexico. The Comanche lived in parts of present-day Oklahoma and Texas. The Pawnee occupied western Nebraska, and the Sioux were scattered from Minnesota to the Dakotas and Montana. The Cheyenne and Arapaho were the principal groups of the central Plains.

In 1850 the American Indian population of the Plains was over 150,000. Although the many groups of the Plains spoke different languages, they had developed a complex and efficient sign language so that all could communicate with one another.

The Plains Indians differed from group to group. Some groups were divided into bands. The Cheyenne, for example, consisted of bands with names like the Hairy Band, the Scabby Band, and the Dogmen Band. The bands were governed by chiefs and councils of elders. Although each band was a separate community, bands at times joined together for religious ceremonies or to fight enemies.

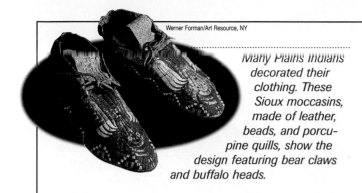

Werner Forman/Art Resource, NY

Many Plains Indians decorated their clothing. These Sioux moccasins, made of leather, beads, and porcupine quills, show the design featuring bear claws and buffalo heads.

Small groups of warriors called **soldier bands** settled disputes between band members, punished those who broke tribal laws, protected the group against attacks, and led hunting expeditions. Within each band, warriors tried to prove their courage and daring on the battlefield. To touch an enemy or capture his weapon—called "**counting coup**"—was proof of a warrior's highest bravery.

The Plains Culture

Most of the Plains groups shared a common culture based on the use of the buffalo and other large game. When Europeans arrived with their horses, guns, and metal tools, the Plains Indians incorporated these new elements into their lives.

Horses on the Plains. Spanish explorers had brought the first horses to America. Some of these animals escaped and ran wild. Eventually, large herds roamed parts of the West, living off the fertile grass of the prairies. Beginning in the mid-1600s the Plains Indians captured and tamed wild horses. Sometimes these horses even came to them, as a Sioux oral history tells of the event that marked the winter of 1781:

Mounted on a horse and armed with a bow and arrows, a Plains Indian would go track down a buffalo herd. It required courage and skill to face a buffalo.

"This year while they were in camp with their ponies in the center of the circle, many wild horses came down from the hills and joined their ponies; so they divided up the wild horses."

Many of the Plains Indians, both men and women, became expert riders. On horseback they could cover large distances swiftly and run down buffalo and other game. Horses became so important to the Plains Indians that many groups went to war against their neighbors to obtain them. Many counted their wealth in horses. Some even paid their debts with horses.

Following the buffalo. Before Europeans came to America, Indians had lived in the hills on the edges of the Plains and would venture down onto the Plains to hunt on foot. They hunted some buffalo, but still relied heavily on agriculture for food. With the introduction of the horse, the Plains Indians were able to hunt buffalo far more successfully. They could travel great distances and spend much more time on the Plains than before. They depended on game of many kinds, but none more than the buffalo to support their way of life.

Hunting parties followed the thundering buffalo herds across the Plains. Men were usually the hunters, although in some groups women also participated. Many Plains Indians carried bows made of wood. Their arrows had

points made of bone, flint, or metal. Galloping on horseback at a high speed, they could shoot arrows so fast that the next would be in the air before the first had found its target. These arrows struck with great force. At short range a hunter could sink the entire shaft of an arrow into the body of a buffalo.

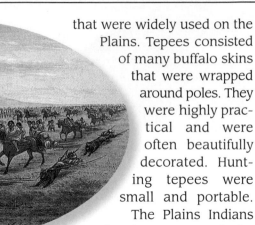

Western artist George Catlin spent years sketching and painting life on the Plains. In this painting he illustrated the Sioux moving with their tepees.

Using the buffalo. After a successful hunt, women were responsible for preserving the meat and processing the hides. This was quite a task because the Plains Indians used all parts of the buffalo. As well as providing fresh meat, the buffalo flesh was dried for future use. They called this dried meat **jerky**. Plains Indian women used buffalo skin to make clothing. The thick buffalo fur made robes that provided protection against the harsh winters. They used tanned buffalo leather to make the shelters, called tepees,

that were widely used on the Plains. Tepees consisted of many buffalo skins that were wrapped around poles. They were highly practical and were often beautifully decorated. Hunting tepees were small and portable.

The Plains Indians used other parts of the buffalo, such as bones, for tools and weapons. Some warriors were armed with long, stone-tipped lances and round shields made of buffalo hide. These shields were smoked and hardened with glue made from buffalo hooves. They were so tough that bullets striking them at an angle would not go through the shields.

With the buffalo providing for most of their needs, the Plains Indians prospered. For close to 100 years, from around 1780 to 1880, the Plains Indians lived and hunted in the midst of an immense grassland, moving freely on their swift ponies.

Section 1 Review

• Glossary

IDENTIFY and explain the significance of the following: Plains Indians, soldier bands, counting coup, jerky

REVIEWING FOR DETAILS
1. How were Plains Indian societies organized?
2. How did the horse change the lives of the Plains Indians?

REVIEWING FOR UNDERSTANDING
3. **Geographic Literacy** In what ways were the Plains Indians dependent on the buffalo?
4. **Writing Mastery:** *Describing* Imagine that you are an early explorer staying overnight at a Plains Indian village. Write a report to the president describing the Plains Indians and their way of life.
5. **Critical Thinking:** *Synthesizing Information* How did the members of Plains Indian societies work together for survival?

Section 2

THE WARS FOR THE WEST

Multimedia Connections

Explore these related topics and materials on the CD-ROM to enrich your understanding of this section:

 Profiles

- Chief Joseph
- Helen Hunt Jackson
- Susette La Flesche
- Sitting Bull

 Media Bank

- Massacre at Wounded Knee
- Ghost Dance
- Sitting Bull
- Chief Joseph
- Slaughtering the Buffalo
- Geronimo
- Crazy Horse
- Sarah Winnemucca

 Biographies

- Geronimo

 Readings

- Nez Percé

The young Cheyenne woman was bathing in the Greasy Grass stream near a Sioux camp when she heard the shouting. "Soldiers are coming!" Kate Bighead liked to watch battles—and her nephew would be fighting in this one—so she hurried to the battle scene. There were about 20 warriors for every soldier. The warriors rained arrows down on the U.S. soldiers for whom there was no escape.

As you read this section you will find out:

▶ **How incoming miners and settlers disturbed American Indian culture.**

▶ **What attempts the U.S. government made to end conflict between Plains Indians and settlers.**

▶ **How the Sioux response to the expansion of settlement changed over time.**

New Treaties

Before the 1850s the Plains Indians seldom came into contact with whites, other than fur traders. For the most part, only the Spanish in the Southwest and the Mormons in Utah had made permanent white settlements in this huge area. In the early 1850s, however, settlers and miners began moving into the Plains. They demanded that the U.S. government remove the Plains Indians.

Much of the Great Plains consisted of land that the United States had recognized as the property of American Indians. To secure safe passage west for settlers and future railroads, the federal government sent agents to negotiate with the Plains Indians. In 1851 the agents met with the northern Plains tribes at Fort Laramie, in present-day Wyoming. The meeting ended with both sides agreeing to the

Many Plains Indians did not want pioneers to cross their territory. In this painting, an Indian leader refuses to let a wagon train pass through tribal land.

● **U.S. Indian Policy**

Fort Laramie Treaty. Two years later, the government signed a treaty with the southern Plains Indians at Fort Atkinson.

Under these treaties, most of the Plains remained Indian land. The treaties encouraged Indians to live in particular areas and paid them fees to do so. The treaties' terms also stated that settlers could pass freely through the territories and that Indian groups would be held responsible for any attacks. In turn, the U.S. government promised to pay for any damages caused by travelers. It was not long before problems arose. The pioneers who crossed the Plains used wood—a scarce resource—for their campfires and killed local game along the trails. The Shoshoni chief Washakie complained:

> "Since the white man has made a road across our land and has killed off our game, we are hungry, and there is nothing for us to eat. Our women and children cry for food and we have no food to give them."

Broken Treaties

The Plains Indians soon found that the U.S. government would not keep its promises. People moving west demanded more and more land for settlement. The treaties were broken first on the southern Plains. The trouble began north of the Pikes Peak area of Colorado, where gold was discovered. By 1859 a seemingly endless stream of wagons was rolling across the Plains. Many of these prospectors, called "fifty-niners," had the slogan "Pikes Peak or Bust!" lettered on their canvas wagon covers.

Close to 100,000 of these "fifty-niners" pushed their way onto Cheyenne and Arapaho land. The Colorado territorial government persuaded federal officials to make new treaties that would move, and restrict, these Indians to **reservations**—federal lands set aside specifically for American Indians. The federal government's **Bureau of Indian Affairs** supervised the reservations and promised money and supplies to support this new way of life. The reservation system would mean the end of the buffalo-hunting culture because it required freedom of movement.

Some Cheyenne and Arapaho agreed to move to reservations. Others fiercely resisted, and between 1861 and 1864 they clashed several times with settlers and miners. Then in November 1864 Colonel John M. Chivington led a surprise attack on a peaceful Cheyenne encampment at Sand Creek in the Colorado Territory. The Cheyenne, under Chief

American Indians often decorated their buffalo-hide tepees, tools, and weapons, such as this Cheyenne warrior's shield.

The Granger Collection, New York

Black Kettle, tried to surrender by first raising an American flag and then a white flag of truce.

Chivington ignored these flags. "Kill and scalp all, big and little," he ordered. The U.S. soldiers killed around 200 Cheyenne during this **Sand Creek Massacre**. Others, including Black Kettle, escaped. Some of the Cheyenne bands later struck back with equally bloody attacks on settlers.

War on the Plains

The Sand Creek Massacre enraged many American Indians throughout the Plains. As more whites crossed Indian land, the conflict intensified. Soon, many other Plains Indians were at war with the U.S. Army and settlers.

The Indian Wars then spread to the northern Plains after the Pikes Peak gold rush that had triggered the conflict on the southern Plains proved to be a bust. About half the miners returned East. This time the signs on their wagons read "Busted, By Gosh!" The miners who remained in the West spread north through the mountains. Many followed the route pioneered by John M. Bozeman, a prospector from Georgia. This **Bozeman Trail** branched off the Oregon Trail west of Fort Laramie and ran north into Montana. It cut through the rolling foothills of the Big Horn Mountains, the hunting grounds of the western Sioux.

Red Cloud, a Sioux chief, protested angrily when miners and settlers began to appear on the trail. Red Cloud warned that the Sioux would fight to protect their hunting grounds, which were alive with deer, buffalo, elk, antelope, and bear.

In 1865 Sioux warriors made repeated attacks on trespassing white parties. The U.S. Army responded by building forts along the trail. In December 1866 Ta-sunko-witko (tuh-SUHN-koh WIT-koh), known as "Crazy

Global Connections

European Expansion in Southern Africa

Much like American Indians, the native peoples of southernmost Africa battled to save their homelands from European settlers. When the first Europeans came, many native Africans fell victim to European diseases. Then in the 1800s, many native Africans lost their land to German, Dutch, British, French, and other European settlers.

At first British settlers and Afrikaners, descendants of the early Dutch settlers, lived on the coast. Over time, mining and farming interests drew them inland. As these pioneers moved onto native Africans' land, conflicts broke out. Native Africans gained some ground when they used rifles, but few had access to European weapons. In the end the settlers and their weapons overpowered native Africans. Entire groups of some native peoples, such as the San and the Khoikhoi, were wiped out. By 1900, many native Africans had been killed, and those that remained had lost most of their power and their lands.

Horse," led an attack on an army supply caravan. When a troop of soldiers commanded by Captain W. J. Fetterman appeared, the Sioux retreated. Fetterman followed them and fell right into their well-laid trap. The Sioux defeated Fetterman, killing him and every man in his troop. A few months later John Bozeman was killed crossing the Yellowstone River on the very trail he had marked.

Prospectors stopped crossing Sioux land. Both sides were ready to end the fighting. In 1867 the southern Plains Indians had signed the **Treaty of Medicine Lodge**, agreeing to give up their lands and move to reservations in Indian Territory. The Sioux signed a second

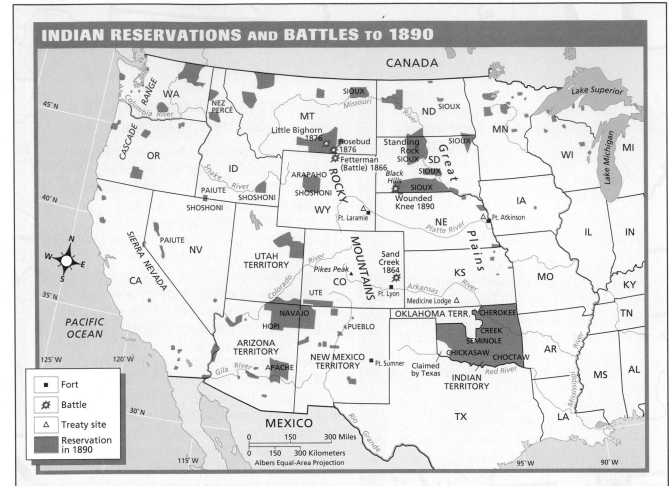

INDIAN RESERVATIONS AND BATTLES TO 1890

CANADA

Legend:
- ■ Fort
- ✹ Battle
- △ Treaty site
- ▓ Reservation in 1890

0 150 300 Miles
0 150 300 Kilometers
Albers Equal-Area Projection

Learning from Maps. Despite early treaties that guaranteed American Indians full control of their lands, later agreements relocated many tribes to reservations.

▶ **Location.** In which state did federal officials and southern Plains Indians sign the treaty of Fort Atkinson?

• Maps

treaty at Fort Laramie in 1868. The federal government agreed to abandon its forts along the Bozeman Trail in exchange for an end to Sioux raids. To ensure that the government kept its word, the Sioux burned down all the forts. Then they agreed to live on a reservation in the Black Hills of the Dakota Territory.

Sioux chief Red Cloud and his great-granddaughter, Burning Heart

The Sioux War of 1876

This move to the reservation did not end the fighting, however. In 1869 Civil War hero General William Tecumseh Sherman became commander of the U.S. Army. He pursued a policy of total war against the Plains Indians. Between 1869 and 1875 more than 200 clashes between Plains Indians and army units took place.

Sitting Bull. Tatanka Iyotake (tuh-TAHN-kuh ee-yuh-TAH-kay), also known as Sitting Bull, was one of the most important leaders of the northern Plains Indians. He was a **shaman**, or

American Letters

Ten Bears's Speech from 1867

The Comanche of the southern Great Plains fought to keep their lands and stay off of reservations. Ten Bears was an important chief of the Yamparika Comanche. In this 1867 speech, Ten Bears describes the conflicts in Texas.

My people have never first drawn a bow or fired a gun against the whites. There has been trouble on the line between us, and my young men have danced with war dance. But it was not begun by us. It was you who sent out the first soldier and we who sent out the second. Two years ago I came upon this road, following the buffalo, that my wives and children might have their cheeks plump and their bodies warm. But the soldiers fired on us, and since that time there has been a noise like that of a thunderstorm. . . . The blue-dressed soldiers and the Utes came from out of the night when it was dark and still, and for campfires they lit our lodges. Instead of hunting game they killed my braves, and the warriors of the tribe cut short their hair for the dead. So it was in Texas. They made sorrow come in our camps, and we went out like buffalo bulls when their cows are attacked. When we found them we killed them, and their scalps hang in our lodges. The Comanches are not weak and blind, like the pups of a dog when seven sleeps old. They are strong and farsighted, like grown horses. We took their road and we went on it. The white women cried and our women laughed.

. . . You said that you wanted to put us upon a reservation, to build us houses and make us medicine lodges [places of religious practice]. I do not want them. I was born upon the prairie, where the wind blew free and there was nothing to break the light of the sun. I was born where there were no enclosures and where everything drew a free breath. I

This 1875 photograph was taken in Indian Territory. Comanche and Kiowa Indians are in the process of painting their history on buffalo robes.

want to die there and not within walls. I know every stream and every wood between the Rio Grande and the Arkansas. I have hunted and lived over that country. I lived like my fathers before me, and, like them, I lived happily.

When I was at Washington the Great White Father told me that all the Comanche Land was ours, and that no one should hinder us in living upon it. So, why do you ask us to leave the rivers, and the sun, and the wind, and live in houses? Do not ask us to give up the buffalo for the sheep. . . .

If the Texans had kept out of my country, there might have been peace. But that which you now say we must live on is too small. The Texans have taken away the places where the grass grew the thickest and the timber was the best. Had we kept that, we might have done the things you ask. But it is too late. The white man has the country which we loved, and we only wish to wander on the prairie until we die.

medicine man, of the Sioux. Fiercely proud and independent, Sitting Bull urged the Sioux to keep their lands and customs. He refused to sign a treaty with the United States no matter how favorable the terms seemed. He firmly believed that compromise was impossible with a people he did not trust. "What treaty that the whites have kept has the red man broken? Not one. What treaty that the white man ever made with us have they kept? Not one." Sitting Bull's views made him extremely popular with many Plains Indians.

The Battle of the Little Bighorn.
In 1874 Sioux territory was invaded again, this time by prospectors looking for gold in the Black Hills. Sitting Bull advised the Sioux to resist any attempts to be moved from their sacred Black Hills, and war soon broke out.

Lieutenant Colonel George Armstrong Custer was in command of the U.S. 7th Cavalry when it rode into southern Montana in search of the Sioux. American Indians called Custer "Long Hair" because of his long, flowing blond hair. Custer often wore buckskin trousers, red-topped boots, and a broad-brimmed hat. A Civil War veteran, Custer was sometimes too daring, deliberately leading his troops into dangerous situations in hopes of winning what he called "glory."

On June 25, 1876, Custer led a troop of around 250 men toward what he believed to be a small Sioux camp. Instead, at a site near the Little Bighorn River, called Greasy Grass by the Sioux, he stumbled upon a very large group of Sioux.

The war chiefs Crazy Horse and Gall commanded the Sioux that now surrounded Custer's force. Racing around and around on their ponies, the Sioux warriors poured a deadly fire upon the troops. The desperate soldiers dismounted and tried to keep their horses from running away. In a short time, the entire company, including Custer, was dead. Sitting Bull's vision of a great Sioux victory was fulfilled. Often called Custer's Last Stand, the **Battle of the Little Bighorn** was the U.S. Army's worst defeat in the West.

The Sioux triumph at the Little Bighorn was short-lived, however. A few months later, the U.S. Army defeated the Sioux. When Crazy Horse surrendered with 900 other Sioux, he was stabbed fatally in the back with a bayonet. Sitting Bull led a group of Sioux into Canada and held out until 1881. He finally surrendered because the Sioux were starving—white hunters had killed off most of the buffalo on which the Sioux depended. In 1883 Sitting Bull was confined to Standing Rock Reservation in the Dakota Territory.

The Granger Collection, New York

At the Battle of the Little Bighorn, a troop from the U.S. 7th Cavalry was quickly surrounded and suffered an overwhelming defeat at the hands of the Sioux.

● **George Armstrong Custer**

Many of the U.S. Army troops assigned to the West were Civil War veterans. Among these soldiers were several African American regiments. These African American troops were nicknamed "buffalo soldiers" by American Indians.

The Ghost Dance

The final bloodshed in the wars on the Plains took place in South Dakota. In 1889 an American Indian religious movement, which whites called the **Ghost Dance**, swept through the Plains. Plains Indians performed this Ghost Dance to fulfill the prophecy of a Paiute Indian named Wovoka. The prophecy said that an Indian leader would come to drive white settlers from Indian lands, bring back the great buffalo herds, and unite Indians with their ancestors.

The Ghost Dance spread rapidly among Plains Indians. Government agents, alarmed by the energy and the mystery of the ritual dance, ordered the army to put an end to the Ghost Dance and also to arrest Sitting Bull, who had joined the Ghost Dance movement. When reservation police came to arrest Sitting Bull, they shot and killed him.

Many Sioux fled the reservation with the U.S. Army in pursuit. In December 1890, at Wounded Knee Creek in South Dakota, the U.S. 7th Cavalry encountered a band of Sioux families who were traveling in search of food. Suddenly, a shot rang out. Without warning the U.S. troops opened fire with rifles and Hotchkiss guns, a type of cannon. They massacred around 300 men, women, and children.

Many settlers saw Wounded Knee as revenge for Custer's earlier defeat. Other Americans, however, were horrified by it and demanded an investigation into the massacre. This **Massacre at Wounded Knee** marked the end of more than 25 years of the Plains Indians' armed resistance.

Section 2 Review

• Glossary

IDENTIFY and explain the significance of the following: Fort Laramie Treaty, reservations, Bureau of Indian Affairs, Sand Creek Massacre, Bozeman Trail, Treaty of Medicine Lodge, Sitting Bull, shaman, George Armstrong Custer, Battle of the Little Bighorn, Ghost Dance, Massacre at Wounded Knee

REVIEWING FOR DETAILS

1. How did the U.S. government try to end conflicts between Plains Indians and settlers who were moving west?
2. How did the Sioux gradually change their response to the settlers' expansion?

REVIEWING FOR UNDERSTANDING

3. **Geographic Literacy** How did incoming miners and settlers disturb the Plains Indians' relationship with the land?
4. **Writing Mastery:** *Persuading* Imagine that you are a Sioux chief. Prepare a speech to the Sioux tribal council persuading them either to return to their reservations or to continue resisting the U.S. Army.
5. **Critical Thinking:** *Fact and Opinion* Considering the policies tried by the U.S. government, was war with the Plains Indians unavoidable? Explain your answer.

Section 3

MINERS AND COWBOYS

Multimedia Connections

Explore these related topics and materials on the CD–ROM to enrich your understanding of this section:

 Atlas

- Mining Centers

 Profiles

- Annie Oakley

 Readings

- Cowboy Songs
- Mining Camps and Cattle Towns

 Simulation

- The Gold Rush

 Media Bank

- Cowboy Life
- Prospectors
- Nevada Mining Town
- Nat Love

Mrs. Lee Whipple-Haslam was a young girl when her family moved to the wilderness and built a snug log cabin. There the family was warm, well fed, and full of hope. Before long, however, prospectors found gold near the cabin. Word soon spread that gold had been discovered, and a mining town quickly sprang up, attracting all types of people, including criminals. Less than a year later, Wipple-Haslam's father was found murdered.

As you read this section you will find out:

▶ **How new technology changed the role of the individual prospector.**

▶ **In what ways the cattle industry borrowed from Spanish-Mexican culture.**

▶ **What factors contributed to the end of open-range ranching.**

The Mining Boom

After the California Gold Rush in 1849, the next important strike was in Nevada in 1859. One center of this activity was Gold Canyon, a sagebrush-covered ravine on the southern slope of Mount Davidson in western Nevada. At first the miners panned for gold in the gravel beds of streams. When their yields declined, they moved up the mountain.

The Comstock Lode. Henry Comstock, known as "Old Pancake," and his partner, James Fennimore, called "Old Virginia," began digging at the head of Gold Canyon on a small rise known as Gold Hill. Another pair, Peter O'Riley and Patrick McLaughlin, started digging at Six Mile Canyon, on the northern slope.

O'Riley and McLaughlin soon came upon a dark, heavy soil sprinkled with gold. Just as

These mining cars are coming out of a shaft in the Comstock Mine in the late 1860s.

some 15,000 people swarming into the region. Comstock gained everlasting fame by naming the find the **Comstock Lode**.

New mining technology. Most of the gold and silver was buried deep in veins of hard quartz rock and required heavy machinery to dig it out. Steam-powered drills gouged out massive chunks of earth. Newly developed steam shovels moved the chunks to waiting wagons or rail cars, which carried them to smelters. Huge rock crushers and smelters then separated the ore from the rock. By 1872 a railway wound through the mining communities, bringing coal to fuel the smelters.

Mine owners realized that large smelters, located in Golden or Denver, were more efficient. So the railroad hauled the ore—rich with silver, copper, lead, and gold—to these plants. Tunneling operations called for experienced mining engineers. Powerful pumps were needed to remove groundwater that seeped in as the shafts grew deeper. Miners like Comstock, O'Riley, and McLaughlin did not have the skill or the money that such operations required. Comstock eventually sold his share of the mine for a mere $11,000.

they were shouting news of their discovery, Comstock came riding by. Jumping from his horse, he quickly examined the find. "You have struck it, boys!" he said. Then the old prospector bluffed his way into a partnership:

> **"This spring was Old Man Caldwell's. You know that. . . . Well, Manny Penrod and I bought this claim last winter, and we sold a tenth interest to Old Virginia the other day. You two fellows must let us in on equal shares."**

At first O'Riley and McLaughlin said no. Then they were afraid that they might lose everything, so they agreed. The partners went to work at once. They found very little gold. Instead, they struck large deposits of heavy, bluish sand and blue-gray quartz. Not knowing what that "blasted blue stuff" was, they simply piled it beside the mine. A Mexican miner, however, gathered up a sack of the blue quartz and had it **assayed**, or tested.

The assayers' reports exceeded the partners' wildest dreams. They had hit upon a silver **bonanza**, a large find of extremely rich ore. News of the discovery brought

Prospectors went from one mountain to the next in search of a mining claim that would make them rich. Miners worked hard, but few succeeded in their search for a bonanza.

The Granger Collection, New York

The Cattle Kingdom

While miners were searching for gold and silver, other pioneers were seeking their fortunes in cattle. The land that stretched from Texas into Canada and from the Rockies to eastern Kansas eventually formed the **Cattle Kingdom**. This area, which spanned roughly one quarter of the United States, became dotted with cattle ranches.

Cattle in the Southwest.

Spanish explorers had brought the first cattle into Mexico in the 1500s. Over the years their herds had increased enormously. Many ran wild, and new breeds developed. These great herds spread northward as far as Texas. By the mid-1860s, about 5 million wild cattle were grazing in Texas. Many of these were Texas longhorns, so named because their horns had a spread of as much as seven feet. Longhorns thrived on the Plains because they could survive with little water or grass.

After the Civil War there was a growing demand for beef in eastern cities. Cattle that were worth from $3 to $5 a head in Texas could be sold in the East for $30 to $50 a head. The problem was transporting the herds to the East. Railroads had not yet come to Texas. Joseph G. McCoy, an Illinois meat dealer, thought he had a solution. He hoped to make his fortune by establishing a convenient meeting place for buyers and Texas cattle ranchers.

Cattle towns.

McCoy chose the town of Abilene, Kansas, as this meeting place. There he built a hotel for the cowhands and dealers and built barns, pens, and loading chutes for the cattle. He persuaded officials of the Kansas Pacific Railroad to ship cattle to Chicago—the meat-packing center of the United States—at special low rates.

At first, Abilene was a quiet town, coming to life only during the few months that the ranchers brought in their cattle. Local men and women saw new opportunities for opening businesses such as saloons, restaurants, hotels, and stores. Even children could find work in the rapidly growing town. What had been little more than a railroad station with stockyards for cattle became a town with businesses, schools, and churches. Soon Abilene faced competition from other Kansas cattle towns, such as Ellsworth and Dodge City.

Cattle drives.

To get Texas longhorns to cattle towns meant herding them slowly northward over the Plains. This long trip, called a **cattle drive**, was a journey of several months over hundreds of miles. On the first drive, Texans herded some 35,000 longhorns over the Chisholm Trail to Abilene. Soon ranchers blazed other routes, such as the Goodnight-Loving, Western, and Shawnee Trails. During the next 25 years about 10 million head of cattle were driven north over these trails of open grasslands.

The Granger Collection, New York

Cowboys herded Texas longhorns north on the long drive to market. The drive ended at cattle towns like Dodge City, where the railroad would pick up the cattle and ship them east. In this engraving, Dodge City is suddenly filled with the cowboys driving the longhorns to market.

● **Cowhands and Cattle Drives**

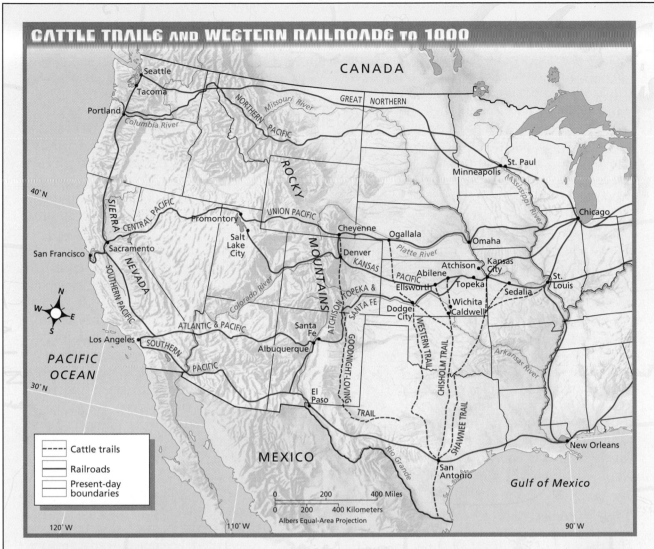

CATTLE TRAILS AND WESTERN RAILROADS TO 1000

Legend:
- - - - Cattle trails
——— Railroads
☐ Present-day boundaries

0   200   400 Miles
0 200 400 Kilometers
Albers Equal-Area Projection

Learning from Maps. By the mid- to late 1800s, cattle trails and railroads had crossed much of the West.

▶ **Movement.** About how many miles was it from New Orleans to Los Angeles on Southern Pacific's railroad route?

• Maps

Open-Range Ranching

The key to the success of the cattle drive was the **open range**, or grass on the public lands, along the trails. Ranchers discovered that prairie grass made an excellent food for their cattle and that the longhorns got along very well in the harsh winters of the Plains.

When the U.S. government turned former Indian land into public lands, cattle ranching spread west and north of Texas. Cattle roamed freely across the unfenced land that was by now nearly empty of buffalo. Ranchers grazed millions of cattle on the Plains without paying a cent to the federal government. Cattle ranching became highly profitable, and soon it attracted investors from the East Coast and Europe who acquired huge ranches.

Range rights. Cattle ranchers needed access to water. **Range rights**, or water rights, along a stream meant control of all the land around it. Ranchers, individually or in a group, quickly bought up all the land around their water supply. By owning a few acres along a river, ranchers could control thousands of acres of surrounding grassland without actually owning it. Although the rest of the range was public property, no other rancher for miles around could graze cattle there because the access to water was on private property.

Roundup. The ranchers who owned the banks of the stream let their cattle mix together. Each spring and fall, cowhands gathered all the animals to a central place—an event known as a **roundup**. Next they sorted each rancher's cattle from the rest by checking every animal's **brand**, or marking. This brand was a scar made by pressing a red-hot branding iron onto the animal's hide. Each rancher's brand had a distinct shape, so it was easy to determine who owned which cattle.

The Cowhand

The success of the drive and the roundup depended upon that colorful figure, the cowboy or cowhand. Many cowhands came from poor families. About one third of the cowhands who worked the herds of cattle on the open range were either Mexican Americans or African Americans.

American Indians and Mexican Americans were the first cowhands. These *vaqueros,* as they were called in Spanish, invented almost all the tools of the cowhands' trade, including the broad-brimmed felt hat, the cotton bandanna, the rope lariat, and the special western saddle.

Every item of the cowhands' clothing and equipment served a necessary function. The wide brims of their hats could be turned down to shade their eyes or drain off rainfall. Their

The Granger Collection, New York
The vaqueros *wore large hats and leather chaps in their work.*

● **Cowboy Music**

bandannas could be tied over their noses and mouths to protect them from the dust raised by the pounding hooves of countless cattle. The bandanna could also serve as a towel, napkin, bandage, and handkerchief.

Cowhands sometimes wore leather protectors, called chaps, over regular pants. Chaps were fastened to a broad belt buckled at the back. They protected a rider's legs from injury if a cowhand fell from a horse or had to ride through cactus, sagebrush, or other thorny plants.

The cowhands' western saddle was heavy but comfortable. It had a sturdy horn, for help in roping powerful steers and horses. At night the saddle could become a pillow and the saddlecloth a blanket when the cowhand stretched out beside the campfire. Before settling down to sleep, the cowhands often sang songs, such as "Home on the Range." These songs have become a rich part of American music.

Most cowhands' had hard lives. They worked from sunup to sundown and received lower wages than most factory workers. Their legs often became bowed from long days in the saddle. They developed permanent squints from peering into the glaring sunlight of the treeless Plains. Their faces were lined and leathery, their hands callused from constantly handling coarse ropes. The time spent on the open range made for a lonely life.

The End of the Open Range

By the end of the 1880s the days of the open range were coming to an end. Ranchers had overstocked the range. As a result, there was a shortage of good grazing land and a surplus of beef, which drove down prices.

Farmers were glad to see the end of the open range. Cattle herds often trampled

The Granger Collection, New York

Barbed wire made fencing off western farmland easier and more affordable, and as a result, put an end to open-range ranching.

In the foothills of the Rockies, sheepherders squared off against local cattle ranchers because sheep cropped the grass so close to the roots that cattle could no longer graze. Many range wars broke out between cattle ranchers and sheep ranchers for control of the grasslands.

Two terrible winters in a row added to the decline of the open range. In 1885–86 and in 1886–87 blizzards howled across the Plains. Theodore Roosevelt, then a "gentleman rancher" in Dakota Territory, wrote:

"Furious gales blow down from the north, driving before them the clouds of blinding snow-dust, wrapping the mantle of death around every unsheltered being."

farmers' crops. The farmers also feared that the free-roaming herds would infect their dairy cows with a disease called "Texas fever." The invention of **barbed wire**, a relatively cheap method of fencing, allowed farmers and ranchers to close off their land, thus shrinking the amount of open land for cattle grazing.

When spring came in 1887, ranchers discovered that the storms had wiped out a large percentage of their herds. The boom times were over. Cattle ranchers had to fence in their herds and feed them hay in the winter. Thus cattle ranchers became cattle feeders, and the days of the long cattle drives came to an end.

Section 3 Review

• Glossary

IDENTIFY and explain the significance of the following: assayed, bonanza, Comstock Lode, Cattle Kingdom, cattle drive, open range, range rights, roundup, brand, barbed wire

LOCATE and explain the importance of the following: Abilene, cattle trails

• Gazetteer

REVIEWING FOR DETAILS

1. How did new mining technology change the role of the prospector?
2. What elements of Spanish-Mexican culture were used by cowhands?

REVIEWING FOR UNDERSTANDING

3. **Geographic Literacy** Why did open-range ranching come to an end?
4. **Writing Mastery:** *Describing* Imagine that you are the sheriff in a western town in 1884. Write an editorial for the local newspaper describing the conflicts between farmers, cattle ranchers, and sheepherders in the region.
5. **Critical Thinking:** *Synthesizing Information* What effects did mining and the cattle industry have on the growth of towns in the West?

Section 4

SETTLEMENT ON THE GREAT PLAINS

Multimedia Connections

Explore these related topics and materials on the CD–ROM to enrich your understanding of this section:

 Media Bank

- U.S. Government and the West
- Cost of Establishing a Farm
- Union and Central Pacific Meet

- Pony Express Rider
- Harvesting Wheat
- "Exodus" Movement

 Atlas

- Oklahoma Land Rush

 Readings

- *A Lantern in Her Hand*

 Profiles

- Willa Cather

Everyday life in the West was often quite difficult. Anne Howard Shaw described her experiences when she was a 15-year-old teacher in a one-room schoolhouse:

> "The school was four miles from my home. . . . During the first year I had about fourteen pupils, of varying ages, sizes, and temperaments, and there was hardly a book in the school-room except those I owned. One little girl, I remember, read from an almanac, while a second used a hymn-book."

As you read this section you will find out:

▶ **Why settlers moved to the Great Plains.**

▶ **What natural obstacles farmers faced on the Great Plains.**

▶ **How farmers adapted to the unique conditions of the Great Plains.**

Railroads Reach West

The federal government encouraged economic growth in the West through important legislation passed in 1862, particularly the **Pacific Railway Act**, the **Homestead Act**, and the **Morrill Act**. These acts gave western land grants to promote the building of a transcontinental railroad, settlements, and educational facilities, respectively.

As miners, ranchers, and settlers went west, companies and individual investors became increasingly interested in the region. It still took people several months to reach California by wagon or clipper ship, however. Faster transportation to the Pacific seemed more important than ever.

Soon after passage of the Railway Act, the Union Pacific Railroad and the Central Pacific Railway began the great task of building a

The Central Pacific Railroad saved millions of dollars by hiring Chinese workers at a rate two thirds of that paid to a white laborer. Chinese railroad gangs of 12 to 20 men usually had a Chinese cook who prepared native dishes.

railroad across the West. In 1869 these companies completed the first transcontinental railroad, meeting at Promontory, Utah.

Other railroad companies soon built more transcontinental lines. These new railroads connected with eastern railroads at Chicago, St. Louis, and New Orleans. This meant a traveler could go from the Atlantic coast to San Francisco and other Pacific coast cities in about a week's time, which was much quicker than ever before.

• Building the Railroads

To offset their building costs, the railroad companies sold their free government land grants—about 130 million acres of public lands. The railroad companies advertised these lands in the East and in Europe and offered discounted and free tickets to settlers who would buy land.

The railroad boom in the West also led to improved communications. Railroad companies often stretched **telegraph** lines alongside tracks. The telegraph, which had been invented by Samuel F. B. Morse in 1837, used a system of dots and dashes to transmit messages over wires. During the late 1800s, businesses came to rely on telegraph communications to make orders and to fix schedules. By 1866 Western Union, the

nation's largest telegraph company, had over 4,000 offices.

The Plains Farmers

Settlers came by the thousands to buy land from the railroad companies. Others claimed their 160 acres under the Homestead Act. Although Homestead land was practically free, settlers needed some financial resources to make the trip west—buying and transporting supplies to start up a farm or a business was quite costly.

Civil War veterans and New England farmers looking for better soil were among those who headed west. Many more settlers came from states such as Illinois, Indiana, and Wisconsin.

Political oppression drove other Americans west. For example, Benjamin Singleton led some 20,000 or more African Americans west from the South in 1879. They hoped to leave behind violence and racial prejudice. These black settlers became known as **Exodusters**.

Other western settlers were emigrants from Europe. Hundreds of thousands of Irish, Germans, Czechs, Ukrainians, Russians, and Scandinavians settled on the Plains. Writer O. E. Rölvaag described one Norwegian family who moved to Dakota Territory because there was "no lack of opportunity in that country!"

Daily Life on the Plains

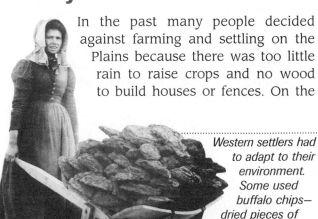

In the past many people decided against farming and settling on the Plains because there was too little rain to raise crops and no wood to build houses or fences. On the

Western settlers had to adapt to their environment. Some used buffalo chips— dried pieces of manure—as fuel.

treeless Plains the pioneers had to build their first homes out of the earth itself. The thick roots of the wild grasses made it possible to cut sod into bricklike chunks. Usually, only the roofs of these sod houses were made of wood. Sod houses were smoky and damp, but they provided shelter until the railroads brought in affordable lumber for building better homes.

Many found that the hardships overshadowed the advantages of free land. The environment offered one of the biggest challenges. In winter, blizzards roared out of Canada. In summer, the thermometer frequently soared above 100 degrees, and tornadoes sometimes swept across the Plains. In addition, pests such as great swarms of grasshoppers descended on the land, eating everything in sight.

Neighbors lent each other their support in this harsh environment. In Willa Cather's novel, *My Ántonia,* the narrator describes a visit to a Czech family who had a new log house:

> **"The neighbors had helped them [the family] to build it in March. It stood directly in front of their old cave, which they used as a cellar. The family were now fairly equipped to begin their struggle with the soil. They had four comfortable rooms to live in, a new windmill—bought on credit—a chicken-house and poultry."**

Farming was hard and risky work. Each member of the family had countless chores. These ranged from plowing, to milking cows, to planting a garden, to taking care of the children. Women often found that their work expanded beyond traditional roles of tending the house and the family. Children also had important duties.

Farming the Plains

Farming on the Great Plains was difficult, but the soil was very fertile. The biggest problem facing the farmers of western Nebraska, Kansas, and the Dakotas was the lack of rainfall. In some years there was plenty of rain to grow wheat and other grain crops. Often, however, there were dry years, and even **droughts**, when almost no rain fell. Well water could be used to irrigate a small plot or a vegetable garden, but it was not enough for any large-scale farming.

Young People In History
Sodbuster Kids

Life on the Plains was hard for young people. They often lived in very cramped quarters with as many as 10 brothers and sisters. Some could attend school. Many, however, spent long, tiring days working in the fields. Despite the hard work, these young pioneers found ways to have fun. Author Laura Ingalls Wilder wrote many novels based on her own childhood on the Plains. In one book, she described the main character, Laura, joyfully riding her pony after the daily chores were done.

Children on the Plains found enjoyment in simple things.

Nebraska State Historical Society

"She and the pony were going too fast but they were going like music and nothing could happen to her until the music stopped. . . . That was a wonderful afternoon. Twice Laura fell off. . . . Her hair came unbraided and her throat grew hoarse from laughing and screeching, and her legs were scratched from running through the sharp grass and trying to leap onto her pony while it was running."

The Granger Collection, New York

Nebraska State Historical Society

Pioneers went west in search of cheap land offered by the government and the railroads. Settlers established farms and built their houses out of sod.

Hardy W. Campbell, a farmer in Dakota Territory, promoted a technique called **dry farming** that made it possible to raise certain crops with very little water. Campbell plowed the land deeply and repeatedly. Rain thus was absorbed easily into the soil, where the roots of the plants could use it. Campbell also planted special varieties of wheat that needed less water than other types. Using dry-farming methods, farmers could raise crops in dry years.

By the 1880s the average Plains farmer was using a great deal of machinery. In 1868 James Oliver of Indiana had begun manufacturing a new type of iron plow. This plow, which later became known as a **sodbuster**, could easily slice through the tough sod of the Plains. In the 1870s John Appleby invented a twine binder. This machine gathered up bundles of wheat and automatically bound them with twine or string, greatly reducing the time needed for harvesting. In 1890 about 5 million people were living on the Great Plains. By the 1890s the land west of the Mississippi Valley had become the breadbasket of America and the greatest wheat-producing region in the world.

Section 4 Review

• **Glossary**

IDENTIFY and explain the significance of the following: Pacific Railway Act, Homestead Act, Morrill Act, telegraph, Exodusters, droughts, dry farming, sodbuster

REVIEWING FOR DETAILS
1. Why did settlers move to the Great Plains?
2. How did farmers adapt to the conditions of the Plains?

REVIEWING FOR UNDERSTANDING

• **Time Line**

3. **Geographic Literacy**   What geographic challenges did farm families face on the Great Plains?

4. **Writing Mastery:** *Expressing*   Imagine that you are a teenager who has recently moved to the Great Plains. Write a letter to one of your friends in the East expressing your feelings about life in your new home.

5. **Critical Thinking:** *Determining the Strength of an Argument*   What were the advantages and disadvantages of the U.S. government granting land to companies in exchange for railroad construction?

CHAPTER 17

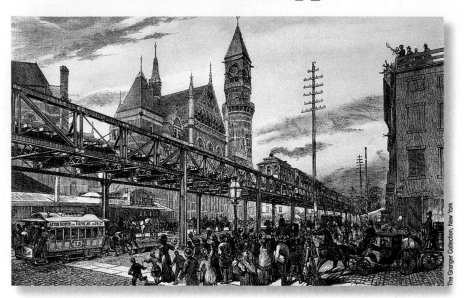

The Granger Collection, New York

Becoming an Industrial Nation (1865–1900)

THEMES IN AMERICAN HISTORY

Technology and Society:
How might new scientific discoveries change people's lives?

Economic Development:
How might industrialization lead to the growth of cities?

Cultural Diversity:
How might large numbers of immigrants affect a society's culture?

*I*n the late 1800s the United States was a land of incredible contrasts. In New York City, mansions stood just blocks away from run-down apartment buildings. Wealthy business owners sat comfortably in fancy offices while their workers labored in dangerous factories. "Never before have the rich been so rich and the poor been so poor," one observer noted.

• Video
Opener

• Skill
Builder

image above: *A city in the late 1800s*

Section 1

INVENTIONS AND THE RISE OF BIG BUSINESS

Multimedia Connections
Explore these related topics and materials on the CD–ROM to enrich your understanding of this section:

 Media Bank

- Inventions, 1850–1900
- Mail-Order Catalog
- Advertising
- Vanderbilt Family

 Glossary

- bankruptcy

 Readings

- The Making of Consumer Culture
- Mark Twain's Criticisms
- Leisure Activities

 Profiles

- Alexander Graham Bell
- Cornelius Vanderbilt
- Elijah McCoy
- Granville Woods
- Thomas Edison

The late 1800s were a time of inventions and industrial expansion. Businesspeople ruled America, and those who controlled the production of essential goods had enormous power. Many Americans hoped the new breed of businessperson would help the country make a successful transition to what some observers called a "modern age."

As you read this section you will find out:
▶ **What new scientific and technological discoveries fueled the Second Industrial Revolution.**
▶ **How entrepreneurs encouraged the growth of business.**
▶ **Why the growth of big business led to government regulations.**

Building the New Industrial Society

Between 1865 and 1900 the United States went through one of the most dramatic periods of change the country had ever seen. Several factors were responsible for this amazing transformation.

Changing iron into steel. Steel was the basic building material of what many called the Second Industrial Revolution. In the 1850s a British inventor named Henry Bessemer perfected an inexpensive way to make steel. The **Bessemer process**, as it was called, made possible the mass production of steel.

Steel had many uses in America's rapidly developing industrial society. After steel rails for railroad tracks came steel skeletons for tall buildings and bridges. Nails, wire, and other everyday objects were also made of steel.

The railroad network. Steel production particularly helped American railroads. The first rails were made of cast iron, but they often wore out quickly. Steel rails lasted much longer than iron rails.

Even after the introduction of steel rails, however, problems in the railroad industry remained. Railroads had been built primarily to serve local transportation needs. Most railroads in the United States were short, averaging only about 100 miles. In 1860, passengers and freight traveling between New York and Chicago, for example, had to change lines 17 times!

Business leaders set out to connect these lines into networks. Cornelius Vanderbilt was a pioneer in this work. Although he quit school at age 11, he had a good head for business. Vanderbilt bought up separate railroad routes and combined them. By 1870 his railroad system extended from New York to Chicago. Passengers could travel between the two cities in less than 24 hours!

Inventions and new practices also contributed to the expansion of railroads. George Westinghouse invented a compressed air brake that made larger, faster, and safer trains possible. Another inventor, African American Granville Woods, improved the design of air brakes and created other useful products as well, including a new telegraph system.

Railroads stimulated the national economy in countless ways. They functioned as a major employer, supplying thousands of new jobs. Railroads also created many other jobs in related industries, such the manufacturing of railroad cars and other materials needed for railroad operation. In addition, railroads allowed for the quick, easy, and inexpensive movement of goods and passengers over long distances. Finally, railroads encouraged urban growth.

Powering the New Industrial Society

Steel and railroads served as the building blocks of the Second Industrial Revolution. Other products and industries powered the new society.

"Black gold." Americans had known about crude oil, or petroleum, for hundreds of years. Oil was very difficult to collect, though, so few people made much use of it. Then in 1859 a retired railroad conductor named E. L. Drake began drilling for petroleum in Pennsylvania. The idea seemed so impractical that

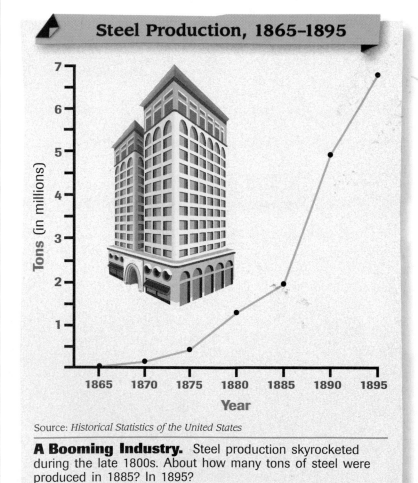

Steel Production, 1865–1895

Tons (in millions)

Year: 1865, 1870, 1875, 1880, 1885, 1890, 1895

Source: *Historical Statistics of the United States*

A Booming Industry. Steel production skyrocketed during the late 1800s. About how many tons of steel were produced in 1885? In 1895?

The expansion of railroad networks in the late 1800s greatly changed the way Americans did business. The Illinois Central Railroad, shown here, was one of the many lines that ran through Chicago.

The revolution in communications. Advances in communications also furthered the growth of American industry. Alexander Graham Bell invented the telephone in 1876. At first, many people considered Bell's invention a joke. Fortunately, others realized its usefulness. Telephone wires soon rose up across the skies. The telephone became an essential part of industrial society, allowing rapid, cheap, long-distance communication by voice.

The Wizard of Menlo Park. In the same year that Bell invented the telephone, Thomas Alva Edison established the nation's first industrial research laboratory in Menlo Park, New Jersey. Although he had received only about five years of on-and-off formal schooling, Edison became known as the greatest inventor of the age because he developed so many products.

Edison's first major invention was the quadruplex telegraph. It could send four messages over one wire at the same time. He also invented the phonograph and made several improvements on Bell's telephone. Edison's early inventions fascinated many Americans.

onlookers called it "Drake's Folly," but when he had drilled down about 70 feet, Drake struck oil. In just a few years, "wildcatters," or adventurous people who searched for oil, flooded into western Pennsylvania to drill for what they called "black gold."

Oil quickly became a big business. By 1861 around 2 million barrels of oil were being pumped from western Pennsylvania annually. Businesspeople opened refineries to purify the crude oil. They sold such finished petroleum product as kerosene to other businesses and communities for use in lighting. Several inventions made oil even more valuable. Elijah McCoy, the son of runaway slaves, invented a lubricating cup that fed oil to parts of a machine while it ran. This breakthrough helped all kinds of machines operate more smoothly and quickly. In the 1890s the internal combustion engine, which burned petroleum in the form of gasoline or diesel fuel, turned oil into one of the nation's major sources of power.

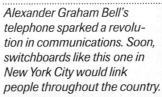

Alexander Graham Bell's telephone sparked a revolution in communications. Soon, switchboards like this one in New York City would link people throughout the country.

The Granger Collection, New York

One writer celebrated the products of Edison's "invention factory" in a popular magazine:

> **"If this can be done . . . what is there that cannot be? . . . We feel that there may, after all, be a relief for all human ills in the great storehouse of nature."**

Edison's most important invention came in the late 1870s, when he developed an electric lightbulb. Edison's basic idea was to pass electricity through a thin wire inside an airless glass globe. The electricity heated the wire, causing it to glow brightly. The wire could not burn up because there was no oxygen in the globe. Soon the "Wizard of Menlo Park" was setting up city lighting companies and power stations to generate electricity. He also sold light bulbs by the millions. In just a few years, electric lights were replacing gas lights in cities across the country.

The Leaders of Big Business

Entrepreneurs (ahn-truh-puh-NUHRZ), or risk-taking businesspeople, played an important role in the Second Industrial Revolution. Some were "robber barons"—rough, greedy businesspeople who cheated and mistreated others to enrich themselves. Some were honest, public-spirited citizens. All were eager to take advantage of the opportunities they saw opening up around them.

New business practices. The entrepreneurs of the late 1800s developed new ways to make more money and operate more efficiently. At around this time, businesspeople began to question traditional forms of business organization. In the early 1800s most businesses were owned by individuals or partners. However, it took huge amounts of money to construct and run a railroad, oil refinery, or research lab.

Therefore, entrepreneurs set up their new businesses as **corporations**. They sold shares called stock certificates to investors. These investors, called **stockholders**, made money when the corporation did well.

Corporations offered a number of advantages over other types of business organization. By selling stock certificates, entrepreneurs could raise a lot of money. Investors benefited as well because they had limited liability. They risked only the money that they had paid for their stock. In a partnership, on the other hand, all the partners were responsible for all the debts of the firm. In addition, corporations allowed a small group of directors to control a very large business operation.

Carnegie and steel. One of the most important business leaders of the late 1800s was Andrew Carnegie. He came to the United States from Scotland as a youth and worked 12 hours a day in a cotton mill. By the time he was 17, he had become the private secretary to a railroad company's superintendent. He soon became a railroad superintendent himself and made a great deal of money from various investments.

Carnegie eventually concentrated his investments in the steel industry. He built the

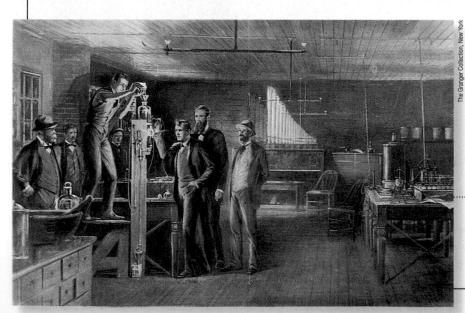

The Granger Collection, New York

Thomas Edison experiments with an electric lightbulb in his Menlo Park laboratory.

• Thomas Edison in Lab

Scottish immigrant Andrew Carnegie made his fortune in the steel business.

The Granger Collection, New York

• **Andrew Carnegie**

first Bessemer factory in America. Using clever business techniques, Carnegie built a vast industrial empire. Carnegie practiced what is known as **vertical integration**, or the attempted ownership of companies that provided the materials and services for his own factories. He bought up businesses that produced iron ore and coal to feed his steel mills, and railroads to move these materials to his factories. When Carnegie sold his company to banker J. P. Morgan in 1901, he became the world's richest man.

Rockefeller and oil. John D. Rockefeller applied the business practices of the late 1800s and created new ones to dominate the oil refining industry. After making a small fortune in the wholesale food business, in 1863 Rockefeller went into oil refining. He organized the Standard Oil Company in 1870. Like Carnegie, he used vertical integration to increase his profits. Rockefeller also practiced **horizontal integration**, or the attempted ownership of all the companies in a particular field. He targeted oil refining firms.

One scholar has described Rockefeller as having "a ruthlessness that never failed to impress his subordinates [employees]." He took business competition very seriously. He would do almost anything to beat out other companies. He forced railroad companies to give him special discounted rates on the oil he shipped with them by threatening to take his business to their competitors.

He sold his oil below cost in some areas to win business from smaller local oil companies. Then he forced the local refiners to either sell out to Standard Oil or face **bankruptcy**, a state of extreme financial ruin. If they refused to sell, he forced them out of business. Though harsh, Rockefeller's methods succeeded. By the late 1870s he controlled almost 90 percent of the American oil business.

Hoping to strengthen his grip on the industry even further, Rockefeller established a **trust**—a legal agreement under which several companies grouped together to regulate production and eliminate competition. To do this, stockholders of the separate companies turned control of their shares over to a group of directors called trustees. By controlling the stock of so many companies, the trustees could control an industry and thus collect huge profits. This resulted in a **monopoly**, or complete domination of an industry.

The Antitrust Movement

The trust idea soon spread to other businesses. By 1900 a small number of wealthy and powerful business owners controlled many

Oil towns like this one in Pennsylvania became increasingly more common sights with the development of the refining system. John D. Rockefeller's Standard Oil Company dominated the industry beginning in the late 1800s.

• **John D. Rockefeller**

Popular political magazines like Puck *criticized the power of trusts in a humorous way.*

• Corporate Mergers

important branches of the nation's manufacturing industries.

The size and power of these trusts alarmed many Americans. They feared that the trusts would not only destroy small companies but also cheat consumers by charging high prices once competition had been eliminated. Eventually, these people formed the antitrust movement. They wanted to break up large businesses into smaller companies to restore competition.

Like other entrepreneurs, Rockefeller defended the trusts: "Only . . . by such an industrial combination is America to-day enabled to utilize the bounty which its land pours forth." Despite these arguments, the demand for government regulation of the economy increased steadily. Then in 1890 Congress passed the **Sherman Antitrust Act**. This law banned combinations "in the form of trust or otherwise" that restricted interstate trade or commerce. Violators faced fines or jail sentences.

The Sherman Antitrust Act had little effect on big business at the time, however. Most judges still stressed the right of companies and individuals to run their affairs more or less as they pleased. In addition, the law was hard to enforce because it did not offer specific definitions of trusts or monopolies.

Section 1 Review

• Glossary

IDENTIFY and explain the significance of the following: Bessemer process, Cornelius Vanderbilt, Granville Woods, Elijah McCoy, Alexander Graham Bell, Thomas Alva Edison, entrepreneurs, corporations, stockholders, Andrew Carnegie, vertical integration, John D. Rockefeller, horizontal integration, bankruptcy, trust, monopoly, Sherman Antitrust Act

REVIEWING FOR DETAILS

1. How did advances in science and technology encourage the Second Industrial Revolution?
2. How did entrepreneurs affect business growth after the Civil War?

REVIEWING FOR UNDERSTANDING

3. **Geographic Literacy** How did changes in transportation and building methods transform the country's landscape in the late 1800s?
4. **Writing Mastery:** *Persuading* Imagine that you are an ordinary citizen in the late 1800s. Write a letter to your local newspaper persuading readers to support or oppose more government regulation of big business.
5. **Critical Thinking:** *Drawing Conclusions* What were some of the negative effects of big business on society? In what ways do you think big business benefited ordinary citizens?

Section 2

WORKERS AND LABOR UNIONS

Multimedia Connections

Explore these related topics and materials on the CD-ROM to enrich your understanding of this section:

 Media Bank

- Samuel Gompers
- Homestead, Pennsylvania

 Profiles

- Samuel Gompers

 Biographies

- Mary "Mother" Jones

 Atlas

- Labor Strikes, 1870–1900

The "Captains of Industry" had succeeded in building a new society—at least in their own factories, shops, and mines. Some people praised this society. "The factory system," one author insisted, "is vastly superior as an element in civilization." Others were more uneasy. They surveyed the world around them, so different from that of their grandmothers and grandfathers, and found it lacking. "Absolutely injurious," one observer complained. "A positive evil."

As you read this section you will find out:

▶ **What working conditions were like for the average worker.**

▶ **How labor unions developed.**

▶ **What methods workers and factory owners used in dealing with labor issues.**

The New Workplace

The industrial changes that took place after the Civil War greatly affected the men and women who worked in American factories. Many factory owners insisted on specialization. This meant that each worker performed one task over and over, hundreds of times each day. In a steel plant, for example, some workers shoveled ore. Others moved the finished steel. No single worker could make steel alone. Instead, each worker contributed to one part of the process. Specialization had become a more efficient way to produce goods.

Workers also labored in a workplace that relied on machines. Machines greatly increased the amount a worker could produce, which tended to raise wages and lower prices. Lower prices helped to bring more goods within the reach of the average family.

Most factory workers, like these in New York City, worked with dangerous machinery that had no protective equipment. As a result, workers were often injured on the job.

Machines made work less interesting, however, because most required few skills to operate.

Workers faced very strict working conditions. To control a growing workforce and maximize profits, businesspeople created many rules regulating the behavior of workers. Breaks were often limited, even just to get a drink of water. Some bosses would not even allow workers to talk to one another while on the job.

The industrial workplace was also dangerous. Every year between 1880 and 1890 about 35,000 railroad workers were killed and more than 500,000 injured. Businesses did not pay much attention to safety, and they usually did not offer any help to those who suffered job-related injuries. Sometimes companies asked hurt workers to sign a release, or papers that removed all responsibility from the corporation. In a typical accident, a worker had been badly injured by falling rocks in a mine. He explained why he agreed to a release:

Frank J. Farrell (left), a member of the Knights of Labor, introduces union leader Terence V. Powderly (center) at a meeting. Powderly promoted acceptance of African Americans at a time when most unions were strictly segregated.

"If I don't sign . . . I can never get a day's work under that company or any other round here, for if I get well I'll be blacklisted. [Then] what will my wife and my babies do?"

Unionization

Many workers did not just accept low pay and dangerous working conditions. Some joined labor unions, seeking to improve their workplaces.

The Knights of Labor.   One of the first large unions to emerge in the United States after the Civil War was the **Knights of Labor**. Uriah Stephens, a tailor, founded the union in 1869. The Knights quickly organized workers into a "great brotherhood." The union generally admitted only white men, ignoring thousands of other workers. Still, by 1881 the Knights claimed to have 20,000 members.

In 1879 Terence V. Powderly, the son of Irish immigrants, became the union's top official. When he was a boy, Powderly went to work for a railroad and soon joined a labor

Mary "Mother" Jones shown here at age 76, was one of the best-known women in the Knights of Labor.

organization. He helped the Knights develop a strategy. They called for the eight-hour workday and strict regulation of trusts.

Under Powderly's direction the Knights increased the admission of African Americans, women, some European immigrants, and unskilled workers to the union. Most other unions continued to reject these workers. African American labor leader Isaac Myers praised Powderly's move, explaining the importance of union membership for black workers, "American citizenship for the black man is a complete failure if he is proscribed [forbidden] from the workshops of the country."

Women also played active roles in the Knights. Mary Harris Jones served as a union organizer. She accepted the job readily, stating that she belonged wherever there was a "good fight against wrong." She became known as "Mother" Jones because of her warm, comforting manner.

The Knights prospered under Powderly's leadership. In the 1880s local leaders organized and won several important strikes against railroad companies. Union membership soared. About 700,000 workers belonged to the organization by 1886. The union eventually ran into trouble, however. Local unions called strikes recklessly, and many of these failed. Workers became discouraged and dropped out of the Knights.

Then the Knights were blamed, quite unfairly, for a terrible bombing incident that occurred in May 1886. To protest an earlier conflict between local strikers and police, radicals called for a meeting to take place in Chicago's Haymarket Square. The gathering was peaceful, but the police tried to break it up anyway. In the scuffle that followed, someone threw a bomb, killing seven police officers. Public opinion turned against unions after what became known as the **Haymarket Riot**.

The AFL. In 1881, a few years before the Knights of Labor began to decline, representatives from a number of craft unions founded a new labor organization. In 1886 this group officially became the **American Federation of Labor** (AFL).

Samuel Gompers, a cigarmaker, was president of the AFL. The organization concentrated on working for higher wages, shorter hours, and better working conditions. The way to obtain these benefits, Gompers and other leaders of the AFL maintained, was through **collective bargaining** with employers. This meant that union leaders would negotiate with employers to determine employee working conditions and benefits. Unlike the Knights, the AFL consisted only of skilled workers. AFL members were organized by particular crafts, such as printers, bricklayers, and plumbers.

This wood engraving shows the confusion following the bombing at Haymarket Square. The bombing killed seven police officers and caused a decline in support for unions.

Strike!

One of the most violent strikes in American history involved an AFL member union, the Amalgamated Association of Iron and Steel Workers. This powerful union had more than 24,000 members. Some worked at the Carnegie steel factory in Homestead, Pennsylvania. In 1892, when the company reduced wages, the union called a strike.

Carnegie was in Scotland when the **Homestead strike** began. His associate, Henry Clay Frick, ran the company in his absence. Frick was a tough executive and a bitter opponent of unions. With Carnegie's approval, Frick announced that he would hire strikebreakers, or people to replace the workers out on strike. To protect the new workers, Frick hired private police from the Pinkerton Detective Agency.

The Pinkerton Agency sent 300 armed officers to Homestead. They approached the plant from a nearby river at night. But the strikers had been warned. They met the Pinkerton force at the docks with gunfire and dynamite. When the fighting ended, seven Pinkerton men and nine strikers were dead.

The governor of Pennsylvania then sent 8,000 National Guard troops to Homestead to

Private police officers from the Pinkerton Detective Agency square off against striking union members at the Homestead strike.

The Granger Collection, New York

keep the peace. The strikers held out for more than four months, but the union finally gave in, and the workers went back to the plant on Frick's terms. Although the Homestead strike inspired thousands of workers across the country, it also showed how hard it would be for unions to win against big business, which had the support of the government.

Section 2 Review

• Glossary

IDENTIFY and explain the significance of the following: Knights of Labor, Terence V. Powderly, Haymarket Riot, American Federation of Labor, Samuel Gompers, collective bargaining, Homestead strike

REVIEWING FOR DETAILS

1. What were working conditions like for ordinary workers in the late 1800s?
2. How did labor unions organize?
3. How did workers and factory owners deal with labor problems?

REVIEWING FOR UNDERSTANDING

4. **Writing Mastery:** *Creating* Imagine that you are a union worker at the Homestead strike. Write a song or poem to boost workers' morale by reminding them why they are on strike.

5. **Critical Thinking:** *Drawing Conclusions* How might workers and factory owners have solved labor problems without violence?

Section 3

IMMIGRANTS AND THE GROWTH OF CITIES

Multimedia Connections

Explore these related topics and materials on the CD-ROM to enrich your understanding of this section:

 Atlas

- Largest Cities, 1900

 Gazetteer

- China
- Japan
- Russia
- Poland
- Greece

 Media Bank

- Centennial Exposition
- Brooklyn Bridge Construction
- Immigrant Neighborhood
- Trolley Cars
- Asian Small Business
- Early Baseball Game
- Immigrant Music

 Interactive Map

- Development of a Modern City

 Readings

- Immigrant Voices
- Jacob Riis and Urban Reform

L ee Chew, the owner of a store in New York, reflected on life in America. "I, too, [wanted] to go to the country of the wizards and gain some of their wealth," he recalled, explaining why he left China. Chew described dangerous times in America—running a laundry service on the mining frontier and fighting off the white men who tried to steal from him. Many Chinese immigrants faced severe persecution. Realizing this, Chew asked, "How can I call [America] my home?"

As you read this section you will find out:

▶ **Why people came to America.**

▶ **What efforts the U.S. government made to limit immigration.**

▶ **What problems many immigrants faced in large cities.**

The New Immigrants

Many of the people who worked in the new factories—or even owned them, like Andrew Carnegie—were immigrants. Between 1860 and 1900 about 14 million newcomers arrived in the United States. It seemed as though the country was an enormous magnet drawing people from every direction.

A land of opportunity. Many immigrants came to America to find work. To millions of poor people in other parts of the world, industrial expansion made the United States seem like a pot of gold at the end of a rainbow. Other immigrants left home to escape political, religious, or economic troubles. For example, Jewish immigrants had faced religious persecution in eastern Europe. Some Chinese

These immigrants were among the thousands who passed through Ellis Island in New York Harbor on their way to a new life in the United States.

immigrants had suffered decades of political chaos and economic depression in China's southern provinces.

Most of the immigrants settled in large cities. In 1880 around 85 percent of Chicago's residents were either immigrants or the children of immigrants. New York, San Francisco, and many other major American cities had similarly large immigrant populations. The flood of immigrants into the United States meant that American culture was growing increasingly richer and more diverse.

Through Others' Eyes
The Golden Land

As the new immigrants flooded into the United States during the late 1800s, their impressions of the country filtered back home through postcards and letters. Southern and eastern Europeans formed their own impressions of America from these letters. Many pictured it as both fearsome and promising. Miriam Shomer, a Jewish teenager from eastern Europe, recorded her thoughts as she journeyed across the ocean to America.

"We were going to a land of wonders, and we were prepared for all manner of miracles. There were very few women in America, we were told; . . . and, it was whispered, there was a class of Cyclops—people who had only one eye in the middle of their foreheads. It was a strange, wonderful land! . . . When we sailed into the harbor, the crowd of Jewish immigrants . . . wept with joy. . . . One and all dedicated their hearts to America. They had left nothing but tears and pain behind. Now they were America's, to do with as she chose."

European immigrants. Before the 1880s most immigrants came from western and northern Europe, particularly from Britain, Ireland, Germany, and the Scandinavian countries. These groups became known as the **old immigrants**.

In the 1880s, however, immigration trends changed. Many people from southern and eastern Europe began to arrive. Thousands of Italians, Poles, Hungarians, Russians, and Greeks flocked to the United States. Since they came later and originated from different areas than the earlier groups, they were known as the **new immigrants**. They practiced a wide variety of faiths, such as Greek Orthodox, Eastern Orthodox, Roman Catholic, and Jewish.

Asian immigrants. Asian immigrants also made the long trip to the United States, though in smaller numbers than the new immigrants from Europe. Between 1862 and 1882 some 160,000 Chinese immigrants came to the United States. Most Chinese immigrants practiced Buddhism, a religion little understood in America. Some Japanese immigrants also made the journey to the United States in the middle and late 1800s.

Life in a New Country

Like the old immigrants, those who came in the late 1800s believed in the golden dream of American opportunity. When a 13-year-old Russian girl learned that her father had asked the rest of the family to join him in America, she wrote:

> "So at last I was going to America! Really, really going, at last! The boundaries burst. The arch of heaven soared. A million suns shone out for every star. The winds rushed in from outer space, roaring in my ears, 'America! America!'"

Entering a new home. Immigrants' first glimpse of America came at the processing centers where they officially entered the United States. Many European newcomers passed through Ellis Island in New York Harbor, where they were awed by the sight of the Statue of Liberty. Most Asian immigrants stopped at Angel Island in San Francisco Bay. The processing centers were crowded and noisy. Tired workers interviewed the immigrants and examined them for disease. Sometimes they could not pronounce immigrants' names and thus changed them. A name like Martinisian, for example, might be shortened to Martin.

Although many immigrants thought that the United States was much better than their native land, others wondered if America would live up to their hopes. Another young Russian girl, Anzia Yezierska, wrote:

> "Between the buildings that loomed like mountains, we struggled with our bundles. . . . I looked about the narrow streets of squeezed-in stores and houses, ragged clothes, dirty bedding oozing out of the windows, ashcans and garbage cans cluttering the sidewalks. A vague sadness pressed down on my heart—the first doubt of America."

Many Asian immigrants found work on farms on the Pacific Coast.

Harsh realities The backgrounds of many old immigrants helped them adjust to their new home. British and Irish immigrants spoke English. Many German immigrants were well educated and skilled in useful trades. Scandinavians usually knew how to farm and often came with enough money to buy land in the West. Except for the Irish and some of the Germans, most of the old immigrants were Protestants, as were the majority of native-born Americans.

The backgrounds of those who came to America in the late 1800s differed considerably. Unlike the old immigrants, the new immigrants often had little education and few special skills. Most knew no English. Their habits, cultures, and religions were different from those of most native-born Americans. These factors made it difficult for the new immigrants to adjust to life in the United States. Most could get only low-paying jobs. Whole families worked to survive.

Charitable organizations often set up **benevolent societies** to help immigrants.

Courtesy The Bancroft Library

These groups offered all kinds of assistance, like business loans and money for health care. In addition, local politicians often aided newly arrived immigrants.

Immigrants also created their own communities, which provided assistance and comfort. Newcomers from particular countries or areas tended to cluster together in the same neighborhood. In 1890 a New York reporter imagined a city map that used different colors to represent inhabitants' nationalities. He said it would have "more stripes than the skin of a zebra, and more colors than any rainbow." These ethnic neighborhoods were like cities within cities. They offered immigrants a chance to hold on to a few fragments of the world they had left behind. There they could find familiar foods, people who spoke their language, and churches and clubs based on old-country models.

• Immigrants and Political Machines

Immigrants like Russian-born composer Irving Berlin made many contributions to American music, such as this popular tune, "Alexander's Ragtime Band." One of Berlin's best-known songs is "God Bless America."

Efforts to Limit Immigration

Many native-born Americans disliked immigrants. Nativist workers resented their willingness to work long hours for low wages. Nativists believed that this massive new immigration would weaken their political, social, and religious power. In addition, they also claimed that the immigrants were physically and mentally inferior. The nativists said immigrants were dangerous radicals who wanted to destroy American democratic institutions. In his poem "Unguarded Gates," writer Thomas Bailey Aldrich expressed these fears. "Wide open and unguarded stand our gates," he claimed, "And through them presses a wild motley throng [rowdy group]."

As the number of immigrants grew, nativists launched efforts to limit immigration or end it completely. Some Americans targeted Chinese immigrants. When a depression swept the country, native-born Californians worried that Chinese workers would steal their jobs. In 1882 Congress responded to these fears by passing the **Chinese Exclusion Act**. This law prohibited Chinese

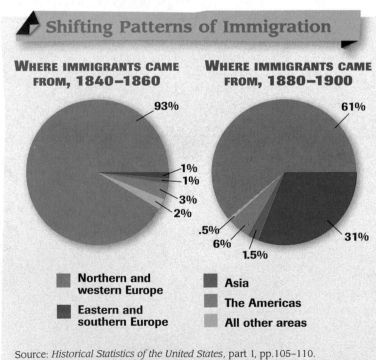

Shifting Patterns of Immigration

WHERE IMMIGRANTS CAME FROM, 1840–1860

93%
1%
1%
3%
2%

WHERE IMMIGRANTS CAME FROM, 1880–1900

61%
.5%
6%
1.5%
31%

■ Northern and western Europe
■ Eastern and southern Europe
■ Asia
■ The Americas
■ All other areas

Source: *Historical Statistics of the United States*, part 1, pp.105–110.

The New Immigrants. Toward the end of the 1880s immigration patterns changed drastically. What immigrant group experienced the largest increase between 1840–1860 and 1880–1900?

• Graphs

workers from entering the United States for a period of 10 years. The ban was later extended well into the 1900s. It caused a sharp drop in the Chinese population in the United States.

In the 1890s some nativists formed the **Immigration Restriction League**. This group called for a law preventing immigrants who could not read or write any language from entering the United States. A literacy test would keep out many people from southern and eastern Europe, where public schools were scarce.

Congress passed a literacy test bill in 1897, but President Grover Cleveland vetoed it. He insisted that the United States should continue to be a place of refuge for the world's poor and persecuted. Many employers, for less humane reasons, opposed any check on immigration. They favored unlimited immigration because it would assure a steady source of low-paid but hardworking laborers.

The Rise of American Cities

The growth of cities after the Civil War was both rapid and widespread. In 1865 places like Denver and Seattle were no more than small towns. By 1900, however, they were major urban centers. In that year there were 38 American cities that had 100,000 or more inhabitants.

A number of factors contributed to urban growth. Immigrants, of course, played an essential role, but thousands of native-born Americans also flooded into the cities. Some southern African Americans tried to escape prejudice and limited economic opportunities by moving to northern cities such as Chicago, Detroit, and New York. In addition, many rural whites headed for cities.

Troubling living conditions. The new city-dwellers faced a serious shortage of housing and other facilities. As more people streamed into towns, land values soared. Because of the high cost of property, builders put up large overcrowded apartments called **tenements**. These tenements were crowded so closely together that they blocked out the sunlight and air.

A five- or six-story tenement usually had four apartments on each floor. Front apartments contained four rooms, rear apartments three. Many of the rooms had no windows. In most cases, two families had to share a single

Urban immigrant neighborhoods like this one were often overcrowded, but they helped immigrants preserve ties to their heritage and culture.

bathroom located in a dark, narrow hallway. Musty, garbage-cluttered "air shafts" separated one tenement building from the next and often caused health problems. As one resident told the New York State Tenement House Commission in 1900, "the air shaft is a breeder of disease."

Jacob Riis, a social reformer, wrote *How the Other Half Lives* to describe the terrible living conditions of poor people. He had this to say about one New York City tenement:

This cartoon expressed the sentiments of many opponents of immigration, who wanted to keep foreigners off American soil. Many of those who were opposed to immigration blamed the new immigrants for the many problems facing the growing cities.

The Granger Collection, New York

> **"Suppose we look into [a tenement] on Cherry Street. . . . Here is a door. Listen! that short hacking cough, that tiny helpless cry—what do they mean? . . . The child is dying of measles. With half a chance it might have lived. But it had none. That dark bedroom killed it."**

Many cities lacked basic public services. Police and fire protection remained inadequate in most cities. Garbage collection was infrequent at best, and city water was often impure. Open sewers, clogged with trash, trickled slowly through the streets. Disease could spread quickly under these conditions.

Improving the cities. Many people were disturbed by books like *How the Other Half Lives* and what they saw around them every day. These people tried to improve urban living conditions. Boards of health made studies and established standards for sewage and garbage disposal. Elaborate systems of pipes and reservoirs brought pure water from distant lakes and rivers. Bit by bit, cities started to improve.

Section 3 Review

• Glossary

IDENTIFY and explain the significance of the following: old immigrants, new immigrants, benevolent societies, Chinese Exclusion Act, Immigration Restriction League, tenements, Jacob Riis

REVIEWING FOR DETAILS
1. Why did many immigrants come to America?
2. How did the U.S. government attempt to limit immigration?

REVIEWING FOR UNDERSTANDING
3. **Geographic Literacy** What were some positive and negative factors for immigrants living in large cities?
4. **Writing Mastery:** *Describing* Write a short story describing the life of a typical immigrant to the United States in the late 1800s.
5. **Critical Thinking:** *Synthesizing Information* How did America live up to the expectations of many immigrants? In what ways was it a disappointment?

— Section 4

POLITICAL REFORM AND POPULISM

Multimedia Connections

Explore these related topics and materials on the CD–ROM to enrich your understanding of this section:

 Atlas

- Agricultural Regions, 1900

 Profiles

- Benjamin Harrison
- Chester Arthur
- Grover Cleveland
- James Garfield
- William McKinley

 Media Bank

- Mark Twain

Putting pencil to paper, an African American farmer addressed those who criticized the new Populist Party. "We don't want to rule the government; we don't want to come into your family," he reassured them. Then he went on to outline a list of supposedly "radical" demands—good wages, equality, a life free of crippling debt. Like many others, he believed that active membership in a new political party could accomplish these goals.

As you read this section you will find out:

▶ **What issues caused farmers to form a political movement.**

▶ **How the Populist movement affected government decisions.**

▶ **What effect the Populist movement had on presidential elections.**

Calls for Political Reform

National, state, and local politics after the Civil War were often characterized by scandal and corruption. Many politicians used their positions to gain wealth for themselves and their friends.

Several scandals developed during the presidency of Ulysses S. Grant, for example. One of the most serious scandals involved Grant's vice president, Schuyler Colfax. Colfax and several members of Congress collected huge sums of money from a railroad company that had greatly overcharged on a government contract. Many critics claimed that the scandal was caused in large part by the well-established spoils system— the practice of awarding civil service (government) jobs to loyal political supporters.

• Civil Service Reform

Throughout the 1880s, the issue of civil service reform increasingly divided national politics. When Republican James A. Garfield was elected president in 1880, many people hoped that reform would soon follow. They were shocked, however, when Garfield was assassinated only a few months after taking office. In 1883 Chester Arthur, Garfield's successor, signed the **Pendleton Civil Service Act**, which established competitive examinations as the basis for awarding some government jobs.

The fight for civil service reform was not over. When Democrat Grover Cleveland won the presidency in 1884, he pushed for further civil service reform. After Cleveland lost the election of 1888, however, his successor, Republican Benjamin Harrison, reversed Cleveland's efforts, and the Republicans appointed many supporters to public office.

Farmers Seek Change

It is not surprising that in the years following the Civil War, many Americans felt ignored by national politicians, who seemed concerned only with their own wealth. Small farmers in particular looked for ways they could have more voice in their government.

In addition, economic conditions in the late 1800s were extremely hard for American farmers. As the number of farms grew, huge amounts of food flooded the market, causing prices to fall. This resulted in serious financial problems for farmers. Many had to borrow money just to keep going; some lost their homes when they could not repay these debts.

In the 1870s many farmers joined the **National Grange** for assistance. The Grange was originally a social club, but it soon became a political organization as well. Branches sprang up all over the country, particularly in the Midwest. The organization founded banks and campaigned for local politicians. It also set up cooperatives, which allowed farmers to buy supplies wholesale and sell directly to stores, thus avoiding costly middlemen.

Granger members also criticized what they saw as the unfair practices of railroads. They believed that freight and storage rates were too high. An angry rural newspaper editor explained:

"**There are three great crops raised in Nebraska. One is a crop of corn, one is a crop of freight rates, and one is a crop of interest. One is produced by farmers who by sweat and toil farm the land. The other two are**

Presidential Lives

Grover Cleveland

The Granger Collection, New York

Many Americans referred to Grover Cleveland as "ugly-honest." The term referred to his principles, not his physical appearance. During his long political career, Cleveland acquired a reputation for careful, absolute honesty. The *New York World* convinced many readers to vote for Cleveland with this short list: "1. He is an honest man; 2. He is an honest man; 3. He is an honest man; 4. He is an honest man."

In the harsh world of American politics, Cleveland's honesty sometimes brought him cruel enemies. Quiet and determined, he normally suffered them in silence. A friend glimpsed his true feelings, however, when a stray dog bounded into Cleveland's home in New Jersey. People started to run and shout, assuming that Cleveland would be upset. As his friend ran to get the dog out of the house, Cleveland joked, "No, let him stay. He at least likes me."

The Granger Collection, New York

In an increasingly industrial world, the Grangers celebrated the agricultural way of life. They wanted the government to regulate big business to promote a fair and competitive environment.

produced by men who sit in their offices and behind their bank counters and farm the farmers."

Granger leaders demanded government regulation of freight charges. In several states, their efforts led to the passage of laws that helped protect farmers.

The Granger laws led to a debate over whether state governments could regulate businesses like railroads for "the public interest." In the 1877 case of *Munn* v. *Illinois* the Supreme Court ruled that state governments could indeed regulate businesses such as railroads. The Court reasoned that companies that provided broad public services could not be considered completely private.

After a later Supreme Court decision scaled back *Munn* v. *Illinois*, Congress passed the **Interstate Commerce Act** to help farmers.

This 1887 law provided that railroad rates must be "reasonable and just." To oversee the affairs of railroads and to hear complaints from shippers, Congress also established the **Interstate Commerce Commission** (ICC), a board of examiners appointed by the president. This was the first of the many modern federal regulatory agencies. However, the ICC had no real power to enforce the regulations it established.

The Money Issue

In addition to criticizing high freight charges, farmers also came together to fight a political battle over the nation's money supply. Before the Civil War, both gold and silver had been minted into coins and used to back bank notes. In 1873, however, Congress voted to stop coining silver. This left only the **gold standard**, a monetary system in which the government backed each dollar with a set amount of gold. The amount of gold in the U.S. Treasury determined the supply of money. The gold standard tended to keep the quantity of money in public circulation fairly low because the supply of gold was limited.

Farmers, however, wanted as much silver coined as possible in order to increase the money supply. They hoped this would create inflation, thus raising the prices for farm products while easing their debt burden. These farmers urged **free coinage**—that is, a law requiring the government to coin silver freely. If this was done, farmers reasoned, there would finally be enough money in circulation.

The Populist Party

Even as they fought for the silver cause, farmers looked for other ways out of their financial hard times. First in Texas, and then elsewhere in the South and Midwest, a new movement, called the **Farmers' Alliance**, was spreading. Like the National Grange before it, the Alliance quickly became an important political force. Its leaders campaigned against high railroad freight rates and high bank interest rates.

Attorney William Jennings Bryan became an outspoken supporter of Populist causes, particularly the coining of silver. Bryan and others felt that poor farmers would never be able to survive in business unless there was more money in circulation.

• **William Jennings Bryan**

Alliance members also began to run for local and national offices. In 1890 more than 50 Alliance supporters were elected to Congress. Encouraged by these successes, Alliance officials decided to establish a new political party and run a candidate for president. To broaden their appeal, they persuaded labor unions to join them. They named their new organization the People's Party, or **Populist Party**.

In July 1892 the first Populist nominating convention met in Omaha, Nebraska. The delegates adopted a platform that called for government ownership of railroads and the telegraph and telephone network. They also supported a federal income tax and government loans for farmers. To win the support of native-born industrial workers, they called for immigration restrictions and the eight-hour workday. Populists politicians also demanded the "free and unlimited coinage of silver and gold."

The Populists chose James B. Weaver of Iowa, a former Union general, as their candidate for president. Weaver faced Republican President Benjamin Harrison and Democrat Grover Cleveland.

The 1892 election was an exciting one. Though Cleveland won, Weaver received more than 1 million votes, a large number for a third-party candidate. In addition, the Populist Party won many local contests.

The End of an Era

Shortly after the 1892 election, the United States entered perhaps the worst period of economic hard times it had ever experienced in what became known as the Panic of 1893. Business activity slowed, and unemployment dramatically increased. Farmers had trouble selling their products at almost any price. President Cleveland found something to blame for the economic decline—silver.

An election approaches. The money issue continued to play an important role in national politics. As the presidential election of 1896 drew near, the Democrats had to make a difficult decision. The Populist Party was making large gains in several areas by calling for free coinage. If the Democrats again chose Cleveland, who defended the gold standard, they seemed sure to lose.

The Republican Party nominated Ohio governor William McKinley for president. The Republicans' platform was simple—they "opposed . . . the free coinage of silver." This position infuriated farmers. Since many farmers normally voted Republican, Democrats saw a chance to hold on to the presidency.

The money question was the key issue at the Democratic convention. In a formal debate on the topic, former Nebraska congressman William Jennings Bryan gave a speech in support of free coinage. He praised western farmers as "hardy pioneers" who had "made the desert to bloom." He concluded by likening the supporters of the silver standard to Jesus Christ, saying to the defenders of the gold standard: "You shall not crucify mankind upon a cross of gold."

After cheering this "Cross of Gold" speech, the Democrats adopted a platform calling for the free coinage of both silver and gold and nominated the "Great Commoner," Bryan, for the presidency. After much debate the Populists also nominated Bryan. The fact that many Democrats and Populists agreed on several important issues effectively ended the Populist Party. Bryan ran as a Democrat and the Populists ran no other candidate, hoping that Bryan's popularity would carry him to victory.

The election of 1896. The election reflected major shifts in voting patterns. Populists in the South and West solidly voted for Bryan. In the mountain states, where silver mining was important, Bryan won easily. However, thousands of formerly Democratic industrial workers now voted Republican. McKinley had convinced them that free silver would be bad for the economy. The election was a solid Republican triumph. The electoral vote was 271 for McKinley, 176 for Bryan.

Activist Mary Elizabeth Lease fought for many political causes, but she was best known for her work on behalf of Populists. She wrote about her views in the 1895 book The Problem of Civilization Solved.

The Granger Collection, New York

Section 4 Review

IDENTIFY and explain the significance of the following: Pendleton Civil Service Act, National Grange, Interstate Commerce Act, Interstate Commerce Commission, gold standard, free coinage, Farmers' Alliance, Populist Party, William McKinley, William Jennings Bryan

• **Glossary**

REVIEWING FOR DETAILS

1. Why did people see a need for civil service reform?
2. How did farmers influence government decisions?

• **Time Line**

3. What role did the Populist movement play in the presidential elections of 1892 and 1896?

REVIEWING FOR UNDERSTANDING

4. **Writing Mastery:** *Persuading* Imagine that you are a farmer living in the late 1800s. Write a letter to your senator explaining the conditions you are currently facing, the need for free silver, and what you feel the government should do to help you.

5. **Critical Thinking:** *Determining Cause and Effect* How did the wide diversity of American voters affect the 1896 election? How might political parties try to appeal to a widely diverse voting public?

Immigrants and Cities

The growth of American industry in the late 1800s brought millions of immigrants to the United States. By 1900 huge numbers of immigrants—including Greeks, Italians, Russians, Czechs, Poles, and Hungarians—had begun arriving from southern and eastern Europe. Thousands of Chinese and Japanese immigrants also arrived from Asia.

Most immigrants flocked to America's cities seeking factory jobs and a chance for a new start. Many settled in cities that already had immigrant communities. The largest numbers of immigrants, and the greatest variety, were concentrated in New York City and Chicago. In 1860 Chicago's population was just a little more than 100,000. By 1900 it was nearly 1.7 million. Immigrants accounted for much of this growth. Other major industrial cities that benefited from the growth of their immigrant communities included Philadelphia, Detroit, and Boston.

America's Geography AMERICA'S GEOGRAPHY

Population Changes

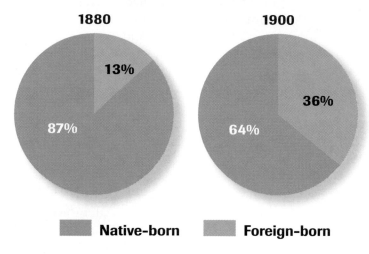

1880

13%
87%

1900

36%
64%

■ Native-born   ■ Foreign-born

Percentage of Population Living in Very Large Cities in 1900

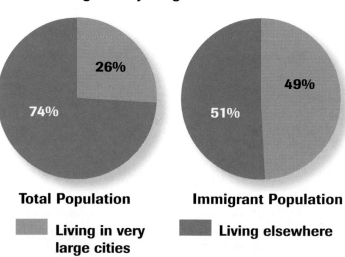

26%
74%

49%
51%

Total Population   **Immigrant Population**

■ Living in very large cities   ■ Living elsewhere

By 1900 around 75 percent of all foreign-born residents of the United States were living in urban areas. Although the majority of Americans still resided in rural areas, few of the new immigrants had enough money to buy land.

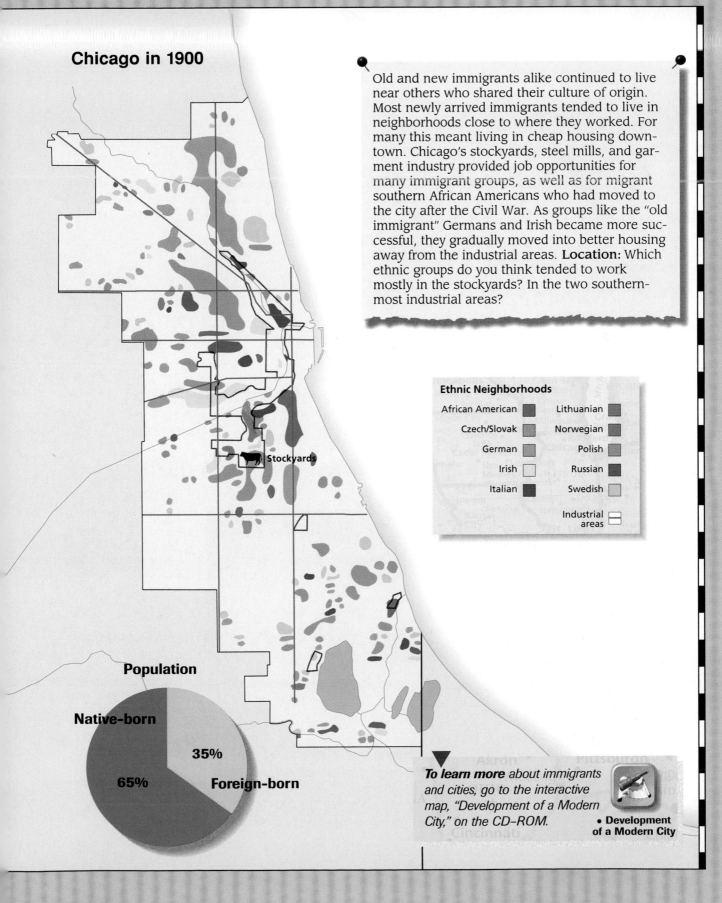

Chicago in 1900

Old and new immigrants alike continued to live near others who shared their culture of origin. Most newly arrived immigrants tended to live in neighborhoods close to where they worked. For many this meant living in cheap housing downtown. Chicago's stockyards, steel mills, and garment industry provided job opportunities for many immigrant groups, as well as for migrant southern African Americans who had moved to the city after the Civil War. As groups like the "old immigrant" Germans and Irish became more successful, they gradually moved into better housing away from the industrial areas. **Location:** Which ethnic groups do you think tended to work mostly in the stockyards? In the two southernmost industrial areas?

Ethnic Neighborhoods

African American	Lithuanian
Czech/Slovak	Norwegian
German	Polish
Irish	Russian
Italian	Swedish

Industrial areas

Stockyards

Population

Native-born

65%

35%

Foreign-born

To learn more about immigrants and cities, go to the interactive map, "Development of a Modern City," on the CD-ROM.

• Development of a Modern City

u n i t **7**

AMERICA BECOMES A WORLD POWER (1865–1920)

Chapter 18
Progressives and Reform (1890–1920)

Chapter 19
Involvement in World Affairs (1865–1914)

Chapter 20
America and the Great War (1914–1920)

The Grand Canyon is one of the most beautiful sights on the American landscape. Reformers in the late 1800s and early 1900s fought to preserve such scenic beauty for future generations.

LINKING *P*AST TO PRESENT
National Parks

In the Florida Everglades a middle-school-aged group of campers gets ready to break down its tents after sleeping out in the damp air, surrounded by palm trees. Farther north, in the Great Smoky Mountains, another group goes horseback riding on trails that wind through areas once traveled by Daniel Boone. Across the country in Yellowstone National Park, another group prepares to watch as Old Faithful bursts forth with water.

All of these students are enjoying the benefits of areas that have been preserved as national parks. Millions of people visit the country's many national parks every year. National parks provide places for people to hike, swim, camp, or just enjoy some of the most beautiful scenery in the country. For students studying the natural environment, the parks provide a live observation area.

In addition to the national parks, many other areas have been set aside as protected land. The National Park Services manages this land and today is responsible for more than 350 sites on some 80 million acres of land.

For people who live in cities, the parks offer a refreshing break from the hustle and bustle of urban life. Some conservationists, however, worry that the national parks are too popular, arguing that tourists are "loving the parks to death." Environmentalists are searching for ways to balance the need to protect the parks with people's desire to enjoy their natural beauty. In many ways this debate goes back to the concerns that originally led to the creation of the national parks system.

As you read this unit, you will learn about the reform movements that helped to create systems like the national parks. In the late 1800s many people became concerned that Americans were using up all of their available natural resources. Many areas were set aside as protected land. Thanks to their efforts, today Americans can enjoy natural scenery that might otherwise have been destroyed.

These teenagers are hiking in one of the many parks in the United States.

CHAPTER **18**

Progressives and Reform (1890–1920)

THEMES IN AMERICAN HISTORY

Constitutional Heritage:
Why might reformers work for constitutional amendments rather than state laws?

Cultural Diversity:
How might members of oppressed groups seek reform?

Economic Development:
How might reformers try to protect workers?

 • Video Opener

 • Skill Builder

As a new century dawned, one writer described a special sort of American— the "progressive." This "political person" has "new organs," he informed readers. Progressives wished to "be in the service of the people . . . to secure for them progress in the struggle of life and justice at the hands of their fellows." Progressives carried out this ideal by trying to improve American society in many ways.

image above: *An ideal progressive city*

Section 1
PROGRESSIVE IDEALS

Multimedia Connections

Explore these related topics and materials on the CD–ROM to enrich your understanding of this section:

 Readings

- Muckrakers

 Gazetteer

- Chicago

 Media Bank

- Degrees Earned, 1890–1920

 Glossary

- political bosses

 Profiles

- Ida Tarbell
- Lincoln Steffens

Young Ida Tarbell considered her father's bad news. His oil business had failed, and he was facing financial disaster. Ida's father blamed John D. Rockefeller. Rockefeller's gigantic company ate up one small business after another, her father complained bitterly. Ida vowed to do something about the problem. More than 30 years later, she did. She became a journalist and used the pen as her weapon.

As you read this section you will find out:

▶ **What types of people became progressives.**

▶ **What goals the progressives hoped to accomplish.**

▶ **What problems the muckrakers worked to change.**

The Progressive Mood

Many Americans surveyed the last years of the 1800s with dismay and anger. Despite the efforts of reformers, serious problems continued to affect the government, the economy, and society itself.

Signs of trouble. In great American cities millionaire manufacturers ruled over dirty, often unsafe factories where their employees labored for pitifully low wages. Many Americans greatly benefited from the goods these business giants produced, but sometimes the rich seemed too powerful, the poor too weak.

The continued growth of great corporations and trusts provided another cause for concern. In the year 1899 alone, big companies swallowed up more than 1,000 small firms. Even the largest corporations merged with each other to form giant monopolies. Many Americans considered these "super-companies" dangerous because they were so powerful.

The reforming spirit. These problems inspired large numbers of Americans to work for reform. Observers called these people **progressives** because they tried to make progress.

Progressives did not suddenly appear as the 1900s approached. Social reformers had been active for years. The desire to improve America became particularly strong, however, during the years between 1890 and 1920. Historians now call this period the Progressive Era. Progressivism was a point of view about society and politics, not a particular political organization. Progressives came from the Republican, the Democratic, and the Socialist Parties.

Progressives came largely from the growing American middle class. Most of them had been born in the United States, and many had gone to college. They worked as teachers, ministers, and social workers, among many other professions. Unlike the earlier Populists, progressives tended to live in cities and to focus on urban problems.

Though progressives did not form a united social or political movement, most supported several common goals. They hoped to limit the power of big businesses, which they considered greedy special interests. They also wanted to improve the hard lives of children, elderly people, and the poor.

Some progressives believed that government—local, state, and national—should play an active role in society. One writer defined their view:

> **"The term 'Progressive,' as it engages the public mind to-day, suggests certain ideas of government. . . . Governments were established among men to protect the weak from the strong. . . . A Progressive . . . suggests the appropriate governmental action to prevent . . . further abuse."**

In addition, many progressives wanted to end political dishonesty and make the political system more democratic.

The Muckrakers

Progressives depended heavily on newspapers, magazines, and books to reach the American people. A small army of progressive writers and researchers helped with this task. One politician called them "**muckrakers**" because they saw the "filth on the floor" and "scraped [it] up with the muck-rake" in order to make people aware of it. This name stuck and became well known.

Muckrakers often dug into public records. They also interviewed politicians and businesspeople, city clerks and police officers, factory workers and immigrant laborers. Then they published their results in hard-hitting books and articles. They were specific. They named names and demanded that something be done.

Muckraking photographers often took pictures of poor children in large cities, like these two girls. • **Jacob Riis**

American Letters

The Jungle
Upton Sinclair

Upton Beall Sinclair wrote novels, articles, and pamphlets for years to support himself and his family. None of his early pieces attracted much attention or success. His 1906 novel The Jungle, *a muckraking examination of Chicago's meat-packing plants, however, stunned Americans. "I aimed at the public's heart," Sinclair explained, "and hit it in the stomach." The novel's graphic descriptions, as in the following excerpt, pushed the book up the bestseller lists—and prompted reform in the food processing industry.*

Upton Sinclair originally intended for his novel The Jungle *to focus attention on the problems facing immigrants in the cities. Instead, it led to massive reforms in the food processing industry.*

. . . And then there was the condemned meat industry, with its endless horrors. The people of Chicago saw the government inspectors in Packingtown, and they all took that to mean that they were protected from diseased meat; they did not understand that these . . . inspectors had been appointed at the request of the packers. . . . The packers . . . [eventually] compelled [forced] the mayor to abolish the whole bureau of inspection; so that since then there has not been even a pretense [claim] of any interference with the graft [bribes]. There was said to be two thousand dollars a week hush money from the tubercular steers alone . . . which you might see any day being loaded into box cars and hauled away to a place called Globe, in Indiana. . . .

. . . It seemed that they [the packers] must have agencies all over the country, to hunt out old and crippled and diseased cattle to be canned. There were cattle which had been fed on "whiskey malt," the refuse of the breweries, and had become what the men called "steerly"—which means covered with boils. It was a nasty job killing these, for when you plunged your knife into them they would burst and splash foul-smelling stuff into your face. . . . It was stuff such as this that made the "embalmed beef" that had killed several times as many United States soldiers as all the bullets of the Spaniards. . . .

. . . The workers in each of them [the packing plants] had their own peculiar diseases. . . . The worker bore the evidence of them about on his own person—generally he had only to hold out his hand. . . .

. . . There were the wool pluckers, whose hands went to pieces even sooner than the hands of the pickle men; for the pelts of the sheep had to be painted with the acid to loosen the wool, and then the pluckers had to pull out this wool with their bare hands, till the acid had eaten their fingers off. . . . As for the other men, who worked in tank rooms full of steam, and in some of which there were open vats near the level of the floor, their peculiar trouble was that they fell into the vats; and when they were fished out, there was never enough of them left to be worth exhibiting—sometimes they would be overlooked for days, till all but the bones of them had gone out to the world as Durham's Pure Leaf Lard!

Muckrakers exposed a wide variety of problems. They described terrible living conditions in the slums, for instance, and showed children laboring in factories and sweatshops. Improvements in printing and better ways of reproducing photographs added greatly to the effectiveness of their style of journalism.

Lincoln Steffens and Ida Tarbell were two of the best-known muckrakers. Steffens specialized in exposing corrupt city and state governments. He published many articles in *McClure's Magazine*, one of many important muckraking periodicals. Steffens reported on conditions in Minneapolis, St. Louis, and other cities ruled by greedy political bosses. In 1904 he republished these pieces in a book, *The Shame of the Cities.*

McClure's Magazine

Ida Tarbell was both a journalist and a historian. Before she turned to muckraking, she wrote biographies of Napoleon and Abraham Lincoln. Then she focused her attention on John D. Rockefeller's Standard Oil Company. Her critical study of his business methods ran in monthly installments in *McClure's Magazine.* She claimed Rockefeller "employed force and fraud to obtain his end."

Ray Stannard Baker was one of the few muckrakers who called attention to the problems of African Americans. Baker reported on segregation and racial discrimination in America. His magazine articles eventually formed the basis of his book, *Following the Color Line.*

Famous muckraker Ida Tarbell is shown here working at her desk, where she wrote many articles for McClure's Magazine.

Section 1 Review

• Glossary

IDENTIFY and explain the significance of the following: progressives, muckrakers, Lincoln Steffens, Ida Tarbell, *McClure's Magazine,* Ray Stannard Baker

REVIEWING FOR DETAILS
1. What kinds of people became progressives?
2. What did the progressives hope to change?
3. What did the muckrakers criticize?

REVIEWING FOR UNDERSTANDING
4. **Writing Mastery:** *Persuading* Imagine that you are a muckraking journalist. Write a brief article to draw your readers' attention to a particular social problem, such as child labor, poor living conditions, or powerful businesses.
5. **Critical Thinking:** *Drawing Conclusions* What do you think motivated middle-class progressives to work to improve conditions of people poorer than themselves?

Section 2

THE PROGRESSIVE AGENDA

Multimedia Connections

Explore these related topics and materials on the CD–ROM to enrich your understanding of this section:

 Media Bank

- Union Membership, 1864–1921
- Art of the Reform Movement
- Ashcan School Depiction
- Immigrant Workers on Strike
- Louis Brandeis

 Profiles

- Louis Brandeis
- Lugenia Burns Hope
- Joseph Mayer Rice

 Gazetteer

- Ohio
- Wisconsin
- Oregon

 Readings

- Reform Efforts

 Glossary

- political machines

 Simulation

- The Political Machine

The "army" wound through the streets of Philadelphia. Its soldiers, however, carried no guns. They were children, many under 10 years of age. These child toilers were on their way to see the president of the United States. They wanted to tell him about working in mines and on factory lines, and show him their twisted shoulders and scarred hands. As the protestors moved forward, they wondered if progressives would do something to end "the enslavement of children."

As you read this section you will find out:

▶ **How progressives worked to improve city life.**

▶ **How progressives made state governments more democratic.**

▶ **What legal changes led to improved working conditions in factories.**

Reforming the City

Many progressives concentrated their efforts on reforming the poor living and working conditions that were common to many American cities. Progressive activist Jane Addams described the problems cities faced:

"Insanitary housing, poisonous sewage, contaminated water, infant mortality, the spread of contagion [disease], adulterated [contaminated] food, impure milk, smoke-laden air, ill-ventilated factories, dangerous occupations, juvenile crime, unwholesome crowding . . . are the enemies which the modern city must face and overcome would it survive."

Alarmed and determined to make a difference, progressives soon developed different ways to improve city life.

The fight for better living conditions. Some progressives established community centers called **settlement houses** to help slum-dwellers better their lives. The settlement houses provided day nurseries for children, gymnasiums and social activities for young and old, English classes for immigrants, and many other services.

Perhaps the most famous American settlement house was **Hull House** in Chicago, founded by Jane Addams. The daughter of a wealthy businessman and dedicated abolitionist, Addams had a deep commitment to social reform from a young age. In 1889 she opened Hull House, which served as a model for later settlement houses.

Many of the workers in Hull House were young female college graduates. They lived in the building and tried to become members of the neighborhood. They believed that they could benefit personally and also help others by getting involved in local affairs.

Progressives also campaigned for laws to improve the health and housing of poor city-dwellers. In New York City, for example, progressives fought for a stronger tenement house law. One was passed in 1901 that required better plumbing and ventilation in all new tenements. Older buildings had to be remodeled to meet the new standards. During the Progressive Era more than 40 other cities passed similar laws.

The drive for better governments. Progressives also tried to reform city governments, by becoming politicians or by working as reformers. Progressives hoped to destroy the power of the corrupt political machines that controlled many cities. Samuel M. Jones was one notable progressive mayor. He was a Welsh immigrant who grew up poor but eventually made a fortune drilling for oil. Then he became a manufacturer of oil-drilling equipment in Toledo, Ohio.

Jones set out to apply the Golden Rule—"Do unto others as you would have them do unto you"—in his factory. He raised wages and reduced the workday of his employees to eight hours. He offered employees paid vacations and annual bonuses. He created a park and gave picnics for his employees.

In 1897 "Golden Rule" Jones became mayor of Toledo. His election was a victory for honest government. He stressed political independence rather than party loyalty. He established the eight-hour workday for many city employees. He also built playgrounds and provided kindergartens for children.

Other progressives organized reform movements in such cities as Philadelphia, Cleveland, Chicago, and Los Angeles. In San Francisco a newspaper editor named Fremont Older and Rudolph Spreckels, the son of a wealthy sugar manufacturer, led local reformers. Spreckels's family had once held a monopoly on the sugar business.

Jane Addams is shown here celebrating the 40th anniversary of Hull House with children from the settlement house. Many people were served by settlement houses throughout the country.

• Jane Addams

Samuel "Golden Rule" Jones set a precedent for running an honest city government.

A movement for better utilities.

Progressives put pressure on local and state governments to play active roles in solving urban problems. Some city politicians responded with a form of **socialism**, the idea that the government should own all the means of production—the raw materials, factories, and money required to produce goods. Some city leaders took over waterworks that had been privately owned, hoping to lower the cost of water to customers. A few socialist progressives extended this policy to the public ownership of gas and electric companies and streetcar lines. Those progressives who believed in socialist ideas thought the best way to protect the public against high charges and inefficiency was to have their local governments own all public utilities and even some public transportation.

Reforming State Governments

Progressives also worked on the state level. They tried to make state governments more democratic by putting more power in the hands of the people.

Wisconsin sets an example.

Many progressives admired the Wisconsin Idea, a set of policies established by Governor Robert M. La Follette. To give voters more control over who ran for public office, La Follette persuaded the legislature to pass a direct primary law. Instead of being chosen by politicians, candidates had to campaign for party nominations in primary elections. The people selected the candidates who would compete in the final election.

La Follette also worked to limit the amount of money candidates for office could spend and to restrict the activities of **lobbyists**, or people hired to influence legislators on behalf of special interests.

La Follette had great faith in the good judgment of the people. He also realized that state governments had to perform many tasks that called for considerable technical knowledge. He therefore created commissions of experts to handle complicated matters such as the determination of tax rates and the regulation of railroads. There were railroad and public utility commissions in many states before 1900, but such organizations spread rapidly during the Progressive Era.

More states enact progressive reforms.

Other states copied the Wisconsin Idea to try to expand democratic practices to more people. Many passed direct primary laws. Others authorized important voting practices—the initiative, the referendum, and the recall. The **initiative** enables voters to initiate, or propose, laws. If a certain number of voters in a state sign a petition in favor of a particular proposal, the legislature has to consider it. Under the **referendum**, a legislative proposal is put before the citizens, who vote for or against the measure at a regular election. The **recall** allows voters to remove an elected politician from office before the person's term expires.

Robert M. La Follette's Wisconsin Idea was copied by other state governments across the nation.

Global Connections

The Secret Ballot

One progressive reform—the secret ballot—came to the United States from Australia. Until the 1850s, Australia had used a system of "oral voting." At the public polls, voters would simply call out the name of a candidate, and officials would record it. Many Australians believed this method led to "bribery, a great deal of rioting, and broken heads."

In 1856 the state of South Australia approved a ballot on which voters made a cross in a box beside a particular candidate's name. This ballot later became widespread in the United States. The Australians also developed other ways to ensure voting privacy. They used ballots that contained only candidates' legal names and that listed all of the candidates on one sheet. The Australian government also appointed election officials to hand out the ballots, which further helped to guarantee secrecy in the voting process.

American progressives eventually looked to the Australian secret ballot to decrease corruption and increase democracy. In 1888 Massachusetts became the first state to widely use the secret ballot. Most of the states followed within 10 years.

Amending the Constitution. Another progressive attempt to expand democracy was the **Seventeenth Amendment**. The Constitution had provided that U.S. senators would be elected by members of the state legislatures. However, the Seventeenth Amendment, ratified in 1913, changed the system by providing that the people of a state would elect senators. Supporters of the amendment believed that this would give more political power to the people rather than to the local political machines.

Reforming Society

Progressives were deeply moved by the problems of industrial workers. Many progressives tried to reform working conditions for American laborers by lobbying state legislatures. Progressives also brought cases before state and federal courts to accomplish these goals.

The workplace and workers. A terrible tragedy known as the **Triangle Fire** highlighted the need for workplace reform. In March 1911 a fire broke out in the upper floors of the Triangle Shirtwaist Company factory in New York City. The workers, mostly female immigrants, tried to escape. Many of the exit doors were locked, however, and there had been little preparation for fighting a fire. More than 140 women died in the blaze.

Rose Schneiderman, a local union organizer, blamed the Triangle Fire on greedy employers and an uncaring society:

"This is not the first time girls have been burned alive in the city. Each week I must learn of the untimely death of one of my sister workers. Every year thousands of us are maimed. The life of men and women is so cheap and property is so sacred. There are so many of us for one job it matters little if 143 of us are burned to death."

Despite Schneiderman's fear that the women's "blood" would go unnoticed, the Triangle Fire did lead to reform. New York State responded by passing numerous new factory inspection laws. Other states also approved stronger laws improving the safety of factories. Many states began requiring manufacturers to insure their workers against accidents.

Progressives also fought to change child labor laws. They argued that employing children

The tragic deaths of more than 140 women in the Triangle Fire shocked people throughout the country. Many began to demand reforms to make sure that similar tragedies would not occur again.

The Granger Collection, New York

disrupted schooling, thereby blocking a way out of poverty and condemning child laborers to a life of often backbreaking work. Urged on by progressives, most states eventually outlawed the employment of young children, but many businesses simply ignored the laws.

A shorter workday.

Many states also limited the hours that women, older children, and people in certain dangerous occupations could work. Many employers and some workers claimed that these laws were unconstitutional. They noted that the Fourteenth Amendment says a state

Progressives were concerned about the many children who worked instead of going to school, like this West Virginia boy who worked in a coal mine.

may not "deprive any person of life, liberty, or property." Business executives insisted that laws placing restrictions on their operating practices took away their "property." Some employees claimed that such laws deprived them of their "liberty."

Progressives and others who favored reforms responded by stressing the power of the state to protect the public. They argued that laws preventing people from working long hours or under unhealthy conditions protected their families and society in general, not just the workers themselves.

The Court's response.

Business owners and employees eventually challenged the new laws in court. Some of these cases went to the U.S. Supreme Court. In the 1905 case of *Lochner* v. *New York,* the Court decided that a New York law limiting bakers to a 10-hour workday was unconstitutional. Such laws represented "meddlesome interferences with the rights of the individual," the justices ruled.

Three years later, however, the Court took a different position. This time the case involved an Oregon law that limited female laundry workers to a 10-hour workday. Louis Brandeis served as the head lawyer for the state of Oregon. He presented a detailed brief, or argument, showing that long workdays injured the health of women and thus damaged the public welfare. Two progressives, Florence Kelley and Josephine Goldmark, did much of the research for this "Brandeis brief."

In the 1908 case *Muller* v. *Oregon,* the Court decided that the law was a proper use of the state's power. Many female laundry workers were also mothers. If working too long injured their health, their children's health might also suffer. Therefore, said the Court, "the physical well-being of woman becomes an object of public interest and care."

This case was particularly important. For the first time the Court paid attention to economic and social statistics, in addition to legal arguments. This changed the way future cases of this type were argued and decided but did not end the controversy about the power of a state to protect its citizens. By the end of the Progressive Era, many more laws had been passed to help workers and the poor.

These women canned olives at a factory in California. Progressives argued that many female workers and their unborn children were put at great risk by the long hours and harsh conditions in some factories.

Section 2 Review

• Glossary

IDENTIFY and explain the significance of the following: Jane Addams, settlement houses, Hull House, Samuel M. Jones, socialism, Robert M. La Follette, lobbyists, initiative, referendum, recall, Seventeenth Amendment, Triangle Fire, Louis Brandeis

REVIEWING FOR DETAILS

1. How did progressives change state governments to make them more democratic?
2. What legal changes improved conditions for industrial workers?

REVIEWING FOR UNDERSTANDING

3. **Geographic Literacy** How did progressives work to improve people's lives in the cities?
4. **Writing Mastery:** *Persuading* Imagine that you are the owner of a New York City garment factory in 1912. Write a letter to the newspaper to justify the working conditions in your factory or to explain how and why you plan to change these working conditions.
5. **Critical Thinking:** *Synthesizing Information* Why do you think progressives had so much success in improving conditions on a local level?

Section 3

THE PROGRESSIVE PRESIDENTS

Multimedia Connections

Explore these related topics and materials on the CD–ROM to enrich your understanding of this section:

 Atlas

• National Parks

 Media Bank

• Bull Moose Party
• Meatpacking Plant

 Profiles

• Theodore Roosevelt
• William Howard Taft

The messenger rushed toward Vice President Theodore Roosevelt. "The president appears to be dying," the messenger relayed sadly, "and members of the cabinet . . . think you should lose no time coming." Roosevelt climbed down the mountain and traveled through a terrible thunderstorm. When he finally made it to a railroad station, he was informed that President William McKinley was dead. America had a new president who was a progressive. The nation would never be the same again.

As you read this section you will find out:

▶ **How Theodore Roosevelt carried out his progressive ideas.**

▶ **Why Roosevelt ran for president in 1912 as a third-party candidate.**

▶ **How Woodrow Wilson tried to limit the power of big business.**

Roosevelt Becomes President

Progressives found a colorful ally in the new president, Theodore Roosevelt. He loved hunting, boxing, and writing history books. He also loved politics and had served in many city, state, and national offices.

One newspaper reporter explained why Roosevelt had so much success in politics and life in general:

"**Roosevelt, more than any man I ever knew, is 'energizing' to the full extent of his capacities. . . . In talking with many people who have met Roosevelt for the first time I have been impressed by their comments upon his 'familiarity.' . . . The marvelous thing in his career is the way in which he has used his commonplace qualities—in every possible direction.**"

Presidential Lives

Theodore Roosevelt

The public admired Theodore Roosevelt for his enormous stores of energy. "Get action," he told Americans, and he set a fine example. As a child, Roosevelt had suffered frequent asthma attacks. He later remembered his father "carrying me in my distress, in my battles for breath, up and down a room all night." After his father advised him to "make your body," Roosevelt began a physical fitness plan and became quite strong.

As president, he loved to go on "obstacle walks," or rough hikes, with important foreign visitors. The French ambassador appeared in formal dress and a silk hat for one such outing. Roosevelt showed up in a "tramping suit" and promptly led the Frenchman across an overgrown field. When they came to a river, the president took off all his clothes "so as not to wet our things in the creek." Shocked but determined to uphold the honor of France, the ambassador removed everything but a pair of purple leather gloves. Then they crossed the river, dressed, and continued their walk.

In 1900 Roosevelt had been elected vice president under William McKinley. When an assassin killed McKinley in 1901, Roosevelt became president.

Roosevelt's approach to the presidency. Roosevelt, whom Americans called "TR" or Teddy, believed that the president should play an active role in politics and society. Early in his presidency he demonstrated his approach to the office.

In 1902 Roosevelt got involved in a national coal strike by forcing mine owners and miners into **arbitration**, or negotiations led by a neutral party. He threatened to take over the mines unless the owners agreed to a settlement. Then he appointed a commission to arbitrate the dispute.

Roosevelt takes on the trusts. Roosevelt soon developed a reputation for being a "trust buster." He accused a railroad organization, the Northern Securities Company, of violating the Sherman Antitrust Act. The Northern Securities Company controlled three railroads, whose lines carried most of the rail traffic between the Midwest and the Pacific Northwest. Roosevelt argued that the combination blocked the natural course of trade and should be broken up. He instructed the attorney general to start legal proceedings against the company.

When the *Northern Securities* case reached the Supreme Court in 1904, the justices ordered the combination dissolved. Roosevelt then brought antitrust suits against such giants as the meatpackers, the tobacco, and the Standard Oil trusts.

Roosevelt did not want to break up all trusts, however. There were, he insisted, "good" trusts and "bad" trusts. "Bad" trusts were those that did nothing for the public good. Roosevelt believed that all large companies had to operate under government regulations.

Roosevelt's other reforms. Roosevelt continued to fight for progressive reforms after he won a second term in 1904. Like many others, he had been horrified by *The Jungle*, Upton Sinclair's novel about conditions in the Chicago stockyards. At Roosevelt's urging,

Progressive President Theodore Roosevelt "tames" the lions of trusts and other unfair business practices.

THE LION-TAMER

Congress passed the **Pure Food and Drug Act** of 1906 as well as a meat inspection law. The act provided for federal control of the quality of most foods and drugs. It also called for the regulation of slaughterhouses.

Taft Becomes President

After he completed his second term, Roosevelt used his influence to get the Republican presidential nomination for his secretary of war, William Howard Taft. Taft easily defeated Democrat William Jennings Bryan in the election of 1908.

Taft tried to continue the progressive policies of the Roosevelt administration. He supported a law increasing the powers of the Interstate Commerce Commission. He also continued Roosevelt's policy of attacking "bad" trusts under the Sherman Antitrust Act.

However, Taft also allowed conservative Republicans to influence his policies in many ways. He mismanaged a well-meaning attempt to get Congress to lower the tariffs on manufactured goods, for example.

Taft's actions angered many progressives. Eventually, they persuaded Roosevelt to run for the presidency again in the 1912 election. He sought the Republican nomination, but when the nomination went to Taft, Roosevelt formed a new political organization—the Progressive Party—and secured its nomination. The Democrats selected New Jersey governor Woodrow Wilson. The socialists selected Eugene V. Debs, a labor leader. The election was an exciting one, and Wilson came out on top.

● **Presidential Election of 1912**

Wilson as President

When he took office, President Wilson first urged Congress to lower the high protective tariff. The resulting **Underwood Tariff** of 1913 decreased tariffs significantly. It provided for an income tax to make up lost revenue. This step was possible because the **Sixteenth Amendment**, a progressive reform that authorized a federal income tax, had just been added to the Constitution.

Wilson next targeted the banking system for improvement. He explained the need for a new structure:

> **"Control of the system of banking . . . which our new laws are to set up must be public, not private, [and] must be vested in [the responsibility of] the Government itself, so that the banks may be the instruments, not the masters, of business and of individual enterprise and initiative."**

Although President Taft supported many progressive policies, he appeared to struggle with issues more than the confident Roosevelt, as this cartoon shows.

In 1913 Congress passed the **Federal Reserve Act**. This law created 12 Federal Reserve banks in different sections of the nation. These were banks for banks, not for businesses or individuals.

The Federal Reserve Board in Washington, D.C., supervised these banks. The board regulated the country's money supply by controlling interest rates. When the board members believed the economy was expanding too rapidly, they encouraged banks to increase the interest rate they charged on loans to businesses. This would discourage borrowing and slow down economic expansion. During depressions or slumps, the Board could lower interest rates so that businesses could borrow money more cheaply. This would encourage businesses to expand.

In practice, the Federal Reserve system often did not work quite so smoothly. It was not always easy to know whether to stimulate the economy or slow it down. However, the system was a great improvement over the old national banking system. It is still an important part the national economy today.

In 1914 Congress passed the **Clayton Antitrust Act**. This law made it illegal for directors of one corporation to be directors of other corporations in the same field. It also stated that labor unions were not to be considered "combinations . . . in restraint of trade under the antitrust laws," meaning that labor unions were legal organizations.

Congress also established the **Federal Trade Commission** in 1914. This commission conducted investigations of large corporations. If the commission found a corporation acting unfairly toward competitors or the public, it issued a "cease and desist order" to stop the corporation's activities.

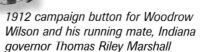

1912 campaign button for Woodrow Wilson and his running mate, Indiana governor Thomas Riley Marshall

• **Election of 1912**

Section 3 Review

• Glossary

IDENTIFY and explain the significance of the following: Theodore Roosevelt, arbitration, Pure Food and Drug Act, William Howard Taft, Woodrow Wilson, Underwood Tariff, Sixteenth Amendment, Federal Reserve Act, Clayton Antitrust Act, Federal Trade Commission

REVIEWING FOR DETAILS

1. How did Theodore Roosevelt advance progressive ideas?
2. Why did Roosevelt form a third party for the election of 1912?
3. What federal legislation did Woodrow Wilson pass to limit the power of big business?

REVIEWING FOR UNDERSTANDING

4. **Writing Mastery:** *Persuading* Imagine that you are a speech writer for one of the candidates in the 1912 election. Write a short speech convincing people that your candidate deserves to be elected.
5. **Critical Thinking:** *Drawing Conclusions* How might Roosevelt's formation of a third political party have hurt Taft's chances of re-election?

Section 4

SUCCESSES AND SHORTCOMINGS

Multimedia Connections

Explore these related topics and materials on the CD–ROM to enrich your understanding of this section:

 Atlas

- Lynchings, 1890–1920

 Biographies

- Susan B. Anthony
- Ida B. Wells-Barnett

 Media Bank

- Suffragettes Marching
- American Suffragette Parade

 Glossary

- suffragette
- suffragist

 Profiles

- Booker T. Washington
- Elizabeth Cady Stanton
- W. E. B. Du Bois
- Annie Bidwell

Alice Paul and Lucy Burns sighed with excitement and relief. They had received permission to hold a suffrage parade on the day before Woodrow Wilson's presidential inauguration! They flew into action, hoping the event would persuade Americans to support full voting rights for women. When Wilson rolled into town for his opening ceremonies, he discovered that his "greeters" had gone to see the women's rights parade. Paul and Burns had succeeded. But would women's suffrage triumph as well?

As you read this section you will find out:

▶ **How women sought more political power.**

▶ **Why and how prohibition came about.**

▶ **How some progressives worked for African Americans' rights.**

The Suffrage Movement

Female progressives like Jane Addams played a large part in bringing about many progressive reforms. Even so, male progressives often attempted to limit women's roles and influence in particular organizations and even in the government itself.

Many progressives—some men, but mostly women—hoped to accomplish reform by giving American women the right to vote. They faced powerful opposition. Many people of both sexes agreed with former president Grover Cleveland, who felt women's suffrage would create "social confusion and peril [danger].

Most progressives insisted that women deserved suffrage. "Give the women a Square Deal," they demanded. Some also argued that women would help "purify" the political process if allowed to vote. One female minister,

Reverend Anne Garlin Spencer, wrote:

> "The instant . . . the State took upon itself any form of educative, charitable, or personally helpful work, it entered the area of distinctive feminine training and power, and therefore became in need of the service of woman."

In 1890 a group of women founded the **National American Woman Suffrage Association** (NAWSA) to lead the fight for the right to vote. First run by Elizabeth Cady Stanton and then by Susan B. Anthony, the organization worked primarily on the local level. It tried to use progressive reforms like the initiative and referendum to place the suffrage issue before state legislatures and voters. Early on, the NAWSA found little support for its ideas among local politicians.

Carrie Chapman Catt worked out a successful strategy that slowly won support for the women's suffrage movement by working up from the local and state levels.

A dynamic leader named Carrie Chapman Catt helped revive the suffrage group. She had worked for women's rights in her home state of Iowa and became president of the NAWSA in 1900. Catt encouraged suffragists to broaden their base of support by rallying lower-middle-class and poor women to the cause of women's suffrage. Her strategy worked, and many more people began to support suffrage rights for women. By 1912 women had full voting rights in nine states.

A then-radical group of suffragists soon stepped up the call for political equality. They were led by Alice Paul. She had left the NAWSA in 1913 and founded what became the **National Woman's Party**. This group called for a constitutional amendment guaranteeing women's suffrage. Members of the organization used attention-getting techniques such as parades, hunger strikes, and picketing to achieve their goal.

With both the National Woman's Party and the NAWSA working hard for suffrage, the tide slowly turned. In 1918, women had full voting rights in 15 states. The following year Congress passed the **Nineteenth Amendment** to give women voting rights. The amendment was ratified in 1920.

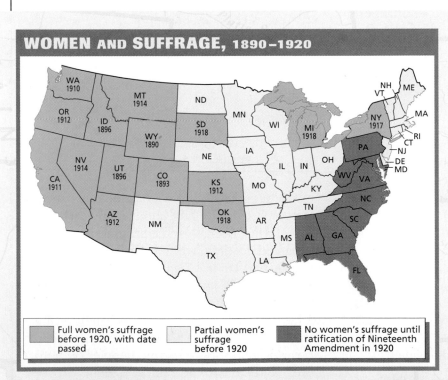

WOMEN AND SUFFRAGE, 1890–1920

WA 1910
OR 1912
MT 1914
ND
MN
NH
VT
ME
ID 1896
SD 1918
WI
MI 1918
NY 1917
MA
WY 1890
NE
IA
OH
CT
RI
NJ
NV 1914
UT 1896
CO 1893
IL
IN
PA
DE
MD
CA 1911
KS 1912
MO
KY
WV
VA
AZ 1912
NM
OK 1918
AR
TN
NC
SC
MS
AL
GA
TX
LA
FL

| Full women's suffrage before 1920, with date passed | Partial women's suffrage before 1920 | No women's suffrage until ratification of Nineteenth Amendment in 1920 |

Learning from Maps.
Organizations such as the National American Woman Suffrage Association and the National Woman's Party led a successful battle for women's suffrage.

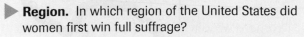

• Maps

▶ **Region.** In which region of the United States did women first win full suffrage?

The Temperance Movement

Female progressives also played a large role in the temperance movement. Joined by some male progressives, they worked for prohibition, or an end to the manufacture, transportation, and sale of alcoholic beverages. They argued that drinking caused immorality, family troubles, poverty, and social disorder.

Progressives joined organizations to work for prohibition. The **Women's Christian Temperance Union**, begun in 1874 and led by Frances Willard, staged protests against very heavy drinking. The **Anti-Saloon League**, begun by progressives in 1895, urged state legislatures to pass prohibition measures.

Individual reformers, such as Carry Nation, fought for the cause as well. She first supported temperance with public prayer sessions. Then she attacked what she saw as the heart of the problem—saloons. With her ax in hand, she entered bars across the country and chopped beer kegs and liquor bottles to bits.

• **Dry States**

This temperance poster shows the positive qualities of a life without alcohol.

The prohibition movement gradually gained strength. By 1915 more than a quarter of the states had enacted prohibition laws. These "dry" states, as they were often called, were located mostly in the South and West. In 1919 the states ratified the **Eighteenth Amendment** to make the entire nation dry. The **Volstead Act** gave the government the power to enforce the amendment.

Progressives and Immigrants

Progressives accomplished many other political, social, and economic reforms. They had prejudices and blind spots, however, that limited their achievements. Most had mixed feelings about immigrants, for example.

Some progressives who felt alarmed about corruption in politics blamed this problem on the immigrants who supported big-city political bosses and machines. Social workers and others who tried to help the poor argued that the country could not absorb so many immigrants so quickly. More generally, many progressives feared that immigrants were destroying the special character of American life.

Some progressives worked to slow or end immigration. Others attempted to assimilate, or absorb and familiarize, immigrants with

Because they attacked and destroyed supplies of alcoholic beverages, Carry Nation and other temperance leaders were often compared to fierce warriors on a holy crusade.

American culture and values. These progressives wanted immigrants to be like native-born white Americans.

Racial Equality in the Progressive Era

The most glaring weakness of the progressive reformers was their attitude toward race relations. Very few progressives believed in racial equality. Most thought that nonwhite racial groups, including Asian Americans and African Americans, deserved second-class citizenship at best. Many progressives shared the attitude of an Alabama reformer who said that African Americans were meant "to be protected by Government, rather than to be the directors of Government."

Clashes over strategy. African American leaders created their own reform agenda during the Progressive Era. Booker T. Washington remained an important figure. He raised a great deal of money for African American schools. He also worked behind the scenes to fight racial discrimination and to help African Americans gain access to political jobs.

Washington believed that the key to African Americans gaining more rights lay in their economic improvement. Washington argu-

Some African American leaders, like Harvard-educated W. E. B. Du Bois, argued that greater political freedom was needed to improve life for African Americans. Du Bois expressed many of his ideas in his well-known book The Souls of Black Folk.

ment was that African Americans must first learn trades and skills, which would help them hold good jobs and improve their living conditions. Only through economic progress, he insisted, could African Americans seek more political and social equality with whites.

Younger leaders took a different approach to race relations, however. W. E. B. Du Bois was the most important of the new African American figures. He had grown up in Massachusetts and was a brilliant and hard-working student. He won scholarships and eventually earned a doctorate degree in history from Harvard University. Du Bois was proud to be an African American. "Beauty is black," he said. He urged other African Americans to be proud of their African origins and culture.

At first Du Bois admired Washington and supported his policies. Du Bois, however, soon became convinced that more radical action was necessary. Washington "apologizes for injustice," Du Bois wrote in 1903. He argued that African Americans would never get their "reasonable rights" unless they stopped "voluntarily throwing them away." He explained the danger of Washington's approach:

"Mr. Washington is especially to be criticized. His doctrine [belief] has tended to make the whites, North and South, shift the burden of the problem to the Negro's

As head of Tuskegee Institute, Booker T. Washington became one of the best-known African American leaders in the country. He worked tirelessly to promote economic improvement for the African American community.

shoulders and stand aside as critical and rather pessimistic spectators when in fact the burden belongs to the nation."

Du Bois encouraged all African Americans to speak up for their rights.

African American progressives form organizations. At a 1905 meeting in Niagara Falls, Canada, Du Bois and other African American leaders founded the **Niagara Movement** to work for a variety of issues. They demanded equal economic and educational opportunities, an end to segregation, and protection of voting rights. Four years later, Du Bois joined with Jane Addams and other progressives to form a new organization—the **National Association for the Advancement of Colored People** (NAACP). Du Bois became editor of its journal, *Crisis*. The NAACP attempted to end lynching, or mob murder. Lynching had a long history in the United States. Ku Klux Klan mobs had killed many African Americans since Reconstruction.

After the Civil War lynching became a means of controlling and frightening African Americans. Throughout the Progressive Era about 80 percent of lynch victims were African American. In the 1890s Ida B. Wells-Barnett, a black journalist, studied the records of many lynchings. She found that most of the victims were killed for "no offense, unknown offense, offenses not criminal, misdemeanors, and crimes not capital [those which did not call for the death penalty]."

The NAACP did not succeed in significantly reducing the number of lynchings, which remained high until the early 1920s. Yet the organization grew rapidly both in members and influence. It also won impressive court victories that affected voting rights and housing codes in the South. By the end of the Progressive Era more African Americans started to speak out for their rights.

Though the pace of progressive reform had slowed by the 1920s, progressivism did not come to an end. Indeed, many of the progressives' basic beliefs still influence American life today.

Section 4 Review

• **Glossary**

• **Time Line**

IDENTIFY and explain the significance of the following: National American Woman Suffrage Association, Elizabeth Cady Stanton, Susan B. Anthony, Carrie Chapman Catt, Alice Paul, National Woman's Party, Nineteenth Amendment, Women's Christian Temperance Union, Anti-Saloon League, Eighteenth Amendment, Volstead Act, W. E. B. Du Bois, Niagara Movement, National Association for the Advancement of Colored People

REVIEWING FOR DETAILS

1. What methods did women's suffrage organizations use to achieve their goals?
2. What ideas and events led to the passage of the Eighteenth Amendment?
3. In what ways did progressives try to achieve more rights for African Americans?

REVIEWING FOR UNDERSTANDING

4. **Writing Mastery:** *Describing* Imagine that you are a moderator for a debate between Booker T. Washington and W. E. B. Du Bois. Write a brief transcript for a dialogue between the two leaders on the issue of improving rights for African Americans.
5. **Critical Thinking:** *Cause and Effect* How might the success of earlier progressive legislation have influenced the supporters of women's suffrage, prohibition, and equality for African Americans?

CHAPTER 19

The Granger Collection, New York

Involvement in World Affairs (1865–1914)

THEMES IN AMERICAN HISTORY

Economic Development:
What economic influences might lead a country to expand its power?

Global Relations:
What might be some advantages and disadvantages of controlling colonies?

Cultural Diversity:
How might territorial expansion increase cultural diversity?

 • **Video Opener**

 • **Skill Builder**

During the late 1800s, while many European powers were building overseas empires, the United States tended to keep to itself. Some Americans, however, came to believe that the country had a special duty to expand. "We cannot retreat from any soil where Providence [divine guidance] has placed our flag," declared Senator Albert J. Beveridge in 1898. "It is up to us to save that soil for liberty and civilization."

image above: *Spreading America's Wings*

Section 1

EXTENDING AMERICA'S INFLUENCE

Multimedia Connections

Explore these related topics and materials on the CD–ROM to enrich your understanding of this section:

 Media Bank

- U.S. Foreign Trade, 1865–1915
- Political Cartoon on Expansion

 Gazetteer

- Hawaii
- Alaska

 Profiles

- William McKinley

 Biographies

- Liliuokalani

 Readings

- Viewpoints: Alaska and Hawaii

n March 1893 a ship docked in New York Harbor. Aboard the ship was 17-year-old Princess Kaiulani of the Hawaiian Islands. The princess had recently received news that a group of Americans had overthrown Hawaii's monarchy in a peaceful revolt. She came to New York to plead for her country's right to rule itself. She asked Americans to "refuse to let their flag cover . . . mine." However, the princess could not stop the new voices of expansion that were slowly growing louder in the United States.

As you read this section you will find out:
▶ **Why the United States did not expand its territory much in the late 1800s.**
▶ **How the country acquired Alaska.**
▶ **What events led to the annexation of Hawaii.**

Isolationism and Expansionism

By the 1850s the American people had spread more than 3,000 miles across the North American continent. By the late 1800s, however, the open frontiers on the continent had almost entirely disappeared. What did the closing of the frontier mean to America?

Many powerful European nations, particularly Great Britain, greatly expanded their overseas empires during the late 1800s. For most of this period, American officials called for **isolationism**—keeping out of foreign affairs and halting further expansion of U.S. borders.

By 1900 some people believed that the western frontier was closing because of increasing white settlement. These Americans came to believe that the same manifest destiny that had brought the West into the Union should eventually bring much more of North and South America under the Stars and Stripes. Some argued that this might even include some islands of the Pacific Ocean. This attitude was known as **expansionism**.

The Purchase of Alaska

One of the few territorial additions to the United States in the late 1800s was Alaska. Americans knew little about Alaska when Secretary of State William H. Seward purchased it from Russia in March 1867 for $7.2 million.

News of the Alaskan purchase surprised almost everyone in the United States. Congress knew little about the negotiations

Alaska's beautiful scenery and natural resources would come to be highly valued by many Americans, though some originally considered its purchase to be a bad deal.

until it was presented with the treaty. To win support for the purchase, Seward launched a nationwide campaign. Alaska's fish, furs, and lumber were very valuable, he claimed. Gaining control of Alaska would increase U.S. influence in the northern Pacific. As Seward explained in one of his speeches:

> "**Alaska has been as yet but imperfectly explored; but enough is known to assure us that it possesses treasures. . . . The entire region of Oregon, Washington Territory, British Columbia, and Alaska seems thus destined to become a shipyard for the supply of all nations.**"

Arguments such as these persuaded Congress to approve the deal, even though many Americans thought buying Alaska was a mistake. They called the new territory "Seward's Folly," "Frigidia," and "President Andrew Johnson's Polar Bear Garden."

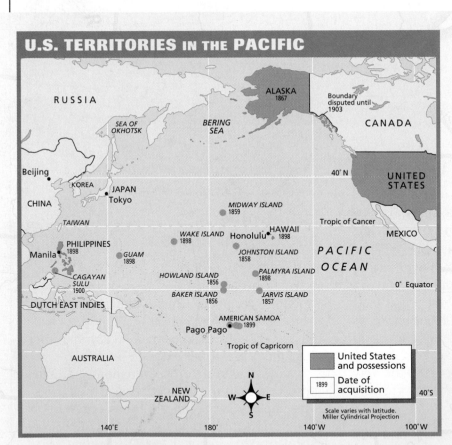

U.S. TERRITORIES IN THE PACIFIC

RUSSIA

ALASKA
1867

Boundary disputed until 1903

CANADA

SEA OF OKHOTSK

BERING SEA

40° N

UNITED STATES

Beijing

KOREA
JAPAN
Tokyo

CHINA

TAIWAN

MIDWAY ISLAND
1859

Tropic of Cancer

MEXICO

WAKE ISLAND
1898

Honolulu HAWAII
1898

PACIFIC OCEAN

PHILIPPINES
1898
Manila

GUAM
1898

JOHNSTON ISLAND
1858

PALMYRA ISLAND
1898

CAGAYAN SULU
1900

HOWLAND ISLAND
1856

0° Equator

DUTCH EAST INDIES

BAKER ISLAND
1856

JARVIS ISLAND
1857

AMERICAN SAMOA
1899
Pago Pago

Tropic of Capricorn

AUSTRALIA

United States and possessions

1899 | Date of acquisition

NEW ZEALAND

40°S

Scale varies with latitude.
Miller Cylindrical Projection

140°E   180°   140°W   100°W

Learning from Maps.

In the mid- to late 1800s, the United States acquired many territories in the Pacific.

▶ **Location.** Which American territories were located along latitude 0°?

• **Maps**

Still, Seward made quite a bargain. For about two cents an acre he obtained a region twice the size of Texas. Alaska contained huge amounts of lumber, gold, copper, and other metals. A gold rush in the 1890s brought thousands of eager miners to Alaska. More recently, rich deposits of oil and natural gas have been discovered there.

Hawaii

Some Americans also became interested in the Hawaiian Islands, located in the Pacific about 2,000 miles southwest of San Francisco. The first Americans to reach these beautiful, sunny islands had been New England traders and whalers. Beginning in the late 1700s, they stopped in Hawaii on their lonely Pacific voyages for rest and fresh supplies.

American influence. These sailors were followed by missionaries who came to the islands hoping to convert Hawaiians to Christianity. Most of the missionaries settled down, built houses, and raised various crops. In the mid-1800s the second generation of these American missionary families began to cultivate sugar. By the time of the U.S. Civil War, the missionary families dominated the islands' economy and government.

The Hawaiians were ruled by a monarch. Originally, he or she made all the decisions and owned all the land. As foreign influence increased, however, the power of the monarchy declined as rulers adopted American practices. In 1840 Hawaii established a constitution that drew from parts of the U.S. Constitution.

By the 1870s, however, many Hawaiians were becoming concerned with foreign influence in the islands. King Kalakaua (kah-LAH-KAH-ooh-ah) had close ties to the American sugar planters, and his own government was corrupt. Whenever the king's advisers opposed his decisions, he usually replaced them with foreigners.

In 1875 the United States and Hawaii signed a treaty allowing Hawaiian sugar to enter the United States without payment of a tariff. In exchange, King Kalakaua agreed not to give territory or special privileges in the islands to any other nation.

This treaty greatly stimulated sugar production and further increased U.S. power in the islands. The leading American families formed corporations and imported thousands of low-paid Chinese and Japanese workers to toil on their plantations.

History Makers

Queen Liliuokalani (1838–1917)

For many years former Hawaiian ruler Queen Liliuokalani [li-lee-uh-woh-kuh-LAHN-ee] continued to hope that her country would regain its independence. In 1894 she was placed under house arrest for supporting a counterrevolution. Two years later she traveled to Washington, D.C., to voice her opposition to annexation.

In her later years Queen Liliuokalani became somewhat of a celebrity. The Hawaiian government continued to support her with a generous pension. She lived in Honolulu until her death in 1917. For many Hawaiians she was a symbol of traditional Hawaiian culture. Her autobiography, published in 1898, only increased public fascination with her. So did the many popular songs she wrote, such as "Aloha Oe" (Farewell to Thee).

Between 1875 and 1890 the amount of Hawaiian sugar shipped to the United States increased dramatically. The sugar boom came to a sudden end, however, when Congress passed the **McKinley Tariff** of 1890, a law that, in effect, took away the special advantage of the Hawaiians. The law granted sugar producers in the United States a **subsidy**, or government bonus, of two cents per pound. Prices fell, and the Hawaiian economy suffered.

Workers labor in the fields of a Hawaiian sugar plantation.

Political disputes. Along with Hawaii's economic crisis came a political crisis. A group of U.S. businessmen formed a secret organization to ensure that the United States eventually annexed Hawaii. In 1887 the group forced King Kalakaua to accept a new constitution that essentially put all the power of the government in American hands.

In 1891 the king died. The new ruler was his sister, Queen Liliuokalani (li-lee-uh-woh-kuh-LAHN-ee). Liliuokalani was fiercely patriotic and resented the influence Americans were having in her country. Her attitude was expressed in the slogan "Hawaii for the Hawaiians." She pleaded:

"**Americans, . . . hear me for my downtrodden [oppressed] people! Their form of government is as dear to them as yours is**

precious to you. Quite as warmly as you love your country, so they love theirs."

The queen was determined to break the power of the foreign-dominated Hawaiian legislature. In January 1893 she announced a new constitution that strengthened the power of the monarchy. In the meantime, the Americans were organizing a revolution.

John L. Stevens, the U.S. minister to Hawaii, ordered 150 U.S. Marines ashore from an American warship in Honolulu Harbor. They did not have to fire a shot to persuade Liliuokalani and her supporters not to resist. With U.S. military support, the revolutionaries promptly raised the American flag. Because of objections to the revolution, however, the United States did not annex the islands until 1898.

Section 1 Review

• **Glossary**

IDENTIFY and explain the significance of the following: isolationism, expansionism, William H. Seward, McKinley Tariff, subsidy, Queen Liliuokalani

REVIEWING FOR DETAILS
1. Why was there little U.S. territorial expansion in the late 1800s?
2. How did Alaska become part of the United States?
3. How did the United States take control of Hawaii?

REVIEWING FOR UNDERSTANDING
4. **Geographic Literacy** What characteristics made Alaska so appealing to Americans such as William Seward?
5. **Critical Thinking:** *Recognizing Point of View* Why might Queen Liliuokalani have resented American influence in her country?

Section 2

THE SPANISH-AMERICAN WAR

Multimedia Connections

Explore these related topics and materials on the CD–ROM to enrich your understanding of this section:

 Profiles

- José Martí
- Joseph Pulitzer
- Lola Rodríguez de Tió

 Media Bank

- José Martí
- Yellow Kid
- Female Revolutionary

 Gazetteer

- Cuba
- Spain

 Readings

- Rough Riders

In January 1898 riots swept Havana, in the Spanish colony of Cuba. To protect U.S. citizens, President William McKinley sent in a battleship, the USS *Maine*. On February 15, while the *Maine* lay at anchor in Havana Harbor, an explosion rocked the ship. Of the 350 men aboard, some 260 were killed. Demands for war against Spain swept across the United States. "Remember the *Maine*!" became a battle cry similar to "Remember the Alamo!" during the Texas Revolution of the 1830s.

As you read this section you will find out:

▶ **Why Cubans rebelled against Spain.**

▶ **What led the United States to enter the conflict.**

▶ **What course the fighting took in the Spanish-American War.**

Cuba and Spain

Cuba was one of the few Spanish colonies that had not rebelled in the early 1800s. It was Spain's last important colonial possession in the Americas. In 1868 a revolution had begun on the island that lasted 10 years. The revolution had failed, but in 1895 Cuban patriots took up arms once again.

With independence as their objective, the rebels engaged in surprise attacks and guerrilla warfare. They burned sugarcane fields, blocked railroads, and ambushed small parties of Spanish soldiers.

The Cuban patriots were inspired by José Martí, a tireless critic of Spanish rule in Cuba. He had been forced out of Cuba in 1879 for opposing colonial rule. Living in exile in New York, he wrote many poems, articles, and speeches that were printed in numerous

American newspapers. In these works, Martí urged other exiled Cubans to return home to support the revolution:

> **"Nations are not founded upon mere hopes in the depths of a man's soul! . . . Down there is our Cuba, smothered in the arms that crush and corrupt it for us! . . . Let us rise up for the true republic, those of us who . . . know how to preserve it."**

When the fighting broke out, Martí returned to Cuba to help but was soon killed. He instantly became a national hero.

In an effort to regain control over the Cuban countryside, the Spanish governor-general, Valeriano Weyler, began herding farmpeople into what were called *reconcentrados*, or concentration camps. He imprisoned several hundred thousand Cubans in these camps. Weyler did this so that Cubans in the camps could not supply the rebels with food and assistance. At least 100,000 Cubans died in the concentration camps. Most were victims of disease and malnutrition.

Swaying Public Opinion

Most people in the United States sympathized with the Cubans' wish to be independent and were horrified by the stories of Spanish cruelty. Encouraged by American support, Cuban revolutionaries established committees called **juntas** in the United States to raise money, spread propaganda, and recruit volunteers for the struggle.

This cartoon calls on the United States to save Cuba from the evil ruler Spain.

• Fighting Spanish Imperialism

The Granger Collection, New York

As tension mounted, the publisher of the *New York Journal,* William Randolph Hearst, sent artist Frederic Remington to Cuba to draw pictures of the revolution. Hearst supported the idea of the United States entering a war with Spain on behalf of Cuba. Remington complained that he could find no signs of revolution and asked to be allowed to come home. Hearst telegraphed him:

> **"PLEASE REMAIN. YOU FURNISH THE PICTURES AND I'LL FURNISH THE WAR."**

On February 9, 1898, Hearst published a letter written by the Spanish minister to the United States. The private letter had been intercepted by a Cuban spy. In it the minister insulted President McKinley, calling him "a would-be politician." Americans were outraged by the letter.

Less than one week later the USS *Maine* exploded in Havana Harbor. To this day the cause of the explosion remains a mystery. The Spanish government claimed the disaster was caused by an explosion inside the *Maine*. Many Americans assumed that the Spanish had sunk the ship with a mine, a kind of underwater bomb. Emotions ran high on both sides.

American reporters, like those who wrote for the New York Journal, *helped stir up American anger against Spain after the explosion aboard the USS* Maine.

$50,000 REWARD.—WHO DESTROYED THE MAINE?—$50,000 REWARD.

EDITION FOR GREATER NEW YORK

NEW YORK JOURNAL

AND ADVERTISER

DESTRUCTION OF THE WAR SHIP MAINE WAS THE WORK OF AN ENEMY.

$50,000!

$50,000 REWARD!
For the Detection of the Perpetrator of the Maine Outrage!

Assistant Secretary Roosevelt Convinced the Explosion of the War Ship Was Not an Accident.

The Journal Offers $50,000 Reward for the Conviction of the Criminals Who Sent 258 American Sailors to Their Death. Naval Officers Unanimous That the Ship Was Destroyed on Purpose.

$50,000!

$50,000 REWARD!
For the Detection of the Perpetrator of the Maine Outrage!

In the United States, support for war grew However, President McKinley, a Civil War veteran, wanted to avoid war. He told a friend, "I have been through one war. I have seen the dead piled up, and I do not want to see another." McKinley did not let the sinking of the *Maine* cause an immediate diplomatic break with Spain.

War Is Declared

McKinley was still determined to stop the fighting in Cuba. He believed the Spanish must do away with the concentration camps and negotiate a truce with the Cuban rebels. He also felt that more self-government should be granted to Cuba. After the sinking of the *Maine,* Spain seemed at last willing to take these steps in order to avoid going to war with the United States.

The rebels, however, wanted total independence. The Spanish government did not dare give in completely. Any government that "gave away" Cuba would surely be overthrown. Perhaps the king himself would be deposed. These thoughts made the Spanish stand firmly against Cuban independence.

McKinley finally decided that Spain would never give up control of Cuba voluntarily. On April 11, 1898, the president told Congress that he had "exhausted every effort" to end the "intolerable" situation in Cuba. He then asked Congress to give him the power to secure a stable government on the island.

Congress had been thundering for war for weeks. By huge majorities, Congress passed a

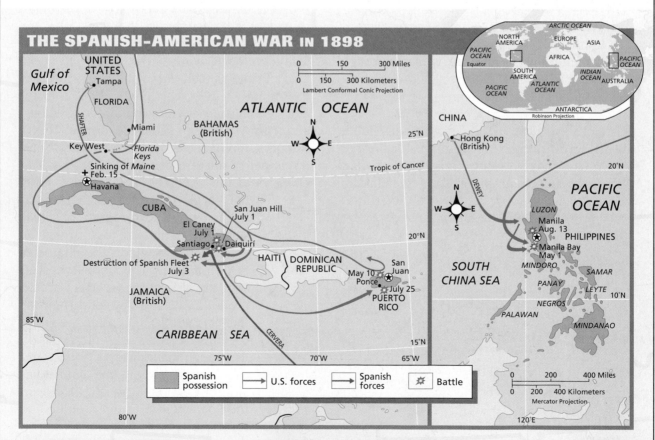

THE SPANISH-AMERICAN WAR IN 1898

Learning from Maps. Naval warfare and strategy played an important role in the Spanish-American War.

▶ **Movement.** What route did the U.S. forces take to attack the Cuban port of Daiquirí?

• **Maps**

joint resolution stating that the people of Cuba "ought to be free and independent." If the Spanish did not withdraw from the island "at once," the president should use "the entire land and naval forces of the United States" to drive them out.

Congress then tried to protected itself against being accused of going to war for selfish reasons by approving a resolution proposed by Senator Henry M. Teller of Colorado. The **Teller Amendment** stated that the United States had no intention of taking Cuba for itself or trying to control its government. McKinley gave the Spanish government three days to accept his terms or face war. Unwilling to yield, the Spanish broke off relations with the United States.

Battling the Spanish

The two powers did not limit their conflict to the Caribbean. In fact, the first important battle of the Spanish-American War was fought not in Cuba but on the other side of the world in the Spanish-held Philippines.

The Philippines. The United States had a naval squadron led by Commodore George Dewey stationed in Hong Kong. Weeks before war had been declared, Assistant Secretary of the Navy Theodore Roosevelt had ordered Dewey to prepare for battle. As soon as war broke out, Dewey steamed swiftly across the China Sea to the Philippine capital of Manila.

Dewey's fleet entered Manila Bay late on the night of April 30, 1898. Early the next morning, Dewey gave the captain of his flagship the command "You may fire when you are ready, Gridley." The U.S. fleet far outgunned the Spanish warships guarding Manila. By half past noon the Spanish fleet had been smashed, yet not one single American sailor had been killed.

Fighting in Cuba. The war in Cuba did not begin so quickly. President McKinley called for volunteers to fight and received an enthusiastic response. Some 200,000 recruits soon enlisted. Theodore Roosevelt resigned his position as assistant secretary of the navy to organize a regiment to fight in Cuba. He was appointed a lieutenant colonel in the 1st Volunteer Cavalry.

Roosevelt's call for volunteers brought forth many eager applicants. The colorful colonel enlisted several hundred cowboys, several American Indians, some Texas Rangers, lumberjacks, ranchers, hunters, and a number of Harvard and Yale graduates. The chaplain of the regiment was a former football player. The outfit became known as the **Rough Riders**. One observer noted that this odd assortment of soldiers represented, "the character of its founder." Theodore Roosevelt drew on his experience as a Harvard graduate, western adventurer, athlete, and politician to bring the group together. After a brief training period the Rough Riders were ready to fight the Spanish. Before the land invasion of Cuba could begin, however, the Spanish fleet in the Atlantic had to be located and defeated.

The Battle of Manila Bay secured U.S. control of the Spanish Philippine Islands.

The *Wranger* Collection, New York

The 9th and 10th Colored Cavalry lent support to the Rough Riders as they took San Juan Hill, near the important harbor of Santiago.

met stiff Spanish resistance. Major battles were fought at El Caney and San Juan Hill. At El Caney a member of the U.S. 2nd Massachusetts regiment reported:

> **"[The Spaniards] are hidden behind rocks, in weeds and in underbrush, and we just simply can't locate them. They are shooting our men all to pieces."**

The Rough Riders and African American soldiers of the 9th and 10th Cavalries took San Juan Hill by storm on July 1. Now U.S. artillery could be moved within range of Santiago Harbor, but the Spanish fleet had sailed. When it did, the powerful American fleet swiftly destroyed every one of the Spanish vessels.

The Spanish commander, Admiral Pascual Cervera, tried to avoid the American navy by seeking shelter in the harbor of Santiago, on the southeastern coast of Cuba. By late May an American squadron had discovered this fleet and blockaded the entrance to the harbor.

American strategy called for an attack on Santiago. The U.S. invasion force, commanded by General William R. Shafter, landed first at Daiquirí, a town to the east of Santiago. Once ashore, it began its advance, assisted by Cuban rebels. The U.S. and Cuban forces soon

On July 17 the Spanish army commander surrendered Santiago. Less than two weeks later another U.S. force completed the occupation of the Spanish island of Puerto Rico, about 500 miles east of Cuba. Within a month after the battle at Santiago, the remaining Spanish forces in Cuba surrendered. The war was over.

• **The United States and Cuba**

Section 2 Review

• **Glossary**

IDENTIFY and explain the significance of the following: José Martí, *juntas,* William Randolph Hearst, Teller Amendment, Rough Riders

LOCATE and explain the importance of the following: Philippines, Santiago, El Caney, San Juan Hill

REVIEWING FOR DETAILS
1. Why did Cubans launch a revolution against Spain?
2. What events prompted the United States to enter the war on Cuba's behalf?

• **Gazetteer**

REVIEWING FOR UNDERSTANDING
3. **Geographic Literacy** Where did most of the early fighting in the Spanish-American War take place, and why did the fighting occur there?
4. **Writing Mastery:** *Expressing* Imagine that you are a Cuban political writer like José Martí. Write a poem expressing why you feel Cuba should gain its independence.
5. **Critical Thinking:** *Drawing Conclusions* Do you think the news media influenced U.S. entry into the Spanish-American War? Explain you answer.

Section 3
AMERICA EXPANDS FURTHER

Multimedia Connections

Explore these related topics and materials on the CD–ROM to enrich your understanding of this section:

 Media Bank

- Great White Fleet
- Public Schools in Puerto Rico
- Perry in Japan
- Filipino Patriots

 Gazetteer

- Puerto Rico
- Guam
- Japan
- China
- Beijing

 Profiles

- Emilio Aguinaldo
- Yung Wing
- Luis Muñoz Marin

At relatively little cost in money and lives, the United States had met its goal of freeing Cuba from Spanish control. But the thrill of victory encouraged some Americans to now create a colonial empire, starting with the Philippines. President McKinley argued that this was necessary "to educate the Filipinos, and uplift them and civilize and Christianize them." The Philippines, however, had already been shaped by centuries of Spanish rule. And the vast majority of Filipinos were already Christians!

As you read this section you will find out:

▶ **Why some people opposed the treaty that ended the Spanish-American War.**

▶ **How Filipinos reacted to the treaty.**

▶ **How the United States expanded its influence in East Asia.**

The Treaty Controversy

In late July 1898, President McKinley sent his peace terms to the Spanish government. At the peace conference the U.S. delegates demanded possession of the Philippines in addition to the islands of Puerto Rico and Guam. The Spanish strongly objected, but finally gave in. To make it easier for them, the United States agreed to pay $20 million for the islands.

Many people in the United States opposed the treaty with Spain. They insisted that **imperialism**—controlling overseas colonies by force—was un-American. Some Americans who opposed U.S. colonization formed the **Anti-Imperialist League** to oppose the proposed treaty. Despite their objections, the Senate approved the treaty.

• Treaty Fight

Fighting in the Philippines

The Filipino people would not agree to American rule. After his victory at Manila Bay, Commodore Dewey had helped the exiled leader of the Filipino patriots, Emilio Aguinaldo, return to the islands. Dewey also encouraged Aguinaldo to resume his fight against Spanish rule. Aguinaldo thus assumed that the United States intended to help liberate his country.

After the Spanish forces had been defeated, Aguinaldo declared the Philippines independent and started drafting a new constitution. When it became clear that the United States was planning to take over the islands, Aguinaldo organized a revolt against U.S. rule. He warned that if U.S. troops invaded, "upon their heads will be all the blood which may be shed."

Bloody jungle fighting broke out as 70,000 U.S. troops were sent to the islands. Many Americans opposed the war. Peace was not fully restored until 1902. By that time, more than 4,000 American troops and at least 200,000 Filipinos had been killed. The revolt was over, but opposition to imperialism was growing in the United States.

The Open Door Policy

Despite such growing opposition, controlling the Philippines made the United States a power in East Asia. Most importantly, it gave the country a base near China. For many years Great Britain, France, Germany, and Russia had been seizing **spheres of influence**—regions where foreign countries controlled trade and natural resources—in China. If this trend continued, Americans feared that they might not be able to expand their share of the Chinese market.

● Opening of Japan

Global Connections

Roosevelt and Japan

By 1907 President Theodore Roosevelt had become concerned that Japan, an emerging world power, might be getting too strong. He was particularly worried that the Japanese might try to take control of the Philippines away from the United States. To remind Japan of America's military might, Roosevelt sent a fleet of U.S. naval ships on a 46,000-mile global cruise. All of the ships were painted a brilliant white. When this "Great White Fleet," as it was nicknamed, sailed into a Japanese harbor it sent a stern but silent warning.

Earlier that same year Roosevelt had negotiated a secret "Gentleman's Agreement" to limit informally Japanese immigration to the United States. Roosevelt promised to try to stop discrimination against Japanese Americans if Japan halted immigration to the United States. Both the Gentleman's Agreement and the Great White Fleet sent a message that the United States wanted the Japanese to stay within their present boundaries.

WELL, I HARDLY KNOW WHICH TO TAKE FIRST!

This cartoonist made fun of the American imperialists' appetite for more land, showing President McKinley ready to take their order.

In the 1850s the United States had reacted to the situation by forcing Japan open to U.S. trade and creating its own sphere of influence. The United States, however, was unable to gain such influence in China.

In 1899 Secretary of State John Hay asked the European nations and Japan to agree that all countries should be allowed to trade with China on equal terms. Hay's so-called Open Door note was intended to protect U.S. trade. None of these discussions included the Chinese, whose trade and territory were being carved up. To protest, members of a secret society of Chinese nationalists known as the "Fists of Righteous Harmony," or Boxers, launched an attack on foreigners in the capital city of Beijing (Peking) and in other parts of China.

Armed with swords and spears, the Boxers destroyed foreign property and killed missionaries and businesspeople. Frightened foreigners fled for protection to the buildings that housed their governments' representatives in Beijing. They remained there for weeks, basically prisoners cut off from the outside world.

The Western nations organized an international army to put down this **Boxer Rebellion**. A force that included some

These participants in the Boxer Rebellion opposed foreign interference in China.

2,500 Americans was rushed to the area. They rescued the trapped foreign civilians and defeated the Boxers.

Hay feared that the European powers would use the rebellion as an excuse to expand their spheres of influence. He sent off a second Open Door note stating that the United States opposed any further carving up of China by foreign nations. The **Open Door Policy** thus stated that all nations would have equal trade rights in China. None of the European nations officially rejected these principles. American businesses were able to trade freely throughout the Chinese Empire.

Section 3 Review

• Glossary

IDENTIFY and explain the significance of the following: imperialism, Anti-Imperialist League, Emilio Aguinaldo, spheres of influence, John Hay, Boxer Rebellion, Open Door Policy

REVIEWING FOR DETAILS

1. Why did some people in the United States oppose the treaty that ended the Spanish-American War?

2. How did the United States expand its trade in East Asia?

REVIEWING FOR UNDERSTANDING

3. **Geographic Literacy** How might the location of the Philippines have influenced the decision to retain American control of the islands?

4. **Writing Mastery:** *Expressing* Imagine that you are a Filipino shortly after the end of the Spanish-American War. Write a letter to the U.S. president expressing your reaction to the peace treaty.

5. **Critical Thinking:** *Determining the Strength of an Argument.* Was John Hay justified in calling for the Open Door Policy? Why or why not?

Section 4

POLICING THE WESTERN HEMISPHERE

Multimedia Connections

Explore these related topics and materials on the CD–ROM to enrich your understanding of this section:

 Media Bank

- Fighting Mosquitos in Panama

 Atlas

- Panama Canal Zone
- U.S. Interests in Latin America

 Gazetteer

- Panama
- Dominican Republic
- Veracruz

 Profiles

- Francisco "Pancho" Villa

I n 1913 American writer Frederic Haskin described what would become one of the seven wonders of the modern world, thanks to American politics:

> **"Now stretches a man-made canyon across the backbone of the continent; now lies a channel for ships through the barrier; now is found . . . the gate through the West to the East. . . . It is majestic. It is awful. It is the Canal."**

As you read this section you will find out:

▶ **Why the Panama Canal was built.**

▶ **How the Roosevelt Corollary and "dollar diplomacy" shaped foreign policy.**

▶ **What policy Woodrow Wilson followed toward Mexico.**

The Panama Canal

The Spanish-American War increased interest in linking the Atlantic and Pacific Oceans with a canal across Central America. During the war, one U.S. battleship had to steam 12,000 miles from the West Coast around South America in order to get to Cuba. At top speed that voyage took 68 days. A canal would have shortened the trip down to 4,000 miles.

In the 1880s a private French company had obtained the right to build a canal across Panama, which was then part of the Republic of Colombia. The company had spent a fortune but had made little progress and ended up bankrupt. The company then offered to sell to the United States its right to build a canal for $40 million.

In 1903 Secretary of State John Hay and a Colombian representative negotiated a treaty

In this cartoon Philippe Bunau-Varilla is shown sparking Colombia to release Panama. The free Republic of Panama then hands over control of the canal zone to President Roosevelt.

in which Colombia would lease a canal zone across Panama to the United States. Colombia would receive $10 million up front and a rent of $250,000 a year.

The U.S. Senate approved this treaty, but the Colombians rejected it. They wanted more money. President Theodore Roosevelt was furious with the Colombians. Roosevelt got word to Philippe Bunau-Varilla, a representative of the now bankrupt French canal company that he would not look unfavorably on a rebellion in Panama. Bunau-Varilla soon led the Panamanians in a revolt against the Colombian government.

When Colombian troops landed at the port of Colón to put down the revolt, they found themselves faced by the guns of the USS *Nashville*. The Colombians were forced to return to their base without firing a shot.

Thus was born the Republic of Panama. Three days later, on November 6, 1903, the U.S. government officially recognized Panama. On November 18, Secretary of State Hay signed a canal treaty with Bunau-Varilla,

now the representative of the new nation. The **Hay–Bunau-Varilla Treaty** granted the United States a 10-mile-wide canal zone under the same financial agreement Colombia had turned down. Work on the long-awaited canal could now begin.

From 1906 to 1914, a large force of workers drilled, blasted, dug, and scooped. They had to cut a long channel through mountains of solid rock. To remove the 105 million cubic yards of earth required about 6 million pounds of dynamite each year. Writer Frederic Haskin described how the difficult task progressed:

"**Here the great barrier of the continental divide resisted to the utmost the attacks of the canal army; here disturbed and outraged Nature conspired with gross [huge] mountain mass to make the defense stronger and stronger. . . . Grim, now, but still confident, the attackers fought on. The mountain was defeated.**"

It took many years to dig out the land for the Panama Canal. The task took some 43,000 workers, of which about 6,000 died during the project from disease and accidents.

• **Building of the Panama Canal**

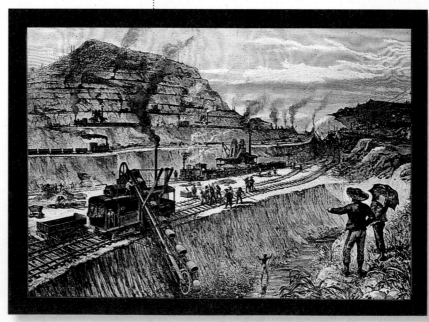

President Roosevelt enforces his policy to "speak softly and carry a big stick" in the Caribbean by ordering the U.S. Navy to patrol the area and keep foreigners out.

The **Panama Canal** was finally finished in 1914, a truly magnificent achievement. Some people in the United States and in many Latin Americans, however, believed that Roosevelt had stolen the canal zone away from Colombia. In 1921 Congress gave Colombia $25 million to make up for the loss of Panama.

Involvement in the Americas

The Panama Canal was one of the many ways in which President Roosevelt expanded U.S. involvement throughout the Americas. Roosevelt was particularly interested in keeping European nations from interfering in the domestic affairs of Latin American governments. Increasing numbers of American and European businesspeople looked to Latin America as a source of investment. These investments often took the form of high-risk loans. When these governments did not make their loan payments, European governments sometimes sent in troops to force the countries to pay.

Roosevelt decided that any European interference in nations in the Western Hemisphere violated the Monroe Doctrine.

He believed that if a nation in the Western Hemisphere could not pay its debts, then the United States must make it do so. This policy became known as the **Roosevelt Corollary** to the Monroe Doctrine.

Early on, Roosevelt said that he applied the Corollary with great reluctance. Before he sent marines into the Dominican Republic in 1905, he insisted that he had no more desire to make that nation a colony of the United States than a snake would have to swallow a porcupine backward.

After William Howard Taft became president in 1909, the United States began to try to control the nations of the region indirectly. By investing money in countries like Cuba and the Dominican Republic, more stable economies and governments might result. This policy came to be known as "**dollar diplomacy**" since it focused on using economic methods more than military force.

Wilson and Mexico

Even before his election to the presidency in 1912, Woodrow Wilson held strong opinions about how to deal with foreign nations. He reasoned that the United States did not need any more territory since it had no foreign enemies. Wilson also believed that the United States had a duty to help its neighbors.

One of Wilson's first foreign policy challenges came from America's closest neighbor to the south—Mexico. A revolution had begun there in 1910. The **Mexican Revolution** was against the dictator Porfirio Díaz, who had allowed foreign companies to take advantage of his country's resources. The revolution concerned U.S. officials because American investments were threatened by the troubles. Also, many Mexican refugees were crossing the border illegally into the United States.

In 1911 a reform-minded rebel leader, Francisco Madero, forced Díaz to resign and leave Mexico. Madero became president but early in 1913 he was murdered by General Victoriano Huerta, who set up a military dictatorship. President Wilson called Huerta's government "a government of butchers" and refused to recognize him as the official leader of Mexico.

Many Mexicans agreed with President Wilson. A new revolt soon broke out, led by Venustiano Carranza. Wilson asked Huerta to order free elections and to promise not to be a candidate himself. If Huerta agreed, the United States would then try to persuade the Carranza forces to stop fighting.

Supporters of both Huerta and Carranza resented Wilson's interference. If Mexicans agreed to U.S. interference, said an official of the Huerta government, "all the future elections for president would be submitted to the veto of any president of the United States."

In April 1914 a group of U.S. sailors were arrested in Mexico. They were soon released, but their arrest flared into an international incident that further divided the United States and Mexico. Wilson tried to use the incident to overthrow Huerta. He sent a naval force to seize the port of Veracruz.

Wilson expected his "show of force" to lead to the downfall of Huerta. Unfortunately, 19 American sailors and more than 100 Mexicans were killed before Veracruz was captured. Again, Carranza joined his enemy, Huerta, in speaking out against the interference of the United States in Mexican affairs.

Fortunately, a group of ambassadors from the **ABC Powers**—Argentina, Brazil, and Chile—offered to find a peaceful settlement. Wilson eagerly accepted their offer, and the crisis ended. By August Carranza had forced Huerta from power. The United States then withdrew its naval force from Veracruz.

The Pursuit of Pancho Villa

No sooner had Carranza defeated Huerta than one of his own military commanders, Francisco "Pancho" Villa, rebelled against him. Resenting Carranza's criticism of the U.S. policy, Wilson supported Villa. Villa also seemed to be interested in improving the lives of poor Mexicans. Supporting Pancho Villa soon became a serious

Mexican rebel leader Pancho Villa (third from right) inspects the rifles of his troops. Although the United States supported Villa at first, he soon became the country's sworn enemy.

problem for the Wilson administration. Villa was strongly anti-American, and Carranza's forces were considerably stronger than Villa's. Carranza's troops soon drove the Villistas into the mountains of northern Mexico.

In October 1915 Wilson realized that the best policy for the United States was to let the Mexican people decide for themselves how they wanted to be governed. Thus, he officially recognized the Carranza government.

This decision angered Pancho Villa, who quickly planned his response:

"We have decided not to fire a bullet more against Mexicans, our brothers, and to prepare and organize ourselves to attack the Americans in their own dens and make them know that Mexico is a land for the free and a tomb for thrones, crowns, and traitors."

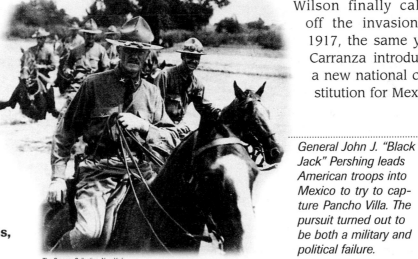

The Granger Collection, New York

In January 1916 Villa's forces stopped a train in northern Mexico and killed 18 Americans on board. Then in March, Villa and his men crossed the border and attacked the town of Columbus, New Mexico. They killed 17 more Americans and set the town on fire.

President Wilson then ordered troops under General John J. Pershing to capture Villa. This meant invading Mexico. Pershing's men pursued Villa vigorously, but they could not catch him on his home ground. This U.S. interference again angered Carranza. Wilson finally called off the invasion in 1917, the same year Carranza introduced a new national constitution for Mexico.

General John J. "Black Jack" Pershing leads American troops into Mexico to try to capture Pancho Villa. The pursuit turned out to be both a military and political failure.

Section 4 Review

• Glossary

• Time Line

IDENTIFY and explain the significance of the following: Hay–Bunau-Varilla Treaty, Panama Canal, Roosevelt Corollary, dollar diplomacy, Mexican Revolution, Victoriano Huerta, Venustiano Carranza, ABC Powers, Pancho Villa

REVIEWING FOR DETAILS
1. How did the Roosevelt Corollary and dollar diplomacy influence U.S. foreign policy?
2. How did President Wilson respond to the Mexican Revolution?

REVIEWING FOR UNDERSTANDING
3. **Geographic Literacy** Why would the construction of a canal across Panama be a benefit to the United States?
4. **Writing Mastery:** *Persuading* Imagine that you are a member of Woodrow Wilson's cabinet. Write a memo to Wilson explaining why the United States should or should not get involved in Mexican affairs.
5. **Critical Thinking:** *Making Comparisons* How did the role of the United States in the revolution in Panama differ from its role in the Mexican Revolution?

Imperialism

The rapid industrialization that occurred during the late 1800s and early 1900s was closely tied to imperialism. As their industries expanded, the United States and other industrial nations hoped to dominate foreign regions to gain sources of raw materials and new markets for their products. The resource-rich continent of Africa was quickly taken over by European nations looking to build overseas empires. By 1914 Liberia, the country founded by American abolitionists, and Ethiopia stood alone as the only independent nations left on the continent.

Although the United States possessed few overseas colonies, it invested millions of dollars in overseas business ventures and trade. Likewise, European countries continued to invest in businesses in North and South America. The Monroe Doctrine helped prevent Europeans from trying to build new colonies in the Americas, but it did not prevent them from investing money there. With such economic influence often came political influence over foreign governments.

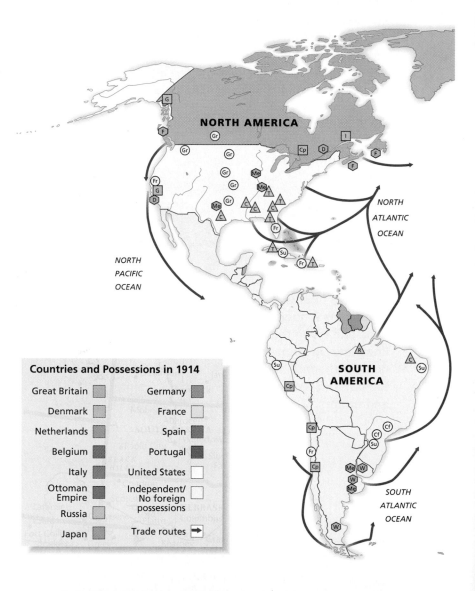

Countries and Possessions in 1914

Great Britain	Germany
Denmark	France
Netherlands	Spain
Belgium	Portugal
Italy	United States
Ottoman Empire	Independent/ No foreign possessions
Russia	
Japan	Trade routes ➡

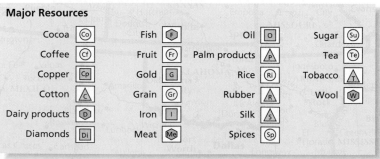

Major Resources

Cocoa	Co	Fish	F	Oil	O	Sugar	Su
Coffee	Cf	Fruit	Fr	Palm products	P	Tea	Te
Copper	Cp	Gold	G	Rice	Ri	Tobacco	T
Cotton	C	Grain	Gr	Rubber	R	Wool	W
Dairy products	D	Iron	I	Silk	S		
Diamonds	Di	Meat	Me	Spices	Sp		

Global Possessions in 1914

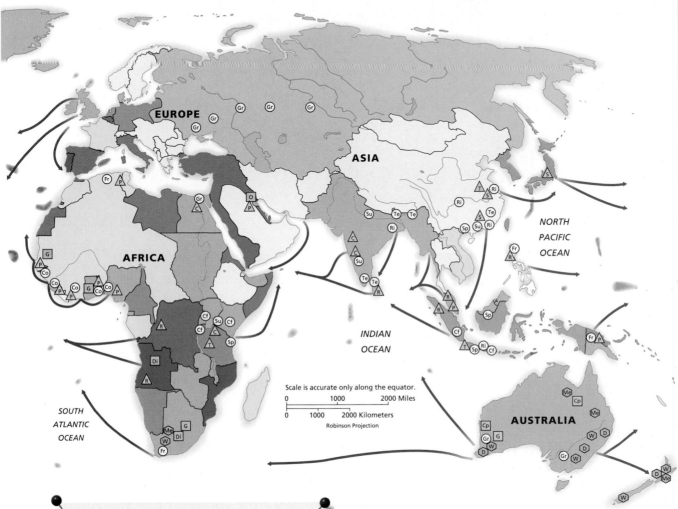

The United States benefited greatly from the resources of its colonies and areas of financial investment. For example, its major possession in Asia—the Philippine Islands—was rich in rubber used to supply U.S. industries. Financially, the United States focused its attention on Latin America, as U.S. businesses invested more money in South America than in any other continent. **Region:** What were the three major resources of South America? What other areas had these same resources?

To learn more about imperialism, go to the interactive map, "U.S. Imperialism in Latin America," on the CD–ROM.

• U.S. Imperialism in Latin America

CHAPTER **20**

America and the Great War (1914–1920)

THEMES IN AMERICAN HISTORY

Global Relations:
Why might a country be drawn into an international conflict when its safety is not directly threatened?

Democratic Values:
How might democratic values shape a country's foreign policy?

Technology and Society:
What effect might technological advances have on warfare?

*S*ongwriter George M. Cohan penned the following tune in 1917 as an anthem to American soldiers who were entering a bloody conflict that had spanned the globe:

*"***Over there, over there, . . .**
Send the word, send the word to
beware,
We'll be over, we're coming over,
And we won't come back till it's
over over there.*"*

• Video
  Opener

• Skill
  Builder

image above: *Fighting in World War I*

Section 1

WAR ENGULFS EUROPE

Multimedia Connections

Explore these related topics and materials on the CD–ROM to enrich your understanding of this section:

 Atlas

• Trench Warfare

 Glossary

• nationalism
• imperialism
• neutrality

 Profiles

• Woodrow Wilson

 Readings

• Life in the Trenches

 Media Bank

• German Artillery

 Gazetteer

• Bosnia and Herzegovina
• Austria-Hungary
• Bulgaria
• Ottoman Empire
• Russia

On July 29, 1914, the headline of the *New York Tribune* read: "AUSTRIA DECLARES WAR, RUSHES VAST ARMY INTO SERBIA." A month earlier, an Austrian prince and his wife had been murdered in the Bosnian city of Sarajevo (sahr-uh-YAY-voh). The killer was a member of a terrorist organization from neighboring Serbia. What did these events have to do with Americans? Plenty, as the murders in Sarajevo soon led to one of the largest wars the world had yet seen.

As you read this section you will find out:

▶ **What the fundamental causes of World War I were.**

▶ **Why many Americans supported a policy of neutrality.**

▶ **How the early years of the war progressed.**

The Spark Is Lit

At first there seemed to be no reason why the murder of Austro-Hungarian archduke Franz Ferdinand and his wife would lead to a long and terrible war. There had not been a major war in Europe since 1815. Below the surface, however, tensions among the European powers were simmering.

Nationalism and imperialism. In the years before 1914, several dangerous pressures were building in Europe. The most important of these was nationalism—the pride or loyalty that people have for their country or for a shared language or custom.

Nationalism had helped the German-speaking states unite to form the Austro-Hungarian and German empires in the late 1800s. Yet nationalism also united the Slavic peoples of southeastern Europe in resentment against Austria-Hungary, which ruled them. This resentment led to the assassination of Archduke Franz Ferdinand in Sarajevo. The city was in Bosnia and Herzegovina (hert-suh-goh-VEE-nuh), a Slavic region controlled by Austria-Hungary.

How did the nationalist fight between Austrians and Slavs come to affect so many other nations? One reason was imperialism, or the controlling of overseas colonies by force. Some European nations had built colonial empires in Asia and Africa. Others, such as Germany and Italy, envied these empires and wanted to build empires of their own. These attempts brought them into conflict with the established imperialist powers.

By 1900 the German **kaiser**, or emperor, Wilhelm II, had made Germany's army the best-trained fighting force in Europe. The other nations of Europe also began to strengthen their forces and to believe that the use of military force was a good solution to international problems, an idea known as **militarism**. Before long, a dangerous arms race was under way in Europe.

Alliances.   To further increase their military strength, European powers signed a complicated network of treaties. Two groups known as the **Triple Alliance** (Germany, Austria-Hungary, and Italy) and the **Triple Entente** (Great Britain, France, and Russia) were eventually created. European leaders claimed that these alliances maintained a **balance of power**—that is, they kept the two rival groups of nations at nearly equal strength.

Alliances, however, proved to be a grave danger. When a member of one alliance was threatened, the other members pledged to support it. When Franz Ferdinand was killed, the event created a ripple effect throughout the world because of the alliances. Austria-Hungary blamed Serbia for the assassination. The Austrians declared war on Serbia, whose ally Russia came to its aid.

Since Germany was an ally of Austria-Hungary, it joined in the fight and declared

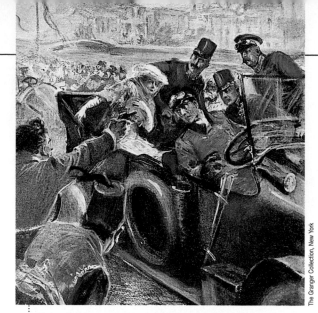

Felix Schwarmstadt painted this image of the assassination of Archduke Franz Ferdinand and his wife in 1914.

war first on Russia, then on France, Russia's ally. The German army requested permission to march through neutral Belgium to reach France. When the Belgians refused, Germany invaded. In an earlier treaty, Great Britain had promised to protect Belgian neutrality. Thus, when the Germans invaded, Britain also declared war on Germany and its allies. Soon, practically all the members of Europe's alliances were swept into war.

Germany, Austria-Hungary, and their allies, Bulgaria and the Ottoman Empire, became known as the **Central Powers**. Opposing them were the Triple Entente nations and their allies, which were known collectively as the **Allied Powers**.

American Neutrality

Americans were surprised by the outbreak of the Great War, which later generations came to call World War I. For most Americans the obvious policy for the United States was neutrality, or not taking either side. Europe was far away, and its rivalries had always been viewed by Americans with distrust.

President Woodrow Wilson expressed this attitude clearly on August 20, 1914. Every American ought to "act and speak in the true spirit of neutrality," he said. This meant behaving with a lack of favoritism "and fairness and friendliness" toward all the nations at war.

The Course of the War

World War I quickly became one of the bloodiest conflicts ever fought. Imperialist expansion had allowed European powers to gain colonies throughout the world, and these colonies were also drawn into the war.

On the eastern front, Russian troops clashed with Austrian and German armies in a series of seesaw battles. Fighting also broke out in the Ottoman Empire and Serbia. Allied troops in Africa clashed with German colonial

forces. In May 1915 Italy entered the war on the side of the Allies and attacked Austria-Hungary from the south. Italian leaders claimed that because Austria-Hungary had declared war on Serbia first, Italy was not required to support Austria-Hungary.

The United States was most interested in the fighting in Belgium and France—the western front—and on the high seas. When Germany invaded Belgium in 1914, the Belgians resisted bravely, but they could not stop the invaders. By September 1914 the German armies were within 30 miles of Paris. There, in the **Battle of the Marne**, French and British troops stopped the Germans.

Learning from Maps. The British established a naval blockade that stretched from Spain into the Atlantic Ocean north of Great Britain. The British hoped their blockade would cut off Germany from the supplies it needed to continue the war.

▶ **Place.** Which battles took place along the western front trench line?

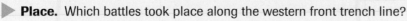

 • **Maps**

The Granger Collection, New York

French troops march through the muddy trenches in World War I.

The two armies then dug trenches to protect themselves from bullets and artillery shells. They also put up mazes of barbed wire in front of their positions. Lines of these trenches soon ran all the way across northern France from the sea to Switzerland. Between the opposing trenches lay a narrow strip of territory known as **no-man's-land**. Charles Carrington, a British soldier, described what a trench was like from the inside:

> **"When moving about in the trenches you turn a corner every few yards, which makes it seem like walking in a maze. . . . When the trenches have been fought over the confusion becomes all the greater."**

Trench warfare was both uncomfortable and dangerous. Soldiers ate and slept in the gravelike damp. First one side, then the other would try to break through the line. The artillery would begin the attack by firing exploding shells at the enemy trenches for hours. Soldiers would then climb from their trenches and rush with fixed bayonets toward the enemy line. The defenders' artillery would rain shells upon them while sharpshooters and machine gunners assaulted them with a hail of bullets. The armies reached a **stalemate**—neither side could win a clear victory despite repeated assaults that cost hundreds of thousands of lives. No-man's-land often looked like the surface of the moon. No tree or house remained.

Section 1 Review

• **Glossary**

• **Gazetteer**

IDENTIFY and explain the significance of the following: kaiser, militarism, Triple Alliance, Triple Entente, balance of power, Central Powers, Allied Powers, Battle of the Marne, no-man's-land, trench warfare, stalemate

LOCATE and explain the importance of the following: Sarajevo, Serbia, eastern front, western front

REVIEWING FOR DETAILS

1. What factors contributed to the outbreak of World War I?
2. Why did many Americans hope to remain neutral in the war?

REVIEWING FOR UNDERSTANDING

3. **Geographic Literacy** How did the early years of the war progress on the western front?
4. **Writing Mastery:** *Expressing* Imagine that you are an American-born son or daughter of a German immigrant living in the United States in 1915. Write a diary entry expressing your feelings about the war in Europe.
5. **Critical Thinking:** *Synthesizing Information* How did the assassination of Archduke Franz Ferdinand draw all of Europe's major powers into war?

Section 2

AMERICA ENTERS THE WAR

Multimedia Connections

Explore these related topics and materials on the CD–ROM to enrich your understanding of this section:

 Atlas

• Convoy System

 Profiles

• Jeannette Rankin

 Media Bank

• German Zeppelin
• Wilson Asks for War
• European War Refugees
• American Peace Advocates
• Wilson's 1916 Campaign

 Gazetteer

• Germany
• Mexico

As time passed it became more difficult for the United States to remain neutral. In January 1917, British intelligence intercepted a note from one German official to another. The note spelled out a plan to ask Mexico for its help should the United States enter the war against Germany. In exchange for its help, Mexico would receive "the lost territory in Texas, New Mexico, and Arizona." Americans were enraged. Such incidents soon drew the United States into the war.

As you read this section you will find out:

▶ **What tactics the British and German navies used in the Atlantic.**

▶ **How the war affected the election of 1916.**

▶ **What events finally drew the United States into the war.**

The War in the Atlantic

While European land forces were stalled on the western front, a new kind of struggle was developing in the Atlantic Ocean. This struggle would greatly affect the United States.

Great Britain's navy was far stronger than Germany's. The British attempted to blockade all northern European ports in order to keep Germany from obtaining supplies from neutral nations, including the United States. The British even tried to limit the amount of goods shipped to neutral countries like Norway and Sweden. Otherwise, the British claimed, those nations could import more products than they needed for themselves and ship the surplus to the Central Powers.

The Germans, in turn, tried to keep supplies from the Allied Powers by using submarines, which they called "Undersea boats,"

German U-boats like this one, the U 53, attacked many merchant ships during World War I. In this painting the U 53 is shown attacking a British commercial ship.

Collection Claus Bergen, Bergen, Germany, Photograph by Erich Lessing/Art Resource, NY

or **U-boats**. Germany did not have enough surface ships to operate in the Atlantic against the Allied fleets. U-boats were thus the best naval weapon the Germans could use. German U-boats roamed the seas looking to attack vessels that were suspected of carrying war materials for the Allies. These attacks often caused heavy losses to civilian lives when the targets were merchant ships. When they sighted enemy warships, the U-boats slipped away beneath the surface.

Both the British blockade and the German submarine campaign hurt American businesses. These activities on the high seas also violated the long-held U.S. interpretation of the rights of neutral nations. British warships stopped American ships and forced them to enter Allied ports for inspection. Goods headed for Germany were seized.

The Germans refused to follow the international rules for stopping merchant ships in wartime. These rules provided that ships could be stopped and their cargoes examined. Enemy vessels and neutral ships carrying war materials to enemy ports could be taken as prizes or sunk. Before destroying a merchant ship, however, the attacker was supposed to take the crew prisoner or give them time to evacuate the vessel in lifeboats.

It was extremely dangerous for submarines to obey these rules. If a submarine surfaced and ordered a merchant ship to stop, the ship might turn suddenly and ram the submarine before it could react. Some merchant ships also carried cannons. A single cannon shell could send a submarine to the bottom of the ocean in minutes.

Therefore, the U-boats attacked their targets without warning from below the surface, firing torpedoes packed with powerful explosives. Many sailors and passengers lost their lives when their ships went down after being hit by a U-boat torpedo.

Wilson and Neutral Rights

President Wilson protested strongly against both British and German violations of neutral rights. The British would probably have obeyed the rules if he had threatened to cut off trade with Great Britain. The British depended upon war supplies from the United States. However, Wilson was unwilling to go that far, in large part because the profitable trade with the Allies was extremely important to the United States.

Wilson took a much stronger position against Germany. When U-boats began to sink ships without warning, he announced in February 1915 that Germany would be held to "strict accountability" for any American lives lost or property destroyed. Diplomatically speaking, the phrase "strict accountability" was a polite way of saying, "If you don't do what we ask, we will probably declare war."

The danger of war over submarine attacks suddenly became much more critical on May 7, 1915, when a German U-boat torpedoed the British liner **Lusitania** without warning. The *Lusitania* was crowded with civilian passengers. About 1,200 of them, including 128 Americans, were killed in the sinking.

Technically, the Germans could defend their sinking of the *Lusitania*. The ship was carrying a cargo of guns and ammunition. Alice Hamilton, an American doctor, recalled that many Germans felt the sinking was totally justified:

> **"Even the very best of them accepted the *Lusitania* incident without questioning. She [the *Lusitania*] was carrying munitions, the passengers had been warned, she was rightly doomed. One [German] . . . woman told us that the day the news came she declared a holiday and took her children on a picnic to the country to celebrate."**

The American public was shocked and angered. President Wilson demanded only that the Germans apologize, pay damages, and promise not to attack passenger ships in the future. Long negotiations followed. In March 1916, after other passenger vessels, including the *Sussex,* were torpedoed with the loss of more American lives, Germany finally promised not to sink any more passenger or merchant ships without warning. This promise was known as the ***Sussex* pledge**.

The Election of 1916

By late 1916 an increasing number of Americans, including former president Theodore Roosevelt, were arguing that the United States should enter the war on the side of the Allies. Many believed that the United States should at least prepare for war by building up its armed forces. Still, a majority of the American people

The sinking of the Lusitania *is re-created in this drawing by Charles Dixon, based on survivors' descriptions of the event. Media coverage of the tragedy helped stir up anti-German feelings in the United States.*

The Granger Collection, New York

wanted to remain neutral. They appreciated Wilson's patient attempts to avoid involvement and his efforts to persuade the warring nations to make peace.

The 1916 presidential campaign brought out the depth of these feelings among the American people. The Democratic campaign slogan, "He kept us out of war," proved to have enormous appeal. The presidential election was very close. Wilson won 277 electoral votes to 254 for Republican candidate Charles Evans Hughes. Many people agreed that the president's success in keeping the United States out of the war saved him from defeat. President Wilson knew, however, that if the Germans eventually decided to ignore the *Sussex* pledge and sink merchant ships again without warning, the United States could not stay neutral.

"Peace Without Victory"

Wilson's fear of being forced into the war led him to strive to end the war by negotiation. On January 22, 1917, he made a moving speech calling for "peace without victory." If either side tried to profit from the war by taking land or money from the other, Wilson said, the only result would be hatred that would cause more wars. All the nations, including the United States, must try to make a peace based on "justice throughout the world."

Unfortunately, neither the Allies nor the Central Powers would settle for such a peace. The cost in lives and money had been so great after two and a half years of war that neither side could face the idea of all that expense having been for nothing. At the very least, each side probably wanted the other to accept blame for causing the war.

The German government had also secretly decided to resume its unrestricted submarine warfare. The Germans realized that unleashing their U-boats would probably cause the United States to declare war. Nevertheless, they expected that submarine warfare would keep food and munitions from reaching Great Britain, and the British would have to surrender. The war would be over before the United States could raise and train an army and get its soldiers across the Atlantic.

Less than two weeks after his great "peace without victory" speech, President Wilson broke off diplomatic relations with Germany over the U-boat activities. He ordered the German ambassador out of the United States and recalled the U.S. ambassador from Germany.

Through Others' Eyes

The Great Gamble

In early 1917 Germany was confident that it could defeat the Allies. Even though it did not want the United States to join the war, Germany took the risk and broke its *Sussex* pledge. On February 1, 1917, the German navy resumed unrestricted submarine warfare. Two days later the United States broke off relations with Germany. A German sailor reacted to this news:

"I almost suffered a heart attack when I read this terrible . . . news. If America does not hesitate at the last minute and declares war against us, our situation . . . will be extremely critical. I have always looked upon the United States as a source of reserve strength for the world and hoped that it would give . . . Europe a transfusion of new blood. We were all agreed that the United States would not significantly strengthen the military position of our enemies but that it would make them economically indestructible. Just think what enormous gold reserves they hold on the other side of the great pond!"

War Is Declared

Late in February 1917 the president learned that the German foreign secretary, Arthur Zimmermann, was trying to form an alliance with Mexico in the event that the United States declared war on Germany. In the **Zimmerman Note**, the foreign secretary revealed that:

> **"We [the German government] intend to begin unrestricted submarine warfare. . . . We shall endeavor [try] in spite of this to keep the United States neutral. In the event of this not succeeding, we make Mexico a proposal of alliance. . . . Inform the President [of Mexico] . . . most secretly as soon as the outbreak of war with the United States is certain."**

When this note was made public, many Americans called for war against Germany.

In February and March the number of merchant ships sunk by German U-boats increased steadily. Against this dark background the president took the oath of office for his second term. Outraged by the continued German submarine attacks, on April 2, 1917, he asked Congress to declare war. The reason, he said, was to make a just and lasting peace possible. "The world," he added, "must be made safe for democracy."

IF NOT BY FAIR MEANS, THEN—

This political cartoon shows the German kaiser plotting against the United States by offering an alliance to Mexico. This plan, revealed by the Zimmerman Note, was the final straw that drove many Americans to support entering the war against Germany.

Section 2 Review

• Glossary

IDENTIFY and explain the significance of the following: U-boats, *Lusitania*, *Sussex* pledge, Zimmerman Note

REVIEWING FOR DETAILS

1. What tactics did the British and Germans use in the Atlantic?
2. What effect did World War I have on the U.S. presidential election campaign of 1916?
3. How was the United States drawn into the war?

REVIEWING FOR UNDERSTANDING

4. **Writing Mastery:** *Describing* Imagine that you are a German U-boat captain in 1917. Write a typical day's entry in your ship's log as you cruise in the Atlantic.
5. **Critical Thinking:** *Determining the Strength of an Argument* Was Germany's use of unrestricted submarine warfare its best hope for victory? Explain your answer.

Section 3
ON THE HOME FRONT

Multimedia Connections

Explore these related topics and materials on the CD–ROM to enrich your understanding of this section:

 Profiles

- Oliver Wendell Holmes

 Biographies

- Bernard Baruch

 Media Bank

- Labor Unions Against the War

 Readings

- The Migration North

 Glossary

- propaganda
- American Federation of Labor

A mericans from all walks of life joined the war effort. Mary Carolyn Davies, who was from a poor neighborhood in New York City, rolled bandages alongside a wealthy woman from Fifth Avenue. Before the war they would have had little in common. Now they found themselves united by the star-shaped pins they wore to indicate that they had a loved one in the war. "We're sisters," Davies wrote, "while the danger lasts."

As you read this section you will find out:

▶ **How the United States raised troops.**

▶ **How the U.S. government organized to distribute goods and food.**

▶ **What groups benefited from wartime labor needs.**

Mobilizing an Army

When the United States declared war on Germany, thousands of young men volunteered for military service. Volunteers alone were not enough, however. In order to raise the huge force that the United States needed to fight in Europe, Congress passed a draft law, the **Selective Service Act** of 1917. This law required all men aged 21 to 30 (later changed to 18 to 45) to register with local draft boards, who then decided which of them would go to war. Some 24 million American men registered before the end of the war. About 2.8 million of the 4.8 million American men who served in the war were draftees.

The Selective Service System drafted men of all races, but soldiers were still segregated. Many African Americans hoped that by fighting to "make the world safe for democracy"

Many civilians aided the war effort, such as this nurse, who helps a soldier from Senegal write a thank-you letter to the American Red Cross. He is writing with the use of new artificial limbs after losing both of his arms in combat.

they would be able to gain fairer treatment at home. Most of the nearly 370,000 African Americans who served in the war were given more opportunities than those who had served during the Spanish-American War. About 1,400 became officers. Emmett J. Scott of the Tuskegee Institute was appointed an assistant to the secretary of war.

Although women were not drafted under the Selective Service Act, many served the war effort as army or navy nurses, clerks, switchboard operators, and ambulance drivers. Juliet Goodrich explained why she volunteered:

> **"I had always been strongly pro-ally, believing that Germany represented the negation of those principles of freedom and democracy. . . . Now with my own country fighting for Liberty, I felt that I had a right, a duty indeed, to take a more direct part in the struggle."**

Overall, some 25,000 American women served in Europe. Many others did volunteer work in hospitals and for such organizations as the Red Cross.

Not all Americans were eager to serve in the war, however. As during the Civil War, some opposed the draft as an intrusion on civil liberties. To encourage support for the war, the government launched a massive media campaign and tried to limit the activities of groups that opposed the war.

• **Opposing the War**

Organizing Wartime America

Building an army and supplying it quickly was a huge task. Many changes had to be made in the way goods were manufactured and businesses were run.

The War Industries Board. The U.S. government took over the management of all the nation's railroads, in order to move the many goods that were needed in the war effort. Wilson appointed Secretary of the Treasury William G. McAdoo to run the entire railroad system. The president also established a **War Industries Board** to oversee the production and distribution of manufactured goods. The head of this board was Bernard Baruch, a millionaire stockbroker. Baruch was active in Democratic Party politics at a time when most wealthy stockbrokers were Republicans.

After Baruch took control of the board, the agency performed brilliantly. He organized industry as though it were one big factory. The board decided what was to be made and where the raw materials were to come from. The board also controlled the distribution of scarce resources and in some cases even set the price at which they were sold. The effort was successful in part because most producers were eager to cooperate with the board.

The Granger Collection, New York

ON THE JOB FOR VICTORY
UNITED STATES SHIPPING BOARD   EMERGENCY FLEET CORPORATION

American propaganda, such as this poster from the United States Shipping Board, helped encourage support for war industries.

BOYS and GIRLS!
You can Help your Uncle Sam Win the War

W.S.S.

Save your Quarters
BUY WAR SAVINGS STAMPS

The Granger Collection, New York

Americans of all ages were encouraged to help with the war effort, including buying stamps, which helped raise funds.

The Food Administration. Baruch's board had to provide for the needs of the home front as well as those of the Allied nations. Great Britain in particular depended on American products, such as wheat and meat, for its survival. As head of the **Food Administration**, it was Herbert Hoover's job to make sure that enough food was produced and that it was distributed fairly. Hoover set out both to increase food production and to reduce domestic consumption. At the same time, it was important to keep prices from skyrocketing.

Hoover had little trouble increasing production. The demand for crops was enormous. American farmers raised 620 million bushels of wheat in 1917 and 904 million bushels in 1918.

Getting Americans to consume less proved to be more difficult. Hoover organized a vast campaign to convince the public of the need to conserve. Catchy slogans carried his message. "Food will win the war" was one of the best known.

Hoover also promoted "meatless Mondays" and "wheatless Wednesdays" to encourage the American public to cut down on eating meat and bread. President Wilson allowed sheep to graze on the White House lawn to set a good example. Hoover encouraged all American families to plant vegetable gardens, which he called "victory gardens." Hoover's rules, however, could not be easily enforced. He depended on voluntary cooperation. He made it clear that patriotic citizens were *expected* to obey the rules. Hoover was very proud that most Americans voluntarily obeyed these rules. This prevented the government from having to enforce rationing.

Labor in Wartime

Organizing the human resources of the nation was also complicated. During the war, the U.S. Employment Service directed millions of people to new jobs. The war provided many benefits to men and women working on the home front. Wages rose, and unskilled workers were able to get better jobs.

These women went to work in a munitions factory in Detroit, Michigan, to help with the war effort. War industries helped boost the economy and provide jobs for many people who previously had trouble finding employment.

Regulating labor. It was important to the war effort to try to prevent strikes from slowing down the production of vital goods. A **National War Labor Board** was set up to try to settle disputes between workers and their employers. This board also tried to make sure that workers were not fired for trying to organize unions. The board heard some 1,200 disputes between workers and their employers. In most instances the board ruled in favor of the workers. This support boosted interest in unions, which grew rapidly during the war. Most unions like the American Federation of Labor (AFL), which grew to about 3 million members by 1918, cooperated with the board.

New opportunities. The need for workers helped many people who had been discriminated against in the job market in the past. Thousands of women found jobs they could not have hoped to get before the war. They worked in such diverse occupations as truck driving, auto repair, bricklaying, and metalworking.

In all, some 1.5 million women held industrial jobs during the war. This led the leader of the National Women's Trade Union League to declare in 1917, "This is a woman's age! Women are coming into the labor [movement] on equal terms with men." Although this was an exaggeration, female workers did make important gains. Recognizing how necessary women had been to the war effort, in 1920 the Wilson administration established a women's bureau in the Department of Labor.

Moving north. Wartime job opportunities influenced many people—particularly southern African Americans and Hispanics—to move north. Thousands of descendants of slaves had already migrated from the South to northern cities before the war began.

Half a million more followed between 1914 and 1919. This mass movement of southern African Americans became known as the **Great Migration**.

Many northern black newspapers, such as the *Chicago Defender,* encouraged this movement. They noted that most northern newcomers could earn far more money in war plants than they could raising cotton or tobacco in the South. NAACP official Walter White advised southern planters, who were worried about losing their source of cheap

Young People In History
Scouting and the War Effort

World War I poster

During World War I, thousands of young Americans helped the war effort by selling war bonds—known as Liberty Bonds—rolling bandages, and collecting scrap materials. Two important youth groups that helped were the Boy Scouts and the Girl Scouts. During the war, Scouts were praised as good examples of young people who were prepared in times of crisis. Images of Scouts appeared on many government materials to promote support for the war.

As a result of their efforts, interest in scouting soared. The Girl Scouts received a particular boost. Before the war, many people had criticized the Girl Scouts for their military-style uniforms and for teaching girls skills usually reserved for boys. The Girl Scouts' efforts in the war ended many of these criticisms. As a result, membership in the Girl Scouts rose during the war years from about 5,000 to 50,000.

farm labor to the North, that they could stop the massive migration by granting equal rights to African Americans:

> "[The South] has the opportunity now to clean house and prevent further migration by wiping out the abuses which exist. . . . It remains to be seen whether the better element among the whites can (and will) gain the ascendancy [control] over the larger element."

Few southern planters heeded White's advice. As a result, the Great Migration continued. Hundreds of thousands more African Americans moved north in the decade after the war.

Mexican immigrants also benefited from the labor shortage in the United States. Beginning in 1910, thousands had crossed the border to escape the confusion of the Mexican Revolution. Many more came after World War I began. Most Mexican immigrants settled in the Southwest. Many worked in the cotton fields of Texas and Arizona or on farms in Colorado and California. Others became railroad laborers, construction workers, or miners.

Some immigrants settled in northern cities, attracted by jobs in war plants. The jobs were low paying, but unskilled workers could earn much more than they could in farming. By the end of the war, Mexican immigrant communities had sprung up in major northern cities, such as Chicago and Detroit.

Many Mexican immigrants like these refugees of the Mexican Revolution found jobs in the United States during and after World War I.

Section 3 Review

• Glossary

IDENTIFY and explain the significance of the following: Selective Service Act, War Industries Board, Bernard Baruch, Food Administration, Herbert Hoover, National War Labor Board, Great Migration

REVIEWING FOR DETAILS
1. How did the United States fill its military ranks during the war?
2. What wartime organizations were created to distribute goods and food?

REVIEWING FOR UNDERSTANDING
3. **Geographic Literacy** How did World War I affect African Americans?
4. **Writing Mastery:** *Describing* Write a short newspaper article describing how various groups have benefited from wartime labor needs.
5. **Critical Thinking:** *Drawing Conclusions* How do you think the Great Migration affected the lives of those who migrated?

Section 4

WINNING THE WAR

In a letter home, U.S. soldier E. J. Canright tried to describe the feeling of being at the western front. "Try and picture the very worst thunderstorm you have ever heard. Then multiply it by about 10,000 . . . ," he wrote. "The roar and crash of the guns just seems to tear the air to pieces, and explosions shake the ground." Despite the dangers, he assured his family that he was glad to be "taking part in this—one of the greatest battles the world has ever known."

As you read this section you will find out:

▶ **What new weapons were used in World War I.**

▶ **How new technology affected casualty rates in the war.**

▶ **What battles finally ended the stalemate and led to peace.**

"Over There"

President Wilson put General John J. Pershing in command of the **American Expeditionary Force** (AEF) that would fight in Europe. The first units of the AEF reached France during the summer of 1917, but it took many months before enough Americans were in position to affect the outcome of the war.

The American troops who arrived at the front were shocked at the conditions. Soldiers spent weeks in muddy trenches. One soldier, Norman Roberts, described his introduction to the fighting:

"Started for the front at 6 P.M. Raining and wind blowing. Very cold. All boys wet to the skin. . . . No one allowed to talk. . . . [We] finally found the trench which we had been allotted [assigned]. Some mud. Over

Wounded British soldiers walk back to safety alongside a German prisoner after a harsh battle.

Weapons of War

World War I was a new experience even for U.S. veterans of previous wars. After nearly four years of fighting, the war had become more and more mechanized. The British and French were the first to use tanks. The first tanks were tractorlike vehicles—slow, clumsy, and unreliable, but they protected advancing troops as they moved toward the enemy.

Another new weapon was poison gas. The Germans used gas first, but the Allies soon copied them. Gas was a horrible weapon, choking and blinding its victims. It could also prove dangerous for those who released it. If the wind shifted, it might blow back on them.

Airplanes were used increasingly as the war progressed. Most planes were used to locate enemy positions and to signal artillery units where their shells were hitting so they could aim more effectively. Some planes were capable of dropping bombs but none were powerful enough to carry heavy loads of bombs for great distances.

the knees. . . . Oh, what a morning. Machine gun bullets flying past you as the wind. Whistling as a bird going [by]. Dead and wounded all around you. Comrades falling directly in front and you not allowed to assist them. The command *onward*. Every minute looking for the next to be gone to the great beyond."

The Allies' problems were soon compounded when Russia, caught up in a revolution, pulled out of the war in January 1918. In March the Germans launched a tremendous attack at the section of the western front closest to Paris. With the help of thousands of veterans transferred from the eastern front after the Russians left the war, the Germans advanced as far as Château-Thierry, a town northeast of Paris. There, in June 1918, Americans entered into battle to reinforce French troops. The German advance was stopped. The number of Americans in the trenches increased daily.

Control of the skies was important. There were many deadly air battles, known as **dogfights**, between Allied and German pilots. In this huge war of faceless fighters, pilots were often heroes. Those pilots who shot down many enemy planes were known as **aces**. Paul-René Fonck, a French ace, shot down 75 enemy planes.

The most famous of the German aces was Baron Manfred von Richthofen,

The fierce weapons and unsanitary conditions in World War I left many soldiers who survived with severe injuries. This American soldier, who lost a leg during the war, talks to a civilian observing a postwar parade.

who claimed 80 "kills." Richthofen was known as the "Red Baron" for the color of his plane. He was killed in action in 1918. Captain Edward "Eddie" Rickenbacker was the leading American ace. He was awarded a Medal of Honor after shooting down 26 German planes.

By far the deadliest weapons were still artillery and machine guns. By 1917 each side had tens of thousands of cannons ranged behind the lines. To prepare for one offensive, the French fired 6 million shells into an area only 20 miles long. The number of machine guns increased even more rapidly.

The tremendous advances in weapons technology greatly increased the war's deadliness. Red Cross nurse Katrina Herzer described the effects of such weapons on her wounded patients at the eastern front:

> **"Hospital trains brought them filthy, hungry, exhausted to us. Many of them had their faces blown away; pus flowed down their chests. . . . Hideous mutilation was the rule, not the exception."**

U.S. Navy nurse Mary Elderkins put it this way: "I don't believe one of us had ever imagined men could be so absolutely 'shot to pieces.'"

Final Battles and Armistice

None of these deadly weapons gave either side enough advantage to end the long strug-

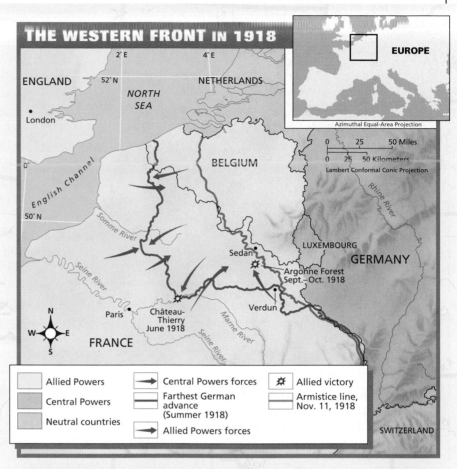

THE WESTERN FRONT IN 1918

Map legend:
- Allied Powers
- Central Powers
- Neutral countries
- → Central Powers forces
- ▬ Farthest German advance (Summer 1918)
- → Allied Powers forces
- ✳ Allied victory
- ▬ Armistice line, Nov. 11, 1918

Locations shown: England, London, North Sea, Netherlands, Belgium, Luxembourg, Germany, Rhine River, Somme River, Seine River, Sedan, Argonne Forest Sept.–Oct. 1918, Verdun, Marne River, Château-Thierry June 1918, Paris, France, Switzerland, English Channel

Learning from Maps.
In early and mid-1918, German forces pushed into France.

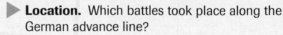 **Location.** Which battles took place along the German advance line?

• Maps

gle quickly. Throughout June and July of 1918, the fighting continued with little movement in either direction.

This stalemate finally ended in mid-September when U.S. and French forces pushed the Germans back at the desperate **Battle of the Argonne Forest**. The Argonne was a rocky, hilly region crisscrossed by streams and blasted by years of constant shelling. Between September 26 and mid-October, U.S. forces struggled through this wilderness. German artillery rained powerful explosives upon them from the hills. Beyond the Argonne the Allies continued to advance against the retreating German army.

Deaths in World War I

Source: *Encyclopedia of World History.*

The Human Costs. In all, some 10 million people died in World War I. Of the major powers shown here, which one suffered the most deaths? The least?

In early November U.S. troops finally broke through the German defenses. They then advanced toward Sedan, a city near the Belgian border. All along the front, French and British armies were also driving the Germans back, rapidly gaining ground. On November 11, 1918, the Germans gave up the hopeless fight. They signed an **armistice**, or cease-fire.

The United States fought in World War I less than a year and a half, yet some 112,000 Americans died during the conflict. More than 200,000 others were wounded. However, American war losses were much smaller than those of any of the other major warring nations, who had been fighting for more than four years. Even so, during the last few months the United States bore a great deal of the fighting and suffered enormous casualties.

Section 4 Review

• Glossary

IDENTIFY and explain the significance of the following: American Expeditionary Force, dogfights, aces, Manfred von Richthofen, Edward "Eddie" Rickenbacker, Battle of the Argonne Forest, armistice

LOCATE and explain the importance of the following: Paris, Château-Thierry

• Gazetteer

REVIEWING FOR DETAILS
1. What new weapons did the armies use in World War I?
2. How did advances in technology affect wartime casualties?

REVIEWING FOR UNDERSTANDING
3. **Geographic Literacy** Which battles finally led to an armistice, and how were these battles different from earlier fighting on the western front?
4. **Writing Mastery:** *Describing* Imagine that you are a soldier on the western front in the summer of 1918. Write a letter home to your family describing your daily life, including your thoughts about the future course of the war.
5. **Critical Thinking:** *Drawing Conclusions* What effect do you think the new weapons had on civilians during World War I?

Section 5

THE SEARCH FOR PEACE

Multimedia Connections

Explore these related topics and materials on the CD–ROM to enrich your understanding of this section:

 Media Bank

- League of Nations
- Events of WWI
- Influenza Epidemic

 Gazetteer

- Poland
- Czechoslovakia

 Glossary

- arbitration

 Readings

- Wilson's Fourteen Points

 Profiles

- Henry Cabot Lodge

After the signing of the armistice, Woodrow Wilson became a world hero. In January 1918 he had delivered a speech to Congress describing his plans for peace. "The world . . . [must] be made safe for every peace-loving nation," he said. Millions of people believed that Wilson's idealism, backed by the power of the United States, would bring about basic changes in international relations. A new era of worldwide peace and prosperity seemed about to begin.

As you read this section you will find out:

▶ **What ideas Wilson's Fourteen Points contained.**

▶ **What was included in the Treaty of Versailles.**

▶ **Why the treaty was not ratified by the United States.**

Wilson's Fourteen Points

President Wilson began preparing for peace even before the United States entered the war. He believed that to achieve "peace without victory" the terms must not be so hard on the Central Powers that they caused those countries to begin planning another war to regain what they had lost. Unless all the nations are treated fairly, he argued, *none* can count on being treated fairly. In this respect "all the peoples of the world are in effect partners," said Wilson.

The president listed **Fourteen Points** that he said made up "the only possible program" for peace. One of Wilson's points dealt with the future of European colonies overseas. Several points were more like ideals than practical proposals. These called for freedom of the seas, disarmament, and the lowering of national protective tariffs.

Most of Wilson's other points concerned redrawing the boundaries of European nations and ensuring the right of **self-determination**. This meant that the people of every region should be able to decide for themselves what nation they belonged to.

Wilson believed that the final point was the most important. It called for the creation of an "association of nations." The purpose of this international organization would be to guarantee the independence and the territory of all nations "great and small . . . alike." This **League of Nations**, as it was soon named, would be a kind of international congress that would settle disputes between nations. When necessary, the members of the League would use force against any nation that defied its rulings.

The Versailles Peace Conference

In January 1919, representatives of the victorious Allies gathered at the Palace of Versailles, outside Paris, to write a formal treaty of peace. President Wilson headed the U.S. delegation himself. The chief British representative was Prime Minister David Lloyd George. The French premier, Georges Clemenceau [kle-mahn-soh], and the Italian prime minister, Vittorio Orlando, completed the Council of Four, popularly called the **Big Four**.

Wilson had a difficult time persuading the other leaders to accept his idea of "peace without

victory." Clemenceau wanted to make Germany pay the entire cost of the war. France in particular had suffered terribly in the war. Much of the fighting had taken place on French soil. The northern part of the country was devastated. In addition, almost 1.4 million French soldiers—out of the country's total population of about 40 million people—had been killed.

Lloyd George and Orlando also put the interests of their own nations first. Wilson was forced to agree to a clause in the treaty stating that Germany alone had caused the war. He even accepted a clause making Germany pay "for all damage done to the civilian population of the Allies and their property."

The calculation of these payments, called **reparations**, was so greatly debated that the Allies were not able to decide on an actual amount. They made the Germans sign a "blank check," thus agreeing to pay whatever the victors finally demanded. The amount eventually named was $33 billion, which was more than the Germans could pay. This was certainly not the "peace without victory" Wilson had promised.

The final **Treaty of Versailles** did, however, embrace some of the goals Wilson had aimed for in his Fourteen Points speech. Poland and Czechoslovakia became new countries based on the principle of self-determination. Moreover, the new map of Europe probably placed continent under the flag of their choice than had ever been done before. The treaty included what Wilson considered his single most important objective—the covenant of the League of Nations. All League members were required to protect one another's territories against attack. Serious disputes between members were to be submitted to arbitration.

President Wilson waves at supporters after returning from a trip to Europe following the armistice.

FPG International Corp.

Nations that did not obey League decisions could be punished by penalties. These could take the form of a ban on trade with the violating country or even the use of military force.

The creation of the League of Nations was Woodrow Wilson's proudest accomplishment. He believed that its founding marked the beginning of an era of permanent world peace. He knew that the Treaty of Versailles was not the true "peace without victory" that he had hoped for. Yet he was absolutely certain that the League would be able to deal with the problems the treaty had created. In July 1919 Wilson submitted the treaty to the U.S. Senate.

Republican Opponents

Wilson had counted on the Democrats still being in control of the Senate in 1919. However, the Republicans had won majorities in both the House and the Senate in the 1918 congressional elections. After the election, Wilson made matters worse for himself by not including any Republican senators among the peace delegation at Versailles.

Wilson now needed the support of a large number of Republican senators to get the two-thirds majority necessary to approve the Versailles Treaty. The president seemed to assume that the peace treaty would be so

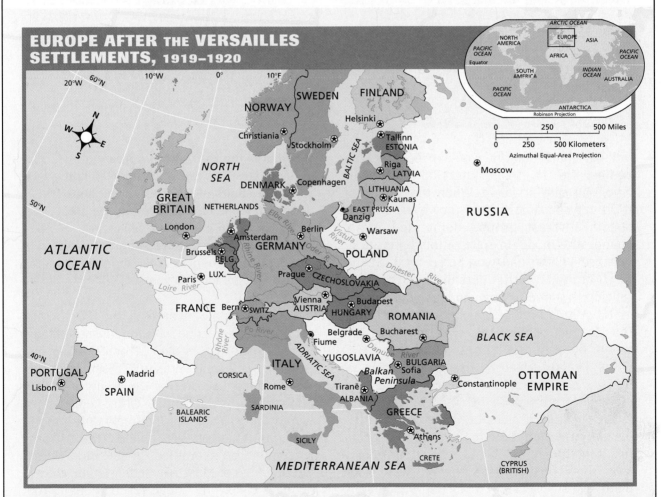

EUROPE AFTER THE VERSAILLES SETTLEMENTS, 1919–1920

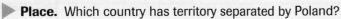

Learning from Maps. The Treaty of Versailles reflected the principle of self-determination and created several new countries. Many of these countries, such as Poland, were located in eastern Europe.

▶ **Place.** Which country has territory separated by Poland?

• **Maps**

World leaders meet to work out the details of the Treaty of Versailles. Although Woodrow Wilson hoped to play a large role in shaping the treaty, the leaders of European countries that had suffered the most during the war rejected many of his suggestions.

popular that senators would not dare vote against it. "The Senate must take its medicine," he said privately. When the details of the treaty became known, however, various special-interest groups demanded many changes be made. In spite of this opposition, because Wilson had worked so hard on the negotiations of the Versailles Treaty, he refused to agree to any changes whatsoever.

The most important criticism involved the League of Nations. The United States would be only one among many members. If the League voted to use force against a nation, many people wondered, would U.S. troops be forced to go into battle? The U.S. Constitution gives Congress the right to declare war. Many congressional leaders worried that the new League of Nations might take this constitutional power away from them. Old suspicions of tricky European diplomats and entangling foreign affairs began to reappear. Senator William Borah, a leading opponent of the League of Nations, stated the problem this way:

"What is the result of this Treaty of Versailles? We are in the middle of all of the affairs of Europe. . . . We have surrendered, once and for all, the great policy of 'no entangling alliances' [advised by George Washington] upon which the strength of this Republic has been based for 150 years."

In the Senate nearly all the Democrats supported the League without question. Many Republican senators also favored joining the League. Some, known as mild reservationists, were willing to vote for the treaty if a few minor changes were made. Other Republicans were willing to vote for the treaty only if more important changes were made. These strong reservationists were led by Senator Henry Cabot Lodge of Massachusetts. He introduced changes called the Lodge reservations to the treaty. The most important of these stated that U.S. armed forces could not be sent into action by the League of Nations until Congress gave its approval.

If Wilson had been willing to accept the Lodge reservations, the Versailles Treaty might have been approved easily. Only a small group of senators, known as the irreconcilables, refused to vote for it on any terms. The president probably could have received the two-thirds vote needed for approval by making some small compromises with the mild reservationists alone. Wilson, however, refused to budge. He felt that he could not compromise on the treaty terms any more than he already had at the negotiations.

Final Defeat

Wilson set out on a long tour of the United States in early September 1919 to try to persuade people to support the League. At the beginning of the tour, he stated what he felt was at the heart of the matter:

"**If we do not end wars, we are unfaithful to the loving hearts who suffered in this war. . . . The League of Nations is the only thing that can prevent another dreadful catastrophe [disaster] and fulfill our promises.**"

While he was trying to rally support for the League, the president suffered a serious stroke. His left side was partially paralyzed. For weeks, Wilson was isolated in the White House.

On November 19, 1919, the treaty, with the Lodge reservations attached, came to a vote in the Senate. It was defeated primarily by Democratic votes. Then the treaty was voted on without reservations. This time the Republicans defeated it. The following March, after further debate, the Senate again voted on the treaty with reservations. For the third and final time the treaty was rejected.

President Wilson's League of Nations was unpopular with many members of Congress.

The Granger Collection, New York

Section 5 Review

• Glossary

• Time Line

IDENTIFY and explain the significance of the following: Fourteen Points, self-determination, League of Nations, Big Four, reparations, Treaty of Versailles, Henry Cabot Lodge

REVIEWING FOR DETAILS
1. What were the main ideas of Wilson's Fourteen Points?
2. What were the main terms of the Treaty of Versailles?
3. Why was the Treaty of Versailles rejected by the U.S. Senate?

REVIEWING FOR UNDERSTANDING
4. **Writing Mastery:** *Describing* Imagine that you are one of the American delegates to the Versailles Conference. Write a memo to your supervisor describing the debates among the Allies over the proposed settlement.
5. **Critical Thinking:** *Recognizing Point of View* Do you think the Allies were justified in forcing Germany to accept sole responsibility for the outbreak of the war? Explain your answer.

u n i t **8**

*G*OOD TIMES AND WORLD CRISES (1919–1945)

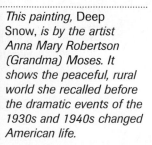

This painting, Deep Snow, *is by the artist Anna Mary Robertson (Grandma) Moses. It shows the peaceful, rural world she recalled before the dramatic events of the 1930s and 1940s changed American life.*

Grandma Moses: *Deep Snow* Copyright © 1998, Grandma Moses Properties Co., New York. Photo: Edward Owen/Art Resource, NY

LINKING PAST TO PRESENT
History Within a Lifetime

Ever since she was a young girl Kathy has been listening to her grandfather talk about his experiences during his lifetime, which has spanned more than 90 years. In that time he has lived through a century of amazing transitions for the United States. Today he passes on stories of those experiences to his grandchildren.

In 1906 Kathy's grandfather was born to a family of homesteaders. They traveled long distances by covered wagon. As a boy he earned extra money by hunting for animal furs. As a young man in the 1930s, he faced economic disaster along with the rest of the country. Unable to find work in his profession as a mining engineer, he traveled as far as Alaska, Chile, and the Philippine Islands in search of employment.

In the 1940s he was still in the Philippines when world war broke out. He spent most of that time as a civilian prisoner of war. He tells his granddaughter stories of the daily struggles and of the encounters with the enemy he had during his imprisonment.

As Kathy's grandfather passes along these stories to his grandchildren, they can only imagine what life was like in the first half of the 1900s. Although they live in the same country, it is as if he is describing an entirely different world.

As you read this unit, you will learn about the era that Kathy's grandfather is describing—one that saw devastating events both at home and abroad. Through economic turmoil and world war, the generation you will learn about grew up in a time of extreme uncertainty about the future.

Almost no one in the country was untouched by the hardships. Out of the period emerged a changed society with very different ideas about the role of the American government in daily life and international affairs.

These teenagers are getting a tour of military airplanes used during World War II from a man who lived during the era.

CHAPTER 21

A Decade of Change
(1919–1929)

THEMES IN AMERICAN HISTORY

Technology and Society:
How might new technology change people's lives?

Economic Development:
What might governments do to help economic growth?

Cultural Diversity:
How might ethnic groups respond to discrimination?

 • Video Opener

 • Skill Builder

*I*n the 1920s America's economy was booming. Many people thought the good times would continue. Others believed the economy was seriously flawed. Supreme Court justice Louis D. Brandeis wondered:

"I can't understand where all this . . . money comes from. We are certainly not earning it as a nation. I think we must be exploiting [taking advantage of] about 80 percent of Americans, for the benefit of the other 20 percent."

image above: *Howard Thain's* The Great White Way

Section 1

RETURNING TO "NORMALCY"

Multimedia Connections

Explore these related topics and materials on the CD–ROM to enrich your understanding of this section:

 Media Bank

- Workforce, 1910, 1920, 1930
- Women Voting
- Harding Campaigning
- Sacco and Vanzetti Protest

 Profiles

Warren Harding

 Atlas

- Influenza and Pneumonia

 Readings

- Vanzetti's Last Statement

Charlotte Woodward was a young working woman when she went to the Seneca Falls Convention in 1848. There Woodward listened to speakers discuss women's issues, including the fight for the right to vote. It would be more than 70 years, however, before Woodward could cast her ballot in a presidential election. Of the 26 million American women who could vote in 1920, Woodward, age 91, was the only living signer of the Declaration of Sentiments.

As you read this section you will find out:

▶ **How postwar economics affected workers in the United States.**

▶ **How a fear of radicals and communism led to the Red Scare.**

▶ **What foreign policy advances the United States made during the 1920s.**

The Economics of Peace

The shift from war to peace was difficult for American industry. When the government no longer needed supplies for World War I, many plants shut down temporarily or cut back on production. Hundreds of thousands of wage earners lost their jobs. Of the more than 4 million soldiers returning to civilian life, many had a hard time finding work.

Many women had entered the workforce as part of the war effort. After the war, to make room for returning veterans, employers and some unions forced many women to quit their jobs. Some women took their cases to court. According to one government report, women questioned:

"the right of a group of men to demand the discharge [firing] of women who had been

The lives of many women changed in the 1920s. For some, it meant voting for the first time; for others, it meant working away from home. Women's fashion also changed. Women shortened their skirts and bobbed their hair, like these typists.

in troops to restore order in the city. Coolidge's stand that "there is no right to strike against the public safety by anybody, anywhere, any time" made him a national hero.

The Red Scare

engaged [employed] in good faith, had performed their work in a satisfactory manner, and who had fulfilled all of the items of their contract."

These women claimed that laws limiting the employment of women were discriminatory. They hoped to gain more equal rights through their fight.

Those workers who did hold jobs, both men and women, found that their wages bought them less and less as the cost of living rose. Many workers faced layoffs, wage cuts, and discrimination against union members. Workers protested, and a wave of strikes spread throughout the country.

A general strike paralyzed Seattle when thousands of local workers walked off their jobs. In Boston even the police went on strike. With the streets of Boston unprotected, looters began breaking into stores. The governor of Massachusetts, Calvin Coolidge, finally called

Many people believed the strikes were a warning sign that **Communists** were trying to start a revolution in the United States. Communists wanted to overthrow the capitalist economic system and replace it with a society where all individuals shared wealth equally, and where all private ownership of property was abolished. There were only about 70,000 Communists, called Reds, in the United States. However, Americans were well aware that a tiny group of Communists, called Bolsheviks, had taken over much of Russia in 1917.

In the United States, Communists tried to recruit support among workers. **Anarchists**, who wanted all governments abolished, also tried to stir up workers. Then a series of bombings by terrorists took place. To this day, no one knows who was responsible for most of the bombings. Most people, however, blamed the Reds, by which many meant Communists and anarchists, as well as socialists. A widespread **Red Scare** swept over America.

● **Labor in the 1920s**

These Chicago steelworkers were among the thousands of workers who went on strike in 1919. Strikes continued throughout the 1920s.

The Palmer raids. President Wilson's attorney general, A. Mitchell Palmer, feared that there was a massive communist plot to overthrow the federal government:

> **"Like a prairie-fire, the blaze of revolution was sweeping over every American institution of law and order . . . eating its way into the homes of the American workman, its sharp tongues of revolutionary heat were licking the altars of the churches, leaping in the belfry of the school bell, crawling into the sacred corners of American homes, . . . burning up the foundations of society."**

Palmer ordered raids on the headquarters of suspected radical groups. These **Palmer raids** were often conducted without search warrants. The government took many suspected Communists and anarchists into custody, holding them for weeks without filing formal charges. Others were forced to leave the country.

In 1920 Palmer warned that a communist-led revolution would take place on May 1, the communist Labor Day. When May 1 passed quietly, Americans realized that the danger of a revolution had been exaggerated.

Sacco and Vanzetti. Two Italian male anarchists, Nicola Sacco and Bartolomeo Vanzetti, found, however, that the hostility toward immigrants and radicals remained. In April 1920 two men killed a paymaster and a guard in a robbery of a shoe factory in Massachusetts. Shortly thereafter, authorities charged Sacco and Vanzetti with the crime. In 1921 they were convicted of murder despite there being little physical evidence linking them to the crime.

People in the United States and in other countries protested against the unfair trial. Noted lawyer Felix Frankfurter even helped establish the **American Civil Liberties Union**

(ACLU) to fight for the two men. In August 1927, however, Sacco and Vanzetti were electrocuted. Fifty years later, Massachusetts governor Michael Dukakis reviewed the case and declared that "any . . . disgrace should be forever removed from their names."

The Election of 1920

Both isolation from international events and **xenophobia**—the dislike and fear of foreigners—were aspects of a larger U.S. postwar reaction. Wilson had hoped that the 1920 presidential election would prove that Americans wanted to join the League of Nations. The Democratic candidate, Governor James M. Cox of Ohio, and his running mate, Franklin D.

Global Connections
The Women's Vote

The United States was not the first country to grant women the right to vote. In fact, women in many parts of the world gained the right to vote before American women did in 1920. Women in New Zealand voted for the first time in 1893, and Australian women voted in 1902. Between the years 1913 and 1919, women in 17 European countries voted in national elections.

As a significant percentage of the population, women greatly increased the number of eligible voters. For example, when women first voted in Britain in 1918, they added 8.5 million voters, or 40 percent of all those eligible. In exercising their new political power, women in the 1920s influenced not only the selection of national leaders but also the passage of legislation. In addition to becoming voters, women became elected officials. In 1919, German women voted for the first time and also ran for public office. They gained 41 of the 423 seats in the Reichstag, Germany's national assembly, and won more than 1,500 state and local offices.

Roosevelt, a distant cousin of Theodore Roosevelt, campaigned on a platform that called for joining the League.

The Republicans ran Ohio senator Warren G. Harding for president and Governor Calvin Coolidge of Massachusetts for vice president. Harding was skilled at avoiding controversial questions. He refused to take a clear position on the League of Nations. Instead, he urged Americans to vote for a "return to normalcy," meaning that the nation should turn away from Europe and concentrate on domestic issues. The new Nineteenth Amendment, which gave women the right to vote in national elections, caused a large voter turnout. When the votes were counted, Harding had won by a huge majority.

Foreign Policy in the 1920s

After the war, America had become the leading industrial and financial power in the world. Other nations owed the United States more than $10 billion for huge wartime loans.

The presidents of the 1920s tried to follow a middle road between the narrow view of isolationism and the broader view of internationalism. In 1921 Harding invited delegates from nine

The Philadelphia Inquirer *ran this Red Scare editorial cartoon in 1919.*

European and Asian nations to Washington, D.C., to discuss how to avoid conflict in East Asia. The delegates drafted several treaties at this **Washington Conference**. The most important was the **Five-Power Naval Treaty**, which limited the size of navies.

Harding insisted that the Washington Conference had not committed the United States "to any kind of alliance, entanglement, or involvement." This satisfied most Americans. They could accept the treaties and still believe that they could remain isolated from foreign commitments.

Section 1 Review

• Glossary

IDENTIFY and explain the significance of the following: Communists, anarchists, Red Scare, A. Mitchell Palmer, Palmer raids, Sacco and Vanzetti, American Civil Liberties Union, xenophobia, Warren G. Harding, Washington Conference, Five-Power Naval Treaty

REVIEWING FOR DETAILS

1. What problems did workers in the United States face after World War I?
2. What were the causes and effects of the Red Scare?
3. What role did the United States play in foreign affairs during the 1920s?

REVIEWING FOR UNDERSTANDING

4. **Writing Mastery:** *Persuading* Write a letter to a newspaper to convince others that the government should or should not continue the Palmer raids.
5. **Critical Thinking:** *Synthesizing Information* How did the actions of A. Mitchell Palmer and the Sacco and Vanzetti case bring up issues about American civil rights? What events raise similar issues today?

Section 2
POLITICS AND PROSPERITY

Multimedia Connections

Explore these related topics and materials on the CD–ROM to enrich your understanding of this section:

 Profiles

- Calvin Coolidge
- Henry Ford

 Media Bank

- Assembly Line
- Model T Ford
- 1920s Politics

 Readings

- Women in the 1920s

enry Ford knew he could build cars. His "999" racing car proved it. Yet he wanted cars to be more than a symbol of wealth or a racing machine. He wanted to create a car "so low in price that no man making a good salary will be unable to own one." To achieve his dream, Ford formed his own company with $100,000. In a small factory outside of Detroit, workers began putting together a simple but inexpensive car. Many people predicted that Ford would go bankrupt, but he proved them wrong.

As you read this section you will find out:

▶ **How scandals affected the administration of Warren G. Harding.**

▶ **How Presidents Harding and Coolidge encouraged business and prosperity.**

▶ **How the automobile affected America.**

Harding and Coolidge

Warren G. Harding was friendly, good-looking, firm jawed, and silver haired, but he was not an energetic or creative leader. He also carelessly appointed people to important public offices. Some people he chose were incompetent, others were clearly dishonest. His friends from Ohio, known as the **Ohio Gang**, used their connections to him for their own gain.

A series of government scandals was discovered after Harding died suddenly in 1923. Various members of his administration had stolen money intended for a veterans' hospital, mishandled government property, and accepted bribes.

The Teapot Dome scandal. The worst corruption case, the **Teapot Dome scandal**, involved Albert Fall, Harding's secretary of the

Clifford. K. Berryman's political cartoon (c.1922) shows the Teapot Dome scandal ready to roll over the fleeing Washington politicians.

interior. Fall had leased government-owned land containing rich deposits of oil to private companies. This leased land included the Elk Hills reserve in California and the Teapot Dome reserve in Wyoming. In return, the oil companies gave Fall bribes amounting to $400,000. Fall was convicted of accepting bribes and put in prison.

Coolidge takes office. It was fortunate for the Republican Party that President Harding died before the scandals came to the public's attention. Calvin Coolidge, Harding's successor, had nothing to do with the scandals. Coolidge's personality was almost the exact opposite of Harding's. He was quiet and very private, and he hated to spend money. Coolidge was also thoroughly honest. His no-nonsense attitude made it much more difficult for the Democrats to take political advantage of the scandals that had occurred under Harding, and Coolidge easily won the 1924 election.

Business Growth in the 1920s

Harding had worked for conservative policies that favored big business. Reduction of the national debt, high protective tariffs on manufactured goods, and lower taxes on high incomes were standard Republican policies. Coolidge was even more conservative. He led one of the most business-minded administrations in U.S. history, believing that "the business of America is business," and that "the man who builds a factory builds a temple."

Coolidge's policies were designed to help business interests and large investors. Andrew Mellon, Coolidge's secretary of the treasury, sponsored a tax cut that favored the wealthy by reducing their taxes, in some cases by as much as 60 percent. To make up for the reduced revenues, the government raised tariffs and slightly increased excise taxes—taxes on goods produced and consumed inside a country. These higher tariffs were intended to help American businesses by cutting down on foreign competition. The slight increases in excise taxes on consumer goods and a new tax on automobiles were paid primarily by the middle class.

These federal government policies encouraged businesses to invest in larger factories and more efficient machines. Once industries completed the switch back to peacetime production, the U.S. economy prospered. Thus, this was generally a period of a prosperous economy. Americans experienced high employment and low inflation.

To many Americans, Coolidge's calm dignity and reputation for honesty was a welcome relief from the scandals that had shadowed Harding's presidency.

The Expansion of Industry

Many industries established before World War I expanded rapidly in the postwar boom. For example, telephone companies thrived as the number of telephones in use in the United States doubled between 1914 and 1930. Dial phones and improved switchboards sped up communication and cut costs.

Electric companies also prospered greatly. Electricity became an important source of power for industry. In addition, electricity became widely used in homes. By 1930 the United States was using more electricity than the rest of the world combined.

With almost two thirds of U.S. homes hooked up for electricity, a large electric appliance industry developed. Many families had electric vacuum cleaners, washing machines, and refrigerators.

The growth of other new industries was also very impressive. Chemical plants began turning out many more **synthetics**, artificial materials, such as rayon for clothing and Bakelite™, a hard plastic, for radio cases. Other new mass-produced products included such items as wristwatches, improved cameras, and glassware for cooking.

These goods were meeting consumer demands for new products. With a prospering economy, many American workers, both men and women, had more money to spend than ever before. Those who could not pay in cash could purchase products on the **installment plan**. This idea, first adapted by the auto industry, let customers make monthly payments, along with interest, on a product until it was paid for in full.

Companies were producing the latest technological wonders, and advertisers were there to spread the word. The advertising industry boomed. By 1929 it was nearly a $2 billion business. Ads were everywhere—on radio and billboards, and in newspapers and magazines. Many ads were aimed at women because, according to advertising experts in 1927:

> **"Whether married or getting pay for their work, women are the nation's purchasing agents. Woman is generally admitted to be directly responsible for four out of every five sales."**

Advertisers used psychology to convince people to buy their products. Ads advised and informed women about products such as beauty aids, electric appliances, and numerous other household goods.

The Granger Collection, New York

America was busy modernizing everything from transportation to industry in the 1920s. Perhaps one of the biggest changes that could be seen in a modern home was in its kitchen, where electricity and new appliances made cooking and cleaning a bit easier.

Many of these goods were purchased in the growing number of chain stores. For example, the A & P grocery chain expanded from 400 outlets in 1912 to 15,000 in 1932. Woolworth opened dozens of "five and ten" stores, which sold items for the price of a nickel or a dime. By the end of the decade, Americans were buying about 25 percent of their food and clothing in chain stores.

The Model T

In the 1920s many businesses bombarded Americans with not only a growing choice of household items but also advertisements for the ultimate consumer good—the automobile. The first gasoline-powered vehicles in the United States were built in the 1890s. When the United States entered World War I, the auto industry was producing well over 1 million cars a year. In the 1920s the industry turned out an average of more than 3 million cars a year.

Henry Ford. Many inventors and engineers contributed to the development of the automobile, but Henry Ford was the key American figure in this new industry. Ford grew up in rural Michigan, but he chose not to become a farmer. He had a talent for all kinds of mechanical projects. In the 1890s, while working in Detroit for the Edison Illuminating Company, he designed and built an automobile in his home workshop. A short time later he built a racing car—the "999," which set

Some Woolworth stores were very large, while others were more like a neighborhood corner shop. It was common for a store's manager and family to live on the floor above the shop.

several speed records. In 1903 he founded the Ford Motor Company.

The first American automobiles were very expensive and were mostly toys for the rich. Ford dreamed of producing cars so cheaply that ordinary people could own them:

> **"I will build a motor car for the great multitude. It will be large enough for the family but small enough for the individual to run and care for. It will be constructed of the best materials, by the best men to be hired, after the simplest designs that modern engineering can devise."**

In 1908 Ford achieved his goal with the **Model T**, popularly called the "Tin Lizzie." It sold for only $850. By 1925 Ford had reduced the car's cost to $290. A secondhand Model T still capable of good service sold for $25 to $50. For many Americans, owning a car became financially possible for the first time.

In 1921 this Model T had already been around for more than 10 years. Many Americans, however, were eager to try out a different type of automobile.

The Granger Collection, New York

The assembly line. With low costs and high volume, Ford captured over 50 percent of the American car market. Ford's secret was mass production achieved through the use of the moving **assembly line**. His cars were assembled on a conveyor belt, which moved past a line of workers. Each worker or team performed one fairly simple task. This method of production was highly efficient. As a result, in 1925 the Ford plant was producing one car every 10 seconds!

Ford also kept prices low by making the same basic model year after year. According to a joke of the day, you could have a Model T in any color you wanted, as long as you chose black.

Other automobile manufacturers, such as General Motors and Chrysler, copied Ford's assembly methods but made more expensive cars. In prosperous times, many customers were willing to pay more for larger and more comfortable cars than the Model T. In addition, wealthy customers wanted a car with a bit more personality, so car companies brought out new models in different styles and colors every year. General Motors offered an installment plan to help customers purchase these more expensive cars.

In 1927 Ford finally retired the Model T and brought out the Model A, available in a variety of colors. It was too late, however. By the end of the 1920s Ford was no longer the largest U.S. automobile manufacturer; General Motors had taken the lead.

The Automobile Revolution

The automobile created an economic boom. A huge rubber industry sprang up to produce tires, belts, and hoses for cars. Manufacturers of steel, glass, paint, and dozens of other products greatly increased their output as well.

The automobile also revolutionized the petroleum refining industry. Before World War I, the most important petroleum product was kerosene. By the 1920s, however, gasoline had passed kerosene in importance. In

The Modern Household

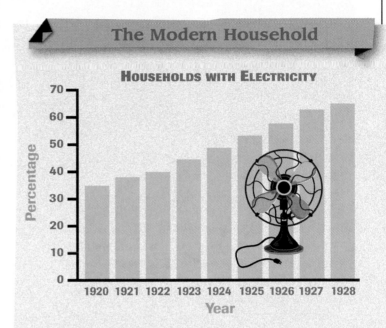

HOUSEHOLDS WITH ELECTRICITY

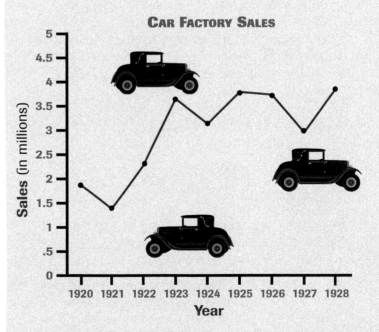

CAR FACTORY SALES

Source: *Historical Statistics of the United States*

A Better Standard of Living. Household electricity use and automobile ownership steadily increased in the 1920s. During what years did automobile sales decline in the 1920s?

The Granger Collection, New York

The automobile meant summer family vacations and weekends at the park. On Sunday afternoons, the streets were frequently jammed with people using their cars for a family outing.

1929 the United States was producing 1 billion barrels of petroleum products a year.

The automobile also affected road construction and tourism. By the end of the 1920s, ordinary cars could speed along at 50 to 60 miles per hour or more. Such speeds were impossible on uneven surfaces. Thus, hundreds of thousands of miles of smooth paved roads had to be built.

Companies manufactured an enormous amount of asphalt and concrete to surface the roads. Engineers designed and constructed new types of road-building machinery. This expanded road-building industry created thousands of new jobs.

Better roads meant more traveling—both for business and pleasure. Gasoline stations appeared alongside each new highway. Roadside restaurants opened side by side with motor hotels, more commonly known as motels.

Automobiles gave Americans the power to travel farther and faster. They could live in suburbs outside of cities, surrounded by trees and green fields, and drive daily to jobs in the cities. They could visit places hundreds of miles away on weekends or cover thousands of miles on a two-week summer vacation. The American automobile revolution was truly under way.

Section 2 Review

• **Glossary**

IDENTIFY and explain the significance of the following: Ohio Gang, Teapot Dome scandal, Calvin Coolidge, synthetics, installment plan, Henry Ford, Model T, assembly line

REVIEWING FOR DETAILS

1. What problems plagued the Harding administration?
2. How did the policies of Presidents Harding and Coolidge affect big business?

REVIEWING FOR UNDERSTANDING

3. **Geographic Literacy** How did the automobile change the American landscape in the 1920s?
4. **Writing Mastery:** *Describing* Write a short essay describing how the automobile industry affected American society.
5. **Critical Thinking:** *Drawing Conclusions* What might be some advantages and disadvantages of working on an assembly line?

Section 3

THE ROARING TWENTIES

Multimedia Connections

Explore these related topics and materials on the CD–ROM to enrich your understanding of this section:

 Biographies

• Zora Neale Hurston

 Readings

• Langston Hughes's Poetry

 Media Bank

• Jazz Age Music
• Langston Hughes
• Charlie Chaplin
• Art of the 1920s
• Countee Cullen

 Interactive Map

• The Harlem Renaissance

 Profiles

• Walter "Walt" Disney
• William Faulkner
• F. Scott Fitzgerald
• Langston Hughes
• Charles Lindbergh
• George "Babe" Ruth
• Sinclair Lewis

Every fall weekend, Americans jammed football stadiums to cheer for their favorite team. One Saturday afternoon in 1924 the excitement in the stands mounted when Harold "Red" Grange, the "Galloping Ghost" of the University of Illinois, came onto the field. Grange returned the University of Michigan's opening kickoff 95 yards for a touchdown. He scored three more touchdowns in the first quarter and another before the game ended. Illinois won 39–14.

As you read this section you will find out:

▶ **What new forms of entertainment became popular in the 1920s.**

▶ **How radio, movies, and other pastimes changed American life in the 1920s.**

▶ **How musicians and writers of the 1920s influenced American society.**

Mass Media

As industry expanded, it produced new wealth and provided more leisure time for millions of people. Many Americans sought new ways to enjoy life. The creators of movies and radio programs set out to entertain them.

Motion pictures. Both the motion picture as an art form and the film industry as a business came to maturity in the 1920s. Early movie theaters were often opened in vacant stores. Many of these "**nickelodeons**"—so called because the usual admission charge was five cents—showed jerky, badly lit scenes. Even so, by 1922, 40 million people a week were going to the movies. Soon, every large city had its movie palaces—elaborate theaters seating several thousand people. By 1930 weekly attendance was averaging 100 million.

The Granger Collection, New York

Clara Bow was a movie star by her early twenties. She starred mainly in roles about flappers, the modern young women of the 1920s. In Wings, *Bow played an ambulance driver in World War I.*

Movies became a leading national industry. The town of Hollywood, California, was the motion picture capital of the world. The city's warm, sunny climate was perfect for outdoor moviemaking.

Americans flocked to every kind of film: historical pictures, love stories, mysteries, and the most popular of all movies—westerns. Movie fans followed the careers and personal lives of their favorite film stars as though they were family members. Movies influenced the way people dressed and talked. Women styled their hair like Greta Garbo or Mary Pickford, and men tried to copy the fashions of Rudolph Valentino or Douglas Fairbanks. One young woman recalled that as a child, she would see a movie with friends and afterward they:

"immediately enacted the parts interesting us most. And for weeks I would attempt to do what that character would have done until we saw another movie and some other hero or heroine won us over."

For years the movies were silent. In theaters, pianists usually played appropriate mood music to accompany the action on the screen. Then in 1927 Warner Brothers, a major film company, released the first "**talkie**," a film that projected the actors' voices as well as their movements. This film was *The Jazz Singer,* starring Al Jolson. Jolson sang three songs and then told the film audience, "You ain't heard nothin' yet, folks." The next year Walt Disney made the first sound cartoon, *Steamboat Willie,* which introduced Mickey Mouse to the world.

Radio. Radio had an even more powerful hold on the public than film. Like the movies, it was one of the most remarkable technological advances of the time.

The first commercial radio station was KDKA in Pittsburgh, Pennsylvania. It was operated by the Westinghouse Electric Company. KDKA began broadcasting in 1920. Three years later there were more than 500 commercial stations. In 1926 the National Broadcasting Company (NBC) began combining local stations into a nationwide radio network. A year later the Columbia Broadcasting System (CBS) created a competing network. Thereafter, people all over the country could hear the same program at the same time.

Audiences grew in the millions. By 1924 more than 1 million American families had radios. In the single year of 1929, more than 4 million sets were sold. Large companies

● **Households with Radios**

Groups such as the 'Professor Ambrose Weems' and the Cuckooo Program players would gather in costume to perform their radio program.

The Granger Collection, New York

sprang up to manufacture radio sets and broadcasting equipment. Department stores devoted entire floors to selling radios. Repairing radios became an important business. Advertising increased as manufacturers tried to reach radio's large audiences by bombarding them with commercials. These advertisers paid large sums of money to broadcast their "sales pitches." Soap companies in particular sponsored dramatic series, which thus became known as soap operas.

Everyone could enjoy radio. People could listen to radio in the privacy of their homes without paying admission. It was also "live." What people heard was taking place at that very moment: a politician making a speech, the crack of the baseball bat, the roar of the crowd at a football game, the sound of a band or a symphony orchestra.

New Sports Heroes

In this new age of mass entertainment, audiences and the media were constantly searching for new heroes. Athletes were among the most popular national figures. Spectator sports boomed. The magic of radio created larger-than-life performers who attracted thousands to follow sporting events. The 1920s was truly the golden age of sports.

Babe Ruth

Football, boxing, tennis, and basketball drew large crowds across the country. Baseball was the national game. Its most famous hero was George Herman "Babe" Ruth, the "Sultan of Swat." He was a tremendous hitter. Ruth was originally a pitcher—and a very good one—but the Boston Red Sox quickly made him an outfielder so he could play every day. In 1920 Ruth joined the New York Yankees, where he continued his outstanding career. Year after year, he was baseball's home-run leader. In 1927 he hit 60, a record that stood for over 30 years. By the end of his career, Ruth had knocked out 714 home runs.

In 1927 Abe Saperstein created another sports legend when he formed what would become one of the most famous traveling basketball teams in the world. He recruited most of his players from Chicago's South Side, but he called his team of African American athletes the **Harlem Globetrotters**. The Globetrotters were magicians with the basketball and drew fans wherever they went.

History Makers

Charles Lindbergh, 1902–1974

The most popular American hero of the 1920s was not a movie star or sports star but a young

The Granger Collection, New York

pilot named Charles Lindbergh. He was the first aviator to fly nonstop across the Atlantic Ocean—and he did it alone. His historic flight began on May 20, 1927. At 7:55 A.M., he took off from a muddy, rain-drenched airfield near New York City in a tiny, one-engine plane, the *Spirit of St. Louis*. He was headed for France. Alone, hour after hour, Lindbergh guided his plane eastward across the Atlantic for some 3,600 miles. About 33 and a half hours after takeoff he landed safely at Le Bourget Airfield on the outskirts of Paris.

Lindbergh returned home a hero. New York City gave him a tremendous ticker-tape parade. The newspapers hailed him as "The Lone Eagle." He was also known as "Lucky Lindy," but his success was because of his courage and skill rather than luck.

In the 1920s the achievements of women were often the cover stories of magazines and newspapers. Tennis star Helen Wills is shown on the cover of this issue of Vanity Fair.

The Granger Collection, New York

Americans enjoyed many other sports as well. Tennis players William Tilden and Helen Wills won many national and international championships. Johnny Weissmuller held a dozen world swimming records. At the 1924 Olympics, swimmer Gertrude Ederle won several medals and set new world records. In 1926, at the age of 19, she became the first woman to swim across the English Channel, breaking the world record at the same time.

The Jazz Age

While thousands of Americans were following sports, others were listening to a new music called **jazz**. Black musicians, primarily in New Orleans, created jazz in the late 1800s. It grew out of the "blues"—music that reflected the

● Bessie Smith

● Louis Armstrong

Bessie Smith (left) and Louis Armstrong (right)

difficult lives of most African Americans. W. C. Handy of Alabama was considered to be the "father of the blues." Bessie Smith, a leading singer of the 1920s, became known as "the Empress of the Blues."

Blues music was popular, but it was jazz that came to symbolize the decade. The 1920s are sometimes called the Jazz Age because jazz was the music that many Americans listened to and danced to during that decade. Jazz spread from New Orleans to Chicago and New York, and then throughout most of the world. Louis "Satchmo" Armstrong was probably the most famous jazz musician of the day. He won fame as a trumpeter, a singer, and an ambassador of goodwill to other countries.

Jazz also symbolized the way many young people of the time felt about life in general. They sought to break away from strictly observed rules and traditions, just as jazz trumpeters and saxophonists departed from written notes in order to express themselves.

Postwar American Writers

Some American artists focused on freer ways of expression, while others turned to critically examining their country. World War I had shocked and disappointed people all over the world. This appeared particularly true of the many Americans who had resisted the war at first, only to be drawn into it later by promises of a world that would be made "safe for democracy."

The Lost Generation. The American writers who had supported the war effort were perhaps the most bitter. Gertrude Stein, a writer who had left the United States to live permanently in Europe, gave these young people a name. She told a young American writer, Ernest Hemingway,

"All of you young people who served in the war, you are all a lost generation."

To this **Lost Generation**, the progressive ideals that had been so important before the war seemed less so afterward. Many writers expressed this sense of loss of values in their works. In his book *Exile's Return,* critic Malcolm Cowley wrote:

> **"Life in this country is joyless and colorless, universally standardized, tawdry [cheaply showy], uncreative, given over to the worship of wealth and machinery."**

Other writers agreed with him and became **expatriates**—people who voluntarily leave their country to live abroad.

● **The Lost Generation**

The Harlem Renaissance. While some American authors exiled themselves in Europe, another group of well-known writers lived in Harlem, a black neighborhood in New York City. Harlem was a place where African Americans could be themselves. Harlem was also the largest urban black community in the United States, and thus was mostly free of white prejudice and mistreatment. Newspapers and magazines as well as theater troupes and libraries—all owned and operated by African Americans—prospered.

In several places around the country, and particularly in Harlem, musicians and artists found their artistic voice. Poets and writers such as Langston Hughes, Claude McKay, James Weldon Johnson, Countee Cullen, Nella Larsen, and Zora Neale Hurston became part of a movement known as the **Harlem Renaissance**. These writers urged respect for African American culture. They tried to bring the spirit of Harlem—of African American confidence and pride—alive. Langston Hughes captured this idea best when he wrote, "Harlem! I . . . dropped my bags, took a deep breath, and felt happy again."

The Granger Collection, New York

Author Zora Neale Hurston

Section 3 Review

● **Glossary**

IDENTIFY and explain the significance of the following: nickelodeons, talkie, Walt Disney, Babe Ruth, Harlem Globetrotters, jazz, W. C. Handy, Bessie Smith, Louis Armstrong, Gertrude Stein, Lost Generation, expatriates, Langston Hughes, Harlem Renaissance

REVIEWING FOR DETAILS
1. What new forms of entertainment became popular during the 1920s?
2. How did new forms of entertainment change American life?
3. What impact did the works of musicians and writers have on the United States during the 1920s?

REVIEWING FOR UNDERSTANDING
4. **Writing Mastery:** *Expressing* Write a song, poem, or short story about life in America during the 1920s.
5. **Critical Thinking:** *Making Comparisons* Some people called the decade the "Roaring Twenties." For others, the generation of the 1920s was "lost." Compare and contrast these descriptions of the same period.

Section 4

A DIVIDED NATION

Multimedia Connections

Explore these related topics and materials on the CD–ROM to enrich your understanding of this section:

 Profiles

• Marcus Garvey

 Media Bank

• Aimee Semple McPherson
• Race Riots in 1919
• American Indians
• Rural Life in the 1920s
• African American Population

 Readings

• Marcus Garvey and the UNIA

In the 1920s some Americans believed that the country's problems were so great that the only solution was to emigrate. For African Americans this feeling gained force in a "Back to Africa" movement. Emily Christmas Kinch, a missionary to Africa, urged her fellow African Americans to return to their ancestral land. Africa would welcome them, she explained. It was a place where success awaited them—even presidents were black.

As you read this section you will find out:

▶ **What prejudices many Americans held, and how African Americans reacted to these prejudices.**

▶ **What role religious Fundamentalism played during the 1920s.**

▶ **What events shaped the presidential election of 1928.**

Prohibition America

America was rapidly changing in the 1920s. Prohibition—forbidding the sale, manufacture, or transportation of alcohol—was proving extremely difficult to enforce. People called **bootleggers** smuggled alcohol into the country. Crime statistics soared. Many individuals privately drank liquor at home or in local "**speakeasies**"—secret clubs that served alcohol. Gangsters such as Al "Scarface" Capone of Chicago controlled most liquor sales.

Armed with guns, criminal gangs fought for territory, at times killing innocent bystanders as well as their gang rivals. Despite this violence, powerful "dry" forces kept politicians in both major political parties from proposing an end to prohibition. By the late 1920s, however, even former supporters came to agree that prohibition had led to the growth

Acting Lieutenant Frank Aldenhover (left) took 21 year old Matthew Capone (right) into custody. The young man arrested was the brother of Ralph and Al "Scarface" Capone, two "public enemies."

of crime. Thus, in December 1933 the **Twenty-first Amendment** to the U.S. Constitution repealed prohibition.

For many Americans, problems such as crime, gambling, and dishonesty seemed all too common, particularly in the cities. The nation was becoming increasingly urban. In 1920 for the first time more people lived in cities than on farms. Many resented the look and feel of the changing nation. Some Americans reacted against the wave of new immigrants, the growing voices of African American communities, and the vision of a modern urban nation.

America for Americans

The conservative postwar reaction against immigrants continued throughout the decade. Both the U.S. government and private citizens pursued a nativist policy.

New immigration restrictions. In 1921 Congress responded to the isolationism of the times by taking steps to control the entry of foreigners into the United States. The passage of the **Quota Act** limited the number of immigrants by nationality, reducing the number of newcomers from eastern and southern Europe. Congress later passed an even stiffer quota law, the **Immigration Act of 1924**. By July 1929, a total of only 150,000 immigrants per year could enter the United States. The actual number of immigrants fell below 100,000 every year from 1931 to 1946.

The Ku Klux Klan. The nativist mood of the 1920s also took other forms. One was a

revival of the Ku Klux Klan. Between the years 1920 and 1923, Klan membership grew from about 5,000 members to several million. Like the Klan of Reconstruction days, the new Klan continued to attack African Americans. It also started attacking immigrants and religious minorities, particularly Jews and Catholics. The new Klan threatened, beat, and even murdered innocent citizens. The Klan's Imperial Wizard, Hiram Evans, said:

"We believe that the pioneers who built America bequeathed [gave] to their own children a priority right to it, the control of it and of its future, and that no one on Earth can claim any part of this inheritance except through our generosity."

The Klan's influence soon spread, and it became an important political and social force in some cities. When the corruption of its top members came to the public's attention, however, membership in the Klan declined.

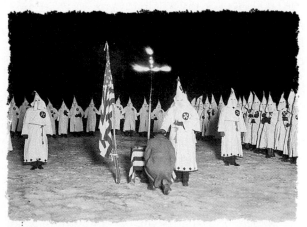

In the 1920s the Ku Klux Klan gained in strength and held rallies across the nation.

The New Negro

Many African American organizations formed in response to race discrimination from groups like the Klan. African Americans in the 1920s, often called the "New Negro," were determined to build a better life for themselves and their children. Langston Hughes, one of the great poets of the era, expressed what life was like for African American children in his poem "Merry-Go-Round":

Poet Langston Hughes

The Granger Collection, New York

> **"*Colored child at carnival:*
> Where is the Jim Crow section
> On this merry-go-round,
> Mister, cause I want to ride?
> Down South where I come from
> White and colored
> Can't sit side by side.
> Down South on the train
> There's a Jim Crow car.
> On the bus we're put in the back—
> But there ain't no back
> To a merry-go-round!
> Where's the horse
> For a kid that's black?"**

The North, in contrast to the segregated South, seemed to be a land of opportunity to many African American southerners. During the 1920s about 800,000 black southerners moved north. African American communities sprang up in all the major northern cities.

African Americans, however, found some of the same problems of prejudice and economic hardship in the North. Like many workers after World War I, African Americans had difficulty finding work. Many could find only low-paying jobs in service industries.

Race riots. African Americans were often the targets of violence after the war. In 1919 mobs, mainly in the South, lynched more than 70 African Americans, 10 of them World War I veterans. Race riots erupted in many cities, including Washington, D.C., and Chicago.

Organizations such as the NAACP were quick to respond to the violence. The NAACP protested the lynchings and encouraged African Americans to defend their rights.

Marcus Garvey. Millions of African Americans felt that progress toward equality was too slow. Some even doubted the possibility of achieving equality in the United States. Black nationalists thought the solution was a nation of their own.

Black nationalist Marcus Garvey's proposal for a black homeland was popular among many African Americans. This photograph shows Garvey (second from right) with his supporters.

Brown Brothers

The most famous black nationalist was Marcus Garvey. Garvey had seen racial discrimination in Central America, Europe, and his native Jamaica. He decided that African Americans' best hope for equality was to move to a black homeland in Africa. He also wanted to promote black economic independence. While living in Jamaica, Garvey founded the **Universal Negro Improvement Association** (UNIA).

Garvey moved to Harlem in 1916, and the UNIA continued to grow. Garvey claimed it had 6 million members by 1923. He also started several African American businesses, including the Black Star Line steamship company and a company that manufactured black dolls. Garvey worked to boost the pride and dignity of his followers. "Up you mighty race," he urged, "you can accomplish what you will." For Garvey the time had come to assert black independence.

The Scopes Trial

Many Americans searching for security in this decade of change found it in the Protestant religious movement called **Fundamentalism**. The Fundamentalist movement was strongest in rural and small-town America, where people blamed society's problems on modern urban culture.

Fundamentalists, who took every word of the Bible literally, believed that God had made the world in six days. They therefore rejected naturalist Charles Darwin's **theory of natural selection**, the idea that all forms of life had developed gradually over millions of years. They campaigned for laws against the teaching of evolution in schools. In 1925 the state of Tennessee passed a law forbidding instructors in the state's schools and colleges to teach "any theory that denies the story of the Divine Creation of man taught in the Bible."

Many people felt that this law restricted the freedom of speech. The American Civil Liberties Union offered to defend any Tennessee teacher who would challenge the law's constitutionality. John T. Scopes, a biology teacher in Dayton, Tennessee, agreed to do so. When Scopes continued to teach natural selection, he was arrested and put on trial.

The **Scopes trial** attracted national attention. The prosecuting attorney was William Jennings Bryan, a three-time Democratic candidate for president. Clarence Darrow, a famous trial lawyer, defended Scopes.

During the trial the prosecution took every opportunity to state its view of the literal meaning of the Bible. The judge even allowed Bryan to testify as an expert witness. Under intense questioning by Darrow, Bryan rejected modern scientific thought.

Scopes was found guilty and fined $100. The Tennessee Supreme Court soon overturned the decision, but the Scopes trial stood for something larger than a controversy over Darwin's theory of natural selection. It emphasized the growing divisions within American society—rural versus urban and traditional versus modern.

"When Shall We Three Meet Again?"

The Granger Collection, New York

The monkey standing between William Jennings Bryan (left) and Clarence Darrow (right) represented Darwin's theory. Many people mistakenly believed that this theory proposed that humans had evolved from monkeys, thus it became known as the Scopes monkey trial.

"Sick" Industries

American industry also showed signs of division. Despite the expansion of the 1920s, there were several weak areas in the economy. The coal industry faced stiff competition from oil, natural gas, and electricity. Many coal mines shut down in the 1920s, and around 600,000 miners went on strike over pay cuts. Manufacturers of cotton and woolen cloth did not prosper either. Partly because of competition from rayon, a new synthetic textile, there was too much unsold cotton cloth on the market. Profits from cotton shrank, and the number of unemployed textile workers grew.

American agriculture also suffered. After World War I ended, European farmers quickly recaptured their local markets. The price of wheat and other farm products fell sharply. Farmers' incomes declined, but their expenses for mortgage interests, taxes, tractors, harvesters, and supplies did not.

In 1921 a group of congressmen from the South and West organized an informal **Farm bloc**. (A bloc is a common interest group.) They hoped to obtain legislation favorable to agriculture. Twice the Farm bloc pushed through a farm aid bill, which would have required that the government purchase farm surpluses to stabilize prices and assist farmers. And twice President Coolidge vetoed the legislation.

The Election of 1928

Coolidge played down the problems of farmers and workers in the "sick" industries. He also ignored the social unrest. The 1920s were a time when politics and politicians seemed to have little connection to how most people lived and thought. While society was changing in dramatic and significant ways, most political leaders were conservative, slow moving, and lacking in imagination.

President Coolidge believed that America's future was bright. "No Congress has met with a more pleasing prospect than that which appears at the present time," he said in his 1928 State of the Union message.

Most people agreed with Coolidge. Americans were enjoying the greatest period of prosperity in their history. Most were earn-

Thomas Hart Benton, who painted Cotton Pickers, *was the best-known American muralist of the 1930s and 1940s. He painted scenes of the real lives of ordinary people. Much of his work focused on the challenges of everyday life in the American Midwest.*

The Granger Collection, New York

ing more money and working shorter hours than ever before. They had cars, radios, and household appliances. They went to movies and sporting events and followed the lives of their favorite star. Life was easy, and it seemed likely to become even easier. The Republican Party naturally took the credit for the good times. In the 1928 presidential campaign, Herbert Hoover, the secretary of commerce, received the Republican nomination. Hoover campaigned on a vision of increasing national prosperity:

> **"The poorhouse is vanishing among us. We have not yet reached the goal."**

Hoover promised that if reelected, he would "go forward with the policies of the last eight years," and the country would see an end to poverty.

The Democratic candidate was Alfred E. Smith. Smith had a record of solid accomplishment as governor of New York. His Catholic faith and his "big city" background hurt him in the campaign, however. Many American Protestants were prejudiced against Catholics and would not vote for a Catholic for president. Some feared that a Catholic president would be a servant of the pope rather than of the American people. Many rural residents disliked Smith because he had been raised "on the sidewalks of New York." They viewed Smith's candidacy as a symbol of the shift from a rural to an urban nation.

Hoover won the election with 21 million votes to Smith's 15 million. The electoral vote was 444 to 87. Smith even lost in his own state of New York as well as in several states in the traditionally Democratic South. The majority of Americans now believed that the Republican Party was the symbol of economic progress and the guardian of good times.

Earlier in his career, Herbert Hoover had worked as a mining engineer all over the world. During World War I, he headed up agencies to help people in need throughout Europe. He continued this work even after the war had ended.

Section 4 Review

• Glossary

IDENTIFY and explain the significance of the following: bootleggers, speakeasies, Twenty-first Amendment, Quota Act, Immigration Act of 1924, Marcus Garvey, Universal Negro Improvement Association, Fundamentalism, theory of natural selection, Scopes trial, Farm bloc, Herbert Hoover

• Time Line

REVIEWING FOR DETAILS

1. How did many people treat African Americans and new immigrants in the 1920s? How did some African Americans react to this treatment?

2. What were some of the economic problems of the 1920s?

3. How did the trial of John Scopes demonstrate social divisions during the 1920s?

REVIEWING FOR UNDERSTANDING

4. **Writing Mastery:** *Describing* Write a short essay describing how the presidential election of 1928 reflected the social, political, and economic divisions of the times.

5. **Critical Thinking:** *Drawing Conclusions* How do you think the prejudices of many Americans were related to the economic conditions of the 1920s?

AMERICA'S GEOGRAPHY

African Americans and The Great Migration

Despite the racism that still existed in the South, relatively few African Americans left the region before 1900. In 1910 almost 90 percent of all African Americans still lived there. Today just under half of all African Americans live in the South. The large majority of African Americans who migrated from the South to the North and the West did so in the early to mid-1900s.

The Great Migration began during World War I as northern job opportunities opened to southern African Americans. The migration continued after the war as more African Americans sought job opportunities in the booming 1920s economy. Many also hoped to find greater civil freedoms outside of the South, which was plagued by racial violence during the 1920s. Some African Americans who hoped for a better life outside the South were disappointed, however, when they found that discrimination existed all over the country.

African American Migration, 1910–1930

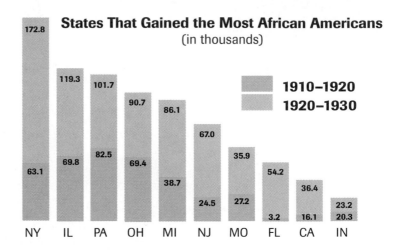

States That Gained the Most African Americans
(in thousands)

1910–1920
1920–1930

	NY	IL	PA	OH	MI	NJ	MO	FL	CA	IN
1910–1920	63.1	69.8	82.5	69.4	38.7	24.5	27.2	3.2	16.1	20.3
1920–1930	172.8	119.3	101.7	90.7	86.1	67.0	35.9	54.2	36.4	23.2

The southern states all lost significant numbers of African Americans to the North and the West from 1910 to 1930. Most went in search of better jobs in major cities like New York and Chicago. **Movement:** How many African Americans moved to New York between 1910 and 1930? How many left Georgia during that same period?

States That Lost the Most African Americans
(in thousands)

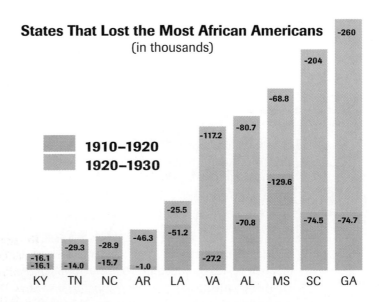

1910–1920
1920–1930

	KY	TN	NC	AR	LA	VA	AL	MS	SC	GA
	-16.1	-29.3	-28.9	-46.3	-25.5	-117.2	-80.7	-68.8	-204	-260
	-16.1	-14.0	-15.7	-1.0	-51.2	-27.2	-70.8	-129.6	-74.5	-74.7

Discrimination Against African Americans, 1930

Many African Americans moved away from the South in search of more freedom as well as job opportunities. Although discrimination existed throughout the country, it was still most strongly enforced in the southern states. States that had few or no state laws discriminating against African Americans gained the most migrants from 1910 to 1930. Racism still existed in many of these states on a local level, however, as city laws and customs were often used against African American migrants. **Place:** How many states had no state-sponsored discrimination in all four areas of education, transportation, marriage, and voting? Which of these states were among the top 10 that gained African American migrants?

State-Enforced Discrimination Against African Americans

Schools segregated	◯
Transportation segregated	●
Interracial marriage outlawed	●
Voting restricted	◯
No state laws enforcing discrimination in these 4 areas	◉

To learn more about African Americans and the Great Migration, go to the interactive map, "The Harlem Renaissance," on the CD–ROM.

• The Harlem Renaissance

CHAPTER **22**

The Great Depression
(1929–1939)

THEMES IN AMERICAN HISTORY

Geographic Diversity:
How might an economic depression affect a rural area differently than an urban one?

Economic Development:
How might government spending help develop a region?

Constitutional Heritage:
How does the Supreme Court fit into the system of checks and balances?

• Video Opener   • Skill Builder

*J*n 1928 Herbert Hoover predicted:

"We in America today are nearer to the final triumph over poverty than ever before in the history of any land. We shall soon . . . be in sight of the day when poverty will be banished from this nation."

Less than one year later, disaster struck, and millions of Americans became victims of poverty during Hoover's presidency.

image above: *St. Peter's Mission in New York City*

Section 1

THE END OF PROSPERITY

Multimedia Connections
Explore these related topics and materials on the CD–ROM to enrich your understanding of this section:

 Readings

• Global Depression
• The Donners

 Media Bank

• Personal Income, 1929–1941
• N.Y. Stock Exchange
• A Casualty of the Crash

 Profiles

• Herbert Hoover

Throughout most of the 1920s, Wall Street had been buzzing with stock tips and tales of the latest rise of stock prices. By the end of October 1929, however, this excitement had turned to gloom. Many people had lost their entire fortune. "If men will only keep their heads on their shoulders and their shirts on their backs," a New York *World* editorial advised, "the real business of America will go forward without serious hesitation." People's hopes that the economy would be roaring again soon turned to despair.

As you read this section you will find out:

▶ **What caused the Panic of 1929.**

▶ **What the basic causes of the Great Depression were.**

▶ **How the Great Depression was different from other economic downturns.**

The Great Crash

The prosperity of the late 1920s created a "get-rich-quick" attitude in the United States. More and more people set out to make fortunes in the stock market. They followed the prices of stocks in the newspapers as closely as they followed Babe Ruth's batting average. By mid-1929 stock prices had been climbing steadily for months. A newspaper writer of the day poked fun at the stock-buying fever:

"**Nowadays the bores I find**
 Are of a single, standard kind:
 For every person I may meet
 At lunch, at clubs, upon the street,
 Tells me, in endless wordy tales,
 Of market purchases and sales;
 Of how he bought a single share
 Of California Prune and Pear;

Or how he sold at 33
A million shares of T. & T. . . .
In herds, in schools, in droves, in flocks
The men and women talk of stocks."

Many people getting involved in the stock market were **buying on margin**—purchasing stock with borrowed money. Speculators, or people who make risky investments in hopes of large profits, could buy stock with as little as 10 percent of the total price down. When the stock rose in price, they could sell it, pay off the loan, and pocket the profit. During the booming **bull market**, a continuing rise in stock prices, margin buying seemed a quick way to wealth. A **bear market**, a steady drop in stock prices, would mean disaster for anyone who bought stock on margin. Most people thought that the bull market would never end.

The market reached a peak in September 1929. Then on October 24—"Black Thursday"—thousands of investors decided to sell stocks instead of buying them. Many economic factors, including rising interest rates, had made them nervous. Frightened investors jammed telephone lines and crowded into brokers' offices, desperate to turn their stocks into cash. With many sellers and few buyers, the prices of stocks plunged. For example, General Electric Company stock dropped from $315 to $283 per share—a major loss, considering the stock's recent growth.

The stock market crash made headlines across the country. Even the entertainment newspaper, Variety, *picked up the story and made it front-page news.*

On October 29—"Black Tuesday"—came an even steeper decline. "When the closing bell rang, the great bull market was dead and buried," recalled one journalist. He went on:

> "**Not only the little speculators, but the lordly, experienced big traders had been wiped out. . . . Many bankers and brokers were doubtful about their own solvency [financial well-being].**"

Day after day the drop continued in this **Panic of 1929**. By the middle of November, General Electric stock was down to $168 a share. The prosperity of the 1920s was over.

From Crash to Collapse

The stock market crash was the start of the worldwide economic downturn known as the **Great Depression**. At the time, some Americans, including the president, Herbert Hoover, blamed the depression on economic conditions in Europe. European countries had built up staggering debts during World War I. Such debts—owed mainly to the United States—greatly handicapped these countries' postwar economic recoveries.

Cartoonist Rollin Kirby predicted three weeks before the crash that a bear market would take hold of Wall Street.

Bank failures. The reasons the depression was so severe, however, lay closer to home. Many investors, including banks, who had bought on margin were left holding worthless stock and were unable to pay their debts. In addition, when farm prices fell in the 1920s, farmers were unable to make their loan payments. By the decade's end, other industries, such as mining, textiles, and construction had also experienced financial problems.

When businesses were unable to pay their debts, hundreds of banks failed throughout the country. Fearing more banks would fail, many depositors withdrew their savings. Between the loss of unpaid loans and the withdrawal of deposits, the banking system almost completely collapsed. Over 5,000 banks failed between 1930 and 1933. Millions of people lost their entire savings.

Business closures. Other Americans had no savings or were in debt before the crash. Many consumers, lured by installment plans and easy credit, had bought items that they could not afford. When the economy took a downswing, they had a hard time paying for the goods they owned and had no resources to purchase new ones.

The boom of the 1920s had enabled a relatively small number of people to obtain a very large percentage of the nation's purchasing power. After a time, the mass of consumers could not afford to buy the goods pouring forth from the factories. Production had increased more rapidly than the income of the average family.

Factories slowed down production and laid off workers. Then, in 1930, Congress passed high tariffs to protect U.S. companies from foreign competitors. International trade declined and the economy shrank even more. As a result, many more people lost their jobs. Production fell off further, more businesses closed, and unemployment grew even worse.

The Business Cycle

When the depression first became noticeable, few people expected it to be very serious. Americans had come to accept tough economic times as a regular part of the **business cycle**—recurring periods of depression and prosperity.

Until the Great Depression, the business cycle had followed a particular pattern. During the prosperous part of the cycle, economic activity expanded, and companies produced more goods. When demand rose, factories hired more workers. Eventually, factory output increased faster than goods were being sold. Surpluses piled up in warehouses and in retail stores. Manufacturers then reduced their production, lowered prices, and laid off some of their workers. These unemployed people had

Global Connections
The Global Depression

The Great Depression was not felt merely in the United States; it affected countries throughout the world. Most industrial nations experienced high unemployment. In Germany, Norway, and Denmark, for example, over 30 percent of the workforce was unemployed in 1932. Those Latin American countries whose economies depended on exporting raw materials were particularly hard-hit by the global depression. For example, from 1928 to 1932, exports fell by more than 50 percent in Chile and Bolivia. Two of Chile's most important exports, nitrates and copper, dropped by 89 percent.

The economies of agricultural nations were also hard-hit. Australia, a large exporter of wheat, and Argentina, which was one of the world's leading beef exporters, suffered greatly. The price of Brazilian coffee fell so low that farmers there burned the coffee beans in cookstoves, because coffee made a cheaper fuel than coal or kerosene.

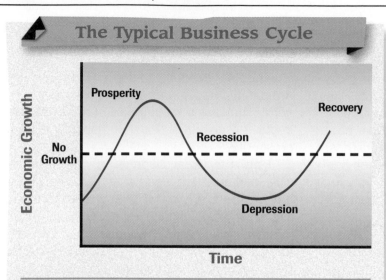

The Typical Business Cycle

Economic Growth

Prosperity

Recovery

No Growth

Recession

Depression

Time

Economic Trends. At first, most Americans thought the depression of the 1930s was only a temporary downswing in the economy. What do you think a graph of the business cycle during the Great Depression would look like?

increased output and rehired workers. These workers, with wages in their pockets, increased their purchases. The economy then entered the recovery stage. Recovery eventually led to prosperity—a time of high profit, full production, and low unemployment once again.

A complete business cycle usually lasted from about three to five years. What made the Great Depression different was that it lasted for 10 years. The economy declined steeply from late 1929 until the winter of 1932–33. Then it appeared to be stuck. Recovery was slow and irregular. Through the 1930s unemployment remained very high—more than 20 percent from 1932 to 1935.

less money to buy goods. More manufacturers laid off more workers, and some companies went out of business. At this point, the economy was in a state of depression.

When factory output became very low, the surpluses were gradually used up. Then producers who had not gone out of business

Workers with years of experience found themselves out of work. Shopkeepers who had devoted their careers to developing their businesses lost everything. Students graduating from schools and colleges could find no one to hire them. The Great Depression affected most Americans in some way.

Section 1 Review

• Glossary

IDENTIFY and explain the significance of the following: buying on margin, bull market, bear market, Panic of 1929, Great Depression, business cycle

REVIEWING FOR DETAILS
1. Why did the U.S. stock market crash in 1929?
2. What were the main causes of the Great Depression?
3. In what ways was the Great Depression part of the normal American business cycle, and how was it unique?

REVIEWING FOR UNDERSTANDING
4. **Writing Mastery:** *Creating* Imagine that it is November 1, 1929, and you are a banker in a small rural town. Create a dialogue between yourself and a local farmer, discussing the events of the day as you meet for lunch at a cafe.
5. **Critical Thinking:** *Cause and Effect* How might the economic changes caused by the Great Depression have affected the ideas, values, and outlooks of the people who lived through it?

Section 2

THE EARLY YEARS OF THE GREAT DEPRESSION

Multimedia Connections

Explore these related topics and materials on the CD ROM to enrich your understanding of this section:

 Atlas

- Unemployment Relief

 Media Bank

- Victims of the Depression
- Unemployment, 1929–1941

 Readings

- The DiMarcos

A nn Rivington was a music teacher, and her husband played in an orchestra. Used to "comfort and apparent security," she, like many Americans, had little idea what it meant to be poor. Then the depression struck. The Rivingtons lost their jobs and their savings soon ran out. "For all my education, my training in thrift and cleanliness, I am become one of them [the poor]." Ann Rivington realized. "From my new place in society I regard the problems and misery of the poor with new eyes."

As you read this section you will find out:

▶ **How President Hoover tried to end the depression.**

▶ **Why Hoover's efforts did not work.**

▶ **What happened to the Bonus Army.**

Hoover Fights the Depression

It was up to President Hoover to deal with the national crisis. When he realized that the country had entered a serious depression, he took steps to stimulate recovery quickly. So that people would have more money to spend on goods and services, he urged Congress—unsuccessfully—to lower taxes. In addition, he called for increased government spending on **public works**, such as constructing roads or building dams. He hoped these measures would stimulate a demand for goods and put jobless people back to work.

The depression hit farmers particularly hard. Farm prices had been low during most of the 1920s, but after the crash the price of most farm products fell even more sharply. Hoover

During the depression, many Americans lost their homes. Some people moved in with relatives; others found space to put down a mattress or cot in a crowded rooming house.

supported a measure to provide lending institutions, including farm mortgage associations, with emergency aid. He hoped this would help stop people from losing their homes and farms. In addition, he urged farmers to form cooperatives and to raise smaller crops until prices rose. Few bankers or farmers followed Hoover's voluntary guidelines, however.

Hoover believed that voluntary cooperation was the best way to tackle the hardships of the depression. He did not want the federal government to greatly expand its role in Americans' lives just because times were hard. Hoover believed that large corporations, state and local governments, and private organizations such as the Red Cross and the Salvation Army—not the federal government—were responsible for distributing charity.

Even after many local communities proved unable to raise enough money to take care of the unemployed, Hoover continued to oppose federal grants for **relief**—money or aid for the needy. He said such aid would destroy the "national character."

Instead, Hoover supported federal assistance to banks and large corporations. He believed these loans were sound investments. Companies could use the money to produce goods, earn profits, and then repay

their loans. Hoover also supported farm aid, such as lending a farmer money to buy seed or livestock feed to keep the farms running. He would not, however, lend farmers money to help feed their children.

The president recognized that Americans had lost confidence in the economic system. He tried to encourage them to have faith in the future. "Prosperity," he said, "is just around the corner." When Hoover's policies failed to end the depression, people stopped believing him. As the depression dragged on, Hoover became increasingly unpopular. To many Americans, he appeared hardhearted because he did not seem to care about the sufferings of the poor.

Breadlines and Soup Kitchens

Both state and local governments and private charities raised money to feed the poor and provide them with a little cash. Churches and other public-spirited organizations conducted charity drives to collect clothing for the unemployed and their families. There were soup kitchens and breadlines, where the hungry could get a free meal, and lodging houses, where the homeless could spend the night. One teenager during the Great Depression recalled her experiences:

The Great Depression affected both the young and the old. Children whose parents were poor and unemployed often ended up hungry and homeless.

"If you happened to be one of the first ones in line, you didn't get anything but the water that was on top. So we'd ask the guy that was putting the soup into the buckets . . . to please dip down to get some meat and potatoes from the bottom of the kettle. But he wouldn't do it. . . . One place had bread, large loaves of bread. Down the road just a little way was a big shed, and they gave milk. My sister and me would take two buckets each. And that's what we lived off for the longest time."

Many Americans found themselves homeless when they were no longer able to make mortgage or rent payments. The urban landscape became dotted with Hoovervilles. In these temporary dwellings, people struggled to carry on in the depression.

Victims of the depression often received help from relatives and friends. Malcolm Little, a well-known civil rights leader who later took the name Malcolm X, recalled such assistance in his *Autobiography*:

"No one we knew had enough to eat or live on. Some old family friends visited us now and then. At first they brought food. Though it was charity, my mother took it."

Many families felt ashamed that they could not support themselves. Americans wanted to work rather than accept charity, but the lack of jobs left them little choice.

As the number of people in need grew, it overwhelmed the capacity of local governments and institutions. Many unemployed Americans had no one to turn to for help. Some stood on street corners trying to sell apples or pencils. Others simply held out their hands, begging for a few pennies. Desperation drove a few to become thieves.

Unable to continue making mortgage payments or rent, many of the unemployed lost their homes. Tramps wandered around the country hitching rides on railroad freight cars. In cities, flimsy shantytowns sprung up. They were called Hoovervilles, after the president many Americans blamed for the depression.

One citizen asked of Hoover, "Can not you find a quicker way of Executing us than to Starve us to death?" Some people did die of starvation. In 1931, for example, New York City hospitals reported treating 238 cases of severe malnutrition, and 45 of these patients died, victims of the depression.

In another New York City case, police arrested 54 homeless men for sleeping in the subway. They told a reporter from the *New York Times* that they were lucky because being in jail had meant "free meals yesterday and shelter last night."

The Bonus Army

Public opinion turned further against Hoover in 1932. Some years earlier Congress had passed a law giving World War I veterans a bonus. Its purpose was to **compensate**, or make up for, the low pay that soldiers had received during the war while workers were earning high wages. The government was not due to pay the bonus until 1945.

During the depression, veterans began to demand that their bonus be paid at once. Hoover angered the public by refusing to ask Congress to change the law. "Why is it," the wife of one veteran complained:

"that it is always a bunch of overly rich, selfish, dumb, ignorant money hogs that persist in being Senators, legislatures, representatives. Where would they and their possessions be if it were not for the Common Soldier, the common laborer that is compelled [forced] to work for a starvation wage?"

World War I veterans from states across the country marched to Washington, D.C. On the Capitol steps, they voiced their demands for immediate compensation for their service to the nation.

In May of 1932 around 10,000 veterans and their families, called the **Bonus Army**, marched on Washington, D.C., to demonstrate before the Capitol. When Congress refused to change the law, some of the marchers settled down on vacant land on the edge of the city. They set up camps of tents and flimsy tar-paper shacks, and they said they intended to stay until the bonus was paid.

Hoover ordered army units to assist police in driving out the veterans. Troops under the command of General Douglas MacArthur went into action. Infantry backed by cavalry units and tanks began to clear the camps. Tear gas used by the army killed one child. The troops also fired shots that killed two veterans. Americans across the country were shocked by the events in Washington, D.C., and Hoover's popularity fell even lower.

Section 2 Review

• Glossary

IDENTIFY and explain the significance of the following: public works, relief, compensate, Bonus Army

REVIEWING FOR DETAILS

1. How did President Hoover try to cope with the problems of the depression?
2. What were the results of Hoover's efforts?
3. What did the Bonus Army want, and what was the result of its protest?

REVIEWING FOR UNDERSTANDING

4. **Writing Mastery:** *Describing* Imagine that you are a volunteer worker in a soup kitchen. Write a letter to Hoover describing how the depression has affected people's lives.
5. **Critical Thinking:** *Synthesizing Information* How did Hoover's actions as president affect his popularity?

Section 3

ROOSEVELT OFFERS A NEW DEAL

Multimedia Connections

Explore these related topics and materials on the CD–ROM to enrich your understanding of this section:

 Profiles

- Franklin D. Roosevelt
- Frances Perkins

 Media Bank

- Fireside Chat
- Harry Hopkins
- CCC Men at Work

 Readings

- The Coreys

In 1921 Franklin D. Roosevelt and his family vacationed at their summer home in Canada. One day Roosevelt helped put out a brushfire while on an outing with his children. He returned home tired and chilled in his wet swimming suit. That night he burned with fever. Within a few days his legs were almost completely paralyzed. He had a severe case of polio. Though he recovered from the disease, he would never again walk without the aid of metal braces and two canes. More often he was carried or used a wheelchair.

As you read this section you will find out:

▶ **What the basic ideas behind Roosevelt's New Deal were.**

▶ **How Roosevelt rescued the banks.**

▶ **What key agencies were established during the Hundred Days.**

The Election of 1932

It is safe to say that in the 1932 election just about any Democratic presidential candidate could have defeated Herbert Hoover. Between 13 and 16 million workers were unemployed. The combined income of all Americans had fallen from over $80 billion in 1929 to below $50 billion in 1932. People demanded change.

The Democrat who challenged Hoover was Franklin D. Roosevelt, the governor of New York. Roosevelt was a distant cousin of former president Theodore Roosevelt and the husband of Theodore Roosevelt's niece, Eleanor.

Franklin D. Roosevelt had a privileged upbringing. After graduating from Harvard University, he went on to study law and enter into politics. In 1920 he ran for vice president on the ticket with James M. Cox, who was defeated by Warren G. Harding.

Franklin D. Roosevelt

The following summer, Roosevelt contracted a severe case of polio. He survived the disease but suffered paralysis in his legs. With his wife's support, Roosevelt went on with his political career and was elected governor of New York state in 1928. Two years later, he was easily re-elected by a huge majority.

Roosevelt then won the 1932 Democratic presidential nomination. He was an extremely effective political campaigner with tremendous energy. At a time when most people were deeply depressed, his cheer encouraged and uplifted millions. The crowds that gathered when he campaigned inspired him as well. "I have looked into the faces of thousands of Americans," he confided to one friend. "They are saying: 'We're caught in something we don't understand; perhaps this fellow can help us out.'"

Roosevelt offered a point of view, not a specific plan, to end the depression:

> "The country demands bold, persistent experimentation. It is common sense to take a method and try it. If it fails, admit it frankly and try another. But above all, try something."

He called this policy a "**New Deal**." In a card game, no one can know how the cards will fall. If one is dealt a poor hand, there is always the chance that the next hand, the new deal, will be better.

This hopeful approach was what millions of voters wanted to hear. In November Roosevelt defeated Hoover with an electoral majority of 472 to 59. The popular vote was 22.8 million to 15.8 million. Voters also gave the Democrats large majorities in both houses of Congress.

Nothing to Fear but Fear Itself

The economy continued its steep downward trend between election day and inauguration day on March 4. Industrial production had fallen sharply once again. About 25 percent of Americans were without jobs. The deepening depression caused Americans to panic. People rushed to withdraw their savings from the banks. Throughout the nation, even the soundest banks closed their doors.

In this dark hour Roosevelt's inauguration speech came like a ray of summer sunshine. "This great nation," he said, ". . . will revive,

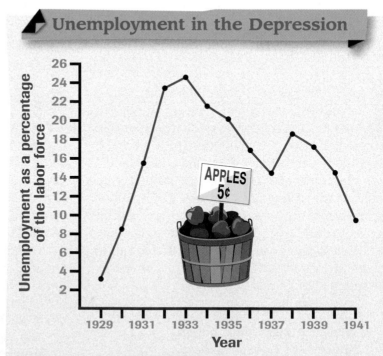

Unemployment in the Depression

Source: *Historical Statistics of the United States*

Jobless Americans. At the peak of the depression, more than 12 million Americans were unemployed. During what year was unemployment highest?

and will prosper. So, first of all, let me assert [strongly state] my firm belief that the only thing we have to fear is fear itself."

Roosevelt took an aggressive approach to fighting the depression. For advice, he turned to experts, mostly college professors, in the areas of law, economics, and social welfare. These close advisers were known as the **Brain Trust**. The president selected Frances Perkins, a well known reformer who sought the improvement of the lives of working-class families and workers' rights, as his secretary of labor. She became the nation's first female cabinet member. For secretary of the interior, Roosevelt chose Harold Ickes, who soon had a lot of influence in both the New Deal and the nation's environmental conservation policy.

Roosevelt Saves the Banks

Roosevelt's first action was to deal with the bank panic by declaring a "bank holiday." He closed all the banks in the country so that a general plan to protect the public's savings could be developed. Inspectors went around to all of the closed banks to determine if they were sound enough to reopen or if they needed financial assistance from the federal government.

Roosevelt then went on the radio to explain the bank holiday. He spoke in terms that everyone could understand. He assured his listeners that the reopened banks would be sound and that investors' money would be safe. Roosevelt managed to restore public confidence. Runs on banks stopped. By the end of March, customers had deposited more than $1 billion back in the banks. As one of Roosevelt's advisers said:

> **"The bank rescue of 1933 was probably the turning point of the Depression. When people were able to survive the shock of having all the banks closed, and then see the banks open up, with their money protected, there began to be confidence. Good times were coming."**

Worried depositors gather outside the closed doors of the Union Bank of New York City. They, like many Americans during the banking crisis, feared losing all of their savings.

Throughout the depression, Roosevelt frequently spoke on the radio. In these "**fireside chats**," the president seemed to be right in the room with listeners. He explained what problems lay before the nation, how he proposed to deal with them, and what Americans could do to help.

The Hundred Days

In his inaugural address the president had called upon the Congress to meet in a special session on March 9, 1933, to deal with the depression. This special session ended 100 days later on June 16. It became known as the **Hundred Days**. The name made clear how much Congress and the president accomplished. Congress approved 15 major New Deal measures to combat the depression.

The New Deal had three general goals—relief, recovery, and reform. Relief came first and was aimed at all Americans in economic distress. Recovery would then get the economy moving again. Reform would prevent another severe depression.

Relief. The New Deal directed its greatest efforts toward helping the unemployed and the poor. Many faced overwhelming problems—

no jobs, little food, and no homes. Soon after Roosevelt took office, Congress created the **Federal Emergency Relief Administration** (FERA). Harry Hopkins, a New York social worker, headed this agency. It distributed $500 million in federal grants among state organizations that cared for the poor.

In addition to direct aid, Roosevelt wanted to create jobs. Regular work, not just charity, would do much to raise Americans' spirits. The Civil Works Administration (CWA), also headed by Hopkins, created jobs for more than 4 million unemployed men and women.

Congress also established the Civilian Conservation Corps (CCC). This agency put unemployed young men from poor families to work on various conservation projects. CCC workers lived in camps run by the army. They cleared brush, planted trees, built small dams,

Frances Perkins had been a public official in New York before she joined Roosevelt's cabinet.

and performed dozens of other useful tasks across the country.

The CCC is a good example of how swiftly New Deal measures were put into effect. The law that created the program passed Congress on March 31, 1933. Within two years, there were over 500,000 corpsmen at work in 2,500 camps.

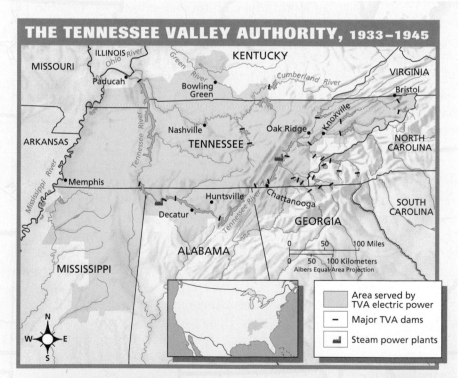

THE TENNESSEE VALLEY AUTHORITY, 1933–1945

MISSOURI
ILLINOIS
Ohio River
KENTUCKY
Green River
VIRGINIA
Paducah
Bowling Green
Cumberland River
Bristol
ARKANSAS
Nashville
Oak Ridge
Knoxville
NORTH CAROLINA
Tennessee River
TENNESSEE
Mississippi River
Memphis
Huntsville
Chattanooga
SOUTH CAROLINA
Decatur
GEORGIA
ALABAMA
MISSISSIPPI

0   50   100 Miles
0   50   100 Kilometers
Albers Equal-Area Projection

N W E S

Area served by TVA electric power
– Major TVA dams
Steam power plants

Learning from Maps.
The TVA provided electricity to a wide area, minimized flooding, and helped lessen poverty.

▶ **Location.** What state had the most dams built in it from 1933 to 1945?

● **Maps**

Recovery. Congress passed laws intended to stimulate business activity and to help farmers recover. The most controversial measure was the **National Industrial Recovery Act** (NIRA). The purpose of the act was to stimulate private business. The act allowed manufacturers in the same field to cooperate with one another without fear of violating any of the antitrust laws. Firms in every industry drew up rules called codes of fair competition. The codes established prices, minimum wages, maximum hours of work, and production limits.

To enforce these new codes, the government next created the National Recovery Administration (NRA). Its symbol was a picture of a blue eagle. Giant factories and small shops all over the country displayed blue eagle stickers in their windows and on their product labels. Despite the NRA's efforts, workers and employers alike criticized the new system. They were unhappy with government regulation of their affairs.

Another section of the NIRA established the Public Works Administration (PWA). The PWA hoped to both stimulate the economy and provide jobs by spending millions of dollars on construction projects such as parks, airports, and public buildings.

Congress tried to solve the farm problem by passing the Agricultural Adjustment Act (AAA). The AAA authorized giving payments to farmers to grow smaller crops. The resulting shortages pushed farm prices and income up.

In addition, Congress established the **Tennessee Valley Authority** (TVA) to start revitalizing the area along the Tennessee River. The TVA built dams and

In this 1933 cartoon, the government, using the NRA, brings employees and employers together to fight the depression.

power stations to stop the frequent flooding and bring electricity to the valley. It developed a network of parks and lakes for recreation. The TVA also helped fight poverty by providing jobs throughout the region. Workers replanted forests and developed other conservation projects. Over time, the TVA and many other New Deal public works projects greatly helped southern and western states in their economic development.

Reform. Congress also established the **Federal Deposit Insurance Corporation** (FDIC) to prevent another banking crisis. The FDIC insured deposits up to $5,000. The U.S. government hoped that guaranteeing deposits would encourage people to keep their money in the banks and enable banks to have money to loan out. In addition, the passage of the new Federal Securities Act regulated the way companies issued and sold stock.

Section 3 Review

• **Glossary**

IDENTIFY and explain the significance of the following: New Deal, Brain Trust, Frances Perkins, Harold Ickes, fireside chats, Hundred Days, Federal Emergency Relief Administration, Harry Hopkins, National Industrial Recovery Act, Tennessee Valley Authority, Federal Deposit Insurance Corporation

REVIEWING FOR DETAILS

1. What did President Roosevelt hope to accomplish with the New Deal?
2. What measures did Roosevelt take to save the banks?
3. What were some of the agencies established during the Hundred Days, and what were some of their functions?

REVIEWING FOR UNDERSTANDING

4. **Writing Mastery:** *Creating* Imagine that you are the president and have just taken office. Write a fireside chat to be broadcast to the American people.
5. **Critical Thinking:** *Drawing Conclusions* What were the advantages and dangers of Roosevelt allowing the federal government to assume so much power during the New Deal?

Section 4

THE NEW DEAL AT ITS HEIGHT

Multimedia Connections

Explore these related topics and materials on the CD–ROM to enrich your understanding of this section:

 Media Bank

- Rural Electrification
- Women on Strike
- Unionized Tenant Farmers
- Mary McLeod Bethune
- Court Packing

 Profiles

- Eleanor Roosevelt
- Huey Long
- Mary McLeod Bethune
- Ralph Bunche

 Simulation

- A Plan for Prosperity

 Atlas

- Labor Strikes of the 1930s

 Readings

- Sit-Down at General Motors

---

n Ohio an 11-year-old farmgirl saved her few pennies to send a letter to the first lady. Perhaps she had some old clothing the girl's family could use. "Mrs. Roosevelt is just a godmother to the world," her mother had said, ". . . an angel for doing so much for the poor." The girl wrote that her father had lost his job, but they had food. She added, "My Papa likes Mr. Roosevelt, and Mother said Mr. Roosevelt carries his worries with a smile."

As you read this section you will find out:

▶ **What the purpose and programs of the Second New Deal were.**

▶ **How Roosevelt changed his political tactics during his second term.**

▶ **What the long-term impact of the New Deal was.**

Criticism of the New Deal

The laws passed during the Hundred Days greatly increased the power of the federal government, particularly that of the president. Some people found this trend alarming. Business leaders objected to restrictions placed on how they conducted their affairs. They charged that the New Deal was destroying the free enterprise system. Opponents of the New Deal formed the **American Liberty League**. They claimed the new laws were unconstitutional. In 1935 and 1936 the Supreme Court ruled that the NIRA and the AAA, respectively, were indeed unconstitutional.

While conservatives argued that the government was doing too much, other critics argued that it was doing too little. Francis Townshend, a California doctor, called for granting a pension to every American over 60.

Senator Huey Long drew great crowds when he spoke. He is photographed here as he helps Senator Hattie Caraway's campaign in Magnolia, Arkansas.

Even some people who had originally supported Roosevelt turned against him. One was a Catholic priest, Father Charles E. Coughlin, who spoke to millions in his weekly radio broadcasts from Detroit. He criticized the New Deal and made bitter personal attacks on Roosevelt. Another was Senator Huey Long of Louisiana, who ruled like a king in his home state. The "Kingfish," as he was called, claimed that the president had become a tool of Wall Street investors.

Long wanted to greatly increase taxes on the wealthy. With these funds, he said, the government could give every family enough money to buy a house and a car and have a minimum income of at least $2,500 a year. The **Share-Our-Wealth** organization, which had been created to carry out Long's plan, had over 4.6 million members. Long hoped to run for president and boasted:

> **"I can take him [Roosevelt]. He's a phony. . . . He's scared of me. I can outpromise him, and he knows it. People will believe me and they won't believe him. . . . He's living on an inherited income. I got nothin', so I don't have to bother about that."**

An assassin's bullet took Long's life before he could test his claim in an election.

The Second New Deal

Most Americans continued to support the New Deal. It relieved much of the human suffering caused by the depression and made people feel that the government was trying to help them. "I think we'd just pack up and move out and leave our stock to starve if the government hadn't stepped in," said one cattle rancher. "This gives us new hope to try again."

The 1934 congressional elections demonstrated the public's support of Roosevelt's New Deal policies. The Democrats increased their majorities in both houses of Congress. One commentator said that Roosevelt was "all but crowned by the people." Now the president could push through more reform legislation. As Harry Hopkins believed:

> **"This is our hour! We've got to get everything we want—a works program, social security, wages and hours, everything— now or never. Get your minds at work on developing a complete ticket to provide security for all the folks of this country up and down and across the board."**

This **Second New Deal** addressed issues that Roosevelt's critics had raised.

Social security. In 1935 Congress passed the **Social Security Act**. This law set up a

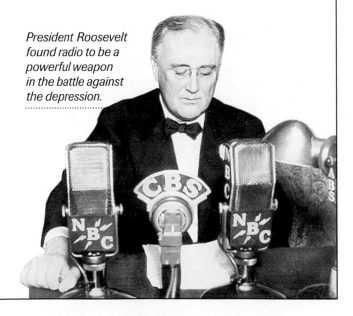

President Roosevelt found radio to be a powerful weapon in the battle against the depression.

system of old-age insurance, which was paid for by workers and their employers. The act also supplied money for disabled workers and for the unemployed.

The Social Security Act did not cover all workers, however. The millions of household servants, agricultural laborers, and other independent workers did not receive these benefits.

WPA. In 1935 the government also established the **Works Progress Administration** (WPA). This program put millions of men and women to work. "Give a man a dole [handout] and you save his body and destroy his spirit," said the WPA's head, Harry Hopkins. "Give him a job and pay him an assured wage, and you save both the body and the spirit." Nationwide, WPA workers built more than 150 airports, 1,000 schools, and 8,000 recreational facilities.

In the city of Boston, for example, major WPA projects included a subway system and an expanded airport. WPA workers taught in nursery schools, cataloged books in the Boston Public Library, and read to the blind. College students employed by the National

In the late 1930s artist Vera Bock created this poster for the Works Progress Administration's Federal Art Project.

Photographer Dorothea Lange documented the depression in California. She became known as one of the world's most talented photographers.

Youth Administration graded papers and did office chores in the Boston schools.

In addition, the WPA employed thousands of artists. They designed posters and painted murals on the walls of many schools and post offices. Musicians gave concerts. Troupes of actors put on plays in big cities and small towns all across America. The Federal Writers' Project collected oral histories, including slave narratives, and prepared regional histories and guidebooks.

Additional acts. In 1935 Congress passed many laws that marked a change of tactics in the battle against the depression. These measures included a higher income tax rate on the wealthy and stricter banking regulations. To lower rates, one law was aimed at breaking up utility company trusts. Congress also passed laws to aid farmers and industrial workers.

• **Workers and Farmers**

The Election of 1936

During the Second New Deal, Roosevelt gave up on holding the support of many industrialists, bankers, and wealthy people. When he campaigned for re-election against Governor Alfred Landon of Kansas in 1936, Roosevelt attacked these groups, whom he called "an enemy within our gates."

Roosevelt built a broad base of support, which included laborers, farmers, women, African Americans, and Hispanics. Before the New Deal, most African American voters had supported the Republican Party—"the party of Lincoln." In 1936, however, a majority of African Americans voted for Roosevelt and other Democrats—one of the most significant political shifts of the 1900s.

In the 1936 election Roosevelt won every state except Maine and Vermont. He did so even though the New Deal had not ended the depression. Unemployment remained very high. Industrial production had picked up, but only slowly. The personality of FDR, as the newspapers called him, had won support for the New Deal and given him a landslide victory.

● **Black Brain Trust**

Roosevelt and the Supreme Court

Roosevelt knew from his victory in 1936 that Americans were behind the New Deal. He feared, however, that the Supreme Court would declare much of the important Second New Deal legislation unconstitutional. The more conservative justices on the Supreme Court believed, for example, that Congress had no right to force workers to contribute to an old-age pension program.

To protect New Deal legislation, Roosevelt asked Congress to increase the size of the Supreme Court. Such an increase would allow him to appoint enough pro–New Deal judges to ensure that the Court would uphold key legislation.

For once Roosevelt misjudged public feeling. Most Americans thought that this "court packing" plan threatened the independence of the judicial branch. After a lengthy, drawn-out debate, Congress rejected the plan.

In time, however, the justices who had opposed New Deal laws either died or resigned. Roosevelt then replaced them with justices who favored the New Deal. The new Court upheld the constitutionality of the Social Security Act and other New Deal legislation. Nevertheless, the Court fight cost Roosevelt much support for his New Deal programs in Congress.

The End of the New Deal

Another setback soon followed. The president never had given up the hopes of cutting

---

History Makers

Eleanor Roosevelt (1884–1962)

The Granger Collection, New York

When she was still a shy young woman, Eleanor Roosevelt attended exclusive private schools and spent holidays with wealthy friends and relatives in high society. Then she married her distant cousin, Franklin, and raised five children.

Early in life, Roosevelt decided to dedicate herself to social service. In the 1920s she began to speak in public. She was a leader in women's rights organizations, a promoter of consumer protection, a friend of the working people, a believer in the rights of young people, and a supporter of better conditions for African Americans.

After she became first lady, Roosevelt continued to be a voice for all the people. During the New Deal, few, if any, white Americans worked harder in the struggle for racial equality. She traveled throughout the country to discover the mood of the people. "You must be my eyes and ears," the president told her.

government expenses and balancing the federal budget. He disliked **deficit spending**—having the government spend more than it takes in—even though most of his New Deal programs required him to follow this policy. During 1936 and early 1937 the economy gradually began to improve and recovery seemed sure. In response, in June 1937, Roosevelt decided to cut back sharply on federal money spent for relief.

This reduction in federal spending brought the recovery to a sudden stop. A recession then followed, business activity fell off, and unemployment increased. Roosevelt quickly agreed to increase government spending again and the economy picked up. For the most part, however, the New Deal Era had ended.

All of the laws passed by Congress during the New Deal and all the new agencies and boards did not end the Great Depression. Why then is the New Deal considered so important?

The New Deal programs created a limited **welfare state**—a system of government institutions that provides for basic social needs of citizens, such as health care and retirement pensions. In addition, the New Deal increased the power of the federal government and gave it greater control over private organizations and individuals. New federal agencies became involved in more aspects of everyday life.

The New Deal years also saw a shift in the balance of power among the branches of the federal government. Congress came to have less power and the presidency more. The crisis of the Great Depression encouraged Congress to put more responsibility on the shoulders of Roosevelt and his appointees. Roosevelt's power and remarkable popularity made the presidency the strongest single force in the national government.

Migrant Mother, *Dorothea Lange's most famous photograph, shows the dignity with which people lived through the difficult times.*

Section 4 Review

• Glossary

IDENTIFY and explain the significance of the following: American Liberty League, Huey Long, Share-Our-Wealth, Second New Deal, Social Security Act, Works Progress Administration, deficit spending, welfare state

REVIEWING FOR DETAILS

1. What programs made up the Second New Deal, and why were they created?
2. What new tactics did Roosevelt use to help win the election of 1936?
3. If the New Deal came to an end in the late 1930s, why is it still considered important?

REVIEWING FOR UNDERSTANDING

4. **Writing Mastery:** *Persuading* Write a short essay persuading others to support or reject Roosevelt's court-packing plan.
5. **Critical Thinking:** *Drawing Conclusions* Why might Roosevelt have thought that appealing to the poor and the working people during the 1936 election was a better strategy than appealing to the wealthy?

Section 5

AMERICANS IN THE DEPRESSION

Multimedia Connections

Explore these related topics and materials on the CD–ROM to enrich your understanding of this section:

 Profiles

- John Steinbeck
- Richard Wright

 Biographies

- Josefina Fierro de Bright

 Readings

- *The Grapes of Wrath*
- The Beuschers

 Media Bank

- Women in Government

n early 1939 the singer Marian Anderson was planning a concert in Constitution Hall in Washington, D.C. The hall's owners, the Daughters of the American Revolution (DAR), canceled the concert. It soon became clear that they did so because Anderson was an African American. In response, Eleanor Roosevelt resigned from the DAR and persuaded the president to arrange for Anderson to sing at the Lincoln Memorial. Anderson gave a performance that brought repeated cheers from the audience of 75,000.

As you read this section you will find out:

▶ **How the depression affected families.**

▶ **How the depression affected many Americans.**

▶ **How people tried to escape the depression.**

The Human Costs

Statistics tell little about the human suffering that the Great Depression caused. Many employed people had trouble making ends meet because of shorter working hours and lower pay. Poor people sank deeper into poverty. Unemployment meant more than the loss of a job—it could mean the loss of a home and the breakup of a family.

Family life. The depression changed the lives of many families. Children of the unemployed had to assume more household responsibility and try to find odd jobs to bring in extra money. Families were split apart when members moved away in an attempt to find employment. In many cases, women became solely responsible for the family while their husbands went to another city in search of work. This separation often put a great strain on family life. One woman told a social worker:

"**My husband went north about three months ago to try his luck. The first month he wrote pretty regularly. . . . For five weeks we have had no word from him. . . . Don't know where he is or what he is up to.**"

The government hired many artists to produce posters for the Works Progress Administration.

Women in the workforce.
Many thousands of women managed to find work when their husbands or fathers lost their jobs. While the number of employed women increased during the depression, so too did discrimination against them. Most of the time women were paid less than men for the same work. Many married women whose husbands were employed lost their jobs because employers, including the federal government, thought these women did not need to work.

Another Side of the Depression

The depression affected the entire nation, but it hit some Americans particularly hard. For example, unemployment was far higher among African Americans, Mexican Americans, and American Indians than among other groups.

African Americans.
The Great Depression struck African Americans with cruel force. As had happened previously during hard times, they were "the last hired and the first fired." By 1932 more than 30 percent of all black workers were unemployed.

Many New Deal programs did little or nothing to help them. Unemployed African Americans rarely got a full share of federal relief money or public works jobs. The Social Security Act did not cover the types of jobs that most African Americans could obtain. NRA industrial codes permitted employers to pay lower wages to African Americans than to whites. The CCC and TVA segregated black workers.

New Deal farm policy actually made conditions worse for black tenant farmers and sharecroppers. The AAA payments were given to landowners. When landowners took tobacco and cotton fields out of production, it meant that the tenants and sharecroppers who had farmed these acres lost their jobs and often their homes as well.

Despite the limitations of the New Deal, most African Americans supported it. The new federal relief programs seemed particularly important to them because so many African Americans were unemployed and poor during the depression. Many believed that the fact that they were merely included in New Deal programs was a sign of progress.

In addition, important New Deal officials treated African Americans fairly. For example, Roosevelt ordered state relief officials not to "discriminate . . . because of race or religion or politics" in distributing government aid. This order was not always followed, but Harry

These men are working in the kitchen of the "Royal Blue" diner car of the Baltimore & Ohio railroad.

Mexican Americans were hard-hit by the depression. Many were forced to leave the country, while others faced poverty and unemployment.

Hopkins and other key WPA officials made sincere efforts to enforce it.

Mexican Americans. Before the depression, thousands of Mexicans had come to the United States to find jobs. In the expanding economy of the 1920s, employers eagerly hired them. Most ended up as farmworkers in the Southwest and the West. When times got tough, however, they no longer were welcome.

During Hoover's presidency, deportation became public policy. Thousands of Mexican-born farm laborers and their families were gathered up by federal authorities and shipped back to Mexico. Officials tried to justify this policy by arguing that there was not enough relief money to care for them. Officials also argued that Mexican workers were taking jobs that American citizens needed—even though some of their children had been born in the United States and were citizens!

Roosevelt's New Deal did little to help Mexican Americans. They were often denied relief and federal jobs. In addition, they were paid lower wages than most other employees. They faced discrimination almost everywhere.

American Indians. American Indians received their own "new deal." Back in 1924 Congress had passed the Indian Citizenship Act granting citizenship to American Indians. Ten years later the **Indian Reorganization Act** (IRA) further changed federal Indian policy.

This law encouraged the revival of tribal life. It provided Native Americans with more protection for their property and better control over their local communities and their culture. The Bureau of Indian Affairs no longer discouraged Indians from studying their history and exploring their culture. Indian schools began to teach Indian languages and history. American Indians relearned and developed their traditional arts and crafts. In addition, to combat the depression the government provided work on New Deal projects and offered loans to start businesses. Indian women benefited from new employment and education opportunities.

The Dust Bowl

During the depression, sometimes even the land seemed to turn against the farmers. The

• The Plow that Broke the Plains

An amateur photographer waited until the cloud of dust was upon him before taking a picture of one of the worst dust storms to hit New Mexico.

hardest-hit were the farmers of the Great Plains—the land from Texas and Oklahoma to South and North Dakota. This region rarely gets much rain. In the early 1930s almost no rain fell.

By 1934 the drought had become so bad that winds picked up the powder-dry topsoil and blew it away in dense black clouds. It was impossible for farmers to grow anything on this dry, shifting land that came to be known as the **Dust Bowl**.

Poor and discouraged, many farm families, from Oklahoma in particular, loaded their possessions into their cars and trucks and headed for California. Once there, these Okies, as they were called, usually became migrant workers. They followed the harvest, picking fruit, vegetables, cotton, and other crops. They spent

Woody Guthrie entertained Americans throughout the depression.

their nights in roadside camps. Old people died alongside unfamiliar roads. Babies grew up constantly hungry.

One of these Okies, a young folksinger named Woodrow Wilson (Woody) Guthrie, moved to California in 1937. "In most towns . . . it is a jailhouse offense to be unemployed," Guthrie wrote. In one of his songs, Guthrie expressed the poor conditions of the migrant workers this way:

> **"California is a garden of Eden,**
> **A paradise to live in or see.**
> **But, believe it or not, you won't find it so hot,**
> **If you ain't got the do-re-mi [money]."**
>
> From "Do Re Mi" ©1961, 1963 TRO.

Images of the Depression

Many artists and writers tried to describe life during the depression. They captured the misery in the faces of people—from the unemployed in urban soup kitchens and breadlines to poor sharecroppers in the South, from farmers in the Dust Bowl, to the migrant laborers in the Far West.

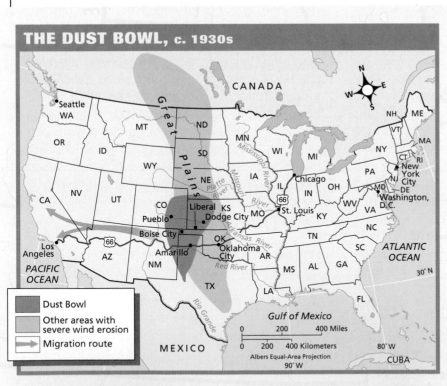

THE DUST BOWL, c. 1930s

Dust Bowl
Other areas with severe wind erosion
Migration route

• **Maps**

Learning from Maps.
The drought devastated farmers in the Dust Bowl and forced many to leave their homes.

▶ **Movement.** What highway route might a family living in or around Oklahoma City take if they were migrating to California?

John Steinbeck's novel *The Grapes of Wrath* is one of the best descriptions of the depression experience. It traces the Joad family's travels from the Dust Bowl to the migrant camps in California. Ma Joad vows, "They ain't gonna wipe us out. Why, we're the people—we go on." In 1962 Steinbeck won the Nobel Prize for literature.

Photographer Walker Evans and writer James Agee recorded the lives of poor tenant farmers. They spent months talking with farmers about their opinions and experiences. Evans and Agee published their pictures and interviews in *Let Us Now Praise Famous Men.* The government employed many other writers and photographers to create similar projects.

Escaping the Depression

While some people were busy recording the depression, others were trying to escape it. Every week, millions of Americans went to the movies to try to forget their troubles for an hour or two. Musicals starring dancers Fred Astaire and Ginger Rogers were incredibly popular. For laughter, audiences depended on comedians like the Marx Brothers, Mae West, and W. C. Fields.

In 1936 Margaret Mitchell's southern epic *Gone with the Wind* became the best selling novel in U.S. publishing history. Three years later, MGM Studios turned the novel into a movie starring Vivian Leigh as Scarlett O'Hara and Clark Gable as Rhett Butler. The film was a huge hit. It won 10 Academy Awards and became MGM's most successful film ever.

When they were not at the movies, Americans spent a lot of time listening to the radio. Programs like *The Shadow* and *Stella Dallas* kept listeners glued to their sets. Orson Welles caused a panic when he broadcast "The War of the Worlds," a program that sounded like a news report describing an army of martians landing in New Jersey to attack Earth. Duke Ellington and Benny Goodman kept radio listeners dancing to their music. Programs such as these, however, provided only a temporary distraction from the depression.

The Granger Collection, New York

King Kong was one of the many movies that Americans saw in the 1930s.

Section 5 Review

• **Glossary**

• **Time Line**

IDENTIFY and explain the significance of the following: Indian Reorganization Act, Dust Bowl, Woody Guthrie, John Steinbeck

REVIEWING FOR DETAILS
1. What impact did the depression have on families?
2. How were the 1930s particularly hard for some Americans?
3. How did people try to forget their problems during the depression?

REVIEWING FOR UNDERSTANDING
4. **Writing Mastery:** *Creating* Write a poem, folk song, or short story about life during the depression.
5. **Critical Thinking:** *Cause and Effect* How did the depression affect discrimination against various groups?

CHAPTER 23

America and World War II (1930–1945)

THEMES IN AMERICAN HISTORY

Global Relations:
How might a country be drawn into a war among other countries?

Technology and Society:
How might the development of new technology change warfare?

Cultural Diversity:
How might a country's involvement in a war affect different groups of people at home?

 • Video Opener

 • Skill Builder

African American Staff Sergeant Johnnie Stevens won the Bronze Star for bravery in 1945. He said of fighting in World War II:

"If any soldier tells you he wasn't afraid, he's a liar. But . . . it's a job. . . . You do what you've been trained to do, and you do it without thinking. You're concentrating on what's there, which takes your mind off being afraid or being brave. In combat, five minutes is like a year."

image above: *American anti-Nazi poster, 1940s*

Section 1

THE WORLD GOES TO WAR

Multimedia Connections

Explore these related topics and materials on the CD–ROM to enrich your understanding of this section:

 Atlas

- Prelude to War: Germany, 1939
- Prelude to War: Italy, 1939
- Prelude to War: Japan, 1941

 Media Bank

- World War II Radio Bulletin
- World War II Alliances
- U.S. Entry into World War II
- Battle of Britain
- Japan's Invasion of China
- Evacuation of Dunkirk
- 1940 Election

 Profiles

- Hirohito
- Benito Mussolini
- Joseph Stalin
- Edouard Daladier

 Readings

- Declarations of War

t was a quiet Sunday morning in Hawaii. At 7:55 A.M. the Japanese struck. Screaming dive-bombers swooped down for the kill. Explosions shattered the air. The destruction was terrible. The Japanese attack on Pearl Harbor was by far the worst defeat the U.S. Navy had ever suffered. The next day President Roosevelt asked Congress for a declaration of war on Japan. He called December 7, 1941, "a date which will live in infamy."

As you read this section you will find out:

▶ **What forms of government arose in Italy, Germany, and Japan.**

▶ **How the attempts of Germany, Italy, and Japan to conquer and control new territories led to war.**

▶ **How the United States was drawn into World War II.**

The Totalitarian States

Many people thought that World War I had been the "war to end all wars." Just 20 years after the signing of the Versailles Treaty, however, they were proven wrong. The treaty had left many people in Germany, Italy, and Japan feeling angry and cheated out of territory. The drive of these three nations to build powerful empires eventually led to the outbreak of World War II.

Italy and Germany. After World War I Germany, Italy, and Japan each developed forms of government known as **totalitarianism**. Their basic principle was that national governments were everything, the individual citizens nothing. These governments stamped out their opposition. The only political party was controlled by the state, and power was concentrated in the hands of one leader. These dictators allowed no criticism of their policies.

Totalitarianism appeared in Italy in the 1920s when Benito Mussolini became the country's dictator. He called his political system **fascism**, named after an ancient symbol of Rome. Mussolini dreamed of controlling the entire Mediterranean region. His views were enormously popular with the Italian people.

In Germany the National Socialists, or **Nazis**, led by Adolf Hitler, established a totalitarian government in 1933. To win followers, Hitler used inspiring speeches reminding

Germans of the harsh Versailles Treaty and the postwar depression. Like Mussolini, Hitler also gained widespread popularity.

● **Between the Wars**

Japanese warlords. In Asia the nation seeking territorial expansion was Japan. There the official head of the government was the emperor, Hirohito, who was considered by the Japanese people to be a god. Hirohito, however, left much of the day-to-day running of the government to Japanese military leaders. In the late 1920s those in power dreamed of seizing foreign lands in order to obtain raw

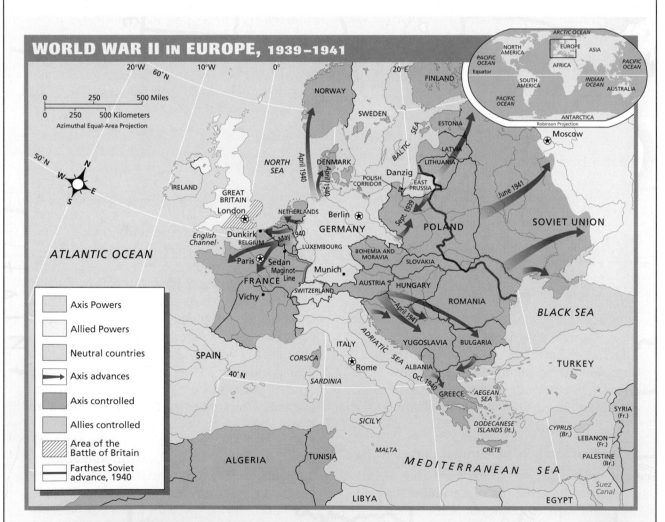

WORLD WAR II IN EUROPE, 1939–1941

Legend:
- Axis Powers
- Allied Powers
- Neutral countries
- → Axis advances
- Axis controlled
- Allies controlled
- Area of the Battle of Britain
- Farthest Soviet advance, 1940

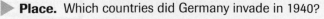

Learning from Maps. Germany's push into Poland in 1939 brought Poland's allies—France and Great Britain—into the conflict and started World War II.

▶ **Place.** Which countries did Germany invade in 1940?

● **Maps**

materials for rapidly growing Japanese industries. They eventually hoped to control all of East Asia and the islands of the Pacific.

In 1931 the Japanese army invaded Manchuria, a province in northern China rich in coal and iron ore deposits. President Herbert Hoover announced that the United States would never recognize Japan's right to any Chinese territory seized by force.

In the mid-1930s Japan began a massive naval buildup. In July 1937 Japanese and Chinese forces clashed near Beijing. The incident led to an all-out war, as Japanese troops poured into northern China.

Roosevelt's Foreign Policy

Japan's attacks on China worried President Roosevelt. Still, he could not ignore the strong isolationist and antiwar feelings in the United States. Famous pilot Charles A. Lindbergh later expressed the sentiments of many isolationists of the 1930s:

> **"If we are forced into a war against the wishes of an overwhelming majority of our people, we will have proved democracy such a failure at home that there will be little use fighting for it abroad."**

In August 1935 Congress passed the first in a series of neutrality acts. This law prohibited the sale of weapons to either side in any war. The law also directed the president to warn American citizens that if they traveled on the ships of warring nations, they did so at their own risk.

Before the passage of the first neutrality act, Italian troops had invaded the African nation of Ethiopia. As the conflict dragged on, Roosevelt applied the neutrality laws. Most Americans sympathized with the Ethiopians, who had done nothing to anger Italy. Yet because the Ethiopians had few modern weapons to use against the heavily

The Granger Collection, New York

This image from a 1934 German magazine shows Adolf Hitler as the savior of Germany, which is how many of his supporters viewed him.

• **Adolf Hitler**

armed Italian invaders, the neutrality acts harmed the Ethiopians far more than their foreign enemies.

Seeing what had happened in Ethiopia, Roosevelt got around the neutrality laws when Japan invaded China. Noting that Japan had not formally declared war, he allowed the Chinese to buy weapons from Americans. Roosevelt was looking for a way to stop the totalitarian nations without getting directly involved in a war.

Hitler's War Machine

After he gained power, Hitler systematically violated the Versailles Treaty. In 1936 his troops occupied the Rhineland, a region that had been controlled by France after World War I. In 1938 Hitler annexed Austria and part of Czechoslovakia called the Sudetenland. Many European leaders were particularly outraged by the move against Czechoslovakia, but few wanted to go to war with Germany.

In September 1938 French and British leaders met with Hitler in Munich, Germany, to work out a solution to the conflict. At the **Munich Conference**, France and Britain agreed to let Germany take the Sudetenland if Hitler agreed that it would be his last territorial claim in Europe. This policy of **appeasement**, or giving in to avoid a larger conflict, would only give Hitler more confidence.

In the summer of 1939 Hitler and Joseph Stalin, the leader of the Soviet Union, signed a **nonaggression pact**, agreeing not to attack one another. With the Soviets no longer a threat, the German army invaded Poland on

As Hitler expanded his military power, he also increased his attacks on European Jews, whom he blamed for most of Germany's troubles. These people observe the results of Kristallnacht (the Night of Broken Glass), when rioters encouraged by Nazi anti-Jewish propaganda attacked Jewish businesses and synagogues in early November 1938.

September 1. This time appeasement would not be tried. Two days later Poland's allies— Great Britain and France—declared war on Germany. World War II had begun.

In a little more than a month, Poland was swallowed up. The mighty German war machine rolled on. In April 1940 the Germans invaded Denmark and Norway. On May 10, German tanks swept into the Netherlands and Belgium. A few days later German troops broke through the French defenses at Sedan. They soon reached the English Channel, trapping thousands of British, French, and Belgian troops at Dunkirk. Between May 26 and June 4, British ships managed to rescue about 340,000 soldiers from the beach at Dunkirk and carry them to England. Still, it was a crushing defeat.

As they had in Poland, in a maneuver known as Blitzkrieg, or "lightning war," the German armored divisions swept on through France. Late in June the French surrendered. Hitler was the master of most of western Europe. Only Britain stood between him and total victory.

Hitler expected to crush British resistance with massive air raids and then invade the shattered country. German U-boats and air bombers had sunk many British merchant vessels. In May 1940 British prime minister

Winston Churchill appealed to President Roosevelt for help. He needed American aid to strengthen the British fleet.

Roosevelt knew that it would take time to get the Senate to act. Therefore, he issued an executive order turning over 50 destroyers to the British in exchange for 99-year leases on naval and air bases in the Caribbean.

The Lend-Lease Act

In the November election, Roosevelt did what no other president had ever done—he ran for a third consecutive term. His opponent was Republican Wendell Willkie. Willkie played up the third term issue as well as the possibility of the United States going to war, but Roosevelt pledged not to join in the conflict. Roosevelt received 449 electoral votes to Willkie's 82.

Roosevelt interpreted his re-election as approval of his policy of aiding Great Britain. The British were now running desperately short of money to pay for American supplies. In addition, German submarines had been threatening American shipping in the Atlantic. Roosevelt therefore proposed lending the British the weapons and goods they needed. In a radio address he told the American people that the United States "must become the great arsenal of democracy."

In January 1941 Roosevelt asked Congress to pass the **Lend-Lease Act.** This measure gave the president authority to sell or lend war supplies to any nation whose defense was considered to be essential to America's security. The Lend-Lease Act aroused fierce opposition. "Lending war equipment is a good deal like lending chewing gum," said Ohio senator Robert A. Taft. "You don't want it back." The majority of Americans, however, favored the Lend-Lease Act, which Congress passed in March.

On June 22, 1941, Hitler broke his 1939 nonaggression agreement with Stalin and invaded the Soviet Union. Roosevelt quickly announced that lend-lease aid would also be extended to the Soviets. In July he ordered 4,000 U.S. Marines to Iceland. This move pushed the area under American protection farther into the Atlantic.

Pearl Harbor

Meanwhile, Japan continued to expand its control over East Asia. President Roosevelt hoped to stop Japanese aggression with economic weapons. In July 1940 he halted the exportation of aviation fuel to Japan. In September 1940 Japan, Germany, and Italy signed a mutual defense treaty. In July 1941, after Hitler invaded the Soviet Union, Japanese troops invaded the southern regions of French Indochina. They were preparing to attack the Dutch East Indies, where there were important oil supplies. At that point, Roosevelt froze all Japanese funds in the United States, making it almost impossible for the Japanese to purchase U.S. oil.

These actions shocked and angered the Japanese. They would either have to come to terms with the United States or find a new oil supply. As the United States insisted that Japan withdraw from China and Indochina, Japan decided to attack the United States.

The Japanese planned a surprise air raid to destroy the U.S. Pacific Fleet stationed at Pearl Harbor in Hawaii. Japanese leaders believed that by the time the United States could rebuild its Pacific forces, Japan would have expanded its control over East Asia. Then Japan could defeat any American counterattack. The raid was set for Sunday, December 7.

On that morning, Japanese warships were in position about 200 miles north of the Hawaiian Islands. The crews of their aircraft carriers sent their planes off with shouts of

Presidential Lives
Franklin Roosevelt

Franklin Roosevelt is the only United States president to ever serve more than two terms. When the Democratic convention met in Chicago in 1940, not even Roosevelt's closest advisers knew if he would seek renomination,

since no one had even attempted a try at a third consecutive term. However, Roosevelt felt that the critical international situation called for continuity of leadership. He won the nomination easily.

Roosevelt's personable style helped build diplomatic relations during the war. Rather than just sending advisers to work out war plans, Roosevelt traveled widely to meet with Allied leaders. He formed a close relationship with British and Soviet leaders. He had a difficult time winning over Soviet leader Joseph Stalin, however, who appeared cold and distant during their first meeting. Roosevelt soon had Stalin laughing loudly at his jokes and treating him as a friend. From that day forward Roosevelt jokingly referred to Stalin as "Uncle Joe."

"Banzai!"—the Japanese battle cry meaning "Long live the emperor." The first wave of 183 planes headed for Pearl Harbor.

Fortunately, the American aircraft carriers were all at sea. But eight battleships were lined up on "Battleship Row" in the harbor. The bombers came so low over these ships that sailors could see the faces of Japanese pilots as they released their bombs. Civilian Cornelia MacEwen Hurd described the view from her home near the harbor:

The Granger Collection, New York

The USS West Virginia *and the USS* Tennessee, *shown here, were hit during the Japanese attack on Pearl Harbor.*

• **Pearl Harbor**

"**I saw the most dreadful thing I ever saw in my life. The fire, the blasting of the ships, just one after the other, in flames! . . . A Japanese plane passed right in front of my yard, not more than forty feet from where I was sitting. . . . It was so vivid I could see the face, the profile, and the rising sun on the plane.**"

The Japanese planes rained bombs on ships in the harbor. They ranged up and down the coast, attacking airfields and barracks. In less than two hours, 18 warships were sunk or disabled. The worst blow came when the USS *Arizona* blew apart and sank, trapping more than 1,000 men inside. Nearly 300 planes were destroyed or damaged, most of them while on the ground.

The next day Congress declared war on Japan. On December 11 Germany and Italy decided to support their ally, Japan, by declaring war on the United States. The nations that fought the **Axis Powers** of Germany, Italy, and Japan were known as the **Allied Powers**. Chief among the Allies were the United States, Great Britain, France, the Soviet Union, China, Australia, and Canada.

Section 1 Review

• **Glossary**

IDENTIFY and explain the significance of the following: totalitarianism, Benito Mussolini, fascism, Nazis, Adolf Hitler, Hirohito, Munich Conference, appeasement, Joseph Stalin, nonaggression pact, Winston Churchill, Lend-Lease Act, Axis Powers, Allied Powers

• **Gazetteer**

LOCATE and explain the importance of the following: Manchuria, Poland, Dunkirk, Dutch East Indies, Pearl Harbor (see map on page 541)

REVIEWING FOR DETAILS

1. What type of governments came to power in Germany, Italy, and Japan during the 1920s and 1930s?
2. What were the causes of World War II?
3. How did the United States become involved in the war?

REVIEWING FOR UNDERSTANDING

4. **Geographic Literacy** Why did Japanese leaders launch a policy of expansion during the 1930s and 1940s?
5. **Critical Thinking:** *Drawing Conclusions* What might have happened had the United States not extended aid to Great Britain or become involved in the war?

Section 2
THE WAR ON THE HOME FRONT

Multimedia Connections

Explore these related topics and materials on the CD–ROM to enrich your understanding of this section:

 Atlas

- Urban Population, 1940
- Relocating Japanese Americans

 Profiles

- Jacqueline Cochran
- Benjamin O. Davis, Jr.

 Readings

- Memories of Internment

 Media Bank

- Jessie Owens at the Olympics
- African Americans in Industry
- Norman Mineta

A fter Pearl Harbor, people throughout the country pitched in to help the war effort. Families that did a particularly good job were rewarded with a "V-Home Certificate." The criteria for becoming a V (for "Victory")-Home reflected the changes the war brought to everyday life, such as conserving items that the armed forces needed. Even as most Americans were united in supporting the war, however, prejudice fueled discrimination against some fellow Americans.

As you read this section you will find out:

▶ **How the attack on Pearl Harbor united Americans behind the war effort.**

▶ **How women and ethnic minorities were affected by the war.**

▶ **What factors led to the internment of Japanese Americans.**

Mobilization

The United States was somewhat better prepared to fight World War II than it had been to fight World War I. In September 1940 Congress had voted to draft men between the ages of 21 and 36 for military service—the first peacetime draft in American history. The draft proved helpful when it became necessary to raise a fighting force quickly.

About two thirds of the 15 million Americans who served in the armed forces during World War II were draftees. Outraged by the Japanese surprise attack on Pearl Harbor, millions eagerly volunteered to serve their country. More than 300,000 of these volunteers were women—over 10 times the number that had served in World War I.

• **Women in Military Service**

During the war, all Americans were encouraged to ration goods and to recycle materials that could be used by the military.

• **Children and Rationing**

The Granger Collection, New York

Hundreds of thousands of additional workers were needed to produce the tools of war. Unemployment ceased to be a national problem for the first time since 1929. Men and women flocked to East Coast shipyards, to midwestern steel plants and former automobile factories, and to western aircraft plants.

About 6 million women went to work in defense plants during the war. Government propaganda and the entertainment industry used the image of "Rosie the Riveter" to encourage women to take jobs traditionally held by men. One woman remembered her job as a riveter and the pride it brought her:

"I worked on that job for three months, ten hours a day, six days a week, and slapped three-eighths or three-quarter-inch rivets by hand that no one else would do. I didn't have that kind of confidence as a kid growing up, because I didn't have that opportunity."

The wartime labor shortage also strengthened the gains that organized labor had made under the New Deal. The National War Labor Board, first created during World War I, was re-established in 1942 to regulate wages and prevent labor disputes. Farmers also experienced boom times. The demand for food to feed U.S. troops and their allies caused farm income to double.

Long before the attack on Pearl Harbor, President Roosevelt had established councils to oversee the production and distribution of war materials. After war was declared, similar boards controlled the distribution of raw materials to manufacturers and stopped the production of nonessential goods.

Steel, aluminum, rubber, and other raw materials needed to make weapons were in extremely short supply. There was no serious shortage of gasoline, but gas was rationed in order to discourage unnecessary travel. The government also rationed scarce foods, such as meat, butter, and sugar.

The huge demand for weapons and supplies finally ended the Great Depression. Many companies shifted away from the production of consumer goods to weapons. Automobile companies turned out tanks, trucks, and even airplanes. Manufacturers of airplanes in the United States produced some 300,000 aircraft by the end of the war.

Discrimination and Segregation

As had been the case during World War I, the labor shortage benefited African American and Mexican American workers. Racial discrimination did not end, however. Many nonwhites continued to face prejudice, both on the home front and overseas.

The Granger Collection, New York

Many civilians, like this woman who worked in a California aircraft plant, found jobs in war-related industries.

American Letters

"Recuerdo: How I Changed the War and Won the Game."

Mary Helen Ponce

Americans on the home front paid close attention to the war news. In Los Angeles, young Mary Helen Ponce, who later became a successful writer, kept adults in her Mexican American neighborhood informed of events by translating English news reports into Spanish.

During World War II, I used to translate the English newspaper's war news for our adopted grandmother Doña Luisa and her friends. All of them were *señoras de edad*, elderly ladies who could not read English, only their native Spanish.

Every afternoon they would gather on Doña Luisa's front porch to await Doña Trinidad's son who delivered the paper to her promptly at 5 P.M. There, among the *geranios* [geraniums] and pots of *yerba buena* [peppermint] I would bring them the news of the war.

At first I enjoyed doing this, for the *señoras* would welcome me as a grown-up. They would push their chairs around in a semicircle, the better to hear me. I would sit in the middle, on a *banquito* [stool] that was a milk crate. I don't remember how I began to be their translator but because I was an obedient child and at eight a good reader, I was somehow coerced [forced] or selected.

I would sit down, adjust my dress, then slowly unwrap the paper, reading the headlines to myself in English, trying to decide which news items were the most important, which to tell first. Once I had decided, I would translate them into my best Spanish for Doña Luisa and her friends.

The news of a battle would bring sighs . . . from the ladies. They would roll their eyes toward heaven, imploring [begging] our Lord to protect their loved ones from danger. . . . Once I had read them the highlights of the war I was allowed to play ball with my friends.

Mexican American writer Mary Helen Ponce accepts an award in Los Angeles.

One day we had an important ball game going, our team was losing, and it was my turn at bat. Just then Doña Luisa called me. It was time for *las noticias* [the news]. Furious at this interruption yet not daring to disobey, I dropped the bat, ran to the porch, ripped open the paper, pointed to the headlines and in a loud voice proclaimed [declared]: *"Ya están los japoneses en San Francisco . . . los esperan en Los Angeles muy pronto,"* or "The Japanese have landed in San Francisco; they should be in Los Angeles soon."

". . . *Purísima* [Goodness gracious]," chanted las señoras as I dashed off to resume my game. . . .

After that I was able to translate according to whim [when it was convenient]—and depending on whether or not I was up to bat when the paper arrived.

The workforce. Beginning in late 1940 African American labor leader A. Philip Randolph planned a march on Washington to protest continued discrimination in the workplace. President Roosevelt feared that such a demonstration would divide public opinion at a time when national unity was essential. Hoping to persuade Randolph to cancel the march, Roosevelt issued an executive order prohibiting racial discrimination in defense plants. This rule was enforced by a **Fair Employment Practices Committee** (FEPC). Randolph then called off the march.

This did not mean that African Americans received equal treatment, however. Many whites resented what they saw as the deals Roosevelt had made with African Americans. There was a good deal of racial conflict within the armed services and in industrial plants. In 1943 riots involving attacks on African Americans erupted in New York City and Detroit. More African Americans were demanding their rights as members of a democratic society. It was clear that when the war ended, demands for fair treatment would increase.

The war also brought conflict as well as some economic opportunities for Mexican

Americans. In July 1942 the United States and Mexico signed a treaty that allowed **braceros**, Mexican farmworkers, to enter the United States temporarily. Their efforts helped keep up vital food production during the war. Mexican American men and women also found jobs in many industries, particularly in the West and the Southwest.

As with African Americans, however, the increased number of Mexicans and Mexican Americans in the workforce led to increased racial tensions. In 1943 the **zoot-suit riots** broke out in Los Angeles when U.S. sailors and others went around the city attacking Mexican American youths dressed in flashy "zoot suits" popular during the time.

The fighting forces. During the war about 1 million African Americans enlisted or were drafted. Compared to earlier wars, there was some improvement in conditions for African American service members. Still, they were kept in segregated units and frequently treated with disrespect by both white officers and enlisted men.

A number of African Americans became pilots in the air force. The most highly decorated African American flying unit was the 99th Pursuit Squadron under the leadership of Colonel Benjamin O. Davis, Jr., son of the first African American brigadier general. These pilots were called the "Tuskegee Airmen" because they trained at Tuskegee, Alabama, home of Booker T. Washington's Tuskegee Institute.

During the war approximately 400,000 Hispanic Americans served in the armed forces. One of the most famous Hispanic units was the mainly Mexican American 88th Division, known as the "Blue Devils." Seventeen Mexican Americans earned the Congressional Medal of Honor.

One of the most interesting minority units was the Navajo Code Talkers, which served in the Pacific. This branch of the Marine Signal Corps sent secret messages based on the Navajo language, which proved impossible for the Japanese to

East Los Angeles deputy sheriff Bartley Brown inspects the haircut of prisoner Alex Rodriguez, who is wearing a "zoot suit." Rodriguez was arrested during the zoot-suit riots of 1943.

These members of the 99th Pursuit Squadron, who trained at Tuskegee, Alabama, were the first African American fighter pilots to see action in World War II. They shot down eight German aircraft in their first battle.

decode. The Code Talkers made breaking the code even more difficult by substituting seemingly ordinary words for military terms. For example, when the Code Talkers used the Navajo words for "chicken hawk," "hummingbird," and "iron fish," they were really referring to a dive-bomber, a fighter plane, and a submarine. More than 400 Navajo marines served in this select unit by the war's end. They were instrumental in helping win some of the most important battles in the Pacific campaign.

Suspicion of Japanese Americans

The major stain on the American civil liberties record during the war was in the treatment of Japanese Americans. The government suspected that some Japanese Americans were disloyal and would try to interfere with the war

effort, even though thousands of Japanese Americans volunteered for and served in combat positions. Government officials forced some 112,000 Japanese Americans who lived on the West Coast to move to internment [confinement] camps in interior sections of the country.

Many white Americans on the West Coast had always been suspicious of the Chinese and Japanese Americans who settled there. This was partly the dislike of immigrants with different customs, but it was also a matter of racial prejudice. These suspicions greatly increased after Japan's surprise attack on Pearl Harbor. Many people were convinced that all people of Japanese descent were spies.

There was no evidence that Japanese Americans were any less loyal than other

Navajo Code Talkers Corporal Henry Bake, Jr., (left) and Private First Class George H. Kirk (right) prepare to send secret messages to American forces during the fighting on the Solomon Islands.

Americans. Most of them had been born in the United States after immigration from Japan was restricted in the early 1900s. Nevertheless, they were forced to give up their homes and property and leave for the camps. One woman, a college student in Seattle, Washington, at the time of her confinement, described a typical internment camp:

> **"Camp Minidoka was located in the south-central part of Idaho, north of the Snake River. It was a semidesert region. When we arrived I could see nothing but flat prairies, clumps of greasewood shrubs, and jack rabbits. . . . Our home was one room in a large army-type barracks, measuring about 20 by 25 feet. The only furnishings were an iron pot-belly stove and cots."**

Many carried the memories of internment with them for years. Some 40 years later Daniel Kuzuhara still recalled "the pain of being labeled a 'dirty Jap' and a 'dangerous enemy.'" After the war many Americans greatly regretted the treatment Japanese Americans received. In 1948 Congress passed an act to help those who had been interned recover part of their financial losses. Court decisions in the 1980s awarded additional benefits to the relocated Japanese American families.

This woman was one of 300 Japanese Americans from Bainbridge Island, near Seattle, Washington, who were forced to relocate to an internment camp. She is assisted by two members of the U.S. Army Medical Corps after collapsing during the relocation.

● **Japanese American Relocation**

Section 2 Review

● **Glossary**

IDENTIFY and explain the significance of the following: A. Philip Randolph, Fair Employment Practices Committee, braceros, zoot-suit riots, Benjamin O. Davis, Jr.

REVIEWING FOR DETAILS
1. How did the Japanese attack on Pearl Harbor influence the American war effort?
2. How did the war affect women and minority groups in the United States and overseas?

REVIEWING FOR UNDERSTANDING
3. **Geographic Literacy** Why were Japanese Americans relocated to areas away from the West Coast?
4. **Writing Mastery:** *Describing* Imagine that you are an American teenager in 1943. Write several diary entries describing how the war is affecting your life.
5. **Critical Thinking:** *Generalizations and Stereotypes* Why do you think people in the United States reacted so strongly toward Japanese Americans?

Section 3

FIGHTING IN ASIA, AFRICA, AND EUROPE

Multimedia Connections

Explore these related topics and materials on the CD–ROM to enrich your understanding of this section:

 Readings

- Soldier's Story
- Technology and Advancements

 Atlas

- D-Day Invasion

 Media Bank

- Combat in Europe
- Fighting in Asia
- War in North Africa

 Profiles

- Winston Churchill
- Douglas MacArthur
- George Patton

n November 1943 the 2nd Marine Division waded ashore on the island of Tarawa, in the Pacific. Sergeant John Bushemi noticed a hand gripping the side of one of the boats. "It was the hand of a marine, frozen in the grip of death." Two months later, U.S. troops landed at Anzio, Italy. The city had once been a resort. Now, reported Sergeant Burgess H. Scott, "the sea washes up equipment that wasn't made for peacetime pleasure but for war."

As you read this section you will find out:
▶ **How the United States planned to defeat Japanese strategy in the Pacific.**
▶ **How the war progressed in North Africa and Europe.**
▶ **Why the Normandy invasion was a major event of the war.**

Early War in the Pacific

Early in the war the Allied strategy in Asia was simply to prevent further Japanese advances until Germany was defeated. After Pearl Harbor Japan had conquered the Philippine Islands, capturing large numbers of U.S. troops. General Douglas MacArthur, the commander in the Philippines, was evacuated before his troops surrendered. "I shall return," MacArthur promised.

Coral Sea and Midway. The Japanese, confident of victory, next prepared to invade New Guinea. However, in the great naval **Battle of the Coral Sea** in May 1942 the Japanese fleet was badly damaged. As a result, the Japanese were forced to give up their planned invasion.

Then in June 1942 a powerful Japanese fleet advanced toward the Midway Islands, a U.S. possession west of Hawaii. The plan was to force a showdown with the U.S. Pacific Fleet, but the Japanese ships never reached Midway. The Americans broke their secret codes, and scout planes spotted their movements. On June 4, U.S. planes sank four Japanese aircraft carriers and destroyed 275 planes. Again the Japanese fleet had to withdraw. This **Battle of Midway** gave the United States control of the central Pacific.

General Douglas MacArthur, shown here with troops in 1944, led the drive to recapture the Philippines.

Island-hopping. When the Allies' position in Europe improved, they started to focus more on Japan. To win the war in the Pacific, American strategists believed that the Japanese home islands must be invaded. The question was how to get there. The Japanese controlled thousands of small Pacific islands. Capturing all these islands would be costly and time-consuming.

The military planners in Washington decided on a two-pronged campaign. General MacArthur, now commander of Allied forces in the southwest Pacific, was to take control of the Bismarck Islands and then head for the Philippines. Meanwhile, Admiral Chester W. Nimitz, commander of the Pacific Fleet, would attack key Japanese-held islands in the central Pacific and press on toward Japan. This strategy of attacking only key islands on the way toward Japan was called **island-hopping**.

American forces tried to capture the Solomon Islands first. As they advanced, the Japanese defended every island with equal determination. Both sides fought desperately for every inch of ground. On the island of Tarawa U.S. forces were opposed by some 4,500 Japanese troops. Few Japanese soldiers were taken prisoner. Almost all the rest died in battle.

Early in August 1942, U.S. troops quickly captured three of the Solomon Islands. But on the island of Guadalcanal, some of the harshest fighting of the Pacific war took place. For six months the Americans spent much of the time inching ahead through dense jungles. By the time Guadalcanal was finally secured for the Americans in February 1943, some 20,000 Japanese troops had been killed.

The Tide Turns in North Africa and Europe

The most serious Allied concern during the early years of the war was the advance of the German army. By early 1942 Hitler controlled nearly all of Europe and much of North Africa.

In June 1942 President Roosevelt put General Dwight D. Eisenhower in command of U.S. troops in Europe, who had begun arriving earlier that year. "Ike" was a first-rate military

The Battle of Midway marked a significant victory for the American forces in the Pacific.

These members of the Women's Army Corps arrive in North Africa to assist the Allied campaign there.

planner. He also got along well with people. Managing and directing the huge and complicated Allied war machine required as much diplomacy as military talent.

Allied leaders did not think an invasion of Europe was possible until more troops and supplies had been gathered in Britain. The first major campaign that Eisenhower directed was Operation Torch, an attack in North Africa, where the British had been battling the Axis Powers for two years. On November 8, 1942, about 110,000 troops, mostly American, went ashore in Morocco. They met little resistance. Morocco and Algeria were soon under Allied control.

In October 1942 British general Bernard Montgomery had led a successful attack in Egypt against the German Afrika Korps, commanded by the brilliant general Erwin Rommel. Rommel was known as the "Desert Fox" for his keen military strategy. In the Battle of El Alamein, Rommel's troops were finally pushed out of Egypt into Libya. Shortly thereafter, the Germans were driven out of the rest of North Africa.

At that same time in eastern Europe, Soviet troops attacked German forces in the **Battle of Stalingrad.** By the time the Germans at Stalingrad finally surrendered in February 1943,

they had lost some 200,000 soldiers. This victory at Stalingrad finally halted the German advance to the east.

The victories in North Africa and at Stalingrad slowed the momentum of the Axis Powers. In July 1943 Eisenhower's forces invaded the Italian island of Sicily. In a little more than a month, Sicily was conquered. In the meantime, the Italians had revolted against Mussolini and tried to surrender, but the German army in Italy took control of the

Through Others' Eyes
A North African View of Americans

The North African country of Morocco was a French colony during World War II. It was in a difficult position after France fell to Germany in 1940. Morocco's leader, Sultan Muhammad V, feared Hitler's army would plow through North Africa. The sultan's son, who later became King Hassan II, remembered the Allied offensive:

"Operation Torch came as a complete surprise to us all. . . . The Americans continued pouring immense quantities of war material into Morocco. They behaved not like conquerors, but friends. I soon had the opportunity to get to know personally some of their great military leaders. . . . These Generals were delighted to show us their armaments—the latest aircraft, armored vehicles, guns, special ships, landing craft, etc. To my father and his advisers it was clear that this army was irresistible. And so it proved to be."

country. Nevertheless, the Americans were able to make a successful landing on the Italian mainland. The conquest of Italy against fierce German resistance was a long and bloody process. The capital city of Rome did not fall until June 1944.

D-Day

As the Allied conquest of Italy came to a close, Operation Overlord, the long-awaited invasion of France, began. For months, U.S. and British air forces had been bombing industrial

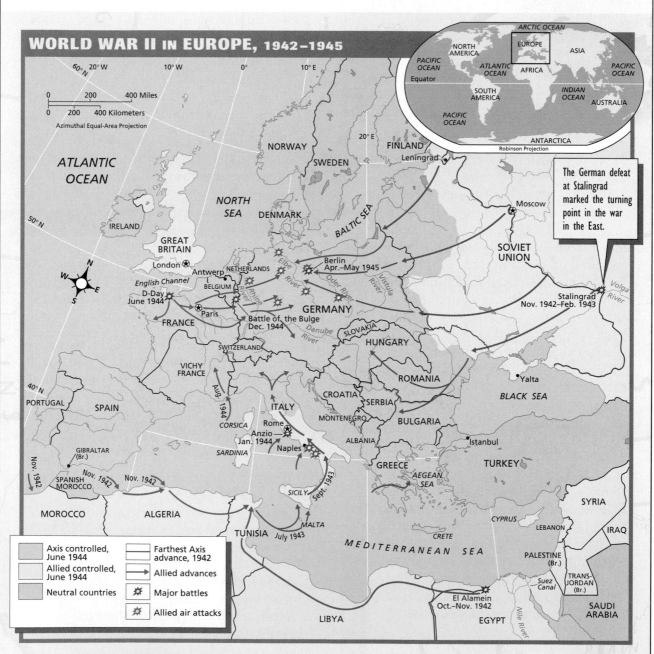

WORLD WAR II IN EUROPE, 1942–1945

The German defeat at Stalingrad marked the turning point in the war in the East.

Axis controlled, June 1944	Farthest Axis advance, 1942
Allied controlled, June 1944	Allied advances
Neutral countries	Major battles
	Allied air attacks

Learning from Maps. In late 1942, the Allies began their campaign to take control of North Africa. Once North Africa was secure, they planned to launch an attack on Italy from the south. The push to retake France and land in eastern Europe would come later.

▶ **Place.** After taking Tunis in Tunisia, what was the Allies' next goal?

● **Maps**

Allied troops prepare to hit the beaches of Normandy on D-Day, when some 6,000 Americans were killed or wounded.

Channel. The troops went ashore at several beaches along the coast of Normandy, a region in northern France. Naval guns and 11,000 planes bombarded the German defensive positions. American war correspondent Ernie Pyle described the approach:

"As one officer said, the only way to take a beach is to face it and keep going It is costly at first, but it's the only way. If the men are pinned down on the beach, dug in and out of action, they might as well not be there at all. They hold up the waves behind them, and nothing is being gained."

By nightfall more than 130,000 troops were ashore. By the end of June, more than 850,000 troops, 148,000 vehicles, and 570,000 tons of supplies had been ferried across the Channel.

targets and railroad yards in Germany and France in preparation for the invasion.

On **D-Day**—June 6, 1944—about 4,000 landing craft and 600 warships carried some 176,000 Allied soldiers across the English

The opening of this second major front was the beginning of the end for the Germans. In addition, the Allies increased their bombing campaign against German cities. The German armies were now on the defensive.

Section 3 Review

• Glossary

IDENTIFY and explain the significance of the following: Douglas MacArthur, Battle of the Coral Sea, Battle of Midway, Chester W. Nimitz, island-hopping, Dwight D. Eisenhower, Battle of Stalingrad, D-Day

LOCATE and explain the importance of the following: Philippine Islands, Midway Islands, Guadalcanal, El Alamein (see map on page 541)

• Gazetteer

REVIEWING FOR DETAILS
1. What events helped the Allies in Europe and North Africa?
2. What was the importance of D-Day?

REVIEWING FOR UNDERSTANDING
3. **Geographic Literacy** How did the United States plan to defeat Japan?
4. **Writing Mastery:** *Describing* Imagine that you are an American soldier during World War II who landed on the Normandy beaches during D-Day. Write a letter home describing your experiences, and explain what effect you think the landing will have on the war.
5. **Critical Thinking:** *Drawing Conclusions* Why do you think the Allies waited until 1944 to invade France? What might have happened if they had invaded sooner?

Section 4
DEFEATING THE AXIS POWERS

Multimedia Connections

Explore these related topics and materials on the CD–ROM to enrich your understanding of this section:

 Readings

• *Diary of Anne Frank*
• Survivors' Voices

 Media Bank

• Holocaust Camps
• Devastated Germany
• President Truman
• Celebration in America

 Atlas

• German Concentration Camps

On August 6, 1945, an event unimaginable before World War II proved that after four long years of fighting, the world would never be the same. A writer described one witness's experience:

"**As Mrs. Nakamura stood watching her neighbor, everything flashed whiter than any white she had ever seen. . . . Something picked her up and she seemed to fly into the next room . . . pursued by parts of her house.**"

As you read this section you will find out:

▶ **What events led to the end of the war in Europe.**

▶ **What occurred in the Nazi concentration camps.**

▶ **How the war against Japan was brought to an end.**

The Allies Enter Paris

In August, after fierce fighting, the U.S. 3rd Army under General George S. Patton swept through a gap in the German defenses in Normandy and raced toward Paris.

Allied troops entered Paris amid great rejoicing in late August 1944. By the end of September almost all of France had been liberated from German occupation. With victory in sight, President Roosevelt had to decide whether to run for a fourth term in 1944. He was in very poor health. He had heart trouble and high blood pressure. Still, he was determined to bring the war to a victorious conclusion.

Democrats nominated the president with little opposition. Senator Harry Truman of Missouri was chosen as his running mate. The Republican candidate was Governor Thomas E. Dewey of New York.

These American troops remove the bodies of prisoners killed by German troops in the drive through Belgium. Some soldiers had to sweep snow off the frozen bodies to uncover them.

Dewey was not an effective campaigner; even so, it would have been nearly impossible to defeat Roosevelt on the eve of victory in the war. The popular vote was 25.6 million for Roosevelt, 22 million for Dewey. The electoral count was 432 to 99.

The Battle of the Bulge

In December 1944 Allied armies were poised all along the German border from the Netherlands to Switzerland. On December 16, before the Allies could attack, Hitler ordered his last reserves—some 250,000 troops—to make a desperate counterattack. The Germans hoped to break through the Allied line and to capture the Belgian port of Antwerp. That would split the Allied forces in two and make it difficult for the Allies to receive supplies.

The German attack came as a total surprise. Within 10 days they had driven a bulge 50 miles deep into the Allied lines. American troops of the 101st Airborne Division were surrounded at the important road junction of Bastogne (ba-STOHN). The Germans then demanded that the American commander, General Anthony C. McAuliffe, surrender his troops. "Nuts!" replied the American general.

Bastogne held out and the strong German advance was stopped.

Every available U.S. and British soldier was thrown into this **Battle of the Bulge**. For the first time, black and white soldiers fought side by side. By January 1945 the bulge had been flattened. The Allies were now ready to storm into Germany.

The Holocaust

One of the most shocking aspects of the entire war was revealed when Allied forces liberated Nazi concentration camps, such as Auschwitz and Treblinka in Poland and Dachau in Germany. To carry out what Hitler called the "Final Solution" to rid Europe of Jews—what the rest of the world would call the **Holocaust**—the Nazis had constructed numerous concentration camps, mostly in occupied eastern Europe. Inmates of these camps were forced to work under terrible conditions. Many were literally worked to death. Other camps were designed for the express purpose of killing millions of Jews and other "nondesirables."

Many children were imprisoned and murdered in Nazi concentration camps. One of the worst camps was Auschwitz, where between 1.2 and 1.5 million people were killed. These children were among the survivors of the camp.

These innocent people had been rounded up, crammed into freight cars, and transported to the camps. When inmates arrived in the Nazi death camps, they were lined up and examined by officials. Those who were sick, old, or too young to work were usually sent to the gas chambers, where they were immediately murdered. Others were forced to work long hours under brutal conditions. When they became too weak to work, they were also killed. Concentration camp survivor Sophia Litwinska recalled how she almost died in the gas chamber (before being saved at the last minute):

> **"We were led into a room which gave me the impression of a shower-bath.... People were in tears; people were shouting at each other; people were hitting each other.... Suddenly I saw fumes coming in through a very small window at the top. I had to cough very violently, tears were streaming from my eyes, and I had a sort of feeling in my throat as if I would be asphyxiated [suffocated]."**

By the end of the war, about 6 million Jews had been murdered in the camps. The Nazis also executed millions of Poles, Slavs, gypsies, political opponents, and other groups.

• **Anti-Semitism and the Holocaust**

Victory in Europe

In March 1945, Allied forces crossed the Rhine River into Germany. By the middle of April, U.S., British, and French troops were within 50 miles of Berlin, the German capital. Soviet armies were approaching the city from the east. On April 25, American and Soviet troops met at the Elbe River. Five days later Adolf Hitler committed suicide in Berlin. On May 8 Germany officially surrendered.

Americans' joy at the ending of the war was restrained, for President Roosevelt was dead. On April 12, while working at his winter home in Warm Springs, Georgia, he had died of a massive stroke. The burdens of the presidency were now upon the shoulders of Harry Truman. Many people, including Truman himself, wondered whether he would be "big enough" to fill Franklin Roosevelt's shoes.

President Truman was quite different from Roosevelt. He had grown up on a Missouri farm and had been an artillery captain in World War I. During the 1920s Truman became involved in Missouri politics. He served as a local judge and in 1934 was elected to the U.S. Senate.

Truman had a reputation for being honest and somewhat liberal, but he seemed a rather ordinary politician. Still, no one had ever accused him of being unwilling to accept responsibility. For example, when he became president he put a sign on his desk at the White House that read "The Buck Stops Here." Truman's willingness to accept responsibility for big decisions would be crucial in the months to come.

Iwo Jima and Okinawa

Before the war in Europe was completely over, the United States began to focus more of its attention on winning the war in the Pacific. MacArthur's army launched an invasion of the Philippines in October 1944. In the **Battle of Leyte Gulf** the U.S. Navy destroyed the last major Japanese fleet. Now the United States had complete control of Philippine waters.

U.S. Marines raise the American flag above Mount Suribachi, on Iwo Jima. The top of the mountain was leveled by Americans after the war.

The next step was to secure the bases needed for a direct invasion of Japan. The Americans first needed to capture the tiny island of Iwo Jima, 750 miles south of Japan. The fight for Iwo Jima was bitter and extremely costly. On February 23, 1945, marines reached the top of Mount Suribachi, a volcano on the southern tip of the island.

As they crawled toward the rim of the crater, they came under fire from Japanese soldiers dug in on the other side of the volcano. A fierce fight developed. To rally his men, one marine picked up an iron pipe, bound a small American flag to it, and held it for the men to see. Later another marine arrived with a larger flag and pole. The victorious marines proudly planted the flag at the top of the mountain. A photographer took a picture of this now-famous second flag-raising over Iwo Jima. That photograph has become the most reproduced image of World War II.

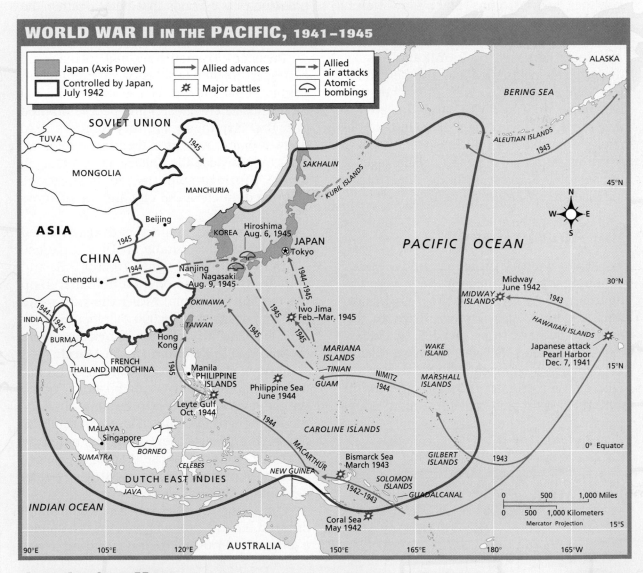

WORLD WAR II IN THE PACIFIC, 1941–1945

Japan (Axis Power)

Controlled by Japan, July 1942

Allied advances

Major battles

Allied air attacks

Atomic bombings

Learning from Maps. By 1942 Japan's control stretched far into the Pacific and stretched across much of East Asia, including Manchuria and other areas in China. Countries under British, French, and Dutch colonial rule had also fallen to the Japanese.

▶ **Movement.** What islands did the Allies take after reaching the Marshall Islands?

• Maps

Two weeks after taking Iwo Jima, U.S. troops went ashore on Okinawa, a much larger island only 350 miles from Japan. By the time this island was secured for the Americans in June 1945, the Japanese lost some 130,000 troops, the Americans about 12,500.

The United States now had complete control of both air and sea. From airfields near Japan, American planes bombed Japanese targets mercilessly. U.S. battleships and cruisers moved in closer to pound industrial targets with their heaviest guns. Soon, almost every important Japanese city had been hit.

As U.S. forces neared Japan, they were repeatedly harassed by **kamikaze** attacks. These suicide pilots tried to crash their bomb-filled planes into U.S. warships. They took their name from a "divine wind" believed to have prevented an invasion of Japan centuries before. Some 1,500 kamikazes were involved in the battle for Okinawa. They damaged a number of U.S. vessels during that struggle and killed many American sailors.

The Atomic Bomb

An Allied victory now seemed certain. Although some Japanese leaders were trying to arrange a surrender, progress was extremely slow. Military experts expected that Japan would have to be invaded, at tremendous cost, to end the war. Japanese soldiers had demonstrated repeatedly that they would fight every battle to the last man. Some authorities estimated that the United States would suffer an extremely high number of casualties before Japan was conquered.

This was the situation President Truman faced when he learned that American scientists had produced a new weapon—the **atomic bomb**. On orders from President Roosevelt, these scientists had been working on the top-secret **Manhattan Project** since early 1942. They had produced a weapon with the explosive force of 20,000 tons of TNT. This tremendous power was released by the breaking of the bonds that held together the atoms of uranium and plutonium, two highly radioactive elements.

President Truman now had to make an extremely difficult decision. Dropping an atomic bomb on a Japanese city would kill thousands of civilians. Some people pointed out that Japanese military leaders had harmed many civilians in their quest for land. After they invaded the Chinese city of Nanjing in 1937, for example, the Japanese troops destroyed much of the city and killed some 250,000 people.

The Japanese military had also treated prisoners of war brutally. In 1942 Japanese soldiers had forced some 70,000 U.S. and Filipino troops to go on a 60-mile march up the Bataan Peninsula. Along the way some 600 Americans and 10,000 Filipinos died or were killed by the Japanese. Many others were brutalized in this **Bataan Death March**.

Despite such examples of Japanese brutality, it was possible that use of the atomic bomb on civilians would turn international sentiment against the United States. In the end, however, Truman believed that the only way to convince the Japanese that further resistance was useless was to use this powerful new bomb against them.

On August 6, 1945, an American plane dropped the first atomic bomb on Hiroshima, a city of 344,000. In one blinding flash

The dropping of the first atomic bomb on Hiroshima, Japan, on August 6, 1945, ushered in a new era in warfare. Until that moment, such a weapon would have been unimaginable to most people throughout the world.

75,000 people died. An observer described some of the bomb's effects:

"**Beyond the zone of utter death in which nothing remained alive houses collapsed in a whirl of beams, bricks, and girders. . . . Those who were inside were either killed or wounded. . . . And the few who succeeded in making their way to safety generally died twenty or thirty days later from the delayed effects of the deadly gamma rays.**"

When the Japanese still hesitated to surrender, another atomic bomb was dropped on the city of Nagasaki. Japanese officials estimated that the total number of deaths caused by both bombs—including those who died later—was 240,000. On August 14, Japan agreed to surrender. On September 2, the Japanese signed the peace agreement finally ending World War II.

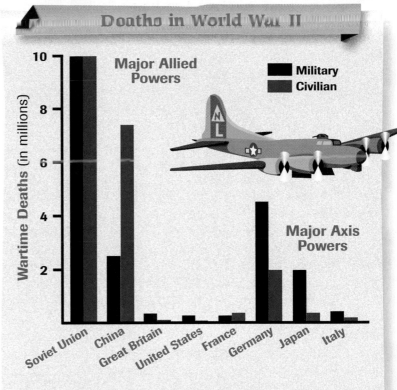

Source: *The Oxford Companion to World War II*

The Costs of War. In all, some 50 million people died in World War II. Many were civilians. Which country suffered the most total losses? Which countries lost more civilians than military personnel?

Section 4 Review

• Glossary

• Time Line

IDENTIFY and explain the significance of the following: George S. Patton, Battle of the Bulge, Holocaust, Harry Truman, Battle of Leyte Gulf, kamikaze, atomic bomb, Manhattan Project, Bataan Death March

REVIEWING FOR DETAILS

1. How did the Allied Powers defeat Germany?
2. What was Hitler's "Final Solution"?
3. What were the immediate effects of the bombing of Hiroshima and Nagasaki?

REVIEWING FOR UNDERSTANDING

4. **Writing Mastery:** *Expressing* Imagine that you are an Allied soldier participating in the liberation of Germany. Write a diary entry expressing your feeling about what you have seen in the concentration camps.

5. **Critical Thinking:** *Determining the Strength of an Argument* What were some of the arguments for and against dropping the atomic bombs on Japan? Which arguments seem the most convincing to you? Explain your answer.

u n i t **9**

*A*SSUMING GLOBAL RESPONSIBILITIES (1945–1969)

Anticommunist images like these were common during the early years of the Cold War.

LINKING PAST TO PRESENT
Television and International News

The students in an eighth grade social studies class begin their day by watching the news. The young reporter on the broadcast, who is only a few years older than the viewers, shows them scenes from a civil war taking place halfway around the world. The reporter's car gets stuck in the jungle mud, which gives a chuckle to some student viewers. Then the reporter comes across startling evidence of a massive slaughter of civilians. It is a chilling scene for both the reporter and the viewers.

Millions of young Americans today learn about international events by watching television news. Sometimes, as in the case of this particular broadcast, viewing such events can send a powerful message to American viewers about disasters and violence happening to people who may not be much different from themselves.

Getting information from television news, however, requires being a critical viewer. Sometimes newscasts are not com-pletely objective. Modern viewers must keep in mind that media reports of international events may be influenced by the perspectives of those presenting the reports. Thus, people must educate themselves about history and current events to be critical viewers.

As you read this unit, you will learn how television became an important medium for news and information in the United States. Before the widespread use of television, most people got their information about international events from newspapers or radio reports. Television was revolutionary in that it helped people sitting right in their homes see what was going on in distant parts of the world.

As you will learn, this ability to see the world right at home helped shape people's views of international events more than any other medium had ever done. As a result, it also affected how Americans viewed their own political leaders and American policies at home and abroad.

A newscaster shows students how his local news program is put together.

CHAPTER 24

Returning to Peace
(1945–1955)

THEMES IN AMERICAN HISTORY

Global Relations:
How might countries' differing ideas on government lead to conflicts?

Democratic Values:
Under what circumstances might a government choose to violate the civil rights of its citizens?

Economic Development:
Why might one country extend economic aid to another country?

General Douglas MacArthur encouraged Americans in September 1945 to "Preserve in peace what we won in war." Preserving peace would prove to be a challenging task in the years following the second global war. Only a short time after the end of World War II, American leaders struggled with how to prevent another massive war from breaking out in the age of nuclear weapons.

 • Video Opener

 • Skill Builder

image above: *U.S. soldiers in Korea*

Section 1

FROM WAR TO COLD WAR

Multimedia Connections

Explore these related topics and materials on the CD–ROM to enrich your understanding of this section:

 Profiles

- Harry S Truman

 Atlas

- Israel, 1949
- The Marshall Plan

 Readings

- Battle for Palestine

 Media Bank

- UN Decision-Making Bodies
- Yalta Conference
- Rebuilding Japan

 Gazetteer

- Israel
- Palestine
- Greece
- Czechoslovakia

African American doctor Leon Bass was one of the soldiers who helped liberate the Nazi concentration camps at the end of World War II. Later, he recalled his thoughts upon having seen one of the most inhumane sides of the war: "If this could happen here, it could happen anywhere." After the war many world leaders shared Bass's fears. They began to take steps to make sure that another tragedy of this size could never occur again.

As you read this section you will find out:

▶ **How Allied nations tried to promote peace after World War II.**

▶ **What problems arose from the Yalta Conference.**

▶ **What foreign policy goals the United States pursued in postwar Europe.**

The Search for World Peace

Any war as widespread and destructive as World War II was bound to cause difficulties and conflicts that did not disappear simply because the shooting had stopped. President Franklin Roosevelt and other Allied leaders realized this. Even before the war ended they began to take steps to create institutions that could deal peacefully with these conflicts.

The United Nations. Representatives of the major Allied Powers met in Washington, D.C., in 1944 to begin designing an international organization called the **United Nations** (UN) that would promote world peace and settle international disputes. President Roosevelt avoided the mistake Woodrow Wilson had made when he did not consult the Republicans about the League of Nations. Roosevelt appointed Senator Arthur Vandenberg of Michigan, a leading Republican, as a delegate to the San Francisco Conference to draft the UN Charter in April 1945.

The 50 nations that sent delegates to San Francisco represented the majority of the world's population. After weeks of discussion and debate, the delegates finally agreed on the wording of the charter. It was then ratified by the separate nations. By an overwhelming majority, the U.S. Senate approved the treaty that made the United States a member of the UN.

War crimes trials. Soon after the United Nations officially came into existence on October 24, 1945, many of the most terrible events of World War II came to the public's attention. The shocking revelations of the Holocaust and of Japanese abuses against American and Chinese prisoners of war led to a series of war crimes trials. These trials were intended to punish those who had carried out "crimes against humanity" during the war.

The first of the trials began in Nuremberg, Germany, in November 1945. An international group of judges presided over these trials. During the **Nuremberg Trials** numerous witnesses testified about how Nazis tortured and killed people during the war. Concentration camp survivor Marie Vaillant summed up the Nazi attitude toward prisoners:

> **"There was the systematic and implacable [unstoppable] urge to use human beings as slaves and to kill them when they could work no more."**

In the initial trials, 11 Nazi leaders were sentenced to death for their part in the war crimes. Seven others received prison terms and three were found not guilty. More trials followed in which thousands of Nazis were eventually punished for their crimes.

In 1948 international desires to help the Jewish community led to the creation of a Jewish homeland in Palestine called Israel. Thousands of Holocaust survivors moved to Israel, despite continued opposition from Arabs already living in the area.

That same year, Japanese military leaders were tried for war crimes in Tokyo. Seven received the death sentence, while 16 were sentenced to life in prison.

The Yalta Conference

During World War II President Roosevelt and Prime Minister Winston Churchill had worked closely on military and diplomatic problems. Both had also consulted frequently with Soviet dictator Joseph Stalin. The most important meeting of the **Big Three**, as Churchill, Roosevelt, and Stalin were called, took place at the Soviet resort of Yalta in February 1945.

At the time of the **Yalta Conference** the war in Europe was almost over. Roosevelt hoped to convince the Soviets to join the other Allies in defeating Japan after Germany surrendered, and Stalin agreed to do so. Roosevelt and Churchill also wanted to restore an independent government in Poland, which had been invaded by Germany in 1939.

These Nazi officials were the first of many to be tried for war crimes. Seated on the far left is Hermann Goering, head of Hitler's secret police, which sent many people to concentration camps.

• **War Crimes Trials**

Many Jewish refugees, like this family, moved to Israel after the nation was founded in 1948.

By 1945, however, Poland was occupied by Soviet troops, and Stalin had hand-picked the new Polish government. Many times in the past, foreign enemies had crossed Poland to attack Russia. Stalin was now determined to prevent any government unfriendly to the Soviet Union from coming to power in Poland.

No freely elected Polish government was likely to be friendly to the Soviet Union, however. The Soviets had joined Germany in dividing up Poland in 1939. Soviet troops had treated the Poles brutally. Several thousand Polish officers had been murdered by the Soviets in the Katyn Forest Massacre of 1940.

After considerable discussion the Big Three worked out a compromise. After the war the Soviet Union would add a large part of eastern Poland to its territory. In the rest of Poland, free elections would be held. The people could choose whomever they wished to govern them.

However, Stalin did not keep his promise to permit free elections in the new Polish republic. Instead, he maintained a pro-Soviet government that he could control. The vast majority of the Polish people bitterly resented this "puppet" government. Growing tensions between the two countries over Poland and other postwar issues contributed to an ongoing struggle for global power between the United States and the Soviet Union that became known as the **Cold War**.

President Roosevelt died soon after returning from Yalta. In May 1945 Germany surrendered. In July Truman, Churchill, and Stalin met at the **Potsdam Conference** to plan Germany's future. They decided to divide Germany into four zones, each controlled by a different country—the United States, Great Britain, France, and the Soviet Union. Berlin, the capital city, would be located in the Soviet zone, but it too was divided into four zones.

Global Connections

Jewish Americans and Israel

The United States was the first country to recognize Israel as an independent nation. The founding of Israel was a long time in coming. Zionists—people who favored having a Jewish homeland in Palestine—had fought for many years to make their dream a reality.

Many Jewish Americans lent their support to the Zionist cause, both before and after the creation of Israel. Eddie Jacobson, a friend of President Truman's, arranged meetings between the president and Zionist leaders. These efforts increased Truman's support for the founding of Israel and for helping relocate Jewish refugees who wanted to move there.

Many Jewish Americans also provided financial aid to the new nation. Golda Meir, a Russian-born Zionist who had lived in the United States before moving to Palestine, raised some $50 million for Israel from the American Jewish community. Many important schools, research centers, and other social and cultural institutions in Israel have been heavily funded by Jewish Americans.

Allied leaders (seated, left to right) Clement Attlee, Harry S Truman, and Joseph Stalin meet at Potsdam to plan for the postwar world. Attlee replaced Winston Churchill as prime minister when, in the middle of the conference, his party won in Britain's national elections.

After Germany surrendered, Stalin kept his promise at Yalta and declared war on Japan. The Soviet military contribution to the defeat of Japan was not needed, however, since the United States ended the war by dropping atomic bombs on Hiroshima and Nagasaki.

The Truman Doctrine

The new U.S. president, Harry S Truman, was even more suspicious of Soviet motives than Roosevelt had been. Because he distrusted Stalin, Truman worried a great deal about the dangers of Soviet expansion and the spread of communism.

In Europe the change from war to peace had not been easy. While the American economy had expanded during the war, large parts of Europe had been devastated. Millions of Europeans had been killed. The loss of so many potential workers was a terrible blow to the European nations' economies.

In every European country, railroads had been wrecked, bridges blown up, factories smashed. About 30 percent of the Soviet Union's industrial capacity had been com-

pletely destroyed. Millions of Europeans were homeless and hungry.

These poor economic conditions contributed to a rapid increase in the strength of the Communist Parties in many European countries. President Truman believed that once the Communists gained control of a government they would do away with free elections. He believed that it was absolutely necessary to protect democracy and to stop the spread of communism in Europe.

How could this be done without starting another war, people wondered. The question became urgent in early 1947 when Greece seemed about to fall behind what Churchill called the "**Iron Curtain**." He used this striking image to describe the political division between democratic Western Europe and communist Eastern Europe.

Guerrillas in Greece, backed by the communist governments of both Yugoslavia and Bulgaria, were seeking to overthrow the conservative Greek government. Great Britain had been providing aid to that government, but in February 1947 the British informed Truman that because of their economic problems they could no longer afford to help Greece.

Truman believed that if Greece became communist, its neighbor, Turkey, might also fall under Soviet influence. Similarly, the Communist Parties in Italy and France would grow more powerful unless these countries received U.S. aid. Truman therefore asked

American and foreign officials observe as a shipment of sugar is loaded to be carried overseas as part of the Marshal Plan.

● **Marshall Plan**

Congress for $400 million to aid Greece and Turkey, declaring.

> **"It must be the policy of the United States to support free peoples who are resisting attempted subjugation [enslavement] by armed minorities or by outside pressures. . . . I believe that our help should be primarily through economic and financial aid."**

This idea became known as the **Truman Doctrine**. Truman was suggesting that the Soviet Union was directly supporting the Greek Communists, which was not actually the case. Congress took no chances, however, and provided the money. The communist threat to Greece and Turkey was stopped.

The Marshall Plan

The Truman Doctrine appealed to both liberals and conservatives in the United States. Many liberals liked the idea of helping the people of other countries defend their independence and rebuild their war-torn economies. Conservatives liked the idea of resisting communism and thus preserving individual rights and the free enterprise system.

Critics of the Truman Doctrine argued that it would be far too expensive. Besides, they insisted, the United States had no business meddling in the internal affairs of other nations. Some also thought that the doctrine did not focus enough on helping people in need.

In response to these objections, George C. Marshall, whom Truman had appointed secretary of state, proposed an economic solution known as the **Marshall Plan**. All the nations

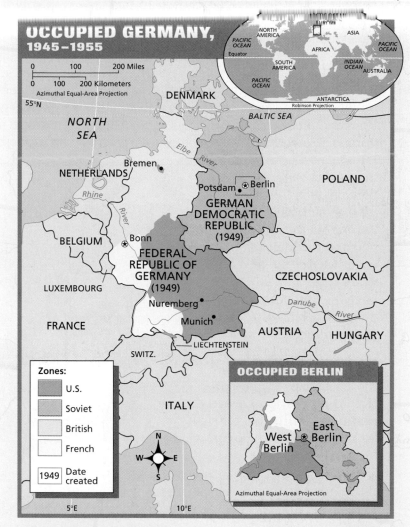

OCCUPIED GERMANY, 1945–1955

Zones:
- U.S.
- Soviet
- British
- French
- 1949 Date created

OCCUPIED BERLIN

Learning from Maps.
The United States and the Soviet Union occupied the largest portions of Germany.

▶ **Place.** Which country controlled the zone in which Bonn was located?

• Maps

of Europe, including the Soviet Union, needed American help in rebuilding their war-damaged societies, Marshall said, but they also ought to help themselves. No aid plan could be imposed on Europeans from the outside. The United States would provide help only if the European nations themselves developed a broad plan for economic recovery.

Marshall did not exclude the Soviet Union from the plan. This was a bluff, or at least a gamble. If the Soviets had chosen to participate in the plan, Congress would probably not have provided enough money to make it work. But Marshall did not think the Soviets would accept this plan, and he was right. They had no desire to accept aid from the capitalist nations. The Soviets also did not want the United States to gain influence in Eastern Europe. Therefore, they also forced the Eastern European countries under their control to refuse to participate in the plan.

The nations of Western Europe, on the other hand, adopted the Marshall Plan eagerly. Over the next few years the United States gave the European nations about $13 billion to carry out their recovery.

The Marshall Plan was a brilliant success. By 1951 the economies of the participating nations were booming. Still, the plan had further divided Europe

The Granger Collection, New York

into two competing systems. In 1948, when Czechoslovakia had showed signs of wanting to accept some Marshall Plan aid, the local Communist Party had seized power with Soviet support.

Czechoslovakia thus joined Poland, Hungary, and the other states of Eastern Europe in the Soviet "orbit." The countries that were dominated by the Soviet Union became known as **satellite nations**. In all of these nations, the communist governments deprived citizens of basic human rights such as freedom of speech, assembly, and religion.

• George C. Marshall

In this cartoon Europe pulls itself up with the help of the Marshall Plan. Supporters of the plan hoped that it would do just that.

Section 1 Review

• Glossary

IDENTIFY and explain the significance of the following: United Nations, Nuremberg Trials, Big Three, Yalta Conference, Cold War, Potsdam Conference, Iron Curtain, Truman Doctrine, Marshall Plan, satellite nations

REVIEWING FOR DETAILS

1. How did Allied nations hope to ensure peace after World War II?

2. What problems arose out of the decisions made at the Yalta Conference?

3. How did the Truman Doctrine and the Marshall Plan help shape U.S. foreign policy after the war?

REVIEWING FOR UNDERSTANDING

4. **Writing Mastery:** *Describing* Imagine that you are the leader of a postwar Western European nation. Write a letter to President Truman describing what you will do with Marshall Plan funds.

5. **Critical Thinking:** *Determining the Strength of an Argument* Joseph Stalin maintained that it was necessary for the Soviet Union to control Eastern European countries to protect itself from future invasions. How strong of an argument do you think this was? What other motives might Stalin have had?

Section 2

LIFE IN POSTWAR AMERICA

Multimedia Connections

Explore these related topics and materials on the CD-ROM to enrich your understanding of this section:

 Profiles

• A. Philip Randolph

 Biographies

• John L. Lewis

 Media Bank

• Rosie the Riveter
• Workers on Strike
• Civil Rights in the Truman Era
• A Call for Civil Rights
• Jackie Robinson

 Atlas

• Election of 1948

Minister Harold Toliver wondered, "What are we going to do about life as we try to re-establish it in our community?" After the joy of victory wore off, Americans had to adjust to life in peacetime. As American Jack Altshul observed, "The war was the dividing line between the depression and the prosperity that followed." For many people, however, economic prosperity did not bring freedom from all problems.

As you read this section you will find out:

▶ **How the government tried to change the country over to a peacetime economy.**

▶ **How President Truman worked to improve civil rights.**

▶ **Why people thought Truman would lose the election of 1948.**

Getting Back to "Normal"

One reason President Truman was so suspicious of the Soviets was that he believed the United States might suffer another serious economic depression after the war. If it did, the Soviets would "take advantage of our setback," Truman predicted.

Fortunately, the depression that Truman feared did not occur. While thousands of workers lost their jobs when military contracts were canceled, many quickly found new ones. Most workers were much better off than they had been before the war. Millions had saved money during the war when there were few civilian goods to buy. Their savings would help fuel a postwar consumer boom.

The demand for everything from nylon stockings and washing machines to automobiles and housing was enormous. This widespread desire for goods greatly helped the U.S. economy, and returning soldiers as well as laid-off war workers soon found new jobs.

In 1944 Congress had passed the Servicemen's Readjustment Act in part to boost morale. This **GI Bill of Rights** made low-cost loans available to veterans to buy houses and farms, and to start new businesses. The bill also helped those who wished to improve their education, by providing money for tuition and books. This created a boom in university enrollment. As American Nelson Poynter observed, "Millions of people whose parents or grandparents had never dreamed of going to college saw that they could go."

As veterans returned to work, many groups who had benefited from the wartime job boom, such as women, African Americans, and Mexican Americans, feared they would once again be shut out of the job market. Such fears increased when Congress abolished the Fair Employment Practices Committee, which had helped prevent discrimination in hiring.

Women were particularly open to job losses. During the war, advertisements had encouraged women to join the war effort by

These students are just a few members of the Veteran Students' Association at Texas A & M College in 1947. Such organizations sprang up on many college campuses as former soldiers used the GI Bill to fund their educations.

working in factories. The message was clear, however, that after the war these women were expected to work only in their homes and leave the paid jobs open to men. Many did, but others wanted to continue working. One female steelworker explained:

> **"If [women] are capable, I don't see why they should give up their position to men. . . . The old theory that a woman's place is in the home no longer exists. Those days are gone forever."**

After the war, a higher percentage of women continued to work outside of the home than before the war. However, they often found themselves limited to less challenging jobs that paid lower wages than they had made during the war.

Immediately after the war thousands of factory workers found themselves out of work. These recently laid-off workers are turning in job applications with the U.S. Employment Service in late August 1945.

● **GIs Return to Work**

Dealing with Labor

Many male workers were also unhappy with their wages. Workers' wages had not kept up with business profits during the war. Millions joined unions to express their concerns. After the war, many labor unions demanded wage increases to help workers keep up with the inflation that soon hit. When the huge demand for goods could not be satisfied quickly, shortages developed, followed by high prices. In 1946 alone some 5 million workers in various industries went on strike.

President Truman feared that work shutdowns would damage the economy. Nearly two months after the **United Mine Workers** (UMW) struck in April 1946, Truman ordered a government takeover of the mines when strike negotiations broke down. UMW president John L. Lewis complained of the forced government takeover, "You can't dig coal with bayonets." After the courts sided with the government, Lewis ordered the workers back to their jobs.

Labor troubles and other similar problems dealt a heavy blow to people's confidence in Truman. By the fall of 1946, many people—even large numbers of Democrats—had decided that Truman was incompetent. "To err is Truman," became a commonly heard wisecrack. "Had enough?" Republican candidates asked during the 1946 congressional campaign, "Vote Republican." A majority of the voters in 1946 did just that. The Republican Party won control of both houses of Congress for the first time since the 1920s.

This new Congress set out to reverse the trend toward liberal legislation that had begun with the election of Franklin Roosevelt in 1932. One of the most controversial measures of the congressional session was the **Taft-Hartley Act**, passed in June 1947 to curb the power of labor unions.

This act outlawed what many people saw as unfair practices of unions, such as the clause in many labor contracts that required job applicants to join the union before they could be hired. The act also allowed courts to

for full employment after the war
REGISTER · VOTE
C I O POLITICAL ACTION COMMITTEE

The Granger Collection, New York

Unions like the Congress of Industrial Organizations encouraged wartime workers to vote for candidates who promised to keep the postwar economy strong.

halt a strike if it threatened national interests. Truman vetoed the Taft-Hartley Act, but Congress passed it over his veto.

Addressing Civil Rights Concerns

After the war African American labor leader A. Philip Randolph pressed President Truman to address the continuing problem of racism in America. In December 1946 the president set up a **Committee on Civil Rights** to report on the status of race relations.

The committee issued its report, entitled *To Secure These Rights,* in October 1947. It described numerous civil rights abuses after the war, including discrimination against African American veterans and increased violence by the Ku Klux Klan. The committee recommended that Congress pass new laws protecting the right of African Americans to vote and banning racial segregation on railroads and buses. It also called for a federal antilynching law and the creation of a permanent government Fair Employment Practices Committee.

Truman urged Congress to adopt almost all these recommendations. When Congress delayed, Randolph threatened to organize a

National Portrait Gallery, Smithsonian Institution, Washington, DC/Art Resource, NY

Labor leader A. Philip Randolph, who had successfully pressured President Roosevelt into ending discrimination in defense plants, continued to press President Truman on racial issues.

massive protest movement unless Truman at least desegregated the military. With World War II over, Randolph warned:

> **"Negroes will not take a jim crow [segregated] draft lying down. . . . I personally will advise Negroes to refuse to fight as slaves for a democracy they cannot possess and cannot enjoy."**

In 1948 Truman issued executive orders ending segregation in the armed forces and prohibiting job discrimination in all government agencies.

The Election of 1948

Truman's support for civil rights helped him win the votes of African Americans in the presidential election of 1948. The campaign took place while the Democratic Party was badly divided. Almost none of its leaders wanted to renominate Truman.

The campaign. Despite these divisions, the Democratic convention nominated Truman and made his civil rights proposals part of the party platform. A group of southern Democrats later known as the **Dixiecrats** opposed Truman because of his civil rights policies. They marched out of the convention and organized the States' Rights Party. When asked why they took such a strong position against Truman when Roosevelt had also expressed support for civil rights, Dixiecrat presidential nominee Strom Thurmond replied, "Truman really means it."

The Democrats were further divided when Henry A. Wallace, who had been Truman's secretary of state, ran as the presidential candidate for a new Progressive Party. Much of Wallace's support came from Democrats. With Democrats so divided, the Republican candidate, Thomas E. Dewey, seemed sure of victory. Many political observers and public polls predicted that he would be elected. In fact, the editor of the *Chicago Daily Tribune* was so sure that Dewey would win that he approved the headline "DEWEY DEFEATS TRUMAN" and went to press on election night before all the votes had been counted.

The results. The polls were wrong. Truman received over 2 million more popular votes than Dewey and won a solid majority in the electoral college. The States' Rights ticket won in only four southern states. Wallace's Progressive

Campaign button for Republican presidential candidate Thomas Dewey and his running mate, Earl Warren

Party was soundly defeated everywhere Observers wondered what had happened.

Truman had conducted a hard-hitting campaign. While on an exhausting "whistle-stop" train tour, he attacked the record of what he called the "do-nothing" Republican-controlled Congress. The Republican Party, he claimed, wanted to "turn the clock back" and do away with all the reforms of the New Deal Era.

This tactic worked well. Organized labor, African Americans, farmers, and other supporters of the New Deal all backed Truman. The president's energy, courage, and determination in fighting so hard when his cause seemed completely hopeless was another reason for his success.

The Fair Deal. Encouraged by his victory, Truman set out to extend the reforms of the New Deal. He proposed a group of reforms that he called the **Fair Deal**. It called for an extension of social security

benefits, a national health insurance plan, a higher minimum wage, increased spending on public housing, more financial aid to farmers, and a continuation of the Fair Employment Practices Committee.

Some of these proposals were adopted. Between 1949 and 1953 Congress extended social security benefits to some 10 million people who were not previously covered by the program. Congress also raised the minimum wage from 40 cents an hour to 75 cents an hour. Some Fair Deal proposals, such as a national health insurance plan, were rejected. In the late 1940s most members of Congress, however, were far more concerned with foreign policy issues related to the Cold War than with domestic issues.

President Harry Truman proved political experts wrong with his stunning victory over Thomas Dewey in 1948. Many observers fully expected Dewey to win.

Section 2 Review

• Glossary

IDENTIFY and explain the significance of the following: GI Bill of Rights, United Mine Workers, Taft-Hartley Act, Committee on Civil Rights, Dixiecrats, Fair Deal

REVIEWING FOR DETAILS

1. How did the U.S. government try to return the economy to "normal"?
2. What did President Truman propose to improve civil rights?
3. What was the outcome of the election of 1948? Why were people surprised?

REVIEWING FOR UNDERSTANDING

4. **Writing Mastery:** *Persuading* Imagine that you are a woman who worked in a factory during the war. Write a speech to persuade factory owners that you should be allowed to keep your job.
5. **Critical Thinking:** *Synthesizing Information* How did the return to "normal" after World War II have both positive and negative effects for Americans?

Section 3

THE COLD WAR TURNS HOT

Multimedia Connections

Explore these related topics and materials on the CD–ROM to enrich your understanding of this section:

 Media Bank

- Nuclear Threat to Peace
- USSR Closes Berlin
- Chairman Mao

 Readings

- Intelligence Agencies
- The Berlin Airlift
- China's Communists

 Gazetteer

- Berlin
- China

n the summer of 1948, the United States dispatched several squadrons of B-29 bombers to strategic points in Europe. Nikolai Chervov, a young Soviet officer, noted that the planes could be carrying a total of some 200 atomic bombs. Chervov feared that could mean "two hundred Hiroshimas." Fortunately, the world was not then on the brink of nuclear war. The bombers were preparing to deliver supplies, not bombs, to civilians in Berlin, which was cut off from the Western world by a Soviet blockade.

As you read this section you will find out:

▶ **How the United States responded to the threat of Soviet expansion.**

▶ **How Western nations reacted to Soviet development of nuclear weapons.**

▶ **Why China became communist.**

Containment

For American leaders, the main objective of the Cold War was to prevent the expansion of Soviet influence without resorting to all-out war. To prepare for this new kind of conflict, Congress reorganized the country's system of defense.

In July 1947 Congress established the Department of Defense as well as the Joint Chiefs of Staff, which combined the leadership of the army, navy, and air force. Later that same year, Congress created the **Central Intelligence Agency** (CIA) under the direction of the National Security Council. The CIA was authorized to carry out secret spy operations against foreign enemies of the United States.

The goal of American Cold War policy was defined by George F. Kennan, a professional diplomat who had served for many years at the U.S. embassy in Moscow. Kennan believed that the Soviet Union was trying to dominate the world by slowly expanding communism into more and more countries. He declared:

"**In these circumstances it is clear that the main element of any United States policy toward the Soviet Union must be that of a long-term, patient but firm and vigilant [watchful] containment of Russian expansive tendencies.**"

Kennan said the United States should build up its armed forces and be prepared to contain Soviet expansion wherever it was attempted. American officials maintained that this policy of **containment** was defensive in purpose. The Soviets, however, felt that the containment policy was a hostile act and thus a form of aggression.

The Berlin Airlift

Cold War tensions increased in 1948 when the United States, Great Britain, and France announced plans to create an independent Federal Republic of Germany from the zones of Germany under their control. The Soviets responded by closing all the roads leading across their zone to Berlin. They could not block the formation of the West German republic, but they might force the Allies to give up their zones in the capital city.

The plan The Soviet action caused a serious dilemma. If the Americans tried to ship supplies to Berlin by truck or train, they would run into Soviet roadblocks. Then they would have to either turn back or fight. Truman therefore decided to *fly* supplies to Berlin.

The **Berlin Airlift** turned the tables on the Soviets, forcing them to decide whether to allow the supplies to reach West Berlin or to start fighting. The Soviets chose to do nothing. They probably believed that it would be impossible to keep the 2 million residents of West Berlin supplied with food and other necessities by air alone.

The U.S. and British air forces proved them wrong. Over the next 11 months, American and British planes flew more than 270,000 missions into Berlin. One Berlin resident recalled that the airlift provided a boost to morale as well as a means of survival:

"**When we woke up, the first thing we did was listen to see whether the noise of aircraft engines could be heard. That gave us the certainty that we were not alone, that the whole civilized world took part in the fight for Berlin's freedom.**"

The response. In May 1949 the Soviets gave up trying to squeeze the Western powers out of Berlin. They lifted the land blockade. Even though the Berlin crisis had been resolved, months later the Soviets sent a chilling

These children from Berlin cheer as American planes prepare to drop supplies to their city.

message to the West by testing their first atomic bomb. The Soviets had been trying to create their own atomic weapons for years, but now the American monopoly on nuclear weapons was broken. The age of the nuclear arms race had begun.

The United States and other Western European nations responded to concerns about the Soviets by strengthening their own alliances. In 1949 the United States, Great Britain, France, Italy, and eight other nations established the **North Atlantic Treaty Organization** (NATO).

Members of NATO pledged to defend one another in case of attack and to form a unified military force for this purpose. To help protect its NATO allies from communist expansion, the United States gave extensive military aid to Western Europe. In 1955 the Soviet Union and its satellites signed the **Warsaw Pact**, pledging mutual defense against attack.

The Fall of China

The policy of containment was significantly challenged in 1949. Not only did the Soviets test an atomic bomb, but China was shaken by a communist revolution. The establishment of the communist People's Republic of China was the result of years of conflict in the country.

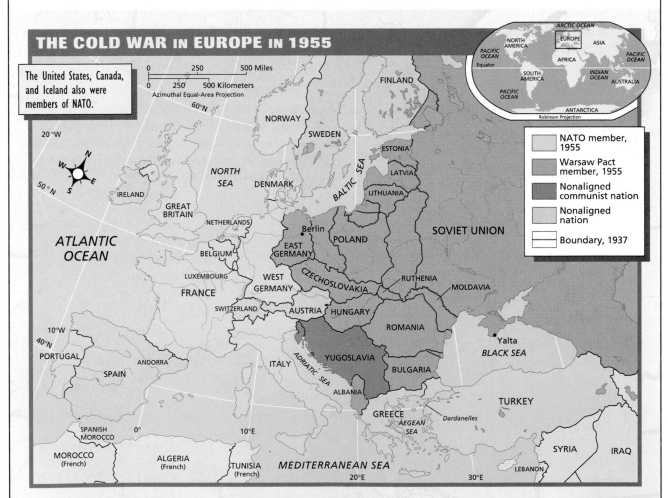

THE COLD WAR IN EUROPE IN 1955

The United States, Canada, and Iceland also were members of NATO.

0   250   500 Miles
0   250   500 Kilometers
Azimuthal Equal-Area Projection

Legend:
- NATO member, 1955
- Warsaw Pact member, 1955
- Nonaligned communist nation
- Nonaligned nation
- Boundary, 1937

Learning from Maps. The majority of European nations were allied with either NATO or the Warsaw Pact.

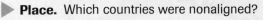

▶ **Place.** Which countries were nonaligned?

• Maps

By the early 1900s more and more Chinese people had come to believe that the ruling monarchy was corrupt and out of touch with the ordinary people. In 1911 the emperor was overthrown. For the next several years, various groups struggled for power in China.

Some nationalists wanted China to have a more modern government styled after the capitalist democracies. They formed the Chinese Nationalist Party to fight for control of the country. In 1928, after several years of war, the Nationalists established a new government led by Chiang Kaishek.

Some Chinese people embraced the ideas of communism. The Chinese Communist Party, led by Mao Zedong, battled Chiang's government. In the late 1930s the Nationalists and Communists agreed to a truce for the duration of the war against Japan. Once the war was over, however, fighting between them resumed. By this time the Communists had a great deal of popular sup-

port. Mao had redistributed land among the poor. This policy appealed to many Chinese people, the vast majority of whom were very poor peasants. Although Chiang had improved transportation and built numerous factories, these actions did little to ease the poverty of most Chinese people. Also, his government was plagued by corruption.

During the internal conflict in China, the United States aided the Nationalists even though State Department experts reported that Chiang's government was hopelessly corrupt and inefficient. When the Chinese Communists defeated the Nationalist armies, Chiang and his supporters were forced to flee to the island of Taiwan (Formosa). China was now part of the communist world.

Chiang Kaishek, shown here with his wife, Madame Chiang, ruled China from 1928 until 1949. After many years of war he could not stop the forces of the Chinese Communist Party.

Section 3 Review

• Glossary

IDENTIFY and explain the significance of the following: Central Intelligence Agency, containment, Berlin Airlift, North Atlantic Treaty Organization, Warsaw Pact, Chiang Kaishek, Mao Zedong

REVIEWING FOR DETAILS

1. How did the Western Allies plan to counter the Soviets' development of nuclear weapons?
2. How did China become a communist nation?

REVIEWING FOR UNDERSTANDING

3. **Geographic Literacy** How did the United States respond to Soviet actions in Berlin?
4. **Writing Mastery:** *Expressing* Imagine that you are a resident of West Berlin. In several diary entries, express your feelings about the importance of the Berlin Airlift.
5. **Critical Thinking:** *Cause and Effect* Why might the communist victory in China have caused concern among many people in the West?

Section 4
COLD WAR FEARS

Multimedia Connections

Explore these related topics and materials on the CD–ROM to enrich your understanding of this section:

Media Bank

- Displaced Koreans
- Firing of General MacArthur
- Alger Hiss
- Cold War Movie Poster

Readings

- Fighting in Korea

Profiles

- Alger Hiss
- Ethel and Julius Rosenberg

Gazetteer

- North Korea
- South Korea

A s the Cold War continued, Americans found themselves drawn into more conflicts, at home and abroad. In explaining his decision to send troops to a small Asian country to prevent a communist takeover, Truman explained that if that country fell "the Communist leaders would be encouraged to override nations close to our own shores." Many began to fear that Communists were already operating within the United States. The enemy seemed to be everywhere.

As you read this section you will find out:

▶ **What caused the Korean War.**

▶ **How President Truman and General MacArthur differed over the conduct of the Korean War.**

▶ **How the U.S. government reacted to the communist threat at home.**

The Korean War Begins

The fall of China to communism heightened Americans' concerns about the future of Asia. These concerns would soon draw the United States into a war to prevent a similar outcome in the small Asian country of South Korea.

Japan had taken over the Kingdom of Korea in 1910. At the end of World War II Korea was freed from Japanese control, but the Allies treated it much like postwar Germany. U.S. troops occupied the southern part of the country and Soviet troops occupied the northern part. Korea was divided between the two forces along the 38th parallel of north latitude.

In 1948 North Korea and South Korea each established separate national governments. Communist North Korea, known as the Democratic People's Republic of Korea, was led by Kim Il Sung. Noncommunist South

Korea, known as the Republic of Korea, was led by Syngman Rhee. In 1949 the United States and the Soviet Union pulled their troops out of Korea. Both North and South Korea laid claim to the entire country.

The Soviets had left behind a well-armed North Korean army, a force much superior to that defending the South. On June 25, 1950, the North Korean army struck across the border.

President Truman assumed that the Soviet Union was behind this invasion. An emergency session of the United Nations Security Council demanded a cease-fire. When North Korea did not pull back its troops, two days later the Council called on UN members to support South Korea. In the name of the United Nations, Truman ordered American air, naval, and ground forces into Korea. Fifteen other members of the United Nations joined in the defense of South Korea.

Senator Robert A. Taft, a leading Republican, strongly objected to the president's actions. He argued that under the Constitution, only Congress had the power to declare war. Truman, however, did not ask Congress to declare war, and Congress took no steps to prevent the military action.

The War Expands

The North Koreans had the advantage of surprise. By September they had conquered nearly all of South Korea. But the UN army, which consisted mainly of Americans and South Koreans, finally halted their advance. General Douglas MacArthur, commander of the UN forces, then executed a brilliant counterattack.

MacArthur landed a large number of troops at Inchon, far behind the North Korean lines. The tide of battle turned swiftly. The North Koreans, being attacked from two sides, retreated. Soon the UN forces had driven them back into North Korea.

However, instead of stopping at this point, MacArthur had Truman's approval to invade North Korea. By November his troops were approaching the boundary between North Korea and China, despite China's warning to stay back.

This action caused the Chinese to enter the war. Striking suddenly and with tremendous force, they drove MacArthur's troops back into South Korea. Chinese foreign minister Zhou Enlai (JOH EN-LY) argued that the Chinese only entered the conflict to protect themselves against a possible American invasion of Chinese territory. They feared that the

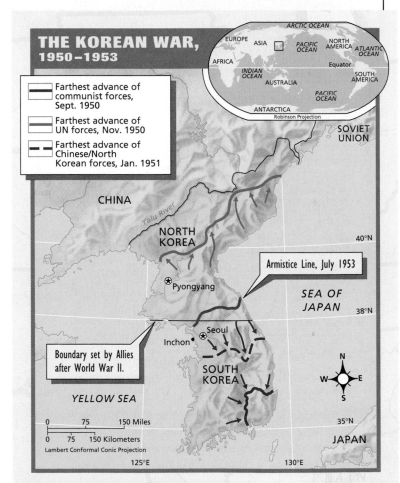

THE KOREAN WAR, 1950–1953

Farthest advance of communist forces, Sept. 1950

Farthest advance of UN forces, Nov. 1950

Farthest advance of Chinese/North Korean forces, Jan. 1951

SOVIET UNION

CHINA

Yalu River

NORTH KOREA

40°N

Pyongyang

Armistice Line, July 1953

SEA OF JAPAN

38°N

Seoul

Inchon

Boundary set by Allies after World War II.

SOUTH KOREA

YELLOW SEA

0   75   150 Miles
0   75   150 Kilometers
Lambert Conformal Conic Projection

125°E

35°N

JAPAN

130°E

N W E S

ARCTIC OCEAN
EUROPE ASIA PACIFIC OCEAN NORTH AMERICA ATLANTIC OCEAN
AFRICA INDIAN OCEAN Equator SOUTH AMERICA
AUSTRALIA PACIFIC OCEAN
ANTARCTICA
Robinson Projection

Learning from Maps.
Both North and South Korea made deep advances into each other's territory.

▶ **Movement.** Which country gained more territory with the Armistice Line of 1953?

• Maps

Americans would take advantage of the war to overthrow the communist government of China:

> **"The U.S. imperialists have adopted a hostile attitude towards us. . . . They wanted to calm China first and after occupying North Korea, they will come to attack China."**

Finally, in the spring of 1951, the battle line was stabilized roughly along the 38th parallel. MacArthur then requested permission to bomb China and to use anticommunist Chinese troops from Taiwan in Korea. President Truman decided not to allow this expansion of the war. MacArthur continued to argue publicly for his plan, which attracted considerable support. MacArthur's outspokenness hurt Truman's efforts to negotiate a peace settlement. Truman therefore exercised his authority as commander in chief of the armed forces to remove MacArthur from his position. The fighting in Korea continued.

The New Red Scare

Although many of the events of the Cold War took place overseas, almost every American was touched by Cold War tensions in some way. Fears of a communist takeover of the United States produced widespread abuses of civil liberties similar to the Red Scare of 1919–20.

When some Republicans accused Truman of allowing Communists to work for the federal government, the president established the Loyalty Review Board to investigate the backgrounds of federal employees. By March of 1952 some 20,000 federal employees had been investigated. Some were fired as "security risks," while many more resigned rather than risk being fired for suspected disloyalty.

Federal employees were not the only people targeted for investigation. In 1947 the **House Un-American Activities Committee** (HUAC) began a series of hearings to investigate citizens who belonged to a number of liberal organizations, from peace activist groups to labor unions.

Members of the Hollywood movie industry particularly became targets. Numerous actors, writers, directors, and producers were questioned about their possible affiliation with some Communists. Many who refused to cooperate with the committee were **blacklisted**—that is, no one in the

Young People in History
The Red Scare in Schools

Even schools were affected by the Red Scare. School boards investigated many teachers

Anticommunist book

and administrators suspected of being Communists. More than 60,000 teachers were investigated; some 5,000 resigned or were fired. Many were blacklisted from teaching altogether.

Students also came under suspicion. For example, Becky Jenkins's father was investigated by the government for his involvement with a school for worker training and education. The investigation started when Becky was in junior high and lasted several years. Jenkins was often teased by other students who accused her of being a Communist. She recalled one incident in a social studies class in which she suggested that the United States should not get involved in the Korean War. "The class started to laugh and scream and hoot at me, yelling 'Commie!'" Jenkins recalled. "I ran home from school sobbing, just humiliated."

entertainment industry would hire them. Some even went to jail for refusing to cooperate with the committee.

• **Hollywood Blacklist**

Spies Among Us

In addition to tracking down members of the Communist Party, HUAC also investigated people suspected of spying for the Soviets. One of the most sensational trials was that of Alger Hiss, a former State Department official. In 1948 former Communist Party member Whittaker Chambers charged that Hiss had given him secret State Department documents to pass on to the Soviets.

Hiss denied the charges and then sued Chambers for slander. Many officials defended Hiss. Then Chambers produced evidence he had been hiding inside a pumpkin on his farm. These "pumpkin papers" seemed to prove that Hiss had lied. As a result, Hiss was found guilty of perjury, or lying under oath. He was sentenced to five years in prison. After the Hiss case, many people panicked. Some believed that Soviet spies were everywhere. In 1950 Congress passed the **Internal Security Act**, which required all communist organizations to register and open their financial records to government inspectors.

Fears about nuclear war and spying came together when several Americans were accused of turning over to the Soviets secret information about the manufacture of atomic bombs. In 1951 Ethel and Julius Rosenberg were convicted of passing atomic secrets to the enemy. Many people believed they were innocent victims of the Red Scare. Despite widespread protests against their conviction, they were both executed for treason in 1953.

Although Ethel and Julius Rosenberg were convicted and executed for treason, many people believed they were innocent.

Section 4 Review

• **Glossary**

IDENTIFY and explain the significance of the following: Kim Il Sung, Syngman Rhee, House Un-American Activities Committee, blacklisted, Alger Hiss, Internal Security Act, Ethel and Julius Rosenberg

LOCATE and explain the importance of the following: North Korea, South Korea, 38th parallel

• **Gazetteer**

REVIEWING FOR DETAILS
1. How did the Korean War begin?
2. What different ideas did President Truman and General MacArthur have about the Korean War?
3. How did the U.S. government respond to the communist threat at home?

• **Time Line**

REVIEWING FOR UNDERSTANDING
4. **Writing Mastery:** *Persuading* Write a newspaper editorial supporting or rejecting the U.S. government's investigations of suspected Communists.
5. **Critical Thinking:** *Drawing Conclusions* Why do you think Truman did not want to follow MacArthur's policy in the Korean War?

CHAPTER 25

Power and Prosperity
(1952–1960)

USA THEMES IN AMERICAN HISTORY

Democratic Values:
How might members of a minority group use democratic methods to challenge inequality?

Economic Development:
How might rapid economic growth change a society?

Technology and Society:
How might a technological advance like television affect society?

• Video Opener

• Skill Builder

African American singer Bernice Johnson Reagon grew up in Albany, Georgia, in the 1950s. She remembered it as "a society where there were very clear lines." She explained how one of the decade's greatest legacies—the civil rights movement—defied those restrictions and changed the world she had once known: "[The movement] gave me the power to challenge any line that limits me."

image above: *Rosa Parks after her arrest*

Section 1

TROUBLES AT HOME AND ABROAD

Multimedia Connections

Explore these related topics and materials on the CD–ROM to enrich your understanding of this section:

 Profiles

- Joseph R. McCarthy
- Margaret Chase Smith
- John Foster Dulles

 Atlas

- Nuclear Technology

 Media Bank

- Candidate Eisenhower
- Khrushchev Visiting America
- *Sputnik*

 Gazetteer

- Soviet Union
- Egypt

 Simulation

- Race to the Moon

In the days after the Soviet Union successfully launched the first artificial satellite, called *Sputnik,* nearly every American had an opinion of the matter. One scientist dismissed it as "a useless hunk of iron." One White House official called it "a silly bauble [trinket] in the sky," while another presidential adviser confidently predicted that Americans would not want to join "an outerspace basketball game." Others, however, feared it was a sign that the United States was losing the Cold War.

As you read this section you will find out:

▶ **Why Dwight Eisenhower was a popular American president.**

▶ **How the fear of communism affected American society during the 1950s.**

▶ **What events and policies shaped the ongoing Cold War.**

Eisenhower Wins the 1952 Election

As the election of 1952 approached, the public's concerns about conditions at home and abroad grew. Inflation was high, and the Korean War dragged on.

Believing he could not win under these circumstances, President Truman decided not to seek re-election. Instead, the Democrats nominated Illinois governor Adlai Stevenson. While he was a witty and thoughtful speaker, many people thought Stevenson was too intellectual and out of touch with the "real world." More importantly, voters seemed ready for political change. After all, the nation had not elected a Republican president since Herbert Hoover won the office in 1928.

The Republicans nominated Dwight D. Eisenhower, leader of the Allied forces in

Dwight D. Eisenhower inspired many Americans who felt that his skills as a general would make him a fine president.

• **Dwight Eisenhower**

Europe during World War II, as their candidate. In addition to Eisenhower's fame as a general, his warm personality appealed to millions. Moreover, Eisenhower had the advantage of being new to party politics. Americans who usually voted Democrat could vote for him without feeling that they were betraying the party. As a matter of fact, Truman had even tried to persuade Eisenhower to run on the Democratic ticket! Eisenhower's campaign slogan—"I like Ike"—captured people's reaction to his candidacy.

When Eisenhower announced that if elected he would go to Korea to negotiate a settlement of the war, his victory seemed certain. He easily won the contest.

Eisenhower kept this campaign promise before he was even sworn into office. In December 1952 he flew to Korea to meet with American commanders and discuss strategy. Then in July 1953, perhaps because Eisenhower had hinted he might use nuclear weapons to end the war if peace talks did not succeed, the parties finally reached a kind of truce. Under the terms of this agreement, communist North Korea and anticommunist

South Korea accepted their prewar border at the 38th parallel. Their armies have continued to face each other across a narrow demilitarized zone at that point ever since.

Fears of Communists

The New Red Scare, which had begun as Cold War tensions grew in the late 1940s, continued in the 1950s. A Republican senator from Wisconsin, Joseph R. McCarthy, played a significant role in increasing fears of communism at home.

McCarthy's rise. Early in 1950 McCarthy charged that the U.S. State Department was filled with secret traitors. He claimed to have a list of 205 Communists who held policy-making posts in the State Department.

This accusation caused a sensation, and the previously unknown McCarthy made headlines in newspapers all over the country. He quickly took advantage of this attention by coming up with more astonishing charges. For example, General George Marshall had been a

Senator Joseph McCarthy "sweeps" Communists out of the Capitol, using a broom sent to him by his supporters in Wisconsin.

special ambassador to China after World War II. Now McCarthy accused him of helping turn China over to the Communists.

Many people believed McCarthy's claims, though his "evidence" did not prove anything. McCarthy justified his tactics by arguing that the country was engaged in a moral fight, "a final, all-out battle," McCarthy declared. "The modern champions of communism have selected this as the time. . . . The chips are down—they are truly down."

In this atmosphere of reckless charges and persecutions, commonly called **McCarthyism**, the senator did not have to provide hard facts. Nevertheless, many of the men and women whom he accused of being either Communists or "soft on communism" found their careers ruined.

McCarthy was actually a fraud. One of the first Americans to realize this was Edward R. Murrow, a well-known reporter. Another was Senator Margaret Chase Smith of Maine, who criticized McCarthy and his tactics:

> **"I think it is high time that we remembered that the Constitution, as amended, speaks not only of freedom of speech but also of trial by jury instead of trial by accusation."**

Many Americans, however, went along with McCarthy, afraid to speak out against him. Many others actually supported McCarthy's actions, sharing in the fear of communism.

President Eisenhower disliked McCarthy and his tactics. Eisenhower tried to use his influence to control Senator McCarthy, but he avoided openly criticizing a member of his own political party. The president even stiffened the already harsh loyalty program that Truman had set up to get rid of communist sympathizers in the government. Employees found to be "security risks" were discharged even if they had done nothing wrong.

McCarthy's downfall. McCarthy finally carried his reckless charges too far. Late in 1953 the army drafted one of his assistants. McCarthy tried unsuccessfully to get his aide excused from active service. At the same time,

McCarthy's accusations that there were Communists in the State Department shook the country and made the senator one of the most powerful men in Washington, D.C. No one wanted to be branded by his accusations.

the senator was undertaking an investigation into what he called "subversive [treasonous] activities" by the U.S. Army. These **Army-McCarthy hearings**, which were televised, soon destroyed McCarthy's reputation. Day after day, millions of viewers saw both the senator's snarling cruelty and the emptiness of his charges.

McCarthy's spell was soon broken. In December 1954 the Senate resolved that his "conduct . . . is contrary to senatorial traditions and is hereby condemned." McCarthy, ignored if not forgotten, remained in the Senate until his death in 1957.

Eisenhower and the Cold War

When he took office, President Eisenhower and his secretary of state, John Foster Dulles, developed a strategy for dealing with the

Soviets known as **massive retaliation**. Dulles explained the approach in the popular magazine, *Life*:

> "There is one solution and only one: that is for the free world to develop the will and organize the means to retaliate [strike back] instantly against open aggression by Red armies, so that, if it occurred any-where, we could and would strike back where it hurts, by means of our choosing."

The threat of massive retaliation came to be known as **brinkmanship** because it suggested that the United States was willing to go "to the brink" of all-out war, if necessary, to stop communism.

American bluffs.   Brinkmanship was usually a bluff. By 1956 both the United States and the Soviet Union possessed nuclear weapons hundreds of times more powerful than the bombs that had destroyed Hiroshima and Nagasaki. Eisenhower and Dulles seldom considered actually using nuclear weapons against any country. An attack would have been very destructive for both powers and probably the whole world.

These Hungarian freedom fighters burn an image of Joseph Stalin to protest the communist influence on their country. The Soviets brutally put down the anticommunist revolution in Hungary.

Hey Fellows!

Herc Ficklen/Dallas Morning News

As this cartoon shows, diplomats had a difficult time working out foreign policy problems as the massive arms race between the United States and the Soviet Union grew.

• **Nuclear Test**

Yet brinkmanship and Dulles's threats kept Cold War tensions high at a time when the Soviets took a somewhat less aggressive position toward the United States. After Joseph Stalin died in 1953, Nikita Khrushchev (kroosh-CHAWF), the new Soviet leader, claimed to favor "peaceful coexistence" with Western nations. When Dulles did not back off from his hard-line position, it gave the Soviets an advantage in the competition for influence in other countries.

International conflicts.   Hoping to avoid a nuclear catastrophe, Eisenhower generally avoided seeking military solutions to international problems. Dulles had spoken of "liberating" Eastern Europeans living under communist dictatorships. However, when anticommunist revolts broke out in East Germany in 1953 and Hungary in 1956, the United States offered little support to the rebels.

Eisenhower also demonstrated restraint when a crisis erupted in the Middle East in 1956. Egypt had earlier announced that it planned to build a large dam on the Nile River at Aswan. Hoping to secure Egypt as an ally, the United States agreed to help finance construction of the dam. When the Egyptian government asked the Soviet Union for assistance as well, however, the United States withdrew its offer to help.

The Egyptians then seized control of the Suez Canal, an international waterway controlled by France and Great Britain, hoping to build the Aswan High Dam with the tolls it collected. Israel, Great Britain, and France joined together in an invasion of Egypt, hoping to reopen the canal and guarantee access for international shipping.

Eisenhower faced a dilemma. The United States had supported Israel and its independence from the beginning. America also regarded Great Britain and France as important allies. Eisenhower, however, objected to their use of force to regain control of the canal. He demanded that they pull back. So did the Soviets, who threatened a military response. As a result, Israel, Great Britain, and France withdrew their troops, and Egypt kept control of the Suez Canal.

Eisenhower had no desire to let the Soviet Union "interfere" in the Middle East, however. The next year, after his re-election as president, he announced the **Eisenhower Doctrine**. It promised American financial and military assistance to Middle Eastern countries that asked for help to resist the spread of communism.

The United States and the Soviet Union

In the mid-1950s Nikita Khrushchev became the premier of the Soviet Union. He was a difficult leader for Americans to understand. One

moment he talked of peace, the next he threatened to use nuclear weapons against his enemies. Relations between the United States and the Soviet Union varied similarly, going from uneasy coexistance to bitter anger.

Sputnik **stuns Americans.** In October 1957 Soviet scientists shocked the world when they sent the first artificial satellite, called ***Sputnik***, into orbit around the earth. (*Sputnik* means "traveling companion" in Russian.) This amazing technological feat shattered American self-confidence, and it provided a great propaganda boost for the Soviet Union and communism.

"Rocket fever" soon swept the United States as Americans raced to "catch up." Americans might have found themselves even further behind had it not been for the pioneering work of scientist Robert Hutchings Goddard. Although Goddard died in 1945, he had laid the groundwork for nearly all American rocket technology that followed. Years after his death the U.S. government was still granting patents for his inventions.

With Goddard gone, however, the country needed a new group of rocket scientists if the space program was going to succeed. Since many people blamed the educational system for America's failure to reach outer space first, schools and universities soon offered more courses in science and mathematics. More scholarships in these fields were also awarded to promising students. In addition,

The United States launched the rocket Jupiter-C *in January 1958. The rocket sent the first American satellite,* Explorer, *into space.*

the government founded the **National Aeronautics and Space Administration** (NASA) to expand scientific research and development on space exploration.

After several embarrassing failures, in January 1958 the United States finally hurled a small satellite into space. America had reached beyond the earth. But how well would the nation do in the "space race"?

The U-2 affair. Just about the time when Khrushchev and Eisenhower were preparing to attend a summit meeting, an incident occurred that greatly strained U.S.-Soviet relations. In 1960 Khrushchev announced that the Soviets had shot down an American U-2 spy plane while it was taking photographs high over Soviet territory. At first, U.S. officials claimed that the U-2 was only a lost weather plane. Later, when Khrushchev revealed that the pilot, Francis Gary Powers, had survived the crash, Eisenhower admitted that the man had been on a spying mission.

American pilot Francis Gary Powers (center) is tried in the Soviet Union for spying. Powers was originally sentenced to 10 years in prison but was released to U.S. officials in 1962 in exchange for a captured Soviet spy.

Khrushchev called the **U-2 affair** "cowardly" and demanded that Eisenhower apologize for spying on his country and trying to cover it up. When the president refused, Khrushchev angrily walked out of the summit meeting. As a new decade dawned, Cold War tensions continued to run high.

Section 1 Review

• **Glossary**

IDENTIFY and explain the significance of the following: Adlai Stevenson, Joseph R. McCarthy, McCarthyism, Margaret Chase Smith, Army-McCarthy hearings, John Foster Dulles, massive retaliation, brinkmanship, Nikita Khrushchev, Eisenhower Doctrine, *Sputnik,* National Aeronautics and Space Administration, U-2 affair

REVIEWING FOR DETAILS

1. Why did Eisenhower easily win the 1952 presidential election?
2. What were the reasons for the wave of McCarthyism that swept the country in the early 1950s?

REVIEWING FOR UNDERSTANDING

3. **Geographic Literacy** Why might controlling outer space give one side an advantage over the other in the Cold War?
4. **Writing Mastery:** *Describing* Write a short paragraph describing the events and policies that shaped the Cold War in the 1950s.
5. **Critical Thinking:** *Comparing* What do you think were the advantages and disadvantages of Eisenhower and Dulles's brinkmanship policy?

Section 2

A PROSPEROUS NATION

Multimedia Connections

Explore these related topics and materials on the CD–ROM to enrich your understanding of this section:

 Profiles

- Lucille Ball
- Elvis Presley
- Ritchie Valens
- Chuck Berry

 Media Bank

- Baby Boom
- A Commuter's Life
- Middle-Class Consumerism
- Beat Movement

 Readings

- Beat Generation

L ee Mintz, the owner of a Cleveland record shop, noticed a startling change in his business. White teenagers were flooding into his store to buy rhythm and blues records, sometimes known as "Negro music." Mintz soon told disc jockey Alan Freed about the trend. Though not certain that it would draw a large audience, in 1951 Freed started a radio program devoted to the music. His "Moondog Show" was an instant success. What Freed called "rock 'n' roll" had reached the world.

As you read this section you will find out:

▶ **How the growth of suburbs affected American life.**

▶ **Why many Americans moved to the South and West during the 1950s.**

▶ **How popular culture changed during the 1950s.**

A Changing Economy

The 1950s were prosperous years for most Americans. World War II had caused an economic boom that lasted well into the decade. By 1960 more than 60 percent of Americans had reached middle-class status—then defined by an income ranging from $3,000 to $10,000 a year. Economic growth opened up many personal and career opportunities. One man remembered the 1950s as being "like an escalator. You just stood there and you moved up." Not all Americans found it easy to gain financial success, however. In 1960 more than 20 percent of the population lived in poverty.

Finally glimpsing economic security after World War II, many more Americans began to marry and have children. For example, during the Great Depression and World War II, the population increased by about 1 to 1.5 million people a year; shortly after the war the population was increasing by nearly 3 million people per year. The trend continued well into the next decade. This leap in the birthrate is known as the **baby boom**.

A Changing Nation

As their families grew, more Americans began moving from cities to suburbs. These suburbanites hoped to find space, affordable homes, fresh air, privacy, and contact with nature. Still, they needed to remain near the cities where most of them worked. They also wanted to continue to take advantage of the excitement and cultural opportunities of city life. In addition, President Eisenhower began work on a national highway system. This system contributed to suburban growth by making it much easier for people to travel between their city jobs and their suburban homes.

• **Domestic Policies**

The suburbs boom. Builders were an important part of the trend, since they constructed huge housing developments in the suburbs. New York's **Levittown,** a development built by the Levitt Company, was one of the first and best known. It was so big that it became a suburb in itself. Other communities followed Levittown, and between 1950 and 1960 more than 1 million homes were built in the suburbs each year. Schools, shopping

Planned suburbs, like this one in Fairfax, Delaware, became increasingly common in the 1950s.

centers, hospitals, and offices accompanied the housing boom.

The houses in these new communities closely resembled each other, leading some people to complain. One decorating magazine asked, "Is this the American dream, or nightmare?" Residents of the new suburbs largely came from the middle class. The poor could not afford even the smallest suburban homes, and there were almost no suburban apartments or houses to rent.

Consumption and conformity. Suburban life encouraged an increase in consumption as residents purchased cars, televisions, refrigerators, and more to go along with their new homes. Families struggled to "keep up with the Joneses," buying as many shiny new products as their next-door neighbors. Some also used shopping as a way to make friends in their new communities. Tupperware™ parties not only offered homemakers the opportunity to stock up on kitchen goods but also helped create social ties.

For some Americans suburban living also encouraged **conformity**, or fitting in to society. Many suburbanites placed a high value on fitting in and getting along. The failure to do so, *Fortune* magazine noted, "is a source of friction, feuds, and sleepless nights in many of

Popular images in the 1950s often expressed the idea that the main role of women should be taking care of the home.

the newer suburban communities." Writer Lewis Mumford wondered if conformity was good for the nation:

> "Suburban areas . . . [are] inhabited by people in the same class, the same income, the same age group, witnessing the same television performances, eating the same tasteless . . . foods from the same freezers, conforming in every outward and inward respect to a common mold."

Still, Americans continued to flock to the suburbs, viewing the calm streets and neat houses as a welcome escape from city life.

Women in the suburbs. Suburban life demanded much of women, who handled most of the domestic and childrearing duties while their husbands worked at jobs in the city. Countless television shows, magazines, movies, and books told women to be "content in a world of . . . kitchen, . . . babies, and home."

While some women found this role fulfilling, others felt smothered and depressed by the confines of suburban life. According to *Life* magazine, they were "bored stiff with numbing rounds of club meetings and card playing." One woman described her feelings after she

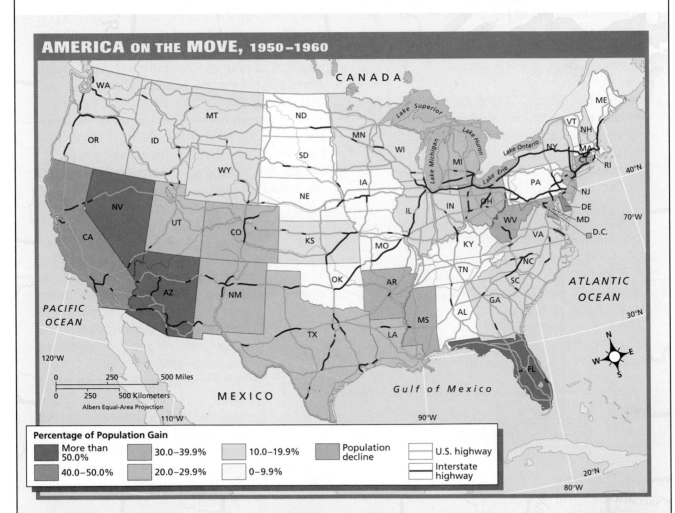

AMERICA ON THE MOVE, 1950–1960

Percentage of Population Gain
- More than 50.0%
- 40.0–50.0%
- 30.0–39.9%
- 20.0–29.9%
- 10.0–19.9%
- 0–9.9%
- Population decline
- U.S. highway
- Interstate highway

Learning from Maps. The creation of a national highway system throughout the continental United States made Americans more mobile.

▶ **Region.** Which of the following Sun Belt states experienced the largest percentage of population gain—Texas, Florida, or Alabama?

● **Maps**

graduated from college and became a full-time housewife:

"**The plunge from the strictly intellectual college life to the 24-hour a day domestic one is a terrible shock. We stagger through our first years of childrearing wondering what our values are in struggling to find some compromise between our intellectual ambition and the reality of everyday living.**"

In order to overcome their feelings of isolation and also provide a second income, more and more middle-class women took jobs outside the home. In nearly every field, however, women continued to be paid lower wages and salaries than men. In addition, women rarely had access to the best jobs or opportunities for advancement.

The inner cities. As middle-class people moved to the suburbs, the percentage of poor people in the cities increased. This strained the finances of city governments because they received fewer tax dollars. The decline in tax revenues had serious results.

Many Mexicans and Mexican Americans moved to cities like Los Angeles in search of jobs in the 1950s.

Many city schools suffered, and general services fell off, which caused still more families to leave the cities. Since many of the people who remained in the cities were African American or Hispanic, a new kind of segregation developed.

The government tried to improve the living conditions of poorer people in the cities by building large **public housing projects**. Usually the income of the tenants determined the rents they paid.

Women in the Labor Force

[Line graph. Y-axis: Percentage of Women in the Civilian Labor Force, ranging from 20 to 60. X-axis: Year, from 1950 to 1980. The line rises steadily from about 34 in 1950 to about 54 in 1980.]

Source: *Statistical Abstract of the United States*

A Changing Workforce. Women's participation in the labor force increased steadily after 1950. About how much did the percentage of women in the labor force increase between 1950 and 1960?

• Graphs

A Changing Population

The national migration to the suburbs was not the only move Americans made during the 1950s. After World War II the population of the United States began a long-term shift to the West and South. Because of their warm climate, these areas of the country came to be known as the **Sun Belt**. Retired people in particular headed to Florida and the Southwest to avoid the harsh northern winters. Home air conditioners, a technological breakthrough in the 1950s, made the southern heat more bearable.

Other factors also contributed to this large migration.

Aircraft, chemical, plastics, and electronics manufacturers located their businesses in the Sun Belt because of low taxes and living costs. Thousands of families followed, attracted by the new jobs and pleasant working conditions these industries provided. The federal government also encouraged the population shift by establishing huge new facilities in the Sun Belt. For example, it created the rocket-launching base at Cape Canaveral, Florida, and NASA headquarters in Houston, Texas.

A Changing Lifestyle

The 1950s also brought an unexpected benefit to many workers—more leisure time. Between 1940 and 1960 the average workweek decreased from 44 to 40 hours. At the same time the average paid vacation increased from one to two weeks. As a result, Americans had more free time during a period in which they also had more money to spend.

Many people used their earnings to purchase automobiles. By 1960 nearly 75 percent of all American families owned a car. These vehicles contributed to the growth of new industries and new types of leisure. Vacationing families climbed into their cars and headed for the beach or the mountains.

Americans also stayed close to home for entertainment and recreation. During the 1950s hundreds of golf courses and bowling alleys were constructed. Attendance at spectator sports like baseball and football grew tremendously as well.

Americans enjoyed another source of entertainment inside their own homes—television. Throughout the 1950s Americans bought about 7 million sets a year. By 1960 most families in America had at least one TV.

The broadcasting industry quickly filled the day with shows. Advertisers soon realized that the public wanted more variety and sponsored game shows, situation comedies, music shows, and children's shows. By the end of the decade the average household watched television for at least five hours each day.

A Changing Youth Culture

Social observers called young people of the 1950s the "**silent generation**." Critics accused them of having a lack of concern about serious problems confronting the United States and the rest of the world. Their only goals appeared to be having plenty of money, a good job, and a comfortable house in the suburbs, commentators complained. Some teenagers and young adults did ignore

Global Connections
Rockin' Around the World

Rock 'n' roll knew no boundaries. Teens all over the world came to identify with its raw, restless themes. Musicians in other countries greeted rock 'n' roll enthusiastically. Britain produced its own rock 'n' roll phenomenon— the Beatles, who were greatly influenced by American artists. By 1964 the "Fab Four" toured the United States with a distinctive mixture of the sounds of Buddy Holly and Little Richard, among others.

In some nations, leaders came to fear the rebellious sound of rock 'n' roll music and worried about its effects on young people. China, North and South Korea, and the Soviet Union banned the broadcasting and sale of rock music. Rock 'n' roll then moved underground and continued to be popular though illegal.

In nations already influenced by African music, musicians have combined American rock rhythms with their own popular tunes. This blending has created rock versions of *ska* in Jamaica, the *samba* in Brazil, and the *makossa* in Cameroon.

The popular television series American Bandstand *featured teenagers dancing to rock 'n' roll music.*

social problems and concentrated on eventually getting a slice of the American pie for themselves. But other young people questioned the values of mainstream society in both bold and subtle ways.

The beats. A small group of young writers and poets called **beats** rebelled against both established literary and social traditions. Many beats lived in San Francisco, where they gathered at bookstores and coffee shops to talk and to read each other's poetry.

Beat writings criticized American society for being meaningless and empty. Poet Allen Ginsberg described society's effects in the opening line of "Howl:" "I saw the best minds of my generation destroyed by madness." Jack Kerouac's *On the Road*, the most influential beat novel, described the author's desire to escape the confines of stifling middle-class stability: "We gotta go and never stop going till we get there."

Rock 'n' roll. Teenagers expressed their desire to be different by listening to a new form of music called **rock 'n' roll**. Rock 'n' roll drew heavily on African American rhythm and blues music and stunned people with its raw,

ear-shattering sound. During the 1950s rock 'n' roll singers like Elvis Presley, Ritchie Valens, and Chuck Berry became very popular.

Countless adults disliked rock 'n' roll and the effect that it produced in teenagers. One psychiatrist even claimed the music caused a "prehistoric rhythmic trance" in listeners! Others objected to the supposed immorality associated with the music, while some did not like to see white and black singers or audiences interacting. Still more did not understand the music's lyrics. Nevertheless, teenagers continued to see rock 'n' roll as a welcome breath of fresh air.

Section 2 Review

• Glossary

IDENTIFY and explain the significance of the following: baby boom, Levittown, conformity, public housing projects, Sun Belt, silent generation, beats, Allen Ginsberg, Jack Kerouac, rock 'n' roll, Elvis Presley, Ritchie Valens, Chuck Berry

REVIEWING FOR DETAILS

1. How did the move to the suburbs affect American society?
2. Why did many Americans migrate across the country in the 1950s?

REVIEWING FOR UNDERSTANDING

3. **Geographic Literacy** What are some changes that might occur in a rural area when it becomes a suburb?
4. **Writing Mastery:** *Informing* Imagine that you are a writer for a popular magazine during the 1950s. Write a short article informing your readers how American culture seems to be changing.
5. **Critical Thinking:** *Making Comparisons* How did the 1950s mark a change for many American families compared to the two previous decades?

Section 3

VOICES FOR EQUAL RIGHTS

Multimedia Connections

Explore these related topics and materials on the CD–ROM to enrich your understanding of this section:

 Gazetteer

- Little Rock
- Montgomery

 Profiles

- Rosa Parks

 Biographies

- Martin Luther King, Jr.
- Earl Warren

 Readings

- Integrating Central High

 Media Bank

- Segregated Drinking Fountains
- Emmett Till
- Earl Warren
- Little Rock Nine
- Linda Brown

The entrance to Central High School loomed before Elizabeth Eckford, an African American student. As she walked to the building, the mob pushed toward her. "Two, four, six, eight, we ain't going to integrate," some chanted. "Lynch her! Lynch her!" others screamed. When she got to the school's doors, an Arkansas National Guard soldier blocked the way. Eckford turned and finally made it to a nearby bus stop.

As you read this section you will find out:

▶ **How U.S. schools were desegregated.**

▶ **How African Americans fought against segregation in public facilities.**

▶ **How individuals like Martin Luther King, Jr., and Rosa Parks rose to national importance.**

The Fight for School Desegregation

After World War II, African Americans increased their demands for political and social equality. Black soldiers had fought and died for the cause of freedom abroad. Now back home, they wanted that same liberty for themselves. African American officer Charles Gates, who had commanded a tank unit, explained how World War II helped the modern civil rights movement. "After the close of hostilities," he said, "we just kept on fighting."

A legal crusade. The NAACP played an essential role in the battle for racial equality. Much of the organization's work concerned the effort to desegregate the nation's schools. Following *Plessy* v. *Ferguson*, the 1896 Supreme Court decision that established the

Attorneys (left to right) George E. C. Hayes, Thurgood Marshall, and James Nabrit, Jr., worked hard to win the landmark case of Brown v. Board of Education.

● **Thurgood Marshall**

"separate but equal" doctrine, many states had created segregated schools. White and black facilities were far from equal, however. Southern states gave white schools much more money than African American schools.

In the early 1950s the NAACP won court victories that opened historically white professional schools, like the University of Texas Law School, to African American students. But widespread segregation continued.

In a 1952 court case the NAACP challenged the very basis of school segregation. The legal suit began when Oliver Brown attempted to enroll his daughter Linda in an all-white grade school in Topeka, Kansas, pointing out that the black school was located on the other side of town from their home. He sued the board of education when it refused to admit her to the nearby white school. **Brown v. Board of Education**, one of the most important cases in U.S. history, soon reached the Supreme Court.

Thurgood Marshall, whose great-grandparents had been slaves, served as the NAACP's head attorney in the case. Marshall

was born in Maryland and went to law school at Howard University. After graduating, he joined the NAACP and began to fight for civil rights. Much of Marshall's early work for the group took him to the South, where he constantly faced danger from white people who opposed racial equality. Nevertheless, he continued his personal and public crusade.

An important decision. Even as *Brown* v. *Board of Education* was on its way to the Supreme Court, the Court itself was undergoing significant changes. In 1953 President Eisenhower appointed a new chief justice, Earl Warren, who had run for vice president with Thomas Dewey in 1948. During World War II, when Warren served as attorney general of California, he supported the internment of Japanese American citizens. Warren later regretted his actions and spent a great deal of time thinking about civil rights. Under his leadership the Supreme Court solidly supported civil rights cases.

The Helicopter Era

The Helicopter Era—from HERBLOCK: A CARTOONIST'S LIFE (Simon & Schuster, 1993)

Critics charged that President Eisenhower tried too hard to stay "above the fray" of controversial issues such as racism.

Thurgood Marshall argued before the Supreme Court in *Brown* v. *Board of Education* that segregation deprived African American students of their civil rights. He used evidence collected by sociologists to show that segregation lowered black children's self-esteem and created lasting psychological harm.

Earl Warren and the other justices reached a unanimous decision in *Brown* v. *Board of Education*. In May 1954 the Court ruled that it was unconstitutional for states to maintain segregated schools. The case overturned the "separate but equal" doctrine established in the earlier case of *Plessy* v. *Ferguson*. "Today education is perhaps the most important function of state and local governments," Warren explained:

". . . To separate [those children] from others of similar age and qualifications solely because of their race generates a feeling of inferiority as to their status in the community that may affect their hearts and minds in a way unlikely ever to be undone. . . . We conclude that in the field of public education the doctrine of 'separate but equal' has no place. Separate educational facilities are inherently [by nature] unequal."

The Court thus ruled that a separate education was an unequal education even if black and white schools were identical. The Court's decision thrilled all Americans fighting for racial equality. The shout "We have won" rang throughout many communities. The *Chicago Defender*, a leading African American newspaper, called the ruling "a second emancipation proclamation . . . more important to our democracy than the atom bomb."

Showdown in Little Rock

The Supreme Court justices knew it would be difficult to put the *Brown* v. *Board of Education* ruling into effect. Few schools integrated immediately after the *Brown* decision. A year after the decision the Court announced that the states had to desegregate "with all deliber-

ate speed." The Court intended that the states had to begin promptly and move steadily toward full integration. Some states took "deliberate" to mean that schools could change slowly. Even in the face of the Court's words, many southern whites refused to accept school integration. Some paid for billboard ads that said "SAVE OUR REPUBLIC! IMPEACH EARL WARREN." There was talk of "massive resistance."

In the wake of *Brown* v. *Board of Education*, some southern whites used violence to try to stop desegregation. White students nearly killed Autherine Lucy, an African American woman, when she attempted to attend classes at the University of Alabama. Even as southern cities slowly began to desegregate their schools, African Americans braced themselves for the fights they knew would come.

In 1957, following a court order to integrate the public schools, the school board of Little Rock, Arkansas, voted to admit nine African American students to the all-white Central High School. Like most of the others in this small group of students, often called the **Little Rock Nine**, Ernest Green saw

Elizabeth Eckford, one of the Little Rock Nine, tries to make her way through an angry white mob opposed to integration. Eckford had missed a message about meeting the other students before going to school and wound up facing the violent protestors all alone.

American Letters

Invisible Man

Ralph Ellison

Ralph Ellison's Invisible Man *affected Americans of all races. The novel followed an African American main character who was "invisible" to the white people around him. Ellison used this character to comment on the blend of harassment and disregard African Americans faced in their lives everyday.*

After the main character's high school graduation speech, a group of well-known white men invite him to deliver it at a social gathering. When he arrives, he learns that they have ordered local black students, including himself, to stage an organized fight for them as "part of the entertainment." After his participation in this fight, the main character gives his speech—with a heartbreaking result.

Writer Ralph Ellison

The M.C. knocked on a table for quiet. "Gentlemen," he said, "we almost forgot an important part of the program. A most serious part, gentlemen. This boy was brought here to deliver a speech which he made at his graduation yesterday . . ." . . .

There was still laughter as I faced them, my mouth dry, my eye throbbing. I began slowly, but evidently my throat was tense, because they began shouting, "Louder! Louder!"

"We of the younger generation extol [praise] the wisdom of that great leader and educator [Booker T. Washington]," I shouted. . . . "And like him I say, and in his words, 'To those of my race . . . who underestimate the importance of cultivating friendly relations with the Southern white man, who is his next-door neighbor, I would say: "Cast down your bucket where you are." . . .'"

I spoke automatically and with such fervor [passion] that I did not realize that the men were still talking and laughing until my dry mouth, filling up with blood from the cut, almost strangled me. . . . I spoke even louder in spite of the pain. But still they talked and still they laughed, as though deaf with cotton in dirty ears. So I spoke with greater emotional emphasis. I closed my ears and swallowed blood until I was nauseated. The speech seemed a hundred times as long as before, but I could not leave out a single word. All had to be said, each memorized nuance [detail] considered, rendered [presented]. Nor was that all. . . . I used the phrase "social responsibility" and they yelled:

"What's that word you say, boy?" . . .

. . . The M.C. rushed forward. They shouted hostile phrases at me. But I did not understand.

A small dry mustached man in the front row blared out, "Say that slowly, son!" . . .

"Social responsibility, sir," I said.

"You weren't being smart, were you, boy?" he said, not unkindly.

"No, sir!"

"You sure that about 'equality' was a mistake?"

"Oh, yes, sir," I said. "I was swallowing blood."

Surrounded by federal troops, the Little Rock Nine walk to school together. Although the school was successfully integrated that year, Governor Faubus would continue to try to stop integration by completely shutting down the Little Rock public school system the following year.

phones, typewriters, and TV studios. Within minutes a world that had been holding its breath learned that the nine pupils, protected by the might of the United States military, had finally entered the 'never-never land.' ”

Even after the Little Rock Nine entered the school, they faced constant harassment. That spring, however, Ernest Green became the first African American student ever to graduate from Central High School.

The Montgomery Bus Boycott

Even before the forced integration of schools, African Americans spoke out strongly against all forms of racial discrimination. NAACP officials looked for other opportunities to challenge segregation and inequality.

The boycott begins. As in many other southern cities, the law in Montgomery, Alabama, forced African American bus riders to sit in the back of city buses. If a bus filled up with white riders, the black riders had to give up their seats and stand.

desegregation as a "personal opportunity to change conditions in Little Rock." Despite the court order, Governor Orville Faubus called out the Arkansas National Guard to prevent the Little Rock Nine from entering the school.

Some government officials pressed President Eisenhower to intervene. Eisenhower said privately that it was "just plain nuts" to force integration. "I don't believe you can change the hearts of men with laws or decisions," he explained. Eisenhower was also concerned about the conflict desegregation would bring. He saw Governor Faubus's act, however, as a direct challenge to federal authority and soon sent 1,000 federal soldiers to Little Rock.

Daisy Bates, the president of the Arkansas chapter of the NAACP, described what happened:

“At 9:22 A.M. the nine Negro pupils marched solemnly through the doors of Central High School, surrounded by twenty-two soldiers. . . . Scores of reporters, photographers, and TV cameramen made a mad dash for tele-

Encouraged by the Montgomery boycott, African Americans in many other cities also protested against segregation on city buses.

One day in December 1955 an African American seamstress named Rosa Parks refused to give up her seat to a white man. When he complained, the bus driver stormed down the aisle and shouted, "I said to move back, you hear?" Parks sat still. Then the police arrived. "Why do you push us around?" she asked them. One officer gave the reply: "I don't know, but the law is the law and you're under arrest."

That night local African American leaders decided to launch what became known as the **Montgomery Bus Boycott**. They asked all African Americans to stay off the buses until the city changed the law requiring them to sit in the rear. Parks also agreed to file a lawsuit against the city.

Jo Ann Robinson, a professor at a local African American college, worked until dawn preparing for the boycott. "As the buses began to roll," she remembered, "we began to realize that the people . . . were going to stay off." The boycott had a successful beginning!

A leader emerges. A young African American clergyman, Martin Luther King, Jr., soon became one of the leaders of the boycott. King believed in nonviolent resistance for religious reasons. He argued that love was a more effective weapon than hate or force. King also had practical reasons for urging nonviolence. To obtain fairer treatment, African Americans needed the help of white liberals and moderates. They were more likely to get that assistance by appeals to reason and decency than by force, King argued.

At first, many white Montgomery residents were sure the boycott would not last. "Comes the first rainy day," the mayor confidently predicted, "[the boycotters] will be back on the buses." He was wrong. Encouraged by a local group called the **Montgomery Improvement Association**, which was headed by King, the vast majority of African Americans supported the boycott through both the spring rain and summer heat. They refused to ride the buses, riding in carpools or walking miles to and from work. Bus boycotter Gussie Nesbitt explained why she walked:

> "I walked because I wanted everything to be better for us. Before the boycott, we were stuffed in the back of the bus just like cattle. And if we got to a seat, we couldn't sit down in that seat. We had to stand up over that seat. I work hard all day, and I had to stand up all the way home, because I couldn't have

History Makers

Rosa Parks (1913–)

Rosa Parks helped spark the civil rights movement when she refused to surrender her seat on a Montgomery bus to a white passenger. Parks was born in rural Alabama in 1913. Her family soon moved to Montgomery, where she attended a private school for African American girls. After graduating, Parks joined the NAACP and soon became the secretary for the Montgomery branch. She explained her 1955 action on the bus with characteristic simplicity and humility. "It was just something I had to do," she said. Parks inspired many people to participate in the Montgomery Bus Boycott. "She was decent," one man recalled. "And she was committed." Shortly after the boycott ended, Parks moved to Detroit, Michigan, where she has been involved in many other civil rights campaigns.

a seat on the bus. . . . I wanted to be one of them that tried to make it better. I didn't want somebody else to make it better for me."

Another African American woman remarked, "My feets is tired, but my soul is rested."

Some white people reacted strongly to the protest. Many African Americans who participated in the boycott lost their jobs. Some, including Rosa Parks, suffered violent attacks. Extremists bombed King's house, and those of many others. But the boycott continued.

The Montgomery Bus Boycott, which lasted for over a year, ended when the Supreme Court ruled that the Montgomery bus law was unconstitutional. A month later, King stepped onto a desegregated bus. "I believe you are Reverend King," said the white driver, smiling. King nodded. "We are glad to have you with us," the driver told him, and pulled away from the curb. "We got our heads up

Martin Luther King, Jr., poses with his wife, Coretta, and their children.

now," an African American janitor commented in the days that followed, "and we won't ever bow down again—no, sir—except before God."

Section 3 Review

• **Glossary**

IDENTIFY and explain the significance of the following: *Brown* v. *Board of Education,* Thurgood Marshall, Earl Warren, Little Rock Nine, Orville Faubus, Rosa Parks, Montgomery Bus Boycott, Martin Luther King, Jr., Montgomery Improvement Association

• **Time Line**

REVIEWING FOR DETAILS

1. How did Supreme Court rulings affect issues of segregation in the public schools?

2. In what ways did African Americans fight for their civil rights in the 1950s?

3. What impact did Rosa Parks and Martin Luther King, Jr., have on the civil rights movement?

REVIEWING FOR UNDERSTANDING

4. **Writing Mastery:** *Expressing* Imagine that you are a member of the Little Rock Nine. Write a paragraph expressing why you want to attend Central High School.

5. **Critical Thinking:** *Drawing Conclusions* Why do you think African American leaders believed that a boycott of city buses would be an effective means of protest?

CHAPTER 26

The Winds of Change
(1960–1969)

THEMES IN AMERICAN HISTORY

Cultural Diversity
Why might some people fear cultural diversity?

Democratic Values:
How might protests help expand democracy?

Global Relations:
How might a country's foreign policy affect its domestic policy?

• Video Opener

• Skill Builder

*W*hile giving a speech in far-away South Africa, Robert Kennedy defined the 1960s: *"Few will have the greatness to bend history itself; but each of us can work to change a small portion of events,"* he said, *"and in the total of all those acts will be written the history of this generation."* By the end of the decade, his words proved to be true. Social and political movements involving millions of citizens had changed the United States.

image above: *Protesting in 1964*

Section 1

THE TORCH IS PASSED

Multimedia Connections

Explore these related topics and materials on the CD-ROM to enrich your understanding of this section:

 Media Bank

- Bobby Kennedy
- Berlin Wall
- Nixon–Kennedy Debate
- Senator Richard Nixon

 Profiles

- John F. Kennedy

 Readings

- Kennedy's New Frontier

 Gazetteer

- Berlin
- Cuba

Surveying the large crowd that had gathered to hear his inaugural address, President John F. Kennedy spoke these inspiring words: "We observe today a celebration of freedom, symbolizing an end as well as a beginning." A large portion of the public welcomed this fresh start and the couple who would lead it. Many Americans openly adored the young president and his stylish wife, Jacqueline. It was, Jacqueline Kennedy later remembered, "one brief shining moment."

As you read this section you will find out:
- ▶ **Why John F. Kennedy was elected president.**
- ▶ **How President Kennedy dealt with foreign policy crises.**
- ▶ **How successful Kennedy's domestic programs were.**

The Election of 1960

As President Eisenhower's second term drew to a close, Americans worried about many national and international problems, including an economic downturn, civil rights conflicts, and the Soviet Union's perceived scientific superiority. The public paid close attention to the coming presidential race.

Republicans nominate Nixon. In 1960 the Republicans nominated Eisenhower's vice president, Richard M. Nixon, as their presidential candidate. He had been a representative and a senator from California before serving under Eisenhower. While in Congress, Nixon was an outspoken opponent of communism who served on the same committee with Senator Joseph McCarthy. After becoming vice president, Nixon toned down his talk about communist agents. Some critics, however, thought he valued victory more than fair play. Nixon once tried to explain his reputation. "I believe in the battle," he said, "it's always been there, wherever I go." He triumphed over crises, he wrote, by being "cool and calm."

Democrats nominate Kennedy.

The Democrats picked Senator John F. Kennedy of Massachusetts as their presidential candidate. He was young, handsome, intelligent, and came from a wealthy family. He was also a World War II hero and an excellent campaigner. Kennedy worked hard to convince people that he was forward-looking and imaginative.

Kennedy and his Democratic advisers believed that one factor—his Catholic faith—could hold him back from the presidency. In the 1928 election Herbert Hoover had defeated Al Smith, a candidate who was also a Catholic, by huge

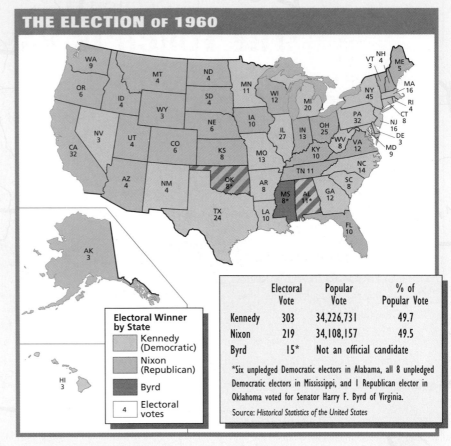

THE ELECTION OF 1960

	Electoral Vote	Popular Vote	% of Popular Vote
Kennedy	303	34,226,731	49.7
Nixon	219	34,108,157	49.5
Byrd	15*	Not an official candidate	

*Six unpledged Democratic electors in Alabama, all 8 unpledged Democratic electors in Mississippi, and 1 Republican elector in Oklahoma voted for Senator Harry F. Byrd of Virginia.

Source: *Historical Statistics of the United States*

Electoral Winner by State
- Kennedy (Democratic)
- Nixon (Republican)
- Byrd
- 4 Electoral votes

Learning from Maps.

The election of 1960 was very close, but John F. Kennedy won the presidency.

▶ **Place.** Which state gave Kennedy the largest number of electoral votes?

• Maps

The Kennedys displayed style and elegance in all their public appearances. Here they are returning from dinner with the president and first lady of France.

margins. Some Democratic leaders felt that the anti-Catholic prejudices of voters in normally Democratic states might be difficult to overcome. Kennedy reassured people who feared that as a Catholic he would not be independent of the influence of the pope by saying that he believed "in an America where the separation of church and state is absolute."

A close election. During the campaign Nixon mainly defended Eisenhower's record and promised to follow the same line. Kennedy, on the other hand, argued that the economy was not growing rapidly enough, and he pledged to "get the country moving again." He called his program to achieve this goal the **New Frontier**.

The election was extremely close. Kennedy won the popular vote by about 118,000, but he took the electoral vote by 303 to Nixon's 219. In his inaugural address he stirred the nation by saying:

> **"The torch has been passed to a new generation of Americans. . . . In the long history of the world, only a few generations have been granted the role of defending freedom in its hour of maximum danger. . . . The energy, the faith, the devotion which we bring to this endeavor [task] will light our country and all who serve it—and the glow from that fire can truly light the world. And so, my fellow Americans—ask not what your country can do for you—ask what you can do for your country."**

The Bay of Pigs

Foreign policy quickly took center stage for President Kennedy. During Eisenhower's second term a communist rebel named Fidel Castro had led a revolution on the island of Cuba, roughly 90 miles south of Florida. Castro took an increasingly unfriendly attitude toward the United States and eventually established a pro-Soviet, communist government.

Many U.S. officials feared the development of a hostile communist base located so close to home. With Eisenhower's approval, the Central Intelligence Agency trained secret forces of Cuban refugees to invade the island and overthrow Castro.

Kennedy learned of the planned invasion after he became president. Initially he hesitated, but eventually he agreed to let the plan go ahead. In April 1961 the force landed on the south coast of Cuba at a place known as the Bay of Pigs. Kennedy decided to cut off American air support for the Cuban exile forces, however. The exiles expected to be joined by other dissatisfied Cubans. Instead, they met only Castro's soldiers, who easily killed or captured all of them.

The failed Bay of Pigs invasion dealt a severe blow to the influence of the United States and to Kennedy in particular. Was the youthful new president a reckless adventurer? Could he stand up to clever communist opponents? People who had voted for Kennedy because they did not trust Nixon felt particularly shocked and betrayed by the mission.

The Berlin Wall

A new challenge soon arose in the divided city of Berlin. Thousands of East Germans had been escaping to the West through Berlin. They left in search of personal freedom and the higher wages they could earn there. Many observers saw their flight as a rejection of the communist system in East Germany.

In August 1961 Nikita Khrushchev, the leader of the Soviet Union, ordered a wall built across the city. The **Berlin Wall**, constructed of concrete and barbed wire, sealed off East Berlin from West Berlin. Kennedy sent 1,500 U.S. troops to West Berlin to protest the "brutal border closing." Over time, tensions in Berlin gradually fell. The Berlin Wall had reduced the flood of dissatisfied East Germans to a trickle. The wall, however, continued to serve as a visible symbol of the Cold War. It reminded the Western world that many people in Eastern European countries were literally prisoners of communism.

In 1963, two years after the wall had

Cuban revolutionary leader Fidel Castro throws out the opening ball for the 1965 Cuban baseball season. Baseball was Cuba's most popular sport, just as it was in the United States.

The building of the Berlin Wall created a great deal of tension between the Western world and the Soviet Union. The wall would remain standing for almost 30 years as a symbol of divided Europe.

divided Berlin, Kennedy visited West Berlin and gave a speech that demonstrated his belief in the importance of liberty:

> **"All free men, wherever they may live, are citizens of Berlin. And therefore, as a free man, I take pride in the words '*Ich bin ein Berliner*' ['I am a Berliner']."**

A huge crowd of Berliners cheered his words.

The Cuban Missile Crisis

Since the United States had let the Berlin Wall stand, the Soviets decided to test Kennedy even further. Once again, Cuba became the focus of dispute.

Alarming discoveries. Despite the failure of the Bay of Pigs invasion, Fidel Castro grew increasingly concerned about the possibility of another American assault. He asked the Soviet Union for weapons to defend his country. Khrushchev agreed to supply them and even offered Castro offensive nuclear missiles, which could reach the United States.

Castro accepted, and Soviet technicians began to build missile bases in Cuba. When Kennedy confronted the Soviets about this activity, they assured him that the weapons were "by no means offensive." Kennedy, however, knew otherwise. In October 1962, American U-2 spy planes had photographed the new installations.

Dangerous days. Now came the most dangerous moment in the Cold War. If the United States attempted to destroy the bases, another world war might result. If the Americans did nothing, they risked destruction.

On October 22 Kennedy went on television to tell the public about the **Cuban missile crisis**. He informed Americans that they were "living daily in the bull's-eye of Soviet missiles." Kennedy demanded that the Soviets remove all offensive weapons from Cuba and close down the missile bases. If the Soviets fired nuclear missiles from Cuba, he warned, the United States would launch an all-out attack. Kennedy also announced the establishment of a U.S. naval blockade around Cuba.

Khrushchev labeled the American blockade "outright banditry." Soviet agents in Cuba armed the missiles there, while American planes readied for an attack. The world held its breath, staring into what Robert Kennedy called "the abyss of nuclear destruction."

On October 24, Soviet ships nearing the American blockade line stopped, then turned back. On October 28, Khrushchev formally agreed to remove the missiles. In exchange, Kennedy promised not to invade Cuba and secretly agreed to remove American missiles from some sites in Italy and Turkey.

Reasons for hope. The resolution of the Cuban missile crisis made the possibility of a nuclear war between the United States and the Soviet Union much less likely. Both sides had stepped back rather than risk destruction. Aware of just how close they had come to a nuclear holocaust, American and Soviet leaders started to work together to prevent another incident like the Cuban missile crisis. They set up a "hot line" telephone connection between Washington and Moscow. In any future conflict American and Soviet leaders could talk to each other directly. They also took a small first step toward nuclear arms control, agreeing to stop testing nuclear weapons above ground, where the explosions released dangerous radioactivity into the atmosphere. With this **Limited Nuclear Test Ban Treaty**, the Cold War had taken a new, more hopeful turn.

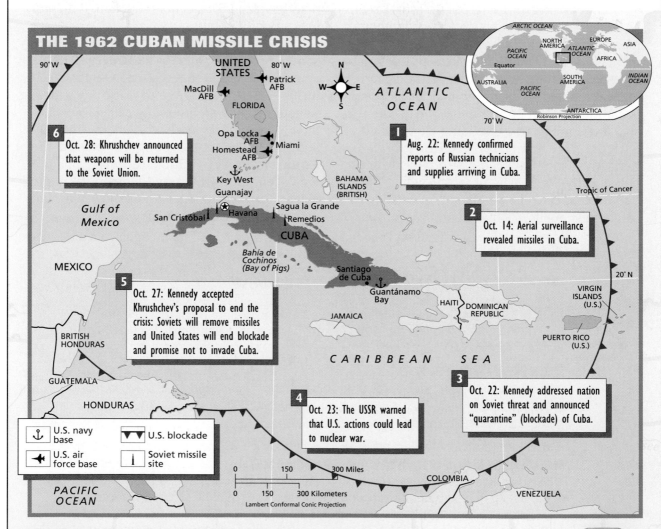

THE 1962 CUBAN MISSILE CRISIS

6 Oct. 28: Khrushchev announced that weapons will be returned to the Soviet Union.

1 Aug. 22: Kennedy confirmed reports of Russian technicians and supplies arriving in Cuba.

2 Oct. 14: Aerial surveillance revealed missiles in Cuba.

5 Oct. 27: Kennedy accepted Khrushchev's proposal to end the crisis: Soviets will remove missiles and United States will end blockade and promise not to invade Cuba.

4 Oct. 23: The USSR warned that U.S. actions could lead to nuclear war.

3 Oct. 22: Kennedy addressed nation on Soviet threat and announced "quarantine" (blockade) of Cuba.

Legend:
- ⚓ U.S. navy base
- ✈ U.S. air force base
- ▼▼ U.S. blockade
- | Soviet missile site

0 150 300 Miles
0 150 300 Kilometers
Lambert Conformal Conic Projection

Learning from Maps. The Cuban missile crisis sent shockwaves throughout the world. Many people feared the crisis would lead to a nuclear war.

▶ **Place.** What U.S. naval base was located on Cuba?

• Maps

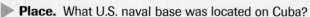

Kennedy's Domestic Programs

Despite his popularity, Kennedy could not get Congress to enact many of his domestic policies. Along with increasing government spending to stimulate the economy, Kennedy's New Frontier proposals called for reducing poverty and providing government-supported medical care. Conservative Republicans and southern Democrats, however, banded together to defeat most of his proposals.

This cartoon shows how President Kennedy successfully stopped the Soviet threat with his stern response to the Cuban missile crisis.

Kennedy's Karate

Kennedy urged Congress to cut taxes, arguing that this would boost the economy by increasing consumer spending and employment. However, many members of Congress objected to lowering taxes while the government remained in debt. The tax cut proposal became stalled in Congress.

In response to increasing demands by African Americans for greater equality, Kennedy also introduced a strong civil rights bill in early 1963. This proposal would have outlawed racial discrimination in all places serving the public, such as hotels, restaurants, and theaters. Like the tax reduction, it did not get through Congress.

The Kennedy administration did have some legislative success, however. After a commission found that working women faced hiring discrimination and low pay rates, Kennedy signed an order that called for equality between men and women in the civil service. In June 1963 Congress passed the **Equal Pay Act**, which required private employers to pay men and women the same wages for the same jobs. The law was not enforced very effectively, however.

Section 1 Review

• Glossary

IDENTIFY and explain the significance of the following: Richard M. Nixon, John F. Kennedy, New Frontier, Fidel Castro, Berlin Wall, Cuban missile crisis, Limited Nuclear Test Ban Treaty, Equal Pay Act

REVIEWING FOR DETAILS

1. How did John F. Kennedy appeal to voters in the 1960 presidential election?
2. What foreign policy crises did the Kennedy administration face, and how were these problems resolved?
3. What domestic political problems did Kennedy face?

REVIEWING FOR UNDERSTANDING

4. **Writing Mastery:** *Using Historical Imagination* Imagine that it is 1960 and you are voting in a presidential election for the first time. Write a short essay explaining why you would or would not vote for John F. Kennedy.
5. **Critical Thinking:** *Drawing Conclusions* Why might the crises in Cuba and Berlin have had an impact on other countries besides the United States and the Soviet Union?

Section 2
THE GREAT SOCIETY

Multimedia Connections

Explore these related topics and materials on the CD–ROM to enrich your understanding of this section:

 Media Bank

- Average Income, 1960–1970
- LBJ as cowhand
- Lyndon Baines Johnson Family

 Profiles

- Lyndon Johnson

 Biographies

- Earl Warren

 Readings

- Johnson's Great Society

 Gazetteer

- Dallas

President Lyndon Johnson once said, "[The] place to build the Great Society is in the classrooms." Through the early years of his presidency, Johnson worked steadily to improve education in America. He finally got Congress to pass a bill that gave more than $1 billion to elementary and high schools. He signed it in the tiny Texas school he had attended. With his former teacher by his side, Johnson moved one step closer to creating what he called a Great Society.

As you read this section you will find out:

▶ **How the assassination of John F. Kennedy affected the nation.**

▶ **In what ways Lyndon Johnson was a successful president.**

▶ **What Johnson's Great Society program included.**

Tragedy in Dallas

As the presidential election year of 1964 approached, President Kennedy prepared for the upcoming race. In November 1963 he and his wife traveled to Texas to smooth out local political matters and to make plans for his re-election campaign.

On November 22 they visited Dallas. The day was warm and sunny, so Kennedy decided not to use the bulletproof plastic bubble top that usually covered his convertible limousine. At about 12:30 P.M., while Kennedy rode through the streets of downtown Dallas with his wife, shots rang out, killing the president. The president slumped into his wife's lap. "My God, they've killed Jack!" Jackie Kennedy screamed. "They've killed my husband!" Texas governor John Connally, traveling in the front of the car, also suffered injuries.

Vice President Lyndon Johnson, two cars behind in the motorcade, was unharmed. He took the presidential oath of office two hours later on *Air Force One* as it carried Kennedy's body back to Washington for burial. "I will do my best," Johnson told the American people. "That is all I can do. I ask for your help, and God's."

Kennedy's death shocked Americans to the core. One columnist later described the feelings of millions:

"**What was killed [in Dallas] was not only the president but . . . youth and the hope of youth, of the beauty and grace and the touch of magic. . . . He never reached his meridian [high point]: we saw him only as a rising sun.**"

The man suspected of shooting the president was Lee Harvey Oswald, a mysterious figure who had once lived in the Soviet Union. Before Oswald could be fully questioned, however, a nightclub owner named Jack Ruby shot and killed him as he was being transferred from one jail to another. This incident, along with many other unanswered questions about the Kennedy assassination, caused many people to believe that Oswald had been murdered

Lyndon Johnson is sworn in as president within hours of Kennedy's assassination. Standing next to him are his wife, Lady Bird Johnson (left), and Jacqueline Kennedy (right).

to keep him from confessing his part in a larger conspiracy to kill the president.

To investigate the assassination, President Johnson appointed the **Warren Commission**, which spent over 10 months analyzing the evidence. The commission, headed by Chief Justice Earl Warren, concluded that Oswald had acted alone. Since the Warren Commission, however, many other theories have been put forward to explain the assassination.

Johnson Becomes President

Few earlier presidents had known more about Washington politics than Lyndon Johnson. He had served for many years as a representative and the Senate leader from Texas, an experience that taught him much about how to get things done in government.

Johnson's first actions. After becoming president, Johnson set out to get Kennedy's legislative programs adopted by Congress. Johnson did this both to honor Kennedy's memory and to establish his own reputation. His long service in Congress gave him an enormous advantage. He bullied, coaxed, and bargained with members of both parties. He brushed aside or smothered hesitating legislators' objections and doubts. Moved by a

Thousands of mourners lined up to watch the funeral of President Kennedy. He was buried at Arlington National Cemetery in Washington, D.C., on November 25, 1963.

combination of awe and fear, lawmakers more often than not voted for what Johnson wanted.

As a result of Johnson's efforts, in 1964 Congress enacted some of Kennedy's proposals. Congress reduced taxes by $11 billion. It also enacted a civil rights law that prohibited racial discrimination in public facilities and made it easier and safer for African Americans in the southern states to register and vote.

Johnson also asked Congress to work toward Kennedy's New Frontier by approving measures aimed at combating poverty. Like Kennedy, Johnson knew that the prosperity of the 1950s had not extended to all Americans. In 1962 about 20 to 25 percent of the population—some 40 million people—lived below the poverty line. Poverty was most alarmingly widespread among children, the elderly, and members of racial and ethnic minority groups.

Reformer Michael Harrington described the scope of the problem in his 1962 book, *The Other America:*

"Tens of millions of Americans are, at this very moment, maimed [injured] in body and spirit, existing at levels beneath those necessary for human decency. If these people are not starving, they are hungry, and sometimes fat with hunger, for that is what cheap foods do. . . . This poverty twists and deforms the spirit. The American poor are pessimistic and defeated, and they are victimized by mental suffering to a degree unknown in Suburbia."

To fight the problem, Johnson announced a **War on Poverty**. He envisioned this fight as "a major long-run effort to weld together a set of measures designed to prevent, remedy, and alleviate [eliminate] poverty in America."

Congress passed the **Economic Opportunity Act** of 1964 at Johnson's

urging. This law was aimed at helping poor people improve their ability to earn money. It established a job training program and it provided loans for those who wanted to start small businesses. Johnson also created an Office of Economic Opportunity (OEO), to develop other programs to reduce poverty. These included Head Start, a program that gave extra help to poor children before they reached school age, and the Job Corps program, which taught essential job skills to school dropouts. In addition, the OEO oversaw the creation of Volunteers in Service to

Presidential Lives

Lyndon Baines Johnson

Lyndon Baines Johnson was born in central Texas in 1908. After a poor but comfortable childhood, he enrolled in Southwest Texas State Teachers College, located near his home. "The enduring lines of my life lead back to this campus," he once said. Johnson first applied his formula for success—hard work, personal contacts, political deals—in his job as secretary to the college president. "You hadn't been in my office a month," his boss later told Johnson, "before I could hardly tell who was president of the school—you or me."

Johnson realized that class prejudices led many to look down on his education—and him. "I do not think that I will ever get credit for anything I do," he once said after he became president, "because I did not go to Harvard." Johnson reacted to this prejudice by driving himself endlessly, striving to be known for his actions rather than his background.

Inspired by the idealism of the Kennedy–Johnson administrations, many volunteers went to work for VISTA, which aided poor Americans, and the Peace Corps, which aided poor people in developing countries. This Peace Corps volunteer teaches children in Kenya.

America (VISTA), which sent workers to impoverished areas of the United States.

The 1964 election. In the months after Kennedy's death, Johnson's popularity soared. Americans admired the smooth but serious way he assumed the presidency. They also supported many of his new social programs. Riding this wave of public support, Johnson easily won the Democratic nomination for president in 1964.

The Republicans chose Senator Barry Goldwater of Arizona to oppose Johnson. Goldwater was not the kind of politician who adjusted his beliefs to appeal to voters. Being very conservative, he spoke critically of such popular institutions as the social security system. He wanted to cut back or eliminate many of the other long-established government programs.

Most voters found Goldwater's ideas too extreme, and Johnson defeated him easily, 486 electoral votes to 52. The Democrats also increased their majority in Congress as well.

Johnson's Great Society

Johnson then forged ahead with what he called the **Great Society** program. He had developed this plan even before winning the 1964 election. He saw his election victory as the green light to push ahead with his programs. Johnson's Great Society was a vast effort to transform American society by eliminating many long-standing social and economic problems. The president saw it as

The War on Poverty sought to help extremely poor families like this one, the Wyatts, who lived near Hazard, Kentucky. Despite the relatively healthy overall economy, there were millions of poor families like the Wyatts throughout the United States.

an improved version of Franklin Roosevelt's New Deal. "This program is much more than a beginning," Johnson once said in a speech. "It is a total commitment . . . to pursue victory over the most ancient of mankind's enemies."

The Great Society called for massive improvements in the economy, the educational system, medical care, housing, and civil rights, among other programs. Johnson tackled all these tasks with typical energy. Congress approved nearly everything he suggested. "Johnson asketh and the Congress giveth," one observer joked.

These new laws included the **Medicare Act** of 1965, which provided health insurance for people over the age of 65. "No longer will older Americans be denied the healing miracle of modern medicine," the president declared. "No longer will illness crush and destroy . . . [their] savings." This law also established **Medicaid**, which provided health insurance for poor people of any age. In addition, Congress passed the Elementary and Secondary

President Johnson was a master at getting legislation passed through Congress. This cartoon shows his "back-slapping" method of getting legislators to do what he wanted.

"Thanks—Thanks A Lot—Thanks Again—Can I Lean Back Now?"

from THE HERBLOCK GALLERY (Simon & Schuster, 1968)

Education Act of 1965, which would provide large amounts of money to improve public schools.

Urged on by Johnson, Congress also worked to improve urban housing. Congress approved a law to develop decent, affordable housing for poor people. Congress also created the Department of Housing and Urban Development (HUD), and Johnson named African American Robert Weaver as its head.

Johnson also encouraged Congress to enact strong civil rights measures. A new law further protected African Americans' ability to register and vote. Johnson's commitment to the Great Society began to slow in the late 1960s, when conflicts overseas demanded more of his time and federal money. Still, the Great Society made a lasting contribution to the United States.

Section 2 Review

• Glossary

IDENTIFY and explain the significance of the following: Lyndon Johnson, Lee Harvey Oswald, Jack Ruby, Warren Commission, War on Poverty, Economic Opportunity Act, Barry Goldwater, Great Society, Medicare Act, Medicaid

REVIEWING FOR DETAILS

1. What impact did Kennedy's assassination have on the country?
2. How was Lyndon Johnson able to achieve his goals as president?
3. What programs were part of the Great Society?

REVIEWING FOR UNDERSTANDING

4. **Writing Mastery:** *Creating* Create a script for a short documentary about how life changed for many poorer Americans during the 1960s.
5. **Critical Thinking:** *Cause and Effect* How do you think Lyndon Johnson's domestic programs affected his popularity?

Section 3
FREEDOM NOW!

Multimedia Connections

Explore these related topics and materials on the CD–ROM to enrich your understanding of this section:

 Biographies

• Martin Luther King, Jr.

 Profiles

• Malcolm X
• Thurgood Marshall

 Readings

• "I Have a Dream"
• Autobiography of Malcolm X

 Media Bank

• James Meredith
• Assassination of King
• Black Panther Party

 Atlas

• School Segregation, 1964

Nervous and excited, African American children waited inside a church on the morning of a 1963 civil rights march in Birmingham, Alabama. They soon opened the church doors, singing as they walked past the segregated facilities that had sparked the protest. Police officers quickly descended on the young demonstrators. They took some 600 teenagers and children—some as young as six years old—to jail. The "children's march" attracted the attention of the nation.

As you read this section you will find out:

▶ **What protest methods African Americans adopted in the 1960s.**

▶ **How African Americans tried to expand their voting rights.**

▶ **What the Black Power movement hoped to achieve.**

The Sit-in Movement

In the late 1950s activists formed new organizations as part of the continuing battle for equal rights. One of these organizations was the **Southern Christian Leadership Conference** (SCLC), founded by Martin Luther King, Jr., and other ministers. Like King, members of SCLC believed nonviolence was the only way to win civil rights for African Americans. They rejected the use of physical force, even to resist attack.

The idea of nonviolence soon spread throughout much of the black community. In February 1960, African American students from North Carolina A&T College in Greensboro decided to challenge racial discrimination by staging a **sit-in**. In this form of nonviolent protest, a group went to a segregated facility and then refused to leave. The students targeted

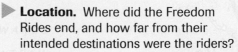

Racist white youths pour food on nonviolent protesters holding a sit-in at a segregated lunch counter in Jackson, Mississippi. Many students who staged sit-ins were called names, beaten, and often arrested.

the local Woolworth's, a drugstore where African Americans could shop but not eat at the "whites only" lunch counter.

On the day of the sit-in, four black students entered the Woolworth's and sat down at the lunch counter. "We do not serve Negroes," a waitress told them. They stayed put and left a few hours later. In less than a week about 1,000 other students—both African American and white—had joined the original protesters.

The sit-in movement quickly spread across the South. Within less than two months of the Greensboro protest, students staged sit-ins in some 54 cities. In most towns, hostile whites tried to end the sit-ins. They screamed, threw rotten food, and launched other attacks against the protesters. The sit-in participants refused to strike back, remaining committed to their nonviolent principles. By 1961 many restaurants and stores, including the Greensboro Woolworth's, had begun to serve African American customers.

Many of the students who had participated in the sit-ins joined a new civil rights organization called the **Student Nonviolent Coordinating Committee** (SNCC). It was founded by Ella Baker, Marion Barry, John Lewis, and other African Americans. Inspired by the earlier successes of

the civil rights movement, SNCC's members continued to challenge segregation.

The Freedom Rides

When restaurants began to serve African American patrons, civil rights activists focused on another area of inequality—bus stations. The Supreme Court had ruled that segregation in bus terminals serving interstate passengers

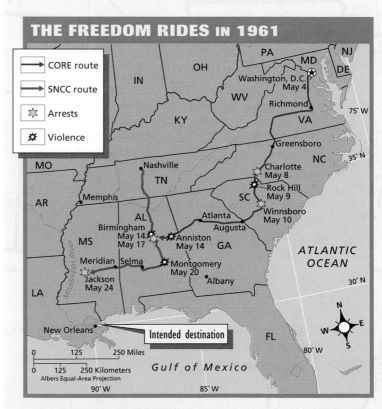

THE FREEDOM RIDES IN 1961

— CORE route
— SNCC route
☆ Arrests
✸ Violence

Washington, D.C. May 4
Richmond
Greensboro
Nashville
Charlotte May 8
Rock Hill May 9
Winnsboro May 10
Memphis
Atlanta
Augusta
Birmingham May 14 May 17
Anniston May 14
Meridian Selma
Montgomery May 20
Albany
Jackson May 24
New Orleans

Intended destination

0   125   250 Miles
0   125   250 Kilometers
Albers Equal-Area Projection

Gulf of Mexico

ATLANTIC OCEAN

Learning from Maps.
The Freedom Rides sparked intense violence, but civil rights workers continued their journey.

▶ **Location.** Where did the Freedom Rides end, and how far from their intended destinations were the riders?

• Maps

Freedom Riders observe the burned-out shell of the bus they had been riding until a white mob in Anniston, Alabama, destroyed it.

As the Freedom Riders left Anniston, Alabama, a mob of angry whites surrounded one of the buses, slashing its tires and setting it on fire. Then they attacked the Freedom Riders as they spilled out the doors. When the second bus arrived in Birmingham, a mob attacked it too. Local police offered no protection. After the governor told the Freedom Riders that he refused to "guarantee the safety of fools" and ordered them "to get out of Alabama as quickly as possible," many riders gave up and went home.

Next, members of SNCC decided to join the Freedom Ride movement. "The future of the movement was going to be cut short," remembered SNCC leader Diane Nash, "if the Freedom Ride had been stopped as a result of violence." Starting in Nashville, Tennessee, they rode once again to Birmingham, Alabama. The city's police chief, Eugene "Bull" Connor, ordered them taken out of the state.

Despite this opposition, the Freedom Riders went on to Montgomery, where another mob attacked them. When they reached Jackson, Mississippi, police officers promptly arrested them. Some of the protesters spent several months in jail. Other civil rights workers attempted to complete the Freedom Rides, however. After months of inaction, the Kennedy administration pushed for tougher desegregation regulations of bus companies.

was illegal. Many southern stations, however, continued to maintain separate waiting rooms, separate water fountains, and separate bathrooms.

Members of the **Congress of Racial Equality** (CORE), a northern civil rights group, set out to challenge segregation in interstate commerce. They developed a simple plan—the **Freedom Rides**. White and black Freedom Riders would travel through the South on buses, intentionally ignoring the signs in segregated stations.

The first Freedom Riders began their journey in May 1961 on two buses. They traveled through Virginia and North Carolina with few problems, but in South Carolina racist whites assaulted an African American man in the group. Although shaken, the Freedom Riders pushed on.

Protesters in Birmingham, Alabama, brace themselves as they are sprayed with fire hoses by police. Images of the Birmingham protesters—many of them young children—being attacked with fire hoses and dogs appeared across the country, increasing national support for the movement.

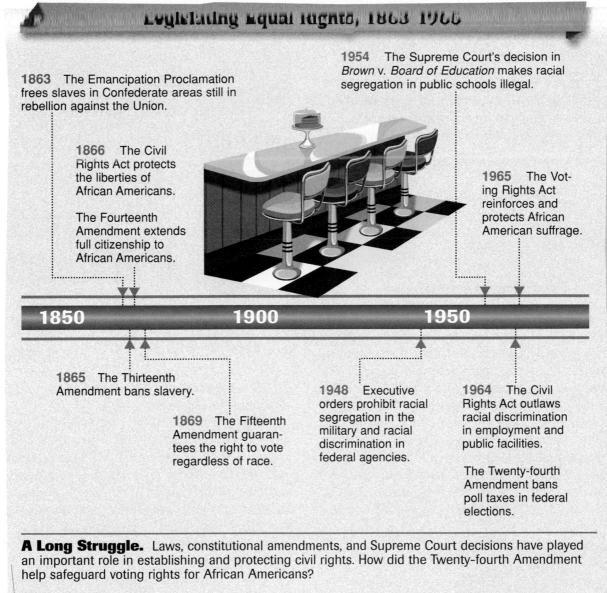

Legislating Equal Rights, 1863–1966

1863 The Emancipation Proclamation frees slaves in Confederate areas still in rebellion against the Union.

1866 The Civil Rights Act protects the liberties of African Americans.

The Fourteenth Amendment extends full citizenship to African Americans.

1954 The Supreme Court's decision in *Brown* v. *Board of Education* makes racial segregation in public schools illegal.

1965 The Voting Rights Act reinforces and protects African American suffrage.

1850   **1900**   **1950**

1865 The Thirteenth Amendment bans slavery.

1869 The Fifteenth Amendment guarantees the right to vote regardless of race.

1948 Executive orders prohibit racial segregation in the military and racial discrimination in federal agencies.

1964 The Civil Rights Act outlaws racial discrimination in employment and public facilities.

The Twenty-fourth Amendment bans poll taxes in federal elections.

A Long Struggle. Laws, constitutional amendments, and Supreme Court decisions have played an important role in establishing and protecting civil rights. How did the Twenty-fourth Amendment help safeguard voting rights for African Americans?

The March on Washington

In April 1963 Martin Luther King, Jr., came to Birmingham to lead a protest against segregation. City police officers drove the protesters from the streets with powerful fire hoses. Many people suffered injuries, and King went to jail. Millions of Americans saw these shocking events on television.

In June 1963 President Kennedy called for a civil rights bill that would end segregation completely. African American leaders were enthusiastic but cautious. Despite his stated belief in racial equality, Kennedy had not been very supportive of the civil rights movement.

Hoping to put pressure on the president, King and others organized a march on Washington to demonstrate peacefully in favor of civil rights. In August 1963 more than 200,000 people gathered near the Capitol. During what is now known as the **March on Washington**, many African American leaders such as labor activist A. Philip Randolph spoke to the crowd. Martin Luther King, Jr., made his famous "I Have a Dream" speech. He looked forward to a time, he told the huge audience, when whites and African Americans could live together in peace and harmony:

> **"I have a dream that one day this nation will rise up and live out the true meaning of its creed: 'We hold these truths to be self-evident, that all men are created equal.'"**

The March on Washington was a huge success. Though Kennedy was soon killed, President Johnson secured the passage of the **Civil Rights Act of 1964**, which outlawed racial discrimination in public facilities and in employment practices.

The Freedom Summer

Even before Congress passed the Civil Rights Act of 1964, black leaders moved to expand and protect voting rights for African Americans. Civil rights workers organized a massive voter registration drive in 1964 known as "**Freedom Summer**." Nearly 1,000 volunteers—many of them white college students—helped with the effort. "It was a tremendous privilege to be allowed to participate in this movement for racial justice," remembered Peter Orris, a white student at Harvard University. Organizers concentrated

Martin Luther King, Jr., waves to the hundreds of thousands of people who gathered for the March on Washington.

• "I Have a Dream"

on Mississippi, a state that had many black residents but few black voters.

Many worried that Freedom Summer would lead to violence. This fear soon proved correct. In June, three civil rights workers—Michael Schwerner and Andrew Goodman, white northerners, and James Chaney, a black southerner—were kidnapped and murdered. Countless other acts of violence and harassment also occurred.

Freedom Summer volunteers bravely continued on, but many local African Americans were too frightened to place themselves on the voting rolls. By the end of the summer, volunteers had registered only 1,600 African American voters.

In January 1965, civil rights workers organized another voter registration drive in the town of Selma, Alabama. Local officials refused to let many African Americans register to vote. As civil rights workers led African Americans to voter registration offices, they faced beatings and arrest. To protest, the organizers called for a 50-mile march from Selma to Montgomery, Alabama. On March 7, some 600 marchers were attacked by the local

A young man marches in Selma, Alabama, for equal voting rights. Many young volunteers risked their lives to register black voters in the South.

• **Black Voter Registration**

police, who sprayed the marchers with tear gas and beat them with clubs. Television cameras captured it all.

The violence in the South so shocked President Johnson that he sent in federal National Guard troops to protect the marchers. He also urged Congress to take action. Five months later, Congress passed the **Voting Rights Act of 1965**. This law prohibited literacy tests for voting, imposed harsh penalties for interference with voting, and provided federal officials to oversee the registration process. Along with the earlier passage of the **Twenty-fourth Amendment**, which banned poll taxes in federal elections, the act finally protected African American voting rights. In just a few years, more than 50 percent of all eligible southern African Americans had successfully registered to vote.

The Black Power Movement

In the early 1960s some African Americans began to question both nonviolence as a tactic and integration as a goal. An African American leader named Malcolm X was one of the first to do so. Born Malcolm Little, as a young man he had served a term in prison for burglary. While in prison, he joined the Nation of Islam, a group whose members call themselves Black Muslims. He also changed his name to Malcolm X, the X standing for his long-lost African ancestor's last name.

When he left prison, Malcolm X rapidly became a leader of the Black Muslims. He insisted that whites were hopelessly racist and said that if necessary African Americans should use violence to protect themselves. In *The Autobiography of Malcolm X,* he wrote:

"I *am* for violence if non-violence means we continue postponing a solution to the American black man's problem. . . . If it must take violence to get the black man his human rights in this country, I'm *for* violence."

In 1964 Malcolm X went on a pilgrimage to Mecca—the most holy Islamic site—in Saudi Arabia. The trip changed his worldview. Before this trip, Malcolm X had believed that whites and African Americans could never live together peacefully, but afterward he saw the possibility of racial harmony within the Islamic religion. In February 1965, months after he broke with the Black Muslims to start his own organization, assassins killed him.

Global Connections
The Irish Civil Rights Movement

The American civil rights movement had a strong impact in Northern Ireland, where religion—not race—formed the basis of discrimination. Many Irish Catholics accused the Protestant government of widespread economic and social oppression. "Like . . . the blacks [in America]," one Catholic woman said, "we were poor, virtually disenfranchised [left out], and very angry."

Irish Catholics borrowed some civil rights strategies from African Americans. They practiced nonviolent resistance, and staged sit-ins. One of the most important demonstrations took place in October 1968, when Catholic students gathered in Derry to protest employment conditions and police harassment. Singing "We Shall Overcome," the African American civil rights anthem, they marched through the streets. The police stopped the marchers outside the city. Some Protestants began to throw rocks at the group, but the marchers remained true to nonviolence. The incident ended peacefully and proved to some Irish Catholics that nonviolent protests could work.

In the mid-1960s increasing numbers of African Americans began to move away from King's ideas and closer to those held by the late Malcolm X. They felt frustrated with the emphasis on nonviolence and integration. "The only way we are going to stop [the whites] from whuppin' us is to take over," Stokley Carmichael of the SNCC declared in 1966. "We've been saying freedom for six years and we ain't got nothin'." He and other leaders called for **Black Power**, a new approach to the civil rights movement.

Those who believed in Black Power wanted African Americans to build their own communities and protect themselves against white racism. To some, this meant group efforts to increase African American political power. To others, this meant complete separation from white society, which they believed was the cause of racism.

The Black Power movement caused great uneasiness among many whites, some of whom reacted against the civil rights movement. The worry and fear of many white Americans was matched by the growing frustration and despair of many African Americans. As news images of race riots filled the country's television screens, the unity between white and black civil rights activists continued to weaken.

• Communities
in Crisis

Malcolm X was a powerful speaker who attracted many people to the Black Power movement. He was highly influenced by the ideas of 1920s black nationalist Marcus Garvey, whom his father had supported.

Section 3 Review

• Glossary

IDENTIFY and explain the significance of the following: Southern Christian Leadership Conference, sit-in, Student Nonviolent Coordinating Committee, Congress of Racial Equality, Freedom Rides, March on Washington, Civil Rights Act of 1964, Freedom Summer, Voting Rights Act of 1965, Twenty-fourth Amendment, Malcolm X, Black Power

REVIEWING FOR DETAILS

1. How did African Americans protest racial inequality during the 1960s?
2. What methods did people use to try to expand voting rights for African Americans?
3. What were the goals and methods of the Black Power movement?

REVIEWING FOR UNDERSTANDING

4. **Writing Mastery:** *Describing* Imagine that you are a Freedom Rider. Describe your experience riding through the South. Include where you were, why you were there, and what your fears and hopes were.
5. **Critical Thinking:** *Making Comparisons* Compare the methods of the Southern Christian Leadership Conference and the Black Power movement. Which approach do you think had the potential to attract more supporters to the civil rights movement? Why do you think so?

Section 4
CHANGING AMERICAN CULTURE

Multimedia Connections
Explore these related topics and materials on the CD–ROM to enrich your understanding of this section:

 Profiles

- Bella Abzug
- Betty Friedan
- Shirley Chisholm

 Readings

- *The Feminine Mystique*

 Atlas

- Urban Unrest
- NASA

 Media Bank

- "The Times They Are A-Changing"
- Music of the 1960s
- Urban Rioting

Sophy Burnham chuckled when she learned what the editors of *Redbook* magazine wanted her to write about— the women's liberation movement! She regarded it as no more than "a lunatic fringe," hardly important enough for a serious article. After four months of researching and learning about the movement, her life took a dramatic turn. "I am now a feminist," she reflected. "I am infused [filled] with pride—in my sisters, in myself, in my womanhood."

As you read this section you will find out:

▶ **What the counterculture revolution was.**

▶ **How the women's liberation movement affected American women.**

▶ **How scientific and technological advances affected American society.**

Protest and Counterculture

During the 1960s young people nurtured earlier seeds of rebellion, like rock 'n' roll music and beat literature, into a full-fledged "**youth revolt**" against American society. Most who took part in this revolution were upper-middle class white youths. Despite their relatively small numbers, however, they had a significant impact on American culture.

Many of these young adults had been involved in or affected by the civil rights movement, which challenged them to question society. Those involved in the youth revolt found a wide range of flaws in American society, such as consumerism and conformity. They openly questioned their parents' values and lifestyles, leading some older Americans to complain about the appearance of a wide "generation gap."

Ott Schatz/FPG International Corp.

During the 1960s many young Americans participated in protests to challenge society, much to the shock of many older Americans.

Student protests. The student protest movement, which drew its inspiration from civil rights demonstrations in the South, spread to many large universities in the 1960s. In 1964, officials at the University of California at Berkeley decided to prevent student organizations from meeting at desirable spots around campus. This denied the groups the space they needed to make speeches and attract new members. In protest, more than 70 percent of the students went on strike. They staged sit-ins and picketed buildings. In the years that followed the Berkeley outburst, student protests spread to other schools as well.

The counterculture. Some leaders of the youth revolt sought to create an entirely new culture—a **counterculture**. Many young people hoped this alternative culture would stand in stark contrast to the world of previous generations. Members of the counterculture placed great emphasis on community, peace, and individual freedom.

Members of the counterculture, sometimes called **hippies**, behaved in ways that shocked and frightened many mainstream Americans. Hippies often used drugs such as marijuana and lysergic acid diethylamide (LSD). Some also engaged in public nudity. While many hippies argued that these practices led to a state of "higher consciousness," many individuals in the counterculture wasted opportunities and suffered from drug addiction.

Music played an important role in the counterculture. Popular musicians drew their inspiration from rock 'n' roll but developed it with new musical styles and messages. New uses of the electric guitar gave rock music an entirely different sound. Guitarist Jimi Hendrix used the instrument to give "The Star-Spangled Banner" a hard, controversial feel. Folk singers such as Joan Baez and Bob Dylan also used their music to comment on American life, filling their lyrics with strong social criticism.

The counterculture reached its musical peak in August 1969, when some 300,000 young people flocked to **Woodstock**, a concert located in upstate New York. It lasted for four days. Despite rain and a shortage of drinking water and basic facilities, the crowd was peaceful and happy.

Many young musicians, like this group, used songs to express the ideals of the 1960s.

Rocco Galatioto/FPG International Corp.

The Women's Liberation Movement

African Americans were not the only group to seek their civil rights during the 1960s. Many women tried to fight inequality based on gender by participating in the **women's liberation movement**. Although women from different backgrounds participated in the movement, most of its early leaders were white, upper middle class and well-educated.

Betty Friedan's *The Feminine Mystique,* published in 1963, helped spark the women's liberation movement. Friedan wrote that American society encouraged women to be completely satisfied with their roles as wives and mothers. Friedan did not claim that caring for a family was a bad thing, but she pointed out that many women felt trapped and depressed by the exclusive focus on being a homemaker. She called this the "problem that has no name," and she described its consequences:

> **"[It] kept us passive and apart, and kept us from seeing our real problems and possibilities. . . . We didn't admit it to each other if we felt there should be more to life than peanut-butter sandwiches with the kids. . . . I and every other woman I knew had been living a lie. . . . If women were really people . . . then all the things that kept them from being full people in our society would have to be changed."**

Many women who read *The Feminine Mystique* were struck by its accurate description of their lives and feelings. They experienced what some called consciousness-raising, or an awareness that their personal doubts and dissatisfactions were shared and had broad social causes. In 1966 Friedan helped found the **National Organization for Women** (NOW). The group wanted "to bring women into full participation in the mainstream of American society now."

Although the 1964 Civil Rights Act had banned discrimination on the basis of sex as well as race, widespread inequality still hurt

Billy Barnes/FPG International Corp.

Activists with the women's liberation movement hold a rally to inform others of their beliefs and goals to end gender discrimination.

women in the workplace and in higher education. NOW hoped to correct this by pushing for an end to legal restrictions on women and fighting for equal employment opportunities in all fields. The organization also argued that the government should provide day-care centers and other assistance for working women with small children. Like some earlier women's groups, NOW pressed for a constitutional amendment to guarantee women's equality.

● **Women's Movement**

Young Women Work for Equal Rights

In the late 1960s, younger women, some only teenagers, began to take part in the women's liberation movement. Many of these women had worked for the civil rights movement or been associated with the counterculture. Yet they found that many of the men in these movements did not welcome women's leadership or even the discussion of women's roles. At one civil rights conference, a male organizer insisted that activist Shulamith Firestone leave the microphone, saying, "Move on little girl; we have more important issues to talk about here than women's liberation."

Angered by such attitudes, many young women joined the fight for equality. The new activists used controversial, attention-getting techniques to bring about change. In 1968, for example, a group of women staged a protest outside the Miss America pageant to criticize the contest's emphasis on physical appearance and traditional female roles. They threw curlers, girdles, and copies of the *Ladies' Home Journal* into a "freedom trashcan."

Gloria Steinem was another person who became active in the women's liberation movement during the late 1960s. After attending Smith College in the 1950s, Steinem had begun to write for magazines and newspapers, usually focusing on women's rights. In 1971 she helped establish the National Women's Political Caucus, a group dedicated to increasing the political participation of women. She also started *Ms.* magazine.

One woman explained her feelings before and after joining the women's liberation movement:

"I had carried . . . the weight of guilt and apology for interests and ambitions that should have been a source of pride. When that weight was lifted, I felt almost literally lighter, certainly more energetic, more concentrated."

Millions of other women shared her experience.

Science and Technology

The 1960s also saw many scientific and technological advances. These stimulated the American economy and had significant social consequences.

The space race continues.   The Soviet Union's early leadership in the space race had shocked and alarmed many Americans. After the Soviets launched *Sputnik,* a small satellite, the United States poured money into aerospace research and development. In the first year of his presidency, Kennedy gave the nation an ambitious

Astronaut Edwin E. "Buzz" Aldrin poses beside the American flag placed on the surface of the moon. The U.S. space program had achieved President Kennedy's goal of putting a person on the moon before the end of the decade.

• Space Race

goal, to put an astronaut on the moon by the end of the 1960s. After Kennedy died, Johnson continued to support this goal.

In 1961 a Soviet spacecraft with a human aboard orbited the earth. Astronaut John Glenn became the first American to accomplish this feat less than a year later.

By the late 1960s the United States had pushed ahead in the space race. In 1969, with a crew of three astronauts—Neil Armstrong, Edwin "Buzz" Aldrin, and Michael Collins—the *Apollo 11* spacecraft settled into orbit around the moon. While Collins remained in lunar orbit, Armstrong and Aldrin landed a small space vehicle on the moon. Millions watching on TV saw them and heard Armstrong say "That's one small step for a man, one giant leap for mankind" as he became the first person to set foot on the moon.

The television effect. Television became a force that not only broadcast public events but also influenced them. This began in the 1950s, when televised hearings exposed Senator Joseph McCarthy as a fraud and a bully, causing public opinion to turn against him. The role of television continued to expand into the 1960s. For example, many observers believed that Kennedy won the 1960 presidential election because he made a better impression on TV than Nixon did.

Television news programs continued to gain even more influence with the public in the 1960s. These shows made increasing use of powerful images, a factor that probably furthered the civil rights movement. Television broadcasts forced viewers to confront the violent reality of segregation and racism on a daily basis.

The computer revolution. The computer revolution also truly began in the 1960s. As early as 1960 there were 5,000 computers in the United States. Compared to computers of today, the first computers were huge, bulky, expensive, and slow. Countless industries depended on computers, however. Laboratories used computers to analyze complex technical information. Banks and many other businesses used them for bookkeeping and billing. The government used computers to prepare statistical reports and check income tax returns. The space program would have been unthinkable before the computer age.

Section 4 Review

• **Glossary**

• **Time Line**

IDENTIFY and explain the significance of the following: youth revolt, counterculture, hippies, Woodstock, women's liberation movement, Betty Friedan, National Organization for Women, Gloria Steinem, Neil Armstrong

REVIEWING FOR DETAILS

1. How did young people form a counterculture in the 1960s?

2. Why did women become involved in the women's liberation movement?

3. What impact did scientific and technological advances have on American society and culture?

REVIEWING FOR UNDERSTANDING

4. **Writing Mastery:** *Creating* Create a flyer to attract people to a 1960s women's liberation rally. The flyer should also give readers an idea of what some of the movement's goals were.

5. **Critical Thinking:** *Drawing Conclusions* How do you think the civil rights movement affected the women's liberation movement?

AMERICA'S GEOGRAPHY

Technology and the Cold War

One of the results of the Cold War for the United States was an increased emphasis on scientific research and technology. Most of the technology that was originally designed to help with military defense was put to use in civilian life.

One of the most important types of military technology to affect Americans was the advanced use of radio waves. Although people had been using radio waves in communication for years, during the Cold War scientists used radio waves to improve radar and satellite systems. Radar sends out radio waves that can track objects too far to see with the human eye. Satellites use very short radio waves, called microwaves, to track objects from far above the earth's surface.

Many items commonly used today rely on these technologies. Meteorologists and airplane pilots track storms using radar and satellites, for example. Even cable television and microwave ovens resulted indirectly from these Cold War technologies.

Defensive Radar Systems, 1959–1964

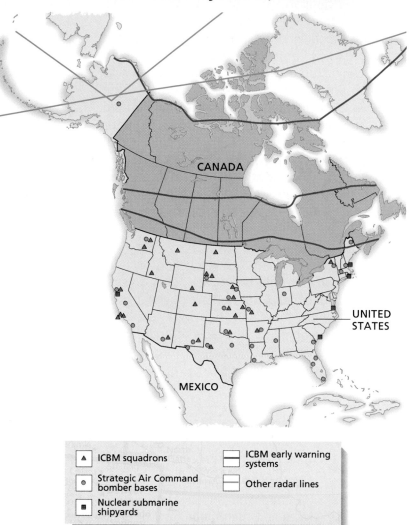

Legend:
- ▲ ICBM squadrons
- ⊙ Strategic Air Command bomber bases
- ■ Nuclear submarine shipyards
- ══ ICBM early warning systems
- ══ Other radar lines

American leaders found that the radar systems used to detect aircraft in World War II were not adequate to keep up with the high-speed jets and missiles developed after the war. An elaborate system of radar stations was established to detect any missiles the Soviets might fire. Since Soviet missiles would travel across the Arctic Circle to reach North America, the United States set up most of these radar stations across Canada. **Movement:** Most intercontinental ballistic missiles (ICBMs) traveled at a rate of 200 miles per minute. If a radar system spotted an ICBM 3,000 miles from its target, how much time would there have been before the missile hit?

Satellite photo of Oklahoma

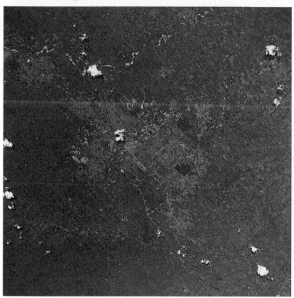

Satellite images reveal amazing details about the earth's geography. Satellite technology was first used to send messages around the globe and to track weapons with the use of microwaves. In 1972 NASA launched what one expert called "the first truly earth observing satellite" to photograph the globe from space using color imagery. The satellite, called *Landsat I,* allowed mapmakers to create maps more accurately than ever before. This image of Oklahoma was used to study land use and the extent of soil erosion in the state.

Distribution of Federal Spending on Space Research in 1960 and 1965

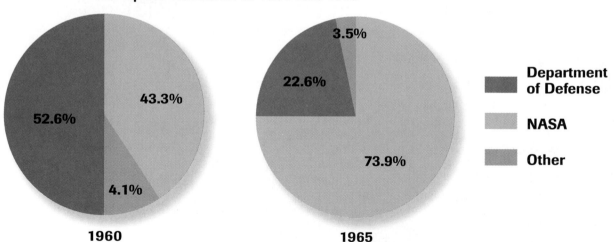

1960
52.6%
43.3%
4.1%

1965
3.5%
22.6%
73.9%

■ **Department of Defense**

□ **NASA**

■ **Other**

In the early years of the Cold War, most space research focused on defense. Thus, the Department of Defense received the majority of federal money for space research. After President Kennedy pledged to send an American to the moon by the end of the 1960s, however, the government began spending more money on space exploration programs run by NASA.

To learn more about technology and the Cold War, go to the interactive map, "Living in the Cold War," on the CD–ROM.

• **Living in the Cold War**

unit 10

$\mathcal{M}$ODERN AMERICA (1954–PRESENT)

These workers enter data into computer programs in 1969. Their computers were among the first with terminals small enough to be used at individual desks.

LINKING Past TO PRESENT
The Electronic Age

Like many other fans of the popular musical group, Steven eagerly anticipates its newest release. He goes to the music store and purchases a small plastic container that holds a shiny, multicolored disc. He brings the compact disc home, puts it into his sound system, and starts to listen.

Steven's parents also enjoyed popular music when they were his age, only they listened to their favorite groups on larger discs that were made of black vinyl. This change in the way most young Americans listen to music is just one of the many ways that the electronic revolution changed everyday life from the 1970s to the 1990s.

Researchers advanced compact disc (CD) technology in the 1970s as a way of storing information with better quality than any previous method. In 1984 the first compact disc musical release, appropriately titled "Born in the U.S.A.," hit record stores. By that time, cassette tapes had already begun to replace vinyl records. CDs, which offered better sound quality, soon began to replace tapes.

Compact disc technology is also used with computers and in home film viewing. Neither of these media were even in homes in the early 1970s. Indeed, the last 30 years has been marked by an explosion in the use of home electronics. Personal computers, cordless telephones, video cassette recorders, and CD players can be found in many homes today.

As you read this unit, you will learn how science and technology became a vital part of almost all aspects of life in the late 1900s. The increasing importance of science and technology

greatly affected the economy as more jobs began to require some technical skill. Companies that manufactured computers and electronic equipment soon became some of the country's largest employers. By 1900 it was virtually impossible for any American to get along without advanced technology.

A young singer records songs that will be put on a compact disc. Such technology has dramatically changed the music industry in recent years.

CHAPTER **27**

War in Southeast Asia

(1954–1975)

THEMES IN AMERICAN HISTORY

Constitutional Heritage:
What might threaten the separation of powers among the branches of the federal government?

Democratic Values:
How might citizens in a democracy protest the government's actions?

Global Relations:
Why might one nation become involved in another's internal affairs?

• Video Opener

• Skill Builder

By the middle of the 1960s, hundreds of thousands of American soldiers found themselves fighting in Southeast Asia. Among them was Philip Caputo, a young marine lieutenant who had come to Vietnam "full of illusions." These were quickly shattered. "Few of us were past 25," he later reflected. "We left Vietnam peculiar creatures, with young shoulders that bore rather old heads."

image above: *The Vietnam Veterans Memorial*

Section 1

WAR IN VIETNAM

Multimedia Connections

Explore these related topics and materials on the CD–ROM to enrich your understanding of this section:

 Gazetteer

- Saigon
- Laos
- Cambodia

 Media Bank

- French at Dien Bien Phu

 Readings

- Vietnam Policy, 1954

 Atlas

- Landscape of Indochina

On September 2, 1945, a crowd of close to half a million Vietnamese anxiously waited for Ho Chi Minh to speak. Just a few days earlier, the emperor Bao Dai had abandoned his throne in favor of Ho's party. Now Ho discussed the nation's future. "We are convinced that the Allied nations which . . . have acknowledged the principle of self-determination and equality of nations," said Ho, "will not refuse to acknowledge the independence of Vietnam."

As you read this section you will find out:

▶ **What happened to French colonial Vietnam after World War II.**

▶ **What caused conflicts between North and South Vietnam in the late 1950s.**

▶ **How the United States supported South Vietnam's government.**

French Colonial Vietnam

Vietnam is a small country about the size of New Mexico. Since the late 1800s, Vietnam and the neighboring countries of Laos and Cambodia made up French Indochina, part of France's colonial empire. A nationalist movement to free Vietnam from French rule arose in the early 1900s.

One of this movement's leaders was Nguyen That Thanh (NY-en TAHT TAHN), or, as he is better known, Ho Chi Minh (HOH CHEE MIN), meaning "He who enlightens." Ho spent many years in exile, mostly in Europe. After he became a Communist, he visited the Soviet Union and China. There he continued to work for Vietnam's independence.

During World War II, Japanese forces invaded Vietnam but kept the colonial government in place. In 1941 Ho slipped back into

Ho Chi Minh spent most of his life working for Vietnam's independence and, then later, its reunification. Ho Chi Minh City, formerly named Saigon, now bears his name.

the country, where he then formed the League for the Independence of Vietnam, or the **Vietminh** (vee-ET-MIN), a Vietnamese group dedicated to resisting the Japanese.

At the end of the war, the Vietminh declared Vietnam's independence. They hoped to gain recognition from the Allied Powers. Ho knew Vietnam would need U.S. support because the French would not be willing to give up Indochina. Ho used words from the U.S. Declaration of Independence when he announced Vietnam's independence before a large crowd in Hanoi on September 2, 1945.

War Breaks Out

In 1946 Vietnam became a battleground again. Instead of receiving American aid as they had hoped, the Vietnamese found that the United States was more interested in containing communism than in toppling French colonialism.

As time passed, events in Asia increased many Americans' fears that communism was spreading. In 1949, Communists under Mao Zedong took over China. One year later, the United States entered the Korean War to defend South Korea from communist North Korea. When communist-led revolts broke out

in other parts of Southeast Asia, U.S. leaders became even more determined to pursue a containment policy in the region.

President Eisenhower warned of a "falling domino" effect if communist expansion were allowed to go unchallenged. "You have a row of dominoes set up," he said. "You knock over the first one, and . . . the last one . . . will go over very quickly." According to this **domino theory**, if Communists gained control of Vietnam, then Laos and Cambodia could easily become communist as well, and the rest of Southeast Asia might follow. Because of its Cold War policy, the United States aided France with money and weapons throughout its war in Vietnam. By 1954 America was footing most of the war bill.

Besides being well financed, France's army was better trained and more experienced than its communist opponents. Despite these advantages, however, they were unable

When the Vietnamese rebelled against French colonial rule, many Vietnamese became refugees, fleeing their destroyed homes and saving just a few possessions.

French casualties rose during the battle at Dien Bien Phu. This battle would be the turning point in the war, causing the French to pull out of Vietnam.

A Temporary Truce

In Geneva, Switzerland, representatives of the People's Republic of China, the United States, Great Britain, the Soviet Union, Laos, and Cambodia joined the French and the Vietminh to work out a treaty. All of these parties had different goals for the new Vietnamese nation. The Americans' concern over the Vietminh's

to defeat the determined Vietnamese. The Vietminh successfully used hit-and-run tactics to wear down the French military. They would strike suddenly at the French and then melt back into the countryside.

The French commanders were hoping to fight a conventional battle against the Vietminh, defeat them, and thus convince them to negotiate an end to the war. In 1954 the French finally got their battle. They had set up a well-fortified outpost at Dien Bien Phu (dyen byen FOO), inside Vietminh territory in the hills of northern Vietnam.

The Vietminh built roads and dug tunnels in the hills around the French position and brought in supplies on foot. When the Vietminh were ready, they launched their attack and pounded the French positions with artillery. The French suffered heavy losses but held out in hope of U.S. air support. It never came, and on May 7, 1954, the Vietminh overran the French. No longer believing that they could win the war, the French agreed to a truce. They had never really understood the war, as one French soldier reflected:

"In prison camp we faced the reality of the Vietminh and we saw that for eight years our generals had been struggling against a revolution without knowing what a revolution was."

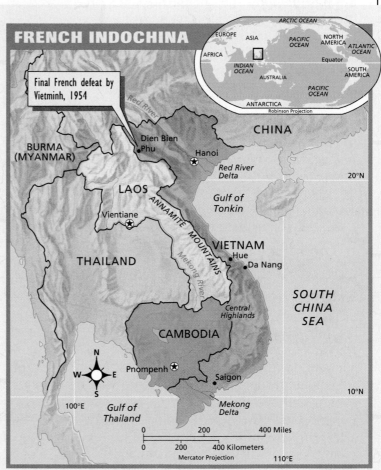

FRENCH INDOCHINA

Final French defeat by Vietminh, 1954

CHINA
BURMA (MYANMAR)
Dien Bien Phu
Hanoi
Red River
Red River Delta
20°N
LAOS
Gulf of Tonkin
Vientiane
ANNAMITE MOUNTAINS
VIETNAM
THAILAND
Hue
Mekong River
Da Nang
SOUTH CHINA SEA
Central Highlands
CAMBODIA
N W E S
Pnompenh
Saigon
10°N
100°E
Gulf of Thailand
Mekong Delta
0   200   400 Miles
0   200   400 Kilometers
Mercator Projection
110°E

ARCTIC OCEAN
EUROPE   ASIA   PACIFIC OCEAN   NORTH AMERICA   ATLANTIC OCEAN
AFRICA
Equator
INDIAN OCEAN   AUSTRALIA   SOUTH AMERICA
PACIFIC OCEAN
ANTARCTICA
Robinson Projection

Learning from Maps.
French Indochina consisted of Laos, Vietnam, and Cambodia.

▶ **Place.** What were the capitals of the countries that made up French Indochina?

• **Maps**

communist connections brought the peace talks to a standstill.

The negotiators in Geneva finally reached a settlement that temporarily partitioned Vietnam along the 17th parallel. The Vietminh were to remain in power in the North, and the Vietnamese connected with the French colonial government were to control the South. These **Geneva Accords** were supposed to be only a temporary solution. In July 1956 North and South Vietnam were to hold general elections and become a single nation. The United States opposed this compromise, fearing that Ho Chi Minh's popularity would guarantee him an election victory. This would make the new unified Vietnam a communist country.

Ngo Dinh Diem posed with his family for this photograph. Many South Vietnamese were angered by the power Diem gave to family members and by their abuse of that power.

South Vietnam

Many U.S. leaders did not intend for the planned elections and reunification to occur. They wanted a pro-Western leader in South Vietnam, so they decided to support Ngo Dinh Diem (en-GOH DIN de-EM), a nationalist and an anticommunist. Having spent some time in the United States in the early 1950s, Diem had political supporters in Washington, D.C., who backed his government.

Diem's government was plagued by corruption, however. Even his election in 1955 to the presidency of the Republic of South Vietnam was rigged. Diem soon became unpopular throughout the country. With his urban, Catholic background, he had little in common with the rural, Buddhist majority. In addition, he appointed members of his family to key positions in the government and did not allow political opposition to his policies. His secret police force, headed by his brother, Ngo Dinh Nhu, harassed, tortured, and imprisoned those who challenged the government.

When the time came for the scheduled election and reunification of North and South Vietnam in 1956, Diem, with the support of the United States, refused to allow it to take place. Instead, he tightened his grip on the South.

The Rise of the Vietcong

Resistance to Diem's policies continued. In 1960 the **National Liberation Front** (NLF) formed to oppose Diem. The NLF included pro-communist South Vietnamese guerrillas, known as the **Vietcong**. But not all members of the NLF were Communists.

President Eisenhower sent a number of American military advisers to South Vietnam to help train its army. The United States also gave military supplies and economic aid to South Vietnam. One visitor to Saigon, South Vietnam's capital, described the many benefits of U.S. support:

"**The stores and market places are filled with consumer goods; the streets are filled with new motor scooters and expensive automobiles; and in the upper-income residential areas new and pretentious [overly fancy] housing is being built.**"

Kennedy and Vietnam

One of Diem's strongest supporters in the United States was Senator John F. Kennedy. In 1956 Kennedy had said that Vietnam:

"is our offspring and if it falls victim to any of the perils [dangers] that threaten its existence—Communism, political anarchy, poverty, and the rest—then the United States, with some justification, will be held responsible; and our prestige in Asia will sink to a new low."

There were about 700 U.S. military advisers in South Vietnam when Kennedy became president in 1961. He continued to back Diem, and he increased the American presence in the country. By 1963 there were more than 16,000 American military personnel in South Vietnam, some of whom were actively participating in the fighting.

Despite increased American aid, Diem was unable to defeat the rebels. The Vietcong used guerrilla tactics similar to those employed by the Vietminh against the French. The longer the conflict continued, the more oppressive Diem's government became.

Many Buddhists in South Vietnam opposed Diem. They became a target for violence by government security forces. On June 11, 1963, to protest Diem's actions, a Buddhist monk named Quang Duc sat down in the middle of a busy Saigon street and set himself on fire.

Americans were shocked by this and other Buddhist protests against Diem. Many Americans pressured Kennedy to take action. He told Diem that he would have to change his tactics or risk losing the support of the United States. When the situation remained unchanged, South Vietnamese army officers, with the active encouragement of the Kennedy administration, overthrew Diem and murdered both him and his brother. What action President Kennedy might have taken in response will never be known because he was assassinated just three weeks after Diem.

Section 1 Review

• Glossary

IDENTIFY and explain the significance of the following: Ho Chi Minh, Vietminh, domino theory, Geneva Accords, Ngo Dinh Diem, National Liberation Front, Vietcong

LOCATE and explain the importance of the following: Vietnam, South Vietnam, North Vietnam (See map on page 621.)

• Gazetteer

REVIEWING FOR DETAILS

1. What happened in French colonial Vietnam after World War II?

2. Why did conflict erupt between the governments of North and South Vietnam in the late 1950s?

3. How and why did Presidents Eisenhower and Kennedy support Diem's government?

REVIEWING FOR UNDERSTANDING

4. **Writing Mastery:** *Describing* In a short essay, describe the role Ho Chi Minh played in Vietnam and the goal he had for the country.

5. **Critical Thinking:** *Cause and Effect* How do you think the events of the Cold War affected the U.S. decision to support a South Vietnamese government? What might have happened if the United States had not supported the South Vietnamese government?

Section 2
THE WAR ESCALATES

Multimedia Connections

Explore these related topics and materials on the CD–ROM to enrich your understanding of this section:

 Readings

- Reporting the War
- Soldiers' Diaries

 Media Bank

- Helicopter Transport
- U.S. Fire Support Base
- Vietcong Trap
- Ho Chi Minh Trail
- Nurse with Vietnamese Child
- LBJ in Vietnam
- U.S. Troops in Rural Vietnam

 Profiles

- Benjamin Spock

On August 2, 1964, U.S. destroyers were patrolling the Gulf of Tonkin when one of the destroyers, the *Maddox,* and three small North Vietnamese boats exchanged fire. Two nights later, the *Maddox* and the *Turner Joy,* again under apparent attack, fired countless shots. James B. Stockdale witnessed the action. He saw "no boats, no boat wakes, no ricochets off boats, no boat impacts, no torpedo wakes—nothing but the black sea and American firepower."

As you read this section you will find out:

▶ **What event led to increased American involvement in Vietnam.**

▶ **What combat conditions U.S. troops faced in Vietnam.**

▶ **How the Vietnam War divided public opinion in the United States.**

Johnson and the War

The tensions in South Vietnam did not diminish after the assassinations of Diem and Kennedy. The new South Vietnamese government soon proved no better at defeating the Vietcong than Diem's had. President Johnson continued to follow his predecessor's course.

The Gulf of Tonkin incident. In early August 1964 Johnson announced that North Vietnamese gunboats in the Gulf of Tonkin had attacked American destroyers. He quickly persuaded Congress to authorize him to "take all necessary measures to repel any armed attack against the forces of the United States" in Vietnam. This authorization became known as the **Tonkin Gulf Resolution**.

Johnson insisted that he "would never send American boys to do the fighting that

Asian boys should do themselves." After winning the 1964 election, however, he stepped up American military activity in Vietnam. He hoped that the presence of more U.S. troops would strengthen the position of South Vietnam.

Johnson made the same basic argument that Truman had in the Korean War and Kennedy had in the Cuban missile crisis. He believed that the way to stop communist aggression was by determination and force:

> **"We could tuck our tails between our legs and run for cover. That would just whet [increase] the enemy's appetite for greater aggression and more territory, and solve nothing."**

Policymakers assumed that the fighting in South Vietnam was between local Vietnamese patriots and "outside" Communists. In reality, the struggle in South Vietnam was a civil war between supporters of the government and the Vietcong, who were mostly South Vietnamese. Later in the war, "outside" Communists from the Soviet Union gradually began supplying the Vietcong with weapons and advice. North Vietnam also became deeply involved. Its objective was the unification of the two Vietnams.

The Americanization of the war.
In February 1965 Johnson made an important decision. The Vietcong had gained control of numerous South Vietnamese villages. Johnson now saw the war as a test of his will. "I will not be the President who saw Southeast Asia go the way China went," he said, referring to the communist takeover in China in 1949. He ordered the U.S. Air Force to begin bombing targets in North Vietnam.

President Johnson and his advisers hoped the bombing campaign—

Operation Rolling Thunder—would hurt the morale of the North Vietnamese and destroy the **Ho Chi Minh Trail**, a jungle route that

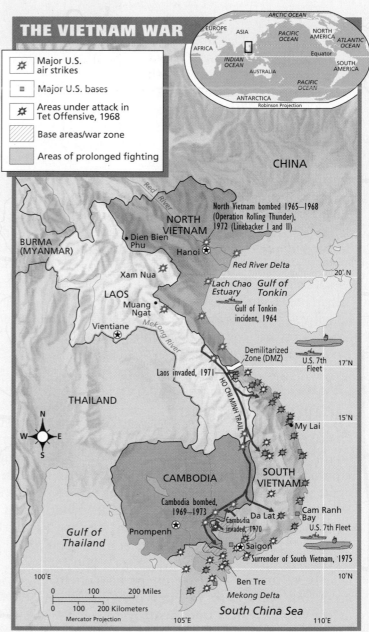

THE VIETNAM WAR

Legend:
- Major U.S. air strikes
- Major U.S. bases
- Areas under attack in Tet Offensive, 1968
- Base areas/war zone
- Areas of prolonged fighting

CHINA

North Vietnam bombed 1965–1968 (Operation Rolling Thunder), 1972 (Linebacker I and II)

BURMA (MYANMAR)

NORTH VIETNAM
Dien Bien Phu
Hanoi
Xam Nua
Red River Delta
Red River
20°N

LAOS
Muang Ngat
Vientiane
Mekong River

Lach Chao Estuary Gulf of Tonkin
Gulf of Tonkin incident, 1964

Demilitarized Zone (DMZ)
U.S. 7th Fleet
17°N

Laos invaded, 1971

THAILAND

HO CHI MINH TRAIL

My Lai
15°N

CAMBODIA

SOUTH VIETNAM

Cambodia bombed, 1969–1973
Pnompenh
Cambodia invaded, 1970
Da Lat
Cam Ranh Bay
U.S. 7th Fleet

Gulf of Thailand

Saigon
Surrender of South Vietnam, 1975

Ben Tre
Mekong Delta
South China Sea

100°E
0   100   200 Miles
0   100   200 Kilometers
Mercator Projection
105°E
110°E
10°N

ARCTIC OCEAN
EUROPE   ASIA
AFRICA   PACIFIC OCEAN   NORTH AMERICA   ATLANTIC OCEAN
INDIAN OCEAN   Equator
AUSTRALIA   SOUTH AMERICA
PACIFIC OCEAN
ANTARCTICA
Robinson Projection

Learning from Maps.
The Tet Offensive surprised American and South Vietnamese forces.

▶ **Movement.** When the Vietnam War eventually expanded beyond Vietnam's borders, which countries did the United States bomb?

• Maps

In July 1965 an Associated Press photographer took this picture of the U.S. soldiers of the 1st Infantry division landing at Cam Rahn Bay in South Vietnam.

started in North Vietnam, snaking through the mountains to South Vietnam. A large portion of the trail ran through Cambodia and Laos. North Vietnam used this trail to bring weapons and supplies to the Vietcong.

The United States dropped more than 600,000 tons of bombs during Operation Rolling Thunder, including firebombs containing the flammable substance napalm and cluster bombs that exploded into thousands of pieces of metal. In addition, planes sprayed chemical defoliants, such as Agent Orange, over the jungles in the South to destroy the vegetation and expose enemy supply lines and bases. These weapons took a terrible toll in human life, killing and injuring many thousands of Vietnamese.

More American Troops in Vietnam

In March 1965 Johnson sent two battalions of marines to Vietnam. Their job was to protect the air bases from which the bombers were operating. Soon more troops had to be sent to the South. When the bombing failed to end the Vietcong's resistance in the South, Johnson decided to send in large numbers of American ground troops.

These troops were given permission to seek out and attack Vietcong units in what were called **search and destroy missions**. Soon, even more troops were shipped to Vietnam. By the end of 1965 there were more than 184,000 U.S. soldiers in the country.

This steady **escalation**, or increase, in U.S. military involvement in Vietnam went on for three years. By the end of 1967 nearly half a million Americans—many of whom were draftees—were fighting in Vietnam.

With thousands of Americans serving in Vietnam, it was now an American war. In addition to the soldiers, thousands of women served as nurses in the army or in volunteer organizations. Despite this U.S. involvement, Congress was never officially asked to declare war. President Johnson was using the Tonkin Gulf Resolution to justify the escalation.

When each escalation of the war proved ineffective at controlling the situation, policymakers hoped just one more increase would do the job. The enormous difference in power and wealth between the United States and Vietnam convinced the president and his advisers that they could win the war whenever they chose. How, they asked, could a nation like North Vietnam successfully resist the more powerful United States?

Political cartoonists often pointed out the contradictions between what politicians said about the Vietnam War and how the war was really progressing.

The Ground War

In large part, the Vietcong were successful because they fought a guerrilla war. The Vietcong wore no uniforms and fought mainly at night using ambush tactics. Americans had difficulty identifying the Vietcong because by day they blended with the rest of the population.

Much of the war was fought in dense jungles and rugged mountains where tanks, and even jeeps, were almost useless. Small squads of American soldiers slowly worked their way through forests and swamps so thick they could see only a few feet in any direction. The enemy could be hiding anywhere. Vietcong snipers would pick off one or two men and then slip away. One soldier recalled an attack in the jungle:

> **"Men all around me were screaming. The fire [shooting] was now a continuous roar. We were even being fired at by our own guys. No one knew where the fire was coming from, and so the men were shooting everywhere. Some were in shock and were blazing away at everything they saw or imagined they saw."**

Mines and booby traps made movement through the countryside—largely controlled by the Vietcong—terrifying.

The fighting in Vietnam was savage. Both sides in the conflict were capable of extreme cruelty. Soldiers often killed civilians suspected only of being enemy sympathizers. Prisoners were sometimes killed or tortured. Many U.S. soldiers who became prisoners of war were treated terribly. Thousands of Vietnamese civilians died in U.S air raids. Through a policy the army called **pacification**, villages were burned to the ground to root out possible Vietcong sympathizers.

Conflict at Home

As American forces struggled in Vietnam, large numbers of citizens at home turned against the war. Television news reports

U.S. soldiers found that moving through the Vietnamese countryside was often difficult and dangerous.

brought the images of the war right into people's homes. Unlike in previous wars, the press was largely free of restrictions and allowed to interview civilians and soldiers—even to follow the latter into battle. As time passed without victory and the body count continued to rise, press reports were increasingly discouraging about the real possibility of winning the war.

Many Americans came to believe that the Vietnam War was a terrible mistake. Some claimed that keeping the weak and unpopular government of South Vietnam in power was criminal, and surely not worth the cost in American lives and money. Others argued that it was wrong for Americans to be killing people in a poor country that was literally on the other side of the world.

Americans who wanted to stop the war were called **doves**, after the traditional bird of peace. People were doves for a wide variety of

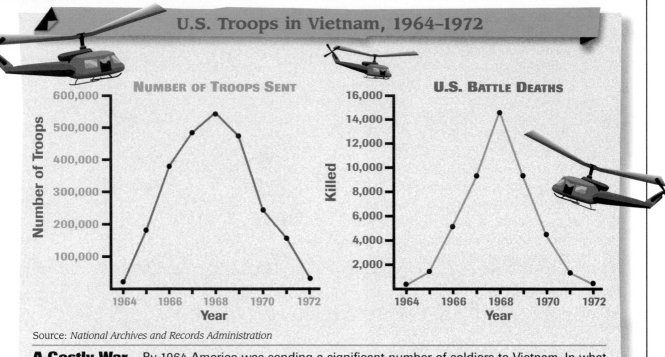

U.S. Troops in Vietnam, 1964–1972

NUMBER OF TROOPS SENT

U.S. BATTLE DEATHS

Source: *National Archives and Records Administration*

A Costly War. By 1964 America was sending a significant number of soldiers to Vietnam. In what year did U.S. involvement in Vietnam peak, and how is that reflected in the number of troops killed?

reasons. Some, like Martin Luther King, Jr., were pacifists. Others did not believe in the domino theory and argued that Vietnam was not vital to American interests. Still others claimed that because many Vietnamese supported the Vietcong, the United States was propping up a government against the will of the majority of Vietnamese.

Those who insisted that the war must be fought until it was won were known as **hawks**. Many hawks were convinced that the United States needed to put a greater commitment into winning the war, including more troops and increased bombing. For many years the hawks shaped U.S. policy. National pride and hatred of communism led many Americans to believe that it would be cowardly and shameful to pull out of South Vietnam before winning the war.

Division in Government

Both sides grew more vocal as the fighting intensified. Early in 1965 Johnson expressed the determination of the U.S. government to seek victory in Vietnam:

"**Americans and Asians are dying for a world where each people may choose its own path to change. Why must we take this painful road?. . . Only in such a world will our own freedom be secure. . . . Why are we in South Vietnam?. . . Over many years have we made a national pledge to help South Vietnam defend its independence. And I intend to keep that promise. . . .**"

Equally determined opponents spoke out against U.S. involvement in the war. Senator J. William Fulbright of Arkansas, chairman of the Senate Foreign Relations Committee, said:

"**One wonders how much the American commitment to Vietnamese freedom is also a commitment to American pride. . . . We may be thinking about our reputation as a great power, fearing that a compromise settlement would shame us before the world, marking us as a second-rate** people with failing courage and determination. Such fears are senseless. They are unworthy of the richest, most powerful, most productive, and best educated people in the world."

Antiwar Protests

While many Americans joined the antiwar movement, one of the best-known groups was the **Students for a Democratic Society** (SDS), formed by college students. On campuses across the country, the SDS held protest meetings, often drawing large crowds.

The SDS opposed more than just the Vietnam War. It also protested against the draft; against companies such as Dow Chemical, the maker of napalm; against the CIA; and against military recruitment on campuses. As early as April 17, 1965, the SDS organized an antiwar protest in Washington, D.C., that drew more than 20,000 people.

The antiwar organizations used a variety of tactics in their protests. At the University of California, students burned draft cards. At Columbia University, they occupied many

campus buildings. Some of the more radical protesters burned American flags, and others even left the country or went to prison rather than respond to their draft notices. Such actions angered many Americans, even some who did not support the war. They thought these activities were unpatriotic.

In the spring of 1965, the SDS staged a series of anti-war events at the White House, the Washington Memorial, and the Capitol.

Section 2 Review

IDENTIFY and explain the significance of the following: Tonkin Gulf Resolution, Operation Rolling Thunder, Ho Chi Minh Trail, search and destroy missions, escalation, pacification, doves, hawks, J. William Fulbright, Students for a Democratic Society

• Glossary

REVIEWING FOR DETAILS

1. How was the Gulf of Tonkin incident significant to the U.S. role in Vietnam?
2. How did the war in Vietnam divide the people of the United States?

REVIEWING FOR UNDERSTANDING

3. **Geographic Literacy** How did Vietnam's geography make it difficult for American soldiers to fight effectively?
4. **Writing Mastery:** *Describing* Imagine that you are a U.S. official in Vietnam. Write a letter to President Johnson describing the pros and cons of U.S. involvement in Vietnam.
5. **Critical Thinking:** *Cause and Effect* How might the media have influenced public opinion during the Vietnam War? In what ways does the media affect public opinion today?

Section 3
1968: A TURNING POINT

Multimedia Connections

Explore these related topics and materials on the CD-ROM to enrich your understanding of this section:

 Atlas

• Election of 1968

 Media Bank

• Protest Folk Music
• 1968 Campaign

 Readings

• Protesting the War

 Profiles

• Richard Nixon
• George Wallace
• Eugene McCarthy

Mark Rudd was the leader of the SDS at Columbia University. He felt that America was headed in the wrong direction and that young people needed to redirect the nation's goals. Rudd and a few other radical students took over the office of Grayson Kirk, the university president. Rudd explained the students' feelings in a letter to Kirk: "You might want to know what is wrong with this society. . . . We can point to your using us as cannon fodder to fight your war."

As you read this section you will find out:

▶ **What the turning point was for U.S. involvement in Vietnam.**

▶ **What events influenced the presidential election of 1968.**

▶ **What happened at the 1968 Democratic National Convention.**

The Tet Offensive

Early in January 1968 the U.S. commander in Vietnam, General William C. Westmoreland, announced that victory was near. The general summed up the previous year, 1967:

> **"The year ended with the enemy increasingly resorting to desperation tactics; . . . and he has experienced only failure in these events."**

Westmoreland believed that the Vietcong soon would be crushed.

On January 30, 1968—the beginning of the Vietnamese New Year's celebration, known as Tet—everyone expected the usual holiday cease-fire. Instead, while most of the South Vietnamese lay sleeping, over 70,000 NLF and North Vietnamese soldiers launched sudden attacks on cities across South Vietnam. They

The Tet Offensive struck at the heart of U.S.-occupied areas of South Vietnam. Even the capital city, Saigon, felt the devastation of the attack.

even gained control of parts of Saigon and threatened the U.S. Embassy there. They held a number of important cities for weeks.

The U.S. and South Vietnamese troops quickly fought back, as one historian put it, "with the fury of a blinded giant." Eventually, they regained control of the cities. In doing so, however, they destroyed even more of Vietnam. In a remark that soon became famous, an American officer justified the smashing of the town of Ben Tre: "It became necessary to destroy the town in order to save it."

The U.S. counterattack crushed the gains made by the **Tet Offensive**. Vietcong and North Vietnamese losses were enormous—more than 40,000 soldiers lost their lives. Westmoreland claimed a victory because combined American and South Vietnamese deaths were estimated at 6,000.

In political terms, however, the Tet Offensive was a defeat for the U.S. war hawks. The American public was deeply shocked at the strength shown by the Communists after so many years of war. Even Saigon was not safe from attack. CBS News anchor Walter Cronkite asked the question that many Americans were now wondering: "What . . . is going on? I thought we were winning the war!"

President Johnson knew the tide of opinion had turned against the war. "If I've lost Cronkite," he said, "I've lost middle America." Even the *Wall Street*

Journal noted: "The American people should be getting ready to accept . . . the prospect that the whole Vietnam effort may be doomed." When Westmoreland asked for 200,000 more troops, Johnson turned him down.

On the Road to the Election of 1968

Johnson continued to try to rally the nation: "Make no mistake about it . . . we are going to

Through Others' Eyes
A Difficult Choice

Many Vietnamese were caught in a war they did not support. Few, however, could remain neutral. Writing to a young American friend, one Buddhist Vietnamese student described the difficulty of choosing the best path for the Vietnamese people:

> "Maybe this is the last letter I send you—because I must make the choice, the choice of my life. I am pushing to the wall. To choose this side or the other side—and not the middle way!
>
> I can no more use my mouth, my voice, my heart, my hands for useful things. All the people here have to choose to manipulate guns—and they have to point straightly in face of each other. One side the Vietnamese city people and Americans, another side Vietnamese rural people and Communists. . . .
>
> What have I to choose? . . .
>
> I can't side even with Americans or Communists. But you have no choice. . . . No it's a desperate situation."

win," he said. Johnson hoped that in the upcoming presidential election the nation would show support for both him and his policy. Senator Eugene McCarthy of Minnesota, a leading dove, had announced that he would oppose Johnson for the Democratic nomination. Before the Tet Offensive, no one gave him any chance of defeating Johnson.

After Tet, however, the situation changed. McCarthy almost defeated Johnson in the important New Hampshire presidential primary. Then Robert F. Kennedy, brother of the slain president, declared that he too was a candidate. Faced with a difficult political fight that would divide the country still further, on March 31, 1968, Johnson announced that he would not seek re-election. He also acknowledged that his Vietnam policy had failed:

"I am taking the first step to de-escalate the conflict . . . unilaterally [alone] and at once. . . . I have ordered our aircraft . . . to make no attacks on North Vietnam, except in the area . . . where the continuing enemy buildup directly threatens allied forward positions. . . . I call upon President Ho Chi

Robert Kennedy opposed the war in Vietnam. When he announced his win in the California primary at a gathering at the Ambassador Hotel in Los Angeles, his supporters excitedly gathered around him to offer their congratulations.

• **Robert Kennedy**

Minh to respond positively . . . to this new step toward peace."

Johnson gave his support to Vice President Hubert Humphrey. As Johnson became more unpopular, Kennedy seemed likely to win the Democratic nomination. Kennedy had a broad base of support and was particularly popular among many African Americans, Hispanics, the poor, and young people. On June 4 he won the California presidential primary. After giving his victory speech, however, Robert Kennedy was fatally shot. The killer was Sirhan Sirhan, a young Jordanian immigrant who objected to the support the United States was giving to Israel. Kennedy's death, which came just two months after the assassination of Martin Luther King, Jr., shocked Americans.

The Democratic Convention

Robert Kennedy's death allowed Humphrey to move ahead in the race for the nomination. Humphrey had loyally supported Johnson's policy in Vietnam. As a result, when the 1968 Democratic National Convention began in Chicago, more than 10,000 antiwar protesters flocked to that city to demonstrate. Mayor Richard Daley, a Humphrey supporter, packed the city's downtown area with police.

Radicals among the demonstrators yelled insults at the police. The police responded by rushing into the crowd, clubs swinging. One British journalist at the scene reported that "the police went berserk, the kids screamed and were beaten to the ground by cops who had completely lost their cool."

Millions of television viewers had tuned in to watch the convention proceedings. Instead, they saw helmeted policemen hitting the demonstrators with their nightsticks and herding them, dazed and bloodied, into waiting police wagons.

Humphrey went on to win the Democratic nomination easily, although thousands of Democrats blamed him for the police riot in Chicago. Most of these same Democrats resented his support of the war in Vietnam.

"Chicago was a catastrophe," Humphrey realized when the convention had ended.

A Republican Victory

This split in the Democratic Party helped the Republican candidate, Richard M. Nixon, the former vice president under Eisenhower, whom John F. Kennedy had defeated in 1960. Few had expected Nixon to run again for president, particularly after he had unsuccessfully run for governor of California in 1962.

Nixon, however, had worked hard for the Republican Party since his defeat. Hundreds of local Republican officials felt that he deserved a second chance for the presidency. When the 1968 Republican convention met, Nixon had a majority of the delegates in his camp and was nominated easily.

Nixon chose Governor Spiro T. Agnew of Maryland as his running mate. Although he was not well known nationally, Agnew had taken a tough stand against civil rights activists and antiwar demonstrators. His record on these issues made him acceptable to many voters who might otherwise have supported Governor George C. Wallace of Alabama, an outspoken opponent of racial integration who was running for president as an independent.

In the three-way contest for president, Nixon won only about 43 percent of the popular vote, less than 1 percent more than Humphrey. Nixon received 301 electoral votes to Humphrey's 191 and Wallace's 46, and thus became president.

Richard Nixon, the Republican candidate for president, waved to the crowd as his motorcade passed through Chinatown in San Francisco.

Section 3 Review

• Glossary

IDENTIFY and explain the significance of the following: William C. Westmoreland, Tet Offensive, Eugene McCarthy, Robert F. Kennedy, Hubert Humphrey, Richard Daley, Richard M. Nixon

REVIEWING FOR DETAILS

1. How did the Tet Offensive affect the Vietnam War?
2. What events affected the 1968 presidential election?
3. What events took place at the 1968 Democratic National Convention in Chicago?

REVIEWING FOR UNDERSTANDING

4. **Writing Mastery:** *Expressing* The year 1968 was a time of "turning points." Write a short essay explaining the event you feel was the most critical that year.
5. **Critical Thinking:** *Synthesizing Information* How was Vietnam different—both at home and abroad—from previous wars the United States had fought?

Section 4

THE WAR UNDER NIXON

Multimedia Connections

Explore these related topics and materials on the CD–ROM to enrich your understanding of this section:

Profiles

• Henry Kissinger

Biographies

• Dith Pran

Media Bank

• Troops Board Plane for Home
• Released POWs
• Fleeing Vietnam
• Vietnamese Refugees
• Bombing of Cambodia
• Kissinger Negotiating
• Presidential Involvement

Readings

• Negotiating With North Vietnam

Diep Thi Nguyen was one of the many desperate people who had come to the U.S. Embassy in Saigon. She was hoping to get her two young daughters out of the country before it fell to North Vietnam. "Late that afternoon, helicopters come, taking people from the roof," she remembered. "We waited all day trying to get aboard, but we could not. People begged, pushed and begged, and there was no way." It would be another 10 years before the Nguyen family found a way to get to America.

As you read this section you will find out:

▶ **How President Nixon planned to end the Vietnam War.**

▶ **Why Nixon decided to invade Cambodia.**

▶ **How the Vietnam War finally ended.**

Nixon's Vietnam Policy

During the 1968 campaign, Richard Nixon had told voters that he had a "secret plan" to end the Vietnam War. Now he had to find a way to fulfill his promise. The difficulty was how to end American involvement without seeming to have lost the war. Nixon vowed:

> **"I won't make it hard for the North Vietnamese if they genuinely want a settlement, but I will not be the first President of the United States to lose a war."**

Like Kennedy and Johnson before him, Nixon wanted to keep the Communists from conquering South Vietnam. He decided to shift the burden of resisting the Vietcong and North Vietnamese back to the South Vietnamese army. As the South Vietnamese army grew stronger, he argued, American troops could be

*Women and children were sometimes evacu-
ated from suspected Vietcong villages before
bombing runs occurred.*

gradually withdrawn. This was called the **Vietnamization** of the war. Nixon hoped it would bring "peace with honor."

Whether Vietnamization would work was doubtful from the start. Over half a million Americans were serving in Vietnam when Nixon took office. In addition, the U.S. military had dropped more than 600,000 tons of bombs on the small country of Vietnam. Even with all this firepower, the United States had not been able to drive the Communists from South Vietnam or weaken their will to fight. It was unlikely that South Vietnam would be able to win the war on its own.

The initial reduction of U.S. troop strength amounted to only 25,000 soldiers. As time passed, Nixon further reduced the size of the U.S. force in Vietnam. By the spring of 1970 it was below 450,000. Nixon proudly announced that he intended to pull out an additional 150,000 troops within a year.

The Invasion of Cambodia

While Vietnamization was taking place, Nixon secretly expanded the war by ordering the bombing of Cambodia and Laos, as well as the increased bombing of North Vietnam. He did this to try to stop the flow of supplies from the North to the Vietcong and to intimidate the North Vietnamese. Even Congress was kept unaware of this secret bombing of neutral countries.

New opposition to the war. On April 30, 1970, a little over a year after the new bombing campaign had begun, President Nixon announced another expansion of the war. He was sending U.S. troops into Cambodia. The reason for this invasion, Nixon said, was that the North Vietnamese were using Cambodia as a base of operations to launch attacks on South Vietnam.

This announcement set off a new storm of protest in the United States. When Americans learned of it, many were outraged. Antiwar protests had slowed somewhat after Nixon began reducing the number of American soldiers in Vietnam, but new demonstrations now suddenly erupted. Americans wondered why, if Vietnamization was succeeding, was it necessary to send U.S. troops into Cambodia. Even many Vietnam veterans began to sympathize with the antiwar movement.

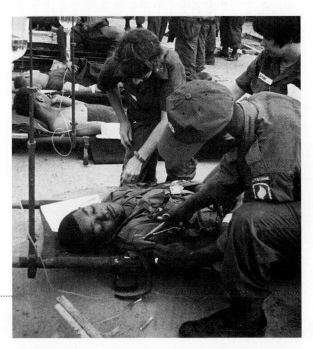

Most of the some 10,000 U.S. servicewomen in Vietnam were nurses. Thousands of other women there volunteered for the Red Cross.

Photographs of the tragic shootings that ended the clash between the National Guard troops and the student protesters at Kent State rocked the nation. Even today, they remain some of the best-known images of the Vietnam era.

The Kent State tragedy.   College students in particular reacted angrily to news of the Cambodian invasion. Throughout the spring of 1970 there were demonstrations on campuses all over the country. Violence broke out at Kent State University in Ohio. Demonstrations there led the governor of Ohio to send National Guard troops to the campus to preserve order.

After several days, a nervous guard unit opened fire on protesting students. Four students were killed and 14 more were wounded. Several days later two students were shot down by Mississippi State Police at Jackson State University, a historically black school. The killings at Kent State and Jackson State caused still more student protests. Many colleges were forced to close down for the remainder of the spring term. Most Americans were shaken by the spectacle of students under fire on their own campuses.

Congressional action.   Many members of Congress were shocked at the Cambodian invasion as well. They had genuinely thought the United States was reducing, not expanding, its role in the war. To challenge Nixon's right to wage the war, Congress repealed the Tonkin Gulf Resolution and threatened to end funding for the war.

The War Drags On

The Cambodian invasion did not result in much heavy ground fighting, and U.S. ground troops in Cambodia were soon pulled back. Nixon also continued withdrawing troops from South Vietnam. By the end of 1972 fewer than 25,000 U.S. troops were still fighting in Vietnam, and the number continued to decline steadily. Nixon depended increasingly on air attacks on North Vietnam to weaken the Communists' will to fight.

While he was withdrawing American soldiers from Vietnam, Nixon was also trying to end the war through diplomacy. His chief foreign policy adviser, Henry Kissinger, had entered into secret discussions with North Vietnamese leaders in Paris.

Nixon also began to back away from a containment policy, hoping instead to establish a balance of power. In 1971 he announced:

"It will be a safer world and a better world if we have a strong, healthy

Protesters against the Vietnam War became a regular sight in Washington, D.C.

United States, Europe, Soviet Union, China, Japan—each balancing the other, not playing one against the other, an even balance."

The Election of 1972

Nixon's renewed efforts to wind down the war in Vietnam increased his popularity at home. He faced little opposition in obtaining the Republican nomination for a second term. The Democrats, on the other hand, had no strong leader in 1972. Hubert Humphrey hoped to face Nixon again. Senator George McGovern of South Dakota campaigned hard in the primaries on an antiwar platform. George Wallace, who was running as a Democrat, was shot while campaigning in Maryland. Wallace's injuries left him paralyzed, and he withdrew from the race. McGovern won the nomination.

Shortly before the November election, Kissinger announced that he had reached an agreement with the North Vietnamese leaders. "Peace is at hand," he said. Largely as a result of this breakthrough, Nixon won an overwhelming victory on election day. He received more than 60 percent of the popular vote and carried every state but Massachusetts.

Americans Leave Vietnam

After Kissinger's "Peace is at hand" announcement, Nixon halted the U.S. bombing of North Vietnam. The agreement Kissinger had negotiated called for a cease-fire, joint North and South Vietnamese administration of South Vietnam, and free elections. Then the last U.S. troops would go home and the U.S. prisoners of war held by the North Vietnamese would be released.

This agreement fell through after Nixon's re-election. The president then resumed the air strikes. This time he sent B-52 bombers, the largest in the air force, to conduct raids on Hanoi, the capital of North Vietnam. While the B-52s pounded Hanoi, peace negotiations resumed in Paris. Finally, in January 1973, an agreement was signed. As far as the United States was concerned, the war was now over. The remaining troops were withdrawn. By the time the last Americans were airlifted out of Vietnam, the war had cost more than 58,000 American lives and more than $140 billion.

Young People In History

Vietnamese Children Come to America

After the war, some Vietnamese children hoped to start a new life in the United States.

Young Mai-Uyen Nguyen and her sister had been unable to escape South Vietnam when it was overrun by North Vietnamese troops. For Mai-Uyen, life in South Vietnam was particularly difficult because she was the daughter of an American soldier who had left the country. Other children picked on her because of her heritage. She later recalled that, even though it was forbidden to do so by the government, she had kept:

"his photograph and the necklace he gave me when I was two years old. . . . My mother had saved it and given it to me. I would never lose it or throw it away."

In 1985 she and her family finally reached America. Many other Vietnamese refugees were also children. Volunteer organizations, churches, and individuals helped to bring them and their families to America.

American Letters

When Heaven and Earth Changed Places

Le Ly Hayslip

Phung Thi Le Ly Hayslip was a Vietnamese teenage girl who struggled to survive the hardships and conflicting loyalties of the Vietnam War. In the midst of the war, she moved to the United States. She raised a family and became a successful businessperson in southern California. In 1986 she returned to visit Vietnam and all of the family she had left behind. When Heaven and Earth Changed Places: A Vietnamese Woman's Journey from War to Peace is her story. In the book's prologue, Hayslip explains the reasons for telling her story:

In 1986, after living for sixteen years in America and becoming a U.S. citizen, I went back to Vietnam—to find out what had happened to my family, my village, my people, and to the man I loved who had given me my first son. I went with many memories and many questions. This book is the story of what I remember and what I found.

It is dedicated to all those who fought for their country, wherever it may be. It is dedicated, too, to those who did not fight—but suffered, wept, raged, bled, and died just the same. . . .

If you were an American GI, I ask you to read this book and look into the heart of one you once called enemy. I have witnessed, firsthand, all that you went through. I will try to tell you who your enemy was and why almost everyone in the country you tried to help resented, feared, and misunderstood you. It was not your fault. . . . Long before you arrived, my country had yielded to the terrible logic of war. What for you was normal—a life of peace and plenty—was for us a hazy dream known only in our legends. Because we had to appease [please] the allied forces by day and were terrorized by Viet Cong at night, we slept as little as you did. We obeyed both

Le Ly Hayslip's books on the Vietnam War have been made into a film.

sides and wound up pleasing neither. We were people in the middle. We were what the war was all about.

Your story, however, was different. You came to Vietnam, willingly or not, because your country demanded it. Most of you did not know, or fully understand, the different wars my people were fighting when you got here. For you, it was a simple thing: democracy against communism. For us, that was not our fight at all. How could it be? We knew little about democracy and even less about communism. . . . How could you hope to end them by fighting a battle so different from our own?

The least you did—the least any of us did—was our duty. For that we must be proud. . . . If you have not yet found peace at the end of your war, I hope you will find it here."

On April 30, 1975, thousands of South Vietnamese and Americans were evacuated before Saigon fell to North Vietnamese troops.

The Vietnamese suffered even heavier losses in lives and property. In the South more than 185,000 soldiers and around half a million civilians had died. The North and the Vietcong had lost an estimated 1 million soldiers. Another 1 million Vietnamese were left orphaned or disabled, some from illness caused by the chemicals used in the war.

• **America After Vietnam**

The Fall of Saigon

Despite its high cost, the war had only delayed what the United States had most feared when it began its involvement: a unified, communist Vietnam. In January 1975, just two years after the U.S. peace agreement, part of South Vietnam fell to North Vietnamese troops. A few months later these troops were threatening Saigon.

In addition to evacuating thousands of American civilians from the capital city, the United States flew out nearly 140,000 South Vietnamese who had worked for the U.S. government and were now in danger. Many Vietnamese who desperately wanted to leave, however, were left behind.

On April 30, 1975, while many people still were trying to leave the country, South Vietnam unconditionally surrendered. In a dramatic moment that same day, people escaped by helicopter from the rooftop of the U.S. Embassy as it was overrun by North Vietnamese troops.

In the decade after the surrender, many more Vietnamese fled the country—in all more than 1.5 million. Many, along with refugees from Cambodia and Laos, risked their lives in small, overcrowded boats. Eventually, more than 730,000 Southeast Asian refugees settled in the United States.

Section 4 Review

• **Glossary**

• **Time Line**

IDENTIFY and explain the significance of the following: Vietnamization, Henry Kissinger, George McGovern

REVIEWING FOR DETAILS

1. What were the goals of Vietnamization?

2. Why did President Nixon decide to invade Cambodia, and how did many people in the United States react?

3. What events brought the war in Vietnam to an end?

REVIEWING FOR UNDERSTANDING

4. **Geographic Literacy** How did the Vietnam War spread in Southeast Asia?

5. **Critical Thinking:** *Synthesizing Information* What do you think has been the lasting impact of the Vietnam War on both the United States and Vietnam?

CHAPTER 28

Searching for Solutions
(1968–1981)

THEMES IN AMERICAN HISTORY

Economic Development:
Why might inflation cause economic problems?

Global Relations:
How might rising oil prices in one region of the world affect others?

Constitutional Heritage:
How might Congress or the Supreme Court attempt to control the power of the president?

One Chicago woman expressed the feelings of many Americans in the 1970s: "You always used to think in this country that there would be bad times followed by good times. Now, maybe it's bad times followed by hard times followed by harder times." The chaos of the previous years had left the country exhausted. Throughout the 1970s Americans struggled to resolve what one leader called a "crisis of confidence."

 • **Video Opener**

 • **Skill Builder**

image above: *Women's rights march*

Section 1

NIXON AS PRESIDENT

Multimedia Connections

Explore these related topics and materials on the CD–ROM to enrich your understanding of this section:

Readings

- Nixon's Visit to China

Media Bank

- Welfare Expenditures
- Supreme Court Appointees
- Nixon Meeting Brezhnev
- Alaska Pipeline
- Cartoon of Détente

Gazetteer

- Chile
- China
- Soviet Union
- Jordan

On July 20, 1969, American astronaut Neil Armstrong stepped down from a ladder onto a land never before visited by human beings. "That's one small step for a man, one giant leap for mankind," he said as millions of people worldwide watched the event on television. President Nixon praised the moon landing as a shining example of American resourcefulness. As the president rejoiced over this triumph, however, he struggled with many problems that troubled the nation.

As you read this section you will find out:

▶ **How President Nixon planned to restore domestic order.**

▶ **What caused the energy crisis.**

▶ **How President Nixon practiced his strategy of realpolitik.**

The Silent Majority

Even as Americans united in joy over the 1969 moon landing, they remained divided over many other issues. The 1960s had left Americans sharply divided over the Vietnam War, civil rights, and the counterculture. When Richard Nixon took office, he said he wanted to represent what he called the **Silent Majority**, those "forgotten Americans" who had not been involved in protests of any sort. Nixon summed up how he and many of the Silent Majority had come to view the events of the 1960s:

> **"I saw the mass demonstrations . . . become a cultural fad. . . . And the new sensitivities to social inequities [inequalities] . . . spawned [created] an intolerance for the rights and opinions of those who disagreed.**

... I had no patience with mindless rioters ... and I was appalled by the response of most of the nation's political and academic leaders to them."

Nixon blamed many of the nation's domestic problems on the enormous size of the federal government. He thus sought to transfer control of many government functions from federal to state and local authorities.

Nixon promised to restore order to the country. He announced his intention to crack down on crime and to reverse many of the changes brought about by the New Deal and Great Society programs.

To help restore "law and order" to the country, Nixon appointed conservative judges to the federal courts. When liberal Chief Justice of the Supreme Court Earl Warren retired in June 1969, Nixon replaced him with conservative Warren Burger.

Nixon's appointments of conservative judges helped him keep his promise not to support any new civil rights legislation. This was part of what he called his "**southern strategy**," to win over traditionally Democratic southern white voters to the Republican Party.

He also slowed federal efforts to help desegregate public schools in the South. This policy appealed to many white southerners who opposed racial desegregation.

Many New Deal and Great Society programs came under fire for having created what Nixon considered to be an inefficient government bureaucracy. He did believe, in principle, that the federal government should help the poor. Nixon himself had grown up in a poor family in California, but he thought that too many government programs wasted money and were easy targets for fraud.

The welfare system, in particular, came under heavy attack. A number of new welfare programs, including food stamps and Medicaid, had been established during the 1960s. Critics claimed that the system was inefficient and discouraged people from working.

The welfare system was administered by the states, so the amount of money families received varied from place to place. Although such noncash benefits as food stamps and medical care were also provided, in most states the money families received was less than what they needed to rise above the poverty level.

Nixon proposed to replace the existing welfare system and the government agencies that ran it with his **Family Assistance Plan** (FAP). Under the FAP, noncash welfare benefits would be abolished. Instead, every family in America would be guaranteed a minimum annual income. Those whose incomes fell below a certain level would receive supplementary cash payments from the government.

The House approved the FAP, but a heated debate broke out when the bill came to the Senate. Liberals opposed the plan because they thought the minimum income guaranteed by the FAP would not be sufficient for most families. Many conservatives felt that the plan did not go far enough to reform welfare. The FAP died in the Senate.

Richard Nixon appealed to many conservative voters, like these supporters of American involvement in Vietnam.

This play money poked fun at President Nixon's policies of dealing with inflation by freezing wages and prices.

The Economy

By the time Nixon became president, many Americans were very concerned about the economy, particularly rising inflation. The country was also experiencing growing unemployment and a recession.

Normally when a nation experiences high unemployment, prices tend to drop. But in the late 1960s and early 1970s both unemployment and inflation rose. Economists describe this unusual situation as **stagflation**—a word coined by combining "stagnation," and "inflation."

In an attempt to improve this situation, Nixon first set out to reduce government spending. He also persuaded the Federal Reserve Board to raise interest rates to discourage borrowing. These policies caused unemployment to increase as well. Meanwhile, prices continued to rise. In August 1971 Nixon ordered wage and price freezes, and he set up new government boards to supervise wages and prices. Labor leader George Meany complained that these wage controls hurt the lowest-paid workers. It was "Robin Hood in reverse," Meany claimed, "because it robs from the poor and gives to the rich."

The wage and price controls did slow inflation, but when Nixon eased these restrictions in 1973, prices shot up again. Inflation continued to plague the country throughout the decade.

The Energy Crisis

One important factor contributing to inflation was the rising cost of fuel. By 1973 the United States was importing 60 percent of all the oil it used. Most of this oil was imported from the Middle East. In 1960 five major oil-producing countries had formed an alliance known as the **Organization of Petroleum Exporting Countries** (OPEC). This group controlled the price of oil flowing from its member countries.

World oil prices were usually affected whenever war broke out in the Middle East. Most of the Arab members of OPEC were enemies of Israel, an ally of the United States. The Israelis and the Arabs had gone to war several times since Israel was established in

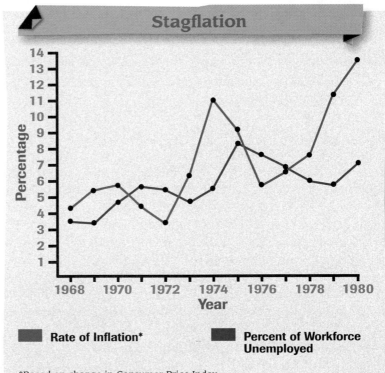

Stagflation

Rate of Inflation*   Percent of Workforce Unemployed

*Based on change in Consumer Price Index
Source: *Statistical Abstract of the United States*

A National Problem. Stagflation, an increase in both inflation and unemployment, flared up periodically from 1968 to 1980. According to this graph, between what two years did stagflation first occur?

• Graphs

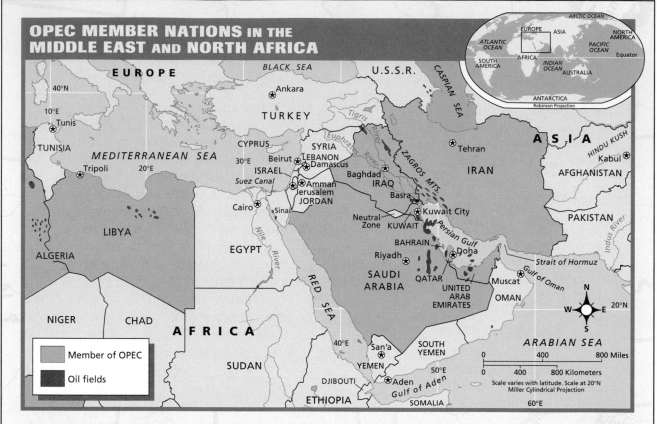

OPEC MEMBER NATIONS IN THE MIDDLE EAST AND NORTH AFRICA

Learning from Maps. OPEC produced much of the world's oil supply.

▶ **Region.** Which countries in the Middle East and North Africa were members of OPEC?

● **Maps**

1948. In the 1967 Six-Day War, Israel won a major victory against Egypt, Jordan, and Syria. In an attempt to regain territory they had lost in that war, Egypt and Syria launched a surprise attack against Israel on the Jewish holiday of Yom Kippur in early October 1973.

The Yom Kippur War lasted for more than three months. During that time OPEC raised the price of oil to four times what it had been before the war. Some Arab nations stopped selling oil entirely to the United States because of its continued support for Israel.

This oil embargo caused serious fuel shortages that produced what became known as the **energy crisis**. Even after the Arab countries agreed

to a cease-fire with Israel and once again began selling oil to the United States, fuel prices remained high. The cost of electricity, gasoline, and home heating oil soared.

The U.S. government tried to encourage Americans to conserve energy by cutting back on heating and cooling their homes, using electrical appliances less, and driving only when necessary. In some places, gasoline had to be rationed. Long lines of cars

Cars wait in line for gas during the energy crisis.

● **OPEC Meeting**

The first Earth Day celebration was held in 1970 to bring attention to the effects of pollution on the environment. Such events helped increase public awareness of environmental issues. Over the years, hundreds of thousands of people have observed Earth Day.

waited their turn at the pumps, sometimes for more than two hours.

The energy crisis made many Americans realize the consequences of relying on foreign oil. Nixon said that the country should attack the energy crisis like it pushed for the *Apollo* space mission. If America could put a man on the moon, then it could rid itself of dependence on foreign oil.

The focus on the energy crisis came at a time when many people had already begun to grow concerned about the damage that pollution was doing to the environment. At the first Earth Day celebration in 1970, Episcopal priest Paul Moore warned:

"We have been fighting nature, and when you fight someone he fights back. . . . Unless we stop stealing, exploiting [taking advantage of], and ruining nature for our own gain, we will lose everything."

Congress responded to the growing concerns of many Americans by establishing the **Environmental Protection Agency** (EPA) in 1970. This agency was responsible for enforcing environmental laws. That same year Congress also approved two new laws providing for cleaner air and water.

Nixon's Foreign Policy

The oil embargo was only one of many ways in which world events affected American life. Foreign affairs were a major focus of Nixon's presidency. Nixon rejected some of the most basic assumptions of the Cold War, namely that the communist nations of the world were united in a struggle against America. He argued that such a position had led the United States into Vietnam. Although Nixon was strongly anticommunist, he and his national security adviser, Henry Kissinger, tried to devise an approach to foreign policy that would not be driven by anticommunism alone.

Realpolitik. Nixon and Kissinger referred to their strategy as **realpolitik**—practical politics. Following this approach, they put practical national interests, such as military security and U.S. financial benefits, above all other considerations when making foreign policy decisions. They also believed that the only way to ensure lasting world peace was to maintain a balance of power between the world's strongest powers—the United States, the Soviet Union, Western Europe, Japan, and China.

Some critics charged that these considerations led the president to make alliances with military dictators who abused human rights in their own countries. For example, Nixon supported a revolt against the socialist president of Chile in 1973. The Chilean president was assassinated and his government was soon replaced by a harsh military dictatorship.

Nixon and China. Despite such concerns, no one could deny that Nixon's approach to foreign policy marked a significant shift in Cold War relations, particularly with the Soviet Union and China. The 1949 takeover of China by the Chinese Communist Party had increased concerns about the expansion of a unified communist power. By the 1970s, however, some American leaders had come to recognize that Soviet and Chinese communism were very different. In fact, China and the Soviet Union had become fierce enemies.

In 1969 a clash occurred on the border between the Soviet Union and China that threatened to turn into a massive military confrontation. Following his theory of practical politics, Nixon sensed that he could turn the Soviet-Chinese feud into an advantage for the United States. Embracing the ancient military saying "The enemy of my enemy is my friend," the president moved to open diplomatic relations with China.

In February 1972 Nixon surprised even many Republicans by visiting China. While there, he reached an agreement with Chinese leaders to open trade between the United States and China and to work together to promote peace.

Arms control. This move alarmed the Soviets, who feared that a U.S.-China alliance would threaten their security. Three months after his visit to China, Nixon went to the Soviet Union to meet with its leader, Leonid Brezhnev. The two worked out an agreement

President Nixon tours the Great Wall of China during his historic visit to the country.

to promote trade and to improve diplomatic relations between their countries.

Perhaps most significantly, the two leaders also began a process to slow the arms race. They signed the **Strategic Arms Limitation Treaty** (SALT), an agreement to limit the numbers of certain types of nuclear weapons their nations produced. Following the signing of SALT came a period known as **détente** (day-TAHNT), where relations improved between the United States and the Soviet Union.

Section 1 Review

• Glossary

IDENTIFY and explain the significance of the following: Silent Majority, southern strategy, Family Assistance Plan, stagflation, Organization of Petroleum Exporting Countries, energy crisis, Environmental Protection Agency, realpolitik, Strategic Arms Limitation Treaty, détente

REVIEWING FOR DETAILS

1. How did President Nixon plan to solve the nation's domestic problems?
2. What conditions led to the energy crisis of the 1970s?
3. How did Nixon pursue his foreign policy strategy?

REVIEWING FOR UNDERSTANDING

4. **Writing Mastery:** *Describing* Imagine that you are a student in the early 1970s. Write a letter to a friend describing how the energy crisis is affecting your life and what you are doing to help.

5. **Critical Thinking:** *Drawing Conclusions* Many people have claimed that Richard Nixon's greatest contributions as president were in the area of foreign policy. Do you agree? Why or why not?

Section 2

WATERGATE AND FORD

Multimedia Connections

Explore these related topics and materials on the CD–ROM to enrich your understanding of this section:

 Biographies

- Walter Cronkite

 Gazetteer

- Cambodia

 Media Bank

- Nixon Resigns
- Nixon's Men
- President Ford
- The *Mayaguez* Incident
- Watergate Demonstrators

 Profiles

- Gerald Ford
- Barbara Jordan

With these words: "I shall resign the Presidency effective at noon tomorrow," on August 8, 1974, Richard Milhous Nixon became the first U.S. president to resign from the office. In less than two years he had gone from winning a landslide re-election victory to giving up the presidency in disgrace. The scandal that led to Nixon's resignation rocked the country and shook many Americans' faith in their government.

As you read this section you will find out:

▶ **How the Watergate investigation unfolded.**

▶ **Why Nixon resigned from office.**

▶ **What challenges Gerald Ford faced as president.**

The Mystery Begins

Richard Nixon's overwhelming victory over George McGovern in the 1972 election made him seem among the most powerful of American presidents. Yet, at the very moment of his success, Nixon's power began to crumble. The cause was a scandal that became known simply as **Watergate**.

On the night of June 17, 1972, shortly before the presidential nominating conventions, five burglars were arrested while breaking into the headquarters of the Democratic National Committee in Washington, D.C. The headquarters were located in an office building and apartment complex on the Potomac River called the Watergate.

The burglars had obviously intended to copy Democratic Party records and to attach listening devices to the office telephones.

Suspicion quickly fell on the Republican Party. One of the men arrested was James W. McCord, a former CIA employee who was now working for Nixon's re-election campaign organization. Two other Nixon campaign officials were also involved in the break-in.

Both Nixon and his campaign manager, former attorney general John Mitchell, denied that anyone on the White House staff had anything to do with the break-in. Most people accepted the president's denial, and the Watergate incident had no effect on the election.

Two reporters for the *Washington Post*, Bob Woodward and Carl Bernstein, however, kept investigating the case. They received a break when a confidential White House source started to leak information to them. The source claimed that many people had been hired by some Republicans to sabotage the Democratic campaign in 1972.

It soon appeared that there had been a cover-up of evidence. The Senate began an investigation early in 1973. James McCord testified that a number of important Republican officials had been involved in planning the Watergate burglary. As the Senate investigation proceeded, witnesses brought out more details about Watergate and other illegal activities connected with Nixon's campaign

Members of the Senate committee investigating Watergate discuss their strategy with Senator Sam Ervin (center), who chaired the committee.

for re-election. Some testified that many large corporations had made secret contributions to Nixon's campaign fund. Such gifts were illegal.

John Dean, a White House lawyer, provided particularly damaging testimony to investigators. Dean testified that the president had helped plan the cover-up from the beginning. According to Dean, the president had

The testimony of White House lawyer John Dean broke the Watergate case wide open, as this cartoon shows.

DOONESBURY   by Garry Trudeau

OKAY, WHO WOULD CARE TO TESTIFY NEXT BEFORE THIS COMMITTEE?

HERE, *ME*, ME! SENATOR, ME!

ME!

TAKE IT *EASY!*. ONE AT A TIME.. YOU'LL ALL GET YOUR TURN... OKAY, *YOU!*.. YES, *YOU*, YOUNG MAN. WHAT DO YOU HAVE TO SAY?

MY NAME IS JOHN W. DEAN III, AND I WANT TO SPILL MY GUTS OUT.

PROCEED.

Special Prosecutor Archibald Cox was given the difficult task of finding the truth behind the Watergate scandal.

lied when he denied that anyone in the White House was involved in the affair. Nixon denied these charges. It seemed to be his word against Dean's.

The Suspicion Grows

Another witness then revealed that Nixon had been secretly recording all the conversations that had taken place in his office. Such tape recordings would almost surely show what Nixon's role in Watergate had been. Senate investigators demanded that the president allow them to listen to these tapes. Nixon refused to release them, claiming **executive privilege**— the president's right to keep information secret when it relates to presidential business.

More people came to believe that Nixon was hiding something. Yet how could the full truth be discovered while people Nixon had appointed ran the Justice Department? To end the criticism, Nixon agreed to the appointment of well-known law professor Archibald Cox as special prosecutor in charge of the case. Cox was promised full control and was told to pursue the truth, wherever the facts might lead.

When Cox demanded that the White House tapes be turned over to his investigators, however, Nixon once again refused. A federal judge then ordered the president to give Cox the tapes. Instead of doing so, Nixon

ordered Attorney General Elliot L. Richardson, head of the Justice Department, to fire Cox!

Rather than carry out Nixon's order, Richardson resigned, as did the assistant attorney general. Finally, a third member of the Justice Department, Robert H. Bork, discharged Cox. These events, which occurred on the evening of Saturday, October 20, 1973, became known as the **Saturday Night Massacre**.

Nixon's entire administration seemed full of scandal. Only 10 days before Cox's firing, Vice President Spiro Agnew admitted that he had cheated on his income taxes. To avoid the national shame of having a vice president in

Through Others' Eyes

Watergate

People around the world watched as the Watergate scandal unfolded. Some foreign observers saw the process that brought about the president's resignation as a sign that the American political process worked to weed out corruption. The day before Nixon announced his resignation, the editors of the Mexican newspaper *Excelsior* wrote:

"Watergate—the complete symbol of the greatness and the misery of the North American nation—cleared up any remaining illusions about the purity of the U.S. electoral process. But, in the opposite sense, it alerted the never fully sleeping consciousness of the majority of the country. Those people who pretend to reduce Nixon's resignation to [simply] a triumph of light over darkness are mistaken. Of the conspiracy itself . . . , however, it cannot be ignored that we are attending [witnessing] a victory for the seeds of liberty and democracy that first came to life in North America two centuries ago."

prison, the Justice Department had allowed him to plead no contest to the charges and to resign from office. Agnew was fined and placed on probation for his crimes. Nixon then chose Congressman Gerald R. Ford of Michigan to replace Agnew.

Nixon Falls from Power

Meanwhile, the Saturday Night Massacre had convinced many people to demand that Nixon be impeached. The House Judiciary Committee began an investigation to see if there were grounds for impeachment. While the committee studied the evidence of Nixon's involvement in the scandal, a new special prosecutor, Leon Jaworski, proceeded against the others involved.

Late in April 1974 Nixon released edited transcripts of some of his taped conversations. These, he said, would prove his innocence. However, important parts of conversations were left out in these printed versions. Nixon would not let others check on the editing. He refused to turn over the complete tapes to either the House Judiciary Committee or to Special Prosecutor Jaworski.

Jaworski therefore asked the Supreme Court to order the president to give him the tapes. On July 24, the Court ruled unanimously that Nixon must turn over the tapes to Jaworski.

Nixon still hesitated. His advisers finally convinced him that if he refused to obey the Court's order, he was sure to face impeach-

Texas congresswoman Barbara Jordan served on the House Judiciary Committee that recommended the impeachment of President Nixon.

• **Impeachment Process**

ment. He therefore gave up the tapes. They proved conclusively that Nixon had known about the Watergate affair from the start. For example, only one day after he had said on television that no one in the White House had anything to do with the affair, Nixon had ordered his chief assistant, H. R. Haldeman, to try to persuade the FBI not to investigate the break-in too vigorously.

On July 27 the House Judiciary Committee passed the first of three articles of impeachment against the president. One accused him of obstructing justice. Another accused him of misusing the powers of the presidency. The third concerned his refusal to let the committee listen to the tapes.

Texas congresswoman Barbara Jordan, a member of the committee, reflected the outrage of many regarding Nixon's actions when she declared:

> **"My faith in the Constitution is whole, it is complete, it is total, and I am not going to sit here and be an idle spectator to the . . . destruction of the Constitution."**

Under the Constitution, the House Judiciary Committee's report would be submitted to the full House of Representatives. If the report was accepted—which was almost certain—the House would then present the articles of impeachment to the Senate. The Senate would act as a court, hearing the charges. If two thirds of the senators voted in favor of any of the three articles, Nixon would be removed from office.

Nixon now had two choices: resign before the House voted to impeach him or go on trial. On August 9, at noon, he officially resigned the presidency. Gerald R. Ford then took the oath of office and became president of the United States.

Gerald Ford Takes Over

Gerald Ford was known as an honest, hardworking politician. Nearly everyone in Congress liked him, and he got along easily with people. Although Ford had never been

With a final wave goodbye and the victory sign, President Richard Nixon leaves Washington, D.C., after becoming the first U.S. president to resign from office.

particularly noted for his vision or originality, many hoped he would be able to heal the wounds of Watergate.

Pardons. Ford quickly lost much public support when, one month after taking office, he issued a full **pardon**, or freedom from punishment, to former President Nixon. This meant that Nixon could not be tried for any crimes he had committed or may have committed while in office. Many people were outraged by the pardon.

Ford did not make things any better when he issued a promise of amnesty, or forgiveness, for those who had avoided the draft during the Vietnam War. They could stay out of prison by pledging their loyalty to the United States and serving two years of public service. Many veterans who had risked their lives in the war took this as an insult. Some draft evaders who felt they had done the right thing to protest what they considered to be an unjust war were equally offended. Dee Knight, who had avoided the draft, said:

"We knew the clemency [mercy] was proclaimed [declared] just to offset the Nixon pardon, which was an insult. We weren't criminals, and Nixon was, but Ford proposed to pardon Nixon unconditionally while offering 'alternative punishment' to us."

The economy. President Ford faced many other problems. The economy was still in a severe recession. By 1974 business activity had slowed down because of cutbacks in government spending and rising inflation. Unemployment reached nearly 10 percent.

The president quickly found himself at odds with Congress over economic issues. The Democratic majority wanted to increase government spending in order to strengthen the economy. As the economy continued to slow down, Ford urged Congress to cut back on such spending, particularly on social welfare programs. To urge support for his policies, Ford issued buttons for supporters to wear that read "WIN," for "Whip Inflation Now."

In the 1974 congressional elections, the Democrats increased their majorities in both the House and the Senate. When the new Congress met, it passed bills designed to help poor people and to create new jobs. Measures providing for construction of public housing, aid to education, and health care were also passed. Ford vetoed all of them. Spending so much more money, he argued, would lead to greater inflation. In most cases the Democrats were not able to get the two-thirds majority needed to override the president's veto.

Finally, in the spring of 1975, Ford reluctantly signed a bill reducing taxes. He had avoided this step for fear it would fuel greater inflation. However, the tax cut did put more money in people's pockets and helped ease the downturn.

Foreign affairs. President Ford also faced challenges in the area of foreign affairs. For the most part he continued Nixon's policies toward the Soviet Union and Vietnam. Then in May 1975, just weeks after South Vietnam fell to communist forces, a U.S. cargo ship, the *Mayaguez,* was stopped in East Asian waters by Cambodian forces. The 39 crew members were then taken to a small island and questioned about American spy activities. By most

Draper Hill/The Memphis Commercial Appeal

accounts, the Cambodians treated the Americans well. One crew member reported that one of their captors who spoke English "greeted us with a handshake."

Still, the taking of an unarmed U.S. ship was serious business. Ford demanded that the Cambodians release the crew of the *Mayaguez* immediately. When the Cambodians did not respond, Ford launched a major military rescue operation. Forty-one Americans died in the assault.

Afterward, it was discovered that the crew of the *Mayaguez* had already been released an hour before the American assault began. Critics argued that if Ford had been just a little more patient, the deaths could have been avoided. Despite this incident, however, Ford did make important progress in improving relations between the United States and the Soviet Union, and with several nations of the Middle East.

Despite his best efforts, President Ford could not escape the many problems left over from President Nixon.

Section 2 Review

• Glossary

IDENTIFY and explain the significance of the following: Watergate, John Mitchell, Bob Woodward and Carl Bernstein, John Dean, executive privilege, Archibald Cox, Saturday Night Massacre, Gerald R. Ford, pardon

REVIEWING FOR DETAILS

1. What events shaped the Watergate investigation?
2. Why did President Nixon decide to resign?
3. What challenges troubled the Ford presidency?

REVIEWING FOR UNDERSTANDING

4. **Writing Mastery:** *Informing* Imagine that you are a newspaper reporter. Write an article informing your readers about the events of the Watergate investigation.
5. **Critical Thinking:** *Synthesizing Information* How was the Watergate affair a test of the separation of powers described in the U.S. Constitution?

Section 3

THE "OUTSIDER" AS PRESIDENT

Multimedia Connections

Explore these related topics and materials on the CD–ROM to enrich your understanding of this section:

 Media Bank

- Carter in Office

 Glossary

- Panama Canal

 Gazetteer

- Afghanistan
- Israel
- Egypt
- Panama
- South Africa

 Profiles

- Jimmy Carter
- Ralph Nader

W atergate destroyed many Americans' faith in their leaders. A poll conducted in March 1975 revealed that 83 percent of Americans agreed with the following statement: "The people running this country (government, political, church, and civic leaders), don't tell us the truth." A new president promised to return honesty and honor to the White House. "Can our government in Washington . . . be decent?" Jimmy Carter asked. "Is it possible for it to be honest and truthful . . . ? I think the answer is yes."

As you read this section you will find out:

▶ **How President Carter's approach differed from those of Nixon and Ford.**

▶ **What advantages and disadvantages Carter had as a Washington "outsider."**

▶ **How Carter pursued foreign affairs.**

The Election of 1976

As the United States celebrated its 200th birthday in 1976, it faced not only serious economic problems but also a loss of faith in its leaders. After Watergate, it looked as if the Democrats would have a good chance of regaining the White House in the upcoming presidential election.

President Ford won a narrow victory at the Republican National Convention. The Democrats nominated a somewhat unknown southern politician named James Earl "Jimmy" Carter, Jr. After graduating from the Naval Academy in 1946, Carter had served for several years as a naval nuclear engineer. He resigned to run his family's peanut farming business in Georgia after his father died. He soon entered politics, serving two terms in the Georgia legislature and one term as governor.

Jimmy Carter reaches out to potential voters. Carter's honesty and "outsider" status made him popular with many voters in 1976.

The Carter Style

In contrast to the closed, secretive nature of the Nixon White House, President Carter stressed that his administration would be open to the people. To emphasize this point, instead of riding to the White House in a limousine after his inauguration, Carter, his wife, Rosalynn, and their children walked down Pennsylvania Avenue, waving and smiling to the crowd.

Once in office Carter continued to stress his informal style. He appeared on television wearing a sweater instead of a suit coat. He had "call-ins" on television and radio during which he answered questions phoned in by citizens. Carter also held a series of "town meetings"—informal gatherings in communities around the country—to discuss his policies and to give people an opportunity to ask him questions face-to-face.

As time passed, however, critics began to claim that Carter was a poor leader. He changed his mind frequently, making it appear that he often lacked direction. Gerald Ford once joked of Carter, "He wavers, he wanders, he wiggles, and he waffles." This criticism centered on Carter's seeming inability to deal

In his presidential campaign, Carter pointed to his role as an "outsider" who was not involved in the corruption and scandal that seemed to surround Washington. He stressed his sincerity, his honesty, and above all, his deep religious faith.

The election was very close. Carter won in the electoral college by 297 to 240 votes. He carried most northern industrial states and most of the South. One reason for his victory was the support that he received from many Mexican Americans and from African Americans. In return for their support, Carter named more African Americans and Mexican Americans, as well as women, to federal appointments than any president before him.

The Carter family walks together down Pennsylvania Avenue on inauguration day to show their closeness to average American people.

effectively with two important issues—the economy and the continuing energy crisis.

At the time of Carter's election, the economy was still sluggish. Unemployment stood at nearly 8 percent overall. Among African Americans and Hispanic Americans it was 13 percent. Carter tried many different approaches to improve the economy, including decreasing taxes for corporations to create more jobs, urging voluntary wage and price controls, and cutting funding for social programs. However, Carter was unable to successfully deal with the persistent problems of inflation and unemployment.

The Energy Crisis Continues

Like Ford and Nixon before him, Carter linked many of the country's economic problems to the energy crisis. He noted that relying on expensive imported oil contributed to inflation and unemployment at home. He praised people who tried to conserve energy, including a young girl named Gwen who wrote him a letter containing this promise:

> **"I am going to try and help with the energy crisis. Every night before I go to sleep, I am going to turn off my TV set even if my mother doesn't yell at me to do it."**

In 1977 Congress created the **Department of Energy** to establish programs for conserving energy and managing the country's energy resources. The following year Congress passed a law encouraging the use of natural gas instead of oil. Even though many members of Congress agreed with Carter on what America's problems were, they could rarely agree with him on how to solve them. The president's "outsider" status was a problem in dealing with Congress. Many legislators considered Carter to be uncompromising. As one observer noted, Carter tended to "equate [match] his political goals with the just and right, and to view his opponents as representative of some selfish or immoral [corrupt] interests."

For example, Carter developed a package of 113 initiatives for tackling the energy crisis.

During the 1970s many people experimented with ways to save energy, like building solar-heated homes.

When he presented his package to Congress for approval, some legislators wanted to amend parts of it. Carter insisted that every part of his plan be approved without change. Faced with the president's stubbornness, Congress rejected his entire energy package.

Carter and Foreign Policy

As with domestic policy, Carter felt that foreign policy should reflect certain moral values, including openness. He called the Nixon and Ford approach a "secretive 'Lone Ranger' foreign policy." Carter felt that concern for human rights—not just national security—should take center stage in determining policy. He argued that the United States should not do business with dictators who violated human rights. Carter also felt that smaller nations, not just the "great powers" of the world, were important to U.S. interests.

The Cold War. Carter believed that respect for human rights should guide Cold War policy. For example, in the 1970s Africa was a focus of struggle between the United States and the Soviet Union. Many African countries that had been colonies of European nations had gained their independence in the 1950s

As the U.S. ambassador to the United Nations, Andrew Young brought American attention to the unjust system of apartheid in South Africa.

and 1960s. Carter determined that the best way to win allies among these nations was to show respect for African self-rule. Rather than dictating how Africans should govern themselves, Carter offered U.S. aid to help African leaders solve their countries' internal problems however they saw fit.

Members of the Carter administration also spoke out against **apartheid**, a legal system of racial and class discrimination in the country of South Africa. Although the majority of South Africans were black, they were ruled by a white minority. Black South Africans had few rights. They were not even allowed to vote. Andrew Young, the U.S. ambassador to the United Nations, supported a movement to issue UN **sanctions**, or official punishments, against the government of South Africa. Young said of those who supported apartheid:

"By their policies of increasing racial oppression, the [white] South African leaders are succeeding in progressively isolating their country from the rest of the world. This process, if allowed to continue, will lead to a situation in which cooperation between South

Africa and the rest of the world . . . will be increasingly difficult, if not impossible."

The Carter administration's approach helped to win many allies in Africa. But the president's sensitivity to the concerns of developing countries was sometimes unpopular at home.

One of Carter's most controversial decisions was to sign a series of treaties that would turn over control of the Panama Canal to Panama by the year 2000. While many Latin Americans praised the move, some Americans opposed it. "We built [the Canal], we paid for it, it's ours," declared Republican Ronald Reagan. Despite such strong opposition, the U.S. Senate ratified the **Panama Canal treaties** in 1978.

Carter's dealings with the Soviet Union were also a source of controversy. In 1979 the Soviets invaded the neighboring country of Afghanistan. Carter condemned the invasion and warned the Soviet Union to withdraw its troops. When the Soviets refused, he cut off all future U.S. grain supplies to the Soviet Union and declared that the United States would boycott the 1980 Summer Olympics in Moscow. While some people praised Carter's position, others complained that the policy unfairly punished American grain farmers and athletes. Carter also withdrew the second Strategic Arms Limitation Treaty (SALT II),

Panamanian students protest against U.S. control of the Panama Canal, which they believed should be controlled by their country.

which was under consideration by the Senate at the time.

Camp David. President Carter's greatest achievement in foreign affairs was helping bring about a series of peace treaties in the Middle East. Many people feared that another war would soon break out between long-time enemies Israel and Egypt.

Egyptian president Anwar Sadat and Israeli prime minister Menachem Begin (BAY-guhn) had tried to negotiate a peaceful settlement between their countries, but they had been unable to reach an agreement. In September 1978 Carter brought Sadat and Begin together at Camp David, the presidential retreat in Maryland. For almost two weeks the group hammered out guidelines for a peace agreement. The document they produced became known as the **Camp David Accords**.

In 1979 Sadat and Begin signed a formal peace treaty ending the long-standing state of

President Carter welcomes Egyptian president Anwar Sadat (left) and Israeli prime minister Menachem Begin (right) to Camp David, marking a turning point for the Middle East.

war between their countries. At the signing of the treaty, President Carter explained how they had been able to get to this point: "Peace," he said, "like war, is waged."

Section 3 Review

• Glossary

IDENTIFY and explain the significance of the following: Jimmy Carter, Department of Energy, apartheid, sanctions, Panama Canal treaties, Camp David Accords

REVIEWING FOR DETAILS

1. How did Jimmy Carter's ideas about the presidency differ from Nixon's and Ford's?
2. How was Carter's position as an "outsider" both beneficial and harmful to his presidency?
3. What goals did Carter pursue in his foreign policy?

REVIEWING FOR UNDERSTANDING

4. **Writing Mastery:** *Creating* Compose a dialogue for one of Carter's radio call-in programs, with callers asking questions about his policies and Carter providing answers.
5. **Critical Thinking:** *Drawing Conclusions* How do you think the Watergate scandal affected Jimmy Carter's election to the presidency?

Section 4

AMERICANS IN THE 1970S

Multimedia Connections

Explore these related topics and materials on the CD–ROM to enrich your understanding of this section:

 Readings

- Equal Rights Amendment

 Media Bank

- Disco Music
- U.S. Immigration, 1971–1993
- Women in the Professions
- Phyllis Schlafly

 Profiles

- César Chávez

 Atlas

- U.S. Asian Population, 1980

Richard Nixon had said he wanted to appeal to the "forgotten Americans" who had not protested during the 1960s. By the 1970s, however, more people who had always felt "forgotten" were protesting. Jessie Lopez de la Cruz organized poor and often mistreated Mexican American farmworkers in California. They did not have to take abuse from their employers, she told them. "We can stand up! We can talk back!" she declared.

As you read this section you will find out:
▶ **What civil rights practices were most controversial.**
▶ **What tactics new civil rights organizations used in the 1970s.**
▶ **Why the Equal Rights Amendment failed.**

Civil Rights Successes and Reaction

The African American civil rights movement continued to expand in the 1970s. With legal segregation abolished in most areas, many African Americans began to see a gradual improvement in their lives.

By the 1970s, high school graduation rates among African Americans were rising along with college attendance. By 1977 more than 1 million African American students were attending college. That was more than five times the number in 1960. Likewise, African American political representation was on the rise. By the end of the 1970s three times more African Americans held public offices than in 1969.

Just as the civil rights movement was making these gains, however, it faced a reaction

The busing crisis in Boston became so dangerous that police had to escort buses carrying African American students to schools that had a majority of white students. The crisis showed that racial tensions were not limited to the southern states.

from some whites who argued that once legal segregation was abolished there was nothing more to be done. Two practices that were intended to reverse the long-term effects of discrimination stirred particular controversy.

In many cities, years of housing discrimination had left neighborhoods and local schools segregated by race. Because of job discrimination, many nonwhite neighborhoods were also poor, thus the schools in these areas had less money than those in wealthier areas. So even in cities where schools were no longer legally segregated, they were often just as "separate and unequal" as schools that had been segregated by law.

In the late 1960s and early 1970s many federal judges began to order school districts to bus students to schools outside of their neighborhoods in order to remedy such indirect school segregation. Many whites strongly opposed such court-ordered **busing**, including people in northern cities who had always considered segregation to be a "southern" problem. Boston experienced some of the most violent protests against busing. African American leader Ruth Batson recalled that some white leaders who opposed busing insisted, "We don't have segregation in Boston."

By the late 1970s much of the opposition to busing had died down. Critics then attacked **affirmative action**. This is the practice by some businesses and government agencies of giving special consideration to non-whites or women when applicants' qualifications are roughly equal to make up for past discrimination. Critics argued that affirmative action was a form of "reverse discrimination."

In 1978 the Supreme Court ruled that some forms of affirmative action were unfair. The case of *University of California* v. *Bakke* involved Allan Bakke, a white man who had been denied admission to a California public medical school. Bakke argued that he would have been admitted to the school if it had not set aside a certain number of places for African American students. The practice of setting aside exact numbers of positions for members of a specific group is called a **quota system**. The Court ruled that while race may be considered in admissions, quota systems were unfair. The medical school was ordered to admit Bakke.

The American Indian Movement

The African American civil rights movement inspired many other groups to organize and to fight for their civil rights. These groups included older Americans, people with disabilities, and other victims of racial discrimination.

Among those who organized were American Indians. Some referred to their movement as "Red Power," after the Black Power movement. In 1968 a group of young American Indians from various tribes formed a protest organization called the **American Indian Movement** (AIM). AIM sometimes used confrontational tactics to draw attention to abuses against American Indians.

In November 1969 AIM members seized control of Alcatraz, an abandoned prison on an island in San Francisco Bay. They offered to buy the island from the government for some beads and cloth—what the Dutch had originally paid American Indians for Manhattan Island. After several months, federal authorities drove the protesters out. The next year AIM members in Plymouth, Massachusetts, seized control of a re-creation of the *Mayflower* during a Thanksgiving Day parade.

Just before the presidential election in 1972, AIM sponsored a march to Washington by Indians from around the country. They called it the "Trail of Broken Treaties," to represent the government's treatment of Indians. At one point a group of the protesters occupied the office of the Bureau of Indian Affairs. They stayed there for days, demanding that the

• Disability Rights Movement

A member of AIM stands guard in front of a church at Wounded Knee, South Dakota, where protesters held off authorities for more than two months.

• American Indian Movement

government address a list of 20 specific points. Protester Mary Crow Dog, of the Lakota (Sioux), recalled a turning point in the protest:

"**For me the high point came . . . [from] Martha Grass, a simple middle-aged Cherokee woman from Oklahoma, standing up to Interior Secretary Morton and giving him a piece of her mind. . . . She talked about everyday things, . . . children's problems, getting down to the nitty-gritty. . . . Morally it had been a great victory. We had faced White America collectively [as a group], not as individual tribes. We had stood up to the government**

One of the greatest concerns of Native American protesters during the 1970s was the extreme poverty that affected many American Indians, like these Navajo children.

and gone through our baptism of fire. We had not run."

In 1973 AIM leader Russell Means led the seizure of a trading post on the Sioux reservation in Wounded Knee, South Dakota—the site of a massacre of Indians by the U.S. Army in 1890. The protesters wanted officials to investigate allegations of corruption in the Bureau of Indian Affairs and to hold hearings on broken treaties of the past. A standoff between the AIM protesters and federal agents lasted 71 days. Two people were killed and one wounded before a compromise was reached.

The Chicano Movement

In addition to the Black Power and Red Power movements, there was also the Brown Power, or **Chicano movement**, among young Mexican Americans. The movement was most widespread among college students, who organized to increase awareness of Hispanic culture and political strength.

The students were inspired by the activism of Hispanic Americans in the 1960s, most notably the Mexican American union activist César Chávez. Like Martin Luther King, Jr., Chávez called for nonviolent protest. During the early 1960s he organized migrant farmworkers in California, most of whom were poor Mexicans and Mexican Americans.

Chávez formed what would eventually become the **United Farm Workers** (UFW). The union focused on improving wages and working conditions for migrant field hands. In 1965 it launched a major campaign against California grape growers. Americans across the country were urged to boycott California grapes. After five years of struggle, the union won its battle with the grape growers. It also launched strikes against other large

The United Farm Workers fought for the rights of laborers like these Mexican field hands who crossed the border to work on California farms.

History Makers

César Chávez (1927–1993)

César Chávez fought for the rights of migrant workers because he had been one himself. His family was originally from Arizona, but they moved so often that Chávez attended nearly 30 different schools before stopping at the seventh grade. He recalled how his family struggled "trying to get enough money to stay alive the following winter, the whole family picking apricots, walnuts, prunes." He also recalled being taken advantage of by those who hired the family.

After serving in the U.S. Navy, Chávez returned to migrant work, then became a labor organizer. He attracted attention to union causes by waging hunger strikes. One of his greatest victories was the passage of the California Agricultural Labor Relations Act of 1975, which, among other things, gave union members the right to use secret ballots in elections.

This mural in Los Angeles celebrates the Chicano movement of the 1970s. The movement sought to give greater political power to the country's growing Hispanic population, which tended to be concentrated in the southwestern states, from Texas to California.

• U.S. Hispanic Population, 1980

agricultural producers who employed migrant workers, such as lettuce growers and citrus growers. The UFW eventually expanded to other areas of the Southwest. It was particularly effective in Texas and Arizona.

These states were centers of activism in the Chicano movement. In January 1970 a group of Chicano activists in Texas organized a Mexican American political party, *La Raza Unida*, "The United People." Since Mexican Americans were becoming a larger part of the overall population, the leaders of *La Raza Unida* felt that having their own party would help them gain political representation.

The purpose of the party was to help register and organize Mexican American voters. The party succeeded in getting many Mexican Americans elected to local offices throughout the Southwest. It also helped to bring national attention to some concerns of the Mexican American community. In 1977 the party successfully lobbied against an immigration bill proposed by President Carter. It also tried to improve relations between the United States and some Latin American countries, such as Cuba and Mexico.

• Changing Population

The Women's Movement Continues

The women's movement also continued in the 1970s. Like the civil rights movement, it experienced some gains as well as setbacks. Some critics blamed the climbing divorce rate on the movement, which encouraged women to seek educations and careers. As more opportunities were opened to them, record numbers of women entered medicine, law, and business. The vast majority of women, however, were still limited to low-paying, low-skilled jobs. Many who were divorced faced severe financial hardships, as the number of poor households headed by women increased. One single mother described the situation she and other women like her faced:

"I work in an office with fifteen fantastic women who are suffering exactly as I am. You want to talk about mad? Everyone of these women is divorced. We come home with a hundred and twenty-three dollars a week. We don't even know how we are going to eat . . . how the kids are going to be fed."

Leaders of the women's movement argued that economic improvements would come only when women had equal rights. The National Organization for Women and other feminist groups thus tried to win passage of an **Equal Rights Amendment** (ERA), which stated: "Equality of rights shall not be denied or abridged [decreased] by the United States or by any state on account of sex."

Congress passed the ERA in 1972. At first, most observers thought the amendment would easily win support from the 38 states needed for ratification. Opponents, however, waged a heated campaign against ratification. Critics of the amendment claimed that it would abolish all distinctions based on gender. Women would have to be drafted into the military, they argued. They would even have to share public restrooms with men! The simple language of the amendment helped make it an easy target for attack, since it might be interpreted many different ways once it became part of the Constitution.

Supporters had 10 years to win the states needed to ratify the ERA. By 1982 they were still short. When the amendment died, one of its most vocal opponents, conservative activist Phyllis Schlafly, declared its failure "the greatest victory for women's rights since the women's suffrage movement."

Opposition to the ERA was part of a larger reaction against the women's movement, which was increasingly accused by critics of being antifamily. Such criticism increased after the Supreme Court handed down a controversial decision in the 1973 case of *Roe* v. *Wade*. The Court said that states could not limit women's access to abortion during the first three months of pregnancy. Many feminists hailed the decision as a show of support for women's rights. Critics argued that it violated the "right to life" of the unborn. *Roe* v. *Wade* touched off a political battle that would rage for many years to come.

New York congresswoman Shirley Chisholm became the first African American woman to run for president when she sought the Democratic nomination in 1972.

Section 4 Review

• **Glossary**

IDENTIFY and explain the significance of the following: busing, affirmative action, *University of California* v. *Bakke*, quota system, American Indian Movement, Russell Means, Chicano movement, César Chávez, United Farm Workers, *La Raza Unida*, Equal Rights Amendment

• **Time Line**

REVIEWING FOR DETAILS

1. Which civil rights practices caused the most controversy in the 1970s?
2. How did civil rights groups try to gain more rights in the 1970s?
3. Why did the ERA fail to win ratification?

REVIEWING FOR UNDERSTANDING

4. **Writing Mastery:** *Creating* Create a poster attracting attention to the Chicano movement or to a United Farm Workers rally.
5. **Critical Thinking:** *Recognizing Point of View* Would you describe the failure of the ERA as a defeat or a victory for the women's rights movement? Explain your answer.

CHAPTER 29

Republicans in Power

(1981–1993)

THEMES IN AMERICAN HISTORY

Constitutional Heritage:
How might a president use the power of appointment to shape public affairs?

Economic Development:
How might a government alter the public's economic behavior?

Global Relations:
How might internal changes affect a nation's foreign relations?

• Video Opener

• Skill Builder

*O*ne television commentator welcomed Ronald Reagan's inauguration and the 1980s as a new chance for a tired nation. "After 20 years of pessimism, after assassinations, Vietnam and Watergate, at last, the burden was off our backs," the commentator cheered. "It was America Reborn, a New America, America All the Way!" Americans waited to see if the decade ahead would live up to these exciting, promising words.

image above: *President and Nancy Reagan*

Section 1

THE REAGAN PRESIDENCY AT HOME

Multimedia Connections

Explore these related topics and materials on the CD–ROM to enrich your understanding of this section:

 Media Bank

- Protest of Reagan's Policies

 Profiles

- Ronald Reagan
- Geraldine Ferraro
- Sandra Day O'Connor

 Gazetteer

- Iran

The people of New York City welcomed the cool, windy weather on the first weekend of July 1986. What's more, it was the hundredth anniversary of the Statue of Liberty! Thousands of Americans gathered in New York to celebrate, and President Reagan was a good host. In one photograph of the party, a spray of background fireworks lit up his smiling face. "[He] has a genius for American occasions," one journalist commented.

As you read this section you will find out:

▶ **What effects the Iran hostage crisis had on America.**

▶ **What President Reagan's approach to government was.**

▶ **How supply-side economics worked in practice.**

The Election of 1980

As the election of 1980 approached, President Jimmy Carter's popularity fell to an all-time low. One poll showed that just 21 percent of Americans approved of his performance in office. The public objected to the steep inflation rate, which rose to more than 13 percent in 1979, and in particular to the high cost of petroleum products like gasoline and heating oil. Americans also came to question Carter's handling of a dangerous situation in Iran.

The Iran hostage crisis. In 1979 Muslim revolutionaries toppled Iran's government and forced the country's shah, or king, to step down. These events alarmed U.S. officials, who regarded Iran as strategically important and who had supported the shah despite charges of his brutality toward his own people.

The Americans taken hostage in Tehran began their 444-day ordeal by being blindfolded and forced to march past a line of their Iranian captors.

Several months after fleeing Iran, the shah asked for permission to enter the United States to receive cancer treatment. Carter agreed despite strong objections from the new Iranian government.

In November 1979 a mob in Tehran, the capital of Iran, invaded the U.S. Embassy and took 53 people hostage to protest Carter's decision. The captors demanded that the United States turn over the shah, but Carter refused to do so. A standoff resulted, and the **Iran hostage crisis** dragged on for months.

As pressure for action mounted, Carter ordered a team of U.S. military commandos to fly into Iran by helicopter at night and try to rescue the hostages. The mission was called off, however, because several of the aircraft involved collided, killing eight servicemen. The hostage crisis continued.

The election. In the midst of the Iran hostage crisis, Carter won the 1980 Democratic presidential nomination. The Republicans nominated the popular former governor of California, Ronald Reagan, for president. During the campaign, Reagan took advantage of the poor state of the economy and Carter's failure to free the captives in Iran. Reagan also put forward a very powerful and popular message. He pledged to help America "stand tall" again by increasing military spending, slashing taxes, cutting back on government activity, and promoting conservative values.

Voters responded to Reagan's campaign mes-

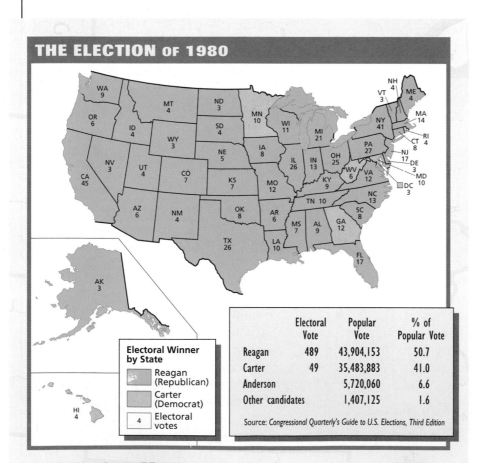

THE ELECTION OF 1980

	Electoral Vote	Popular Vote	% of Popular Vote
Reagan	489	43,904,153	50.7
Carter	49	35,483,883	41.0
Anderson		5,720,060	6.6
Other candidates		1,407,125	1.6

Source: *Congressional Quarterly's Guide to U.S. Elections, Third Edition*

Electoral Winner by State
- Reagan (Republican)
- Carter (Democrat)
- 4 Electoral votes

Learning from Maps.
Ronald Reagan swept the election of 1980.

▶ **Region.** Which state did Reagan lose in the Lower South, and how many electoral votes did it cost him?

• Maps

sage by giving him a sweeping victory—
43.9 million popular votes to Carter's 35.5 million. The Republican Party also made large gains in both houses of Congress and took control of the Senate. Many Americans had made it clear that they were ready for a change.

On January 20, 1981 Reagan took the oath of office as president. Later that same day, he announced that the Iranians had freed the American hostages. After 444 days of imprisonment in Iran, the hostages came home. Bill Belk, an American hostage, described the captives' endless days of boredom and fear:

> **"Our nerves were frayed. We were sick and tired of being hostages. We kept hoping and hoping that we'd be released, but we were still sitting there. Because of that, the degree of frustration was intense. . . . Ahmed [a guard] kept telling me, 'No one is writing to you. Your wife is not writing to you.' I knew that was [a lie], but in the prison I think there were times when all of us felt like we'd been left there and forgotten."**

Reagan Takes Office

President Reagan's victory reflected the growing power of the **New Right**, a loose organization of social and political conservatives. The New Right received much of its support from white Christians who objected to the liberal policies of the 1960s and 1970s.

Members of the New Right opposed the Equal Rights Amendment, abortion, and the use of busing to integrate public schools. They supported prayer in public schools, a smaller federal government, and "family values." They supported Reagan, convinced that he could change the course of American politics.

Reagan came into office with a simple formula for revitalizing America: he wanted to scale back

the role of the federal government while increasing the role of the private sector. Like many in the New Right, he believed that the federal government was too big and too deeply involved in everyday life. He said in his inaugural address, "In this present crisis, government is not the solution to our problems; government is the problem."

Supply-side economics in theory. Reagan wanted to reduce taxes. He also hoped to balance the federal budget and to increase military spending—aims that required huge amounts of money. To accomplish both objectives, he relied on **supply-side economics**, a complex theory that suggests that lower tax rates will lead to economic growth.

Reagan and his advisers argued that if taxes went down, Americans would invest the money they saved in new business enterprises or spend it on new consumer goods. This would cause the economy to boom. More jobs would be created, and business profits would rise. Tax revenues might go up even though tax rates were lower. Reagan hoped that such increased revenues would, at the same time, support higher military spending. He cut back

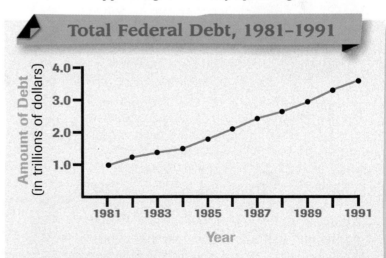

Total Federal Debt, 1981–1991

Source: *Statistical Abstract of the United States*

A Growing Problem. Though President Reagan pledged to balance the federal budget, the total federal debt increased drastically during his time in office. How much did the federal debt rise from 1984 to 1988?

• **Graphs**

some social welfare programs to save money and removed government regulations on many industries to encourage growth.

Democratic leaders in Congress opposed Reagan's programs, but did not have enough votes to block them. By summer 1981 both the Reagan budget and bills drastically reducing federal income taxes had passed Congress.

An assassination attempt. Just months after Reagan took office, a would-be assassin shot the president in the chest. Reagan showed great courage as well as a sense of humor in the face of near death. When he went into the operating room, he said to the doctors, "Please assure me that you are all Republicans." When his wife, Nancy, arrived at his side, he told her, "Honey, I forgot to duck." Fortunately, Reagan recovered quickly.

Supply-side economics in practice. Supply-side economics did not seem to work as well in practice as it did in theory. By Reagan's second year in office, the nation's economic slump had become the worst since the Great Depression. Unemployment rose to more than 10 percent. With tax revenues down and the government still spending huge amounts of money, the deficit—the amount of money borrowed by the federal government each year—went up to around $200 billion in 1983. Cuts in social programs also left many poorer Americans with less support.

Frank Lumpkin, an unemployed African American steelworker, described the effects of the country's economic problems in human terms:

> **"If Reagan thinks he's gonna roll the country back to the old days, he better think again. I see the spirit among the people. . . . There's no way the people is gonna be taken back to where they were before."**

Lumpkin formed a "Save Our Jobs" committee to distribute food and to work for full employment. As the recession continued, other similar groups sprang up around the country.

The Reagan "Revolution"

Despite this economic decline, President Reagan remained extremely popular. After the economy began to recover in the third year of his presidency, he seemed a sure bet to be

Presidential Lives

Ronald Reagan

Before entering politics in the 1960s, Ronald Reagan had a long career as a movie actor. Some Americans argued that he did not have the experience to run for political office. Reagan reacted to such charges with humor, ignoring his critics and revealing his generous nature. When someone once showed him a picture from his 1951 film *Bedtime with Bonzo,* in which he costarred with a chimpanzee, Reagan laughed and said, "I'm the one with the watch." When a reporter asked him whom his wife would pick as president, he brushed the question away with, "She's going to vote for some former actor."

Reagan was very serious, however, on the subject of politics and the state of the nation. "When I was announcing sports I was happy and thought that was all I wanted out of life," he remembered. "Then came the chance at Hollywood and that was even better." But public service gave him an unmatched opportunity to make a difference. "Now I'm doing something that makes everything else I've done seem dull as dishwater."

re-elected in 1984. He waged an effective campaign against Demo- crat Walter Mondale and won by a landslide.

• **Election of 1984**

During his second term, Reagan continued to cut government domestic spending. Congress decreased taxes still further. The **Income Tax Act of 1986** relieved most low-income people from all income taxes and reduced the maximum rate as well.

Hoping to ease the burden caused by the federal deficit, Congress passed the **Gramm-Rudman-Hollings Act** in 1985. This law required spending cuts when the deficit went above a certain amount. It did not apply to the earlier deficits, however, and the total national debt continued to rise.

The president also tried to appoint as many conservatives as possible to public office. He particularly hoped to achieve a long-lasting conservative majority on the Supreme Court. In 1981 Reagan appointed conservative judge Sandra Day O'Connor as the first female Supreme Court justice.

When Chief Justice Warren Burger retired in 1986, Reagan nominated Justice William Rehnquist, a strong conservative, to replace him. Reagan then appointed Antonin Scalia, also a conservative, to fill the vacancy. When another seat opened the next year, Reagan nominated Robert H. Bork, a judge whose statements in the past had raised so much controversy that the Senate refused to confirm him. The Senate then approved the more moderate Anthony Kennedy. The Supreme Court proceeded to hand down a series of conservative decisions.

The attempt on President Reagan's life, which also critically injured Press Secretary James Brady, shocked the country. The gunman, John Hinckley, Jr., was sent to a mental institution after being declared unfit to stand trial.

Section 1 Review

• **Glossary**

IDENTIFY and explain the significance of the following: Iran hostage crisis, Ronald Reagan, New Right, supply-side economics, Walter Mondale, Income Tax Act of 1986, Gramm-Rudman-Hollings Act

REVIEWING FOR DETAILS

1. How did the Iran hostage crisis affect America?
2. What were Ronald Reagan's beliefs about how government should work?
3. What was supply-side economics, and what were its results in practice?

REVIEWING FOR UNDERSTANDING

4. **Writing Mastery:** *Expressing* Imagine that you are an observer at a Reagan election rally. Write a letter to a friend expressing the mood of the rally.

5. **Critical Thinking:** *Determining the Strength of an Argument* Why might a person argue that Reagan's appointments to the Supreme Court were among his most important actions as president?

Section 2

THE REAGAN PRESIDENCY ABROAD

Multimedia Connections

Explore these related topics and materials on the CD–ROM to enrich your understanding of this section:

 Media Bank

- Dismantling Nuclear Weapons
- Beirut
- American Invasion of Grenada

 Readings

- World Terrorism

 Profiles

- Oliver North

 Gazetteer

- Nicaragua
- Grenada
- Lebanon

Senator Daniel Inouye of Hawaii watched the White House press conference with concern. In the early 1970s he had played an important role in the Watergate hearings. Now he heard President Ronald Reagan admitting that he had not been "fully informed" of his administration's actions with respect to Iran. Inouye remembered that afterward "I reached the conclusion that uh-oh, here we go again." What would come of the so-called "Iran-contra scandal?"

As you read this section you will find out:

▶ **How Reagan pursued foreign policy in Central America and the Caribbean.**

▶ **What happened in the Iran-contra affair.**

▶ **How changes in the Soviet Union affected U.S.-Soviet relations.**

Reagan and the Cold War

President Reagan took an aggressive position in the Cold War. His emphasis on military spending reflected his belief that the United States needed a stronger defense against the Soviets. He believed that the Soviet Union was an "evil empire" out to dominate the world. The Soviets would restrain themselves only if they feared U.S. military power, the president insisted.

Hoping to counteract the Soviet Union, Reagan continued to support high levels of military spending. He also urged Congress to build the **Strategic Defense Initiative** (SDI), an advanced space-based system designed to destroy incoming missiles before they could reach the United States.

SDI became very controversial. Many scientists predicted that it would not work and even

Although President Reagan had great confidence that SDI technology would help America in the Cold War, others had their doubts, as this cartoon shows.

tary experts, however, regarded it as the ultimate defense against nuclear war, and the leaders of the Soviet Union were very concerned about the possibility of SDI's completion.

Central America and the Caribbean

President Reagan also hoped to prevent Soviet expansion by fighting communism around the world. Insisting that the Soviet Union supported terrorists and violence overseas, he

called it "Star Wars" after the popular science fiction movie. Other observers thought SDI was simply too expensive given America's economic problems. Reagan, as well as other mili-

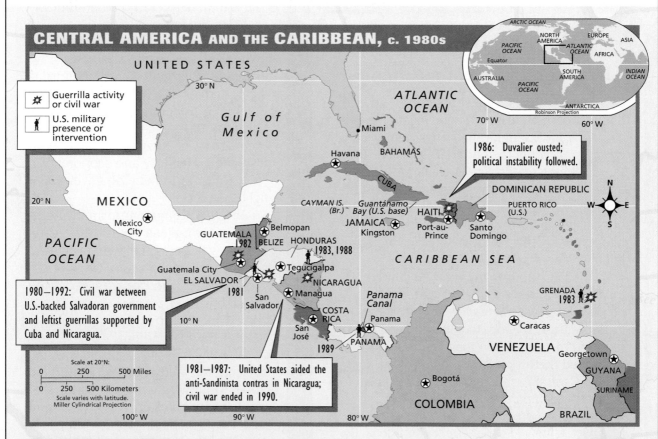

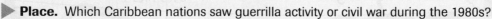

Learning from Maps. The United States sent troops or otherwise intervened in Central America and the Caribbean several times during the 1980s.

▶ **Place.** Which Caribbean nations saw guerrilla activity or civil war during the 1980s?

• Maps

Contra rebels prepared to fight against the Sandinista government in Nicaragua, even after a UN peace-keeping force asked them to disarm.

described the need for the United States to step up its involvement:

> **"Today, our national security can be threatened in faraway places. It's up to all of us to be aware of the strategic importance of such places and to be able to identify them."**

Reagan took a hard line against potential Soviet activity in Central America and the Caribbean.

Global Connections
Democracy in Latin America

Latin America was a focal point for Cold War battles in the 1980s. For years, most of the countries in the region had been controlled by military dictators supported by either the United States or the Soviet Union. Most of these dictators were known to abuse the rights of their own citizens. Throughout the 1980s human rights organizations like Amnesty International drew attention to cases of abuse in Latin America.

By the late 1980s many Latin American countries began to replace their dictators with democratic governments. Central American leaders started to work together to find ways of reducing the violence in their countries. In 1987 the United States joined with most of the countries of Central America in supporting a plan for peace and democracy in Latin America. The sponsor of the proposal, Oscar Arias of Costa Rica, won a Nobel Peace Prize for his efforts. By 1990 all but three Latin American countries—Cuba, Paraguay, and Panama—had replaced their military dictators with civilian leaders.

Nicaragua. In the late 1970s a group of Nicaraguan revolutionaries known as the **Sandinistas** overturned the country's long-standing dictatorship, which had been supported by the United States. The Sandinistas set up a communist-style government friendly to the Soviet Union. Reagan strongly disapproved of the new Sandinista government. Charging that Sandinistas supported leftist rebel forces opposing the ruling government in nearby El Salvador, Reagan cut off all U.S. aid to Nicaragua. The Reagan administration also offered military and economic aid to El Salvador to help the government fight the rebels.

In 1981 Reagan informed members of Congress that the United States was providing weapons and other supplies to rebel Nicaraguan groups called the **contras** (from the Spanish *contra*, meaning "against") who wanted to overthrow the ruling Sandinista government.

Funding for the contras was the subject of heated debate in the United States. Many Americans feared that military intervention in Nicaragua might lead to "another Vietnam." In 1984 Congress moved to limit aid to the contras by passing the **Boland Amendment**, which banned such aid in the future.

Grenada At the same time U.S. aid was flowing to the contras, the United States became involved in a conflict in the Caribbean. In 1983 rebels on the tiny island of Grenada overthrew the national government and killed the prime minister. Reagan thought this group might establish a communist government and seek help from the Soviet Union and Cuba. He also feared for the safety of nearly 800 American medical students on the island.

After several Caribbean nations asked for help from the United States, Reagan decided to invade Grenada. In October 1983, U.S. troops landed on the island. After two days of fighting, the revolutionaries surrendered, and a pro-U.S. government was established in Grenada.

The Iran-Contra Affair

Though militarily successful in Grenada, Reagan soon faced problems connected to the fight against communism in Nicaragua. Since the Boland Amendment banned aid to the contras, the Reagan administration looked for other ways to help the revolutionaries. Marine Lieutenant Colonel Oliver North, a member of the White House national security staff, was given the job of persuading foreign countries and wealthy individuals to contribute money for the contras.

At the same time, U.S. diplomats were trying to negotiate the release of American hostages held in Lebanon by pro-Iranian terrorists. Reagan desperately wanted to win release for the prisoners. In 1986, despite his dislike of bargaining with terrorists, he authorized the secret sale of arms to Iran. He expected that the hostages in Lebanon would be freed in exchange.

Colonel North arranged the arms deal with Iran. He then used the profits of the sale to purchase arms for the Nicaraguan contras. This was illegal because of the Boland Amendment.

Foreign journalists discovered the **Iran-contra affair** in late 1986 and exposed it to the public. Committees established to investigate the incident could not determine whether Reagan knew about the contra aid. Because of the information that came to light in the hearings, North and Admiral John Poindexter, Reagan's national security adviser, were forced to resign.

U.S.-Soviet Relations

The main foreign policy achievement of Reagan's second term in office was the dramatic improvement in U.S.-Soviet relations. When Mikhail Gorbachev became Soviet premier in March 1985, he inherited a nation with severe economic problems and underlying political tensions. He soon realized that the Soviet Union needed drastic internal changes to survive.

Gorbachev established a new policy of **glasnost**, or political openness. He urged the Soviet people to discuss public issues and even criticize government actions. He also instituted **perestroika**, or a massive restructuring of the Soviet government and economy. As part of perestroika, Gorbachev encouraged individual enterprise, cut military spending, and increased foreign trade.

Gorbachev hoped to bring a spirit of relaxation and cooperation to international relations. Though initially somewhat suspicious, Reagan responded favorably, and the Cold War began to thaw. This monumental shift forced many Americans to reconsider their attitudes toward the Soviets.

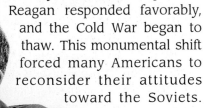

Although Lieutenant Colonel Oliver North broke the law by arranging the Iran-contra affair, many Americans considered him a hero.

(left to right) Nancy Reagan, Ronald Reagan, former Soviet premier Mikhail Gorbachev, and his wife, Raisa, relax at the Reagan's California home in 1992. President Reagan's friendship with Gorbachev during and after their time in office surprised many people, since Reagan had been a longtime enemy of the Soviet Union.

Jean Gump, who had lived through the difficult times of the Cold War, described her feelings:

"Through these years, I found out there's a lot of people that I have to hate. . . . I had to hate the Vietnamese people. I had to hate the commies. . . . But I don't think they're my enemies. I think, God help me, these are people. . . . You know, I have never been so hopeful. If I can change my way of thinking, anybody can."

At a summit meeting in 1987 Reagan and Gorbachev signed the **Intermediate-range Nuclear Forces Treaty** (INF Treaty), in which both sides agreed to completely eliminate medium-range nuclear missiles in Europe. This was a major step toward reducing the possibility and danger of nuclear war between the two superpowers.

Section 2 Review

• Glossary

IDENTIFY and explain the significance of the following: Strategic Defense Initiative, Sandinistas, contras, Boland Amendment, Oliver North, Iran-contra affair, Mikhail Gorbachev, glasnost, perestroika, Intermediate-range Nuclear Forces Treaty

REVIEWING FOR DETAILS
1. Why was the Iran-contra affair a political scandal?
2. How did the United States respond to changes in the Soviet Union?

REVIEWING FOR UNDERSTANDING
3. **Geographic Literacy** Why do you think that President Reagan was so concerned about the spread of communism in Central America and the Caribbean? What did he do to counter this spread?
4. **Writing Mastery:** *Expressing* Imagine that you are a student during Reagan's second term in office. Write a letter to a friend expression your opinion about the thaw in Cold War tensions.
5. **Critical Thinking:** *Drawing Conclusions* Why do you think so many people were concerned about the Reagan administration selling arms to the contras?

Section 3

BUSH'S "NEW WORLD ORDER"

Multimedia Connections

Explore these related topics and materials on the CD–ROM to enrich your understanding of this section:

 Profiles

- Norman Schwarzkopf

 Gazetteer

- Panama

 Media Bank

- Berlin Wall
- U.S. Crime Rate, 1980–1992
- Manuel Noriega
- Boris Yeltsin
- Desert Storm Commanders
- Operation Desert Storm

 Atlas

- Conflicts in the Middle East
- Breakup of the Soviet Sphere

President George Bush stepped into the House of Representatives. Acknowledging the cheers for the successful outcome of the Persian Gulf War, Bush described his vision of international relations. Quoting the words of Winston Churchill, he told the crowd, "'the principles of justice and fair play . . . protect the weak against the strong,'" and offered the chance for "freedom and respect for human rights [to] find a home among all nations."

As you read this section you will find out:

▶ **How the candidates conducted the 1988 presidential campaign.**

▶ **How communism collapsed in the Soviet Union and Eastern Europe.**

▶ **How the Persian Gulf War differed from previous military conflicts.**

The Election of 1988

The presidential election of 1988 was wide open. Hoping to ride Reagan's appeal, the Republicans nominated Vice President George Bush as their candidate. Bush pledged to more or less continue Reagan's policies if elected.

Democratic candidates saw the election as a chance to seize the presidency, and many candidates battled for the Democratic nomination. The field eventually shrank to two—Reverend Jesse Jackson, an African-American leader, and Governor Michael Dukakis of Massachusetts. Despite Jackson's strong showing in early primaries, Dukakis had a majority of the delegates at the convention and won the nomination.

The Democrats hoped to take advantage of the Iran-contra affair. As the race heated up, negative campaign advertisements became

Reverend Jesse Jackson hoped to draw what he called a "Rainbow Coalition" of voters in the 1988 election.

• Jesse Jackson

more common. Bush and Dukakis appeared to not disagree much about really important issues. Yet Bush's campaigning proved more successful. On election day Bush won easily, carrying the electoral college by 426 votes to Dukakis's 112.

Foreign Affairs

President Bush had a long history of service in foreign affairs, including having served as ambassador to China and as head of the Central Intelligence Agency. Not surprisingly, he concentrated heavily on international relations during his administration.

Latin America. Shortly after he took office, Bush announced the beginning of a **War on Drugs**—a comprehensive effort at home and abroad to eliminate the production and use of illegal narcotics. In some South and Central American nations, drug dealers influenced or controlled the governments, making it difficult for U.S. officials to stop the flow of drugs into the United States.

For example, Manuel Noriega, a military dictator and well-known ally of local drug lords, ruled Panama. In late 1989 a U.S. court indicted him on narcotics charges. After Noriega refused to come to the United States to stand trial, Bush ordered U.S. troops to invade Panama. They captured Noriega, but many Panamanians and some American soldiers were killed in the fighting.

The end of the Cold War. As during Reagan's administration, changes within the Soviet Union continued to affect the Cold War while Bush was in office. Encouraged by Gorbachev's liberal policies, the countries of Eastern Europe—Poland, East Germany, Czechoslovakia, Hungary, Romania, and Bulgaria—overthrew their communist leaders. This left what Czech leader Vaclav Havel called "a legacy of countless dead, an infinite spectrum [scale] of human suffering, profound [serious] economic decline and, above all, enormous human humiliation."

Even republics of the Soviet Union, such as Lithuania and Azerbaijan, demanded independence. In November 1989 East and West Germans continued the move toward political freedom by tearing down the Berlin Wall, a longtime symbol of the Cold War. East and West Germany were officially reunified in October 1990.

As communist rule continued to break down throughout Eastern Europe, the Soviet Union kept democratizing its own political system as well. In mid-1991 the Central Committee of the Soviet Union called for a national popular presidential election and announced that the Communist Party would no longer be the only legal political party. In August 1991

President George Bush and his wife, Barbara, wave to supporters at a gathering in their hometown of Houston, Texas.

• George Bush

hard-line Communists in the Soviet Union tried to seize power by arresting Gorbachev. After several tense days their coup failed and they were arrested.

By the end of the year, Ukraine, Belorussia, and Russia had broken away from the old Soviet Union and formed a loose federation called the **Commonwealth of Independent States** (CIS). Other Soviet republics eventually followed, and the Soviet Union itself ceased to exist. Boris Yeltsin, the president of Russia who had courageously defied the hard-liners during the coup, emerged as the leader of the CIS. President Bush declared that "a New World Order" had now emerged.

The Persian Gulf War

At the same time that Eastern European countries were rejecting communism, trouble broke out in the Middle East. In August 1990 Iraqi leader Saddam Hussein ordered his powerful army to invade and occupy Kuwait, Iraq's tiny but oil-rich neighbor. This aggression led the United Nations—encouraged by the United States—to impose an international ban on trade with Iraq. The UN later set a January 15, 1991, deadline for Iraq to withdraw its troops from Kuwait.

The fall of the Berlin Wall marked a turning point in the Cold War, followed by the rapid fall of many communist governments in Eastern Europe.

Refusal. As Iraq ignored the demand of the United Nations and the United States, the leaders of some surrounding Middle Eastern countries became very nervous. At the invitation of Saudi Arabia, which Iraq also threatened to attack, the United States and several other nations sent military forces to the area. The United States was determined to prevent Iraq from seizing any more Middle Eastern oil. Bush addressed the people and Congress:

"I ask for your support in a decision I've made to stand up for what's right and condemn what's wrong—all in the cause of peace. . . . If history teaches us anything, it is that we must resist aggression or it will destroy our freedoms."

Conflict. After the January 15 deadline passed with no action by Iraq, the UN forces launched their attack, which was called **Operation Desert Storm**. The UN force, led by U.S. Army general Norman Schwarzkopf, numbered around 690,000 soldiers, including about 540,000 Americans. For six weeks bombs and guided missiles rained down on Iraqi targets. On February 23, when Saddam still refused to surrender, ground troops swept into Kuwait and Iraq. In just a few days the UN forces soundly defeated Iraq's army and liberated Kuwait from Iraqi control. After feeling the full force of the

UN attack, Saddam agreed to UN terms. These included the payment of reparations to Kuwait and removal of all claims to Kuwaiti territory. The Persian Gulf War had carried a high human cost—more than 100,000 Iraqis as well as some 140 UN troops died in the conflict.

The overwhelming defeat of Saddam's forces did not lead to his overthrow, however. He used what was left of his army to crush his opponents within Iraq and refused to follow many of the terms of the peace agreement.

Critics in the United States argued that the UN army should have used its victory as an opportunity to capture the capital city of Baghdad and overthrow Saddam.

A unique war. The Persian Gulf War differed from other military conflicts in its weaponry and its soldiers. The UN army relied on high-tech devices like computer-controlled missiles and stealth bombers, which were almost impossible to track on radar.

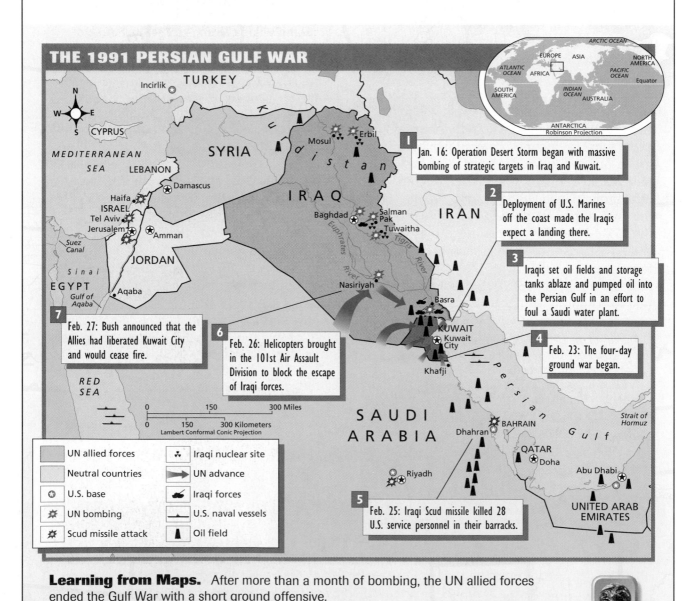

THE 1991 PERSIAN GULF WAR

1 Jan. 16: Operation Desert Storm began with massive bombing of strategic targets in Iraq and Kuwait.

2 Deployment of U.S. Marines off the coast made the Iraqis expect a landing there.

3 Iraqis set oil fields and storage tanks ablaze and pumped oil into the Persian Gulf in an effort to foul a Saudi water plant.

4 Feb. 23: The four-day ground war began.

5 Feb. 25: Iraqi Scud missile killed 28 U.S. service personnel in their barracks.

6 Feb. 26: Helicopters brought in the 101st Air Assault Division to block the escape of Iraqi forces.

7 Feb. 27: Bush announced that the Allies had liberated Kuwait City and would cease fire.

Legend:
- UN allied forces
- Neutral countries
- U.S. base
- UN bombing
- Scud missile attack
- Iraqi nuclear site
- UN advance
- Iraqi forces
- U.S. naval vessels
- Oil field

0 150 300 Miles
0 150 300 Kilometers
Lambert Conformal Conic Projection

Learning from Maps. After more than a month of bombing, the UN allied forces ended the Gulf War with a short ground offensive.

▶ **Movement.** From which country did most of the UN allied troops advance during the ground war?

• Maps

Woman's participation in the Persian Gulf War increased debates about female soldiers serving in combat.

• **Gulf War**

The increasing use of female soldiers sparked intense controversy in the United States. Many Americans thought that women should not be directly involved in warfare. Others disagreed. Rhonda Cornum, a medical officer in the war, argued that women should have access to all combat positions:

"**The war showed that America is ready for Army women, all of whom volunteered, to serve throughout the Army and not be excluded from combat jobs. . . . As a female soldier, I would resent being excluded [from combat]. We preach 'equal opportunity' everywhere. I believe we should also be preaching 'equal responsibility.'** "

The war also saw a larger deployment of female troops than in any previous U.S. war. Nearly 6 percent of the U.S. soldiers were women. Though barred from service in most combat positions, female soldiers performed countless other important tasks, such as serving as doctors, nurses, pilots, mechanics, and truck drivers.

After months of debate, Congress passed a measure that allowed women to serve as military combat pilots.

• **Women in the Military**

Section 3 Review

• **Glossary**

IDENTIFY and explain the significance of the following: George Bush, Jesse Jackson, Michael Dukakis, War on Drugs, Manuel Noriega, Commonwealth of Independent States, Saddam Hussein, Operation Desert Storm, Norman Schwarzkopf

• **Gazetteer**

LOCATE and explain the importance of the following: Iraq, Kuwait, Saudi Arabia

REVIEWING FOR DETAILS

1. How would you describe the 1988 presidential campaign?
2. How did governments in Eastern Europe and the Soviet Union change in the late 1980s and early 1990s?

REVIEWING FOR UNDERSTANDING

3. **Geographic Literacy** How did the collapse of communism change the political boundaries of the Soviet Union?
4. **Writing Mastery:** *Describing* Imagine that you are a U.S. soldier fighting in the Persian Gulf War. Write several diary entries describing your experiences and explain how the war differs from previous conflicts.
5. **Critical Thinking:** *Synthesizing Information* To what extent did President Bush carry on Reagan's foreign policies? How did Bush's policies differ?

Section 4

AMERICA DURING THE 1980s

Multimedia Connections

Explore these related topics and materials on the CD–ROM to enrich your understanding of this section:

 Biographies

- Betty Ford

 Media Bank

- Quilt
- AIDS Cases, 1984–1993
- Stock Market Crash of 1987
- Living Below the Poverty Level
- Homeless in America

 Readings

- Ryan White
- *What For*

O n Friday nights throughout the 1980s, millions of Americans gathered in front of their television sets for a weekly ritual of dreaming. *Dallas* was on, and nearly everyone was watching! The program followed a wealthy Texas oil family and hinted at the values many people held in the decade—money, ambition, and work. A journalist explained the show's effect: "It makes people think that money and material wealth are the only ways to be rich in this world."

As you read this section you will find out:

▶ **What values many Americans held during the 1980s.**

▶ **What technological advances and setbacks unfolded in the 1980s.**

▶ **What challenges President Bush faced in his domestic policies.**

Changes in American Society

The growing gap between the rich and the poor became alarmingly clear in the 1980s. During the decade, the wealthiest 20 percent of the population saw a 19 percent increase in their incomes, while the poorest 20 percent of Americans saw a 9 percent drop. As one segment of American society grew more wealthy, many people seemed to put a greater emphasis on making money and buying things. This caused some observers to label the 1980s a "decade of greed."

A group known as **yuppies**—short for "young urban professionals"—symbolized this social trend. Yuppies earned good money and pursued luxurious lifestyles. Critics called them selfish, more concerned with getting rich than helping others. Despite these charges, yuppies fascinated some Americans during the 1980s. Countless novels, articles, and movies described their lives.

Some Americans used illegal or at least shady means to succeed in their frantic race for wealth. The stock and bond market offered many questionable opportunities to get rich quickly. During the 1980s, thousands of people went to work on Wall Street, hoping to make a financial "killing." Most stockbrokers relied on skill and good luck in their search for wealth. Others indulged in **insider trading**, or the unlawful use of confidential information for personal gain. Many racked up enormous fortunes and showed off their earnings, buying fancy houses and traveling in limousines or private airplanes.

In the mid-1980s a government commission investigated the financial industry and insider trading. A number of stockbrokers and firms pleaded guilty to charges of wrongdoing. Some paid heavy fines; others served jail terms. As news of widespread insider trading broke, Americans began to question the value their society placed on wealth. One young woman offered her opinion: "This craziness of . . . people bending the rules and going to jail shows what happens when you let the greed factor take over."

Wall Street received another blow in October 1987, when the stock market crashed after months of steady growth. Losses totaled nearly half a trillion dollars in "paper" values.

Throughout the decade, the poorest segment of America's population faced tough challenges. Although the number of jobs increased overall during the 1980s, more than half the new positions were in low-paying service occupations. These jobs usually did not pay enough to lift families above the poverty line. Well-paid manufacturing jobs, like those in steel and auto plants, began to disappear.

Given these and other trends, the number of poor Americans steadily increased during the 1980s. By 1990, over 33 million people lived below the poverty line. African Americans, Hispanic Americans, and children were the groups hardest hit. As a result of poverty, homelessness also increased.

Technological Advances and Setbacks

The 1980s witnessed an explosion of new technologies in many fields, such as medicine, computers, and electronics. Along with these advances, however, came a number of disappointing setbacks.

New medical technologies. Many new medical discoveries helped fight diseases. By the late 1980s, for example, extensive research had resulted in lower death rates for certain kinds of cancer.

Genetic discoveries also opened the door to controversial new medical treatments. In 1953 a team of American and British scientists had discovered the structure of deoxyribonucleic

Many Americans like these protesters were upset with economic developments in the 1980s that hurt the poorest workers.

acid (DNA). DNA is made up of **genes**, the tiny segments of chromosomes that determine all of the body's physical characteristics.

In the late 1980s scientists began to use genetic engineering to alter DNA structure and change physical characteristics of plant and animal life. This process had important medical applications, offering the possibility of building new compounds that could help in the war against illness. Many people objected to this sort of genetic tampering, however.

Genetic engineers like this scientist hoped their work would unlock the secrets to fighting serious medical conditions.

Medical challenges. Modern technology did not hold the solution to solving some of the world's most serious health problems. In the early 1980s doctors and scientists became aware of a deadly new disease. They labeled it **Acquired Immune Deficiency Syndrome**, or AIDS, because it destroys the body's capability to ward off illnesses and infections. AIDS nearly always led to death. Later research revealed that it was caused by a virus, which they called the **human immunodeficiency virus**, or HIV.

Reported cases of HIV infection rose dramatically during the 1980s. In the United States alone, the number of people with HIV jumped from some 50,000 in 1987 to more than 150,000 in 1990. Global infection rates kept a similar pace. Scientists have not yet found a cure for the disease, though new medicines have helped with its symptoms.

The *Challenger*. One of the worst technological disasters of the 1980s occurred in the field of space exploration. The incident took place in February 1986, when NASA launched the space shuttle *Challenger*. Shortly after liftoff, the shuttle exploded. All seven crew members on board, including social studies teacher Christa McAuliffe, were killed. The *Challenger* explosion was the most serious disaster ever suffered by the U.S. space program.

Domestic Issues Under Bush

The gap between rich and poor and the concern over new diseases were not the only issues that troubled Americans in the 1980s and early 1990s. Other domestic political and economic events during George Bush's presidency claimed national attention as well.

President Bush largely concentrated his time in office on foreign relations, leading some to criticize him for neglecting affairs at home. He opposed many new domestic proposals. One significant measure Bush did approve was the **Americans with Disabilities Act**, which prohibited discrimination against people with mental or physical disabilities.

The Thomas-Hill hearing. Like Reagan, Bush tried to appoint as many conservative judges as possible to the federal courts. When a vacancy opened on the Supreme Court in 1990, he selected New Hampshire judge, David Souter. He was not well known, but Souter's appointment did not cause controversy.

Supporters of the Americans with Disabilities Act were upset with many of the barriers placed before people with special physical needs.

©55 David Pollack

This was not the case just a year later when another seat on the Court became open. Bush nominated Clarence Thomas, an African American judge who had once headed the Equal Employment Opportunity Commission (EEOC). At Thomas's Senate confirmation hearings, a law professor and former EEOC employee named Anita Hill accused him of sexual harassment, or unwanted sexual language and behavior in the workplace. Like Thomas, she had to testify as the Senate tried to determine the truth of her charges.

Clarence Thomas   *Anita Hill*

Despite Hill's testimony, the Senate confirmed Thomas by a narrow majority. This decision angered many Americans, particularly women, who felt that Hill had told the truth. Thomas's confirmation sparked a national debate about sexual harassment.

The economy. In 1988 Bush had campaigned with the slogan "Read My Lips—No New Taxes!" Just two years after winning the presidency, however, he agreed to raise the top income tax rate to cope with the soaring federal deficit. Bush had predicted that the U.S. economy would boom again. Instead, growth slowed almost to a stop. Unemploy-

ment, which had been declining, rose to more than 7 percent in 1992.

To make matters worse, large numbers of American savings and loan institutions (S&Ls) went bankrupt. A combination of banking deregulation and increasing inflation had led hundreds of S&Ls to invest recklessly in real estate projects and risky, high-interest "junk" bonds. When these bonds failed, many S&Ls went under. Since the federal government insured accounts of the depositors in these institutions, it had to spend hundreds of billions of dollars to repay people.

Section 4 Review

• **Glossary**

IDENTIFY and explain the significance of the following: yuppies, insider trading, genes, Acquired Immune Deficiency Syndrome, human immunodeficiency virus, Americans with Disabilities Act, Clarence Thomas, Anita Hill

REVIEWING FOR DETAILS

1. What values became important to many Americans in the 1980s?

2. What new technological problems and breakthroughs affected the United States during the 1980s?

• **Time Line**

3. Why did some people criticize President Bush on domestic issues?

REVIEWING FOR UNDERSTANDING

4. **Writing Mastery:** *Persuading* Write a short paragraph persuading others why scientists should or should not continue genetic experiments.

5. **Critical Thinking:** *Making Comparisons* Compare the emphasis on earning wealth of the 1980s with the values many Americans hold today. Do you think these values have changed over time? Explain your answer.

Preserving America's Wildlife

Americans share their land with thousands of plant and animal species that serve a valuable function in the environment. As human activity has expanded, however, many species have become extinct. It is estimated that some 500 plant and animal species in what is now the United States have become extinct since 1600. In recent years, many Americans have undertaken a variety of efforts to preserve wildlife and the environment. For example, millions of acres of land have been set aside in national parks and wildlife refuges to protect endangered species from harm.

In 1988 lightning started massive forest fires at Yellowstone National Park. In the end some 45 percent of the park was burned. The following year some of Alaska's shoreline was hard-hit by an oil spill. Some 11.2 million gallons of crude oil gushed into the ocean when the oil tanker *Exxon Valdez* ran aground off the Alaskan coast. The oil slick spread to some 1,000 square miles and washed ashore on some 730 miles of coastland, killing many fish, birds, and land animals.

Yellowstone Fires in 1988

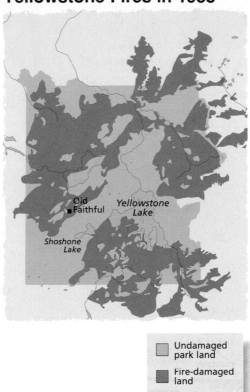

☐ Undamaged park land

☐ Fire-damaged land

Alaskan Oil Spill in 1988

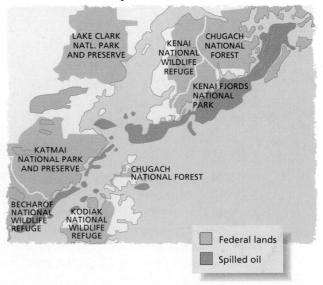

☐ Federal lands

☐ Spilled oil

Human activities such as agriculture, mining, and construction have all contributed to the destruction of the natural environment. The national park system and wildlife refuges began to be established during the Progressive Era to preserve land and wildlife. President Theodore Roosevelt created the first national wildlife refuge in Florida in 1903. In 1966 Congress passed the Endangered Species Preservation Act, which established federal guidelines for overseeing the protection of species in danger of becoming extinct. The law was later strengthened in 1969 and 1973. The agency most responsible for the protection of wildlife is the U.S. Fish and Wildlife Service, which compiles lists of species considered to be in danger of extinction and creates plans for increasing the numbers of these animals. Among other restrictions, it is illegal to kill animals on the endangered species list or to destroy their habitats. **Human-Environment Interaction:** What state with 1–2% of listed endangered species had the most wildlife refuges in 1994?

Wildlife Refuges in the United States in 1994

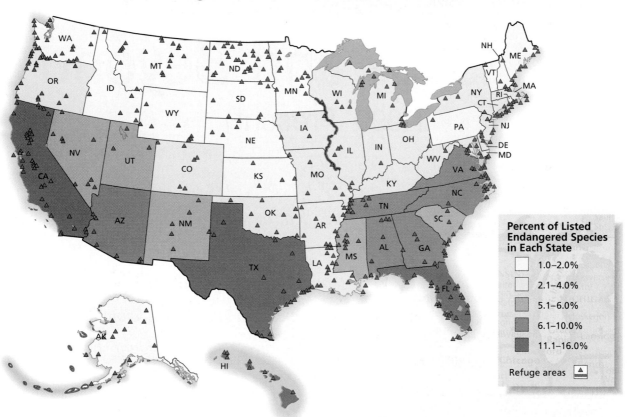

Percent of Listed Endangered Species in Each State

- 1.0–2.0%
- 2.1–4.0%
- 5.1–6.0%
- 6.1–10.0%
- 11.1–16.0%

Refuge areas ▲

To learn more about preserving America's wildlife, go to the interactive map, "Preserving the Wetlands," on the CD–ROM.

• **Preserving the Wetlands**

CHAPTER 30

Court Mast 1992/FPG International Corp.

The 1990s and Beyond
(1990–Present)

THEMES IN AMERICAN HISTORY

Global Relations:
How might trade encourage international cooperation?

Technology and Society:
How might computer technology affect businesses?

Cultural Diversity:
In what ways might cultural diversity enrich a society?

After Bill Clinton was sworn in as president of the United States in 1993, he said: "As we stand at the edge of the 21st century, let us begin anew with energy and hope, with faith and discipline." Clinton was the first U.S. president born after World War II. For many Americans, Clinton became a symbol of the passing of political power to a new generation of leaders.

• **Video Opener**

• **Skill Builder**

image above: *San Francisco in the 1990s*

Section 1

THE CLINTON ADMINISTRATION

Multimedia Connections

Explore these related topics and materials on the CD–ROM to enrich your understanding of this section:

 Readings

- American Political Parties
- Health Care Reform
- How Insurance Works

 Media Bank

- U.S. Health Care
- President Bill Clinton
- Bob Dole Campaigning
- Candidate Ross Perot

 Profiles

- Bill Clinton
- Newt Gingrich
- Robert Dole

They were both raised after World War II. Both came from modest backgrounds, and decided as youths that they wanted to go into politics. Both were southerners. By the early 1990s they were two of the most important people in Washington. Despite their similar backgrounds, Democratic President Bill Clinton and Republican Speaker of the House Newt Gingrich strongly disagreed about how government should be run.

As you read this section you will find out:

▶ **What significant changes occurred in the election of 1992.**

▶ **What Bill Clinton's main goals were.**

▶ **How the Contract with America differed from Clinton's policies.**

The Election of 1992

The victory of UN forces in the Persian Gulf War of 1991 made President George Bush's re-election seem almost certain. Bush's surge in popularity discouraged many well-known Democrats from seeking their party's presidential nomination.

The challengers. One Democrat who did enter the race was Governor Bill Clinton of Arkansas. Clinton went on to win the party's nomination. Senator Al Gore of Tennessee became his running mate. Clinton and Gore represented the baby boom generation born after World War II. As a young man, Clinton had been strongly influenced by the idealism of the 1960s. Like many other young people of his generation, Clinton had also opposed the war in Vietnam.

(left to right) Republican President George Bush, independent candidate Ross Perot, and Democratic nominee Bill Clinton debate each other in 1992.

Ross Perot, a billionaire from Texas, also entered the 1992 race as an independent candidate. Perot emphasized that he was not a professional politician. He also argued that neither the Democrats nor the Republicans truly understood the wishes of the American people. Because of his wealth, Perot did not have to depend on political contributions. He promised to use his business skills to reform the government and improve the economy.

The issues. Perot's economic message was quite timely. By 1992 the country was feeling the impact of an economic recession. As public concerns over the economy increased, support for President Bush declined. Bush downplayed the seriousness of the recession, but he did emphasize the need to reduce the national deficit and to balance the budget.

Clinton accused Bush of failing to develop policies to end the recession. Bush tried to avoid the subject for so long that one Clinton campaign office displayed a sign reading, "The economy, stupid!" to remind Clinton of its importance. Clinton promised to create jobs by developing public works projects and encouraging more private investment. He also promised to reform the nation's health care system.

The candidates ran very personal campaigns, using radio call-in programs and televised "town meetings" to reach out to citizens. Clinton had a very personable style and tended to do better in these types of forums than President Bush.

The November 1992 election witnessed the largest voter turnout since 1960. Clinton defeated Bush by 370 to 168 electoral votes. Clinton received 43 percent of the popular vote. Nearly 19 percent of the voters cast their ballots for Perot. Although he did not win any electoral votes, Perot made the best showing of any candidate to challenge the two major parties since Theodore Roosevelt ran on the Progressive Party ticket in 1912.

Women of 1992. The 1992 election was also significant for the number of women elected to offices throughout the country. Some members of the media labeled 1992 "the year of the woman."

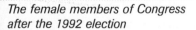

The female members of Congress after the 1992 election

The election marked several firsts for women. Democrat Lynn Woolsey, a divorced mother, became the first person elected to the House to have previously received public welfare. Democrat Carol Moseley-Braun of Illinois became the first African American woman elected to the Senate. California became the first state to fill both its Senate seats with women—Democrats Barbara Boxer and Dianne Feinstein.

By 1993 a record seven women held seats in the Senate. The other female senators were Democrats Patty Murray of Washington and Barbara Mikulski of Maryland and Republicans Nancy Kassebaum of Kansas and Kay Bailey Hutchison of Texas.

Clinton's Policies

President Clinton was committed to the need for a diversified government. He appointed advisers who reflected the ethnic and gender composition of the country. When a position on the Supreme Court came open in 1993 he nominated a female judge, Ruth Bader Ginsberg.

Since the economy had been the main issue of the campaign, Clinton tackled that first. He proposed a plan that would reduce the budget deficit through spending cuts and a tax increase. The idea of raising taxes, however, ran into powerful opposition in Congress. The plan passed by only two votes in the House. The Senate vote on the issue was a tie, so Vice President Gore cast the deciding vote, which was in favor of the plan.

Clinton also proposed a new anticrime bill. Increasing numbers of Americans were concerned about violent crime. In 1994 Congress approved a bill that funded the training of 100,000 new police officers across the country, extended the number of crimes covered by the death penalty, and prohibited the sale and possession of various types of assault weapons. Congress also approved the Handgun Violence Prevention Act, or **Brady Bill**, named after former press secretary James Brady, who was shot during the failed assassination attempt on President Reagan in 1981.

(left to right) Attorney General Janet Reno, President Clinton, James Brady, and his wife, Sarah, celebrate the passage of the Brady Bill.

The Brady Bill required a waiting period and background check in order to buy a handgun.

One of the issues that Clinton had addressed during the campaign was health care, which was growing increasingly expensive. High hospital and doctors' fees and expensive medical technology had made it difficult for many Americans to afford decent health treatment. Clinton put First Lady Hillary Rodham Clinton in charge of the committee that devised a plan for improving the system. Testifying before Congress, she noted:

"There are literally millions of Americans who don't have access to the same quality or quantity [of health care] as millions of others. . . . All too often the decisions about how care is delivered and to whom and at what cost are made on factors other than what is best for the patient."

The committee proposed to overhaul the national health care system by creating a

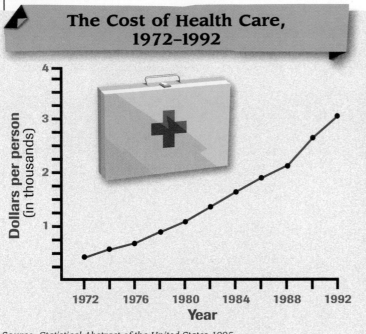

The Cost of Health Care, 1972–1992

Source: *Statistical Abstract of the United States 1995*

Rising Costs. By the 1990s many people were expressing concern over the rising cost of health care. About how many times higher was the average cost of health care per person in 1992 than it was in 1972?

• Graphs

scandal arose over a questionable real estate deal that took place in Arkansas when Clinton was governor there. The deal was also tied to the failure of an Arkansas savings and loan institution. Eventually, several individuals were convicted of wrongdoing in the affair. At the same time, an ongoing congressional investigation looked into Mr. and Mrs. Clinton's roles in Whitewater.

The Contract with America

President Clinton's policies received a further setback in 1994, when the Republicans made huge gains in the 1994 congressional elections. For the first time in 40 years, the Republican Party won majorities in both houses of Congress.

In part, the results of the elections reflected voter frustration with what many people perceived as a federal government in Washington filled with "professional politicians." As one female voter explained:

"I feel like some of the good old boys have been there too long; they're complacent [unconcerned], owe too many people. They're not listening to what we're saying."

government-run insurance program that would guarantee **universal coverage**—health insurance for everyone. Although many people supported health care reform, the Clinton plan ran into a great deal of opposition.

Many critics questioned how the program would be financed. Republicans insisted that the Clinton plan would require huge tax increases, which they strongly opposed. Although numerous health care plans were debated in Congress in 1993 and 1994, none won approval.

Another issue that sparked some criticism of President Clinton was the Whitewater affair. This

First Lady Hillary Rodham Clinton (left) headed the drive to reform health care.

The newly elected Republicans promised to do things differently. During the 1994 campaign many had signed a document written by the new Speaker of the House, Newt Gingrich of Georgia. This **Contract with America** promised to put into effect a comprehensive 10-point program for redirecting the government and the economy. The Contract called for balancing the federal budget with cuts in government spending. The Contract also promised a

Speaker of the House Newt Gingrich led the Republicans who signed the Contract with America.

....

• **Republicans in Congress**

it required would hurt the poor. When Clinton and Congress could not reach a budget agreement, many branches of the federal government had to be shut down temporarily for lack of funds.

The Election of 1996

As the presidential election of 1996 neared, Republicans hoped to continue their winning streak of the 1994 congressional elections. The Republicans nominated Senator Bob Dole of Kansas, a longtime member of Congress and a World War II veteran. The Democrats renominated Clinton.

Dole attacked the Clinton administration on the issues of crime and ethics. The Democrats pointed to the nation's continued economic growth during the Clinton presidency and promised more of the same in the future. President Clinton won with 373 electoral votes to Dole's 124. The Republicans held on to control of both the House and the Senate.

tax cut for the middle class as well as term limits for elected officials.

The Republicans were determined to curb the expansion of the federal government. By the time they were finished they would shift power "back home to state and local governments and to private citizens," Gingrich promised.

President Clinton vetoed several bills that would have made some of the changes promised in the Contract. Late in 1995 he refused to support a proposal that would balance the budget in seven years, arguing that the steep cuts in government spending

Section 1 Review

• **Glossary**

IDENTIFY and explain the significance of the following: Bill Clinton, Ross Perot, Brady Bill, Hillary Rodham Clinton, universal coverage, Newt Gingrich, Contract with America, Bob Dole

REVIEWING FOR DETAILS
1. What changes were brought about by the election of 1992?
2. What changes did President Clinton hope to make in the federal government?
3. What did Republicans hope to achieve through the Contract with America?

REVIEWING FOR UNDERSTANDING
4. **Writing Mastery:** *Persuading* Imagine that you are a campaign worker in 1992. Write a speech you might use to persuade others to vote for one of the presidential candidates.
5. **Critical Thinking:** *Drawing Conclusions* Why might government leaders have a difficult time agreeing on a federal budget?

Section 2

COOPERATION AND CONFLICT

Multimedia Connections

Explore these related topics and materials on the CD–ROM to enrich your understanding of this section:

 Atlas

- Hunger in Africa

 Gazetteer

- Somalia
- Haiti
- Bosnia and Herzegovina
- Oklahoma City

 Media Bank

- Oklahoma City Bombing
- Bombing in Saudia Arabia
- U.S. Troops in Bosnia

At exactly 9:02 A.M. on April 19, 1995, the normal sounds of Oklahoma City were shattered. The front of the Alfred P. Murrah Federal Building was blown off by a bomb. People watched in disbelief as dead and injured people were pulled from the wreckage. "It was just as bad as anything I'd ever witnessed in Vietnam," recalled rescue worker Bobby Johnson in a *Newsweek* interview. "The fact it happened here made it seem even worse."

As you read this section you will find out:

▶ **What President Clinton's foreign policy goals were.**

▶ **How the United States intervened in several foreign countries.**

▶ **How terrorism in the 1990s affected the United States.**

After the Cold War

At the time of Bill Clinton's election, the United States was trying to define its place in a changing world. With the breakup of the Soviet Union, the United States stood alone as the world's military superpower. What its new role should and would be became a source of wide debate.

The Middle East. In some areas the United States continued to act primarily as a mediator. In 1993 President Clinton oversaw the signing of a new Middle East peace agreement. Since 1967 Israel had controlled lands where Palestinian Arabs lived. Palestinian leader Yasir Arafat and Israeli prime minister Yitzhak Rabin (rah-BEEN) signed an agreement allowing Palestinians to regain some control over portions of these lands.

President Clinton observes as Israeli prime minister Yitzhak Rabin (far left) and Palestinian leader Yasir Arafat (far right) sign a new Middle East peace agreement in 1993.

The 1993 agreement resulted from years of work and negotiation by U.S. officials trying to mediate between warring parties in the Middle East. Former secretary of state Cyrus Vance said of the new agreement: "It is, at long last, what all of us who worked on the issue hoped and dreamed might one day come about." Such hopes suffered a serious setback, however, when Prime Minister Rabin was assassinated by an extremist Israeli gunman in November 1995.

Somalia. In other parts of the world, President Clinton faced tough choices over whether to intervene. In December 1992 President Bush had committed U.S. troops to assist with **Operation Restore Hope**, a United Nations relief effort to the African country of Somalia. The country was suffering from a severe famine brought on by years of drought, economic hardship, and political disorder.

The UN forces were there to provide food and supplies to the Somali people, but rivals fighting a civil war made this task almost impossible. One frustrated relief worker declared, "I've become sick and tired of seeing kids dying when I know thieves are taking their food."

A long-term solution to Somalia's very difficult problems required political stability. Many Americans feared that the operation in Somalia could drag out like Vietnam. Pressure to pull out increased when 18 American soldiers were killed and 75 wounded in attacks by warring Somali forces. To help restore order Clinton sent in 15,000 more U.S. troops, declaring that they would soon be recalled. Most of the troops were out by the end of March 1994. In all, 30 U.S. soldiers were killed and 175 wounded in the operation, yet little changed for most Somalis.

Haiti. Another difficult situation had been brewing in the Caribbean nation of Haiti. In 1991 military leaders had overthrown the country's democratically elected president, Jean-Bertrand Aristide (AR-uh-STEED). At that time, the United States and other nations imposed sanctions on Haiti.

The sanctions had little effect on the military leaders. Instead, the sanctions made life even more difficult for the majority of the already poverty-stricken Haitian people. As a result, many Haitians fled the country.

In September 1994 President Clinton ordered U.S. troops to Haiti. Haiti's military leaders quickly agreed to leave office, and President Aristide resumed power in mid-October. Responding

Concern for Somali families, like this one, prompted U.S. involvement in Operation Restore Hope.

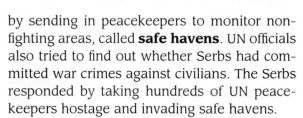

Haitians suffered from such extreme poverty that they were among the poorest people in the Western Hemisphere.

to American concerns that U.S. troops should not be placed at risk for long, Clinton began to withdraw the troops after a newly elected Haitian president took over early in 1996.

Intervention in Bosnia

Discussions over U.S. military intervention were complicated by questions of whether the United Nations or the United States should be in charge of operations that involved U.S. troops. Many critics argued that Operation Restore Hope in Somalia had failed because of poor management by UN officials.

Such concerns made many Americans reluctant to support UN-led operations. When a bloody ethnic war broke out in the African country of Rwanda in 1994, the UN sent in a peacekeeping force, but Clinton refused to send U.S. troops.

Likewise, Clinton resisted committing U.S. troops to the UN's mission in Bosnia and Herzegovina (often referred to as Bosnia), part of what had been Yugoslavia. After the end of the Cold War, Bosnian Serbs tried to drive all Muslims out of their communities. During this process, called **ethnic cleansing**, many Muslims were herded into camps and killed.

The UN tried to intervene in the conflict by placing an arms embargo on the country and by sending in peacekeepers to monitor non-fighting areas, called **safe havens**. UN officials also tried to find out whether Serbs had committed war crimes against civilians. The Serbs responded by taking hundreds of UN peacekeepers hostage and invading safe havens.

International pressure increased for the United States and Western European nations to get involved. Concerned about the safety of U.S. forces, Clinton said he would only commit U.S. troops to a NATO mission led by U.S. military commanders, not the UN. In December of 1995 such an operation was launched. The warring groups in Bosnia signed a peace treaty on December 14.

Terrorism in the 1990s

Even as the Cold War came to an end, terrorist activity around the world continued. **Terrorists** are individuals or small groups that use random violence or threats of violence to advance their political goals. Terrorism has existed for many years. For example, in the Middle East and Northern Ireland, terrorists have carried out deadly attacks against their political enemies for decades.

In some cases, established governments sponsored terrorists who were fighting a mutual enemy. In 1993 the FBI discovered that the Iraqi

A Bosnian woman breaks off wood from a destroyed building to use for firewood as civil war tears her country apart.

government had sponsored a failed plan to assassinate former president George Bush. To discourage such plots, the United States destroyed the Iraqi Intelligence Service headquarters.

In the 1990s the United States experienced a number of terrorist attacks. On February 26, 1993, a bomb exploded at New York's World Trade Center. Six people were killed and more than 1,000 injured. Later that same year, an Arab group linked to the World Trade Center bombing was arrested for plotting to bomb the UN building, the FBI's New York headquarters, and two tunnels under the Hudson River. In 1996, several members of this group were sentenced to life in prison.

Not all suspected terrorists have been foreign enemies. The worst terrorist attack in the United States was the bombing of the large federal office building in Oklahoma City on April 19, 1995. Rudy

Jimenez had just left the building after visiting his wife when an enormous bomb exploded. He recalled:

"I hadn't gone three blocks when I heard this blast. I thought someone had shot me. When I got to the federal building there was smoke everywhere. The first two people I saw were dead."

In all, 168 people died in the Oklahoma City bombing. Initially, many people suspected that foreign terrorists, like the group that had plotted the New York bombings, were responsible. However, the two men arrested for carrying out the Oklahoma City bombing, Timothy McVeigh and Terry Nichols, were native-born Americans. Both had come to resent the U.S. government.

Police officers aid a woman injured in the terrorist bombing of New York's World Trade Center.

Section 2 Review

• Glossary

IDENTIFY and explain the significance of the following: Yasir Arafat, Yitzhak Rabin, Operation Restore Hope, Jean-Bertrand Aristide, ethnic cleansing, safe havens, terrorists

REVIEWING FOR DETAILS

1. What were the major foreign policy goals of the United States after the end of the Cold War?

2. What major terrorist events affected the United States in the 1990s?

REVIEWING FOR UNDERSTANDING

3. **Geographic Literacy** In what areas of the world did U.S. troops intervene in the 1990s, and what were the results of the interventions?

4. **Writing Mastery:** *Expressing* Imagine that you are a television newscaster in Oklahoma City going live on the air for the noon report on April 19, 1995. Prepare a short script for your broadcast, describing the reactions to the explosion and giving any information you can about the incident.

5. **Critical Thinking:** *Determining the Strength of an Argument* Why might America's role in world affairs after the Cold War be a source of debate?

Section **3**

AMERICANS IN THE 1990s

Multimedia Connections

Explore these related topics and materials on the CD–ROM to enrich your understanding of this section:

 Readings

• Baby Boomers and Generation X

 Gazetteer

• Los Angeles

 Media Bank

• Aging America
• Million Man March

 Profiles

• Colin Powell

 Biographies

• An Wang

 Simulation

• New Directions: City Planning

They gathered in Washington, D.C., with hundreds of thousands of other African American men from across the country. Many came to the Million Man March in October 1995 because they believed that average citizens needed to play a larger role in solving problems in their own communities. Army lieutenant colonel Michael Nelson said, "I know how great we can be. This is a great nation, but this could be a greater nation."

As you read this section you will find out:

▶ **What central conflict exists between the baby boomers and Generation X.**

▶ **What arguments were used to try to limit immigration to the United States.**

▶ **What signs indicated divisions and unity in American society.**

Trends in Society

One reason why health care became such an important political issue in the 1990s was that the population was aging. Medical breakthroughs and a higher standard of living were allowing people to live longer than ever before. In addition, the baby boom generation was entering middle age. By 1995 about half of all heads of households were over the age of 45. Many people worried about who would meet the needs of the older population in the years to come, particularly when the baby boomers reached retirement age.

Anxiety about the future was increased by the recession of the early 1990s. The children of the baby boomers, often referred to as the "baby busters" or **Generation X**, faced limited job prospects and decreasing public resources.

Many members of this generation expressed resentment toward earlier generations for wasting the country's resources and leaving them with the consequences, such as a large national debt. Baby buster Suneel Ratan observed that members of the new generation "identify [baby] boomers with the unraveling of American society." Another baby buster, Dana Neilson, agreed:

> **"We're the generation of divorced families and latchkey homes, and that's a big dose of realism. The boomers had elementary schools built for them and then secondary schools and then colleges, and then as they entered the work force, companies made room for them. Now we come along and it seems as if all the resources have been used. . . . Where does that leave us?"**

Many college graduates were particularly discouraged by their bleak job prospects.

Douglas Coupland, *Generation X*

I TRY TO IMAGINE MYSELF IN THIS SAME JOB ONE YEAR FROM NOW...

...BUT I'M JUST NOT SEEING ANY PICTURES

Many members of Generation X worried that they would never have stable employment, as this cartoon from a book about the generation shows.

Salaries for entry-level jobs generally decreased from the 1980s to the 1990s. The high cost of such benefits as health insurance and pension plans made many companies reluctant to invest in full-time workers. Some relied instead on temporary or part-time employees.

Employment in America, 1995–2005

DISTRIBUTION OF EMPLOYMENT BY INDUSTRY, 1995

5%
7%
9%
16%
35%
21%
7%

- Services*
- Public Administration
- Manufacturing
- Finance, Insurance, and Real Estate
- Transportation, Communication, and other Public Utilities
- Agriculture, Mining, and Construction
- Wholesale and Retail Trade

FASTEST GROWING JOBS, 1995 TO 2005

1. Home Health Aides
2. Human Services Workers
3. Personal and Home Care Aides
4. Computer Engineers and Scientists
5. Computer Systems Analysts
6. Physical and Corrective Therapy Assistants
7. Physical Therapists
8. Paralegals
9. Occupational Therapy Assistants and Aides
10. Electronic Pagination Systems Workers

* Includes business and repair, computer, entertainment, health, education, and legal, among others.
Source: *Statistical Abstract of the United States 1995; American Demographics February 1995*

A Changing Workforce. The aging population, health care needs, and the increase in computers has led to an increase in jobs in those areas. Based on the jobs expected to experience the fastest growth between 1995 and 2005, which industry should expand the most?

• Graphs

Even full-time jobs were no longer secure. By the mid-1990s a number of companies were **downsizing**, decreasing the number of employees to keep profits up and stay more competitive. For example, in July 1993 the company International Business Machines (IBM) announced it was cutting 35,000 jobs. Then in January 1996 American Telephone and Telegraph (AT&T) announced it was cutting 40,000 jobs.

Job instability was also accompanied by the rapid increase in the cost of a college education. Between 1968 and 1993 the cost of attending a public university rose by 39 percent after inflation. The cost of attending a private university rose even more rapidly, increasing by 94 percent.

Though job prospects for college graduates were not what many had hoped, the job market increasingly demanded workers with college educations. The number of jobs requiring technical skills rose while the number of manual labor jobs steadily declined. In 1995 the Department of Labor predicted that the largest increase in jobs would be in health and social services.

Despite complaints among college graduates about their job prospects, most graduates were far better off financially than those without a degree. By the mid-1990s the average income for families headed by a college graduate was 76 percent higher than the average income among all families.

To prepare future generations for college and skilled work, more families bought computers in the 1990s. By February 1995 about 31 percent of all American homes had a computer. Almost 4 million home computers were bought in the last six months of 1994 alone.

Immigration

Many Americans anxious about their jobs blamed immigration for hurting the economy. Immigration became a major issue of debate in the 1990s as movement to the United States reached its highest numbers since 1914. From 1990 to 1994, some 4.6 million immigrants arrived in the country.

Many new immigrants were from Latin America, Asia, and the Caribbean. Opponents of immigration argued that immigrants took jobs away from native-born workers. Supporters of immigration noted that many of the recent immigrants, particularly those from Asia, were highly educated and contributed a great deal to American technical industries. At one point, about one third of the engineers in the center of California's thriving computer industry were Asian immigrants. Recognizing these contributions, Congress passed the **Immigration Act of 1990**, which increased the number of skilled workers allowed to immigrate.

California became the site of one of the most heated debates over immigration. In 1994 voters in California approved **Proposition 187**, a measure intended to discourage illegal immigration. At the time of the vote it was estimated that there were some 1.5 million illegal immigrants living in California; most of them were from Mexico.

Technology and health care were two of the fastest growing fields in the 1990s. This medical technician uses skills required in both fields.

Brownie Harris/The Stock Market ©

• Silicon Chip

Many immigrants, like this market owner in Seattle, Washington, make important contributions to the American economy.

In part, the law sought to ban illegal immigrants from attending public schools and from obtaining free health care or welfare benefits. The law required teachers, doctors, and law enforcement officials to report any people they suspected of being illegal immigrants.

Proposition 187 touched off a fierce war of words. Supporters argued that it would save the state billions of dollars and would discourage people from immigrating illegally in order to secure public services.

Opponents called the proposition a racially biased proposal that unfairly targeted Hispanic, or Latino, children and thus increased fear in the community. "People believe that immigration officials will be in front of their schools and their homes, waiting to take them away," declared Latino leader Lorraine Cervantes.

In 1995 a U.S. district judge declared parts of Proposition 187 unconstitutional. The judge ruled that the state could not deny illegal immigrants public services that were funded by the federal government. This ruling set the stage for a national debate on whether the federal government itself should cut off such services to illegal immigrants.

Race Relations

Some observers saw Proposition 187 as only one example of what they believed were growing racial and ethnic divisions in American society. Many people also pointed to the **Los Angeles Riots** of 1992 as evidence of such divisions.

The riots were sparked by a not guilty verdict in the trial of four white police officers who were accused of using excessive force in the beating of African American motorist Rodney King. The officers had been videotaped beating King in front of other officers. The riots that followed the trial lasted for several days. When they were over, 60 people were dead, hundreds injured, and many businesses were destroyed.

Most of the violence was concentrated in South Central Los Angeles, one of the more

A Los Angeles couple observes the rubble left from the violent riots of 1992.

ethnically diverse sections of the city. Most of those affected by the riot were African American and Hispanic American.

Some observers saw the 1992 riots as the result of long-term resentment over poverty, lack of political representation, and ethnic and racial tension in South Central Los Angeles. Years of economic decline had hurt many inner-city neighborhoods. In the 1990s the number of available jobs in Los Angeles was shrinking, while migration to the city, particularly by Hispanic Americans and Asian Americans, was increasing. This situation made competition for already scarce jobs and resources even more fierce.

Despite such conflicts, some observers saw positive developments for race relations in the move to convince retired general Colin Powell to run for president in 1996. Powell had been the first African American to head the Joint Chiefs of Staff. He had received much national attention for his leadership during the Persian Gulf War.

Polls showed that Powell, who had never run for elected office but identified himself as a Republican, enjoyed considerable support from a wide cross-section of voters. Many observers felt that Powell would have had a good chance of beating President Clinton, but Powell declined to run. In announcing that he was not a candidate, Powell said that the strong support he had received was a positive sign for race relations. He noted:

"In one generation we have moved from denying a black man service at a lunch counter to elevating one to the highest military office in the nation and to being a serious contender for the presidency."

Many supporters were disappointed when Colin Powell decided not to run for president in 1996.

Section 3 Review

• **Glossary**

IDENTIFY and explain the significance of the following: Generation X, downsizing, Immigration Act of 1990, Proposition 187, Los Angeles Riots, Colin Powell

REVIEWING FOR DETAILS
1. Why were some members of Generation X unhappy with baby boomers?
2. Why did some Americans want to limit further immigration?
3. Why might some people argue that there were great divisions in American society in the 1990s, while others might say that society has grown more united?

REVIEWING FOR UNDERSTANDING
4. **Writing Mastery:** *Creating* Compose a dialogue between a Generation X-er and his or her parents as the family discusses the younger person's future plans.
5. **Critical Thinking:** *Drawing Conclusions* Why did immigration become such a major issue in the 1990s? What connections did this have to the national economy?

Section 4

LOOKING TOWARD THE FUTURE

Multimedia Connections

Explore these related topics and materials on the CD–ROM to enrich your understanding of this section:

 Media Bank

- U.S. Trade Balance
- Protest Against South Africa
- Environmental Problems
- Three Mile Island Plant
- NAFTA

 Readings

- *Kaffir Boy*
- Importance of Trade

 Profiles

- Bill Gates
- Nelson Mandela

 Atlas

- Wetlands

 Gazetteer

- South Africa

I n 1992 high school senior Dan Helfrich described his hopes for the future: "I have a good feeling about the future," he said. "The people of my generation are more outspoken and more in tune with what's going on, and I'd like to think that when the people of my generation are in [power]," he predicted, "they're going to be more sensitive and more representative of the people of our country."

As you read this section you will find out:

▶ **What environmental concerns gained attention in the 1990s.**

▶ **How international cooperation in economics and communication increased.**

▶ **How democratic movements increased worldwide.**

Environmental Concerns

The world population entering the 21st century will be growing rapidly. By the year 2000 it is expected that there will be about 6.1 billion people on the planet. If current birthrates remain the same, that figure may nearly double by the year 2150.

Damage to the environment. The growing population will put an extra heavy burden on the earth's environment, which is already suffering the effects of so much human activity. Expansion of population and commercial activities have increased concerns over **deforestation**—a process by which the world's forests are disappearing. Around 45 million acres of forest were destroyed in the 1980s alone, most of it in South America, Asia, and Africa.

Pollution also threatens the environment. One serious result of industrial development has been an increase in **acid rain**—rain carrying toxins from air pollution. As this rain falls, it causes more damage to the environment below. Another concern about air pollution is the damage that has been done to the **ozone layer**—a thin shield around the earth's atmosphere that blocks out harmful rays from the sun. It is dangerously thin in some spots.

Although scientists disagree about the exact causes of the thinning of the ozone layer, many countries, including the United States, have taken steps to abolish the use of some products believed to be causing harm to the ozone layer.

Some scientists also fear the problem of **global warming**, a trend in rising temperatures believed to be caused by the "greenhouse effect," in which pollution in the air keeps more heat in the atmosphere, making average temperatures rise. The burning of fossil fuels, such as oil and coal, has possibly contributed to global warming.

Energy and the environment. Since the energy crisis of the 1970s many people have been looking for ways to create energy besides the burning of fossil fuels. Some have experimented with solar energy and new windpower technology. Others have encouraged the increased use of nuclear energy, which is relatively clean to produce. Some critics, however, fear a nuclear accident could spew dangerous radiation into the atmosphere. A nuclear accident at Three Mile Island, Pennsylvania, in 1979 nearly caused such a major disaster.

Even more serious was an explosion at a nuclear power plant in the Soviet town of Chernobyl in 1986. The explosion released radiation into the atmosphere, killing 30 people within two weeks of the accident. Since radiation often kills slowly by causing various cancers, birth defects, and other health problems, scientists estimate that the total death toll from Chernobyl may possibly be in the thousands.

Working for change. Concern about the environment has led to an increase in the number of organizations dedicated to environmental issues. For several years environ-

Young People In History

Young People and the Environment

In the 1990s some of the most outspoken supporters of environmental protection were young people. One group of 20 students appeared before the U.S. Senate to plead for a reduction of harmful emissions into the air. Many of these students promoted environmental issues in their communities by setting up ecology clubs and recycling centers.

Young Americans work together to plant a tree.

Some young people also tried to find new methods for cleaning up the environment. Junior High School student Elizabeth Philip discovered that her city's water supply contained high levels of toxins. She experimented with ways of improving water quality and soon created a simple, inexpensive filter device that used baking yeast to remove almost all of the toxins in the tap water. Elizabeth urged other students to try to make a difference: "Just begin with something you care about, educate yourself, and then go from there."

This artwork from the 1992 Earth Summit reflected universal concerns about the environment, which was an important global topic in the 1990s.

mental political parties, called **Green parties**, gained support, particularly in Europe. In 1996 American environmentalist Ralph Nader ran for president under the Green Party banner.

Several international conferences have been organized to try to expand cooperation between nations on environmental issues. In 1992 the United Nations sponsored an **Earth Summit**, which brought together some 35,000 representatives from all over the world. They put together an agreement that would encourage countries to work toward improving the global environment.

The Information Revolution

Although the world faces many challenges in the future, there are signs that nations are increasingly willing to share information and ideas for finding solutions to common problems. Technology has greatly aided an increase in the exchange and availability of information—a development referred to as the **Information Revolution.**

By the 1990s computers were smaller, more powerful, and much less expensive than ever before. A system of connecting computers worldwide, called the **Internet**, enables people to communicate and acquire vast amounts of information in only a matter of seconds using computers across the globe.

• Internet

Computer specialists referred to improved computer communications systems as the Information Superhighway. Bill Gates, head of the world's largest computer software company, predicted how this "superhighway" might affect the world:

"The information highway is going to break down boundaries. . . . We are watching something historic happen, and it will affect the world . . . the same way the scientific method, the invention of printing, and the arrival of the Industrial Age did. Big changes used to take generations or centuries. This one won't happen overnight, but it will move faster."

The end of the Cold War encouraged many people from different countries to exchange information and ideas on how to solve the world's problems. The 1990s witnessed an increase in cooperation between scientists from America and the countries of the former Communist bloc. In 1995 Russian and American astronauts worked together in a joint space venture. The crew of the U.S. space shuttle *Atlantis* docked with the Russian space

The American space shuttle Atlantis *docks with the Russian space station* Mir.

station *Mir* for five days. In 1996 astronaut Shannon Lucid spent 188 days in space—longer than any American ever—when she went to work with Russian astronauts on the *Mir*.

The Global Economy

Technology has also helped improve business communication worldwide, which is extremely important as the economies of different countries become more closely connected. In recent years, international trade and the rise of **multinational corporations**—corporations that invest in a variety of businesses throughout the world—have shaped the global economy. Today there are several economic superpowers. Some are groups of countries that have formed alliances to strengthen their economic position. Many of the countries of East Asia, for example, have become major exporters of goods to Western countries.

In 1993 a group of countries in Western Europe united to create the **European Union**, which would allow the free movement of goods, labor, and currency between members. Also in 1993 the U.S. Congress approved a trade agreement between the United States, Mexico, and Canada. The **North American Free Trade Agreement** (NAFTA) allowed for a freer flow of goods and labor between those three countries. As a result of the growing importance of international trade, in 1995 the **World Trade Organization** was established to settle trade disputes between nations.

The lowering of trade barriers has helped many multinational corporations expand. However, it has also led to concerns that American workers will lose their jobs if U.S. corporations invest more in foreign countries than they did at home.

The Rise of Democracy

Some people argue that free trade will not bring the world closer together until political oppression is abolished. In many places such as China, North Korea, and Iran, people continue to struggle under oppressive governments. Still, in recent years many countries have made strides toward becoming more democratic, often with aid from the United States. In many Asian and Latin American countries free elections in the 1990s allowed the people to choose their leaders after years of dictatorship.

One of the greatest victories for democracy occurred in South Africa. For years the United States and other countries issued economic sanctions against South Africa to protest the continuation of the racist system of apartheid. In 1990 South Africa's white

Global Connections
The End of Apartheid

The end of apartheid resulted from years of efforts by many people both within South Africa and abroad. Although the system of apartheid had been around for a long time, foreign protests against it began to increase in the 1970s. Many nations began to treat South Africa like "the skunk of the world," said anti-apartheid leader Nelson Mandela.

In the United States protests against apartheid increased in the 1980s, particularly among college students. They pressured their universities to divest, or withdraw, investments in companies that did business with the apartheid government of South Africa. In 1986 Congress banned all new investments in South Africa. Such economic pressure helped convince the white South African leaders to back down. As more businesses divested and foreign banks refused to loan money to South African companies, the country's economy faltered. Finally, South African president F. W. de Klerk admitted that the nation's economy would never recover as long as apartheid continued.

leaders finally began to take some action to end the system. The government legalized the previously outlawed **African National Congress** (ANC), a political group that had fought for the rights of black South Africans.

Nelson Mandela, one of the founders of the ANC, had been imprisoned since 1964 for his political activism. After the apartheid government released him in 1990, Mandela and other black leaders worked with the white government leaders to plan the creation of a democratic government. In April 1994 millions of South Africans waited in long lines, some of them for days, for the chance to vote. Black South African Julius Molawa expressed his feelings about voting for the first time, "My heart tells me it's the best day of my life. I don't have to carry a pass. I can work anywhere in the country I want. I am free."

When the balloting was over, the voters had selected Nelson Mandela as the country's first black president. The country still faced many problems, including a poor economy and fighting among ethnic groups, but the people now had a voice in their government.

The spread of democracy in such countries as South Africa will continue to be important to the United States in years to come. As President Clinton declared in his 1994 State of the Union address, "Ultimately the best strategy to insure our security and to build a durable [lasting] peace is to support the advance of democracy elsewhere."

South African president Nelson Mandela

Section 4 Review

• **Glossary**

IDENTIFY and explain the significance of the following: deforestation, acid rain, ozone layer, global warming, Green parties, Earth Summit, Information Revolution, Internet, multinational corporations, European Union, North American Free Trade Agreement, World Trade Organization, African National Congress, Nelson Mandela

REVIEWING FOR DETAILS

1. What advances helped international trade and communications in the 1990s?
2. How did democracy grow in other countries?

• **Time Line**

REVIEWING FOR UNDERSTANDING

3. **Geographic Literacy** What environmental issues gained more notice in the 1990s?

4. **Writing Mastery:** *Describing* Imagine that you are celebrating your hundredth birthday. Write a speech you might give to a group of students describing the changes you have seen throughout your life and the impact they have made on the world.

5. **Critical Thinking:** *Synthesizing Information* Considering the increasing international cooperation in the areas of trade and communications, what could nations do together to help the environmental problems facing the world?

Booker T. Washington

The Granger Collection, New York

George Washington oversees the Constitutional Convention.

Immigrant neighborhood

Freedman's school in Charleston, South Carolina

The Granger Collection, New York

Plains Indians watch as settlers cross their lands.

Exploring America's Past

Reference Section

Atlas

Cheyenne warrior's shield
The Granger Collection, New York

Elizabeth Cady Stanton (left) and Susan B. Anthony (right)

Civil War camp life

President Franklin D. Roosevelt

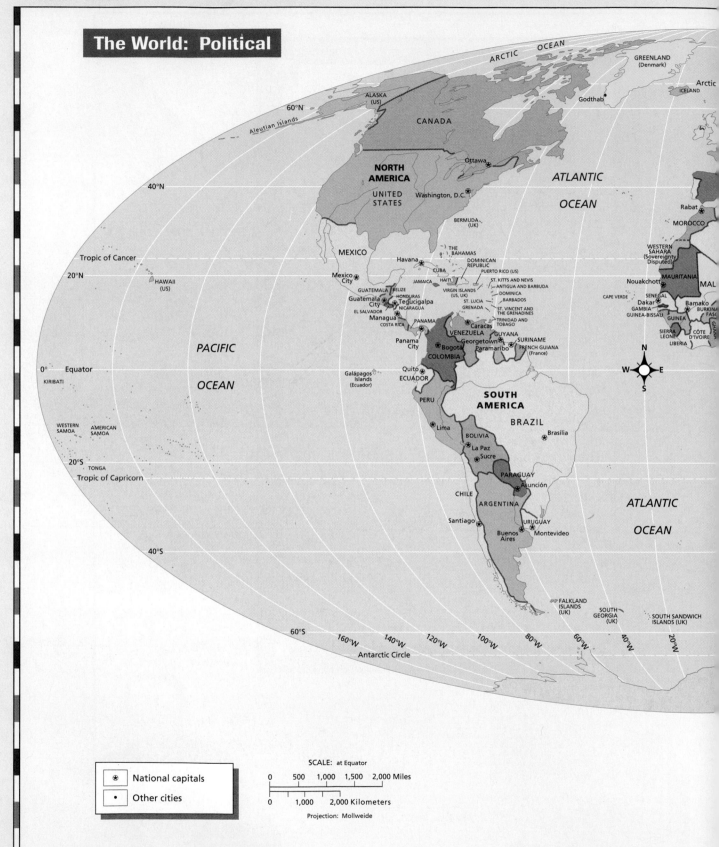

The World: Political

ARCTIC OCEAN

GREENLAND
(Denmark)

Arctic
ICELAND

Godthab

ALASKA
(US)

CANADA

60°N

Aleutian Islands

Ottawa

NORTH
AMERICA

ATLANTIC

OCEAN

40°N

UNITED
STATES

Washington, D.C.

Rabat
MOROCCO

BERMUDA
(UK)

MEXICO

THE
BAHAMAS

DOMINICAN
REPUBLIC

Havana

CUBA

PUERTO RICO (US)

Tropic of Cancer

20°N

HAWAII
(US)

Mexico
City

JAMAICA

HAITI

ST. KITTS AND NEVIS
ANTIGUA AND BARBUDA

WESTERN
SAHARA
(Sovereignty
Disputed)

Nouakchott

MAURITANIA

MAL

GUATEMALA

BELIZE

VIRGIN ISLANDS
(US, UK)

DOMINICA

CAPE VERDE

SENEGAL

Guatemala
City

HONDURAS

Tegucigalpa

ST. LUCIA

BARBADOS

Dakar

Bamako

BURKINA

EL SALVADOR

NICARAGUA

GRENADA

ST. VINCENT AND
THE GRENADINES

GAMBIA

GUINEA-BISSAU

GUINEA

FASO

Managua

PANAMA

Caracas

TRINIDAD AND
TOBAGO

SIERRA
LEONE

CÔTE
D'IVOIRE

COSTA RICA

GUYANA

Panama
City

VENEZUELA

SURINAME

LIBERIA

GHANA

Georgetown

Paramaribo

FRENCH GUIANA
(France)

N

Bogotá

PACIFIC

COLOMBIA

W

E

Quito

Galápagos
Islands
(Ecuador)

ECUADOR

S

OCEAN

0°

Equator

KIRIBATI

PERU

SOUTH
AMERICA

BRAZIL

WESTERN
SAMOA

AMERICAN
SAMOA

Lima

Brasília

BOLIVIA

La Paz

20°S

TONGA

Sucre

Tropic of Capricorn

PARAGUAY

Asunción

CHILE

ATLANTIC

ARGENTINA

OCEAN

Santiago

URUGUAY

40°S

Buenos
Aires

Montevideo

FALKLAND
ISLANDS
(UK)

SOUTH
GEORGIA
(UK)

SOUTH SANDWICH
ISLANDS (UK)

60°S

160°W

140°W

120°W

100°W

80°W

60°W

40°W

20°W

Antarctic Circle

| ⊛ | National capitals |
| • | Other cities |

SCALE: at Equator

0   500   1,000   1,500   2,000 Miles

0   1,000   2,000 Kilometers

Projection: Mollweide

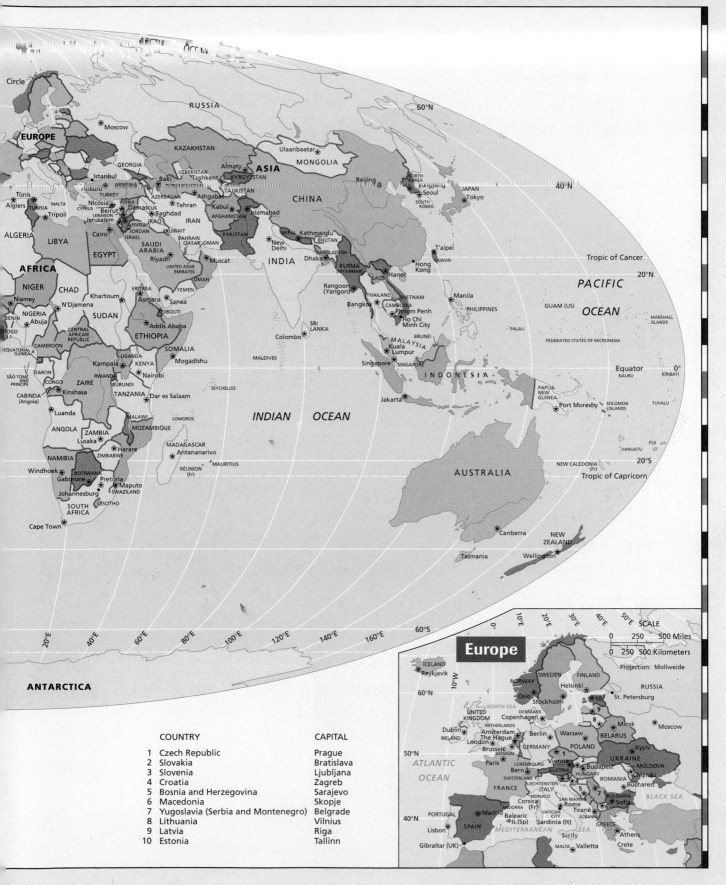

ARCTIC OCEAN

Circle

EUROPE

RUSSIA

60°N

Moscow

KAZAKHSTAN

GEORGIA

ASIA

Ulaanbaatar

MONGOLIA

Almaty

Istanbul

Ankara
ARMENIA
Baki
UZBEKISTAN
Toshkent
KYRGYZSTAN

Beijing

40°N

NORTH
KOREA

JAPAN

Tunis
TURKEY
AZERBAIJAN
Ashgabat
TAJIKISTAN

P'yongyang
Seoul

Tokyo

Algiers
TUNISIA
MALTA
Nicosia
CYPRUS
SYRIA
Damascus
Tehran
Kabul
CHINA
SOUTH
KOREA

Tripoli
LEBANON
Beirut
Jerusalem
IRAQ
Baghdad
IRAN
AFGHANISTAN
Islamabad

Amman
JORDAN
ISRAEL
KUWAIT

ALGERIA

LIBYA

Cairo

EGYPT

SAUDI
ARABIA
BAHRAIN
QATAR
OMAN

PAKISTAN

NEPAL
Kathmandu
BHUTAN

T'aipei

TAIWAN

Tropic of Cancer

AFRICA

NIGER

CHAD

Khartoum

Riyadh

UNITED ARAB
EMIRATES

Muscat

New
Delhi

INDIA

Dhaka
BANGLADESH

Hong
Kong

20°N

PACIFIC

NIGER

Niamey

N'Djamena

SUDAN

ERITREA

Asmara

YEMEN

Sanaa

OMAN

Rangoon
(Yangon)

BURMA
(MYANMAR)
LAOS
Hanoi

OCEAN

GUAM (US)

MARSHALL
ISLANDS

BENIN
NIGERIA
Abuja

CENTRAL
AFRICAN
REPUBLIC

DJIBOUTI

THAILAND

VIETNAM

Manila

TOGO

EQUATORIAL
GUINEA

ETHIOPIA

SOMALIA

Bangkok

CAMBODIA

Phnom Penh
Ho Chi
Minh City

PHILIPPINES

PALAU

FEDERATED STATES OF MICRONESIA

SÃO TOME
AND
PRINCIPE

GABON

CONGO

UGANDA
Kampala

RWANDA

KENYA

Nairobi

SRI
LANKA

Colombo

MALDIVES

BRUNEI
MALAYSIA
Kuala
Lumpur

Singapore
SINGAPORE

Equator

NAURU

0°

KIRIBATI

CABINDA
(Angola)

ZAIRE

Kinshasa

BURUNDI

TANZANIA

Dar es Salaam

SEYCHELLES

INDONESIA

PAPUA
NEW
GUINEA

TUVALU

Luanda

MALAWI

INDIAN OCEAN

Jakarta

Port Moresby

SOLOMON
ISLANDS

ANGOLA

ZAMBIA

Lusaka

MOZAMBIQUE

MADAGASCAR

Antananarivo

VANUATU

FIJI

NAMIBIA

ZIMBABWE

Harare

RÉUNION
(Fr)

MAURITIUS

NEW CALEDONIA
(Fr)

20°S

Windhoek

BOTSWANA

COMOROS

AUSTRALIA

Tropic of Capricorn

Gaborone

Pretoria

Johannesburg

SWAZILAND

Maputo

SOUTH
AFRICA

LESOTHO

Cape Town

Canberra

NEW
ZEALAND

Tasmania

Wellington

60°S

20°E 40°E 60°E 80°E 100°E 120°E 140°E 160°E

ANTARCTICA

	COUNTRY	CAPITAL
1	Czech Republic	Prague
2	Slovakia	Bratislava
3	Slovenia	Ljubljana
4	Croatia	Zagreb
5	Bosnia and Herzegovina	Sarajevo
6	Macedonia	Skopje
7	Yugoslavia (Serbia and Montenegro)	Belgrade
8	Lithuania	Vilnius
9	Latvia	Riga
10	Estonia	Tallinn

Europe

ICELAND
Reykjavik

SWEDEN

FINLAND

RUSSIA

NORWAY

Helsinki

St. Petersburg

SCALE

0 250 500 Miles

0 250 500 Kilometers

Projection: Mollweide

NORTH SEA

DENMARK

Oslo
Stockholm

10

Minsk

Moscow

UNITED
KINGDOM

NETHERLANDS

Amsterdam
The Hague

Copenhagen

Berlin

Warsaw

BELARUS

9

8

Dublin
IRELAND

London

Brussels
BELGIUM

GERMANY

POLAND

Kyiv

UKRAINE

ATLANTIC

OCEAN

Paris

LUXEMBOURG

Bern
SWITZERLAND

1
Vienna
AUSTRIA

2
Budapest
HUNGARY

MOLDOVA

Chisinau

FRANCE

LIECHTENSTEIN

3

4

ROMANIA

Bucharest

MONACO

ITALY

SAN MARINO

7

PORTUGAL

ANDORRA

Corsica
(Fr)

Rome

VATICAN
CITY

5

BULGARIA

Sofia

BLACK SEA

Madrid

Balearic
Is.(Sp)

Sardinia (It)

ALBANIA

6

Tirane

Lisbon

SPAIN

MEDITERRANEAN

GREECE

Athens

Gibraltar (UK)

SEA

MALTA

Sicily

Valletta

Crete

United States of America: Political

WASHINGTON
Strait of Juan de Fuca
Puget Sound
Seattle
Olympia★ Tacoma
Spokane
Franklin D. Roosevelt Lake
Pend Oreille

Portland
Columbia River
Salem★
Eugene
OREGON

PACIFIC OCEAN
Cape Mendocino

Goose Lake
Shasta Lake

Pyramid Lake
Reno
Carson City★ Lake Tahoe

NEVADA

Sacramento
Berkeley
Oakland
San Francisco
San Francisco Bay
San Jose
Monterey Bay

San Joaquin River

Fresno

CALIFORNIA

Santa Barbara
Ventura
Los Angeles
Long Beach
Anaheim
Santa Ana
San Diego
Riverside
Palm Springs
Salton Sea
Channel Islands

Las Vegas
Lake Mead
Colorado River

IDAHO
Boise★
Sun Valley
Snake River
Pocatello

MONTANA
Great Falls
Helena★
Billings
Yellowstone River
Yellowstone Lake

Flathead Lake
Missouri River

WYOMING
Cheyenne

Great Salt Lake
Ogden
Salt Lake City
Snowbird
Utah Lake Provo

UTAH
Green River

Lake Powell

ARIZONA
Flagstaff
Phoenix★
Gila River
Casa Grande
Tucson
Gulf of California

COLORADO
Aspen
Vail
Boulder
Denver★
Colorado Springs
Pueblo

NEW MEXICO
Taos
Santa Fe★
Albuquerque

Las Cruces
El Paso

NORTH DAKOTA
Grand Forks
Bismarck★ Fargo
Lake Sakakawea

SOUTH DAKOTA
Lake Oahe
Pierre★
Rapid City
Sioux Falls
Minnesota River

NEBRASKA
Sioux City
Omaha
Lincoln★
Platte River
Missouri River

KANSAS
Topeka★
Wichita
Arkansas River

OKLAHOMA
Keystone Lake
Tulsa
Oklahoma City★
Eufaula Lake
Amarillo
Lawton
Lake Texoma
Canadian River

TEXAS
Lubbock
Abilene
Fort Worth
Dallas
Midland
Odessa
Waco
Austin★
Houston
Pecos River
Brazos River
Colorado River
San Antonio
Amistad Reservoir
Rio Grande
Laredo
Corpus Christi
PADRE ISLAND

MEXICO

To understand the relative locations of Alaska and Hawaii as well as the vast distances separating them from the rest of the United States, see the world map.

KAUAI
NIIHAU
OAHU
Honolulu★
MOLOKAI
LANAI MAUI
KAHOOLAWE
HAWAII
PACIFIC OCEAN
SCALE
0   75   150 Miles
0   75   150 Kilometers
Hilo
HAWAII
22°N
19°N
155°W
160°W

ARCTIC OCEAN
RUSSIA
Arctic Circle
Bering Strait
Nome
65°N
ST. LAWRENCE ISLAND
ST. MATTHEW ISLAND
NUNIVAK ISLAND
60°N
Yukon River
Fairbanks
ALASKA
Anchorage
Valdez
Skagway
Juneau★
Gulf of Alaska
KODIAK ISLAND
ALEUTIAN ISLANDS
ATTU ISLAND
BERING SEA
SCALE
0   250   500 Miles
0   250   500 Kilometers
Projection: Albers Equal Area
PACIFIC OCEAN
ALEXANDER ARCHIPELAGO
CANADA
140°W
150°W
160°W
170°W
170°E
180
55°N
50°N
55°N
25°N

45°N
40°N
35°N
30°N
130°W
125°W
125°W
120°W

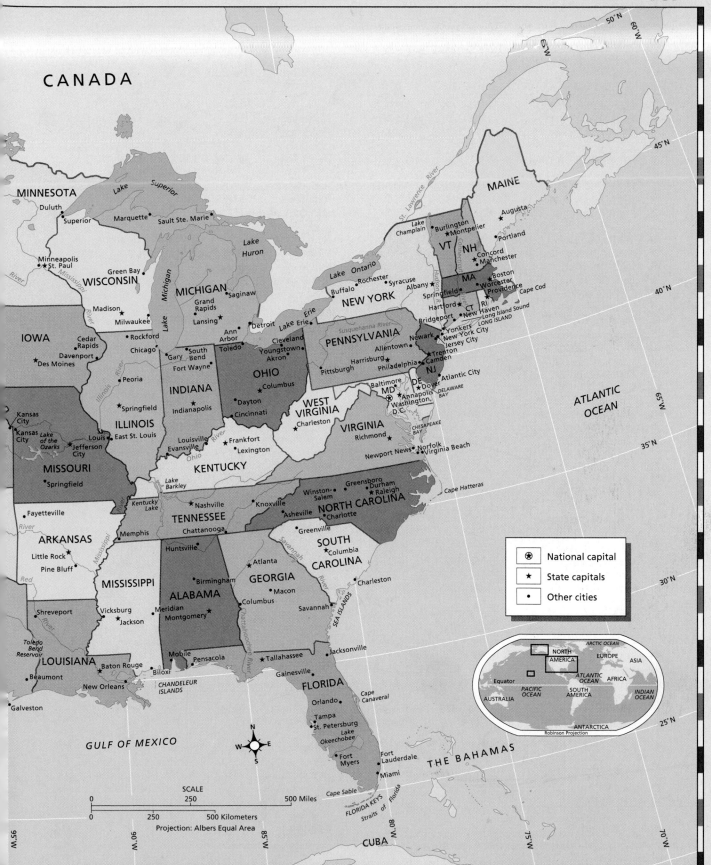

CANADA

MINNESOTA
Duluth
Superior
Marquette
Sault Ste. Marie
Lake Superior

Minneapolis
St. Paul
Green Bay
WISCONSIN
MICHIGAN
Grand Rapids
Saginaw
Lake Huron

Madison
Milwaukee
Lansing
Ann Arbor
Detroit

IOWA
Cedar Rapids
Rockford
Chicago
Gary
South Bend
Fort Wayne
Toledo
Cleveland
Youngstown
Akron

Davenport
Des Moines

Peoria
INDIANA
OHIO
Columbus
Dayton
Cincinnati

Kansas City
ILLINOIS
Springfield
Indianapolis
Louisville
Frankfort
Lexington

Lake of the Ozarks
Louis
East St. Louis
Evansville

Kansas City
Jefferson City

MISSOURI
Springfield

KENTUCKY

Fayetteville
Lake Barkley
Kentucky Lake
Nashville
Knoxville

ARKANSAS
TENNESSEE
Chattanooga
Asheville

Little Rock
Pine Bluff

Memphis

MISSISSIPPI
Huntsville
Atlanta
GEORGIA
Macon
Columbus

Shreveport
Vicksburg
Jackson
Birmingham
ALABAMA
Meridian
Montgomery

Toledo Bend Reservoir
LOUISIANA
Baton Rouge
Biloxi
Mobile
Pensacola
Tallahassee
Jacksonville

Beaumont
New Orleans
CHANDELEUR ISLANDS
Gainesville

Galveston

GULF OF MEXICO

FLORIDA
Orlando
Cape Canaveral
Tampa
St. Petersburg
Lake Okeechobee
Fort Myers
Fort Lauderdale
Miami
Cape Sable
FLORIDA KEYS
Straits of Florida

THE BAHAMAS

CUBA

MAINE
Augusta
Lake Champlain
Burlington
Montpelier
Portland
VT
NH
Concord
Manchester
MA
Boston
Worcester
Providence
Cape Cod
RI
Springfield
Hartford
CT
New Haven
Long Island Sound
Bridgeport
LONG ISLAND

NEW YORK
Buffalo
Rochester
Syracuse
Albany
Yonkers
New York City
Newark
Jersey City
Trenton
PENNSYLVANIA
Allentown
NJ
Camden
Harrisburg
Pittsburgh
Philadelphia
Atlantic City

Baltimore
DE
Dover
MD
Annapolis
Washington, D.C.
DELAWARE BAY

WEST VIRGINIA
Charleston
VIRGINIA
Richmond
CHESAPEAKE BAY

Norfolk
Newport News
Virginia Beach

Winston-Salem
Greensboro
Durham
Raleigh
NORTH CAROLINA
Cape Hatteras

Charlotte

Greenville

SOUTH CAROLINA
Columbia

Charleston

Savannah

SEA ISLANDS

ATLANTIC OCEAN

National capital
State capitals
Other cities

ARCTIC OCEAN
NORTH AMERICA
EUROPE
ASIA
Equator
ATLANTIC OCEAN
AFRICA
PACIFIC OCEAN
SOUTH AMERICA
INDIAN OCEAN
AUSTRALIA
ANTARCTICA
Robinson Projection

SCALE
0   250   500 Miles
0   250   500 Kilometers
Projection: Albers Equal Area

50° N
45° N
40° N
35° N
30° N
25° N

85° W
80° W
75° W
70° W
65° W
60° W
90° W

Presidents of the United States

no.	Name	Born–Died	Years in Office	Political Party	Home State	Vice President
1	George Washington	1732–1799	1789–97	None	VA	John Adams
2	John Adams	1735–1826	1797–1801	Federalist	MA	Thomas Jefferson
3	Thomas Jefferson	1743–1826	1801–09	Republican*	VA	Aaron Burr George Clinton
4	James Madison	1751–1836	1809–17	Republican	VA	George Clinton Elbridge Gerry
5	James Monroe	1758–1831	1817–25	Republican	VA	Daniel D. Tompkins
6	John Quincy Adams	1767–1848	1825–29	Republican	MA	John C. Calhoun
7	Andrew Jackson	1767–1845	1829–37	Democratic	TN	John C. Calhoun Martin Van Buren
8	Martin Van Buren	1782–1862	1837–41	Democratic	NY	Richard M. Johnson
9	William Henry Harrison	1773–1841	1841	Whig	OH	John Tyler
10	John Tyler	1790–1862	1841–45	Whig	VA	
11	James K. Polk	1795–1849	1845–49	Democratic	TN	George M. Dallas
12	Zachary Taylor	1784–1850	1849–50	Whig	LA	Millard Fillmore
13	Millard Fillmore	1800–1874	1850–53	Whig	NY	
14	Franklin Pierce	1804–1869	1853–57	Democratic	NH	William R. King
15	James Buchanan	1791–1868	1857–61	Democratic	PA	John C. Breckinridge
16	Abraham Lincoln	1809–1865	1861–65	Republican	IL	Hannibal Hamlin Andrew Johnson
17	Andrew Johnson	1808–1875	1865–69	Republican	TN	
18	Ulysses S. Grant	1822–1885	1869–77	Republican	IL	Schuyler Colfax Henry Wilson
19	Rutherford B. Hayes	1822–1893	1877–81	Republican	OH	William A Wheeler
20	James A. Garfield	1831–1881	1881	Republican	OH	Chester A. Arthur
21	Chester A. Arthur	1830–1886	1881–85	Republican	NY	
22	Grover Cleveland	1837–1908	1885–89	Democratic	NY	Thomas A. Hendricks
23	Benjamin Harrison	1833–1901	1889–93	Republican	IN	Levi P. Morton
24	Grover Cleveland		1893–97	Democratic	NY	Adlai E. Stevenson
25	William McKinley	1843–1901	1897–1901	Republican	OH	Garrett A. Hobart Theodore Roosevelt
26	Theodore Roosevelt	1858–1919	1901–09	Republican	NY	Charles W. Fairbanks
27	William Howard Taft	1857–1930	1909–13	Republican	OH	James S. Sherman
28	Woodrow Wilson	1856–1924	1913–21	Democratic	NJ	Thomas R. Marshall
29	Warren G. Harding	1865–1923	1921–23	Republican	OH	Calvin Coolidge
30	Calvin Coolidge	1872–1933	1923–29	Republican	MA	Charles G. Dawes
31	Herbert Hoover	1874–1964	1929–33	Republican	CA	Charles Curtis
32	Franklin D. Roosevelt	1882–1945	1933–45	Democratic	NY	John Nance Garner Henry Wallace Harry S. Truman
33	Harry S Truman	1884–1972	1945–53	Democratic	MO	Alben W. Barkley
34	Dwight D. Eisenhower	1890–1969	1953–61	Republican	KS	Richard M. Nixon
35	John F. Kennedy	1917–1963	1961–63	Democratic	MA	Lyndon B. Johnson
36	Lyndon B. Johnson	1908–1973	1963–69	Democratic	TX	Hubert H. Humphrey
37	Richard M. Nixon	1913–1994	1969–74	Republican	CA	Spiro T. Agnew Gerald R. Ford
38	Gerald R. Ford	1913–	1974–77	Republican	MI	Nelson A. Rockefeller
39	Jimmy Carter	1924–	1977–81	Democratic	GA	Walter F. Mondale
40	Ronald Reagan	1911–	1981–89	Republican	CA	George Bush
41	George Bush	1924–	1989–93	Republican	TX	J. Danforth Quayle
42	Bill Clinton	1946–	1993–	Democratic	AR	Albert Gore, Jr.

*The Republican Party of the third through sixth presidents is not the party of Abraham Lincoln, which was founded in 1854.

GLOSSARY

This Glossary contains terms you need to understand as you study American history. After each term there is a brief definition or explanation of the meaning of the term as it is used in *Exploring America's Past.* The page number refers to the page on which the term is introduced in the textbook.

Phonetic Respelling and Pronunciation Guide
Many of the key terms in this textbook have been respelled to help you pronounce them. The letter combinations used in the respellings throughout the narrative are explained in the following phonetic respelling and pronunciation guide. The guide is adapted from *Webster's Tenth New College Dictionary, Webster's New Geographical Dictionary,* and *Webster's New Biographical Dictionary.*

MARK	AS IN	RESPELLING	EXAMPLE
a	alphabet	a	*AL-fuh-bet
ā	Asia	ay	AY-zhuh
ä	cart, top	ah	KAHRT, TAHP
e	let, ten	e	LET, TEN
ē	even, leaf	ee	EE-vuhn, LEEF
i	it, tip, British	i	IT, TIP, BRIT-ish
ī	site, buy, Ohio	y	SYT, BY, oh-HY-oh
	iris	eye	EYE-ris
k	card	k	KAHRD
ō	over, rainbow	oh	oh-vuhr, RAYN-boh
ů	book, wood	ooh	BOOHK, WOOHD
ò	all, orchid	aw	AWL, AWR-kid
òi	foil, coin	oy	FOYL, KOYN
aů	out	ow	OWT
ə	cup, butter	uh	KUHP, BUHT-uhr
ü	rule, food	oo	ROOL, FOOD
yü	few	yoo	FYOO
zh	vision	zh	VIZH-uhn

*A syllable printed in small capital letters receives heavier emphasis than the other syllable(s) in a word.

A

ABC Powers Argentina, Brazil, and Chile. **442**
abolition An end to slavery. **233**
aces Fighter pilots who shoot down many enemy planes. **462**
acid rain Rain carrying toxins from air pollution. **698**
Acquired Immune Deficiency Syndrome (AIDS) A deadly disease that was discovered in the 1980s and that destroys the body's capability to fight off illnesses and infections. **678**
Adams-Onís Treaty (1819) An agreement in which Spain gave up its claims to West Florida and Oregon Country and ceded the rest of Florida to the United States. **195**
affirmative action Practice by some businesses and government agencies of giving special consideration to nonwhites and women when applicants' qualifications are roughly equal to make up for past discrimination. **655**

African National Congress (ANC) A political organization that fought for the rights of blacks in South Africa. **701**
Alamo Old Spanish mission-fort in San Antonio, Texas, that was the site of the most famous battle of the Texas war for independence in 1836; the Mexican victory resulted in the deaths of all the Texan defenders. **265**
Albany Plan of Union (1754) Proposal drafted by Benjamin Franklin for permanently uniting the colonies. **113**
Alien and Sedition Acts (1798) Series of laws passed by Federalists aimed at foreigners in the United States and at Republicans who were supposedly trying to weaken the government. **173**
Allied Powers Great Britain, France, Russia, and their allies in World War I. **448**
Allied Powers The United States, Great Britain, France, the Soviet Union, China, Australia, Canada, and their allies during World War II. **526**

amendments Official changes to a constitution. **118**

American Anti-Slavery Society Group founded in 1833 by William Lloyd Garrison and other abolitionists to support abolition and racial equality. **235**

American Civil Liberties Union (ACLU) Organization founded by lawyer Felix Frankfurter in the 1920s to fight for Italian anarchists Sacco and Vanzetti, who were sentenced to death for a robbery. **475**

American Colonization Society Group organized in 1817 by white citizens to relocate about 1,400 African Americans to what became the African nation of Liberia. **234**

American Expeditionary Force (AEF) American forces led by General John J. Pershing that fought in Europe during World War I. **461**

American Federation of Labor (AFL) Union founded in the 1880s consisting only of skilled workers. **389**

American Indian Movement (AIM) Protest organization formed in 1968 that used confrontational tactics to draw attention to abuses against American Indians. **656**

American Liberty League Organization formed by opponents of the New Deal who claimed the new laws were unconstitutional. **510**

Americans with Disabilities Act (1990) Federal law prohibiting discrimination against people with mental or physical disabilities. **678**

American System Plan developed by Henry Clay to get western members of Congress to vote for high tariffs in exchange for eastern votes for internal improvements. **247**

amnesty Forgiveness. **338**

anarchists People who want all government abolished. **474**

annex To take control of land. **273**

Antifederalists Opponents of the U.S. Constitution who tended to come from rural areas and were generally less wealthy than Federalists. **127**

Anti-Imperialist League Organization formed in June 1898 by Americans opposed to U.S. colonization. **436**

Anti-Saloon League Organization begun by progressives in 1895 to urge state legislatures to pass prohibition measures. **423**

apartheid A legal system of racial and class discrimination in South Africa. **652**

appeasement Policy of giving in to avoid a larger conflict. **523**

arbitration Negotiations led by a neutral party. **418**

armistice Cease-fire agreement. **464**

Army-McCarthy hearings Televised investigation by Senator Joseph McCarthy into "subversive [disloyal] activities" by the U.S. Army. **569**

arsenal Place where weapons are stored. **119**

Articles of Confederation America's first national constitution, drafted in 1777, that stressed the independence of the separate states. **113**

artisans People who craft items by hand. **13**

assayed To have minerals tested for value. **371**

assembly line Method of mass production in which a product is assembled by moving along a conveyer belt past a line of workers. **481**

astrolabe An instrument that helped sailors in the 1400s figure out a ship's latitude. **14**

Atlanta Compromise (1895) Proposal by Booker T. Washington that African Americans should accept American society and try to get ahead within it by learning skilled trades. **355**

atomic bomb Weapon developed by American scientists during World War II that released enormous amounts of energy by breaking the atomic bonds that hold together radioactive elements. **542**

Axis Powers Germany, Italy, and Japan during World War II. **526**

B

baby boom Leap in the birthrate following World War II. **574**

Bacon's Rebellion (1676) Virginia movement led by Nathaniel Bacon to rid the colony of American Indians, in defiance of the royal governor. **54**

balance of power Situation in which rival groups of nations are kept at nearly equal strength. **448**

balance of trade The relationship between what a nation buys from and what it sells to foreign countries, not including its own colonies. **64**

bank notes Paper money produced by banks to represent the money they have on deposit. **162**

Bank of the United States A national bank with branches in major American cities, first proposed by Alexander Hamilton. **162**

bankruptcy A state of extreme financial ruin. **385**

barbed wire A relatively cheap method of fencing that allowed farmers and ranchers to close off their land. **375**

Bataan Death March (1942) The 60-mile forced march of U.S. and Filipino prisoners by Japanese soldiers, in which some 600 Americans and 10,000 Filipinos died. **542**

Battle of Antietam (1862) Civil War battle that resulted in the first major victory for the Union in the East. **325**

Battle of Bunker Hill (1775) Revolutionary War battle in which more than 1,000 British soldiers and some 400 American militiamen were killed or wounded in British victory. **92**

Battle of Fallen Timbers (1794) Battle between U.S. troops led by General "Mad Anthony" Wayne and an Indian confederacy led by Blue Jacket that ended the Indian confederacy's campaign to halt white settlement west of the Appalachian Mountains. **167**

Battle of Gettysburg (1863) One of the bloodiest battles of the Civil War in which the Confederates lost more than 20,000 troops and the Union forces some 23,000. **330**

Battle of Horseshoe Bend (1814) Defeat of Creek Indian forces allied with the British by the Tennessee militia, led by Andrew Jackson, in the War of 1812. **191**

Battle of Lake Erie (1813) U.S. victory led by Oliver Perry in the War of 1812. **190**

Battle of Leyte Gulf (1944) Allied invasion of the Philippines during World War II in which the U.S. Navy destroyed the last major Japanese fleet and took complete control of the Philippines. **540**

Battle of Midway (1942) Naval battle that gave the United States control of the central Pacific during World War II. **534**

Battle of New Orleans (1815) Greatest victory for the United States in the War of 1812, even though it actually took place after the war was officially over. **192**

Battle of San Jacinto (1836) Final battle of the Texas war for independence in which Sam Houston led 800 Texas soldiers to victory against 1,400 Mexican troops led by Santa Anna. **266**

Battle of Saratoga (1777) Turning point of the Revolutionary War in which Americans, led by General Horatio Gates, delivered a crushing blow to British forces led by General John Burgoyne. **105**

Battle of Seven Pines (1862) Civil War battle in which neither side gained an advantage. **320**

Battle of Shiloh (1862) Civil War battle in Tennessee that resulted in Union victory, but a huge loss of life on both sides. **322**

Battle of Stalingrad (1942–43) World War II attack on German forces by the Soviets that halted the German advance to the east. **535**

Battle of the Argonne Forest (1918) Battle in which Allied forces finally pushed back the Germans and ended World War I. **463**

Battle of the Bulge (1944–45) Final offensive assault by the Germans during World War II that ended with an Allied victory. **539**

Battle of the Coral Sea (1942) World War II battle in which the Japanese fleet was damaged so badly that Japan gave up a planned invasion of New Guinea. **533**

Battle of the Little Bighorn (1876) Custer's Last Stand; the U.S. Army's worst defeat in the West when Sioux Indians, led by Sitting Bull, defeated troops led by General George Armstrong Custer. **368.**

Battle of the Marne (1914) World War I battle in which French and British troops stopped the German advance toward Paris. **449**

Battle of the Thames (1813) U.S. victory in the War of 1812 led by William Henry Harrison; allowed the United States to gain back the Great Lakes region and resulted in the death of Tecumseh, which ended the British-allied Indian confederacy. **190**

Battle of Tippecanoe (1811) Indiana battle between Americans, led by William Henry Harrison, against Indian confederacy, led by Tecumseh, that opposed American settlement in the Northwest Territory; defeat weakened the Indian confederacy. **188**

Battle of Trenton (1776) New Jersey battle of the Revolutionary War in which American soldiers overwhelmed Hessians fighting for the British, taking 900 prisoners. **102**

Battle of Yorktown (1781) Final major battle of the Revolutionary War that ended with the surrender of British general Cornwallis. **107**

Bear Flag Revolt (1846) Revolt against Mexico by California settlers who declared the Republic of California during the Mexican War. **275**

bear market A steady drop in stock prices. **498**

beats A small group of young writers and poets who rebelled against both established literary and social traditions in the 1950s. **578**

benevolent societies Groups set up by charitable organizations to help immigrants. **393**

Berlin Airlift (1948) British and American effort to fly supplies to West Berlin after the Soviets closed all ground access to the city. **559**

Berlin Wall Concrete and barbed wire wall built between East Berlin and West Berlin by the Soviets in 1961. **589**

Bessemer process Inexpensive way to make steel, developed by Henry Bessemer in the 1850s. **381**

bicameral Two-house legislature. **121**

Big Four Council of Four; U.S. president Woodrow Wilson, British prime minister David Lloyd George, French premier Georges Clemenceau, and Italian prime minister Vittorio Orlando; leaders of the victorious Allied Powers that gathered to write a formal peace treaty after World War I. **466**

Big Three British prime minister Winston Churchill, U.S. president Franklin Roosevelt, and Soviet leader Joseph Stalin; leaders of the Allied Powers who met at Yalta in 1945 to plan for the end of World War II. **548**

Black Codes Regulations passed by southern state legislators to keep freedpeople in a slavelike condition after the Civil War. **338**

Black Death A deadly disease that first struck in the 1300s and swept across Europe, killing between 25 and 50 percent of the population. **13**

blacklisted Policy, particularly in the entertainment industry, of not hiring people who refused to cooperate with the House Un-American Activities Committee. **564**

Black Power Approach to the civil rights movement that called for African Americans to build their own communities and protect themselves against white racism. **604**

blockade Naval measure that uses ships to cut off a country's trade and supplies. **92**

Boland Amendment (1984) Congressional measure banning future U.S. aid to the Nicaraguan contras. **668**

bonanza A large find of extremely rich ore. **371**

bonds Treasury certificates that represent money the federal government has borrowed from citizens. **160**

Bonus Army (1932) March of about 10,000 veterans and their families to Washington, D.C., to demand immediate payment of bonuses not due until 1945. **504**

bootleggers People who smuggled alcohol into the country during prohibition. **488**

border states Delaware, Maryland, Kentucky, and Missouri; the slave states that did not join the Confederacy. **316**

Boston Massacre (1770) Incident when British soldiers fired into a crowd protesting at a customs house, killing five colonists. **86**

Boston Tea Party (1773) Protest against the Tea Act in which colonists disguised as Mohawk Indians boarded tea ships and threw all the tea overboard. **87**

Boxer Rebellion (1900) Attack on foreigners in Beijing and other parts of China by Chinese nationalists known as the "Fists of Righteous Harmony," or Boxers; an international army organized by Western nations put down the rebellion. **438**

Bozeman Trail Trail for miners, founded by John M. Bozeman, that branched off the Oregon Trail west of Fort Laramie and ran north into Montana. **365**

boycott To refuse to buy goods. **85**

braceros Mexican farmworkers. **530**

Brady Bill (1993) Handgun Violence Prevention Act; Federal law requiring a waiting period and background check in order to buy a handgun. **685**

Brain Trust Close advisers to President Franklin Roosevelt who were experts in law, economics, and social welfare. **507**

brand Scar made by pressing a red-hot branding iron onto a cow's hide. **374**

brinkmanship The threat of massive retaliation that suggested the United States was willing to go "to the brink" of all-out war, if necessary, to stop communism. **570**

Brown v. Board of Education (1954) Supreme Court case that overturned the "separate but equal" doctrine established in *Plessy* v. *Ferguson* and desegregated public schools. **580**

bull market A continuing rise in stock prices. **498**

Bureau of Indian Affairs Government agency that supervised American Indian reservations and promised money and supplies to support their new way of life. **364**

business cycle Recurring periods of economic depression and prosperity. **499**

busing Court-ordered practice in the late 1960s and early 1970s of sending students to schools outside of their neighborhoods in order to end indirect school segregation. **655**

buying on margin Purchasing stock with borrowed money. **498**

C

cabinet Heads of federal departments who advise the president. **158**

California Gold Rush Rush of people to California to prospect for gold after a major gold discovery in 1848. **281**

California Trail Trail to California that branched off south from the Oregon Trail. **271**

Californios Mexican settlers and their descendants in California. **271**

Camp David Accords (1978) Guidelines for a Middle East peace agreement worked out between U.S. president Jimmy Carter, Egyptian president Anwar Sadat, and Israeli prime minister Menachem Begin. **653**

canals Artificial waterways used for transportation. **214**

carpetbaggers Name given to northerners who moved to the South after the Civil War. **344**

causalities People killed, wounded, or missing in combat. **90**

cattle drive Long journey northward to get Texas longhorns to cattle towns. **372**

Cattle Kingdom Area from Texas into Canada and from the Rocky Mountains to eastern Kansas that became dotted with cattle ranches. **372**

cede Surrender. **195**

Central Intelligence Agency (CIA) Organization created in 1947 to carry out secret spy operations against foreign enemies of the United States. **558**

Central Powers Alliance of Germany, Austria-Hungary, Bulgaria, and the Ottoman Empire in World War I. **448**

charter Document granting certain rights and powers to form colonies. **35**

Chicano movement Movement mostly among college students to increase awareness of Hispanic culture and political strength. **657**

Chinese Exclusion Act (1882) Legislation prohibiting Chinese workers from entering the United States for a period of 10 years, which was later extended well into the 1900s. **394**

circumnavigate To travel around the entire world. **24**

Civil Rights Act of 1866 Legislation forbidding southern states from passing laws, such as the Black Codes, restricting freedpeople's rights. **339**

Civil Rights Act of 1964 Legislation outlawing racial discrimination in public facilities and employment practices. **602**

Clayton Antitrust Act (1914) Law that made it illegal for directors of one corporation to be directors of other corporations in the same field. **420**

Cold War Long-lasting struggle for global power between the United States and the Soviet Union after World War II. **549**

collective bargaining Process in which union leaders negotiate with employers to determine employee working conditions and benefits. **389**

colonists People who leave their home countries to establish new settlements. **30**

Columbian Exchange The transfer of ideas, plants, animals, and diseases between the Eastern and Western Hemispheres. **36**

Commercial Revolution A rapid growth in the European economy during the 1400s. **13**

Committee on Civil Rights Organization established by President Harry Truman in December 1946 to report on the status of race relations in the United States. **555**

Committees of Correspondence Group organized by Samuel Adams to share information throughout the American colonies about resistance to the British. **86**

common A plot of public grazing land around which English colonists in North America centered their towns. **48**

Commonwealth of Independent States (CIS) Loose federation of former Soviet republics, formed in 1991. **673**

Communists People who want to overthrow the capitalist economic system and replace it with a society where all individuals share wealth equally and where private ownership is abolished. **474**

compensate To make up for. **503**

Compromise of 1850 Proposal by Henry Clay to allow California to enter the Union as a free state, while the rest of the Mexican Cession would be divided into two new territories where the residents would determine the status of slavery; also prohibited the slave trade in the District of Columbia and created a stronger fugitive slave law. **292**

Compromise of 1877 Proposal that grew out of disputed presidential election of 1876; Democrats agreed to let Republican Rutherford B. Hayes become president if he would remove all federal troops stationed in the South. **349**

Comstock Lode Silver bonanza struck in western Nevada in 1859. **371**

Confederate States of America The Confederacy; central government created by delegates of states that seceded from the Union in 1861. **313**

Confederation Congress Single national governing body created by the Articles of Confederation. **113**

conformity Fitting into society. **574**

conquistadores Soldier-explorers who helped Spain establish and expand its empire in the Americas. **22**

constitution A set of laws that defines the basic structure and powers of a government. **112**

Constitutional Convention (1787) Meeting of state delegates to draw up the Constitution of the United States. **121**

Constitutional Union Party Group formed in 1860 by southerners who wanted to preserve "the Union as it is and the Constitution as it is." **307**

containment Early goal of U.S. Cold War policy, defined by diplomat George F. Kennan, of containing Soviet expansion wherever it was attempted. **559**

Continental Army Official colonial military force created by the Second Continental Congress and led by George Washington. **91**

contrabands Escaped slaves who crossed Union lines during the Civil War. **326**

Contract with America (1994) Republican document that put into effect a 10-point program for redirecting the government and the economy. **686**

contras Rebel Nicaraguan groups who wanted to overthrow the Sandinistas. **668**

Convention of 1818 Agreement that set the boundary between the Louisiana Purchase and British Canada at 49° north latitude from northern Minnesota to the Rocky Mountains; also called for joint control of the disputed area of Oregon Country. **194**

Copperheads Northern Democrats who opposed the Civil War. **327**

Congress of Racial Equality (CORE) A northern civil rights group that set out to challenge segregation in interstate commerce. **600**

corporations Businesses in which entrepreneurs sell shares called stock certificates to investors. **384**

cotton belt A huge agricultural region largely devoted to the production of cotton. **221**

cotton gin Machine produced by Eli Whitney in 1793 that separated cotton seeds from the fibers. **220**

Council of the Indies Group of royal assistants in Spain that nominated colonial officials and drafted and administered laws relating to Spain's colonies in the Americas. **27**

counterculture Alternative culture created by some leaders of the 1960s youth revolt that would stand in stark contrast to the world of previous generations. **606**

counting coup To touch an enemy or capture his weapon; proof of an American Indian warrior's highest bravery. **361**

covenant Sacred agreement. **49**

creditors People to whom money is owed. **119**

crop lien Investors' claim against a crop before it is even harvested. **353**

Crusades A series of religious wars fought between Christians and Muslims for control of Palestine, an area in Southwest Asia that was sacred to Muslims, Jews, and Christians. **12**

Cuban missile crisis (1962) Standoff between the Soviet Union and the United States over missiles in Cuba; resulted in decreasing likelihood of nuclear war. **590**

culture Common values and customs of a society. **4**

culture area A geographic region in which residents share common cultural traits; used to group American Indian societies. **5**

D

D-Day June 6, 1944; beginning of Allied invasion of France during World War II. **537**

debtors People who owe money. **118**

Declaration of Independence Statement by members of the Second Continental Congress, signed on July 4, 1776, explaining the need for independence by the colonies. **95**

deficit spending Situation that results when the government spends more than it takes in. **514**

deforestation Process by which the world's forests are disappearing. **697**

Democratic Party Political party formed in 1828 by Andrew Jackson's supporters who split from the Democratic-Republican Party. **245**

Democratic-Republican Party Republicans; political party led by Thomas Jefferson and formed in the 1790s by those who opposed Alexander Hamilton. **170**

Department of Energy Organization created by Congress in 1977 to establish programs for conserving energy and managing the country's energy resources. **651**

deport To order a person out of a country. **173**

depression A sharp drop in business activity accompanied by high unemployment. **250**

détente Period after the SALT agreement when relations improved between the United States and the Soviet Union. **642**

diplomats Officials who conduct government relations with foreign countries. **113**

dissenters People who disagree with commonly held opinions. **50**

Dixiecrats Southern Democrats who opposed President Harry Truman because of his civil rights policies and who organized the States' Rights Party in 1948. **556**

dogfights Deadly air battles between enemy fighter planes. **462**

dollar diplomacy President William Howard Taft's policy of trying to control nations in the Western Hemisphere indirectly by using economic methods rather than military force. **441**

Dominion of New England Unified group of colonies organized by King James II in 1686 and led by Sir Edmund Andros; was overthrown in 1689. **62**

domino theory President Dwight D. Eisenhower's theory that if Communists gained control of Vietnam, then Laos, Cambodia, and the rest of Southeast Asia might fall to Communists as well. **616**

doves Americans who wanted to stop the war in Vietnam. **623**

downsizing Decreasing the number of employees to keep profits up and to stay more competitive. **694**

draft A system requiring people to serve in the military. **327**

Dred Scott decision (1857) Supreme Court ruling that declared African Americans were not citizens and that the Missouri Compromise had been unconstitutional. **300**

droughts Dry periods when almost no rain falls. **378**

dry farming Technique promoted by Hardy W. Campbell that made it possible to raise certain crops with very little water. **379**

Dust Bowl Region of the Great Plains that suffered a drought in the 1930s so bad that it was almost impossible to grow anything. **518**

duties Import taxes. **84**

E

Earth Summit (1992) Meeting of representatives from all over the world to put together an agreement that would encourage countries to work toward improving the environment. **699**

Eighteenth Amendment (1919) Constitutional amendment that made prohibition legal throughout the nation. **423**

Eisenhower Doctrine (1957) President Dwight D. Eisenhower's promise of U.S. financial and military assistance to Middle Eastern countries who asked for help to resist the spread of communism. **571**

emancipation Freedom. **237**

Emancipation Proclamation Order issued by President Abraham Lincoln to announce that as of January 1, 1863, all slaves in the states rebelling against the Union would be free. **325**

embargo A government order prohibiting trade. **185**

Embargo Act (1807) Law that prohibited all exports from the United States. **185**

empresario Someone who made a business of bringing settlers into the American West. **264**

enclosure movement Process in Great Britain by which many tenant farmers were thrown off their land when owners fenced the land to raise sheep; many of these farmers went to work in factories. **205**

energy crisis Situation in the 1970s when the cost of electricity and gasoline soared due to rising oil prices. **640**

Enlightenment Movement in the 1700s that grew out of the Scientific Revolution and encouraged the use of reason to investigate and try to improve government and society. **112**

entrepreneurs Risk-taking businesspeople. **384**

enumerated articles Products that colonial producers could sell only within English-controlled territory. **64**

Environmental Protection Agency (EPA) Organization established by Congress in 1970 to enforce environmental laws. **641**

Equal Pay Act (1963) Federal law requiring private employers to pay men and women the same wages for the same jobs. **592**

Equal Rights Amendment (ERA) Proposed constitutional amendment stating that equality of rights could not be denied on the basis of gender; passed by Congress in 1972, but failed to be ratified. **659**

Erie Canal Canal completed in 1825, running from the Hudson River across New York to Lake Erie. **215**

escalation Increase. **622**

ethnic cleansing Process by Bosnian Serbs to try to drive all Muslims out of their communities by herding them into camps and killing them. **690**

European Union (EU) Organization created in 1993 by a group of countries in Western Europe to allow the free movement of goods, labor, and currency between members. **700**

excise taxes Taxes on goods produced and consumed inside a country. **161**

executive branch Branch of government that carries out laws. **123**

executive privilege Right to keep information secret when it relates to presidential business. **645**

Exodusters Some 20,000 or more African Americans who moved west from the South in 1879. **377**

expansionism Belief by some people in the late 1800s that the United States should eventually bring most of North and South America under U.S. control. **428**

expatriates People who voluntarily leave their country to live abroad. **487**

export To sell products to another country. **64**

F

54th Massachusetts Infantry African American Union troops that won an honored place in U.S. military history during the Civil War battle for Fort Wagner. **326**

Fair Deal Reforms proposed by President Harry Truman to extend the New Deal after the 1948 election. **557**

Fair Employment Practices Committee (FEPC) Organization created during World War II to enforce President Franklin Roosevelt's executive order prohibiting racial discrimination in defense plants. **530**

Family Assistance Plan (FAP) President Richard Nixon's plan to replace the existing welfare system with one that guaranteed every family a minimum income; the plan died in the Senate. **638**

Farm bloc Common interest group formed by Congress members from the South and the West to obtain legislation favorable to agriculture. **492**

Farmers' Alliance Political group in the late 1800s that opposed high railroad rates and high bank interest rates. **399**

fascism Totalitarian political system founded in Italy in the 1920s by Benito Mussolini. **522**

Federal Deposit Insurance Corporation (FDIC) Organization established by Congress in the 1930s to prevent another banking crisis by insuring deposits up to $5,000. **509**

Federal Emergency Relief Administration (FERA) New Deal agency headed by Harry Hopkins that distributed $500 million in federal grants among state organizations that cared for the poor. **508**

Federal Reserve Act (1913) Legislation that created 12 Federal Reserve banks in different sections of the nation; these banks were for banks, not for businesses or individuals. **420**

Federal Trade Commission Organization established in 1914 to conduct investigations of large corporations. **420**

federalism System established by the U.S. Constitution of dividing power between the state and national governments. **125**

Federalist Party Political party organized in the 1790s by members of Congress who favored Alexander Hamilton's financial policies. **170**

Federalists Supporters of the U.S. Constitution who tended to be wealthy lawyers, merchants, and planters. **126**

Fifteenth Amendment (1869) Constitutional amendment guaranteeing that the right to vote could not be denied on the basis of race, color, or previous condition of servitude. **341**

fireside chats Radio talks by President Franklin Roosevelt. **507**

First Battle of Bull Run (1861) First major battle of the Civil War; made Americans on both sides realize that winning the war might be difficult. **319**

First Continental Congress (1774) Meeting of representatives from all colonies (except Georgia) to express loyalty to Britain but demand the repeal of all British taxation laws and to ban all trade with Britain until Parliament met its demands. **88**

Five-Power Naval Treaty (1921) Agreement drafted at the Washington Conference to limit the size of navies. **476**

folktales Oral stories that help to educate and set a standard of behavior for people. **230**

Food Administration Organization headed by Herbert Hoover during World War I to make sure that enough food was produced and distributed fairly. **458**

Fort Laramie Treaty (1851) Agreement signed between the U.S. government and Plains Indians to allow settlement in the West. **364**

forty-niners At least 80,000 people who flocked to California in 1849 to prospect for gold. **281**

Fourteen Points President Woodrow Wilson's plan for peace after World War I. **465**

Fourteenth Amendment (1866) Constitutional amendment that gave citizenship to all African Americans in the United States. **340**

free coinage Policy requiring the government to coin silver freely, increasing the money in circulation. **399**

Freedmen's Bureau Agency created by Congress shortly before the end of the Civil War to take care of freedpeople and refugees. **339**

Freedom Rides Plan developed by CORE to challenge segregation in interstate commerce by having white and black Freedom Riders travel through the South on buses, intentionally ignoring signs in segregated stations. **600**

Freedom Summer Massive voter registration drive by civil rights workers in 1964. **602**

Freeport Doctrine (1858) Statement by Stephen A. Douglas during the Lincoln-Douglas debates arguing that the people of a territory could outlaw slavery by passing local laws making it impossible for slavery to exist. **304**

Free-Soil Party Political organization founded by antislavery Whigs and northern Democrats to prevent slavery in the new territories. **290**

French Revolution Revolution against the French monarchy that began in 1789. **164**

Fugitive Slave Act (1850) Allowed slave catchers more power to capture suspected runaways. **292**

Fundamentalism Protestant religious movement whose followers took every word of the Bible literally. **491**

G

GI Bill of Rights (1944) Servicemen's Readjustment Act; made low-cost loans available to veterans to buy houses and farms, to start new businesses, and to improve their educations. **554**

Gadsden Purchase (1853) Agreement that added a strip of Mexican land to southern New Mexico and Arizona for $10 million. **276**

Generation X "Baby busters"; children of baby boomers who seemed to face limited job prospects and decreasing public resources in the 1990s. **692**

genes Tiny segments of chromosomes that determine all of the body's physical characteristics. **678**

Geneva Accords (1950) Settlement opposed by the United States that temporarily partitioned Vietnam along the 17th parallel until elections could be held in July 1956 to reunite the country. **618**

Ghost Dance (1889) American Indian religious revival that swept through the Plains. **369**

glaciers Vast ice fields that formed during the Ice Age and caused the water level of the world's oceans to drop sharply. **3**

glasnost Political openness policy established by Soviet premier Mikhail Gorbachev in the 1980s. **669**

global warming A trend in rising temperatures some scientists believe is caused by the "greenhouse effect," in which pollution keeps more heat in the atmosphere. **698**

Glorious Revolution (1688) Revolt against pro-Catholic King James II by Parliament that resulted in James's Protestant daughter Mary and her husband, William of Orange, being crowned leaders of England. **63**

glyphs System of picture writing used by the Maya around A.D. 300–800. **5**

gold standard Monetary system in which the government backs each dollar with a set amount of gold. **399**

Gramm-Rudman-Hollings Act (1985) Federal law requiring spending cuts when the deficit goes above a certain level. **665**

grandfather clauses Laws stating that literacy tests and poll taxes did not apply to persons who had been able to vote before 1867 or to their descendants. **350**

Great Awakening A series of events that began in the 1730s and sparked new interest in Christianity in the American colonies. **71**

Great Compromise (1787) Agreement establishing that population would determine representation in the national legislature's lower house, while each state would have an equal vote in the legislature's upper house. **122**

Great Depression Worldwide economic downturn that began with the stock market crash of 1929. **498**

Great Migration Large movement of English Puritans to the Americas in the 1600s. **49**

Great Migration Mass movement of southern African Americans to northern cities that started during World War I. **459**

Great Society Vast effort by President Lyndon Johnson to transform society by eliminating many long-standing social and economic problems. **596**

Green parties Environmental political parties. **699**

guerrillas Fighters who use hit-and-run tactics. **106**

H

habeas corpus A constitutional protection that prevents authorities from unlawfully jailing people. **327**

Harlem Globetrotters Team of African American basketball players created in 1927. **485**

Harlem Renaissance Movement among black writers in the 1920s who urged respect for African American culture. **487**

hawks People who insisted that the United States must fight the war in Vietnam until it was won. **624**

Hay–Bunau-Varilla Treaty (1903) Agreement granting the United States a 10-mile-wide canal zone across Panama. **440**

Haymarket Riot (1886) Bombing during a union meeting at Chicago's Haymarket Square in which seven police officers were killed; turned public opinion against unions. **380**

headright Land grant of 50 acres per head, or person, given by the London Company to colonists who paid their own way and that of others to America. **53**

hippies Members of the counterculture who behaved in ways that shocked and frightened many mainstream Americans. **606**

Ho Chi Minh Trail Vietcong supply route that started in North Vietnam and wove through the mountains of Laos and Cambodia into South Vietnam. **621**

Holocaust Hitler's "Final Solution," or plan to rid Europe of Jews by placing them in concentration camps, where millions were killed. **539**

Homestead Act (1862) Federal law that gave western land grants to promote settlement. **376**

Homestead Strike (1892) Strike against Andrew Carnegie's steel factory in Homestead, Pennsylvania, which led to violence between strikers and private police from the Pinkerton Detective Agency. **390**

horizontal integration The attempted ownership of all the companies in a particular field. **385**

House of Burgesses The first elected English governing body in the colonies. **54**

House of Representatives Lower house of the United States legislature; assumed to act on behalf of the people. **123**

House Un-American Activities Committee (HUAC) Congressional committee that began a series of hearings in 1947 to investigate citizens who belonged to a number of liberal organizations. **564**

Hull House The most famous American settlement house, founded in 1889 by Jane Addams in Chicago. **412**

human immunodeficiency virus (HIV) The virus that causes AIDS. **678**

Hundred Days (1933) Special session in which Congress approved 15 major New Deal measures to combat the Great Depression. **507**

hunter-gatherers Groups that hunted game and gathered wild plants, traveled in small groups, and lived in caves or tepees. **5**

I

Ice Age Ancient period during which the weather was much colder than it is now, causing snow to fall and form glaciers. **3**

impeachment Bringing formal charges of wrongdoing against a public official. **341**

imperialism Controlling overseas colonies by force. **436**

immigrants Foreign-born people who move to another country. **208**

Immigration Act of 1924 Stiffer version of the Quota Act, restricting immigration to the United States. **489**

Immigration Act of 1990 Federal law increasing the number of skilled workers allowed into the United States. **694**

Immigration Restriction League Organization formed by nativists in the 1890s to call for a law preventing immigrants who could not read or write any language from entering the United States. **395**

immunity Resistance to disease. **26**

import To buy products from another country. **64**

impressment British practice of forcing sailors suspected of being British soldiers to serve in the Royal Navy; strained relations between the United States and Great Britain in the early 1800s. **185**

Income Tax Act of 1986 Federal law relieving most low-income people from all income taxes and reducing the maximum tax rate as well. **665**

indentured servants People who signed contracts to work for others for a set period of time. **53**

Indian Removal Act (1830) Federal law that provided funds to carry out President Andrew Jackson's policy for removing eastern Indian tribes to Indian Territory. **252**

Indian Reorganization Act (1934) Legislation encouraging the revival of tribal life. **517**

Industrial Revolution Period of great industrial expansion that began in Britain in the late 1700s. **200**

Indian Territory Place chosen to relocate eastern Indian tribes in the early 1800s; later, Oklahoma. **252**

inflation A sharp rise in prices. **32**

Information Revolution Increase in the exchange and availability of information aided by technology of the 1990s. **699**

initiative Voting practice that enables voters to initiate, or propose, laws. **413**

insider trading The unlawful use of confidential information for personal gain by stockbrokers. **677**

installment plan Program allowing customers to make monthly payments, along with interest, on a product until it is paid in full. **479**

interchangeable parts Process developed by Eli Whitney in the 1790s to allow broken items to be fixed more quickly by making parts of certain models of an item exactly the same. **203**

Intermediate-range Nuclear Forces Treaty INF treaty; agreement signed in 1987 by President Ronald Reagan and Soviet premier Gorbachev in which both sides agreed to completely eliminate medium-range nuclear missiles in Europe. **670**

Internal Security Act (1950) Required all communist organizations to register and to open their financial records to government inspectors. **565**

Internet A system of connecting computers worldwide. **699**

interstate commerce Business and trade between states. **114**

Interstate Commerce Act (1887) Law that required railroad rates to be "reasonable and just." **399**

Interstate Commerce Commission (ICC) Federal board of examiners who oversaw railroads. **399**

Intolerable Acts (1774) Four laws passed by Parliament in reaction to the Boston Tea Party to reclaim control over the colonies and punish Massachusetts. **87**

Iran-contra affair Illegal purchase of arms for the Nicaraguan contras using money from a secret sale of arms to Iran, arranged by members of the Reagan administration. **669**

Iran hostage crisis (1979–81) Standoff in which 53 Americans were held hostage in Tehran by Iranians opposed to the shah. **662**

Iron Curtain Image used by Winston Churchill to describe the political division between democratic Western Europe and communist Eastern Europe. **550**

Iroquois League The Five Nations; an alliance formed by tribes of the Northeast culture area in what is now New York State. **7**

island-hopping Allied strategy during World War II of attacking only key islands in the Pacific on the way toward Japan. **534**

isolationism Keeping out of foreign affairs and halting further expansion of U.S. borders. **427**

isthmus Small neck of land that connects two larger land masses. **22**

J

Jacksonian Democracy New democratic spirit in America ushered in by the election of President Andrew Jackson in 1828. **245**

Jay's Treaty (1994) Treaty negotiated by John Jay between the United States and Great Britain to ease tensions over trade, western territory, and British seizure of U.S. merchant ships. **166**

jazz Music created in the late 1800s by African American musicians primarily in New Orleans. **486**

jerky Dried meat. **362**

Jim Crow laws Laws that enforced segregation in the South. **350**

John Brown's raid (1859) Incident in which John Brown and his followers took control of an arsenal and government gun factory in Harpers Ferry, Virginia, hoping to spark a slave rebellion. **306**

joint-stock companies Businesses owned by many stockholders who shared in the profits and losses. **41**

judicial branch Branch of the government that interprets laws. **123**

judicial review The right of the courts to declare an act of Congress unconstitutional. **180**

juntas Committees established by Cuban revolutionaries in the United States to raise money, spread propaganda, and recruit volunteers for the struggle for Cuban independence from Spain. **432**

K

kaiser German word for "emperor." **448**

kamikaze Japanese suicide pilots who tried to crash their bomb-filled planes into U.S. warships. **542**

Kansas-Nebraska Act (1854) Federal law allowing residents of each of the territories to decide whether slavery would be legal there. **296**

Knights of Labor One of the first large unions to emerge in the United States after the Civil War; founded by Uriah Stephens in 1869. **388**

Know-Nothings Members of the American Party, formed in 1849 by nativists opposed to immigration. **209**

Ku Klux Klan A secret organization that emerged after the Civil War and used violence and threats to hold back African Americans. **347**

L

labor unions Organizations workers form to improve their conditions. **206**

Land Ordinance of 1785 Congressional plan for the orderly sale of the western territories. **116**

La Raza Unida "The United People"; Mexican American political party organized in Texas in 1970 by Mexican American activists. **658**

latitude The distance north or south of the equator. **14**

League of Nations International congress created after World War I to settle disputes between nations. **466**

legislative branch Branch of government that writes laws. **123**

Lend-Lease Act (1941) Federal law giving the president authority to sell or lend war supplies to any nation whose defense was considered to be essential to America's security. **525**

Levittown New York housing development built by the Levitt Company; one of the first and best known of such developments after World War II. **574**

Lewis and Clark expedition Expedition led by Meriwether Lewis and William Clark starting in 1804 to explore land in the Louisiana Purchase. **183**

Limited Nuclear Test Ban Treaty (1963) Agreement between the Soviet Union and the United States to stop testing nuclear weapons above ground. **591**

Lincoln-Douglas debates Series of debates between Illinois candidates for the U.S. Senate, Republican

Abraham Lincoln and Democrat Stephen A. Douglas. **302**

Line of Demarcation Line established by Pope Alexander VI that divided the ocean about 400 miles west of the Azores. Lands west of the line were to belong to Spain, those east to Portugal. **19**

literacy tests Tests limiting voting to those who could read well; were used primarily against African Americans in the South after Reconstruction. **350**

Little Rock Nine African American students who desegregated Central High School in Little Rock, Arkansas, in 1957. **581**

lobbyists People hired to influence legislators on behalf of special interests. **413**

loose construction Argument that congressional action is constitutional as long as the U.S. Constitution does not clearly forbid it. **162**

Los Angeles Riots (1992) Riots sparked by a not guilty verdict in the trial of four white police officers accused of using excessive force in the beating of African American motorist Rodney King. **695**

Lost Generation Young writers, such as Ernest Hemingway, who had supported the war effort but became bitter after World War I. **487**

Louisiana Purchase (1803) Large American purchase of French land west of the Mississippi River that doubled the size of the United States. **181**

Lowell girls Female employees in Francis Lowell's Massachusetts textile factory. **206**

Loyalists Tories; colonists who strongly supported the British and opposed the Declaration of Independence. **95**

Lusitania British passenger liner torpedoed by a German U-boat on May 7, 1915, killing 1,200 people, including 128 Americans. **452**

M

maize Corn; the most important food crop grown in ancient America. **5**

Manhattan Project Top-secret project among American scientists during World War II that produced the atomic bomb. **542**

manifest destiny Phrase used to describe some Americans' feeling that the entire North American continent could belong to the United States. **271**

manors Sections of land in Europe that were ruled by nobles known as lords. **9**

Marbury v. Madison (1803) Supreme Court case that established the Court's power of judicial review. **180**

March on Washington (1963) Gathering of more than 200,000 people to demonstrate peacefully for civil rights. **601**

Marshall Plan (1948) Economic plan, proposed by Secretary of State George C. Marshall, of providing monetary help to war-torn European nations if they asked for it. **551**

Massacre at Wounded Knee (1890) Killing of 300 Sioux by the U.S. Army; ended armed Indian resistance to white settlement in the West. **369**

massive retaliation Cold War strategy of Secretary of State John Foster Dulles calling for the free world to develop the will and organize the means to retaliate instantly against open aggression by communist armies. **570**

mass production Process of producing large numbers of identical goods more efficiently. **202**

Mayflower Compact (1620) Document drawn up by the Pilgrims to provide a legal basis for Plymouth, their colony in North America. **47**

McCarthyism Atmosphere of reckless charges and persecutions led by Senator Joseph McCarthy in the early years of the Cold War. **669**

McClure's Magazine One of many important muckraking periodicals. **410**

McKinley Tariff (1890) Measure that took away the special advantage of Hawaiians by granting sugar producers in the United States a payment of two cents per pound on sugar; as a result, sugar prices fell and the Hawaiian economy suffered. **430**

Medicaid Program established by the Medicare Act of 1965 to provide health insurance for poor people of any age. **597**

Medicare Act (1965) Federal law providing health insurance for people over the age of 65. **597**

mercantilism Economic program designed to achieve a favorable balance of trade by tightly controlling traded goods. **64**

mercenaries Hired soldiers. **102**

Mexican Cession Territory that Mexico ceded to the United States after the Mexican War. **276**

Mexican Revolution Revolution begun in Mexico in 1910 against dictator Porfirio Díaz. **442**

middle class New social class between the rich and the poor that developed in the 1840s as a result of industrialization. **211**

Middle Passage The transportation of enslaved Africans to the Americas during which many Africans died. **69**

migration Movement from one place to another. **4**

militarism Belief that the use of military force is a good solution to international problems. **448**

militia A group of citizens organized for military service. **78**

Minutemen Colonial members of rebel militias who were ready for action on a minute's notice. **90**

missions Church communities founded by Catholic priests. **30**

Missouri Compromise (1820) Agreement that admitted Missouri to the Union as a slave state and Maine as a free state; it also outlawed slavery in the rest of the Louisiana Purchase north of 36°30' north latitude. **243**

Model T "Tin Lizzie"; car invented in 1908 by Henry Ford; the car's low cost meant that many more Americans could afford to own automobiles. **480**

monopoly Complete domination of an industry. **385**

Monroe Doctrine (1823) Statement issued by President James Monroe declaring that European countries could no longer establish colonies in the Americas and that the United States would stay out of European affairs. **196**

Montgomery Bus Boycott (1955–56) Boycott in Montgomery, Alabama, in which African Americans stayed off city buses until the city changed the law requiring them to sit in the rear and give up their seats to white passengers. **584**

Montgomery Improvement Association Local group led by Martin Luther King, Jr., that supported the Montgomery Bus Boycott. **584**

Mormon Trail Trail on which 15,000 Mormons led by Brigham Young traveled to Utah. **280**

Mormons Members of the Church of Jesus Christ of Latter-Day Saints, founded in 1830 by Joseph Smith. **279**

Morrill Act (1862) Federal law giving western land grants to promote educational facilities. **376**

mountain men Men hired by fur companies to roam the Rocky Mountains and trap beaver and other animals. **267**

muckrakers Progressive journalists who saw the "filth on the floor" and tried to "scrape [it] up with a muckrake." **408**

multinational corporations Corporations that invest in a variety of businesses throughout the world. **700**

Munich Conference (1938) Conference in which France and Great Britain agreed to let Germany take the Sudetenland if Hitler agreed it would be his last territorial claim in Europe. **523**

Muslims Followers of Islam, the religion established by Muhammad in 610. **11**

mutiny Rebellion against the captain of a ship by the crew. **23**

N

National American Woman Suffrage Association (NAWSA) Organization founded in 1890 to lead the fight for women's right to vote. **422**

National Aeronautics and Space Administration (NASA) Agency founded by the U.S. government in the 1950s to expand scientific research and development on space exploration. **572**

National Association for the Advancement of Colored People (NAACP) Progressive organization that attempted to end lynching, or mob murder, and that worked for African Americans' civil rights. **425**

national debt Debt accumulated by the federal government. **160**

National Grange Political organization that represented farmers in the 1870s. **398**

National Industrial Recovery Act (NIRA) New Deal measure to stimulate private business by allowing manufacturers in the same field to cooperate with one another without fear of violating the antitrust laws. **508**

nationalism A spirit of national pride. **197**

National Liberation Front (NLF) Vietnamese group formed in 1960 to oppose Ngo Dinh Diem. **618**

National Organization for Women (NOW) Group founded by Betty Friedan in 1966 to fight for women's rights. **607**

National Road Federal road on which construction started in 1811 in Cumberland, Maryland; the road crossed over the mountains in southwestern Pennsylvania and ended at present-day Wheeling, West Virginia (later extended to Vandalia, Illinois). **214**

National War Labor Board Agency set up during World War I to try to settle disputes between workers and their employers. **459**

National Woman's Party Organization founded by Alice Paul in 1913 to call for a constitutional amendment guaranteeing women's suffrage. **422**

Nat Turner's Rebellion (1831) Failed Virginia slave revolt that resulted in the deaths of 60 whites and at least 120 African Americans. **232**

Navigation and Trade Acts Series of laws passed by Parliament from 1651 to the mid-1700s regulating the buying and selling of goods. **64**

nativists Americans opposed to unlimited immigration because they believed that too many newcomers would destroy American institutions. **209**

Nazis National Socialists; political party led by Adolf Hitler that established a totalitarian government in Germany in 1933. **522**

Neutrality Proclamation (1793) Statement issued by President George Washington to warn Americans not to favor either side in the war between France and Great Britain. **165**

New Deal President Franklin Roosevelt's policy for dealing with the Great Depression. **506**

New Frontier President John F. Kennedy's program to "get the country moving again" by making the economy grow more rapidly. **589**

new immigrants People who came to the United States after the 1880s, mainly from southern and eastern Europe. **392**

New Jersey Plan Rejected set of resolutions written by delegates to the Constitutional Convention from small states that would have continued the one-state, one-vote system of government used under the Articles of Confederation. **121**

New Right Loose organization of social and political conservatives in the 1980s. **663**

Niagara Movement Movement founded by African American leaders in 1905 to demand equal economic and educational opportunities, voting rights, and an end to segregation. **425**

nickelodeons Early movie theaters that usually charged five cents for admission. **483**

Nineteenth Amendment (1920) Constitutional amendment that gave women the right to vote. **422**

no-man's-land Narrow strip of land between opposing trenches during World War I. **450**

nominating conventions Meetings of delegates to choose a political party's presidential and vice-presidential candidates. **246**

nonaggression pact (1939) Agreement between Adolf Hitler and Joseph Stalin agreeing that Germany and the Soviet Union would not attack one another. **523**

Non-Intercourse Act (1809) Federal law that replaced the Embargo Act by restoring trade with all foreign countries except Great Britain and France. **186**

North American Free Trade Agreement (NAFTA) 1993 agreement between the United States, Mexico, and Canada to allow for a freer flow of goods and labor between those countries. **700**

North Atlantic Treaty Organization (NATO) Alliance between the United States and Western European nations in which members pledged to defend one another in case of attack and to form a unified military force for this purpose. **560**

Northwest Ordinance The Land Ordinance of 1787; a plan to create a government for the region north of the Ohio River and west of Pennsylvania. **116**

nullification Idea supported by John C. Calhoun that if a state considered a federal law unconstitutional, it could refuse to accept the law and prevent it from being enforced in that state. **248**

Nuremberg Trials First in a series of war crimes trials intended to punish those who had carried out "crimes against humanity" during World War II. **548**

O

Ohio Gang Friends of President Warren G. Harding who used their connections to him for their own gain. **477**

old immigrants Immigrants mainly from western and northern Europe who came to the United States before the 1880s. **392**

Olive Branch Petition (1775) Offer sent by the Second Continental Congress to King George III asking him to protect the colonies from actions by Parliament until a compromise could be worked out. **92**

Open Door Policy (1898) Statement by U.S. secretary of state John Hay saying that all nations would have equal trade rights in China. **438**

open range Grass on public lands in the West. **373**

Operation Desert Storm (1991) UN military attack on Iraq to drive back Saddam Hussein's invasion of Kuwait. **673**

Operation Restore Hope UN relief effort to the African country of Somalia, which was suffering from a severe famine in the early 1990s. **689**

Operation Rolling Thunder U.S. bombing campaign on North Vietnam meant to hurt North Vietnamese morale of the and destroy the Ho Chi Minh Trail. **621**

Oregon Trail 2,000-mile trail from western Missouri to Oregon. **269**

Organization of Petroleum Exporting Countries (OPEC) Group formed in 1960 by major oil-producing countries to control the price of oil. **639**

ozone layer A thin shield around the earth's atmosphere that blocks out harmful rays from the sun. **698**

P

pacification U.S. Army's policy of burning villages to the ground to root out possible Vietcong sympathizers during the Vietnam War. **623**

Pacific Railway Act (1862) Federal law giving western land grants to promote the building of a transcontinental railroad. **376**

Palmer Raids Raids led by Attorney General A. Mitchell Palmer on the headquarters of suspected radical groups after World War I. **475**

Panama Canal Waterway completed in 1914 linking the Atlantic and Pacific Oceans across the Isthmus of Panama; controlled by the United States. **441**

Panama Canal treaties (1978) Series of treaties turning over control of the Panama Canal to Panama by the year 2000. **652**

Panic of 1837 Sudden collapse of prices and business activity after a boom, followed by many bank and business failures, particularly in the West and South. **249**

Panic of 1929 Drop in stock market prices that began on October 24 and marked the beginning of the Great Depression. **498**

pardon Freedom from punishment. **647**

Parliament The lawmaking body of Great Britain. **61**

Patriots Colonists who favored independence. **95**

Pendleton Civil Service Act (1883) Law that established examinations as the basis for awarding some government jobs. **398**

perestroika Massive restructuring of the Soviet government and economy instituted by Mikhail Gorbachev in the 1980s. **669**

Pickett's Charge (1863) Final, failed Confederate charge, led by General George E. Pickett, in the Battle of Gettysburg. **330**

Pinckney's Treaty (1795) Treaty negotiated by Thomas Pinckney between the United States and Spain establishing a western border for Florida and recognizing American rights on the Mississippi. **167**

pilgrimage A religious journey. **11**

Pilgrims The first English Separatists to come to America seeking religious freedom. **47**

Plains Indians American Indians who lived on the Great Plains, from western Texas to the Dakotas and then on into Canada, in the 1800s. **359**

plantations Large farms. **44**

planters People who owned plantations and who held more than 20 slaves. **222**

Plessy v. *Ferguson* (1896) Supreme Court case that established the doctrine of "separate but equal" facilities for different races. **350**

political parties Groups of people who organize to help elect government officials and to try to influence government policies. **170**

poll taxes Taxes on individuals, which were usually collected at the time of an election. **350**

Pontiac's Rebellion (1763) Failed American Indian rebellion led by Ottawa chief Pontiac to drive white settlers back across the Appalachian Mountains. **84**

popular sovereignty Principle that would let voters in new territories make their own decisions about slavery. **290**

Populist Party People's Party; political party in the 1890s that called for government ownership of railroads, telegraph, and telephone systems, a federal income tax, and loans to farmers. **400**

Potsdam Conference (1945) Meeting between Harry S Truman, Winston Churchill, and Joseph Stalin in which they decided to divide Germany and Berlin into four zones, each controlled by a different country. **549**

Pottawatomie Massacre (1856) Incident in which John Brown and his followers murdered five members of a pro-slavery settlement in Kansas. **298**

precedents Earlier examples. **157**

prejudice Unreasonable opinion unsupported by facts. **122**

privateers Armed private vessels authorized to attack enemy shipping. **165**

Privy Council Group of English royal advisers who made colonial policy and were subject to Parliament. **61**

Proclamation of 1763 Order issued by the British government to close the area west of the Appalachians to colonial settlement. **84**

progressives Americans who worked for reform around 1900. **408**

prohibition The outlawing of the manufacture and sale of alcoholic beverages. **258**

Proposition 187 (1994) A California state measure intended to discourage illegal immigration. **694**

proprietor Single owner of a colony. **55**

prospect To search for. **280**

protective tariffs High duties on imported goods that compete with American products. **247**

public housing projects Apartments built by the government to try to improve the conditions of poor people in the cities. **576**

public works Government projects such as constructing roads or building dams. **501**

pueblos "Towns"; what European explorers called homes of Native Americans in the Southwest culture area. **7**

Pure Food and Drug Act (1906) Law that provided for federal control of the quality of most foods and drugs and for the regulation of slaughterhouses. **419**

Puritans English Protestants who wanted to "purify" the Anglican Church by removing all traces of Catholicism from it. **47**

Q

Quakers Members of a religious sect that settled in Pennsylvania and stressed religious tolerance, simplicity, and kindness toward others. **58**

Quota Act (1921) Federal law limiting the number of immigrants by nationality, reducing the number of newcomers from eastern and southern Europe. **489**

quota system The practice of setting aside exact numbers of positions for members of a specific group. **655**

R

Radical Republicans Members of Congress who were concerned that President Andrew Johnson's plan for Reconstruction would put too much power in the hands of former slaveholders. **338**

range rights Water rights on western lands. **373**

ratification Formal approval by states. **114**

realpolitik "Practical politics"; President Richard Nixon and National Security Adviser Henry Kissinger's policy of putting practical national interests, like military security, above all other considerations when making foreign policy decisions. **641**

recall Practice that allows citizens to remove an elected official from office before the term expires. **413**

Reconstruction The rebuilding of the South's government and society after the end of the Civil War. **337**

Reconstruction Acts (1867) Series of stern measures strengthening military control of the South. **340**

Red Scare Fear of Communists and anarchists, as well as socialists, following World War I. **474**

Redeemers New southern white leaders who claimed they were taking back the powers and duties their class had exercised before Reconstruction. **353**

referendum Practice that allows citizens to vote on a legislative proposal, then vote for or against the measure at a regular election. **413**

Reformation Protestant religious movement of the 1500s that challenged the power of the Catholic Church. **46**

reforms Improvements. **120**

refugees People who flee their homes to avoid danger. **339**

relief Money or aid for the needy. **502**

reparations Payments a nation is required to make for damages done to the property of the victors. **466**

repeal Officially withdraw. **85**

Republic of Texas Government established on March 2, 1836, by Texans who wanted independence from Mexico. **266**

republican Form of government in which the people hold the power and give elected representatives the authority to make and carry out laws. **112**

Republican Party Political organization formed in the North after the passage of the Kansas-Nebraska Act to oppose the spread of slavery into the western territories. **300**

rendezvous Yearly gathering of mountain men where they sold their furs, exchanged stories, and had a rollicking good time. **268**

reservations Federal lands set aside specifically for American Indians. **364**

revivals Spirited religious meetings. **256**

right of deposit The right to transfer goods without paying a duty. **167**

rock 'n' roll Form of music that drew heavily from African American rhythm and blues and initially stunned people with its raw, ear-shattering sound. **578**

Roosevelt Corollary (1904) President Theodore Roosevelt's policy that considered any European interference in nations in the Western Hemisphere a violation of the Monroe Doctrine. **441**

rotation in office Practice of replacing government jobholders to give the party in power more political control. **246**

Rough Riders U.S. regiment in the Spanish-American War made up of an odd assortment of soldiers led by Theodore Roosevelt. **434**

roundup Event that occurs each fall and spring when cattle hands gather all cattle together, then separate them by brand. **374**

Rush-Bagot Agreement (1817) Agreement signed between the United States and Great Britain providing that neither country would maintain a fleet of warships on the Great Lakes. **194**

S

safe havens Nonfighting areas monitored by UN peacekeepers in Bosnia. **690**

sanctions Official punishments. **652**

Sand Creek Massacre (1864) Attack led by Colonel John Chivington on a peaceful Cheyenne encampment in Colorado Territory in which some 200 Cheyenne were killed. **365**

Sandinistas A group of Nicaraguan revolutionaries who overturned the country's long-standing dictatorship in the 1970s. **668**

Santa Fe Trail 780-mile-long route from Missouri to Santa Fe, New Mexico. **271**

satellite nations Countries dominated by the Soviet Union during the Cold War. **552**

Saturday Night Massacre Events that occurred on October 20, 1973, when President Richard Nixon ordered the attorney general to fire Archibald Cox, the special prosecutor investigating Watergate; the attorney general and assistant attorney general both resigned before a third member of the Justice Department fired Cox. **645**

scalawags "Good-for-nothing rascals"; name given to southern white Republicans during Reconstruction. **344**

Scientific Revolution A movement that began in the 1500s in Europe and encouraged people to improve themselves and the world around them by careful study. **72**

Scopes trial (1925) Trial of biology teacher John T. Scopes for violating Tennessee law forbidding the teaching of "any theory that denies the story of the Divine Creation of man taught in the Bible"; trial emphasized the growing divisions within American society. **491**

seadogs English sailors who preyed on Spanish ships in the 1500s. **34**

search and destroy missions Military maneuver used by U.S. ground troops to seek out and attack Vietcong units during the Vietnam War. **622**

secession The act of formally withdrawing as part of a nation. **308**

Second Battle of Bull Run (1862) Civil War battle that resulted in Confederate victory. **321**

Second Continental Congress (1775) Group of delegates who met in Philadelphia after battles of Lexington and Concord; decided not to break with Britain, but did create an official military force. **91**

Second Great Awakening Series of religious revivals that began in the 1790s. **256**

Second New Deal Programs passed after the 1934 elections that addressed issues President Franklin Roosevelt's critics had raised about the New Deal. **511**

sects New religious groups. **47**

segregation Forced separation. **350**

Selective Service Act (1917) Federal law requiring all men aged 21 to 30 (later changed to 18 to 45) to register with local draft boards, who then decided which of them would go to war. **456**

self-determination Right of people of every nation to decide for themselves what nation they belong to; part of President Woodrow Wilson's Fourteen Points. **466**

Senate Upper house of the United States legislature, intended to give the executive advice and consent on appointments and foreign treaties. **123**

Seneca Falls Convention (1848) First American women's rights convention. **261**

Separatists Radical English Protestants who wanted to break with the Church of England. **47**

serfs Peasants who worked for lords on European manors. **9**

settlement houses Community centers established by progressives to help slum-dwellers improve their lives. **412**

Seven Days Battles (1862) Civil War battles that resulted in Confederate victory. **321**

Seventeenth Amendment (1913) Constitutional amendment that allowed the people of a state to elect U.S. senators. **414**

shaman American Indian medicine man. **366**

sharecropping "Sharing the crop": system in which landowners provide farmers with houses, tools, seeds, and other supplies while the sharecroppers provide the skill and labor to produce a crop, which is split at harvest season. **345**

Share-Our-Wealth Organization founded by Huey Long, who wanted to increase taxes on the wealthy to give every family enough money to buy a house, a car and a minimum income of at least $2,500 a year. **511**

Shays's Rebellion (1786–87) Revolt of Massachusetts farmers led by Daniel Shays, sparked by rising taxes and seizure of farms to pay back-taxes. **119**

Sherman Antitrust Act (1890) Federal law banning business combinations "in the form of trust or [that] otherwise restricted interstate trade or commerce." **386**

siege Military strategy of pinning down troops inside a city and waiting for them to surrender. **323**

silent generation What social observers called young people of the 1950s because they seemed to lack concern about serious problems confronting the United States and the rest of the world. **577**

Silent Majority Group that President Richard Nixon called the "forgotten Americans" because they had not been involved in any protests of any sort during the 1960s. **637**

Silk Road Network of trade routes that connected China and the Arab world. **12**

sit-in Form of nonviolent protest used during the civil rights movement in which a group went to a segregated facility and refused to leave. **598**

Sixteenth Amendment (1913) Constitutional amendment that authorized a federal income tax. **419**

slave codes Laws written by white southerners in the early 1800s to control slaves. **228**

slave state A state where slavery was permitted. **243**

socialism The idea that the government should own all the means of production. **413**

Social Security Act (1935) Federal law that set up a system of old-age insurance, which was paid for by workers and their employers. **511**

societies Groups of people who live and work together and who have common values and customs. **4**

sodbuster Plow that could easily slice through the tough sod of the Great Plains. **379**

soldier bands Groups of warriors who settled disputes between different bands of American Indians. **361**

Southern Christian Leadership Conference (SCLC) Organization founded in the late 1950s by Martin Luther King, Jr., and others who believed that nonviolence was the only way to win civil rights for African Americans. **598**

southern strategy President Richard Nixon's plan to win over traditionally Democratic southern white voters to the Republican Party. **638**

Spanish Armada Spanish fleet defeated by England in 1588, opening the way for English settlement in the Americas. **34**

speakeasies Secret clubs that served alcohol during prohibition. **488**

speculators Investors who buy bonds, stocks, or land, gambling that they will be able to make huge profits when they can sell these things at a later date. **161**

spheres of influence Regions where foreign countries control trade and natural resources. **437**

spirituals Deeply moving religious songs that blended Christian and African traditions and provided emotional comfort to slaves. **230**

spoils system Practice by election winners of appointing their supporters to government jobs. **246**

Sputnik The first artificial satellite, sent into space by the Soviets in 1957. **571**

socialism The idea that the government should own all the means of production. **413**

stagflation Situation in which both unemployment and inflation are rising. **639**

stalemate Situation in which neither side can win a clear victory. **450**

Stamp Act (1765) Law approved by Parliament to enable the British to collect money by selling stamps, which had to be purchased and attached to all printed material in the colonies. **84**

staple crops Crops that farmers raise in large quantities to sell. **66**

states' rights Belief that the states, not the federal government, hold ultimate political power. **174**

stockholders Investors in corporations who buy shares and make money when the corporations do well. **384**

Strategic Arms Limitation Treaty (SALT) Agreement between President Richard Nixon and Soviet leader Leonid Brezhnev to limit numbers of weapons their nations produced. **642**

Strategic Defense Initiative (SDI) An advanced space-based system designed to destroy incoming missiles before they could reach the United States. **666**

strict construction Argument that congressional action is constitutional only if the U.S. Constitution specifically says that Congress has the power to carry out that action. **162**

strike A refusal to work until workers' demands for improved conditions are met. **207**

Student Nonviolent Coordinating Committee (SNCC) Civil rights organization founded in the 1960s and made up mostly of students. **599**

Students for a Democratic Society (SDS) Anti–Vietnam War group formed by college students in the 1960s. **625**

subsidy A government bonus in the form of a payment. **430**

suffrage Voting rights. **112**

Sun Belt Area of the West and the South that experienced a long-term population increase due to migration after World War II. **576**

supply-side economics A complex theory suggesting that lower tax rates will lead to economic growth. **663**

Sussex **pledge** (1916) German promise not to torpedo any more passenger or merchant ships without warning. **453**

Sutter's Fort Fort built at the junction of the American and Sacramento Rivers by John A. Sutter. **271**

synthetics Artificial materials. **479**

T

Taft-Hartley Act (1947) Legislative proposal to curb the power of unions. **555**

talkie A film that projects actors' voices as well as their movements. **484**

Tariff of Abominations Name given to a high 1828 tariff by southerners who disliked it. **248**

tariffs Taxes on imported goods. **118**

Tea Act (1773) Law passed by Parliament to allow the British East India Company to sell tea directly to the American colonies; sparked the Boston Tea Party. **86**

Teapot Dome scandal (1926) Worst scandal of the Harding administration, when Secretary of the Interior Albert Fall leased government-owned land containing rich oil deposits to private companies at low rents in exchange for bribes. **477**

technology The use of tools to produce goods or to do work. **202**

GLOSSARY

Tejanos Texans of Mexican descent. **263**

telegraph Invention by Samuel F. B. Morse in 1837 that used a system of dots and dashes to transmit messages over wires. **377**

Teller Amendment (1898) Proposals stating that the United States had no intention of taking Cuba for itself or trying to control its government. **434**

temperance The effort to limit drinking. **258**

tenements Large overcrowded apartments. **395**

Tennessee Valley Authority (TVA) Programs established by Congress in the 1930s to help revitalize the area along the Tennessee River. **509**

terrorists Individuals or small groups that use random violence or threats of violence to advance their political goals. **690**

Tet Offensive (1968) Attack by the NLF that turned American public opinion against the Vietnam War. **627**

textiles Cloth. **200**

theory of natural selection Charles Darwin's idea that all forms of life have developed gradually over millions of years. **491**

Thirteenth Amendment (1865) Constitutional amendment that officially abolished slavery. **338**

Three-Fifths Compromise (1787) Agreement that established a system of counting all free persons and only three fifths of all other persons in figuring a state's population. **122**

total war A strategy to break an enemy's will to fight by destroying the resources of the opposing civilian population and its army. **332**

totalitarianism Forms of government in which the nation-state is everything, the individual citizen nothing. **521**

Toleration Act of 1649 Law passed in Maryland to guarantee religious freedom to all Christians. **55**

Tonkin Gulf Resolution (1964) Congressional orders authorizing President Lyndon Johnson to take all necessary measures to stop armed attacks by anti-American forces in Vietnam. **620**

Townshend Acts (1767) Laws passed by Parliament to put duties on some items that colonists imported from Great Britain. **85**

Trail of Tears (1838) 800-mile forced march of the Cherokee, from the east to Indian Territory, in which 4,000 people died along the way. **254**

transcendentalism Philosophy that stresses an individual's ability to transcend, or rise above, material concerns. **257**

Transportation Revolution Period of rapid growth in transportation during the 1800s that made it easier for people in one region to meet one another and to do business with people in other regions. **217**

Treaty of Dancing Rabbit Creek (1830) Treaty in which the Choctaw accepted removal and ceded their homeland of 10.5 million acres to the United States. **252**

Treaty of Ghent (1814) Agreement signed between the United States and Great Britain, officially ending the War of 1812. **193**

Treaty of Greenville (1795) Agreement signed after the Battle of Fallen Timbers by more than 90 Indian chiefs, turning over the entire southern half of present-day Ohio to American settlers. **167**

Treaty of Guadalupe Hildago (1848) Treaty between the United States and Mexico that ended the Mexican War and gave the United States the Mexican Cession. **276**

Treaty of Medicine Lodge (1867) Agreement signed by Sioux who lived along the Bozeman Trail, agreeing to give up their lands and move to reservations in Indian Territory. **365**

Treaty of New Echota (1835) Agreement signed by a small group of Cherokee leaders agreeing to resettlement. **254**

Treaty of Paris of 1783 Agreement officially ending the Revolutionary War; signaled Britain's recognition of U.S. independence, and enlarged American territory. **115**

Treaty of Tordesillas (1494) Agreement signed by Spain and Portugal to move the Line of Demarcation about 700 miles farther west. **19**

Treaty of Versailles (1919) Peace treaty drawn up by Allied leaders after World War I. **466**

Tredegar Iron Works The largest iron works in the South during the early 1800s, located in Richmond, Virginia. **225**

trench warfare Strategy during World War I when two opposing armies dug trenches to protect themselves from bullets and artillery fire. **450**

Triangle Fire (1911) Fire at the Triangle Shirtwaist Factory in New York in which more than 140 women died. **414**

Triple Alliance Military alliance of Germany, Austria-Hungary, and Italy in the early 1900s. **448**

Triple Entente Military alliance of Great Britain, France, and Russia in the early 1900s. **448**

Truman Doctrine U.S. policy under President Harry Truman to support peoples resisting communism. **551**

trust Legal agreement under which several companies group together to regulate production and eliminate competition. **385**

turnpikes Toll roads that used a pike as a tollgate to block the road until travelers paid the fees to use them. **214**

Twenty-first Amendment (1933) Constitutional amendment that repealed prohibition. **489**

Twenty-fourth Amendment (1964) Constitutional amendment that banned poll taxes in federal elections. **603**

U

U-2 affair (1960) Incident that greatly strained U.S.-Soviet relations when the Soviets shot down an American U-2 spy plane and U.S. officials initially denied it was spying. **572**

U-boats "Undersea boats"; German submarines. **452**

Uncle Tom's Cabin Novel written by Harriet Beecher Stowe in 1852 that increased controversy over slavery. **293**

unconstitutional In violation of the Constitution. **180**

Underground Railroad An informal network that helped between roughly 50,000 and 75,000 slaves escape to freedom. **235**

Underwood Tariff (1913) Federal law decreasing tariffs significantly and providing for an income tax to make up for the lost revenue. **419**

United Farm Workers (UFW) Union led by César Chávez in the 1960s to focus on improving wages and working conditions for migrant farmworkers. **657**

United Mine Workers (UMW) Labor union that struck in April 1946, leading President Truman to order a government takeover of the mines when strike negotiations broke down. **555**

United Nations (UN) International organization formed in 1945 to promote world peace and settle international disputes. **547**

universal coverage Guaranteed health insurance for everyone. **685**

Universal Negro Improvement Association (UNIA) Organization founded by black nationalist Marcus Garvey in 1914. **491**

University of California v. Bakke (1978) Supreme
Court case that declared some Affirmative action
action unfair. **655**
utopian communities Places where transcendentalists
tried to live out their vision of a perfect society. **257**

V

vertical integration The attempted ownership of companies that provide the material and services for the
attempted owner's company. **385**
viceroy Representative of the Spanish monarch who
oversaw Spain's colonies in the Americas. **19**
Vietcong Pro-communist South Vietnamese guerrillas.
618
Vietminh League for the Independence of Vietnam; a
Vietnamese group formed by Ho Chi Minh and dedicated to resisting the Japanese during World War II.
616
Vietnamization President Richard Nixon's plan to
strengthen the South Vietnamese army while gradually withdrawing U.S. troops from the Vietnam War.
631
Virginia and Kentucky Resolutions (1798–99) Statements supported by Thomas Jefferson arguing that the
Alien and Sedition Acts were unconstitutional. **174**
Virginia Plan Proposal drafted in part by James Madison
and presented at the Constitutional Convention by
Edmund Randolph to provide for a central national
government with three separate branches. **121**
Volstead Act (1919) Federal law giving the government
the power to enforce the Eighteenth Amendment. **423**
Voting Rights Act of 1965 Federal law outlawing
literacy tests for voting; imposed harsh penalties for
interference with voting and provided federal officials
to oversee the registration process. **603**

W

War Hawks Members of Congress in the early 1800s
who favored going to war with Great Britain; led by
John C. Calhoun and Henry Clay. **186**
War Industries Board Agency established during World
War I to oversee the production and distribution of
manufactured goods; headed by Bernard Baruch. **457**
War on Drugs A comprehensive effort, announced by
President George Bush, to eliminate the production
and use of illegal narcotics at home and abroad. **672**
War on Poverty Fight waged by President Lyndon
Johnson to prevent, remedy, and eliminate poverty
in America. **595**
Warren Commission Commission appointed by
President Lyndon Johnson and headed by Chief
Justice Earl Warren to investigate the assassination of
President John F. Kennedy; concluded that Lee Harvey
Oswald had acted alone. **594**
Warsaw Pact (1955) Cold War alliance among the
Soviet Union and its satellite nations pledging mutual
defense against attack. **560**
Washington Conference (1921) Meeting in which
President Warren G. Harding invited delegates from
nine European and Asian nations to discuss avoiding
conflict in East Asia. **476**
Watergate Scandal that resulted in the resignation of
President Richard Nixon in 1974. **643**

welfare state System of government institutions that
provide for the needs and the general welfare. **511**
Whig Party Political party founded in 1834 and led by
Henry Clay. **249**
Whiskey Rebellion (1794) Rebellion by western
Pennsylvania farmers protesting a new whiskey tax;
quickly put down by militia organized by President
George Washington. **168**
Wilmot Proviso (1846) Resolution proposed by David
Wilmot of Pennsylvania to declare that "neither
slavery nor involuntary servitude shall ever exist
in" any territory taken from the Republic of Mexico;
passed by the House of Representatives, but defeated
in the Senate. **290**
women's liberation movement Movement started in
the 1960s to end inequality based on gender. **607**
Woodstock (1969) Four-day concert in upstate New
York attended by 300,000 young people. **606**
Worcester v. Georgia (1832) Supreme Court case that
ruled Georgia law did not extend to the Cherokee;
ignored by President Andrew Jackson and the state
of Georgia. **254**
World Trade Organization Body established in 1994 to
settle trade disputes between nations. **700**
Works Progress Administration (WPA) Agency established by the government in 1935 to put millions of
men and women to work. **512**
Women's Christian Temperance Union Prohibition
organization begun in 1874 and led by Frances
Willard. **423**
writs of assistance Special search warrants used by
colonial customs officials. **85**

X

XYZ affair (1797) Scandal in which French agents
reported that the French foreign minister would not
negotiate with U.S. representatives until he received
a large bribe; sparked undeclared naval war between
the United States and France. **172**
xenophobia Fear of foreigners. **475**

Y

Yalta Conference (1945) Meeting between Winston
Churchill, Franklin Roosevelt, and Joseph Stalin in
which Stalin agreed to enter the war in the Pacific
on behalf of the Allies in exchange for a large part
of eastern Poland. **548**
youth revolt 1960s rebellion against American society,
mostly by upper-middle class white youths. **605**
yuppies Young urban professionals; people in the 1980s
who earned good money and pursued luxurious
lifestyles, symbolizing the "decade of greed." **676**

Z

Zimmerman Note (1917) Diplomatic message revealing
that the German foreign secretary was trying to form
an alliance with Mexico in the event that the United
States declared war against Germany. **455**
zoot-suit riots (1943) Riots that broke out when U.S.
sailors and others went around Los Angeles attacking
Mexican American youths dressed in the flashy "zoot
suits" popular at the time. **530**

INDEX

INDEX

U

V

INDEX

ACKNOWLEDGMENTS

For permission to reprint copyrighted material, grateful acknowledgment is made to the following sources:

Africa World Press, Inc.: From "Mali in the Fourteenth Century" by Al Omari, translated by Basil Davidson, from *African Civilization Revisited: From Antiquity to Modern Times* by Basil Davidson. Copyright © 1991 by Basil Davidson. All rights reserved.

Arte Público Press–University of Houston: From *The Squatter and the Don* by Maria Amparo Ruiz de Burton, edited by Rosaura Sanchez and Beatrice Pita. Copyright © 1992 by Arte Público Press.

Bantam Books, a division of Bantam Doubleday Dell Publishing Group, Inc.: Quotation by Gussie Nesbitt from *Voices of Freedom* by Henry Hampton and Steve Fayer. Copyright © 1990 by Blackside, Inc.

Beacon Press, Boston: From "The Gifts of Gold" from *The Broken Spears* by Miguel Leon-Portilla. Copyright © 1962 by Beacon Press.

The Berkley Publishing Group: From "Jack Altshul," from "Cornelia MacEwen Hurd," from "Nelson Poynter," and from "Reverend Harold Toliver" from *Americans Remember the Home Front* by Roy Hoopes. Copyright © 1977, 1992 by Roy Hoopes.

Curtis Brown, Ltd.: From "Death in the Ia Drang Valley" by Jack P. Smith from *The Saturday Evening Post,* January 28, 1967. Copyright © 1967 by Jack P. Smith.

Jonathan Cape Ltd.: From *Warrior Without Weapons* by Marcel Junod, translated by Edward Fitzgerald. Copyright 1951 by Jonathan Cape Ltd.

Peter N. Carroll: From *It Seemed Like Nothing Happened: The Tragedy and Promise of the 1970s* by Peter N. Carroll. Copyright © 1982 by Peter N. Carroll.

Cornell University Press: From *Viet Nam: The Unheard Voices* by Don Luce and John Sommer. Copyright © 1969 by Cornell University Press.

Diario Excelsior: From "Cuando se va un Presidente" from *Excelsior,* August 9, 1974. Copyright © 1974 by Diario Excelsior.

Doubleday, a division of Bantam Doubleday Dell Publishing Group, Inc.: From *When Heaven and Earth Changed Places* by Le Ly Hayslip. Copyright © 1989 by Le Ly Hayslip and Charles Jay Wurts.

Grosset & Dunlap: From letter by Gwen S. from *Kids' Letters to President Carter,* edited by Bill Adler. Copyright © 1978 by Bill Adler Books.

Grove/Atlantic, Inc.: From *Lakota Woman* by Mary Crow Dog and Richard Erdoes. Copyright © 1990 by Mary Crow Dog and Richard Erdoes.

Harcourt Brace & Company: From *444 Days: The Hostages Remember* by Tim Wells. Copyright © 1985 by Tim Wells.

HarperCollins Publishers, Inc.: From "Howl" from *Collected Poems 1947–1980* by Allen Ginsberg. Copyright © 1955 by Allen Ginsberg.

Harvard University Press: From *Hospital Sketches* by Louisa May Alcott, edited by Bessie Z. Jones. Copyright © 1960 by the President and Fellows of Harvard College. Published by The Belknap Press of Harvard University Press, Cambridge, Mass. All Rights Reserved.

David Higham Associates Limited: From "A Chinese View of Mecca (1432)" from *The Overall Survey of the Ocean's Shores* by Ma Huan, translated by J.V.G. Mills. Copyright © 1970 by The Hakluyt Society.

International Marine Publishing Company: From *The Log of Christopher Columbus,* translated by Robert H. Fuson. Copyright © 1987 by International Marine Publishing Company.

Alfred A. Knopf, Inc.: "Merry-Go-Round" from *Collected Poems* by Langston Hughes. Copyright © 1994 by the Estate of Langston Hughes.

Ludlow Music, Inc.: From "Do Re Mi," words and music by Woody Guthrie. TRO, Copyright © 1961 and © 1963 (copyrights renewed) by Ludlow Music, Inc., New York, NY.

David McKay Company, a division of Random House, Inc.: From *The Long Shadow of Little Rock: A Memoir* by Daisy Bates. Copyright © 1962 by Daisy Bates.

W. W. Norton & Company, Inc.: From "Becky Jenkins" from *Red Scare: Memories of the American Inquisition, An Oral History* by Griffin Fariello. Copyright © 1995 by Griffin Fariello. From *Sleepwalking Through History: America in the Reagan Years* by Haynes Johnson. Copyright © 1991 by Haynes Johnson.

Pantheon Books, a division of Random House, Inc.: Quotations by Jean Gump and Frank Lumpkin from *The Great Divide* by Studs Terkel. Copyright © 1988 by Pantheon Books, a division of Random House, Inc.

From *Hard Times: An Oral History of the Great Depression* by Studs Terkel. Copyright © 1970 by Pantheon Books, a division of Random House, Inc.

Mary Helen Ponce: From "Recuerdo: How I changed the war and won the game" by Mary Helen Ponce from *Woman of Her Word: Hispanic Women Write,* edited by Evangelina Vigil. Copyright © 1983 by Mary Helen Ponce.

Presidio Press: From *She Went To War* by Rhonda Cornum and Peter Copeland. Copyright © 1992 by Presidio Press.

Random House, Inc.: From *Invisible Man* by Ralph Ellison. Copyright © 1947, 1948, 1952 by Ralph Ellison. From "People of the North" from *Alaska* by James A. Michener. Copyright © 1988 by James A. Michener.

Rutgers University Press: From *War, Mutiny and Revolution in the German Navy: The World War I Diary of Seaman Richard Stumpf,* edited, translated, and with an introduction by Daniel Horn. Copyright © 1967 by Rutgers, The State University.

St. Martin's Press Incorporated: Quotations by Christopher Columbus and Isabella from *Isabella of Castile: The First Renaissance Queen* by Nancy Rubin. Copyright © 1991 by Nancy Rubin.

The Saturday Evening Post Society: From "I Saw Lee Surrender" by Seth M. Flint from *The Saturday Evening Post,* vol. 245, no. 5, July/August 1976. Copyright © 1976 by The Saturday Evening Post Company.

Time Inc.: Quotes by Suneel Ratan and Dana Neilson from "Hate Boomers" by Suneel Ratan from *Fortune,* October 4, 1993. Copyright © 1993 by Time, Inc.

The University of Alberta Press: Quote by Henri Lancelot-Voisin Sieur de La Popelinière from *The Myth of the Savage: And the Beginnings of French Colonialism in the Americas* by Olive Patricia Dickason. Copyright © 1984 by The University of Alberta Press.

Viking Penguin, a division of Penguin Books USA, Inc.: From "American Bores Common, Ex Div." from *Christopher Columbus and Other Patriotic Verses* by Franklin P. Adams. Copyright © 1931 by Franklin P. Adams.

REFERENCES

From "Mythology of the Oglala Sioux" by Martha Warren Beckwith from *Journal of American Folklore* 43, October–December 1930.

Quotation by an army major from *Big Story: How the American Press and Television Reported and Interpreted the Crisis of Tet 1968 in Vietnam and Washington* by Peter Braestrup. Published by Westview Press, 1983.

Quotation, "Can you not find . . ." from *Who Built America?,* edited by Stephen Brier et al. Published by Pantheon Books, 1992.

From "Death Battle at Tarawa" by Sgt. John Bushemi from *Yank: The Story of World War II as Written by the Soldiers* by the Staff of *Yank,* the Army Weekly. Published by Brassey's (US) Inc., 1991.

Quotation by Lorraine Cervantes from "It's Our Turn Now" by Charles S. Lee and Lester Sloan from *Newsweek,* November 21, 1994.

Quotation by economist Arthur Burns in 1951 about economic equality; quotation by a woman steel worker; quotation by an unidentified female college graduate; quotation by E. D. Nixon, past president of the Alabama NAACP, about Rosa Parks; quotation by a single working mother; and quotation by James Reston about the assassination of John F. Kennedy as printed in *The Unfinished Journey: America Since World War II* by William H. Chafe. Published by Oxford University Press, 1991.

Quotation by Cecil Evans from *Lyndon B. Johnson: A Biography* by Harry Provence. Published by Fleet Publishing Corporation, 1964.

From unpublished autobiographical essay, 8, Juliet Goodrich Papers, Schlesinger Library, Radcliffe College.

Quotation by relief worker Rick Grant from "Aid Workers Plan New Attack on Famine" by Scott Kraft and Mark Fineman from *Los Angeles Times,* December 11, 1992.

Quotation by Andrei Gromyko from *Years of Discord: American Politics and Society, 1961–1974* by John Morton Blum. Published by W. W. Norton & Company, Inc., 1991.

From *The Homefront: America During World War II* by Mark Jonathan Harris. Published by The Putnam Publishing Group, 1984.

From speech by Vaclav Havel from *Mr. Bush's War* by Stephen R. Graubard. Published by Hill & Wang, a division of Farrar, Straus & Giroux, 1992.

Quotation by a television reporter on *Independent News TV*, January 30, 1981, 10:30 P.M.

Quotation by Rudy Jimenez from "Get Me Out of Here!" from *Newsweek*, May 1, 1995.

From "Eirik the Red" from *Eirik the Red and Other Icelandic Sagas*, selected and translated with an Introduction by Gwyn Jones. Published by Oxford University Press, London, 1961.

Quotation by Jackie Kennedy from *The Kennedys: An American Drama* by Peter Collier and David Horowitz. Published by Oxford University Press, 1984.

From *Thirteen Days* by Robert F. Kennedy. Published by W. W. Norton & Company, Inc., 1969.

Quotation about "Black Tuesday" from *Three Years Down* by Jonathan Norton Leonard. Published by J. B. Lippincott Co., 1944.

From "Spirit, Don't Talk So Loud" from *Black Culture and Black Consciousness: Afro-American Folk Thought from Slavery to Freedom* by Lawrence W. Levine. Published by Oxford University Press, 1977.

Quotation by Sophia Litwinska from *The Trial of Joseph Kramer*, edited by Raymond Phillips. Published by Hodge, 1949.

From "In Pursuit of Black Pursuits Excellence" by Avis Matthews from Voice of Youth Advocates 13, October 1990.

From letters by 11-year-old girl to Mrs. Roosevelt and by the wife of a veteran from *Down & Out in the Great Depression: Letters from the "Forgotten Man"*, edited by Robert S. McElvaine. Published by University of North Carolina Press, 1983.

Quotation by Julius Molawa from "Black Power!" by Peter Turnley from *Newsweek*, May 9, 1994.

Quotation about Ronald Reagan from "Yankee Doodle Magic" by Lance Morrow from *Time*, July 7, 1986. Published by Time Inc., 1986.

From "Mier y Terán to Minister of War, Pueblo Viejo, November 14, 1829" from *Terán and Texas: A Chapter in Texas-Mexican Relations* by Ohland Morton. Published by the Texas State Historical Association, 1948.

Quotation by Lewis Mumford from "The House that Levitt Built" by Ron Rosenbaum from *Esquire* 100, December, 1983.

From *This Is London* by Edward R. Murrow. Published by Alfred A. Knopf, Inc., 1941.

Quote by Michael Nelson from "Marching Home" by Jill Smolowe from *Time*, October 30, 1995.

From "All Is Not Lost By Any Means" from *New York World* editorials, October 30, 1929.

From "Foundations of Ghana" by D. T. Niane and J. Suret-Canale from *African Civilization Revisited*, translated by Basil Davidson. Published by Africa World Press, Inc., 1991.

From *Twelve Years A Slave* by Solomon Northup, edited by Sue Eakin and Joseph Logsdon. Published by Louisiana State University Press, 1968.

Quotation by a black janitor from *Let the Trumpet Sound: The Life of Martin Luther King, Jr.* by Stephen B. Oates. Published by HarperCollins Publishers, 1982.

Quotations by a cattle rancher and Harry Hopkins from *Anxious Decades* by Michael E. Parrish. Published by W. W. Norton & Company, Inc., 1992.

From a petition of Antonio María Pico et al., to the Senate and House of Representatives of the United States. Manuscript HM 514 in the Huntington Library, San Marino, California.

From *A Violent Evangelism: The Political and Religious Conquest of the Americas* by Luis N. Rivera. Published by Westminster/John Knox Press, 1992.

From *House Beautiful* magazine quoted in "The House that Levitt Built" by Ron Rosenbaum from *Esquire* 100, December 1983.

From "Forced to Return to the Savage Life" from *The Papers of Chief John Ross*, edited by Gary E Moulton. Published by the University of Oklahoma Press, 1985.

From "A Work of One's Own" by Sara Ruddick from *Working It Out: 23 Women Writers, Artists, Scientists, and Scholars Talk about Their Lives and Work*, edited by Sara Ruddick and Pamela Daniels. Published by Pantheon Books, 1977.

From "Nightmare job at Anzio" by Sgt. Burgess H. Scott from *Yank: The Story of World War II as Written by the Soldiers* by the Staff of *Yank*, the Army Weekly. Published by Brassey's (US) Inc., 1991.

From letter to Jonathan B. H. Smith, March 1–5, 1829, from the Margaret B. Smith Family Correspondence, Manuscript Division, Library of Congress, Washington, D.C.

Quotation by Ruth Smith from "Victories Were Captured by G.O.P. Candidates, Not the Party's Platform" by Richard L. Berke from *The New York Times*, November 10, 1994.

From "Henry's Wedding and a Most Curious Tea Party" from *Nisei Daughter* by Monica Stone. Published by Little, Brown and Company, 1953.

Quote by Simón Planas Suárez from *The Monroe Doctrine: Its Importance in the International Life of the States of the New World* by Alejandro Alvarez. Published by Oxford University Press, 1924.

From "South Vietnam: Lavish Aid, Limited Progress" by Milton C. Taylor from *Pacific Affairs* 34 (1961).

Quotations by Hideko Tamura Friedman and Charles A. Gates from "The Good War": An Oral History of World War II by Studs Terkel. Published by Pantheon Books, 1984.

From *Journey to America* by Alexis de Tocqueville, translated by George Lawrence, edited by J. P. Mayer. Published by Yale University Press, 1962.

Quotation by Garcilaso de la Vega about one woman's journey in South America from *This New World: The Civilization of Latin America* by William Lytle Schurz. Published by Unwin Hyman Ltd., 1956.

PHOTO

Abbreviations used: (t) top, (c) center, (b) bottom, (l) left, (r) right, (bkgd) background, (bdr) border.

TITLE PAGE: i(t,c), Jim Simmen/Tony Stone Images.

TABLE OF CONTENTS: iv(t,c), Jim Simmen/Tony Stone Images; v, © Bob Daemmrich; vi, The Granger Collection; vii, *Emigrants Crossing the Plains*, c1867 by Albert Bierstadt, The National Cowboy Hall of Fame; ix(t), The Granger Collection, New York; ix(b), *Flop House*, 1937 by Edward Millman, National Museum of American Art, Smithsonian Institution, Washington, DC/Art Resource, NY; x(t), Archive Photos; x(b), AP/Wide World Photos; xi, Consolidated News/Archive Photos.

STUDENT GUIDE: xv(t,l), Jim Simmen/Tony Stone Images.

UNIT 1: xx, Courtesy of the Witte Museum, San Antonio, Texas; 1, Travelpix/FPG International.

CHAPTER 1: 2, Corbis-Bettmann; 5(t), Thomas R. Hester, University of Texas at Austin; 5(b), Arrowheads in this image taken from image #1962, Courtesy of AMNH Dept. of Library Services, American Museum of Natural History; 7, National Park Service; 11(b), *Hornblower*, Benin, A.D. 1500–1700, brass/bronze, H 24¼ x W 8½ x D 6" The Brooklyn Museum 55.87, gift of Mr. and Mrs. Alastair B. Martin; 13, Corbis-Bettmann; 16(both), Corbis-Bettmann.

CHAPTER 2: 26, Courtesy Trustees of The British Museum; 28, Archive Photos; 31(t), © Bob Daemmrich; 34(t), Corbis-Bettmann; 38(t), Photograph courtesy The Quilt Complex, San Anselmo, CA; 38(b), Courtesy Peg Thompson; 39, HRW photograph by Sam Dudgeon.

CHAPTER 3: 40, Courtesy The Pilgrim Society; 43(t), Rare Books and Manuscripts Division, The New York Public Library, Astor, Lenox and Tilden Foundations; 45, Courtesy of the John Carter Brown Library at Brown University; 48(t), Massachusetts Historical Society; 48(b), Archive Photos; 50(b), Culver Pictures; 51, Massachusetts Historical Society; 53, Archive Photos; 54(b), Colonial Williamsburg Foundation; 56, Maryland Historical Society, Baltimore; 58(t), Detail from *The Wrath of Peter Stuyvesant*, by Asher B. Durand from The Collection of The New-York Historical Society; 58(b), *Penn's Treaty with the Indians* (1771–72) by Benjamin West, oil on canvas, Courtesy of the Museum of American Art of the Pennsylvania Academy of the Fine Arts, Phildelphia. Gift of Mrs. Sarah Harrison (The Joseph Harrison, Jr. Collection).

CHAPTER 4: 60, Courtesy of the Library of Congress; 64, Hulton Getty/Woodfin Camp & Associates; 65, Courtesy of the Free Library of Philadelphia; 70(t,r), Archive Photos; 73, Historical Society of Pennsylvania; 79, Thornton/Archive Photos.

UNIT 2: 80, Lambert/Archive Photos; 81, Paul S. Conklin.

CHAPTER 5: 82, *Washington Crossing the Delaware* (1851) by Emanuel Leutze, oil on canvas, The Granger Collection, New York; 84(t), Corbis-Bettmann; 85, Courtesy of the John Carter Brown Library at Brown University; 86(b), Corbis-Bettmann; 90(t), *Paul Revere* (1735–1818) by John Singleton Copley, oil on canvas, c 1768–70, The Granger Collection, New York; 92, *The Spirit of '76* (1876) by A. M. Willard, Corbis-Bettmann; 95(l), Historical Society of Pennsylvania; 95(r), *Thomas Paine* (1737–1809) by Auguste Milliere, oil on canvas, The Granger Collection, New York; **Declaration of Independence**: 97–100(all), © Comstock, Inc./Bob Pizaro; 102, Corbis-Bettmann; 103, Courtesy of the Library of Congress; 105, *Surrender of General John Burgoyne at Saratoga, New York, October 17, 1777* by John Trumbull, oil on canvas, The Granger Collection, New York; 106, Corbis-Bettmann; 107, Archive Photos; 108, Photograph courtesy The Quilt Complex, San Anselmo, CA.

CHAPTER 6: 110, Nebraska State Historical Society; 119(both), The Smithsonian Institution, Museum of American History, National Numismatic Collection; 123(t), *Liberty Displaying the Arts and Sciences* (1792) by Samuel Jennings, detail from The Library Company of Philadelphia; 125, Independence National Historical Park; 127, Courtesy of the Library of Congress; 128(b), *Alexander Hamilton* by John Trumbull,

Corbis-Bettmann; 129, Collection of the New-York Historical Society.
Constitution Handbook: 130, © Comstock, Inc./Bob Pizaro; 131(bdr), Images © 1996 PhotoDisc, Inc.; 132 (c) AmStock, Inc./Bob Pizaro; 133(bdr), Images ©1996 PhotoDisc, Inc; 134 © Comstock, Inc./Bob Pizaro; 135, Independence National Historical Park Collection; 135(bdr), Images ©1996 PhotoDisc, Inc.; 136, © Comstock, Inc./Bob Pizaro; 137, © Comstock, Inc./Bob Pizaro; 137(bdr), Images ©1996 PhotoDisc, Inc; 138, © Comstock, Inc./Bob Pizaro; 139, © Comstock, Inc./Bob Pizaro; 139(bdr), Images ©1996 PhotoDisc, Inc.; 140, © Comstock, Inc./Bob Pizaro; 141, © Comstock, Inc./Bob Pizaro; 141(bdr), Images ©1996 PhotoDisc, Inc; 142, © Comstock, Inc./Bob Pizaro; 143, © Comstock, Inc./Bob Pizaro; 143(bdr), Images ©1996 PhotoDisc, Inc.; 144, © Comstock, Inc./Bob Pizaro; 145, © Comstock, Inc./Bob Pizaro; 145(bdr), Images ©1996 PhotoDisc, Inc.; 146, © Comstock, Inc./Bob Pizaro; 147(t), Independence National Historical Park Collection; 147(c), © Comstock, Inc./Bob Pizaro; 147(bdr), Images ©1996 PhotoDisc, Inc.; 148, © Comstock, Inc./Bob Pizaro; 149, © Comstock, Inc./Bob Pizaro; 149(bdr), Images ©1996 PhotoDisc, Inc.; 150, © Comstock, Inc./Bob Pizaro; 151, © Comstock, Inc./Bob Pizaro; 151(bdr), Images ©1996 PhotoDisc, Inc; 152, © Comstock, Inc./Bob Pizaro; 153, © Comstock, Inc./Bob Pizaro; 153(bdr), Images ©1996 PhotoDisc, Inc.; 154, © Comstock, Inc./Bob Pizaro; 155(bkgd), Mountain High Maps® Copyright © 1993 Digital Wisdom, Inc.; 155(bdr), Images ©1996 PhotoDisc, Inc.

CHAPTER 7: 156, From the Collections of Henry Ford Museum & Greenfield Village; 158(b), Corbis-Bettmann; 159, *George Washington, Esq.*, c 1794 by Gilbert Stuart, oil on canvas, Laurie Platt Winfrey Inc./Woodfin Camp & Associates; 160, Daniel Huntington 1816–1906, *The Republican Court* 1861, Oil on Canvas, 167.6 x 277.0 (66 x 109), The Brooklyn Museum 39.536.1, Gift of the Crescent–Hamilton Athletic Club; **Bill of Rights**: 163, © Comstock Inc./Bob Pizaro; 165, Archive Photos; 166(t), Detail from the original, courtesy of The Historic New Orleans Collection; 166(b), Corbis-Bettmann; 167, Corbis-Bettmann; 168, Laurie Platt Winfrey Inc./Woodfin Camp & Associates; 169, Laurie Platt Winfrey Inc./Woodfin Camp & Associates; 171, McAlpin Collection, Miriam and Ira D. Wallach Division of Art, Prints and Photographs, The New York Public Library, Astor, Lenox and Tilden Foundations; 172(t), Archive Photos.

UNIT 3: 176, Corbis-Bettmann; 177, Nancy Shehan/PhotoEdit.

CHAPTER 8: 181(t), *View of the West Front of Monticello and Garden* (1825) by Jane Braddick Peticolas (1791–1852) watercolor on paper, courtesy of the Thomas Jefferson Memorial Foundation, Inc., Photographer: Edward Owen; 186(t), *Portrait of Henry Clay (1777–1852)* c 1845 by George Peter Alexander Healy, National Portrait Gallery, Smithsonian Institution, Washington, DC/Art Resource, NY; 186(b), Corbis-Bettmann; 187, Archive Photos; 191(b), Laurie Platt Winfrey Inc./Woodfin Camp & Associates; 196, Laurie Platt Winfrey Inc./Woodfin Camp & Associates.

CHAPTER 9: 198, Archive Photos; 200, Breton Littlehals/National Geographic Image Collection; 202, Corbis-Bettmann; 203, Corbis-Bettmann; 212, Archive Photos; 216, Corbis-Bettmann; 217, Corbis-Bettmann.

CHAPTER 10: 221(both), Courtesy of The Charleston Museum, Charleston, South Carolina; 225, General Research Division, The New York Public Library, Astor, Lenox and Tilden Foundations; 228(t), Corbis-Bettmann; 228(b), Corbis-UPI/Bettmann; 229, *The Slave Auction* (1862) by Eyre Crowe, 13 x 21″ oil on canvas, photography courtesy of Kennedy Galleries, Inc., New York; 230, Abby Aldrich Rockefeller Folk Art Center, Williamsburg, VA; 231, The Library Company of Philadelphia; 235, Corbis-Bettmann; 237, Corbis-UPI/Bettmann; 238, Photograph courtesy The Quilt Complex, San Anselmo, CA; 239, Photo by Mungier/Louisana State Museum.

UNIT 4: 240(t) Courtesy Museum of American Political Life, University of Hartford, West Hartford, CT; 240(b), The Hermitage/Woodfin Camp & Associates; 241, Robert Brenner/PhotoEdit.

CHAPTER 11: 244, Laurie Platt Winfrey Inc./Woodfin Camp & Associates; 245(t), *Andrew Jackson* c 1800 by Asher B. Durand, Corbis-Bettmann; 248(t) *Henry Clay (1777–1852)* by Charles Bird King, oil, 1821, The Granger Collection, New York; 248(b) Bob Prestwood after a Phillip Dorf illustration; 253(b) *The Trail of Tears* by Robert Lindneux, Woolaroc Museum, Bartlesville, Oklahoma; 259, Corbis-Bettmann; 261, Corbis-Bettmann.

CHAPTER 12: 262, *Grand Canyon of the Yellowstone* (1872) by Thomas Moran, Lent by the U.S. Dept. of the Interior, Office of the Secretary, National Museum of American Art, Washington, DC/Art Resource, NY; 265(t,c), Laurie Platt Winfrey Inc./Woodfin Camp & Associates; 265(b), *Fall of the Alamo* by Robert Jenkins Onderdonk, Courtesy of Friends of the Governor's Mansion, Austin, Texas; 268(t), *Indians and Trappers at Ft. Walla Walla, Oregon Territory*, (1841) by Joseph Drayton, Oregon Historical Society, Negative number OrHi 56364; 268(b), Culver Pictures; 269(t), *Emigrants Crossing the Plains* c 1867 by Albert Bierstadt, National Cowboy Hall of Fame; 270, Corbis-Bettmann; 272, Detail from *Westward the Course of Empire Takes its Way* by Emmanuel Gottlieb, from National Museum of American Art, Washington, DC/Art Resource, NY; 275(b), Sipa Press/Woodfin Camp & Associates; 276(t), *Henry David Thoreau* (1817–1862) by Benjamin D. Maxham, daguerrotype, 1856, National

Portrait Gallery, Smithsonian Institution, Washington, DC/Art Resource NY; 277, Courtesy The Bancroft Library; 278, Corbis-UPI/Bettmann; 280(t), Sipa Press/Woodfin Camp & Associates; 283, Courtesy of the California History Room, California State Library, Sacramento, California; 284, Photograph courtesy The Quilt Complex, San Anselmo, CA.

UNIT 5: 286, Laurie Platt Winfrey, Inc./Woodfin Camp & Associates; 287, David Young-Wolff/PhotoEdit.

CHAPTER 13: 288, Collection of The New-York Historical Society; 303(t), Archive Photos; 307, Kansas State Historical Society; 310, Photograph courtesy The Quilt Complex, San Anselmo, CA.

CHAPTER 14: 312, The Connecticut Historical Society, Hartford, Connecticut; 315, Courtesy of the Library of Congress; 317, Archive Photos/American Stock; 319(c), The Lloyd Ostendorf Collection; 321(t), Virginia Historical Society, Richmond, VA; 321(b), Corbis-Bettmann; 323, Laurie Platt Winfrey Inc./Woodfin Camp & Associates; 325, Missouri Historical Society, St. Louis, Photographer: Alexander Gardner; 326, Courtesy of the Library of Congress; 328, Corbis-Bettmann; 330(t), Corbis-Bettmann; 330(b), *Pickett's Charge at the Battle of Gettysburg*, by Peter F. Roteermel, The State Museum of Pennsylvania, Pennsylvania Historical and Museum Commission; 332(t) The Lloyd Ostendorf Collection; 332(b), Culver Pictures; 333, Corbis-Bettmann; 334, Corbis-Bettmann; 335, Tom Lovell/National Geographic Image Collection.

CHAPTER 15: 336, Nebraska State Historical Society; 338(t), Corbis-Bettmann; 345, Corbis-Bettmann; 348(b), Laurie Platt Winfrey Inc./Woodfin Camp & Associates; 349, Corbis-Bettmann; 350, Corbis-Bettmann; 354(t), Picture Collection, The Branch Libraries, The New York Public Library; 354(b), Corbis-Bettmann; 355, Photographs and Prints Division, Schomburg Center for Research in Black Culture, The New York Public Library, Astor, Lenox and Tilden Foundations.

UNIT 6: 356, The Granger Collection, New York; 357, HRW photograph by Sam Dudgeon.

CHAPTER 16: 360, *Watching the Wagons* by Oscar Berninghaus, Peter Newark's American Pictures; 361(b), Corbis-Bettmann; 362, Detail of Transparency #070.86, George Catlin, *Sioux Indians Moving Their Tents*, Courtesy Department of Library Services, American Museum of Natural History; 364(t), Archive Photos; 366, Archive Photos; 367, Courtesy Oklahoma Historical Society; 369, Corbis-Bettmann; 371(t), National Archives Reproduction by Polaroid Corporation; 377(t), Courtesy, The Bancroft Library; 377(b), Corbis-Bettmann; 378, Nebraska State Historical Society; 379(l) Nebraska State Historical Society.

CHAPTER 17: 385(b), Archive Photos; 386, Culver Pictures; 389(both), Corbis-Bettmann; 392, Culver Pictures; 393 Courtesy The Bancroft Library; 395, Corbis-Bettmann; 400, Corbis-Bettmann; 402, Photograph courtesy The Quilt Complex, San Anselmo, CA,

UNIT 7: 404, Willard Clay/FPG International; 405, Michael Newman/PhotoEdit.

CHAPTER 18: 408, Corbis-Bettmann; 409, Laurie Platt Winfrey Inc./Woodfin Camp & Associates; 410(l), Corbis-UPI/Bettmann; 410(r), Culver Pictures; 412, Corbis-Bettmann; 413(t), Toledo-Lucas County Public Library; 413(b), Corbis-Bettmann; 415(t,l), Corbis-UPI/Bettmann; 415(b), Corbis-Bettmann; 416, Archive Photos; 418, Laurie Platt Winfrey Inc./Woodfin Camp & Associates; 419(t), Corbis-Bettmann; 420, Corbis-Bettmann; 422, Culver Pictures; 423(t), Culver Pictures; 423(b), Corbis-Bettmann; 424(both), Archive Photos.

CHAPTER 19: 428(t), Sydney M. Laurence, *Mount McKinley* c. 1930, Anchorage Museum of History and Art, Gift of Mr. and Mrs. John M. Sorenson, Chris Arend Photographer; 429, Corbis-UPI/Bettmann; 430, Courtesy of the Hawaii Agriculture Research Center; 432(b), Laurie Platt Winfrey Inc./Woodfin Camp & Associates; 442, Corbis-Bettmann; 444, Photograph courtesy The Quilt Complex, San Anselmo, CA.

CHAPTER 20: 446, © ERL/Sipa Press/Woodfin Camp & Associates; 453(b), Hulton Getty/Woodfin Camp & Associates; 455, Newspaper Collection, The Center for American History, The University of Texas at Austin/Reprint Courtesy of the *Fort Worth Star-Telegram*; 457(t), Corbis-UPI/Bettmann; 458(b) Corbis-Bettmann; 459, Corbis-Bettmann; 460, Corbis-UPI/Bettmann; 462(t),© Godard/Sipa Press/Woodfin Camp & Associates; 462(b), Corbis-UPI/Bettmann; 468, © ERL/Sipa Press/Woodfin Camp & Associates.

UNIT 8: 470, Grandma Moses: *Deep Snow:* Copyright ©1998, Grandma Moses Properties Co., New York. Photo: Edward Owen/Art Resource, NY; 471, HRW photograph by Peter Van Steen, courtesy Confederate Air Force.

CHAPTER 21: 472, Laurie Platt Winfrey Inc./Woodfin Camp & Associates; 474(t), Corbis-Bettmann; 474(b), Corbis-UPI/Bettmann; 476, Stock Montage, Inc.; 480(t), Corbis-Bettmann; 485(r), Corbis-Bettmann; 486(b,l), Archive Photos/Frank Driggs Collection; 486(b,r), Hulton Getty/Woodfin Camp & Associates; 489(t) Hulton Getty/Woodfin Camp & Associates; 489(b), Archive Photos; 490(b) Brown Brothers; 493, Corbis-Bettmann; 494, Photograph courtesy The Quilt Complex, San Anselmo, CA.

CHAPTER 22: 496, Corbis-Bettmann; 502(b) Corbis-Bettmann; 503, Culver Pictures; 504, Corbis-UPI/Bettmann; 506, Corbis-UPI/Bettmann;

507, Corbis-Bettmann; 508, AP/Wide World Photos; 511(t), Corbis-UPI/Bettmann; 511(b), Corbis-Bettmann; 514, Dorothea Lange/Hulton Getty/Woodfin Camp & Associates; 516(b), Corbis-UPI/Bettmann; 517(t), Courtesy of the Library of Congress; 517(b), AP/Wide World Photos; 518, AP/Wide World Photos.

CHAPTER 23: 524, AP/Wide World Photos; 525, Corbis-UPI/Bettmann; 529, Photo courtesy of Mary Helen Ponce; 530, AP/Wide World Photos; 531(t), Corbis-UPI/Bettmann; 531(b), National Archives Reproduction by Polaroid Corporation; 532, AP/Wide World Photos; 534(t), AP/Wide World Photos; 534(b), Archive Photos; 535, Corbis-Bettmann; 537, © Trippett/Sipa Press/Woodfin Camp & Associates; 539(t), AP/Wide World Photos; 539(b), Corbis-Bettmann; 540, Corbis-Bettmann.

UNIT 9: 544(both), Archive Photos/Michael Barson; 545, HRW photograph by Peter Van Steen, courtesy KXAN-TV 36, Austin, Texas.

CHAPTER 24: 546, Corbis-UPI/Bettmann; 548, Corbis-UPI/Bettmann; 549, Hulton Getty/Woodfin Camp & Associates; 550(t), Corbis-UPI/Bettmann; 550(b), Hulton Getty/Woodfin Camp & Associates; 554(t), AP/Wide World Photos; 554(b), Corbis-UPI/Bettmann; 556(b), Archive Photos; 557, Archive Photos; 559, Corbis-UPI/Bettmann; 561, AP/Wide World Photos; 564, Archive Photos/Michael Barson; 565, Archive Photos.

CHAPTER 25: 566, AP/Wide World Photos; 568(t), Corbis-UPI/Bettmann; 568(b), AP/Wide World Photos; 570(t), Hulton Getty/Woodfin Camp & Associates; 570(b), Herc Ficklen/*Dallas Morning News*; 571, Corbis-UPI/Bettmann; 572, Archive Photos; 574(t), Corbis-Bettmann; 574(b), Tom Kelley/Archive Photos; 576(t), Corbis-UPI/Bettmann; 578, Archive Photos; 580(t), Corbis-UPI/Bettmann; 580(b), The Helicopter Era—from the HERBLOCK: A CARTOONIST'S LIFE (Simon & Schuster, 1993); 581, Corbis-UPI/Bettmann; 582, Bernard Gotfryd/Archive Photos; 583(both), Corbis-UPI/Bettmann; 584, AP/Wide World Photos; 585, Brown Brothers.

CHAPTER 26: 586, Corbis-UPI/Bettmann; 588, AP/Wide World Photos; 589, Corbis-UPI/Bettmann; 590, AP/Wide World Photos; 592, Les Immel/*Peoria Journal Star*; 594(both), AP/Wide World Photos; 595, Corbis-UPI/Bettmann; 596(t), © Marc and Evelyne Bernheim/Woodfin Camp & Associates; 596(b), "Thanks—Thanks a lot—Thanks again—Can I Lean Back Now?"—from THE HERBLOCK GALLERY (Simon & Schuster, 1968); 599, AP/Wide World Photos; 600(both), Corbis-UPI/Bettmann; 602(t), Hulton Getty/Woodfin Camp & Associates; 602(b), © Dan Budnik 1985/Hulton Getty/Woodfin Camp & Associates; 604, AP/Wide World Photos; 608, Courtesy of NASA; 610, Photograph courtesy The Quilt Complex, San Anselmo, CA.

UNIT 10: 612, Zintgraff Collection, The Institute of Texan Cultures, San Antonio, Texas; 613, HRW photograph by Sam Dudgeon.

CHAPTER 27: 614, © Wally McNamee 1982/Woodfin Camp & Associates; 616(t), © Torregano/Sipa Press/Woodfin Camp & Associates; 616(b), Archive Photos; 617, Sipa Press/Woodfin Camp & Associates; 622(t), AP/Wide World Photos; 622(b), "Our position hasn't changed at all."—from THE HERBLOCK GALLERY (Simon & Schuster, 1968); 623, Archive Photos; 625, AP/Wide World Photos; 627, AP/Wide World Photos; 628, Archive Photos; 629, AP/Wide World Photos; 631(both), Corbis-UPI/Bettmann; 632(t), Corbis-UPI/Bettmann; 632(b), Archive Photos; 633, AP/Wide World Photos; 634, Corbis-Reuters/Bettmann; 635, © Nick Wheeler/Sipa Press/Woodfin Camp & Associates.

CHAPTER 28: 636, © Sylvia Johnson/Woodfin Camp & Associates; 638, Archive Photos/Washington Bureau; 639, Archive Photos; 640, © Robert McElroy/Woodfin Camp & Associates; 641, © Jason Laure/Woodfin Camp & Associates; 642, AP/Wide World Photos; 644(t), Corbis-UPI/Bettmann; 644(b), DOONESBURY copyright 1973 G.B. Trudeau. Reprinted with permission of UNIVERSAL PRESS SYNDICATE. All rights reserved; 645, Corbis-UPI/Bettmann; 646, Corbis-UPI/Bettmann; 647, Corbis-UPI/Bettmann; 648, Draper Hill/*The Memphis Commercial Appeal*; 650(t), Corbis-UPI/Bettmann; 650(b), © Wally McNamee/Woodfin Camp & Associates; 651, © Arthur Tress/Woodfin Camp & Associates; 652(t), © Bernard Gotfryd/Woodfin Camp & Associates; 652(b), Corbis-UPI/Bettmann; 653, Corbis-UPI/Bettmann; 655, Archive Photos; 656(t), AP/Wide World Photos; 656(b), © Michael Heron/Woodfin Camp & Associates; 657(t), Lambert/Archive Photos; 657(c), Frank Mostra/Archive Photos; 658, © Craig Aurness/Woodfin Camp & Associates; 659, AP/Wide World Photos.

CHAPTER 29: 660, © Lester Sloan 1991/Woodfin Camp & Associates; 662, Corbis-UPI/Bettmann; 664, Archive Photos; 665, © Robert Wallis/Sipa Press/Woodfin Camp & Associates; 667(t), SARGENT 1983 Austin American-Statesman. Reprinted with permission of UNIVERSAL PRESS SYNDICATE. All rights reserved; 668, AP/Wide World Photos; 669, AP/Wide World Photos; 670, Corbis-Reuters/Bettmann; 672(t), AP/Wide World Photos; 672(b), Corbis-Reuters/Bettmann; 673, © Guans/Sipa Press/Woodfin Camp & Associates; 675, Bill Gentile/Sipa Press/Woodfin Camp & Associates; 677 Corbis-UPI/Bettmann; 678(t), © Florence Durand/Sipa Press/Woodfin Camp & Associates; 678(b), © 95 David Pollack; 679(both), © Trippett/Sipa Press/Woodfin Camp & Associates; 680, Photograph courtesy The Quilt Complex, San Anselmo, CA.

CHAPTER 30: 682, Court Mast 1992/FPG International Corp.; 684(t), AP/Wide World Photos; 684(b), © Robert Trippett/Sipa Press/Woodfin Camp & Associates; 685, © L. Nark/INE/Sipa Press/Woodfin Camp & Associates; 686(b), AP/Wide World Photos; 687, AP/Wide World Photos; 689(t), Consolidated News/Archive Photos; 689(b), © Nicolas Jallot/Sipa Press/Woodfin Camp & Associates; 690(t), © Nicholas Jallot/Cosmos/Woodfin Camp & Associates; 690(b), Corbis-Reuters/Bettmann; 691, AP/Wide World Photos; 693(t), Douglas Coupland, *Generation X*; 694, Brownie Harris/The Stock Market©; 695(t), © Lindsay Hebberd/Woodfin Camp & Associates; 695(b), © Lester Sloan 1992/Woodfin Camp & Associates; 696, AP/Wide World Photos; 698, Cheryl R. Richter; 699(t), © Frederico Mendes/Sipa Press/Woodfin Camp & Associates; 699(b), Consolidated News/Archive Photos; 701, Corbis-Reuters/Bettmann.

Reference Section: 702(t,l), Archive Photos; 702(t,r), The Granger Collection, New York; 702(c,l), Corbis-Bettmann; 702 (c,r), The Granger Collection, New York; 702(b), Peter Newark's American Pictures; 703(t,c), Tony Stone Images; 703(t), The Granger Collection, New York; 703(c), Corbis-Bettmann; 703(b,l), Corbis-Bettmann; 703(b,r), Corbis-Bettmann.

ART

Abbreviated as follows: (t) top, (b) bottom, (l) left, (r) right, (c) center.

All art, unless otherwise noted, by Holt, Rinehart and Winston.

Text maps, feature maps, Atlas, created by GeoSystems Global Corp.

Illustrations: Leslie Kell; Page xiii (Rendition from Federal Works Agency Photo), xviii(l,r), xix(l,r), 68, 161, 209, 353, 382 (Rendition from Missouri Historical Society), 464 (Rendition from U.S.Signal Corps/National Archives Photo), 481(t) (Rendition from Federal Works Agency Photo), 481(b), 506, 543 (Rendition from U.S. Air Force Photo), 576 (Rendition from Russell Dian/HRW Photo), 601, 624 (Rendition from U.S. Army Photo), 686.